Perspectives from *Historical Archaeology:*

The Archaeology of Plantation Life

Compiled by:

Nicholas Honerkamp

SOCIETY *for*
HISTORICAL
ARCHAEOLOGY

Perspectives from Historical Archaeology is a reader series providing collected articles from the journal of the Society for Historical Archaeology (SHA). Published since 1967, *Historical Archaeology* is the oldest North American scholarly publication on the archaeology of sites and materials from the historic past, and one of the world's premier publications on this subject. Each volume in the *Perspectives* series is developed on either a subject or regional basis by a compiler who selects the articles for inclusion and their order. The compilers also provide an introduction that presents an overview of the substantive work on that topic. *Perspectives* volumes offer non-archaeologists a convenient source for important publications on a subject or a region; an excellent resource for students interested in developing a specialization in a specific topic or area; as well as a convenient reference for archaeologists with an interest in the material.

The *Perspectives* series is managed by the SHA's Journal Editor and Co-Publications Editor and is published through the SHA's Print-On-Demand Press. Individuals interested in compiling a volume for publication through this series are encouraged to contact the Series Editors:

J. W. Joseph, PhD, RPA
Journal Editor, SHA
New South Associates, Inc.
6150 East Ponce de Leon Avenue
Stone Mountain, GA 30083
jwjoseph@newsouthassoc.com

Annalies Corbin, PhD
Co-Publications Editor, SHA
The PAST Foundation
1929 Kenny Road, Suite 300
Columbus, OH 43210
annalies@pastfoundation.org

Formed in 1967, the SHA is the largest scholarly group concerned with the archaeology of the modern world (A.D. 1400-present). The main focus of the society is the era since the beginning of European exploration. SHA promotes scholarly research and the dissemination of knowledge concerning historical archaeology. The society is specifically concerned with the identification, excavation, interpretation, and conservation of sites and materials on land and underwater. Geographically, the society emphasizes the New World, but also includes European exploration and settlement in Africa, Asia, and Oceania. To learn more about the SHA and historical archaeology, visit www.sha.org.

2009 © The Society for Historical Archaeology
ISBN: 978-1-957402-02-4
Library of Congress Control Number: 2009941960

Compiled with an Introduction by Nicholas Honerkamp

Contact information:
Nicholas Honerkamp
Department of Sociology, Anthropology, and Geography
615 McCallie Avenue
University of Tennessee at Chattanooga
Chattanooga, TN 37403

Cover images:
William Macintire and Phil McCormick, Artists, from *Race and the Disciplines of the Plantation*, page 153.

Richard H. Kimmel, Artist, *Notes on the Cultural Origins and Functions of Sub-Floor Pits*, 1993, page 96.

An I-house on the Savannah River Site (AEC Tract J-920) ca. 1950. Photo courtesy of Savannah River Sites Archives, from *Bush Hill: Material Life at a Working Plantation*, page 177.

James A. Delle, Artist, *The Landscapes of Class Negotiations on Coffee Plantations in the Blue Mountains of Jamaica: 1790-1850*, 1999 page 33.

Part I. <u>Introduction</u>

1. *The Trajectory of Plantation Studies in* Historical Archaeology
   Nick Honerkamp..1

Abstract: A summary of some of the major themes and debates in plantation archaeology over the last 40 years is presented, followed by articles selected to illustrate how these themes and debates have been expressed in the pages of Historical Archaeology. A short synopsis of each article is included

Part II. <u>Plantation Landscapes</u>

2. *Spatial Analysis of the King's Reach Plantation Homelot, Ca. 1690-1715*
   Dennis J. Pogue...16

Abstract: This paper considers the spatial arrangement and utilization of the King's Reach plantation homelot (ca. 1690-1715). The primary analytical tool is the interpretation of distributional patterns of plowzone-derived artifacts. The pipe stem distributions have proven to be especially effective in identifying diachronic shifts in refuse disposal. The ceramics, glass, and other materials are not particularly indicative of temporal change, but do provide evidence for functional differentiation. Those patterns point to a typically located and oriented plantation house and quarter, with extensive refuse middens nearby. However, the King's Reach homelot appears unusual in that other outbuildings, almost always found at such sites, have not been discovered. Their absence may be at least partially explained by the presence of a possible outlying quarter and/or workhouse located nearby. An unusual number of cellars were located below the plantation house floor, apparently a result of successive replacement due to collapsing cellar walls. [HISTORICAL ARCHAEOLOGY 22(2):40-56 (1988) (14 printed pages)]

3. *The Landscapes of Class Negotiation on Coffee Plantations in the Blue Mountains of Jamaica: 1790-1850*
   James A. Delle..33

Abstract: Analyzing the material elements of class negotiation should be a focus of historical archaeology. One of the most promising forms of material culture with which to conduct such analysis is landscape. To examine how landscapes shaped the negotiation of class relations in 19th century Jamaica, the material remains of three coffee plantations-Sherwood Forest, Clydesdale, and Chesterfield-are described and analyzed. The archaeological analysis of the landscapes of 19th century class negotiation can shed light on the historical development of capitalist social processes, many of which still impact the negotiation of class relations today. [HISTORICAL ARCHAEOLOGY 33(1):136-158 (1999) (22 printed pages)]

4. *"The little Spots allow'd them": The Archaeological Study of African-American Yards*
   Barbara J. Heath and Amber Bennett...56

Abstract: Yards, like buildings and more portable artifacts, are significant expressions of culture. Yet within African-American archaeology, yards have not been the focus of serious discussions addressing questions of work and leisure activities, community interactions, aesthetics, and culture change. The authors review archaeological, ethnographic, and historical evidence of yards associated with New World slave quarters and present a framework for analysis. Results of recent excavations at a slave quarter at Poplar Forest in central Virginia, occupied from ca. 1790 to 1812, are presented within the context of this framework. The archaeological study of yard spaces provides significant information about cultural meanings and uses of space. [HISTORICAL ARCHAEOLOGY 34(2):38-55 (2000) (17 printed pages)]

Part III. **Plantation Architecture**

Abstract: *If I could do it, I'd do no writing at all here. It would be photographs: the rest would be fragments of cloth, bits of cotton, lumps of earth, records of speech, pieces of wood and iron, phials of odors, plates of food and excrement (Agee and Evans 1969:12).*
Here is an interpretation of what was found in the ruins of a slave cabin. The ruins are on Cumberland Island, Georgia. The cabin was lived in between circa 1834 and 1864. We seek to discover and convey a sense of daily life as it might have been experienced by the people who lived in the cabin. Until now, what slavery was like anywhere has been largely constructed from the writings of slave owning groups (Davis 1966:30). In the case of plantation slavery in Georgia, records and accounts of slave owning farmers often provide information (Flanders 1933). Another general of source of information are the writings of men and women who once had been slaves (Osofsky 1969). Third are materials from excavation. These differ from all writing in the matter in intent. We take it for granted that no one expected us to see or touch the things we unearthed. [HISTORICAL ARCHAEOLOGY 5:3-17 (1971) (14 printed pages)]

Abstract: A review of the current literature demonstrates that subfloor and sub-surface "cellars" occur in many cultural, chronological, and functional contexts, and that many uses may produce pit features reminiscent of the hearth-front slave root cellars documented at Kingsmill Plantation. Recent site documentation at a 19th-century Virginia farmstead indicates that among some groups one original function might be as borrow for hearth fill or chimney mortar. Such pits might then be adapted for use as sub-floor storage. The review leads to several conclusions. First, the presence of a sub-floor pit should not be taken as prima facie evidence of root storage, storage of valuables, or of African-American occupation; instead, the assigning of ethnicity and site function must rely on a broad view of assemblage attributes. Second, the potential importance of subsurface pits is such that Phase I testing strategies should add larger test units to the more typical shovel test research design. Third, problem-oriented research is needed to provide an objective basis for cultural and behavioral interpretations, and to identify the modifying influences of taphonomic factors on abandoned sub-floor pits. [HISTORICAL ARCHAEOLOGY 27(3):102-113 (1993) (11 printed pages)]

Part IV. Social Status and Ethnicity on the Plantation

Abstract: Data recovery at the Spiers Landing site (South Carolina 38BK 160) was directed to the salvage of behavioral information from a construction-threatened, undocumented site which was ceramically datable to the turn of the late 18th/early 19th century. Research focused on the discovery of socioeconomic patterns associated with the occupation. Prehistoric components represented at the site included Archaic, Woodland and Mississippian periods. Analysis of faunal, floral, ceramic and structural remains associated with the historic component indicates that the site reflects a domestic occupation by low-status persons. Archival and documentary evidence strongly suggests that the site was a slave cabin on Fountainhead plantation, a part of property owned by Colonel Robert McKelvey. By 1850 the property as a whole was a small multi-commodity production unit with a focus on subsistence-level agriculture and livestock raising. The Spiers Landing site is seen as an example of low-status occupation against which other small historic surface artifact scatters can be compared in order to develop a series of distributional patterns by which low-status Afro-American and Euro-American sites of the colonial and antebellum periods can be archaeologically defined. [HISTORICAL ARCHAEOLOGY 15(2):58-68 (1981) (10 printed pages)]

Abstract: Previous work on Georgia plantations has provided useful data about life on the large plantations on barrier islands. More recent work on small to mid-sized plantations reveals that slaves' acquisition of ceramics may reflect more of their own decisions on what was purchased and what was used. Coarser ware frequencies indicate food preparation and storage in the slave quarters. Porcelain was often found in greater numbers in the slave quarters than in the plantation bighouse kitchen. Like earlier research, slaves at Kings Bay were found to have relatively more small bowls, but surprisingly they had relatively more plates as well. Comparison of slaves and planters using CC Index revealed that for several vessel forms the slaves had more expensive ceramics than their masters. This suggests that the slaves themselves viewed ceramics as status indicators and purchased them accordingly. [HISTORICAL ARCHAEOLOGY 23(1):69-96 (1989) (27 printed pages)]

Abstract: Ethnic studies have recently received great emphasis in American historical archaeology. Three groups have commonly been studied: blacks or African Americans, Hispanics, and Overseas Chinese (Staski n.d.). Each of these groups is seen as having an emic identity within the historic period being studied, an identity which is connected to the identity held by members of the present groups that descend from these historical ancestors (Staski n.d.). Indeed, a major reason why these three groups are studied is the desire of these present groups to understand their ancestors. Due to problems with biased or incomplete written records (Deetz 1977:7-8), archaeology is embraced as a method of inquiry, of building a bridge of understanding between these present groups and their forebears. [HISTORICAL ARCHAEOLOGY 24(4):20-28 (1990) (8 printed pages)]

Abstract: An interpretation or presentation of the construction of race in plantation society must ultimately grapple with two different, yet not entirely unrelated, forms of discipline" (Foucault 1970, 1979). The first and most obvious connotation is that of labor discipline, the role racial ideology played in the assertion and exercise of control which was not immediately dependent upon physical coercion. The second connotation is the partitioning of knowledge and inquiry into discrete, bounded, and autonomous academic disciplines, a tendency which is particularly problematic since race itself is an ideological assertion of otherness, inferiority, and fragmentation. [HISTORICAL ARCHAEOLOGY 24(4):29-36 (1990) (7 printed pages)]

Abstract: Bush Hill Plantation, located near Aiken, South Carolina, and Augusta, Georgia, along the middle Savannah River valley, was owned by four generations of the George Bush lineal family between 1807 and 1920. Drawing upon the interpretive concept of the working plantation, perceptions regarding material conditions and the standard of living experienced by southern planters are explored in this essay. Economic records indicate that the George was among the top wealth-holding groups within the surrounding community. Although the planter family was affluent, the standard of living revealed archaeologically was economically conservative. The Bush family used inexpensive household items and did not acquire the luxury goods often thought to be archaeological hallmarks associated of genteel society, such as expensive dining sets or tea wear. Conversely, archaeological data revealed that they were aggressive consumers, indicated by the sheer quantity of materials discarded at the site. The example provided by Bush Hill underscores the complexity of planter households in the past and illustrates that the wealth held by former site residents is not always directly discernable in the archaeological record. [HISTORICAL ARCHAEOLOGY 40(4):51-83 (2006) (32 printed pages)]

Abstract: Regional cuisines or foodways have been a topic of interest to both historians and archaeologists for at least the past 30 years. Scholars recognize a regional foodway in the antebellum Upland South that is part of the larger "Upland South" cultural tradition. The agricultural and archaeological data on subsistence in the antebellum Upland South have been woven into an idealized set of subsistence practices that revolved around agricultural practices. The examination of four contemporaneous faunal assemblages representative of different societal classes living in 19th-century Kentucky shows that this generalized version of Upland South foodways does not hold true across economic classes. Instead, a closer look reveals that many people living on Kentucky's antebellum farmsteads struggled regularly for food security and that the idealized version of a shared "Upland South foodway" was restricted to the wealthy planter class that had ready access to the market economy. [HISTORICAL ARCHAEOLOGY 42(4):88-104 (2008) (17 printed pages)]

Part V. African American Lifeways on the Plantation

Abstract: The 1964-65 excavation of the slave quarters at Garrison Plantation near Baltimore, Maryland, yielded groups of objects that display certain 'Africanisms.' The groups of objects are proposed elements of early Afro-American material culture and are compared to items from similar sites in the mid-Atlantic region. [HISTORICAL ARCHAEOLOGY 21(2):112-119 (1987) (7 printed pages)]

Abstract: During the analysis of glass artifacts recovered from undisturbed archaeological contexts at Oakley Plantation, West Feliciana Parish, Louisiana (16WF34), a number of glass sherds were found to have retouching and edge damage consistent with wear found on utilized lithics. Of these, 35 sherds were determined to exhibit significant evidence of use as tools. These tools were recovered from four African-American assemblages dating from the 1840s through the 1930s. This paper discusses the analysis of these tools, whether variations among the tools are representative of distinct types, a review of the occurrence of similar tools at other sites, and whether the tools can be considered to be of uniquely African-American origin. [HISTORICAL ARCHAEOLOGY 30(4):37-49 (1996) (12 printed pages)]

Abstract: In this article, artifacts excavated from 19th-century African-American contexts at the Hermitage plantation near Nashville, Tennessee, are examined in light of their possible use in religious ritual, traditional healing, and other behaviors related to spirituality. While specific spiritual behaviors cannot he determined from the Hermitage archaeological and documentary record, the presence of a distinct African-American belief system at the Hermitage is suggested through comparison of selected artifacts from the Hermitage assemblage with various historical, folkloric, and archaeological sources. This belief system and its associated behaviors may have aided African Americans in achieving limited social and economic autonomy within the system of plantation slavery. [HISTORICAL ARCHAEOLOGY 31(2):63-80 (1997) (17 printed pages)]

Part VI. <u>Method and Theory in Plantation Archaeology</u>

Abstract: South's pattern concept has acquired prominence in archaeological research since its explanation in the late 1970s. Nowhere has this prominence been greater than in plantation archaeology. Unfortunately, the pattern concept is inappropriate for the analysis of plantation remains because its scope is too large and its perspective is mainly synchronic. [HISTORICAL ARCHAEOLOGY 23(2):28-40 (1989) (28 printed pages)]

Abstract: The archaeology of southern plantations promises to provide new data about slave life. This is most welcome, but like all sets of data--whether historical, anthropological, or archaeological, archaeological data require analysis and interpretation before becoming important or even useful. It is well to pause periodically and assess the links between methods of analysis and the theories which shape archaeological interpretations. [HISTORICAL ARCHAEOLOGY 24(4):78-91 (1990) (13 printed pages)]

Abstract: Social relations on the plantations of the South Carolina and Georgia Lowcountry were structured by a series of classifications which in turn expressed and codified plantation ideology. Racism, paternalism, and emergent capitalism have all been demonstrated through archaeological investigations as major constellations within this ideological universe. The expression of these social and ideological relations occurred symbolically within the plantations, as evidenced by settlement systems, architecture, and material remains. This ideology was also expressed in the documentary record in the ways in which planters classified their slaves and other social groups. This article considers the archaeology of ideology among the plantations of the Georgia and South Carolina Lowcountry as expressed through symbolization and classification and examines the evolution of plantation ideology from the 17th century to the end of the Antebellum era. It suggests that the social and ideological structure shifted from one based on racial classification to one dependent on labor specialization and social stratification, in response to changes in the Lowcountry's plantation economy. [HISTORICAL ARCHAEOLOGY 27(3):57-73 (1993) (16 printed pages)]

Abstract: From broken pots, rusted fishhooks, and scraps of bone, archaeologists bring to light aspects of African-American life on antebellum plantations. But it is a dim light, shared by a few through technical reports and scholarly journal articles. This paper examines the distillation of information and ideas from technical reports into publications written specifically for nonarchaeologists. Historical and genealogical society journals, museum newsletters, and church bulletins provide venues through which archaeologists can convey not just what they are doing, but what they have learned. That knowledge has value in the political arena. [HISTORICAL ARCHAEOLOGY 31(3):51-64 (1997) (13 printed pages)]

Abstract: Archaeological data from the Levi Jordan plantation in Brazoria County, Texas, indicate that the African Americans who lived on this plantation participated in many activities, several of African origin, that functioned to insure this community's survival in an increasingly oppressive outside world. Ethnographic data indicate that many descendants of the plantation's residents, African American and European American, still live in the Brazoria area, and that these descendants continue to negotiate issues of power and control. Any public interpretation of this archaeology will necessarily deal with diverse understandings of race and history in present-day Brazoria County. This paper will describe the political and organizational strategies being employed by a team of descendants, archaeologists, and other community members to plan and implement public interpretations that are "inclusive" of the various histories and archaeologies of the plantation's ancestors: pre- and post-emancipation African Americans as well as planters. [HISTORICAL ARCHAEOLOGY 31(3):114-131 (1997) (17 printed pages)]

NICHOLAS HONERKAMP

The Trajectory of Plantation Studies in *Historical Archaeology*: An Introduction

ABSTRACT

A summary of some of the major themes and debates in plantation archaeology over the last 40 years is presented, followed by articles selected to illustrate how these themes and debates have been expressed in the pages of *Historical Archaeology*. A short synopsis of each article is included.

It has been two decades since Theresa Singleton reviewed the state of the art, and science, of plantation archaeology in the pages of *Historical Archaeology* (1990:70-77). At that time she used a single word to describe the previous 15 years of plantation studies: *proliferation*. Another word is appropriate in portraying what has happened since then: *exponential.*

The present volume constitutes a sample of this exponential trajectory, in the form of a compendium of articles published in the journal *Historical Archaeology* that relate to plantations. While there are myriad definitions of a plantation, for the purposes of this reader "an agricultural operation where most of the agricultural products were raised through the use of enslaved labor..." (Cabak and Groover 2004:2-1) circumvents ambiguity concerning "sufficient" acreage and the number of slaves present. Besides distinguishing plantations from farms that lack slave labor, this definition accommodates the dynamic nature of plantation evolution, one that is well illustrated by the 19 plantation archaeology articles presented here. Spanning over 35 years, the earliest contribution is the now-classic interpretation of a Georgia slave cabin by Robert Ascher and Charles Fairbanks (1971), while the latest, by Tanya Peres, offers a comparison of foodways from four contemporaneous antebellum plantation sites in Kentucky (2008). As might be expected in over three-and-a-half decades, a wide range of approaches are represented; as a microcosm of the published output devoted to plantations, *Historical Archaeology* reflects both the growth and the diversity of this subfield. So also does the excellent African diaspora reader compiled by Christopher S. Fennel (2008). Entitled *Perspectives From Historical Archaeology: African Diaspora Archaeology,* Fennel's volume and the present reader intersect and nicely complement each other.

Ignition

Between the appearance of the first plantation article in *Historical Archaeology* by Ascher and Fairbanks until Fairbanks' overview of the field 13 years later (1984), only a single plantation article by Leslie Drucker (1981) was published in the journal. The next six years saw the publication of nine articles, while the decade of the 1990s (including Singleton's overview of the field) generated 45 articles. This trickle-to-flood of interest in plantation-oriented studies, closely linked to African American archaeology, began as an outgrowth of the Civil Rights Movement and historic preservation legislation in the 1960s (Ferguson 1992; Singleton 1995; Agbe-Davis 2007). Black activism was important in the genesis of several early studies, and contributed to an emphasis on the archaeology of slave components and away from the "big house" orientation that had characterized research at (but not necessarily of) plantations up to that point. The "new social history" movement of the 1960s and 1970s and the "vindicationist" scholarship that goes back at least to Du Bois and Herskovits provided an intellectual backdrop for this changing focus in archaeology, one that included studies of a variety of ethnic communities (Singleton 1995:121; Mullins 2008:106-107).

Certainly the seminal work of Charles Fairbanks reflected this trend. As Barbara Heath (2009:1-2) has noted:

"...his [Fairbanks] work was crucial to foregrounding African slaves and the contexts of their lives—plantations—as important subjects of study, and for creating the subfield of plantation archaeology that has focused on understanding African and African-American lifeways, the material patterning of status differences, expressions of inequality, power and resistance, and more recently, African American agency as expressed through the diverse but interrelated realms of spiritual and economic practices and gender."

The foregrounding Heath speaks of is clearly manifest in Ascher and Fairbanks' humanistic presentation of slave lifeways at Rayfield Plantation (1971) and Fairbanks' search for "Africanisms" at Kingsley Plantation (1974). But Fairbanks' involvement in plantation archaeology was also grounded in solid methodological concerns as much as anything else: what could be more prone to intentional and unintentional bias than the emotionally-charged subject of antebellum slavery in the United States? Fairbanks possessed a healthy and abiding skepticism of self-serving documentary accounts of slave life (1984:8), and like Stanley South (1977:16) and James Deetz (1977:7-8), saw archaeology as a necessary corrective for responding to egregious historical errors, biases, and omissions—not to mention outright lies—in the documentary record. The "handmaiden to history" approach (Noël Hume 1964), with its emphasis on documentary verification and architectural reconstruction (read "big house"), was clearly over (Deagan 1982).

While plantation archaeology possesses its own particular sins of omission related to poor preservation, sampling issues, narrow research designs, etc., it nevertheless has made important contributions in two major areas: studies of plantation material culture and history, and studies of plantation slavery and social structure (Orser 1984:3). The first category encompasses the dialectical relationship between above-ground documents and below-ground archaeological remains; early on, this meant that even at a descriptive level historical archaeology provided a necessary reality check on documentary assertions regarding plantation life. This was accomplished by generating original information and insights on the conditions, constraints, and accomplishments of slave groups (and sometimes individuals) that could not be obtained using above-ground sources (see, for instance, Handler and Lange 1978). The second area has come to incorporate quantitative and qualitative material manifestations of plantation status, and more recently the examination of the dynamics of race, identity, self determination, power, resistance, negotiation, and cultural change. It is in this second broad area that plantation archaeology has experienced a pronounced expansion. Whereas early plantation archaeology succeeded in giving a voice to the voiceless, which no doubt contributed to its professional and popular appeal, contemporary studies have moved from a moral mission to social action that contributes to vindicationist goals

(Singleton 1999; Mullins 2008).

Takeoff

Although Fairbanks was certainly not the first archaeologist to excavate a slave site, his slave quarter excavations in the late 1960s at Kingsley and Rayfield plantations (Ascher and Fairbanks 1971; Fairbanks 1974) ushered in a shift in research away from slaveholders and toward slaves; in so doing, this demonstrated that plantation archaeology was a viable and appropriate focus within historical archaeology (Singleton 1990:72; Agbe-Davies 2007:414). Even research at sites like Colonial Williamsburg and Monticello that had traditionally concentrated on planters began to reflect this new direction. Around this time Stanley South introduced his pattern recognition approach to historic site research. While not necessarily concerned with plantation archaeology per se, South had a profound influence on the field with the publication of *Method and Theory in Historical Archaeology* (1977). Incorporating a heavy emphasis on quantification, South's group-class-type format for classifying historic artifacts into functional patterns provided a useful and straightforward analytical approach for historical archaeologists. South had already contributed a valuable tool for dating historic sites in the form of the Mean Ceramic Date Formula (1972). Additionally, the annual meetings of the (now-extinct) Conference on Historic Sites Archaeology, which he organized, were an important forum for annual paper presentations, discussions and debates, and publications for historical archaeologists. It was also one that he used to champion an empirical approach to archaeology.

In the mid to late 1970s John Solomon Otto—one of Fairbanks' students—pretty much single-handedly shifted the focus of plantation archaeology's intellectual landscape in a new direction with his work at Cannon's Point (1975, 1977, 1984). Heavily influenced by South's approach as well as the work of Marxist historian Eugene Genovese (1974), Otto was the first archaeologist to hold status constant while comparing the material correlates of the plantation's slave, overseer, and planter occupations. The utility of this approach for recognizing "status patterning" at other plantations became immediately apparent, and it inspired a plethora of studies, with researchers attempting to replicate Otto's quantitative approach and test his results (Singleton 1990:72). Aiding and abetting this expansion was the explosive growth in cultural resource management (CRM) studies as a result of federal legislation in the 1960s and 1970s (see Joseph 2004 for a comprehensive summary of the contributions of CRM-based archaeology to plantation studies). In essence, Otto gave marching orders to both CRM and academic archaeologists in the form of an explicit research design that extended beyond any particular site and invited intersite comparison. The response, which primarily took the form of comparisons and contrasts, proceeded with a vengeance. Over the years a vast number of CRM reports were produced, along with theses and dissertations that were directly influenced by South and Otto (Orser 1989). This work still reverberates, especially through the continued focus on archaeological and documentary manifestations of status differences (see Cabak and Groover 2006).

However, although it never disappeared, the investigation of class and status, and especially the pattern recognition methodology that Otto championed, eventually fell out of favor with a number of historical archaeologists. As Singleton notes, some rejected the use of the status concept in the study of plantation life because it did "not explain adequately the nature of master-slave social relations nor how this relationship operated and was responded to by those enslaved" (1995:128). Instead, for some researchers dominance and resistance would replace class and status as the focus of research. Others began to reject the notion of archaeology as a generalizing science altogether. In part this was due to the influence of a larger postmodern critique of anthropology, one that eschewed materialist, processual, empirical orientations in favor of an emphasis on subjectivity (Spiro 1996). Acceptance of postprocessualism (Shanks and Tilley 1987), the postmodern equivalent in archaeology, lagged behind cultural anthropology. But delayed or not, the rise of a postmodern perspective in historical archaeology in general and plantation studies in particular could not have gained a theoretical foothold without a certain amount of pattern recognition angst.

One of the unsettling realizations to gradually emerge in this retrenchment was that Otto's results were not being replicated by other researchers; it seemed that every site produced its own quantitative variation on the Cannon Point's theme (Orser 1989:28). One problem with the pattern recognition approach was that it did not specify range of variation parameters, i.e., how similar or different must a site's artifact frequency profiles have to be from another site's "Kitchen" or "Architectural" percentages to constitute a similar or a separate pattern. Many researchers erred on the side of splitting: soon there were any number of proposed patterns based on artifact frequency spikes at individual sites (Farnsworth 1993:116), and no grand synthesis to make sense of it all. The supreme irony of this atomization is that it began to look and sound like a kind of neo-Historical Particularism—exactly the opposite of what South had intended in his search for empirically-based generalizations about cultural evolution (South 1988).

Other chinks in the pattern recognition armor emerged as well. As disquiet over Otto's seemingly unique results continued to grow, his artifact patterns began to be considered as something of a conundrum, as sites that might be expected to show similar results did not. On another front Charles Orser took Otto (and Moore 1981, 1985) to task for simplifying the "exceedingly complex correlation among behavior, power, and material goods [that] existed on plantations" (1988:742). Similarly, Howson (1990) amplified this critique by suggesting that archaeologists needed to recognize that plantation artifact assemblages are imbedded in multiple contexts, requiring "a contextual description of material culture that is conscious of both plantation class relations and historical processes of culture change..." (p. 90). It didn't help that Otto's temporal controls were also criticized. George Miller's somewhat incendiary assessment (1991) on the misuse of a mainstay of historical archaeology— the mean ceramic date formula—was illustrated with examples from Cannon's Point. The larger and more disquieting questions that Miller indirectly raises concerning sampling adequacy at historic sites remain to this day mostly dormant and undisturbed in his article; J. W. Joseph was one of the few archaeologists to face this issue head-on in his thoughtful discussion of the problems and potential of applying South's approach to plantation sites (1989:57-60). In a resounding critique that is reproduced in this volume, Orser questioned the validity of South's pattern recognition approach on theoretical grounds, and flatly declared it to be static and incapable of detecting historical change in plantation artifact assemblages (1989:28). As an example: artifact profiles derived from a site that contained both a planter and then a subsequent slave occupation, as had occurred at the First Hermitage (Smith 1976), would ultimately produce artifact group ratios that were reflective of neither planter nor slave and therefore meaningless. (Today South's group-class-type analytical format is often retained as a classificatory device for presenting site artifact inventories, without reference to patterns.) Suffice it to say that by the mid-1980s, while still strongly influenced by the Southean pattern recognition methodology, numerous alternative approaches began to be developed for investigating plantation sites, and this expansion accelerated in the 1990s.

All the while, the early emphasis on slave living conditions persevered through the paradigmatic shifts in historical archaeology and remained as a consistent theme of plantation research. This is due in part to the fact that any excavation of a plantation's slave component is likely to yield such information, but it also stems from an enduring interest in this theme by archaeologists and the public (Singleton 1995:123). Housing (including landscape studies) and foodways remain the most commonly studied areas. Particularly intriguing has been the recognition (and significance) of African-related construction styles at slave sites, especially early earth-fast, clay-walled cabins that were replaced over time with brick, tabby, log, or frame construction (Drucker 1981; Wheaton et al. 1983; Kelso 1984; Jones 1985; Wheaton and Garrow 1985; Ferguson 1992; Thomas 1998), and the presence of indoor sub-floor pits for various possible functions (Kelso 1984; McKee 1992; Yentsch 1992; Kimmel 1993; Sanford 1994). To contextualize such discoveries required historical archaeology to expand beyond the confines of the United States to Africa and elsewhere, and a global, comparative, and synthetic perspective has developed that is still being robustly expressed through African diaspora archaeology (Fennell 2008).

The initial interest in plantation foodways has likewise remained strong. Early on it became apparent that wild resources must have been self-procured at slave sites and were synonymous with self-reliance (Ascher and Fairbanks 1971; Fair-banks 1974; Otto 1977; Gibbs et. al 1980). Besides simply indicating which wild animal species slaves procured, zooarchaeological remains also reflected availability and choice (Reitz et al. 1985), something that was also confirmed in slave narratives. Surprisingly, what was less clear was the association of faunal remains with plantation status differences (Reitz 1987; see also Bowen 1992). The notion that food is a social construct (McKee 1999) has directed the analysis of slave diets toward additional questions relating to identity, dominance, and resistance as expressed through foodways (Scott 2001)

The study of foodways also includes the material culture associated with the procurement, processing, storage, and serving of food. Ceramics are obviously part of this equation, and an interesting debate has emerged concerning slave production and use of colonoware pottery on southern plantations. This pottery dates primarily to the 17th through early 19th centuries and is most commonly found in the Carolinas and Virginia, with next to none from Georgia (Kelso 1979; Adams 1987; Ferguson 1992). In urban areas and rural areas that experienced heavy European influence, the forms are similar to English prototypes (Deetz 1988; Ferguson 1991). Originally referred to as "Colono-Indian Ware," this unglazed, hand-made pottery was first recognized at Colonial Williamsburg by Noël Hume (1962). He proposed that this ceramic type was Indian made and probably sold to slaves, accounting for their presence on plantation sites. Following a suggestion made by Stanley South, Leland Ferguson noticed that a significant number of these sherds were associated with slave communities that were unlikely to have had any interaction with historic Native American groups, and he ultimately concluded that in the Carolinas the vast majority of these ceramics were made by slaves (Ferguson 1978, 1992). Of course, this does not preclude Native American manufacture: there is a strong likelihood that colonoware, with regional variations in forms, temper, etc., was produced by Native Americans as well (Vernon 1988; Singleton and Bograd 2000), and Ferguson has outlined some of this variation (1992:36-37). Not only the origin of this ceramic ware but also what its presence at slave sites might signify has fueled considerable discussion about acculturation, creolization, spirituality, ethnicity, resistance and separatism, and dominance and control (Babson 1987, 1988; Ferguson 1992; Espenshade and Kennedy 2002). More recently, Laura Galke has argued that the occurrence of colonoware at six sites in 19th-century Manassas "was not an 'ethnic' marker denoting peoples of African descent, but rather a social marker that distinguished enslaved people from free" (2009:303). What is clear about the colonoware discussion is that it is far from over.

Cruising Altitude

Over the last two decades, the acceleration of plantation research has been manifest in both the frequency and multiplicity of approaches that has emerged. From an incipient concern with reconstructing lifeways to an examination of status and class, plantation archaeology has branched out to embrace issues of race (Babson 1990; Epperson 1990; Otto 1980; Joseph 1993; Orser 1998, 2003, 2007), ethnicity and cultural identity (Schuyler 1980; McGuire 1982; Babson 1990; Franklin and Fessler 1999; Orser 2001, 2007), power, resistance and negotiation (Orser 1988; Howson 1990; McKee 1992; Thomas 1998), and separatism, acculturation, and creolization (Ferguson 1992; see also the excellent thematic issue of *Historical Archaeology* edited by Shanon Lee Dawdy [2000]). The development of new perspectives and myriad research questions also allows reconsideration of the results of previous work to be carried out, adding a richer and deeper understanding about the "world the slaves made." At the same time, historical archaeologists are becoming more sensitive to the sociopolitical dimensions of engaging in research on plantation sites, and the intended and unintended use to which archaeological research is put. That sensitivity is reflected in several articles in this reader.

Singleton's speculations in 1990 and 1995 about future directions for plantation archaeology have largely come to pass, although the development of mid-range theory that she called for as necessary for exploring archaeological "questions that count" seems to have lagged behind other initiatives. The expansion of plantation archaeology to a global scale is certainly a step in the right direction, but only so far as comparative data generated from this expansion extends beyond the "just-so

story" level of analysis; establishing the occurrence of, say, a symbolically charged object without examining why it occurs, and whether there are definable contextual patterns of occurrence, is ultimately a sterile exercise. Bridging arguments should actually span the gulf between artifacts and assertions about artifact meaning and significance. Rather than simply noting similarities between Old World and New, archaeologists would do well to concentrate on one of their primary strengths, "the ability to draw inferences from artifacts that share strong temporal and spatial associations" (Heath 2009:4). Inferences that are (literally) grounded in this type of contextualization are simply stronger, more informative, and more credible than inferences that are ungrounded. It has also become clear that bridging arguments and research designs can be enhanced through increased involvement of and partnerships with African Americanists in plantation archaeology. Without such bridging arguments, and without greater inclusion of African American perspectives in archaeological research, the field is in danger of becoming "just another anthropological discourse of an Other" (Singleton 1995:135).

The rest of this book is devoted to archaeological research of and at plantations. The sections that follow relate to five general aspects of plantations, as revealed in articles published in *Historical Archaeology*: plantation landscapes (Part II), plantation architecture (Part III), social status and ethnicity (Part IV), African American lifeways (Part V), and plantation method and theory (Part VI). Astute readers will swiftly realize that the categories the articles appear under are fairly arbitrary, as many of these studies could obviously be placed in more than one section. The final choices were a matter of degree rather than kind.

Plantation Landscapes

The first group of articles is concerned with how space on plantations is used by planters and slaves. Dennis Pogue (1988) examines an early 18th century high-status plantation house site in Maryland that was occupied for a short time. Although the site was heavily plowed, the artifacts retained horizontal integrity, and the synchronic nature of the occupation allowed the researchers to successfully identify specific refuse disposal patterns for a variety of artifact classes. By distinguishing between primary and secondary refuse (Schiffer 1972), an understanding of the layout and functional use of the home site by its owners, if not its slaves, was convincingly revealed. James Delle provides a detailed comparison of how three Jamaican coffee plantations were organized, both pre- and post-emancipation, in order to demonstrate the spatial dynamics of class relations (1999). After a review of landscape studies in historical archaeology, he uses cartographic and archaeological data to describe the settlement structures of the slaves, overseers, and elites at each plantation, including access to and ownership of arable land and the "surveillance points" incorporated into overseer house locations and construction styles. Delle skillfully demonstrates that while "the landscapes of control were designed to maximize efficient production and exert subtle social controls over those forced to toil on Jamaican coffee estates, so too did these landscapes serve as arenas of resistance against these same oppressive social relations of production" (1999:151).

Barbara Heath and Amber Bennett focus on landscapes writ small (2000). In their article they analyze the yard areas of slave quarters, specifically a yard at the Poplar Forest Quarter Site in Virginia, but their insights extend far beyond any one site. By teasing out the multiple meanings that such yards represent, they explore a multiplicity of issues that include class dimensions, group identity and community, religious beliefs, work, and leisure. To do so they survey documentary, ethnographic, and archaeological sources from West Africa, the Caribbean, and the southern United States, and they embrace a multidisciplinary approach through the analysis of botanical and chemical samples from Poplar Forest. Where artifacts do not occur is imbued with as much significance as where they do occur: clean swept areas signify one kind of space, and midden areas denote a quite different meaning to the site's inhabitants. Heath and Bennett persuasively argue that it behooves archaeologists to anticipate and seek out the subtleties and clues that occur in "yardscapes."

Plantation Architecture

While there are only two articles making up

this section, they are both intriguing additions to the reader. In 1971, visual anthropologist Robert Ascher and historical archaeologist Charles Fairbanks produced a seminal anthropological study of a plantation site. "Excavation of a Slave Cabin: Georgia, USA" resonates on several levels. Orser (2007:16) describes this article as an early foray into interpretive archaeology that used multiple voices in the form of "soundtracks" to comment on the rather traditional presentation of archaeological remains from a slave site on Cumberland Island. Although an "archaeologists as storytellers" approach has certainly been explored since Ascher and Fairbanks' pioneering example (for instance, an entire volume of Historical Archaeology [Praetzellis and Praetzellis 1998] was devoted to this topic), perhaps no one except Leland Ferguson has been as successful at presenting an accessible and "scientifically humanistic" account, however brief, of slave life. A measure of this success is seen in the 1979 observation by Fairbanks (personal communication) that he had more requests from non-archaeologists for copies of this article than for any other publication in his entire career. On another level, the concern with slave living conditions in this article fits squarely into the descriptive/moral mission goals of plantation archaeology, as well as reflecting the enduring emphasis on slave housing. Details about architectural construction and materials are prominently reported for the Rayfield cabin, and are coupled with an ahead-of-their-time chemical analysis of soils to indicate how the structure was used over an extended period. At least in the soundtracks, if not in the archaeological descriptions, there is overt attention paid to the impact of racism (Orser 2007:16), which is yet another first for plantation archaeology.

Richard Kimmel's discussion of sub-floor pits at plantations (1993) provides a valuable cautionary tale concerning assumptions regarding "obvious" functions of archaeological features at slave sites. After a review of the literature in which he establishes the wide variety of form, function and chronological contexts for sub-floor pits, he concludes that the presence of such pits cannot provide prima facie evidence of either a storage function or ethnicity. He suggests that the original function of such pits must be identified before their cultural significance can be assessed, and this requires taxonomic, ethnographic, and taphonomic research.

Kimmel's suggestion still resonates—14 years later Patricia Samford (2007) combined ethnographic information related to West African and Igbo spiritual practices with the quantitative and qualitative archaeological data from three Virginia sites to propose symbolic and religious functions for sub-floor pits. The kind of contextualization advocated by both of these studies will no doubt produce a fuller understanding of such features in the future.

Social Status and Ethnicity on the Plantation

Lesley Drucker's analysis of the Spiers Landing Site in South Carolina, published in 1981, is an appropriate article to begin this section. Spiers Landing is a good example of what many archaeologists encounter at one time or another: a site with poor visibility and sparse or ambiguous documentary information on the identity of its inhabitants. It also illustrates the race-class problem that commonly confronts plantation researchers. The artifacts indicated a date range of 1780 to 1830, and based on the modest architectural data and a comparison of ceramic, floral, and faunal remains from contemporaneous sites, she concludes that the residents were low status; the presence of a high proportion of colonoware ceramics supported this assessment. But was it a slave cabin? Drucker carefully enumerates several test implications related to this question, and in so doing wrestles with "the archaeological tangibility of race and class as intertwined vectors of social inequality" (Orser 2007:48).

William Adams and Sarah Bowling (1989) concern themselves with economic status at three small plantation sites at King's Bay, Georgia. They begin by reviewing the documentary evidence related to planter relative status as reflected by land and slave ownership in the antebellum South, in Georgia, and the local region. They then analyze ceramics by type and ware and use Miller's CC Index (1980) to compare assemblages from the three sites. They were surprised to learn that porcelain percentages were higher for the slave than the planter components. They also found relatively more flatware in the slave middens, and to complete their trifecta of unexpected results, the CC Index results indicated that while planter assemblages exhibited a wider variety of vessel forms,

slaves often possessed more expensive ceramics than their masters. These results are interpreted to suggest that the slaves at King's Bay had "considerable" access to and participation in a market system, and that their self-provisioned ceramics may have functioned as internal status markers. In essence, Adams and Bowling are making an argument for a certain amount of slave cultural autonomy at King's Bay. Even so, Parker Potter (1991) produced a stinging postprocessual rejoinder to their article that faults the authors for inadequate self-reflection, and therefore failing to anticipate the social uses, good and harmful, to which their conclusions might be put. (Other researchers like Theresa Singleton, John Otto, and Elizabeth Reitz also share in the guilt of unreflective sin.) Notwithstanding that to suppose that an article published in *Historical Archaeology* might be distorted let alone read by skinheads presumes a great deal about skinhead polemics and their intellectual milieu(s), Potter does usefully highlight some of the sociopolitical dimensions of plantation research and the value and necessity of African American engagement. Interestingly, he never actually disagrees with any of Adams and Bowling's conclusions, but does suggest that native meanings of ceramic artifacts be added to CC Index comparisons. Adams and Bowling (and countless other plantation archaeologists) would no doubt agree, but such an addition is easier said than done.

Some of the issues raised by Potter are reflected in the next two articles. David Babson (1990) points out the vital importance of historical archaeology for correcting documentary biases and connecting present ethnic groups with their historical descendants. At the same time, he indicates potential problems in achieving these worthy goals. For instance, merely identifying an ethnic group archaeologically and then assuming equivalency with this group's descendants precludes an understanding of growth and change of identity through time. Instead, archaeologists should focus on dynamic and changing interactions rather than stopping at the level of static ethnic typologies. Babson provides an insightful discussion of the role of racism in defining ethnic groups, and of resistance of oppressed groups to the imposition of racism. He makes a convincing case for the need to recognize racism as a contextual element of any plantation study.

Like Babson, Terrence Epperson (1990) examines race and resistance by concentrating on how racial ideology was used to maintain discipline on plantations, and how physical and ideological forms of coercion were opposed by enslaved groups. He provides some horrendous documentary examples of plantation racism in action at two adjacent Virginia plantations, and also indicates the often subtle but impressive forms of slave resistance that are present in the documentary and archaeological records for these sites. Epperson is also concerned with disciplinary fragmentation in the study of slavery, and makes a compelling case for the need to resist interdisciplinary autonomy and fragmentation in plantation research.

The last two articles in this section are explicitly concerned with defining status, and both accomplish this goal by debunking myths and stereotypes about the antebellum South. Melanie Cabak and Mark Groover (2006) examine the planter component at the Bush Hill site near the Savannah River in South Carolina. As the title of the article implies, the site consisted of a working plantation rather than stereotypical columned estate, and the authors persuasively demonstrate the relative economic status of the planter family through an exhaustive and systematic analysis of census and probate sources. While the family was certainly affluent, the archaeological record reveals little in the way of luxury goods that might be expected at this site. At the same time, the family was aggressively connected to consumer markets, and what they lacked in quality, they made up in quantity. As with many of the other articles in this reader, Cabac and Groover emphasize the complexity inherent in archaeological interpretation, and provide a valuable caveat concerning one-to-one relationships between artifacts and status. Tanya Peres (2008) takes aim at an idealized Upland South model of foodways in her well-organized study of four contemporaneous sites in eastern Kentucky. She debunks the presumed universality of the model through a careful comparison of faunal assemblages representing three different social classes. Using multiple lines of evidence, Peres demonstrates that both impoverished slaves and middling farmers were faced with food insecurity. Whether due to low social status or simple isolation from markets and domestic livestock, these groups responded similarly by addressing the do-

mestic animal lacuna through a reliance on wild species, as quantifiable measures of species diversity clearly indicate. Peres also cautions against the use of "ethnic faunal indices" that conflate such variables as status, ethnicity, availability and access.

African American Lifeways on the Plantation

The three articles devoted to plantation lifeways seem at first glance to focus on narrow artifact studies, but in reality they reach well beyond a particularizing focus. Eric Klingelhofer (1987) advocates a comparative approach in the definition of "Africanisms." Excavations of a slave quarter in Maryland resulted in the identification of three distinct "elements of material culture" that seem to contrast with European and colonial traditions and are found at other Tidewater slave sites: incised decorations on metal spoons; modifications of glass bottles and gunflints into scraping tools; and objects of ceramic, glass and wood that were fashioned into similar polygonal shapes. The large size, careful shaping, and rare occurrence of these latter artifacts would seem to preclude their use as gaming pieces. Klingelhofer presents a plausible explanation of these three elements as a possible example of a creolization process. Concentrating on one of these elements, Laurie Wilkie (1996) analyzes glass tools knapped from bottles or jars that were associated with four African American components at a Louisiana plantation. Her detailed attribute analysis indicates how most of the tools were used as knives or scrapers, and she also carries out a review of the occurrence of similar tools at other African American sites, although most, like her sample, had postbellum associations. While she is not able to conclusively demonstrate such tools as distinctly African American, she sets the stage for doing so in the future, and she also raises the possibility that the production of these artifacts may have a gender dimension.

Reflecting the growth of interest in ideological systems, Aaron Russell (1997) carried out a study of artifacts from the Hermitage Plantation in Tennessee in terms of their relevance to slave religion, healing, and spirituality. Russell approaches this elusive topic through comparison of specific artifacts with data derived from documents, folklore, and the archaeological record at the Hermitage and elsewhere. Most notable at the Hermitage are the distinctive brass "fist charms" and bead assemblages that this site is well known for, and Russell argues that these items most likely indicate a limited degree of slave economic autonomy. Following Wilkie (1995), he emphasizes the value of these items in maintaining family and community stability in an inherently unstable and hostile social environment. Although no archaeological contexts could be equated with specific ritual behavior at the site, he does see in its overall artifact assemblage indications of a shared belief system that was separate and distinct from the dominant planter ideology. He ends with an excellent suggestion: that archaeologists move beyond the construction of "ideological genealogies" to an examination of the function that beliefs and practices served for enslaved African Americans.

Method and Theory in Plantation Archaeology

The final section on plantation theory contains five stimulating articles. As one of the most prolific researchers in plantation archaeology, Charles Orser is probably best known for his laser-like focus on issues involving race, ethnicity, and power and resistance. He has also invariably demonstrated a keen interest in the theory that drives the practice of historical archaeology. As indicated earlier, he found major theoretical problems with South's pattern recognition approach to plantation archaeology and that salvo, entitled "On Plantations and Patterns" (1989), is reprinted here. In it Orser characterizes pattern recognition methodology as inappropriate for historical archaeology because it is in essence a normative and by extension synchronic formulation of artifact patterns that is incapable of investigating historical change. At the theoretical level Orser argues that South's view of culture is an eclectic one that borrows willy-nilly from Kroeber, Steward, and Malinowski, and this seriously compromises his model of cultural evolution. A drawback of South's theoretical eclecticism is that it results in the definition of "whole culture" patterns that gloss over dynamic processes of class formation and social change. Orser ends with a plea for historical archaeologists to use the dual data base of documents and artifacts to create concepts and ideas that explain the changing nature of plantation relations over time.

A year later, Jean Howson published her critique of plantation archaeology (1990). Like Orser, she saw an obligation for historical archaeologists to emphasize diachronic change in their study of plantation sites, and she advocated that the most appropriate approach for them to take was to pay a good deal of attention to the structure of power relations and how power was maintained and contested. This would include a consideration of the relationship between material culture and ideology, for instance, how planters used material symbols to establish and maintain patriarchal order. Essential to this approach is contextual description that includes "how slaves' interpretations, reinterpretations, and contested interpretations of material things were worked out" (Howson 1990:90). J.W. Joseph's article (1993) also reflects an explicit concern with plantation social relations and their ideological manifestations. He reviews the archaeology of plantation ideology literature for Georgia and South Carolina in order to develop a theory of ideological classification that was originally grounded in racialization. Using documentary materials and archaeological evidence derived from artifacts, architecture, and settlement patterns, Joseph presents a hierarchical classification for the Low Country region that was predicated on the maintenance of plantation order, control and economic success. He then proposes that this race-based ideology shifted in the mid-18th century to one that emphasized labor specialization in the milieu of a strictly capitalist plantation system, and that this ideological change is reflected in the archaeological record. As Joseph explains (1993: 69), "With the shift to tidal rice agriculture, European-American planters stopped emphasizing the differences between Africans and Europeans, to the point that the material evidences of such cultural variation disappeared." While Orser (2007:23-24) criticizes this model for using a "whole-culture" interpretation and for minimizing "the effects of racialization as an enduring fact of plantation life," it does provide a thought-provoking explanation for the puzzling contraction of the material-culture gap between Low Country slave and planter sites over time.

Throughout this introduction, reference has been made to the sociopolitical aspects of plantation archaeology. The last two articles, by James

Gibb (1997) and Carol McDavid (1997), speak to some these aspects. Gibb reviews and affirms Potter's (1991) suggestions concerning reflexiveness, but then points out that however reflexive they may be, plantation studies residing in academic journals and CRM technical reports have a decidedly limited readership. While rigorous scholarship is certainly necessary for plantation studies, it is not sufficient. Since technical reports are often physically and intellectually inaccessible to nonprofessionals, Gibb makes a strong case for the need to transform plantation archaeology contributions into readable publications that are widely available to the public. To this end, Gibb offers two excellent suggestions: know your subject matter, and know your audience. He argues that archaeologists are part of more than just their professional communities, and that we have a responsibility to engage with the public by conveying what we have found, and learned. Since archaeologists have training and expertise that is recognized and acknowledged by the public, we are in a unique position to do so. Although he did not mention it in 1997, modern web access to both technical and nontechnical plantation literature only increases our opportunities and responsibilities for engagement.

It is appropriate to end the reader with a notable example of engagement that takes the form of archaeologists and local communities collaborating in the interpretation of the Levi Jordan plantation in Texas. Although proceeding from a critical theory approach (Leone et al. 1987), McDavid highlights the complex nature of an inclusive interpretation when it involves a variety of constituencies—including both black and white plantation descendants—that sometimes are at odds with each other. Successfully negotiating various family and personal agendas is not an easy thing and is bound to constrain some of the interpretive inclusiveness, as what is "telling the story" for one group is "rewriting history" for another; speaking truth to power can also be harmfully polarizing. McDavid provides a graphic example of this kind of potential conflict when she asks "How can one be 'multivocal' about a [slave] shackle?" (1997:126). There is no easy or simple answer to this question. Using interviews, community meetings, and informal encounters the author eventually was able to identify potential themes for the plantation exhibit(s), themes that were not imposed from on high by archaeologists but were generated by interactions with local residents. More than anything else, McDavid's article illustrates that plantation archaeology matters in the real world.

Vapor Trail

It needs to be emphasized that the articles included in this volume are only a sample of plantation studies available in *Historical Archaeology*. It is a sample that is hopefully representative of the kind of problems, data, interpretations, and issues that have consumed plantation archaeologists to date and that has inspired them to seek publication in the journal. It should also provide a fairly good sense of at least some of the future trajectories the field is likely to take.

References

ADAMS, WILLIAM H. (EDITOR)
1987 Historical Archaeology of Plantations at King's Bay, Camden County, Georgia. Reports of Investigations 5, Department of Anthropology, University of Florida, Gainesville.

ADAMS, WILLIAM H. AND SARAH J. BOLING
1989 Status and Ceramics for Planters and Slaves on Three Georgia Coastal Plantations. *Historical Archaeology* 23(1):69-96.

AGBE-DAVIES, ANNA S.
2007 Practicing African American Archaeology in the Atlantic World. In *Archaeology of Atlantic Africa and the African Diaspora*, edited by Akinuwumi Ogundiran and Toyin Falola, pp. 413-425. Indiana University Press, Bloomington.

ASCHER, ROBERT AND CHARLES H. FAIRBANKS
1971 Excavation of a Slave Cabin: Georgia, USA. *Historical Archaeology* 5:3-17.

BABSON, DAVID W.
1987 Plantation Ideology and the Archaeology of Racism: Evidence from the Tanner Road Site (38BK416), Berkeley County, South Carolina. *South Carolina Antiquities* 19(1&2):35-47.
1988 The Tanner Road Settlement: The Archaeology of Racism on Limerick Plantation. Volumes in Historical Archaeology IV, *Conference on Historic Sites Archaeology*. South Carolina Institute of Archaeology and Anthropology, University of South Carolina, Columbia.
1990 The Archaeology of Racism and Ethnicity on Southern Plantations. *Historical Archaeology* 24(4):20-28.

BOWEN, JOANNE
1992 Faunal Remains and New England Urban Household Subsistence. In *The Art and Mystery of Historical Archaeology: Essays in Honor of Jim Deetz*, Anne E. Yentsch and Mary Beaudry, editors, pp. 267-281. CRC Press, Boca Raton.

CABAK, MELANIE A. AND MARK D. GROOVER
2004 *Plantations Without Pillars: Archaeology, Wealth and Material Life at Bush Hill. Volume 1, Context and Interpretation*. Savannah River Archaeological Research Papers No. 11, Occasional Papers of the Savannah River Archaeological Research Program, South Carolina Institute of Archaeology and Anthropology, University of South Carolina, Columbia.

2006 Bush Hill: Material Life at a Working Plantation. *Historical Archaeology* 40(4):51-83.

DAWDY, SHANNON LEE (EDITOR)
2000 Creolization, Thematic Issue of *Historical Archaeology* 34(3).

DEAGAN, KATHLEEN
1982 Avenues of Inquiry in Historical Archaeology. *In Advances in Archaeological Method and Theory*, Volume 5, edited by Michael B. Schiffer, pp.151-177. Academic Press, New York.

DEETZ, JAMES
1977 *In Small Things Forgotten: An Archaeology of Early American Life*. Anchor Books, New York.
1988 American Historical Archaeology: Methods and Results. *Science* 239:362-367.

DELLE, JAMES A.
1999 The Landscapes of Class Negotiation on Coffee Plantations in the Blue Mountainsof Jamaica: 1790-1850. *Historical Archaeology* 33(1):136-158.

DRUCKER, LESLEY M.
1981 Patterning at an Undocumented Late 18th Century Lowcountry Site: Spiers Landing, South Carolina. *Historical Archaeology* 15(2):58-68.

EPPERSON, TERRENCE W.
1990 Race and the Discipline of the Plantation. *Historical Archaeology* 24(4):29-36.

ESPENSHADE, CHRISTOPHER T. AND
LINDA KENNEDY
2002 Recognizing Individual Potters in Nineteenth Century Colonoware. *North American Archaeologist* 23(3):209-240.

FAIRBANKS, CHARLES H.
1974 The Kingsley Slave Cabins in Duval County, Florida, 1968. *Conference on Historic Site Archaeology Papers* 7:62-93.
1984 The Plantation Archaeology of the Southeastern Coast. *Historical Archaeology* 18(1):1-14.

FARNSWORTH, PAUL
1993 "What Is the Use of Plantation Archaeology?" No Use at All, if No One Else Is Listening! *Historical Archaeology* 27(1):114-116.

FENNELL, CHRISTOPHER C. (COMPILER)
2008 *Perspectives From Historical Archaeology: African Diaspora Archaeology*. Society for His-

torical Archaeology.

FERGUSON, LELAND
1978 Looking for the "Afro-" in Colono-Indian Pottery. *Conference on Historic Sites Archaeology Papers* 12:68-86.
1991 Struggling With Pots in South Carolina. In *The Archaeology of Inequality*, edited by Randall H. McGuire and Robert Paynter, pp. 28-39.
1992 *Uncommon Ground: Archaeology and Colonial African America, 1650-1800*. Smithsonian Institution Press, Washington, DC.

FRANKLIN, MARIA AND GARRETT FESSLER (EDITORS)
1999 *Historical Archaeology, Identity Formation, and the Interpretation of Ethnicity*. Colonial Williamsburg Research Publications. Dietz Press, Richmond.

GALKE, LAURA J.
2009 Colonowhen, Colonowho, Colonowhere, Colonowhy: Exploring the Meaning Behind the Use of Colonoware Ceramics in Nineteenth-Century Manassas, Virginia. *International Journal of Historical Archaeology* 13(3):303-326.

GARROW, PATRICK AND THOMAS WHEATON, JR.
1989 Colonoware Ceramics: The Evidence from Yaughan and Curriboo Plantations. In Studies in South Carolina Archaeology: Essays in Honor of Robert L. Stephenson. *Anthropological Studies* No, 9:175-184. South Carolina Institute of Archaeology and Anthropology, University of South Carolina, Columbia.

GENOVESE, EUGENE D.
1974 *Roll, Jordan, Roll: The World the Slaves Made*. Vintage Books, New York.

GIBB, JAMES G.
1997 Necessary but Insufficient: Plantation Archaeology Reports and Community Action. *Historical Archaeology* 31(3):51-64.

GIBBS, TYSON K., KATHLEEN CARGILL, LESLIE SUE LIEBERMAN, AND ELIZABETH J. REITZ
1980 Nutrition in a Slave Population: An Anthropological Examination. *Medical Anthropology* 4(2):175-262.

HANDLER, JEROME S. AND FREDERICK W. LANGE
1978 *Plantation Slavery in Barbados: An Archaeological and Historical Investigation*. Harvard University Press, Cambridge.

HEATH, BARBARA
2009 Some Thoughts on Plantations: Comments on "Plantation Archaeology: Expanding Perspectives." Paper delivered at the Society for Historical Archaeology Annual Meetings, Toronto.

HEATH, BARBARA AND AMBER BENNETT
2000 "The little Spots allow'd them": The Archaeological Study of African-American Yards. *Historical Archaeology* 34(2):38-55.

HOWSON, JEAN
1990 Social Relations and Material Culture: A Critique of the Archaeology of Plantation Slavery. *Historical Archaeology* 24(4):78-91.

JONES, THOMAS L.
1985 The African American Tradition in Vernacular Architecture. In *The Archaeology of Slavery and Plantation Life*, edited by T. A. Singleton, pp. 195-213. Academic Press, Orlando.

JOSEPH, J. W.
1989 Pattern and Process in the Plantation Archaeology of the Lowcountry of Georgia and South Carolina. *Historical Archaeology* 23(1):55-68.
1993 White Columns and Black Hands: Class and Classification in the Plantation Ideology of the Georgia and South Carolina Lowcountry. *Historical Archaeology* 27(3):57-73.
2004 Resistance and Compliance: CRM and the Archaeology of the African Diaspora. Historical Archaeology 38(1):18-31.

KELSO, WILLIAM M.
1979 *Captain Jones's Wormslow: A Historical, Archaeological, and Architectural Study of an Eighteenth Century Plantation Near Savannah, Georgia*. University of Georgia Press, Athens.
1984 *Kingsmill Plantations, 1619-1800*. Academic Press, New York.

KIMMEL, RICHARD H.
1993 Notes on the Cultural Origins and Functions of Sub-Floor Pits. *Historical Archaeology* 27(3):102-13.

KLINGELHOFER, ERIC
1987 Aspects of Early Afro-American Material Culture: Artifacts from the Slave Quarters at Garrison Plantation, Maryland. *Historical Archaeology* 21(2):112-119.

LEONE, MARK P., PARKER POTTER, JR.,
AND PAUL A. SHACKEL
1987 Toward a Critical Archaeology. *Current Anthropology* 28(3):283-302.

MCDAVID, CAROL
1997 Descendants, Decisions, and Power: The Public Interpretation of the Archaeology of the Levi Jordan Plantation. *Historical Archaeology* 31(3):114-131.

MCGUIRE, RANDALL H.
1982 The Study of Ethnicity in Historical Archaeology. *Journal of Anthropological Archaeology* 1:159-178.

MCKEE, LARRY W.
1992 The Ideals and Realities Behind the Design and Use of 19th Century Virginia Slave Cabins. In *The Art and Mystery of Historical Archaeology: Essays in Honor of Jim Deetz*, Anne E. Yentsch and Mary Beaudry, editors, pp. 195-213. CRC Press, Boca Raton.
1999 Food Supply and Plantation Social Order: An Archaeological Perspective. In *"I, Too am America": Archaeological Studies of African-American Life*, edited by Theresa A. Singleton, pp. 218-239. University of Virginia Press, Charlottesville.

MILLER, GEORGE L.
1980 Classification and Economic Scaling of 19th Century Ceramics. *Historical Archaeology* 14:1-41.
1991 Thoughts Towards A User's Guide to Ceramic Assemblages, Part I: Lumping Sites into Mega-assemblages by Those That Cannot Tell Time. *Council for Northeast Historical Archaeology Newsletter*, No. 18:2-5.

MOORE, SUE
1981 *An Antebellum Barrier Island Plantation: In Search of an Archaeological Pattern*. Ph.D. dissertation, University of Florida. University Microfilms, Ann Arbor.
1985 Social and Economic Status on the Coastal Plantation: An Archaeological Perspective. In *The Archaeology of Slavery and Plantation Life*, edited by T. A. Singleton, pp. 141-160. Academic Press, Orlando.

MULLINS, PAUL R.
2008 Excavating America's Metaphor: Race, Diaspora, and Vindicationist Archaeologies. *Historical Archaeology* 42(2):104-122.

NOEL HUME, IVOR
1962 An Indian Ware of the Colonial Period. Archaeological Society of Virginia, *Quarterly Bulletin* 17:1-14.
1964 Archaeology: Handmaiden to History. *The North Carolina Historical Review* 41(2):215-225.

ORSER, CHARLES
1984 The Past Ten Years of Plantation Archaeology in the Southeastern United States. *Southeastern Archaeology* 3(1):1-12.
1988 The Archaeological Analysis of Plantation Society: Replacing Status and Caste With Economics and Power. *American Antiquity* 53(4):735-751.
1989 On Plantations and Patterns. *Historical Archaeology* 23(2):28-40.
2001 *Race and the Archaeology of Identity*. University of Utah Press, Salt Lake City.
2003 *Race and Practice in Archaeological Interpretation*. University of Pennsylvania Press, Philadelphia.
2007 *The Archaeology of Race and Racialization in Historic America*. University Press of Florida, Gainesville.

OTTO, JOHN S.
1975 *Status Differences and the Archaeological Record: A Comparison of Planter, Overseer, and Slave Sites from Cannon's Point Plantation (1794-1861), St. Simons Island, Georgia*. Ph.D. dissertation, University of Florida. University Microfilms, Ann Arbor.
1977 Artifacts and Status Differences: A Comparison of Ceramics from Planter, Overseer, and Slave Sites on an Antebellum Plantation. In Research Strategies In *Historical Archaeology*, edited by Stanley South, pp. 91-118. Academic Press, New York.
1980 Race and Class on Antebellum Plantations. In *Archaeological Perspectives on Ethnicity in America: Afro-American and Asian-American Culture History*, edited by Robert Schulyer, pp. 3-13. Baywood, Farmingdale, New York.
1984 *Cannon's Point Plantation, 1794-1860 Living Conditions and Status Patterns In the Old South*. Academic Press, Orlando.

PERES, TANYA
2008 Foodways, Economic Status, and the Antebellum Upland South in Central Kentucky. *Historical Archaeology* (4):88-104.

POTTER, PARKER, JR.
1991 What Is the Use of Plantation Archaeology? *Historical Archaeology* 25(3):94-107.

POGUE, DENNIS J.
1988 Spatial Analysis of the King's Reach Plantation Homelot, Ca. 1690-1715. *Historical Archaeology* 22(2):40-56

PRAETZELLIS, ADRIAN
AND MARY PRAETZELLIS (EDITORS)
1998 Archaeologists as Storytellers, Thematic Issue of *Historical Archaeology* 32(1).

RIETZ, ELIZABETH J.
1987 Vertebrate Fauna and Socioeconomic Status. In *Consumer Choice in Historical Archaeology*, edited by Suzanne M. Spencer-Wood, pp. 101-119.

REITZ, ELIZABETH J., TYSON K. GIBBS
AND TED A. RATHBUN
1985 Archaeological Evidence for Subsistence on Coastal Plantations. In *The Archaeology of Slavery and Plantation Life*, edited by Theresa A. Singleton, pp. 163-191. Academic Press, New York.

RUSSELL, AARON E.
1997 Material Culture and African-American Spirituality at the Hermitage. *Historical Archaeology* 31(2):63-80.

SAMFORD, PATRICIA
2007 *Subfloor Pits and the Archaeology of Slavery in Colonial Virginia*. University of Alabama Press, Tuscaloosa.

SANFORD DOUGLAS
1994 The Archaeology of Plantation Slavery in Piedmont Virginia. In *Historical Archaeology of the Chesapeake*, edited by Paul A. Shackel and Barbara J. Little, pp. 115-30. Smithsonian Institution Press, Washington, DC.

SCHIFFER, MICHAEL
1972 Archaeological Context and Systematic Context. *American Antiquity* 37:156-165.

SCHUYLER, ROBERT (EDITOR)
1980 *Archaeological Perspectives on Ethnicity in America: Afro-American and Asian American Culture History*. Baywood, Farmingdale, NY.

SCOTT, ELIZABETH A.
2001 Food and Social Relations at Nina Plantation. *American Anthropologist* 103(3): 671-691.

SHANKS, MICHAEL AND CHRISTOPHER TILLEY
1987 *Re-Constructing Archaeology: Theory and Practice*. Routledge, London.

SINGLETON, THERESA A.
1990 The Archaeology of the Plantation South: A Review of Approaches and Goals. *Historical Archaeology* 24(4):70-77.
1995 The Archaeology of Slavery in North America. *Annual Review of Anthropology* 24:119-140.
1999 An Introduction to African-American Archaeology. In *"I, Too am America": Archaeological studies of African-American Life*, edited by Theresa A. Singleton, pp. 1-17. University of Virginia Press, Charlottesville.

SINGLETON, THERESA A. AND MARK BOGRAD
2000 Breaking Typological Barriers: Looking for the Colono in Colonoware. In *Lines That Divide: Historical Archaeologies of Race, Class, and Gender*, edited by James A. Delle, Stephen Mrozowski and Robert Paynter, pp.3-21. University of Tennessee Press, Knoxville.

SMITH, SAMUEL D. (EDITOR)
1976 *An Archaeological and Historical Assessment of the First Hermitage*. Division of Archaeology, Tennessee Department of Conservation/Ladies Hermitage Association, Nashville.

SOUTH, STANLEY
1972 Evolution and Horizon as Revealed in Ceramic Analysis in Historical Archaeology. *Conference on Historic Site Archaeology Papers* 6:71-116.
1977 *Method and Theory in Historical Archaeology*. Academic Press, New York.
1988 Whither Pattern? *Historical Archaeology* 22(1):25-28.

SPIRO, MELFORD E.
1996 Postmodernist Anthropology, Subjectivity, and Science: A Modernist Critique. *Comparative Studies in Society and History* 38(4):759-780.

THOMAS, BRIAN W.
1998 Power and Community: The Archaeology of Slavery at the Hermitage Plantation. *American Antiquity* 63(4):531-555.

VERNON, RICHARD
1988 17th Century Apalachee Colono-Ware as a Reflection of Demography, Economics, and Acculturation. *Historical Archaeology* 22(1):76-82.

WHEATON, THOMAS JR., AMY FRIEDLANDER,
AND PATRICK GARROW

1983 *Yaughan and Curriboo Plantations: Studies in Afro-American Archaeology*. Atlanta, GA: Archeological. Services Branch, National Park Service.

WHEATON, THOMAS JR. AND PATRICK GARROW

1983 Acculturation and the Archaeological Record in the Carolina Lowcountry. In *The Archaeology of Slavery and Plantation Life*, edited by Theresa Singleton, pp. 239-259. Academic Press, New York.

WILKIE, LAURIE A.

1995 Magic and Empowerment On the Plantation: An Archaeological Consideration of African-American World View. *Southeastern Archaeology* 14(2): 136-148.

1996 Glass-Knapping at a Louisiana Plantation: African-American Tools? *Historical Archaeology* 30(4):37-49.

YENTSCH, ANNE E.

1992 Gudgeons, Mullet, and Proud Pigs: Historicity, Black Fishermen, and Southern Myth. In *The Art and Mystery of Historical Archaeology: Essays in Honor of Jim Deetz*, Anne E. Yentsch and Mary Beaudry, editors, pp. 238-314. CRC Press, Boca Raton.

NICHOLAS HONERKAMP
DEPARTMENT OF SOCIOLOGY, ANTHROPOLOGY,
AND GEOGRAPHY
615 MCCALLIE AVENUE
UNIVERSITY OF TENNESSEE AT CHATTANOOGA
CHATTANOOGA, TN 37403

DENNIS J. POGUE

Spatial Analysis of the King's Reach Plantation Homelot, Ca. 1690–1715

ABSTRACT

This paper considers the spatial arrangement and utilization of the King's Reach plantation homelot (ca. 1690–1715). The primary analytical tool is the interpretation of distributional patterns of plowzone-derived artifacts. The pipe stem distributions have proven to be especially effective in identifying diachronic shifts in refuse disposal. The ceramics, glass, and other materials are not particularly indicative of temporal change, but do provide evidence for functional differentiation. Those patterns point to a typically located and oriented plantation house and quarter, with extensive refuse middens nearby. However, the King's Reach homelot appears unusual in that other outbuildings, almost always found at such sites, have not been discovered. Their absence may be at least partially explained by the presence of a possible outlying quarter and/or workhouse located nearby. An unusual number of cellars were located below the plantation house floor, apparently a result of successive replacement due to collapsing cellar walls.

Introduction

Over the last decade, the spatial arrangement and uses of the plantation homelot has become an increasingly popular field of inquiry. This is especially true for the 17th century Chesapeake, where society was overwhelmingly plantation oriented and, therefore, the plantation household and its associated homelot are primary subjects of study. In addition, since no 17th century plantation complexes, and virtually no 17th century structures of any kind, survive above ground in the region, their study is particularly appropriate for archaeological investigation. The King's Reach site (18 Cv 83), a homelot complex dating to the ca. 1690–1715 period, will be examined below primarily through analysis of patterns in plowzone-derived artifact distributions. Those results will be compared with similar studies of other Chesapeake sites.

The Site

During 1984 and 1985, the Maryland Historical Trust/Jefferson Patterson Park and Museum conducted excavations at the King's Reach Site. The site is located at the Jefferson Patterson Park and Museum, in lower Calvert County, Maryland (Figure 1), in an agricultural field approximately 450 feet from the Patuxent River. The King's Reach Site, along with 35 others, some dating from as early as 9000 years BP, was discovered during a preliminary survey of the 512-acre property undertaken in 1981 (Clark and Smolek 1981). Systematic surface collection of artifacts from the plowed field surface in a 50-by-60-meter area in 1984 allowed more detailed delineation of site boundaries and served as the basis for selecting areas in which to begin excavation. A total of 144 2-by-2-meter square quadrats were then excavated over the ensuing two summers' field work, with 116 of those concentrated in the site core and the remaining 28 systematically distributed in the outlying zone (Figure 2). The plowed stratum of each square was hand-screened through 3/8-inch hardware cloth for uniform artifact retention.

The plantation core was completely exposed, revealing remains of a relatively large post-supported frame dwelling measuring 30-by-30 feet and a smaller 20-by-10-foot quarter with a connecting fenced foreyard (Figure 3). The combination of the architectural and artifact evidence suggests a wealthy household. Based on inventory data, Main (1982:152) indicates that in Maryland for the period 1660–1719 those households with an average of five rooms in the main house ranked in the 70–79th percentile according to wealth. The King's Reach main house had at least five rooms and could well have had more. Preliminary artifact analysis supports that finding, with an assemblage including numerous brass and pewter objects, fine table glass, and matched ceramics. All evidence points to a short-term occupation, dating to the ca. 1690–1715 period. Unfortunately, no documentary data pertaining to the site has survived, largely due to a series of courthouse fires that destroyed most of the county's early land records.

The upper strata of the King's Reach Site have

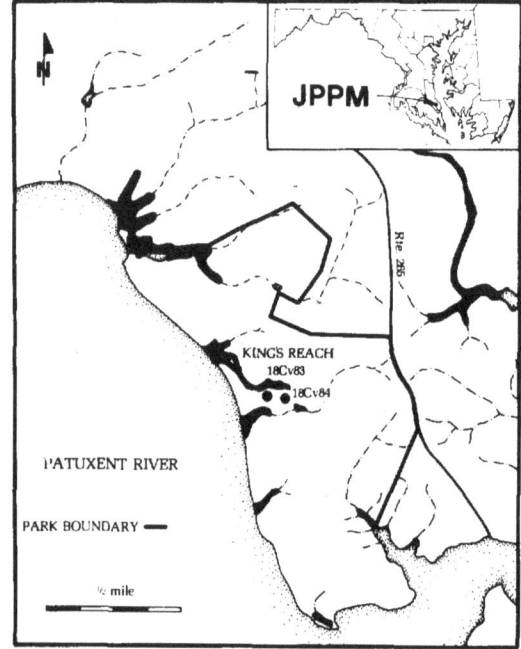

FIGURE 1. King's Reach Site location.

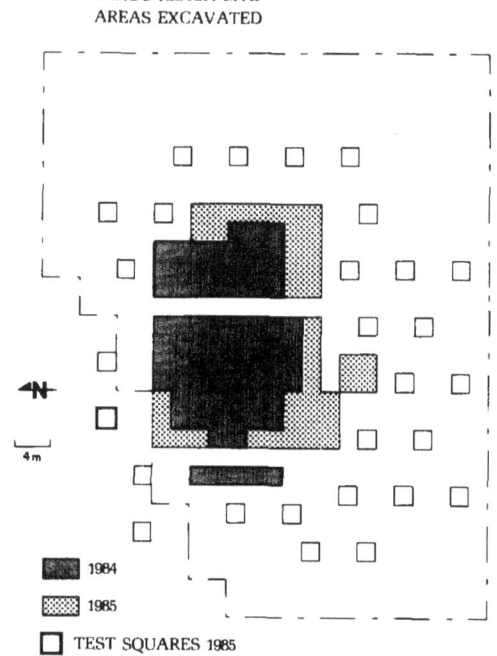

FIGURE 2. King's Reach Site, areas excavated.

been extensively disturbed by almost continuous plowing over the last 300 years. Despite this fact, analysis of the distributions of the artifacts recovered from plowzone is a particularly important tool. Without such evidence, the site interpretation would be dependent on the analysis of the surviving portions of subsurface features alone, which provide only limited data pertaining to homelot use. The distributional analysis is based on the finding that while vertical relationships are destroyed by plowing, the horizontal distributions of plowzone artifacts remain generally intact (Lewarch and O'Brien 1981). Each of the previous studies of households and their homelots that will be referred to below are based on similar analyses of plowzone-derived artifacts. The most comparable of these are the St. John's Site in St. Mary's City, Maryland (Keeler 1978) and The Clifts Plantation in Virginia (Neiman 1980). The Van Sweringen (King and Miller 1984) and Village Center (Miller 1983 and 1986) Sites in St. Mary's City also provide important comparative data. In

each instance broad diachronic trends as well as sometimes extremely minute indications of intra-site spatial patterns were identified.

Unlike most of the other sites mentioned above, however, King's Reach likely was inhabited for no more than a generation. Therefore, King's Reach provides a rare opportunity to interpret synchronic intrasite distributional patterns. In addition, the unusual existence of at least 10 major subsurface features provides an opportunity to examine the correlation of these features with the distribution patterns, and to study the nature and manifestations of the processes of intrasite refuse disposal.

Based on comparison of King's Reach evidence with the results of previous archaeological and documentary research (cf., Carson et al. 1981, Main 1982), the structural spaces have been interpreted as consisting of a main house with a hall-parlor plan and two attached sheds, and a one-room quarter (Figures 3 and 4). The main house was heated by a single fireplace, probably with a brick hearth and fireback, and a flame hood and an interior

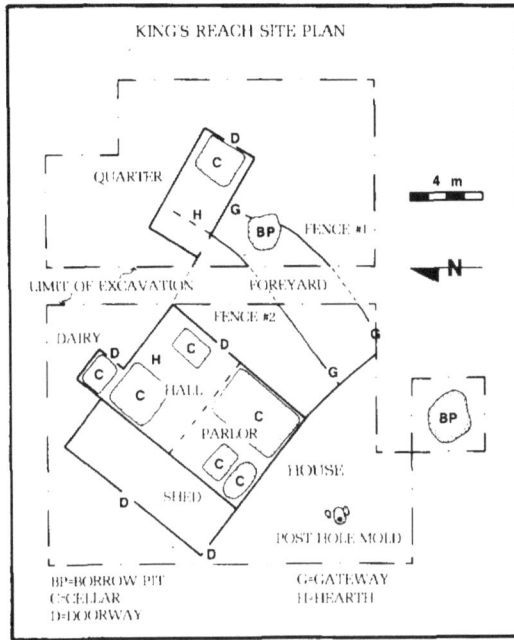

FIGURE 3. King's Reach Site plan.

"Welsh," or mud-and-stud, chimney. The heated room served as the hall or kitchen, partitioned from the parlor or chamber, that may have been further divided into two smaller rooms. A shed, which may also have been partitioned, extended all along the rear and a loft occupied the space over the hall-parlor. A small shed attached to the hall gable probably served as a milkhouse, or dairy, used mainly to store dairy products in a shallow, wood-lined pit. It also may have served as a general storage "closet."

Based on studies of probate inventory evidence from the period (cf., Main 1982), the hall served as the focus of household activity and where food was prepared. The shed probably accommodated a variety of household chores and provided additional sleeping and storage room. The parlor served mainly for dining and sleeping. The loft was used for sleeping and probably for storage. Structural evidence in the form of door posts exists for two doorways in the main house: in the east wall of the long axis entering into the hall and in the corner of the south gable entering into the shed.

The quarter apparently consisted of a single heated room, with a cellar below, and with two doorways. One doorway was located within five feet of the corner nearest the main house and opening onto the foreyard. Evidence for it consists of a slight discoloring of subsoil, apparently caused by foot traffic; the placement of the second foreyard fence also supports that location, as no other would allow direct access to the main house via the foreyard. The second doorway was centered in the east gable. Two posts apparently supporting a porch serve as the direct evidence for its existence. A ditch running parallel to the gable and north wall may have served to channel water run-off from upslope (Figure 4); the posts intrude the ditch, suggesting that the door there may be a later addition. A chimneyless hearth was situated in the west end of the building (Figure 3). The quarter's single room would have served all three major household functions—sleeping, cooking, and general household chores—for the servants and/or slaves residing there. A cellar below probably served a general storage function.

One remarkable feature of the main house is the existence of at least six cellars below the structure. Such a quantity of cellars is unusual, with the only comparable examples being associated with slave sites in Virginia (Kelso 1984:105–128). Excavation has supplied a plausible explanation, however. Two of the six appear to have served specialized functions: a root cellar in front of the hearth, where the radiant heat would help keep root vegetables from freezing, and the attached dairy cooling pit. Root cellars situated in the same position relative to hearths are well known (Kelso 1984:106). Apparently this one proved unsatisfactory, however, as the cellar was found to have been used as a dump for hearth ashes and other household refuse. At least three of the four remaining cellars appear to be successive generations serving the same general storage function. Upon excavation, each was found to have suffered from collapsed walls, apparently necessitating their being replaced in turn. The largest of the three seems to have been the earliest, with the later two dug under the floor boards and fitted neatly between five-foot-spaced floor joists. Therefore, the un-

FIGURE 4. King's Reach plantation interpretive drawing, viewed from the east (Scheirer after Hoang and Stone).

usual number of cellars apparently reflects a difficulty in constructing cellars with stable walls.

Surface collecting the area previously identified as comprising the site revealed a marked artifact concentration. The following distribution maps of plowzone-derived materials serve to reinforce and amplify the surface data. An extensive midden is indicated off the rear of the house that did not show up previously, however, due to its being in the unplowed field margin and, therefore, uncollectable. These maps were created using a three-dimensional spline as the interpolation algorithm, with contour intervals reflecting percentiles of the frequency distribution of artifact counts (Tukey 1977). The maps showing distributions of pipes and ceramics have contour lines at the median and

upper one-quarter and one-eighth quantiles; for the remainder, contours are at the upper one-quarter, one-eighth, and one-sixteenth. The centers of each of the 144 2-by-2-meter units serve as data points.

Refuse Disposal Processes

On domestic sites of the 17th and early 18th centuries, refuse disposal has been identified as primarily occurring in extensive surface middens. These middens generally are located in close proximity to living spaces and adjacent to doorways that served as avenues of disposal (cf., Keeler 1978). Therefore, for the most part, these middens are not primary deposits as defined by Schiffer (1972) and,

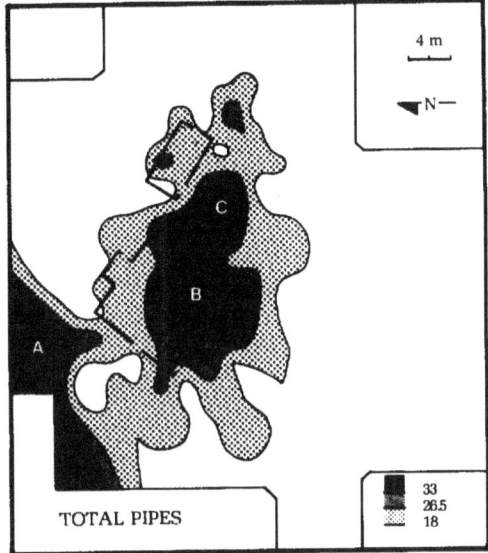

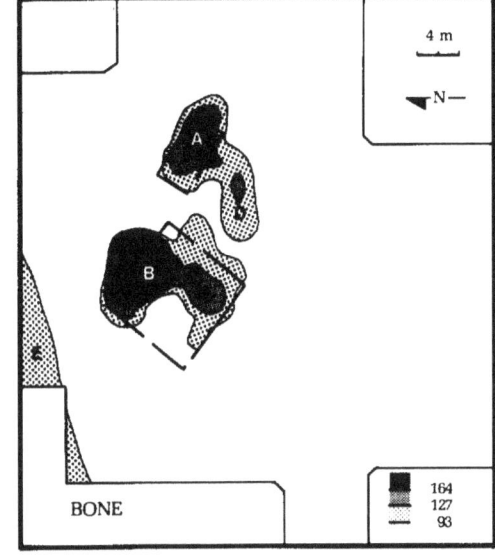

FIGURE 5. Distribution of total measurable pipe stems.

FIGURE 6. Distribution of bone, by weight.

instead, reflect deposition and redeposition from activities occurring elsewhere. Given such a process, and combined with the hurly burly of the myriad homelot activities and the traffic of both people and animals, mixing of debris from separate functional areas must be expected. Of secondary importance for everyday refuse disposal were subsurface features, often dug for a specific purpose such as a borrow pit or storage cellar. After ceasing in their original functions, they usually were filled with domestic and other refuse via a combination of purposeful and natural deposition. This is the pattern that occurs at King's Reach as well.

The distribution of total measurable pipe stems serves to demonstrate the general patterns of artifact distribution at the site (Figure 5). Three major concentrations occur: to the rear of the main house (5a), centering on the house and extending to the south (5b), and between the house and quarter (5c). Based on the succeeding analyses, the rear concentration and that between the house and quarter appear to be extensive sheet middens. The concentration located within the house clearly is not, however, and its

existence is unusual. At sites where similar distributional analyses have been conducted (cf., Keeler 1978, Neiman 1980, Miller 1983 and 1986, King and Miller 1984), the interior of dwellings generally have been found to be areas of low artifact density. The high density within the King's Reach house seems to stem from the existence of the numerous large subsurface features located there. This situation complicates the distributional analyses to follow, but by separating and plotting pipe stems according to bore size and other artifacts by type, more meaningful patterns are discernible.

The distributions of bone, brick, and nails also serve to demonstrate the impact on spatial patterns caused by the various site formation processes at work. Bone is a fragile material that is particularly vulnerable to deterioration due to weathering and, especially, due to plowing. In Figure 6, three major concentrations of bone are apparent, all of which are directly associated with major subsurface features that have yielded great quantities of faunal remains—the quarter cellar (6a), the dairy and hall cellars (6b), and the earliest parlor cellar

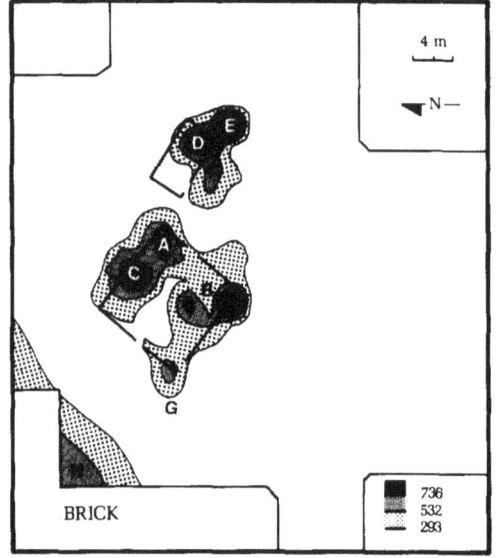

FIGURE 7. Distribution of brick, by weight.

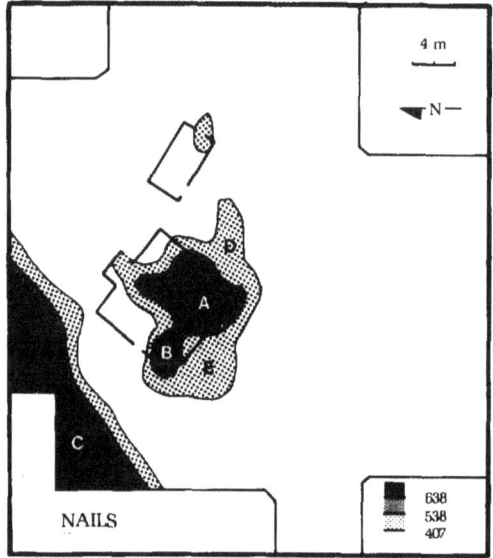

FIGURE 8. Distribution of nails, by weight.

(6c). The fore and back yard surface middens, that show up as major concentrations for more durable types of artifacts, are indicated by smaller concentrations of bone (6d,e). Therefore, in this instance the bone concentrations in plowzone seem to signify the locations of bone-bearing features more than an accurate indication of where food remains had been deposited during the site's occupation.

Brick distributions also seem to be markedly affected by the presence of subsurface features. A concentration of brick occurs in the hall where a brick fireplace base was located (Figure 7a). However, even larger concentrations are located in the parlor (7b), in front of the dairy (7c), in the quarter (7d), and off the quarter's east gable (7e). Three of those concentrations (7b,c,d) are situated directly over major subsurface features, each of which yielded substantial amounts of brick and mortar rubble when excavated. Only the major concentration east of the quarter and two more limited concentrations south of the quarter (7f) and adjacent to the shed (7g), and the rear midden (7h), do not appear directly associated with such features.

Three of those concentrations are located near known or suspected doorways (7e,f,g), however, and may stem from dumping of brick waste generated from periodic fireplace renovations. The rear midden (7h) also apparently served as a dump for renovation refuse.

Nails exhibit a much more focused distribution associated with the house. In this case, some of the cellars under the structure appear to be the main source (Figure 8a). A smaller but substantial concentration also occurs in the corner of the shed (8b), as well as in the rear midden (8c), in the foreyard (8d), and off the south gable (8e). The shed concentration may stem from a carpentry function carried out there; the others appear to reflect surface dumping of refuse.

As doorways and gates served as prominent avenues for refuse disposal, identification of their locations is a necessity in gaining a more precise understanding of disposal patterns at the site. The distribution of gun flint debitage has been identified as particularly indicative of doorway locations (Keeler 1978). Apparently, doorways were pre-

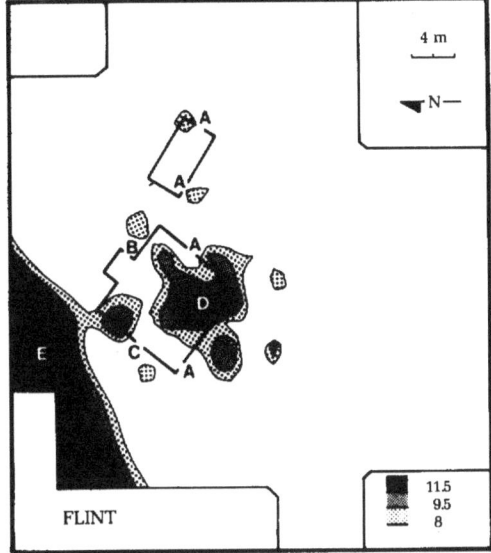

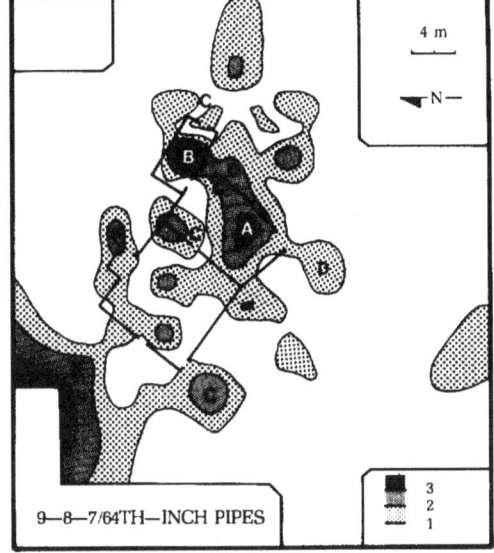

FIGURE 9. Distribution of flint.   FIGURE 10. Distribution of 9-8-7/64th-inch pipe stems.

ferred locations for periodic flint knapping, resulting in concentrations of debitage nearby. At King's Reach, concentrations of flint occur adjacent to all four of the doorways for which other archaeological evidence exists (Figure 9a), and also suggest at least two additional doorways. These are located in the main house hall gable, very likely in the dairy (9b), and in the shed's west wall (9c). As usual, major concentrations also occur within the house and in the rear midden (9d,e).

Pipe Stem Distributions

A total of 2706 measurable pipe stems were recovered from plowzone. These pipes have been plotted according to bore diameter in an attempt to identify diachronic shifts in artifact disposal patterns. Tobacco pipes have been shown to be one of the most sensitive temporal indicators available, and also occur in sufficient quantity to identify midden locations (cf., Keeler 1978, Neiman 1980, Miller 1983 and 1986, King and Miller 1984). The pipe stem distributions serve to reinforce the six

doorway locations described above, as well as several gateways in the foreyard fences. In addition, they also indicate that the foreyard was reduced in size and suggest that the main house and quarter were virtually contemporaneous in construction.

The 9, 8, and 7/64th-inch pipes have been combined, due to the low number of pipes involved (N = 126). Even with such a small sample, however, the distribution of these early pipes serves to reinforce the general patterns revealed by other data. The most significant evidence is for the temporal relationship of the two foreyard fencelines. The concentration of pipes west of the fenceline shown in Figure 10a suggests that it is the earlier of the two, with refuse dumped within the foreyard during the period represented by these pipes. The concentrations of early pipes in association with the shed, dairy, and quarter also support the assessment, based on in-ground structural evidence, that the main house and quarter were contemporaneous in construction. A concentration within the quarter (10b) also suggests that it was used as a domestic space early on.

The early pipe distributions offer additional

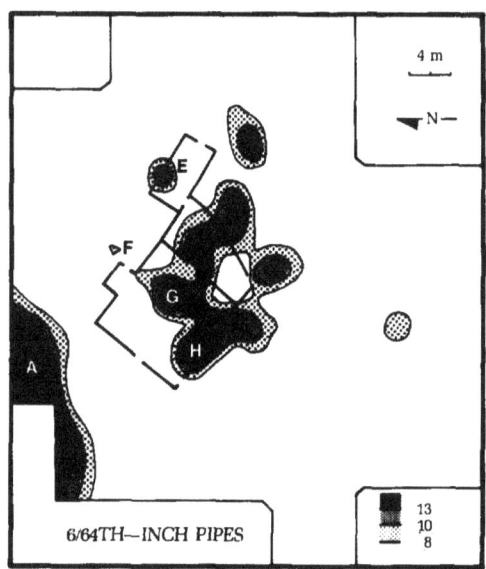

FIGURE 11. Distribution of 6/64th-inch pipe stems.

support for the presence of three of the four doorways for which other evidence also exists—in the quarter front and the main house front door and gable shed door—as concentrations of pipes are located near all three doorways (10c). A concentration also occurs east of the quarter gable door, but based on other data, that doorway may be a somewhat later addition. They also support the presence of the two gates in the fence, which are indicated by structural evidence, as both gates also have nearby pipe concentrations (10d). Finally, the major midden to the rear of the house (10e) suggests the second doorway located in the shed and the concentration adjacent to the attached dairy (10f) suggests a doorway there.

The distribution of 6/64th-inch pipes (N = 765) again reveals the major middens both to the rear and in front of the main house (Figure 11a,b). However, the foreyard midden exhibits a significantly altered shape, with the major concentration outside the second fenceline and directly in line with the front door. The concentration over the fenceline supports the interpretation that this fence

is the second of the two. Concentrations also are located just outside the later gateway (11c) and near the quarter gable door (11d) and inside the quarter (11e). A slight concentration also occurs adjacent to the dairy (11f).

Additional support for the truncation of the foreyard early on is provided by the evidence from a trash-filled pit that intrudes the earlier fence paling ditch. The fill of the pit overwhelmingly consisted of oyster shells, but with domestic materials thoroughly intermixed. Given the extremely irregular shape of the pit itself, and the presence of shovel scars in its sides and bottom, it appears to have served initially as a borrow pit, commonly found on sites with mud-and-stud chimneys that required repair every few years. The lack of strata within the pit suggests that it was quickly filled with the remnants of one or more major oyster feasts. The tobacco pipes recovered support both an early and quick deposition, with 11.9% of the 109 measurable bores 7/64th-inch in diameter, 83.4% 6/64th-inch, and only 4.5% 5/64th-inch. Although the number of pipes is too small to yield a trustworthy result, the Binford (1962) mean date is 1699.5, very close to the year that might be otherwise expected.

A second major difference between the distributions of the early and middle period pipes is the later existence of two major concentrations within the main house. One of those concentrations (11g) may represent primary deposition within the hall sifting through the wooden floor, but the other apparently stems from a subsurface cellar feature located there (11h). What is at least initially puzzling is this cellar's correlation with pipes of the middle period, as it is believed to have been filled at the end of the site's occupation.

The feature's upper stratum includes great quantities of nails and plaster and mortar and brick rubble, suggesting destruction fill. Other artifacts support a late period of deposition as well as a possible catastrophic end for the house. Several virtually complete items were recovered—a padlock, pewter spoon, and tobacco pipe with an "IE" mark, possibly that of Isaac Evans, a Bristol maker operating from 1698 to at least 1701 and probably later (Walker 1977 II(C):1426–27). That pipe and 79.4% of the 39 measurable bores recovered have a 4 or 5/64th-inch diameter, with only 20.5% 6 or 7/64th-inch. Other dating evidence is provided by an "RT"-marked bowl, probably the second Robert Tippett, making pipes from circa 1678 to 1713 (Walker 1977 II(C):1493–97), and a badly worn William III copper halfpenny, of a type minted from 1695 to 1701 (Noel Hume 1970:160). Finally, several other "IE"-marked bowl fragments were recovered from this context and none were retrieved from any other feature on the site. Therefore, based on this evidence and the absence of any artifacts diagnostically dating after circa 1715 at the site, the cellar appears to have been filled at the end of the site occupation.

How then to explain the apparent correlation of the earlier 6/64th-inch pipes and the feature? An answer is suggested by again considering the processes of deposition at the site. In contrast to the borrow pit discussed previously, which gives ample evidence of being purposely filled over a short period, this feature may well have remained open after being partially filled when the house was demolished. Therefore, in addition to materials in use at that time, artifacts that were deposited earlier in nearby middens could continue to find their way into the feature through natural processes such as erosion. Interestingly, six prehistoric pottery sherds dating to the Early Woodland period were recovered there as well, totalling two more than the colonial sherds found. Therefore, it seems plausible that a sufficient quantity of residual 6/64th-inch pipe stems also could have made their way into the feature, in sufficient quantity to show up as a concentration on the distribution map when plowed. These results also support the observation that the presence of extensive subsurface features with significant amounts of artifacts can affect the plowzone distribution patterns.

The map of 4 and 5/64th-inch pipes (N = 1815) points to a second concentration caused by subsurface remains, where the largest cellar is located (Figure 12a). It appears that cellar fell into disuse relatively early in the occupation, but the concentration of late pipes and the presence of rubble within the fill suggests that it was completely capped only late in the site's history. The other patterns shown are by now familiar—a major

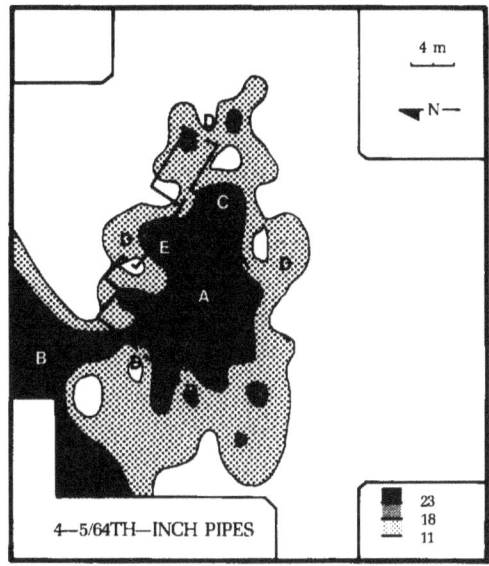

FIGURE 12. Distribution of 4-5/64th-inch pipe stems.

midden to the rear (12b), a second midden across the foreyard fence (12c), and smaller concentrations located adjacent to the other door and gateways (12d). Another marked concentration is located in the corner of the hall (12e), apparently reflecting the primary deposit of pipes there.

The pipe stem distributional analysis has allowed a much more sensitive interpretation of the refuse disposal patterns at the site. It has served as a significant temporal indicator in particular, even though the time span involved is relatively limited.

Analysis of the distribution of other artifact types, principally ceramics and glass, allows additional insight into the process of refuse disposal as well as evidence for functional uses of space. However, as the ceramics span the entire occupation period and glass fragments are difficult to date, their usefulness as temporal indicators is limited.

Ceramic Distributions

A total of 2415 ceramic sherds were recovered from the 144 test units (Table 1). This number is

TABLE 1
PLOWZONE CERAMICS BY WARE TYPE

Ware	Sherds	Percentage
Rhenish Gray Stoneware	254	10.51
Hohr Stoneware	36	1.49
Rhenish Brown Stoneware	90	3.72
English Brown Stoneware	65	2.69
STONEWARES SUBTOTAL	445	18.42
Tin-glazed Earthenware	762	31.55
North Devon Sgrafitto Earthenware	60	2.48
Staffordshire Earthenware	33	1.36
FINE EARTHENWARES SUBTOTAL	855	35.40
North Devon Gravel-tempered Earthenware	63	2.60
Black-glazed Earthenware	52	2.15
Brown-glazed Earthenware	31	1.28
Interior-glazed Earthenware	375	15.52
Exterior-glazed Earthenware	51	2.11
Interior and Exterior-glazed Earthenware	73	3.02
Yellow-glazed Earthenware	338	13.99
Green-glazed Earthenware	59	2.44
Colono Ware	30	1.24
COARSE EARTHENWARES SUBTOTAL	1072	44.38
Other/Unattributable	43	1.78
TOTAL	2415	99.98

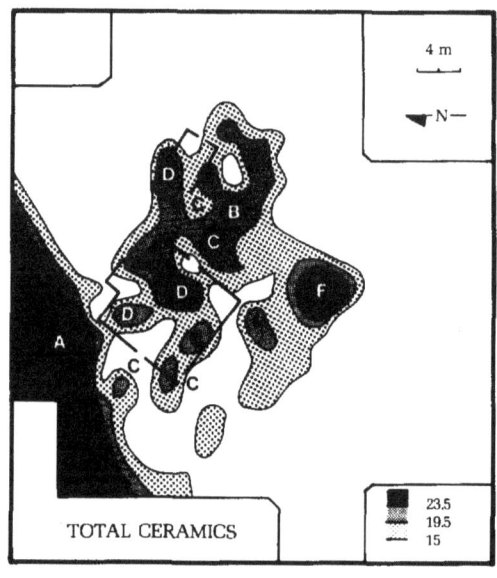

FIGURE 13. Distribution of total ceramics.

small in comparison with the total ceramics recovered at sites such as the Clifts Plantation and at St. Mary's City, again testifying to the site's short occupation span. Examination of the map totalling all ceramic sherds (Figure 13) reveals general patterns similar to those provided by the pipes. To be precise, there is a major midden behind the house (13a), a second major midden between the house and quarter (13b), showing two peaks probably stemming from the shifting of the fenceline, and smaller concentrations near all suspected doorways (13c). Concentrations also occur within the quarter and the house, apparently deriving from domestic activity there (13d), and also correlating with at least one cellar location (13e). Finally, significant concentrations are located off of the house's south gable, one of which correlates with a second borrow pit (13f).

The density and extent of the rear house concentration, as shown on all the maps already examined and those to follow, points to an extensive sheet midden that was a major dump throughout the site's occupation. It is located downslope from the house and adjacent to an existing ravine leading to a stream and the Patuxent River. That location supports the identification of the concentration as a refuse dump rather than a work area. The major avenues for disposal at the midden appear to have been via the shed, through the rear and gable doorways. The foreyard midden also was continuously accreting, with the apparent primary sources of refuse being the house and quarter front doorways. As such, both middens could have received refuse stemming from household activities in the hall and parlor, with quarter refuse confined to the foreyard and shed refuse to the rear.

Separate middens comprised of refuse from the hall, parlor, quarter, and dairy would be expected to vary in composition, reflecting the different functions carried out in the respective areas. Such patterns have been identified most clearly at St. John's (Keeler 1978), The Clifts (Neiman 1980),

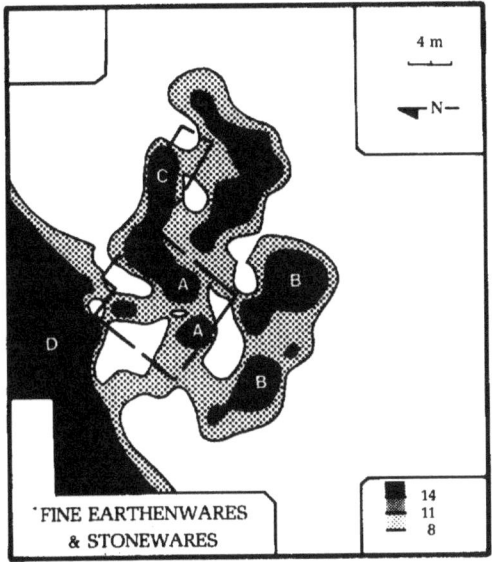

FIGURE 14. Distribution of fine earthenwares and stonewares.

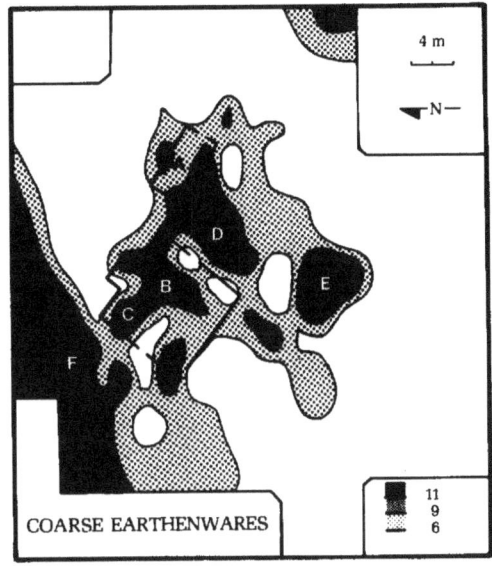

FIGURE 15. Distribution of coarse earthenwares.

and The Country's House (Miller 1986) Sites, where, in general, fine ceramics clustered in middens stemming from the parlor and coarse wares clustered around food preparation and storage areas such as halls, kitchens, quarters, and dairies. At King's Reach, where at least the two major middens identified derived from mixed origins, the analysis of the functional uses of space is necessarily made more complex.

Comparison of coarse earthenwares with fine earthenwares and stonewares does reveal some significantly different patterns, however. Fine table wares concentrate within the parlor (Figure 14a), apparently stemming from primary deposition in one or more of the cellars there. Fine wares also concentrate off the parlor gable (14b), possibly originating in that room and deposited via the shed, over the foreyard fence, and through the later gate. Fine wares are concentrated within and around the quarter as well (14c), apparently pointing to the quarter's use in dining in addition to household chores. Coarse wares concentrate within the quarter (15a), hall (15b), and shed

(15c), as would be expected. In addition, a broad concentration of coarse wares spreads across the foreyard between the house and quarter (15d), suggesting they originated in the quarter and hall. Coarse wares also concentrate over the probable borrow pit (15e), which, when excavated, yielded great quantities of North Devon Gravel-tempered butter pot and milk pan fragments. Finally, both coarse and fine wares concentrate in the rear house midden (14d and 15f), pointing to both parlor and hall/shed refuse deposited there.

The distributions of individual ware types reinforce these observations and also point to the mixed origin of most of the middens. Tin-glazed earthenware, the most common earthenware type recovered and consisting overwhelmingly of table wares, also concentrates off the parlor end of the house (Figure 16a) and in the rear midden (16b), as expected. Interestingly, it also shows a marked concentration within and around the quarter (16c), lending support to the hypothesis that the quarter served a dining function for its inhabitants. Tin-glazed wares also concentrate within the hall and

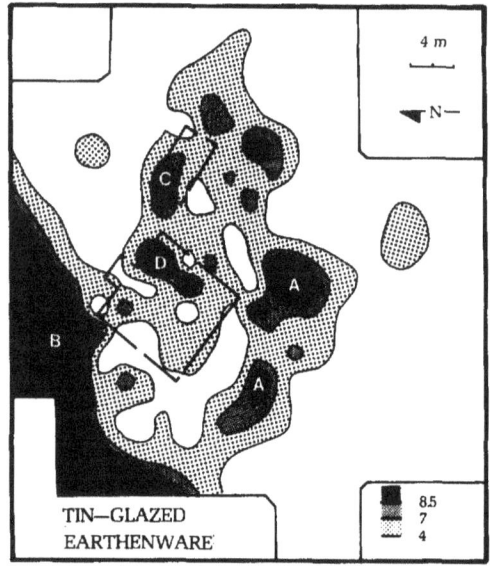

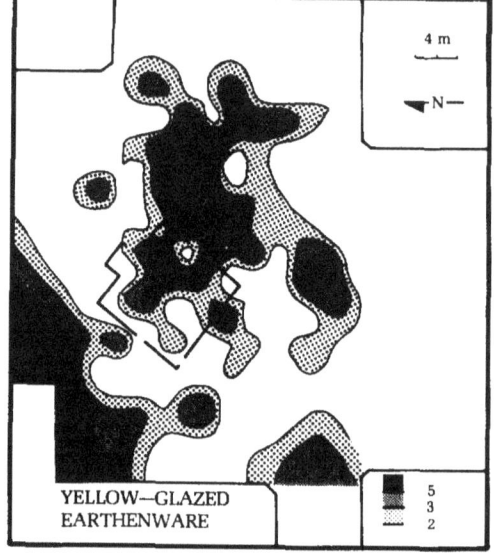

FIGURE 16. Distribution of tin-glazed earthenware.

FIGURE 17. Distribution of yellow-glazed earthenware.

near the dairy (16d). Neiman (1980:123) found significant concentrations of fine wares near a dairy at The Clifts, which, based on inventory data, he attributes to the storage of serving and dining vessels there. The concentration of Tin-glazed wares in the northwest corner of the quarter suggests that it may have served for storage as well.

Yellow-glazed earthenware is second only to Tin-glazed as the most common earthenware recovered, primarily consisting of small shallow bowls. This ceramic has a highly-fired, fine buff paste and yellow lead glaze, and is suggestive of but not identical to wares produced in the Surry-Hampshire district of England (Noel Hume 1970:102). It concentrates within the hall and around the quarter, but its almost universal distribution (Figure 17) suggests it was a multi-purpose vessel type and probably was used in a variety of household and food related functions.

The distribution of Rhenish Blue-Gray stoneware, primarily large round drinking pot/pitchers, shows a marked concentration near the dairy (Figure 18a), as well as in the rear midden (18b)

and elsewhere. This may signify that those vessels were being used for storage of dairy products as well as for drinking. Rhenish brown stoneware bottles provide the clearest pattern of all, however, concentrating around the quarter and pointing to that building's use for beverage storage, probably in the cellar and in the northwest corner (Figure 19). Interestingly, of the 30 ceramic sherds recovered from the nearby borrow pit, 17 are brown stoneware bottle fragments, suggesting that feature may have been filled primarily with quarter refuse.

In addition, 30 sherds of a very coarse, quartz-tempered earthenware with blackened interior and cord-marked surface treatment and vertical, European-style rim have been identified as regionally produced Indian ware of the Potomac Creek tradition (Egloff and Potter 1982:112). According to Clark (1980:8), this type of ware was being produced through the 17th century and suggests trade with one of the Indian groups that survived in the region at that time. Colono Ware, generally attributed to Indian rather than slave manufacture, has been recovered in some quantity in other areas of

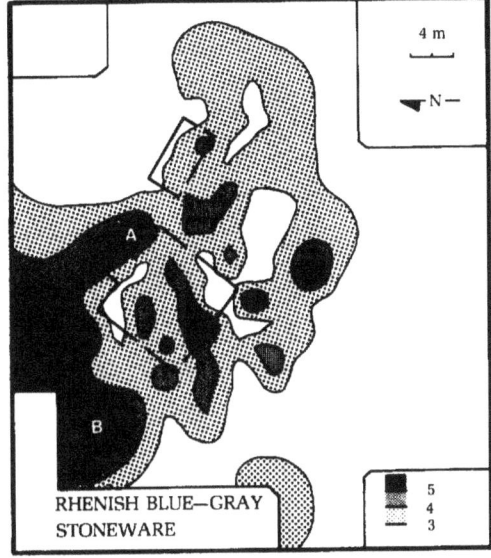

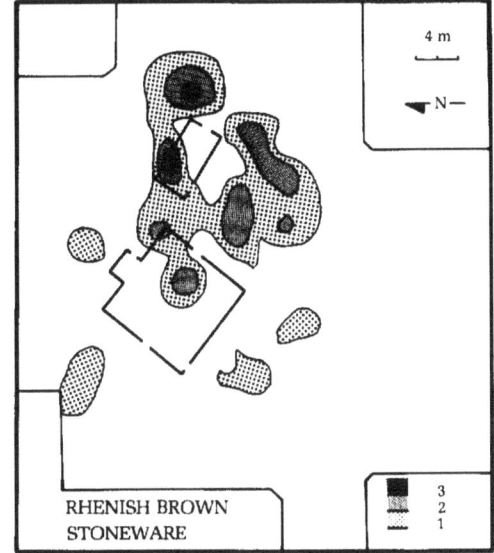

FIGURE 18. Distribution of Rhenish blue-gray stoneware.   FIGURE 19. Distribution of Rhenish brown stoneware.

the Chesapeake, but in limited numbers in Southern Maryland. Since the sample is small, their distribution has been hand plotted (Figure 20), revealing a marked clustering around the quarter. As these sherds are Indian rather than African, their presence alone cannot be used to support occupation of the quarter by slaves. But at the least, the clustering around the quarter does support the identification of that building as a domestic residence and suggests that the occupants were of lower status than the residents of the main house. When analysis of all the feature data is completed and combined with the midden information, it may be possible to identify more substantive differences between the quarter and house refuse reflecting differing status, wealth, and culture between servants, slaves, and masters.

Distribution of Glass

The patterns in wine bottle glass (N = 3268) distribution serve to support the identification of the quarter and hall, with major concentrations of

bottle glass associated with those two areas. A concentration within the quarter in the northwest corner (Figure 21a) again suggests a storage capacity there. A concentration off the east gable (21b) supports the doorway location there and also provides further evidence for the quarter cellar as a beverage store house. A less dense concentration also is located adjacent to the other quarter doorway (21c). The two remaining concentrations are located within the main house, centered on the hall (21d), and in the rear midden (21e). A total of 14 wire wine bottle closers and substantial portions of several bottles were recovered from the borrow pit near the quarter where large quantities of Rhenish brown stoneware, oyster shell, and faunal remains were found. This seems to add support for the hypothesis that the pit was filled primarily with quarter domestic refuse.

In contrast, and possibly due to the relatively small sample recovered (N = 139), the table glass distributions are much more dispersed. Three concentrations occur at the parlor end of the house (Figure 22a), however, testifying to that room's more formal function. As usual, concentrations

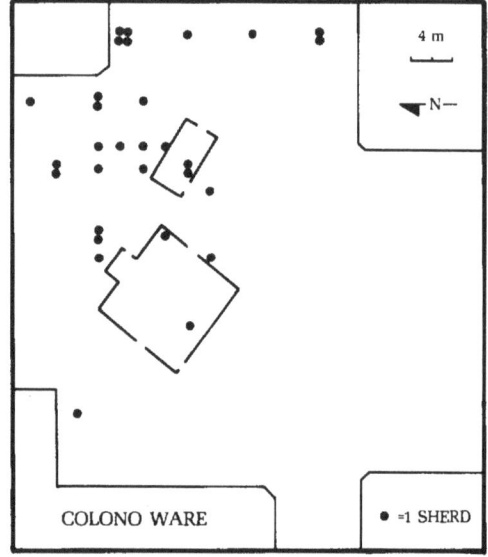

FIGURE 20. Distribution of Colono ware.

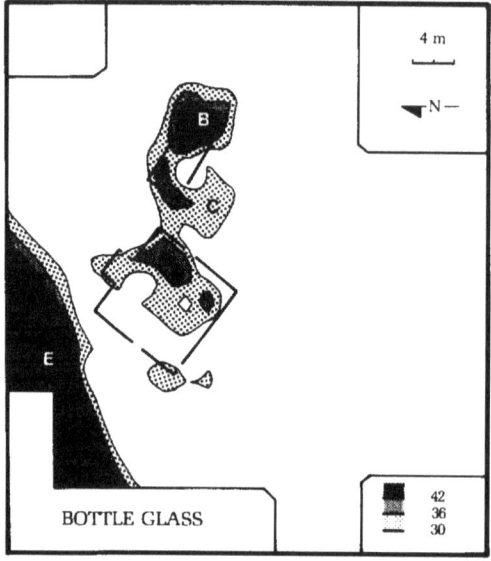

FIGURE 21. Distribution of bottle glass.

also occur in the rear and foreyard middens (22b), reflecting deposition from various origins. Somewhat surprising, however, are the slight concentrations around the quarter (22c), possibly representing the use of handed-down items.

Discussion

Except for gun flint debitage that probably stems from knapping taking place in the various doorways, it appears that the patterns of refuse disposal that these distributions reflect derive almost completely from secondary deposition in the form of purposeful dumping of trash outside the nearest door or, if close enough, over the fence. Therefore, the foreyard midden does not reflect activity actually taking place there, but more likely is a result of refuse deposited from the hall and quarter. The same appears true for the rear house midden and other smaller middens as well. The purposely filled borrow pit near the quarter is a more focused example of such deposition, and because of its limited volume appears to have been quickly filled with refuse stemming from a single source. As a result, very few of these middens are located where the activity which generated the refuse actually occurred. Some of the concentrations within the quarter and house do appear to stem from activity there, but they seem to represent a minority. Finally, the cellars appear to have been filled through a variety of processes—natural erosion, purposeful deposition, and destruction. It is likely that those cellars do contain artifacts that originated nearby, which suggests that detailed analysis of those remains may yield significant differences reflecting the different hall, parlor, and quarter functions.

Little evidence for the types of activities that presumably took place in the surrounding areas has been found. The foreyard clearly served as a major connecting link between the house and quarter and was fenced to keep intruders away from the domestic spaces. That area more than likely also served as a convenient work space for a variety of household chores that may have generated some of the materials examined. The area north of the house and quarter is remarkably clear of refuse, and may be the location of the kitchen garden. The nearby

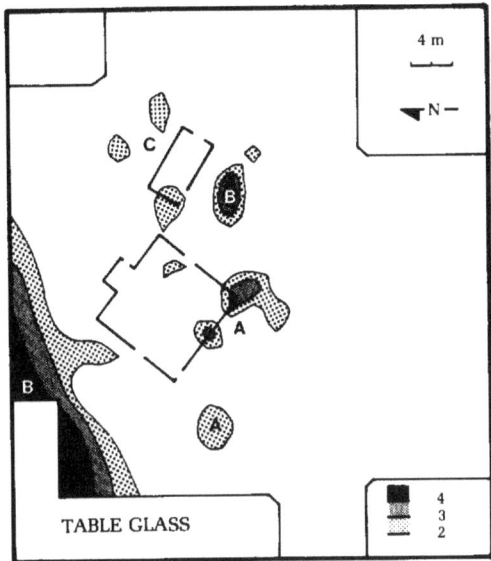

FIGURE 22. Distribution of table glass.

storage cellars and a detached servant and/or slave quarter with storage cellar below. That the detached structure served as a quarter is supported by the existence of remnants of a hearth, associated concentrations of tobacco pipes, ceramics, and glass, and also food remains within the cellar beneath the structure and in the nearby borrow pit. Mixture of the middens with refuse from separate functional areas probably has served to mask some of these patterns, however. The disposal of refuse in convenient pits and in sheet middens via doorways also is common.

Another similarity is the concentration of refuse between the quarter and house. Such a pattern was found at both The Clifts and St. John's Sites as well. At The Clifts, the quarter was located near the hall, similar to King's Reach, but also with a number of smaller outbuildings such as smoke and meat houses and dairies clustered there, which apparently served as the primary service yard (Neiman 1980). At St. John's a marked difference between front and back yard activities has been inferred, with the front apparently functioning as a court yard, with the cluttered back yard and near the kitchen/quarter being the service areas (Keeler 1978:72). The King's Reach foreyard gives little evidence of acting as a court yard. Instead, it served as a major refuse dump and probably was a work area and major thoroughfare between the house and quarter. The uncluttered court yard at St. John's may well stem from the site's location at St. Mary's City and its use as a residence of Charles Calvert, third Lord Baltimore, and as a governmental meeting place throughout much of its existence. As King's Reach was an outlying and more isolated plantation, the occupants may have been less interested in maintaining such a formal space.

A rather surprising feature of the King's Reach plan is the apparent absence of the other, smaller outbuildings that are commonly found on such sites. While it is possible that the smaller structures may have been overlooked as a result of the necessity of sampling outside of the core area, it seems unlikely that they all could have been missed. In addition, the distributions of brick and nails from plowzone do not point to any other

location of a spring would make it a desirable site for that activity and being adjacent to the quarter and hall would allow easy access. It may have been protected using worm rail fencing, which leave no archaeological remains in a plowed context. Finally, the area south of the house exhibits sporadic clusters of refuse, and also is the location of the second apparent borrow pit as well as a single post hole and post supports of unidentified function. Again, it would appear to be a logical location for a number of short-term activities.

In comparing the King's Reach results with those from other sites, several major similarities are apparent. The basic homelot configuration of house, quarter, and connecting foreyard is typical (cf., Keeler 1978). That the foreyard was reduced in size over time appears relatively inconsequential. The house floor plan, while largely inferred from comparison with previous documentary and archaeological research, is supported by the distributional analyses, and also is not unusual, except for the total number of cellars. It consists of a hall, parlor, shed, and attached dairy, with the various

TABLE 2
CERAMICS FROM 18 Cv 84 SURFACE COLLECTION

Ware	Sherds
Rhenish Gray Stoneware	2
Tin-glazed Earthenware	2
Interior-glazed Earthenware	12
Yellow-glazed Earthenware	19
Green-glazed Earthenware	5
TOTAL	40

outbuildings (Figures 7 and 8). Instead, it may be that many of those activities usually carried out in outbuildings were performed in the shed, dairy, and quarter. Finally, there is the possibility that some activities may have occurred at another site (18 Cv 84, Figure 1), located approximately 300 feet to the east, where a second but much less extensive concentration of domestic artifacts dating from the same period has been found. The limited variety of ceramic types and number of sherds recovered (Table 2) suggests a periodically occupied quarter/work house rather than a year-round quarter. Such structures and associated agricultural complexes are often referred to in the documentary record (Main 1982:128). An apparent detached quarter was also found located approximately 140 feet distant from the main house at The Clifts (Neiman 1980:111).

Neiman (1984 and 1986:307–309), among others, has suggested that a major change in homelot usage occurred after circa 1665 in the Chesapeake with the gradual shift away from the main house as the focus of household activities shared by both servants and masters. By the late 17th century, a distinct separation between servant and/or slave and master households is expected. The King's Reach results as demonstrated by the various distribution maps lend support for that trend, as the presence of domestic refuse associated with the quarter points to such a separation from initial occupation of the site.

As for the site location itself, it fits well with the pattern of settlement in the 17th century Chesapeake that has been identified (Smolek et al. 1984). A ravine and spring head where fresh water

could be obtained are located less than 60 feet to the north and the surrounding fields are some of the richest in the area and well-suited to agriculture. The possible outlying field quarter is located on level ground only a short distance from the spring and nearer the center of the cultivateable area where access to and from the crop would be optimized.

Analysis of plowzone-derived artifacts once again has proven to be extremely effective in plotting refuse disposal patterns and, in turn, in understanding the layout and functional use of the plantation homelot. Patterns in the distribution of tobacco pipes by bore diameter were particularly useful in identifying diachronic changes, especially as the ceramic assemblage spans the site's entire occupation period. Analysis of ceramics, glass, and other materials has led to more sensitive identification of functional spaces. The resulting picture of the King's Reach homelot is typical in many ways, but the absence of outbuildings suggests that some of those activities that traditionally were carried out in the surrounding yards may have been restricted to the interior work areas, and/or to an associated quarter and agricultural complex.

ACKNOWLEDGEMENTS

Undertaking a project such as the King's Reach Site investigation necessarily has required the assistance of a great many people. First, I must thank the dozens of volunteers and the 11 students from the 1984 and 1985 St. Mary's College archaeological field schools, without whose labor the excavation and artifact processing simply would not have been possible. The efforts of the members of the Archeological Society of Maryland Southern Chapter are particularly appreciated. Second, my field assistants during the two seasons' excavation performed their duties with enthusiasm and professionalism: Mark Shaffer (1984), and Robert Hurry, Julia King, Patricia McGuire, and Jim O'Connor (1985). Third, and most important in terms of this article, Fraser D. Neiman of Yale University not only generously volunteered his time to generate all the distribution maps, but also enriched my understanding of their meaning with the benefit of his remarkable expertise. Funding support for the 1985 field season was provided by a grant from the

National Endowment for the Humanities through the Maryland Humanities Council; indispensable logistical support was cheerfully provided by the entire Jefferson Patterson Park and Museum staff. Finally, thanks to all who reviewed earlier drafts of this article—your comments and suggestions have been extremely helpful.

REFERENCES

BINFORD, LEWIS R.
1962 A New Method for Calculating Dates From Kaolin Pipe Stem Samples. *Southeastern Archaeological Conference Newsletter* 9(1):19–21.

CARSON, CARY, NORMAN F. BARKA, WILLIAM M. KELSO, GARRY WHEELER STONE, AND DELL UPTON
1981 Impermanent Architecture in the Southern American Colonies. *Winterthur Portfolio* 16(2/3):135–96.

CLARK, WAYNE E.
1980 The Origins of the Piscataway and Related Indian Cultures. *Maryland Historical Magazine* 75(1):8–22.

CLARK, WAYNE E. AND MICHAEL A. SMOLEK
1981 The Patterson Estate on St. Leonard Creek: an Archaeological Site Inventory. *Maryland Historical Trust, Manuscript Series* 16.

EGLOFF, KEITH T. AND STEPHEN R. POTTER
1982 Indian Ceramics from Coastal Plain Virginia. *Archaeology of Eastern North America* 10:95–117.

KEELER, ROBERT W.
1978 *The Homelot on the Seventeenth Century Chesapeake Tidewater Frontier.* Ph.D. dissertation, University of Oregon. University Microfilms, Ann Arbor.

KELSO, WILLIAM M.
1984 *Kingsmill Plantations, 1619–1800: Archaeology of Country Life in Colonial Virginia.* Academic Press, New York.

KING, JULIA A. AND HENRY M. MILLER
1984 Exploring 17th Century Spatial Behavior: Evidence from the Van Sweringen Site, St. Mary's City, Maryland. Paper presented at the Society for Historical Archaeology Annual Meeting, Williamsburg.

LEWARCH, DENNIS E. AND MICHAEL J. O'BRIEN
1981 Effect of Short Term Tillage on Aggregate Provenience Surface Pattern. In Plowzone Archeology: Contributions to Theory and Technique, edited by Michael J. O'Brien and Dennis E. Lewarch. *Vanderbilt University Publications in Anthropology* No. 27:7–50.

MAIN, GLORIA
1982 *Tobacco Colony: Life in Early Maryland, 1650–1720.* Princeton University Press, Princeton, New Jersey.

MILLER, HENRY M.
1983 A Search for the "Citty of Saint Maries": Report on the 1981 Excavations in St. Mary's City, Maryland. *St. Maries Citty Archaeology Series* No. 1.
1986 Discovering Maryland's First City: A Summary Report on the 1981–1984 Archaeological Excavations in St. Mary's City, Maryland. *St. Mary's City Archaeology Series* No. 2.

NEIMAN, FRASER D.
1980 Field Archaeology of the Clifts Plantation Site, Westmoreland County, Virginia. Ms. on file, Jefferson Patterson Park and Museum, St. Leonard, Maryland.
1984 An Evolutionary Approach to House Plans and the Organization of Production on the Chesapeake Frontier. Paper presented at the Society for Historical Archaeology Annual Meeting, Williamsburg.
1986 Domestic Architecture at the Clifts Plantation: the Social Context for Early Virginia Building. In *Common Places: Readings in American Vernacular Architecture*, edited by Dell Upton and John Michael Vlach, pp. 292–314. University of Georgia Press, Athens.

NOEL HUME, IVOR
1970 *A Guide to Artifacts of Colonial America.* Alfred A. Knopf, New York.

SCHIFFER, MICHAEL
1972 Archaeological Context and Systematic Context. *American Antiquity* 37:156–165.

SMOLEK, MICHAEL A., DENNIS J. POGUE, AND WAYNE E. CLARK
1984 Historical Archaeology of the 17th Century Chesapeake: a Guide to Sources. *Jefferson Patterson Park and Museum, Occasional Paper* No. 1.

TUKEY, JOHN
1977 *Exploratory Data Analysis.* Addison-Wesley, Reading, Massachusetts.

WALKER, IAIN C.
1977 *Clay Tobacco Pipes, with Particular Reference to the Bristol Industry* Volume II(C). Parks Canada, Ottawa.

DENNIS J. POGUE
MT. VERNON LADIES' ASSOCIATION
MT. VERNON, VIRGINIA 22121

JAMES A. DELLE

The Landscapes of Class Negotiation on Coffee Plantations in the Blue Mountains of Jamaica: 1790-1850

ABSTRACT

Analyzing the material elements of class negotiation should be a focus of historical archaeology. One of the most promising forms of material culture with which to conduct such analysis is landscape. To examine how landscapes shaped the negotiation of class relations in 19th century Jamaica, the material remains of three coffee plantations—Sherwood Forest, Clydesdale, and Chesterfield—are described and analyzed. The archaeological analysis of the landscapes of 19th century class negotiation can shed light on the historical development of capitalist social processes, many of which still impact the negotiation of class relations today.

> —Free negroes are found to act differently from other free men; not because they differ from others in character, but because their circumstances are different; and just in proportion as they are brought within the reach of those motives by which Europeans are governed, will their conduct resemble that of the natives of Europe (Henry George Grey to the Deputation of the Standing Committee of West India Planters, 1833).

Introduction

In recent years historical archaeologists have begun to seriously consider how material culture functions in the negotiation of the social relations of production. While such endeavors have traditionally focused on the various ways in which capitalist society has historically been stratified through the construction of hierarchies of "status" or "ethnicity" (Otto 1977; Schuyler 1980) only a few historical archaeologists have, to date, risked the challenging task of analyzing the material processes through which class relations are constructed and negotiated (Paynter and McGuire 1991; Wurst 1991; Scott 1994; Hood 1996; Johnson 1996; Mullins 1996; Orser 1996;

Historical Archaeology, 1999, 33(1):136–158.
Permission to reprint required.

Shackel 1996). Given that class is one of the most important organizing structures of capitalist society and that most historical archaeologists study material culture produced and consumed within the capitalist system, it would seem to follow that historical archaeologists are logically situated to analyze the relationships that exist between material culture and the dynamics of class negotiation.

The analysis of class relations remains rare in historical archaeology, however. This may in part be related to the general difficulty archaeologists still have in interpreting dynamic social phenomena from the static archaeological record. Class relations are such dynamic phenomena; although class relations are constructed with material culture, it is the negotiation of the social relations expressed by such material culture, and not the material culture itself, that defines social class. An added barrier to class analysis results from the typical research design which tends to focus on individual sites or even subareas within sites. Interpretations are made on sites in isolation, not in relation to other sites. Such an approach limits what can be said about class dynamics. To convincingly interpret class dynamics from the material record, historical archaeologists must reach beyond traditional methodologies which more often than not fetishize portable artifacts from isolated sites. While quantification and classification of portable artifacts recovered from excavations may reveal the kinds of possessions typical (or atypical) of members of specific social classes, it remains difficult to interpret anything meaningful about the relationships negotiated between members of different classes from such exercises. Class exists within these relationships; a class is only truly meaningful in relation to other classes and to the political economy which shaped them. While such social relations can be interpreted through the analysis of many types of historical material culture, landscapes may be among the most fruitful avenues of research as they materially serve as the arenas in which people negotiate class relations. It thus follows that the emerging specialization of land-

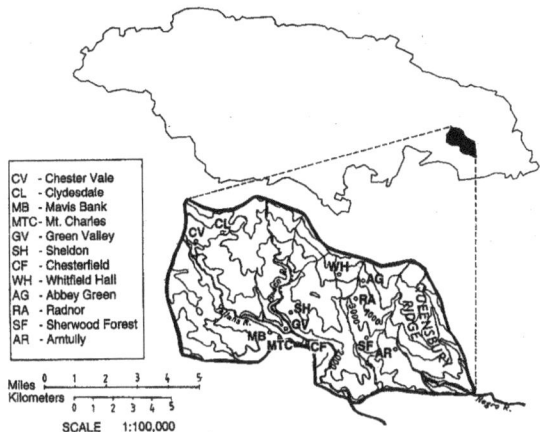

CV - Chester Vale
CL - Clydesdale
MB - Mavis Bank
MTC - Mt. Charles
GV - Green Valley
SH - Sheldon
CF - Chesterfield
WH - Whitfield Hall
AG - Abbey Green
RA - Radnor
SF - Sherwood Forest
AR - Arntully

Miles
Kilometers
SCALE   1:100,000

Figure 1. Location of Yallahs River drainage and plantations mentioned in the text.

scape archaeology provides one means by which archaeologists can shed light on the historical negotiation of class relations.

The ultimate goal of this work is to demonstrate through a case study how landscapes influence the material negotiation of class relations in capitalist society. As a work of landscape archaeology, this article is based on two premises: 1) that material culture plays a significant role in the negotiation of social relations; and 2) that landscape is a form of material culture. Added to this second premise is the idea that landscapes are constructed of various spatial elements, some of which, like buildings, are empirically observable in the archaeological record, while other spatial elements, like land tenure systems, are best interpreted from cartographic and documentary records. To be most successful, an archaeology of historic landscapes should incorporate analyses of all three data sources: material, documentary, and cartographic. This essay attempts to do just that in considering how the organization of coffee plantation landscapes in pre- and post-emancipation Jamaica influenced and directed the negotiation of class relations.

To this end, this paper analyzes class relations as they were negotiated on coffee plantations in

the first half of the 19th century in the upper Yallahs River drainage, located in the Blue Mountains of eastern Jamaica (Figure 1). The Yallahs region incorporates the uplands of two historic parishes: St. David's and Port Royal. This analysis of the negotiation of class in this region will: 1) suggest how landscape archaeology can inform class analysis; 2) describe the class structure of the case study; 3) discuss how land and labor relations were incorporated into the negotiation of this class structure; and 4) analyze how coffee plantation landscapes specifically influenced the negotiation of class relations.

Landscape Archaeology and the Study of Class Relations

Although a relatively new moniker, landscape archaeology has recently emerged from several intellectual traditions which have had a long and profound impact on the practice of historical archaeology, notably settlement pattern analysis and vernacular architecture studies, and should in fact be considered an extension of these types of spatial analysis. While many recent landscape and spatial studies in archaeology have been explicitly designed to inform preservationists on the accurate reconstruction of isolated spaces, particularly gardens (Beaudry 1996), several have demonstrated how landscapes impact the negotiation of class relations on a variety of scales. For example, Robert Paynter (1980, 1981, 1982, 1983, 1985) has demonstrated how regional settlement patterns can be analyzed to interpret change within class structure. In his examination of rural western Massachusetts, Paynter has argued that by controlling access to the flow of surplus and by concentrating surplus at entrepôts, regional elite classes created a spatial system that supported the maintenance of class-based inequality. Although not explicitly concerned with class dynamics, Ken Lewis (Lewis 1984, 1985) has similarly used a settlement pattern study to suggest how spatial analysis can inform the analysis of the dynamic processes of Euroamerican colonialism. Lewis emphasized that colonial expansion on the South Carolina frontier was dependent on a hierarchically arranged system of frontier towns and settlements. He argued for the use of a diachronic model as he hypothesized that economic changes, and thus shifts in class relations, will precipitate changes in spatial forms (Lewis 1984:1-7, 17-27, 107-113).

In examining the spatial dynamics of class relations at a more refined scale, a number of historical archaeologists have focused their analysis on specific villages, towns, or cities. For example, Ed Hood's examination of landscapes in Deerfield, Massachusetts (Hood and Reinke 1989; Hood 1995, 1996) demonstrates how an elite class intentionally manipulated the town landscape in the attempt to create a false impression of past landscapes. This sanitized vision of Deerfield's past served primarily to reinforce the ideology of early 20th-century capitalism by creating a landscape which reflected modern inequality. By suggesting that such landscapes were ancient, 20th-century elites served to justify their class position by projecting its presence into the tangible past.

A major contribution to spatial analysis in historical archaeology has emerged from Mark Leone's long-term archaeology project in Annapolis, Maryland. Leone has argued that in the late 18th century, the so-called Georgian elites manipulated their landscapes to reflect their control over both the natural and social orders, including the class structure (Leone 1984, 1988).

This line of argument has been thoughtfully taken up by Elizabeth Kryder-Reid in her study of the Annapolis garden site known as St. Mary's. She demonstrated that the ability to control the space of the 18th-century garden served to reflect the control of knowledge as well as space; gardens thus served as powerful media "of the colonial elite to communicate and negotiate their social identity," i.e. their class position (Kryder-Reid 1994:132). Paul Shackel (1994) has demonstrated that the baroque city plan of St. Mary's City, Maryland's first capital, was designed specifically to bolster the class status of the administrative elite. When the capital was

transferred from St. Mary's to Annapolis in 1694, this new city was designed so that the Anglican Church and the State House stood on the city's two highest points, visible from any location thus constantly reinforcing the authority of both church and state (Shackel 1994:88). The control of space evident in the town plan and architecture of these two capital cities reinforced social and economic hierarchies constructed on social divisions based not only on class, but on race and religion.

Randy McGuire has examined town and community landscapes to analyze the changing ideology of capitalism in late 19th- and early 20th-century Broome County, New York (McGuire 1988, 1991; Wurst 1991). The differences in the industrial landscapes constructed by the industrialists Jonas Kilmer and George F. Johnson demonstrate transformations in how class relations were materially negotiated through the manipulation of the social landscape. McGuire documents how in the late 19th-century Kilmer constructed his factories and mansion in such a way as to exude power, physically demonstrating the social gulf between himself and the working class. In contrast, and in reaction to two generations of labor unrest, Johnson constructed an industrial landscape that overtly minimized social distance; in building his house in the same style as that of his workers, Johnson sought to obscure class differences by manifesting a sliding scale of relative equality. By constructing an industrial welfare system through which company profits were used to subsidize the construction of parks, hospitals, and other public monuments, Johnson attempted to construct an ideology which emphasized the mutual interests shared by employers and employees and create an illusion of equality between classes (McGuire 1991). Similar material expressions of the changing ideology of capitalism can be read in the mortuary architecture, design, and layout of the cemeteries of Broome County (McGuire 1988; Wurst 1991). Similar questions concerning the relationship between urban industrial landscapes and the negotiation of class relations have been addressed by Steve

Mrozowski and Mary Beaudry in the their long-term study of the Boott Mills industrial complex in Lowell, Massachusetts (Beaudry 1989; Mrozowski and Beaudry 1990; Beaudry, Cook, and Mrozowski 1991; Mrozowski 1991; Mrozowski et al 1996).

Vernacular architecture studies have contributed a great deal to the historical archaeology of landscapes. For example, Dell Upton has demonstrated that the most evident material expression of class relations on 18th-century Chesapeake tobacco plantations are the spatial relationships between the landscapes of the planters and those of the enslaved (Upton 1988). Chesapeake tobacco plantations were generally isolated and self-contained communities, likened to a village, with the planter's house serving as a "town hall" or center of power (Upton 1988:362). To reinforce this authority, planters' houses were physically elevated above other buildings, on a hill for instance, and were segregated from the surrounding countryside by systems of terraces and fences (Upton 1988:362). Plantation houses were thus intentionally constructed to dominate the landscape just as the planters dominated the class structure.

The methodologies of landscape archaeology have also been applied in the examination of how class is negotiated through plantation landscapes (Orser 1988, Armstrong and Kelly 1990; Hudgins 1990; Kelso 1990; Luccketti 1990; Delle 1994; McKee 1996; Pogue 1996). For example, Chuck Orser has demonstrated how landscapes impacted the negotiation of post-emancipation class relations at Millwood, a South Carolina cotton plantation (Orser and Nekola 1985; Orser 1988a, 1991). The owner of Millwood Plantation, James Edward Calhoun, was a well connected member of the southern elite. With the defeat of the Confederacy, planters like Calhoun reorganized the system of labor exploitation and class relations on their plantations. To this end, several new strategies of labor extraction were established, including farm wage labor and systems of time and crop sharing (Orser 1988:45-51). This restructuring of class relations following emancipation resulted in the restructuring of plantation landscapes. Unlike antebellum plantation settlements which put a premium on direct surveillance of the laborers, post bellum plantation settlements tended to be dispersed; each farmer, whether renter or sharecropper, lived with his or her family near the fields they tended. Significantly, where sharecroppers made up the bulk of the plantation tenants, the settlement form more closely resembled antebellum forms in that barns, sheds and other outbuildings were located near the planter's house, providing the planter class with the capability to directly supervise the sharecroppers (Orser 1988:92).

Studies like Orser's demonstrate how historical archaeologists can interpret the role landscapes play in the negotiation of class relations in a plantation context in which, despite the end of slavery, the elite classes manipulated the landscape to implement and reinforce a class structure in which they remained in control of land and production. Jamaica's Yallahs drainage provides an interesting context in which to examine how plantation landscapes shaped the development of class relations in the Caribbean. It is necessary first to characterize the region's class structure as it existed in the 19th century, and then to analyze the role landscapes played in the negotiation of class relationships.

The Class Structure of Coffee Plantations in the Yallahs Region: 1790-1850

In the 19th century Jamaica's political economy was defined by the production and export of agricultural products; the class structure on the island was thus largely defined by access to the agricultural means of production, particularly land. Members of the agrarian elite class in Jamaica referred to themselves as "planters." The planters were not a homogenous group free from internal division. This ruling segment of society included not only the members of the landed oligarchy, but also those employed as estate staff, and other members of Jamaican society involved in the commodities trade and service industries required to maintain it, including merchants, attorneys, and financiers (Pares 1950; Checkland 1957; Lobdell 1972; Davis 1975; Butler 1995; Stinchcombe 1995). The members of the planter classes most closely associated with the production of agricultural commodities were subdivided by social ranking, particularly as that ranking applied to an individual's relationship to the means of production. Heuristically, the planters can be divided into three overlapping classes. The most powerful, which can truly be called the "planter class," was comprised of proprietors who held legal title to estates as well as attorneys or factors who managed the financial affairs of absentee or deceased proprietors. The overseers who ran the daily operation of the estates and their assistants (often called "bookkeepers") can be characterized as an "agrarian middle class." The final group, the "professional middle class," included artisans, merchants, doctors, and other professionals, most of whom lived in the urban centers and some of whom owned plantations (Roughley 1823; Sheridan 1974). As can be seen from this rough outline, class membership was fluid. Members of the professional class could become proprietors of large estates; the occasional overseer ascended to the planter class through the acquisition of land, Hall (1989) presenting a notorious example.

Throughout Jamaica's history, most manual work has been performed by African slaves and their descendants. Until slavery was abolished in 1834 members of this class were not free to sell their labor power in an open market, but were dehumanized and considered commodities, valued by their potential to provide labor power to commercial agricultural estates. Between 1834 and 1838 most able-bodied workers were required to remain on the estates which had previously enslaved them as "apprentices," a transitional social category created by Parliament. The apprenticeship system was designed to teach former slaves the conditions of wage labor; while they were required to work for a certain number of hours each week for the estates, apprentices were free to sell their labor power at other times. In Jamaica this condition was abolished in 1838 and the laborers were nominally free to sell their labor power to the highest bidder.

A key element in the negotiation of this class structure was the planter class's ability to establish and maintain control of surplus production. This involved many social processes, including creating a particularly violent form of racism expressed through cruel dehumanization, physical abuse, and denigration. The planter class sought to exert control over access to land as part of their larger intention to dictate the nature of the social relations of production. It is self-evident that the planter class claimed the legal right to most surplus production under slavery by claiming ownership of the labor power of enslaved workers and most of the commodities they produced. The negotiation of post-emancipation labor relations was an entirely different matter. With the end of slavery the planter class claimed to recognize the former slaves as "free" laborers, yet strove to the best of their ability to limit that freedom by controlling the wages and terms of work. In the decades following the end of slavery, the planter class attempted to reassert their monopoly control over land as a means of production in the attempt to create a landless rural proletarian peasantry alienated from the means of production and thus dependent on wage labor for subsistence (Holt 1992, Butler 1995).

Just as the planter class was divided by an internal hierarchy which separated large proprietors from small, planters from merchants, and proprietors from overseers, the enslaved class was segmented by an internal division of labor which served as the template for the post-emancipation class structure. The nature of this pre-emancipation division of labor on Yallahs region coffee plantations can be interpreted from two sources: *The Coffee Planter of St. Domingo* (1798), an instructive treatise written for Jamaican planters by the Haitian émigré P. J. Laborie, and a surviving day book for Radnor plantation (1822-1826) which, among other things, lists the tasks performed by specific members of the plantation work force.

Laborie provided Jamaican coffee planters with a model for the division of labor to be established among the enslaved population of a working coffee plantation. In Laborie's model the economic roles slaves played in the coffee plantation economy were defined by a clearly articulated division of labor based on the type of labor expected to be performed. Laborie suggested that coffee plantations should have a class structure composed of artisans (which he calls "artificers"), skilled laborers (e.g. coffee-men, midwives, doctresses), various supervisors ("drivers"), and an unskilled labor force, which he calls "the gang in general." According to Laborie, the artisan group, many of whom were highly skilled laborers, should include carpenters, tilers, masons, and saddlers He explicitly listed the duties expected from each of these workers (Laborie 1798:164).

Laborie suggested that the unskilled labor force be divided into at least three work gangs One gang was to be assigned the specialized task of pruning. Another gang, responsible for lighter work such as weeding and gathering coffee, was to be composed of young adolescents between the ages of 12 and 16, while the bulk of the heavy work was to be done by the third group, the great gang. Once elevated into this group, adolescents would be considered adults; significantly, Laborie suggested that this status be affirmed by giving them houses, provision grounds, utensils, and two hens (Laborie 1798:175).

The Radnor plantation book indicates that the division of labor proposed by Laborie in the late 18th century was actualized by the 1820s. The journal indicates that Radnor field workers were organized into three gangs. The first gang was composed of 85 workers, of whom three were drivers. The second gang consisted of 23 people, including a driver and a cook. The third gang was composed 22 workers, again including a driver and a cook. As recommended by Laborie, the vast majority of skilled positions on Radnor were occupied by men: seven carpenters, one doctor, a boatswain, three masons, a saddler and five sawyers. According to the plantation

book, there were only three specialized occupations on Radnor open to women, all characterized by Marietta Morrissey (1989) as "semi-skilled": midwife, nurse, and cook.

The immediate post-emancipation era in the Yallahs region was characterized by dissent over wages and what was then termed the planters' rights to "continuous labor." Underlying the strife between planters and workers in the immediate post-emancipation period was a new logic within the capitalist world order based on the concept of free trade. In 1846, the British Parliament passed the Sugar Duties Act, which lifted protective duties on produce imported from the colonies into Britain. This legislation was intended to stimulate production in the newer British Colonies in the East Indies and the Indian Ocean, particularly Ceylon and Mauritius. The passage of the act reflected the newly dominant ideology of Free Trade which dictated that unimpeded market forces should determine economic relations. The result for the Jamaican planter class was devastating. Without protective duties Jamaican planters could not produce crops cheaply enough to compete with Mauritius sugar and Ceylon coffee, which was being produced with cheap contract labor from the Indian subcontinent; nor could the Jamaican planters compete with producers in Cuba and Brazil, who utilized slave labor into the 1000s (Holt 1992:117) In response to their crisis the planters attempted to minimize the costs of production by keeping wages low and hiring laborers only when needed. It was the hope of the planters not only to create an army of surplus labor by making the people dependent on wages, but to remain in control of the terms by which those wages were paid and when people could work.

One strategy that the planters used in their attempt to control post-emancipation labor was wage capping. Within the various parishes local planter cartels colluded to establish standard wage rates by creating what they called "scales of labor." Due to the reticence and sometimes violent resistance of the Jamaican workers to accept low wages, however, solidarity between the planters quickly broke down, as the laborers forced plant-ers into a wage bidding war to secure sufficient labor to harvest the crops. The planters encour-aged the immigration of new labor pools to break the solidarity of the laboring class. In 1840, Governor Metcalfe of Jamaica appointed immigration agents in North America, Great Brit-ain and elsewhere. These agents met with little success, however, as neither the black populations of the United States and Canada nor the laboring classes of Britain or Ireland showed much inter-est in emigrating to Jamaica (Holt 1992:197).

In 1841 the planter class introduced indentured African labor to Jamaica. It was thought that the introduction of contract labor would serve the planters well, as such laborers would not be at liberty to leave the estates to which they were attached, nor would they have the right to nego-tiate for higher wages. At this same point in time the British imperial government was at-tempting to stem the illicit slave trade, which still operated despite being outlawed by both the American and British governments earlier in the century. As part of the strategy to end the illicit slave trade, British warships seized slavers in the eastern Atlantic and repatriated the captive Afri-cans to Sierra Leone. Knowing that many of these people were being deposited hundreds or thousands of miles from their homes, immigration agents sought to recruit indentured laborers from their numbers. Between 1834 and 1865, Green (1976:284) estimates that approximately 10,000 laborers were recruited to Jamaica from this population. This immigration policy met with public and official resistance, however, as many felt that the policy of recruiting Africans to work under coercive conditions in the West Indies was too reminiscent of slavery. In reaction to the limited success of recruiting African indentured labor, the planter class began recruiting inden-tured laborers from India in 1844. This scheme, too, met with only limited success; the number of Indian laborers transported to Jamaica prob-ably was less than 10,000 (Green 1976:284). In all, it has been estimated that between 1834 and 1865, no more than 25,000 indentured laborers

were recruited to Jamaica, at an expense of £231,488 (Green 1976:284; Holt 1992:202).

The impetus to import indentured laborers into Jamaica was not merely to keep wages low, but to stimulate the development of an agrarian pro-letariat. Since many emancipated laborers were raising their own food on available vacant land, the laborers were not completely dependent on wages. Furthermore, the planters wanted the freedom to hire workers only during those times when they needed them most. Nevertheless, it was difficult for some planters to find workers even at high wages. The planter class thus sought to coerce the development of a proletar-ian work force dependent upon wages. In De-cember of 1842, for example, the Jamaica As-sembly enacted a series of taxes on imports, tar-geting those goods that were most commonly consumed by the laboring classes. Holt (1992:204) reveals, for example, that while no tax was levied on expensive manufactured goods, duties on imported salt beef and pork—staples of the laboring classes—rose by 40%.

The post-emancipation attempts by the planter class to manipulate labor relations affected Yallahs coffee plantations in several ways. For example, an analysis of crop accounts for ten plantations traced from the beginning of the cen-tury through the 1860s revealed that only four of them reported crops after 1839 (Delle 1996). This suggests that from the planters perspective, coffee production entered a crisis stage following emancipation, as it became increasingly difficult for the planters to control labor. This is re-flected in a sworn statement by William George Lowe before a special committee of the Jamaica Assembly appointed in 1847. Lowe, who owned several coffee properties in the Blue Mountains, reported difficulty in obtaining labor to cultivate his estates. When asked about the condition of his properties Lowe reported "[my] property, Green Hill, in St. George's, I have been obliged to abandon for want of labour. When the cof-fee was ripe on the trees, I was unable to find labourers to gather it in. In 1833 there were 52 labourers attached to the property; more than two-thirds of them have purchased or leased lands, and become independent settlers; the other property, Violet Bank, I continue to cultivate, but not now to advantage" (Parliamentary Papers [PP] 1848, 23/3:163).

During the same set of hearings concerning the condition of sugar and coffee cultivation in Jamaica, Hugh Fraser Leslie reported that in 1847 he was in possession of several coffee plantations in the Yallahs region as well as a sugar estate. He reported that while there were 1,268 workers attached to his plantations during slavery, by 1847, fewer than 400 workers remained in his employ (PP 1848, 23/3:167). Leslie complained that he had a difficult time organizing and controlling labor on these estates, hampering his efforts at efficient estate management:

> From the indisposition of the people to work during the Christmas holidays, a great sacrifice of property takes place from the loss of coffee, which falls to the ground from want of hands to pick it during a period of two or three weeks, when no wages, however extravagant, can obtain their labour, this too being the period when the ripening of the coffee is the most general . . . Another difficulty is the refusal of the people to work on Fridays and Saturdays, even when the coffee is ripe on the field (PP 1848, 23/3:167)

Such overt expressions of independence on the part of the laboring class frustrated the attempts of the planters in the Yallahs region to conduct coffee cultivation as they saw fit. The post-emancipation decline in coffee production can in part be explained by the refusal of the African Jamaican population to develop into a rural proletariat dependent on wages paid for work on the estates. As early as 1839 special magistrate Henry Kent reported that Yallahs estates were experiencing difficulty in maintaining a labor force. Kent attributed the labor difficulties to a lack of available capital on the part of the planters, and the increasing economic independence of the workers. On the former development, he reported that the larger estates had more "hands than they can afford to pay at the present rate of wages. . . ." On the latter, he reported that on other properties "great difficulty is found in pro-

curing labour, as the Negroes are certainly more intent in working their own grounds than cultivating the estate, finding it more profitable than any wages that could be offered them . . ." (Colonial Office [CO] 137/242/240).

Landscapes and the Means of Production in the Yallahs Drainage

Just as the economy of the Yallahs drainage in the 19th century was dominated by the production of coffee the landscape of the region was dominated by coffee plantations. To understand how class relations were negotiated on coffee plantations it is now necessary to examine how members of the various classes interacted within coffee plantation landscapes and to describe the relationships members of the various classes had with the primary means of production required for coffee.

In the pre-emancipation era the planter class established hegemonic control over the means of production through the exercise of monopoly control over the legal possession of agricultural land and the knowledge and capital required to construct coffee works. In Jamaica, this monopoly was established by the middle of the 18th century when a mere 467 people, or 2.9% of the white population, held possession of 78% of this land, each holding in excess of 1000 acres (Sheridan 1974:219). This figure seems all the more oppressive when one considers that by 1790 the enslaved population of Jamaica was approximately 211,000 people while the planter classes numbered less than 25,000. Thus approximately 0.002% of Jamaica's estimated population (here considering absentees in the equation) had economic control of over 78% of the island's productive land (Deerr 1950; Higman 1976:255). As the mills and other industrial buildings required for preparing commodities for export were generally located on the individual plantations, one can conclude that this same small minority of landowners controlled approximately the same proportion of the industrial means of production, including the knowledge, raw material, capital and/or the technology required to construct the mill machinery required for export production.

Jamaican planters usually required the enslaved population to produce their own food. Heads of enslaved households were granted access to land known as provision grounds; the food grown in provision ground gardens provided most of the nutritional requirements for the population, as well as the small amount of surplus exchanged in local markets. Prior to emancipation it was recognized by both the planters and the enslaved that these provision grounds were the de facto economic property of the enslaved; that is to say, it was the enslaved who controlled the sale and distribution of produce grown in these garden plots. The historic record for Radnor Coffee Plantation, one of the estates located in the Yallahs drainage (Figure 1), indicates that by the early 1820s a number of the enslaved workers sold produce directly to the white estate staff in exchange for cash (Delle 1996). The actual size of the allotted plots probably varied depending on the individual planter and the quality of land designated for provisions (Mintz 1960). For example, in 1790 the Jamaican plantation observer William Beckford commented that a "quarter acre . . . will be fully sufficient for the supply of a moderate family, and may enable [them] to carry some to market besides . . ."(Beckford 1790:257).

Since provision grounds were spaces occupied and utilized by the enslaved for their own use, little information on pre-emancipation provision grounds appears on period maps or plans of the Yallahs region. Nevertheless, some observations can be made from the cartographic record. A pre-emancipation estate map of Mavis Bank identifies 79 ¾ of the estate's 302 acres, approximately 26% of the estate's acreage, as "Negro Grounds and Provisions." While the boundaries of the "Negro Grounds" are clearly demarcated, no internal subdivision within the general area is rendered. This suggests that the surveyor either was not interested in the exact allocation of that land, or else did not gain access to this particu-

lar area of the plantation. It is also possible, given the use of this space, that the planters were not interested in the exact allocation of the land, but left the allocation and occupation of the land to the enslaved workers themselves. As the enslaved population of Mavis Bank in 1817 numbered 106, it can be estimated that approximately ¾ of an acre was allocated per capita; it remains impossible to say, however, just how much of the land was under cultivation at any given time.

An 1806 depiction of Radnor Plantation gives some further indication of how provision grounds fit into the internal division of material space on coffee plantations (Higman 1986, 1988). Of the estate's 689 acres, 133 acres were in "Negro grounds and provisions," while an additional 222 acres were in "woodland and Negro grounds." There were four separate areas of the plantation designated as "Negro grounds," and a fifth identified as "woodland." As was the case on Mavis Bank, most of this land was located along the periphery of the estate. On Radnor, the distance between the slave village and the provision grounds was between one-third and three-quarters of a mile. Just under one acre of provision ground and woodlot was allocated per capita in 1807 (Higman 1986).

When the British Parliament abolished slavery in 1834, the relationships both the planter and laboring classes had with land changed. The Jamaican planters attempted to create a new class structure which would maintain their hegemonic control over the island's export economy and the laborers' relationship to land. After 1838 many formerly enslaved workers entered into wage relationships with the planter class, selling their labor power to the estates in exchange for a wage. These newly freed tenant farmers were expected by the planters-turned landlords to pay rent both for the houses they occupied (which in many cases were the same houses the occupants had built for themselves while enslaved) and on the provision grounds they tilled. Land that had once been recognized as the economic property of the enslaved was redesignated as the economic property of the planters. To make use of the provision grounds, land in which ironically they were free to produce surplus while enslaved, many emancipated workers were forced into wage relationships with the planters just to be able to afford the rent on their gardens.

The planters' demand for rent often met with resentment, and was resisted by many of the newly freed laborers; the courts were crowded with cases for non-payment of rent (Holt 1992:138). When several cases were decided in favor of the workers, the planter class sought to legislate new conditions through which they could control the land. A notable example of this strategy of domination was the Summary Ejectment Law passed by the Jamaica Assembly in 1840. This law allowed the planters to eject at will people from land they occupied but which they did not hold legally, including provision grounds. The laboring class resisted such efforts by purchasing their own land or squatting on vacant land in areas remote from the centers of white settlement.

By the end of the 1840s it was clear that the planters' strategy to remain in monopoly control over the means of production was failing. For example, while in 1840 there were only 2,830 small freeholds of less than 50 acres in the island, by 1845 this number had increased almost ten-fold to 24,268, and more than doubled again to 60,000 by 1865. Simultaneously, the number of large land holdings of 1000 acres or more declined from 755 in 1850 to 503 in 1880 (Higman 1988:17; Holt 1992:268).

After the abolition of slavery, the planter class began to pay closer attention to how the laborers used their provision grounds. As some records were kept by the planter class concerning acreage tilled and rents paid by emancipated laborers it is possible to say more about the material spaces of African Jamaicans in the post-emancipation period than it is during the time of slavery. For example, a plan of Green Valley (Figure 1) plantation rendered in 1837 was drawn specifically to measure the extent of the provision grounds cultivated by the apprenticed laborers attached to the estate. According to this plan,

the only rendition of provision grounds known to exist for the Yallahs region, that part of the estate utilized for provisions was divided into 18 pieces, ranging in size from 3½ to 13½ acres. This document is all the more significant in as much as it identifies the types of foodstuffs produced on each parcel and identifies the people who worked each piece of land. The heading above the lists of names reads "[the] following are the names of those apprentices who posses grounds . . ." indicating that even from the perspective of the planters the laborers held some claim to possession, if not ownership, of their provision grounds.

The post-emancipation history of Whitfield Hall exemplifies a different course followed by the planter class in the Yallahs region (Figure 1). Crop accounts for this plantation indicate that the formerly enslaved workers and their descendants rented cottages and land from the estate. Unfortunately, the records do not indicate the size of the rented grounds or the number of renters. One can surmise, however, that the renting option was not a popular one with the laboring class. In 1842 the estate collected £36 in rent. The total amount of rent collected declined each year through 1846, when a mere £8..2..0 was collected. No record of rent collected appears in the accounts following this date, which may indicate either that the landlords abandoned the idea of trying to construct tenant farming on the estate, or else the farmers abandoned their rented lands and relocated on better terms on another estate, purchased land for themselves, or else began squatting on one of the many abandoned plantations located in the region.

The Landscapes of Class Negotiation

Historical archaeologists, particularly those involved in landscape archaeology, recognize that particular spaces influence and shape the negotiation of social relations between classes in context-specific ways (Leone 1988, 1995; Mrozowski 1990; Shackel 1994; Hood 1996). Having discussed in general terms how the class hierarchy in Jamaica was constructed socially and in the landscape, we now turn to a consideration of three specific landscapes—those of Chesterfield, Clydesdale, and Sherwood Forest plantations (Figure 1). A description of the material remains of these Yallahs coffee plantations is followed by an analysis of how these spaces mediated the negotiation of class relations in the Blue Mountains.

The Material Remains of Chesterfield, Clydesdale, and Sherwood Forest

As Jamaican coffee plantations were built in accordance to the general logic of estate production, the landscapes of Chesterfield, Clydesdale, and Sherwood Forest were segmented into task specific zones. The estate staff, including the overseers, plantation managers, and owners if they were present, inhabited an elite space dominated by the great house and its appendages, yards, and gardens. The overseer inhabited a space which mediated between the spatial dominance of the great house and the spaces of both coerced labor and the supervised domestic lives of the workers. The estates were further divided into coffee fields, industrial processing and storage areas, and provision grounds (Laborie 1798; Roughley 1823:187-188; Pulsipher and Goodwin

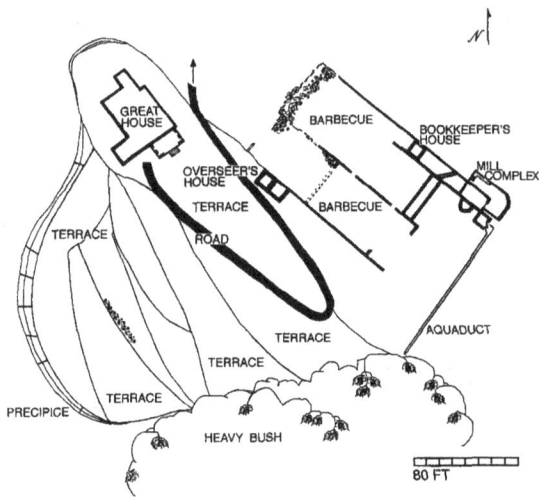

Figure 3. Site plan of Chesterfield.

1982; Higman 1988:80-81; 82; Orser 1988:85-93; Armstrong 1990; Delle 1994; Pulsipher 1994; Reeves 1997).

Coffee works minimally included a pulping mill to extract the beans from the berries, a set of drying platforms known as barbecues, and a second machine for removing a thin skin, known as parchment, from the dried beans. The process of pulping required a vast amount of water, not only to power the machinery, but also because the process of separating the beans from pulp required suspending the pulp in water and then separating the beans from the solution. Coffee works thus required holding tanks or vats and an aqueduct system to divert water from a river, stream, or spring to the coffee works (Laborie 1798; Higman 1988; Montieth 1991).

The pulping mill at Clydesdale is located within a massive two-story stone structure, which measures 26 ft. 8in. x 54 ft. 10 in. The ground floor of the structure contains the mill machinery; the pulping mill and water wheel are located on the western side of the large single room composing the ground floor. The vertical overshot water wheel was originally powered by an aqueduct which transported water from the Clyde River into the mill complex. The upper floor

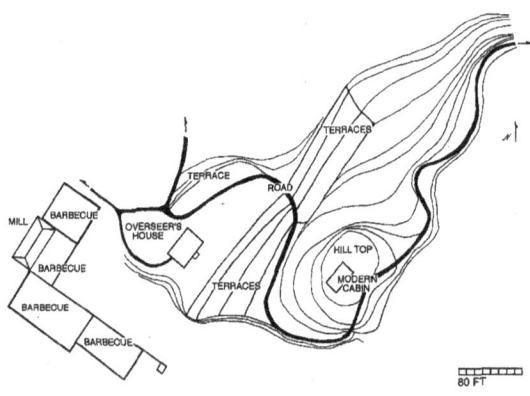

Figure 2. Site plan of Clydesdale.

contains two large rooms that may have been occupied by members of the estate staff, but given that these rooms are located within the mill building, and that they were probably never finished, it is likely that they were used as a warehouse space or coffee store. The mill is flanked to the west by a linear series of barbecues (Figure 2).

The mill complex at Chesterfield is in a poor state of preservation (Figure 3). Nothing remains of the pulping mill save a foundation. From this scanty evidence, however, several observations about the material space of the mill can be drawn. The ruins of an aqueduct indicate that water from the Fall River was diverted to power the mill and to fill the several cisterns surrounding the foundation ruin. As was the case with Clydesdale, the mill was a distinct structure, located away from the overseer's house. Unlike the Clydesdale barbecues, which were located on level ground abutting the Clyde River, a series of barbecues at Chesterfield were terraced into a hillside which overlooks the confluence of the Yallahs River and the Fall River.

The original pulping mill at Sherwood Forest differs from those at Clydesdale and Chesterfield as it was actually located within the overseer's house. The mill was housed in one room of this structure, while the overseer's domestic space

was located in the other. Like the mills at Clydesdale and Chesterfield, the pulping mill was water powered. Unlike the other two estates, however, Sherwood Forest is not situated below a river, but rather is located above the Negro River. To compensate for this, the mill complex contains a spring-fed cistern, which serves as a sort of "mill pond." During the pulping process, water from the cistern was channeled to the mill by means of a small aqueduct, which survives today, but is not functional. The barbecues at Sherwood Forest are similar to those at Chesterfield, as they are terraced into a hillside. Above the terraced barbecues is a series of smaller terraces which are currently used as a coffee nursery. It is possible that this was the original function of these terraces, as coffee plants require careful nurturing for several years before they can be transplanted into the coffee fields. It is likely that each plantation had some kind of nursery facility (Figure 4).

Although the European population on each coffee plantation was small, there was nevertheless a distinct class structure in place incorporating planter/owners, overseers, and bookkeepers. The class structure was reified by the spaces reserved for members of these distinct classes; this class-stratified space was manifested most directly in the creation of the material spaces of overseers' houses and great houses.

As was the case during the actual production of coffee, the production of plantation space was supervised by the overseer. The overseer was the de facto manager of the estate, responsible for organizing labor and supervising the production and distribution of coffee as an agricultural commodity (Stewart 1971 [1808]:129–130; Hall 1989; Walvin 1994:239). As resident managers, overseers served as intermediaries between the planter-owners and the laborers; their houses both reflected and created this relationship. To interpret the material space of this class of supervisor, we can turn to the archaeological record of the Yallahs region, which retains several examples of overseers' houses in various stages of preservation.

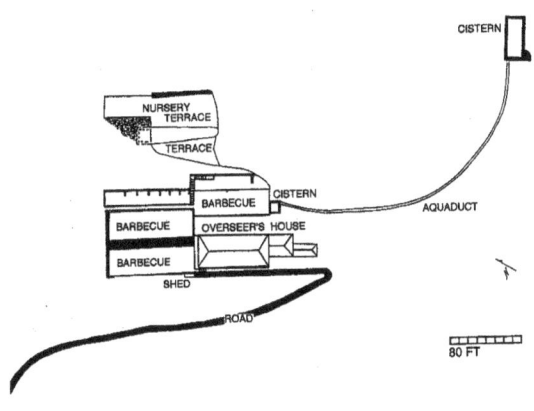

Figure 4. Site Plan of Sherwood Forest.

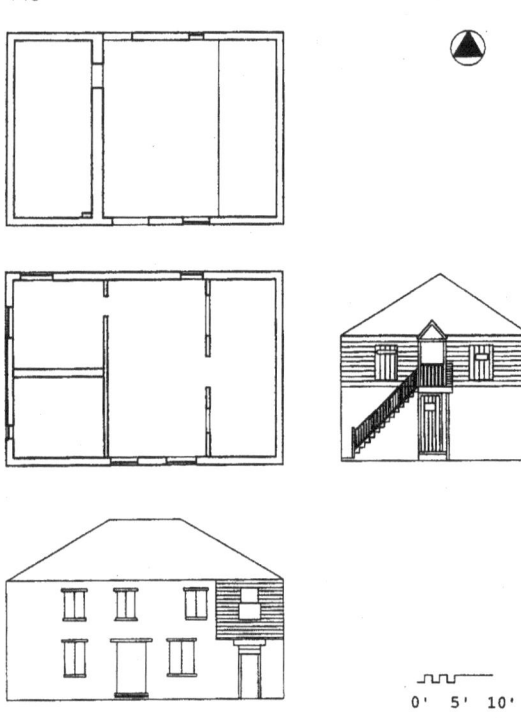

Figure 5. Architectural drawing of Clydesdale overseer's house.

Perhaps the best example of an extant overseer's house is that located on Clydesdale (Figure 5). The Clydesdale overseer's house is located within the industrial complex of the plantation. This is a two story building; however, the only access to the second story is an exterior staircase, originally constructed of wood. The upper story is finished, suggesting that this area was the domestic space of the overseer, while the lower story is not, suggesting that this area was used for either storing tools, equipment, or coffee. The upper story is divided into three rooms and originally included a second floor veranda, now sheathed in clapboards. It is likely that the largest of the three rooms served as a social area in which the overseer would entertain guests and conduct business, while the other two served as bedrooms. The veranda overlooked the coffee works, allowing the overseer to supervise the pulping and drying of coffee without having to

leave the comfort of this house. The walls of this building are constructed of cut stone, and are two feet thick. Clearly, the overseer was able to isolate himself and his family with a significant physical buffer between them, the elements, and the enslaved workers. Since the exterior stairway was the only access to the domestic quarters of the upper story, once the door was bolted the overseer was in a virtually impenetrable fortress.

The overseer's house at Sherwood Forest exhibits two phases of construction, with the older section actually serving as part of the foundation for the later house. As was the case with Clydesdale, the earlier overseer's house is a relatively small structure built with massive stone walls. This structure is divided into two rooms which housed the domestic space of the overseer and the pulping mill, respectively. In this case, the overseer was in direct sensual contact with the first stage of coffee processing. The other key architectural feature of this building was a veranda, oriented toward the barbecues. From this vantage point, the overseer had the capability to continuously observe the drying beans. At Sherwood Forest, the domestic space of the overseer, at least during the first phase of the plantation's existence, was inseparable from the space of production.

Another example of an overseer's house survives at Chesterfield. This small house also exhibits two phases of construction (Figure 6). In the first phase it was a squat, two story building, with one room on each floor. The interior rooms each measure 10 x 10 ft. and the 2 ft. thick walls are made from field stone covered with lime plaster. Both this building and the plantation experienced a second phase of construction, probably beginning in 1824. During this phase of expansion, a 10 x 12 ft. room was added to the second story, atop a massive stone foundation. The walls of this new room were far more gracile than the massive field stone walls of the original. The new walls were a mere 7 in. thick, constructed with a technique which local informants described as "nag"— which is little more than a sophisticated form of wattle and daub. The wattle is a mesh of iron wire, which would be attached to studs. A type of lime mortar or concrete would be poured between the studs, forming, in effect, a seven inch thick plaster wall. The remains of the Chesterfield Great House, located nearby, demonstrate that this building, too, was constructed with the nag technique. The historic record of the plantation indicates that in 1824 the planter hired a "jobbing gang" from a nearby plantation to assist with the construction of these buildings. It seems likely that given the expense of such hired labor in the mid 1820s, the two buildings indicate a considerable investment in the improvement of elite space on Chesterfield.

As was the case at Sherwood Forest, the overseer at Chesterfield was in direct contact with production. Although the pulping mill was not located in the house, it was oriented in such a way as to allow the overseer to supervise the coffee crop as it dried on the barbecues. He was in visual contact with the mill, so that although not as intimately linked to the production process, the overseer was indeed in a position to

watch production as he saw fit, without having to leave his own domestic space.

Although it is possible that these structures were massively built out of stone to protect the overseers from hurricanes, an ecologically-based explanation for the massive construction is unsatisfactory. At least two nearby plantations, Abbey Green and Whitfield Hall, had overseers' houses built of timber. Both of these houses are still standing, and are actually in better shape than the Chesterfield house. In addition, the second phase of construction at Sherwood Forest was also a timber-framed house. It is notable that both Whitfield Hall and Sherwood Forest had smaller laboring populations than did Clydesdale or Chesterfield (Delle 1996). The fact that timber-framed buildings existed in the Yallahs region suggests that the construction of stone overseers' houses was a choice not a necessity based on ecological constraints. Massive stone walls may have been built to provide a more secure buffer between the overseers and the enslaved population on the larger estates.

In contrast to the number of standing overseers' houses in the Yallahs region, there are very few surviving great houses. For example, while the locations of the great houses for both Sherwood Forest and Whitfield Hall are known by local residents neither remains standing. It is unclear why this is the case, although it may be speculated that 1) the cost of maintaining larger houses in the post-emancipation era prohibited their reuse after the coffee industry failed or 2) since these houses were often vacant even prior to emancipation they fell to ruin more quickly than overseers' houses which would have been continuously occupied. Regardless of the cause, of the three plantations under consideration, visible ruins of a great house exist only at Chesterfield.

The great house at Chesterfield was much larger than any of the overseers' houses in the region, reflecting the class distinction between estate proprietors and their white employees. The floor plan of the great house indicates that the structure contained a 15 ft. 6 in. x 18 ft.

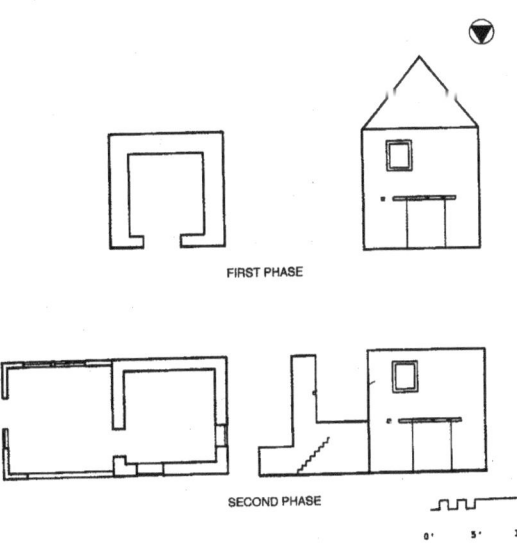

FIRST PHASE

SECOND PHASE

0'   5'   10'

Figure 6. Architectural drawing of Chesterfield overseer's house.

hall, three chambers, and an attached kitchen with a store room. A small 4 x 9 ft. room with its own attached veranda may have served as the planter's office. Two additional rooms in the back of the house, near the kitchen, may have served as the quarters for domestic servants. This house also had a veranda, which overlooked the river valley, the industrial works, the overseer's house, and the coffee fields; the cartographic record of Chesterfield indicates that the latter were located on the opposite side of the Yallahs River.

Enslaved workers in the Yallahs region probably lived in nucleated villages clustered in areas defined by the planters as marginal to coffee production. Unlike the industrial and elite housing on the estates, the domestic houses of the workers were constructed of perishable materials, and thus were impermanent structures. In the attempt to locate the villages surface surveys of Chesterfield, Sherwood Forest, and Clydesdale were conducted in 1994. Comparing location information obtained from the historic maps to modern topographic maps and the actually existing landscapes, the locations of slave villages at Radnor and Clydesdale were identified; unfortunately the presence of modern coffee trees at the former and severe bulldozer disturbance at the latter prohibited excavation. Surface reconnaissance at Chesterfield did not reveal the location of a village. Attempts to locate this village were thwarted not only by the relative silence of surface record for the structures, but by erosion and other depositional processes which have undoubtedly removed surficial evidence of the village. Furthermore, as both Clydesdale and Sherwood Forest were under coffee cultivation during the 1992-1994 field seasons, the areas available for subsurface testing were limited.

Nevertheless, some preliminary observations can be made about the layout of slave villages based on an analysis of two cartographic representations of pre-emancipation villages. The first such representation is Barry Higman's (1986, 1988) reproduction of an 1806 plan of Radnor. In 1806 the entire slave village, a cluster of 30

buildings located in a meadow, which occupied 2.7 acres of land (Higman 1986) housed 252 people (Delle 1996). If one assumes that the plan reproduced by Higman accurately depicted the number of houses, and that the relevant slave return data accurate, then an average of 8 people occupied each structure. Regardless of the actual number of houses, if all 252 people were indeed living in the 2.7 acre meadow, the village would have been a very densely populated place indeed. It should be noted that this densely populated zone only incorporates the area encompassing the slave village. It is likely that many people spent much of their time in the provision grounds. The only other representation of a slave settlement on a coffee plantation map that can be confidently dated to the pre-emancipation period is a depiction of Clydesdale dated 1810. According to this map, 10 houses were located in a 10-acre field. In 1818 it was reported that 109 laborers were attached to the plantation. If we accept that there were 10 houses in the village, this information suggests that there were approximately 11 people per house.

Features of post-emancipation villages can be interpreted from historic estate plans of two nearby estates, Ayton and Abbey Green, rendered by the surveyor James Smith in the 1850s. These indicate the location of "Negro Houses"; in each case, the houses appear clustered together, much as they had in the pre-emancipation villages. The Abbey Green plan shows the relative location of 17 individual buildings; in January of 1839, special magistrate Henry Kent reported that there were 108 laborers residing on the estate (CO137/242/241). Assuming the accuracy of the house counts and Kent's figures, each structure on Abbey Green housed an average of about 6 people; those at Ayton between 2.1 and 3.5 people per house. These numbers are consistent with a variety of possible household membership structures, including both nuclear family and extended family structures. The maps may thus represent the number of houses and hence the household size in the post-emancipation Yallahs region.

Negotiating the Landscape

As should be clear by now, members of the various classes perceived and experienced Yallahs plantations landscapes differently. The planter class who designed the estate landscapes actively constructed plantation spaces—or more accurately, had enslaved workers create the plantation spaces according to the planters' designs—as an active part of their strategy of social control. It was within these landscapes that class relations were negotiated; as such, the planter classes designed spaces with which they could most effectively control the lives and labor of African Jamaican workers, and thus better create profits for them-selves. Just as these landscapes of control were designed to maximize efficient production and exert subtle social controls over those forced to toil on Jamaican coffee estates, so too did these landscapes serve as arenas of resistance against these same oppressive social relations of production.

As Upton (1988, 1992), Orser (1988b), and Leone (1995) have argued, under capitalism the position of structures and the division of social space on a landscape express power and class relations. The archaeological evidence of the Yallahs plantation landscapes indicates that such power was negotiated particularly through surveillance over the plantation population both at home

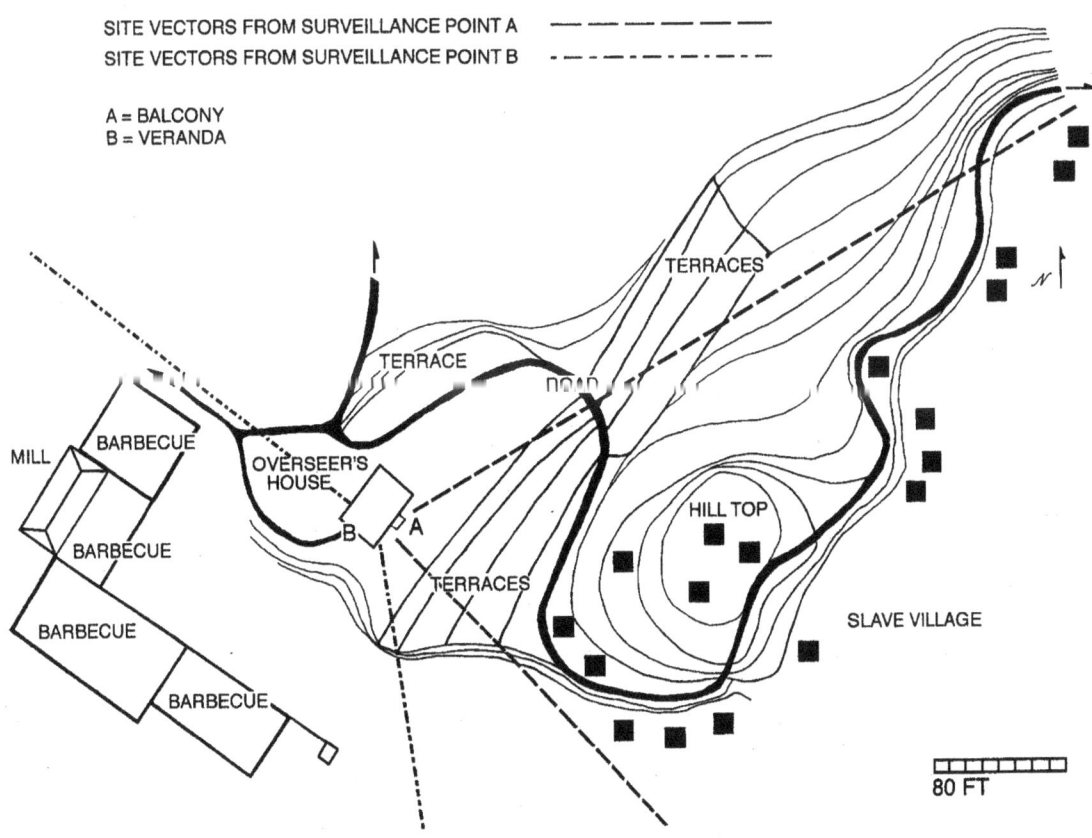

Figure 7. Composite site plan of Clydesdale

and at work; maximizing panoptic viewscapes was key to landscape design. In the Yallahs context such landscapes of surveillance are best considered at Clydesdale, given the superior preservation of the plantation's buildings and the extent of its cartographic record. Using these two data sources, it is possible to create a composite map which can usefully reconstruct the landscape of surveillance (Figure 7). The overseer's house featured two surveillance positions. The first was the entrance door to the overseer's house, which probably had a small landing at the top of a wooden stair. From this point, the overseer could monitor the slave village, which was located uphill from the house, within the viewscape of this position. The path from the village to both the coffee fields and the industrial works passed directly by this point. Thus, without leaving the material confines of his house, the overseer could survey the domestic quarters of the workers, and supervise the morning procession to work as the laborers passed below him on their way to the fields and mill.

The second surveillance point was the veranda of the overseers house. The coffee works and barbecues were located downhill and within the viewscape of this vantage point. From the comfort of his veranda the overseer could supervise the coffee works and any activity occurring on the barbecues. During those times when the overseer wanted to exert the greatest measure of control over the workers, he could practice panoptic surveillance over the population. This method of social control relied equally on the direct observation of the watcher and on creating the perception that the workers were being constantly observed, whether the overseer was watching them directly or not. By locating the overseer's house in such a way that the overseer could survey both the village and works from the veranda, or even by simply gazing out of one of the house's windows, the workers could never be entirely sure when they were being watched. The purpose behind the construction of this landscape was the construction of an internalized discipline in the work force; the logic of the

panopticon dictated that the workers would cooperate if they thought there were a possibility that their behavior at any given moment was under scrutiny (Foucault 1979).

Changes in the domestic spaces of the elites, particularly the overseer's houses, reflect the changes in social relations that occurred following emancipation. For example the form of the overseer's house at Sherwood Forest changed considerably over time. The original overseer's house was constructed with 21 in. thick stone walls. A veranda provided the overseer with a southern view which encompassed the coffee drying platforms while an 18 in. thick interior wall separated the overseer's room from the pulping mill which was contained in the same building as the overseer's domestic space. Although contained within an imposing fortress-like structure, as long as he was in his room or on his veranda, the overseer could directly supervise the production of coffee. From the veranda the overseer could monitor the coffee crop as it dried, while from his room he could watch the coffee as it was pulped and channeled to the drying platforms. This spatial arrangement created an intensive capacity for surveillance over production while simultaneously and physically segregating the overseer from the work force.

The second phase of construction at the overseer's house was much more gracile, and served to remove the overseer from the direct surveillance of production. The second house was literally built on top of the first; the older house served as part of the foundation for the newer structure. This later building was timber framed, and itself experienced several phases of construction. The pulping and grinding mills remained in the building, but were now located on a lower floor, separating the overseer's domestic space somewhat from the direct activity of production. Interestingly, the veranda of the second building is oriented to the east. The viewscape from this perspective encompasses a scenic view of the valley and surrounding hills and not the barbecues. To directly see what was happening on the barbecues, the overseer would have to crane his neck as it takes more than a casual effort to supervise production from this vantage point.

This new spatial arrangement reflects the change in the relations of production which developed after emancipation. Beginning in the late 1840s, Sherwood Forest began acquiring the estates which bounded it to the east and south; the previously independent estates of Arntully and Eccleston were defined in the crop accounts of the 1850s as appendages to Sherwood Forest. The comfortable wooden structure may have developed into a post-emancipation great house from which the affairs of the several plantations were managed. In his discussion of Arntully, Higman (1988:175) notes that no great house was indicated in the 1839 plan of this Yallahs region estate; this may substantiate the hypothesis that during the 1840s at least, the affairs of Arntully may have been directed from Sherwood Forest.

Conclusion

By the middle of the 1850s, the Jamaican coffee industry was on the verge of collapse. In 1855 special magistrate Henry Kent remarked: "[i]t is difficult now to procure labour, the able bodied people having mostly left the estates" (CO 137/327/97). An unsigned dispatch from 1857 reveals that the newly developing class structure was such that the planter class could no longer control the landscapes of production: ". . . there is great difficulty experienced in carrying on cultivation; the able bodied Negroes having left the estates and idlying their time away upon their small freeholds . . ." (CO137/334/24).

A final blow to the Jamaican coffee industry was the leveling of colonial duties. In the late 1840s and 1850s the Jamaican planters could not compete with the cheaper coffee produced with the fresher soils and contract labor of Ceylon and the vast slave-labor production of Brazil. When asked by a Parliamentary committee to account for the rapid abandonment of Jamaican coffee plantations, the coffee planter Alexander Geddes testified that "the great cause for the abandonment of the coffee plantations is the low price now obtained . . . owing to the introduction of slave and Ceylon coffee" (PP 1847-1848, 23/2:20). According to Geddes's testimony, the abandonment of coffee estates had begun immediately following the end of apprenticeship, a time when the planter class had great difficulty controlling the negotiation of class relations between themselves and the newly freed workers. It is quite evident that changes in the global economy were directly effecting changes both in class relations and the form of plantation landscapes in the Yallahs region at this time.

The class dynamics of the Yallahs region changed dramatically in the first half of the 19th century, as both the conditions of labor and land tenure, two key factors in the negotiation of class relations, were radically reconstructed with the end of slavery. It was, of course, relatively simple for the planter class to maintain its virtual monopoly over land and labor prior to the abolition of slavery, a time when the planters exerted great control over the conditions of labor, the class structure, and thus the relations of production. With emancipation, however, the planters' quest to retain control over both the means and the social relations of production became much more difficult. Even before the abolition of slavery, many of the estates that had previously been productive during the boom years of the Napoleonic wars had failed; hundreds of estates were abandoned by the planters following emancipation. As a result, there were literally hundreds of thousands of acres of land lying unoccupied when slavery was fully abolished in 1838. Following emancipation, many African-Jamaican people abandoned both the land on which they had lived and their role in the production of export crops, opting instead to carve a subsistence living on small plots in the interior, supplementing their domestic economy by producing small surpluses to be sold in local town and city markets. They were acting in such a way as to take control over the material negotiation between themselves as working people, and the landowners, who attempted to construct from their numbers a wage-earning rural proletariat.

If, as Leone and Potter (1988) argued a decade ago, historical archaeologists need to be aware of the social context in which they work, and make their analyses of the past relevant to the present, we are given no choice but to confront the issue of class. The unequal accumulation of material wealth holds a place of central importance in the structure of capitalist society; one's relative ability to accumulate that material wealth plays a large part in the negotiation of class relations. As society is increasingly fragmented into specialized markets based on a given demographic group's ability to purchase material goods, as citizens continue to be redefined as consumers, as the largest corporations continue to control more wealth than most national governments, as capitalism penetrates into the final hidden corners of Amazonia, Central Asia, and Eastern Europe, and as these phenomena increasingly define the shape of global society, we as social scientists would do well to focus our studies on the processes that resulted in the historical trajectories which created the world of the late 20th century. At the head of this list of processes is the definition and negotiation of social classes.

The landscapes of coffee plantations in eastern Jamaica were but one arena in which class relations were historically negotiated. In many ways the landscapes of these plantations were designed and lived in such a way as to maximize the planter class's ability to control the work force through technologies of surveillance. In the years following the end of slavery, these landscapes of surveillance, despite the best efforts of the planter class, became less useful in the maintenance of the severe class hierarchy imposed under the slave regime. The newly freed workers found ways to resist the planter class by creating new landscapes of their own, in which they exerted control over both meanings of and production from landscapes. It was only by the creation of oppressive government controls over

vacant land, like the Summary Ejectment Law, and the enforcement of legislation controlling the amount of surplus production which the laboring class was allowed to export, that the post-emancipation planter class was able to dictate the terms of the landscapes of class hierarchy and maintain their control over Jamaica's political economy.

The late 20th century is witnessing two not unrelated phenomena. While communication and surveillance technologies are becoming increasingly sophisticated, an ever-increasing percentage of the world's population is being incorporated into the global capitalist system, most as members of the working class. As the number of people in the working class is growing exponentially, manufacturing and financial corporations are creating new and better technologies with which to create and direct the flow of surplus wealth and to exert control over the dynamics of class negotiation. Specific forms of material culture play a central role in this process; for example internet hardware, cellular phones, and automatic surveillance cameras are increasing the ability of the wealthier classes to supervise and direct the production and distribution of goods by the working classes. Such phenomena did not spontaneously appear in a vacuum but are the result of specific and complex historical trajectories, including the creation and negotiation of coffee plantation landscapes in 19th-century Jamaica. As scholars interested in the ways that material culture mediates social relations, historical archaeologists would do well to examine how various forms of material culture, including such landscapes, influenced the shape of class relations in the recent past to better understand how and why the current class structure emerged.

ACKNOWLEDGMENTS

I would like to thank all of those who assisted me in constructing this paper. I am grateful to LouAnn Wurst and Rob Fitts for inviting me to participate in this volume; especially LouAnn who read through numerous drafts and always offered sound advice for the paper's improvement. The HA reviewers also provided helpful comments. I would also like to thank Bob Paynter, Martin Wobst, and Ben Howatt who advised me on the larger project from which this paper sprung. A number of individuals assisted my research in Jamaica, including Doug Armstrong, Matt Reeves, Dorrick Gray, Spider Walters, Dr. Charles Deichman, John Allgrove, Lance Douglas, Mike Volmar, Jim Dooley, Jackie Watson, and especially Mary Ann Levine. I am grateful for the assistance extended me by the staffs of the Jamaica National Heritage Trust, the Jamaica Forestry Department, the Jamaica Archives, and the National Library of Jamaica. This research was funded by the Wenner-Gren Foundation for Anthropological Research.

REFERENCES CITED

ARMSTRONG, DOUGLAS V.
   1990   *The Old Village and the Great House: An Archaeological and Historical Examination of Drax Hall Plantation, St. Ann's Bay, Jamaica.* University of Illinois Press, Urbana.

ARMSTRONG, DOUGLAS V. AND KENNETH G. KELLY.
   1990   Settlement Pattern Shifts in a Jamaican Slave Village, Seville Estate, St. Ann's Bay, Jamaica. Paper Presented at the Annual Conference on Historical and Underwater Archaeology, Tucson, AZ.

BEAUDRY, MARY C.
   1989   The Lowell Boott Mills Complex and Its Housing: Material Expressions of Corporate Ideology. *Historical Archaeology* 23 (1):19-32.
   1996   Why Gardens? In *Landscape Archaeology: Reading and Interpreting the American Historical Landscape*, edited by Rebecca Yamin and Karen B. Methony, pp. 3-5. University of Tennessee Press, Knoxville.

BEAUDRY, MARY C., LAUREN COOK, AND STEPHEN A. MROZOWSKI
   1991   Artifacts and Active Voices: Material Culture as Social Discourse. In *The Archaeology of Inequality*, edited by Randall H. McGuire and Robert Paynter, pp. 150-191. Basil Blackwell, Oxford.

BECKFORD, WILLIAM
   1790   *A Descriptive Account of the Island of Jamaica.* T. and J. Egerton, London.

BUTLER, KATHLEEN M.
   1995   *The Economics of Emancipation: Jamaica & Barbados, 1823-1843.* University of North Carolina Press, Chapel Hill.

CHECKLAND, S. G.
   1957   Finance for the West Indies, 1780-1815. *Economic History Review* 10:461-469.

COLONIAL OFFICE RECORDS (CO)
   1839   Colonial Office Records. Public Records Office of
   -1857 England, Kew.

DAVIS, DAVID BRION
   1975   *The Problem of Slavery in the Age of Revolution, 1770-1823.* Cornell University Press, Ithaca, NY.

DEERR, NOEL
   1950   *The History of Sugar.* Chapman and Hall, London.

DELLE, JAMES A.
   1994   A Spatial Analysis of Sugar Plantations on St. Eustatius, Netherlands Antilles. In *Spatial Patterning in Historical Archaeology: Selected Studies of Settlement*, edited by Donald W. Linebaugh and Gary G. Robinson, pp. 33-62. King and Queen Press, Williamsburg, VA.
   1996   *An Archaeology of Crisis: The Manipulation of Social Spaces in the Blue Mountains of Jamaica, 1790-1865.* Ph.D. dissertation, Department of Anthropology, University of Massachusetts, Amherst. University Microfilms International, Ann Arbor, MI.

FOUCAULT, MICHEL
   1979   *Discipline and Punish: The Birth of the Prison.* Vintage Books, New York.

GREEN, WILLIAM
   1976   *British Slave Emancipation: The Sugar Colonies and the Great Experiment, 1830-1865.* Clarendon Press, Oxford, England.

HALL, DOUGLAS
   1989   *In Miserable Slavery: Thomas Thistlewood in Jamaica, 1750-86.* Macmillan, London.

HIGMAN, BARRY
   1976   *Slave Population and Economy in Jamaica, 1807-1834.* Cambridge University Press, London, England.
   1986   Jamaican Coffee Plantations 1780-1860: A Cartographic Analysis. *Caribbean Geography* 2:73-91.
   1988   *Jamaica Surveyed: Plantation Maps and Plans of the Eighteenth and Nineteenth Centuries.* Institute of Jamaica, Kingston.

HOLT, THOMAS
   1992   *The Problem of Freedom: Race, Labor, and Politics in Jamaica and Britain, 1832-1938.* Johns Hopkins University Press, Baltimore, MD.

HOOD, J. EDWARD
   1995   Some Observations on Interpreting the Archaeology of a New England Village to the Public. Paper Presented at the Annual Meeting of the Society for American Archaeology, Minneapolis, MN.

1996 Social Relations and the Cultural Landscape. In *Landscape Archaeology: Reading and Interpreting the American Historical Landscape*, edited by Rebecca Yamin and Karen B. Metheny, pp. 121-146. University of Tennessee Press, Knoxville.

HOOD, J. EDWARD AND RITA REINKE.
1989 Manipulating the Landscape: Some Evidence from Deerfield, Massachusetts. Paper Presented at the Annual Meeting of the Eastern States Archaeological Federation, East Windsor, CT.

HUDGINS, CARTER L.
1990 Robert "King" Carter and the Landscape of Tidewater Virginia in the Eighteenth Century. In *Earth Patterns: Essays in Landscape Archaeology*, edited by William Kelso and Rachel Most, pp. 59-70. University Press of Virginia, Charlottesville.

KELSO, WILLIAM
1990 Landscape Archaeology at Thomas Jefferson's Monticello. In *Earth Patterns: Essays in Landscape Archaeology*, edited by William Kelso and Rachel Most, pp. 7-22. University Press of Virginia, Charlottesville.

KRYDER-REID, ELIZABETH
1994 "As Is the Gardener, So Is the Garden": The Archaeology of Landscape as Myth. In *The Historical Archaeology of the Chesapeake*, edited by Paul A. Shackel and Barbara J. Little, pp. 131-148. Smithsonian Institution Press, Washington.

LABORIE, P.J.
1798 *The Coffee Planter of Saint Domingo*. T. Caddell and W. Davies, London.

LEONE, MARK P.
1984 Interpreting Ideology in Historical Archaeology: The William Paca Garden in Annapolis, Maryland. In *Ideology, Power and Prehistory*, edited by Daniel Miller and Christopher Tilley, pp. 25-35. Cambridge University Press, London, England.
1988 The Georgian Order as the Order of Merchant Capitalism in Annapolis, Maryland. In *The Recovery of Meaning: Historical Archaeology in the Eastern United States*, edited by Mark P. Leone and Parker B. Potter, Jr., pp. 219-229. Smithsonian Institution Press, Washington.
1995 A Historical Archaeology of Capitalism. *American Anthropologist* 97(2):251-268.

LEONE, MARK P. AND PARKER B. POTTER, JR.
1988 Introduction: Issues in Historical Archaeology. In *The Recovery of Meaning: Historical Archaeology in the Eastern United States*, edited by Mark P. Leone and

Parker B. Potter, Jr., pp. 1-20. Smithsonian Institution Press, Washington.

LEWIS, KENNETH
1984 *The American Frontier: An Archeological Study of Settlement Pattern and Process*. Academic Press, New York.
1985 Plantation Layout and Function in the South Carolina Lowcountry. In *The Archeology of Slavery and Plantation Life*, edited by Theresa Singleton, pp. 35-66. Academic Press, San Diego.

LOBDELL, R.
1972 Patterns of Investment and Sources of Credit in the British West Indian Sugar Industry. *Journal of Caribbean History* 4:31-53.

LUCCKETTI, NICHOLAS
1990 Archaeological Excavations at Bacon's Castle, Surry County, Virginia. In *Earth Patterns: Essays in Landscape Archaeology*, edited by William Kelso and Rachel Most, pp. 23-42. University Press of Virginia, Charlottesville.

McGUIRE, RANDALL H.
1988 Dialogues with the Dead: Ideology and the Cemetery. In *Recovery of Meaning*, edited by Mark Leone and Parker B. Potter, Jr., pp. 435-480. Smithsonian Institution Press, Washington.
1991 Building Power in the Cultural Landscape of Broome County, New York, 1880 to 1940. In *The Archaeology of Inequality*, edited by Randall H. McGuire and Robert Paynter, pp. 102-124. Basil Blackwell, Oxford, England.

McKEE, LARRY
1996 The Archaeology of Rachel's Garden. In *Landscape Archaeology: Reading and Interpreting the American Historical Landscape*, edited by Rebecca Yamin and Karen B. Metheny, pp. 70-90. University of Tennessee Press, Knoxville.

MINTZ, SIDNEY AND DOUGLAS HALL
1960 The Origins of the Jamaican Internal Marketing System. *Yale University Publications in Anthropology*. New Haven, CT.

MONTIETH, KATHLEEN
1991 The Coffee Industry in Jamaica, 1790-1850. Master's thesis, Department of History, University of the West Indies at Mona.

MORRISSEY, MARRIETTA
1989 *Slave Women in the New World: Gender Stratification in the Caribbean*. University of Kansas Press, Lawrence.

MROZOWSKI, STEPHEN
1991 Landscapes of Inequality. In *The Archaeology of Inequality*, edited by Randall. McGuire and Robert Paynter, pp. 79-101. Basil Blackwell, Oxford, England.

MROZOWSKI, STEPHEN A. AND MARY C. BEAUDRY
1990 Archaeology and the Landscape of Corporate Ideology. In *Earth Patterns: Essays in Landscape Archaeology*, edited by William Kelso and Rachel Most, pp. 189-208. University Press of Virginia, Charlottesville.

MROZOWSKI, STEPHEN A., GRACE H. ZIESING, AND MARY C. BEAUDRY
1996 *Living on the Boott: Historical Archaeology at the Boott Mills Boardinghouses, Lowell, Massachusetts.* University of Massachusetts Press, Amherst.

MULLINS, PAUL R.
1996 *The Contradictions of Consumption: An Archaeology of African America and Consumer Culture, 1850-1930.* Ph.D. dissertation, Department of Anthropology, University of Massachusetts, Amherst. University Microfilms International, Ann Arbor.

ORSER, CHARLES E., JR.
1988a *The Material Basis of the Postbellum Tenant Plantation: Historical Archaeology in the South Carolina Piedmont.* University of Georgia Press, Athens.
1988b Toward a Theory of Power for Historical Archaeology: Plantations and Space. In *The Recovery of Meaning*, edited by Mark Leone and Parker Potter, Jr., pp. 235-262. Smithsonian Institution Press, Washington.
1996 *A Historical Archaeology of the Modern World.* Plenum Press, New York.

ORSER, CHARLES E., JR. AND ANNETTE M. NEKOLA
1985 Plantation Settlement from Slavery to Tenancy: An Example from a Piedmont Plantation in South Carolina. In *The Archeology of Slavery and Plantation Life*, edited by Theresa Singleton, pp. 67-94. Academic Press, San Diego.

OTTO, JOHN S.
1977 Artifacts and Status Differences: A Comparison of Ceramics for Planter, Overseer, and Slave Sites on an Antebellum Plantation. In *Research Strategies in Historical Archeology*, edited by Stanley South, pp. 91-118. Academic Press, New York.

PARES, R.
1950 *A West-India Fortune.* Longmans, Green and Co., London.

PARLIAMENTARY PAPERS (PP)
1847 Parliamentary Papers. British Library, London.
-1848

PAYNTER, ROBERT
1980 *Long Distance Processes, Stratification and Settlement Pattern: An Archaeological Perspective.* Ph.D. dissertation, Department of Anthropology, University of Massachusetts, Amherst. University Microfilms International, Ann Arbor.
1981 Social Complexity in Peripheries: Problems and Models. In *Archaeological Approaches to the Study of Complexity*, edited by S. E. van der Leeuw, pp. 118-141. A. E. van Giffen Institute, Amsterdam, The Netherlands.
1982 *Models of Spatial Inequality.* Academic Press, New York.
1983 Expanding the Scope of Settlement Analysis. In *Archeological Hammers and Theories*, edited by James Moore and Arthur Keene, pp. 234-277. Academic Press, New York.
1985 Surplus Flow between Frontiers and Homelands. In *The Archeology of Frontiers and Boundaries*, edited by S. W. Green and S. M. Perlman, pp. 163-211. Academic Press, Orlando.

PAYNTER, ROBERT AND RANDALL H. MCGUIRE
1991 The Archaeology of Inequality: Material Culture, Domination and Resistance. In *The Archaeology of Inequality*, edited by Randall H. McGuire and Robert Paynter, pp. 1-27. Basil Blackwell, Oxford, England.

POGUE, DENNIS
1996 Giant in the Earth: George Washington, Landscape Designer. In *Landscape Archaeology: Reading and Interpreting the American Historical Landscape*, edited by Rebecca Yamin and Karen B. Metheny, pp. 52-69. University of Tennessee Press, Knoxville.

PULSIPHER, LYDIA
1994 The Landscapes and Ideational Roles of Caribbean Slave Gardens. In *The Archaeology of Garden and Field*, edited by Naomi Miller and Kathryn Gleason pp. 202-221. University of Pennsylvania Press, Philadelphia.

PULSIPHER, LYDIA AND CONRAD GOODWIN
1982 A Sugar and Boiling House at Galways: An Irish Sugar Plantation in Montserrat, W. I. *Post-Medieval Archaeology* 16:21-27.

REEVES, MATTHEW
1997 *"By Their Own Labor": Enslaved Africans' Survival Strategies on Two Jamaican Plantations.* PhD dissertation, Department of Anthropology, Syracuse University, Syracuse, NY. University Microfilms International, Ann Arbor, MI.

ROUGHLEY, THOMAS.
1823 *The Jamaican Planter's Guide.* Longman, Hurst, Rees, Orme and Brown, London.

SCHUYLER, ROBERT (EDITOR)
  1980   *Archaeological Perspectives on Ethnicity in America:
         Afro-American and Asian American Culture History.*
         Baywood, Farmingdale, NY.

SCOTT, ELIZABETH (EDITOR)
  1994   *Those of Little Note: Gender, Race, and Class in
         Historical Archaeology.* University of Arizona Press,
         Tucson.

SHACKEL, PAUL A.
  1994   Town Plans and Everyday Material Culture: An
         Archaeology of Social Relations in Colonial Maryland's
         Capital Cities. In *Historical Archaeology of the
         Chesapeake,* edited by Paul A. Shackel and Barbara J.
         Little, pp. 85-100. Smithsonian Institution Press,
         Washington.
  1996   *Culture Change and the New Technology: An
         Archaeology of the Early American Industrial Era.*
         Plenum, New York.

SHERIDAN, RICHARD B.
  1974   *Sugar and Slavery: an Economic History of the British
         West Indies, 1623-1775.* Johns Hopkins University
         Press, Baltimore, MD.

STEWART, JOHN
  1971   *An Account of Jamaica and its Inhabitants.* Books for
         Libraries Press, Freeport. Reprint of 1808 edition.

STINCHCOMBE, ARTHUR
  1995   *Sugar Island Slavery in the Age of Enlightenment.*
         Princeton University Press, Princeton, NJ.

UPTON, DELL
  1988   White and Black Landscapes in Eighteenth-Century
         Virginia. In *Material Life in America, 1600-1860,*
         edited by Robert B. St. George, pp. 357-369.
         Northeastern University Press, Boston, MA.
  1992   The City as Material Culture. In *The Art and Mystery
         of Historical Archaeology,* edited by Anne Yentsch
         and Mary C. Beaudry, pp. 51-74. CRC Press, Boca
         Raton FL.

WALVIN, JAMES
  1994   *Black Ivory: A History of Black Slavery.* Howard
         University Press, Washington.

WURST, LOUANN
  1991   "Employees Must Be of Moral and Temperate Habits":
         Rural and Urban Elite Ideologies. In *The Archaeology
         of Inequality,* edited by Randall H. McGuire and Robert
         Paynter, pp. 125-149. Basil Blackwell, Oxford,
         England.

JAMES A. DELLE
DEPARTMENT OF ANTHROPOLOGY
FRANKLIN AND MARSHALL COLLEGE
LANCASTER, PA 17604

Barbara J. Heath
Amber Bennett

"The little Spots allow'd them": The Archaeological Study of African-American Yards

ABSTRACT

Yards, like buildings and more portable artifacts, are significant expressions of culture. Yet within African-American archaeology, yards have not been the focus of serious discussions addressing questions of work and leisure activities, community interactions, aesthetics, and culture change. The authors review archaeological, ethnographic, and historical evidence of yards associated with New World slave quarters and present a framework for analysis. Results of recent excavations at a slave quarter at Poplar Forest in central Virginia, occupied from ca. 1790 to 1812, are presented within the context of this framework. The archaeological study of yard spaces provides significant information about cultural meanings and uses of space.

Introduction

Early archaeological studies of plantation slavery attempted to define the material conditions of life common to enslaved men and women and to trace the persistence of African cultural retentions through time. More recent studies have addressed questions of status and hierarchy within plantation communities, the negotiation of relationships between planters and enslaved people, the creation of an African-American ethnic identity, and the symbolic representations of belief systems (Singleton and Bograd 1993:14-29). Nearly all of these studies of plantation slavery are based on the analysis of individual households; indeed, most have focused on the physical remains of quarters and the artifacts associated with them.

In the preface to Richard Westmacott's *African American Gardens and Yards in the Rural South*, Theresa Singleton referred to the use of space as "the most monumental aspect of material culture" (Singleton 1992:x). Studies of the use of architectural space have been of enormous benefit in understanding symbolic and functional aspects of daily life in the past (Upton 1985; Vlach 1991;

Deetz 1996). Similarly, investigations focusing on the ways in which people appropriated external space, or crafted and used the spaces allotted to them, define the emerging subdiscipline of landscape archaeology. Like the structures they surround, yards and gardens have the ability to instruct scholars about the lives of their inhabitants.

The yard is defined here as the area of land, bounded and usually enclosed, which immediately surrounds a domestic structure and is considered an extension of that dwelling. A yard is set aside for particular personal or group uses, including, but not limited to, food production and preparation, care and maintenance of animals, domestic chores, storage, recreation, and aesthetic enjoyment. It is at once a part of the domestic compound and a mediating space between the natural, public world and the constructed, private world of the dwelling.

This definition includes garden areas, which are used for small-scale, personal production of useful and ornamental plants, but excludes larger provision grounds, which were often located some distance from the quarters. This broad definition of yard allows for the acknowledgment of regional differences in yard construction and use. Particular examples of yard spaces must be understood both within this broad framework and as individual products of time and place.

As modern ethnographers have demonstrated, the shaping of one's yard is an action laden with meaning. Through their yards, enslaved African Americans spoke to many audiences: ancestors, family members, neighbors, overseers, planters, and outsiders. While yards cannot be studied independently of the houses they surround, the authors believe it is time to develop tools and to frame questions that take advantage of the unique perspective these external spaces have to offer. Archaeologists must learn to read the multiple messages enslaved men and women sought to express in their yards since the study of these spaces provides information about past lives which can be obtained nowhere else. The focus of this work, thus, is on both the construction of a broadly useful archaeological perspective of African-American yards and its application

Historical Archaeology, 2000, 34(2):38—55.
Permission to reprint required.

to a specific site located in Bedford County, Virginia.

Historical Evidence of Yards

The evidence of the nature of yard spaces includes historical, ethnographic, and archaeological information drawn from Africa, the Caribbean, and the United States. While each of these sources has particular biases, taken together, this body of evidence provides a starting point for a contextualized understanding of slave yards in the American South.

In general, historical documents offer few detailed descriptions of West African yards or of the yards of bondsmen in the Caribbean and the American South. This may be the result of a number of factors: authors may have overlooked yards in favor of house descriptions; they may have deliberately ignored aspects of the day-to-day lives of the enslaved; or they may have seen few distinctions between African-American yards and those of poor whites. The primary descriptions are few in number and are seldom free of bias. Still, available contemporary descriptions offer valuable clues regarding the appearance, use, and development of African and African-American yard spaces over time.

West Africa

Traveler's accounts of West Africa were consulted for historic descriptions of yards. These include Mungo Park's search for the source of the Niger in 1795, Rene Caillie's travels to Timbuktu and Hugh Clapperton's expedition to Soccatoo in the 1820s, and Paul du Challu's explorations of equatorial Africa in the 1850s and 1860s. From the late-18th through the mid-19th centuries, these travelers described domestic architecture and yard spaces in areas encompassing what is today The Gambia through Senegal to Mali and Nigeria.

Broad patterns can be identified despite regional variation in house styles and yard layouts. Free people often lived in compounds consisting of several individual buildings enclosed within a fence. While some enslaved people were housed within these compounds, others lived in individual structures at the edges of villages or in villages of their own. "The houses consist of circular huts, or coozies, built of clay and thatched: a number

of these, enclosed in a square fence of matting, generally form but one house," commented one observer (Clapperton 1829:73). Connected by a wall, the structures enclosed an open and airy courtyard. Here, amidst their flocks of fowl, men sat to exchange news and greet neighbors and friends, and women performed daily chores, including cooking and spinning (Clapperton 1829:92, 141, 214; Caillie 1968:202-203, 205, 302-304; Miller 1969:138). The courtyards, as well as the houses, were routinely kept clean and sprinkled with water every morning (Clapperton 1829:142). This treatment was so customary that special note was taken by Clapperton (1829:162) in the town of Roma, where the chief's courts "were overgrown with weeds and grass." Adjacent to houses, free women and children and enslaved people planted gardens in which they cultivated fruit and nutbearing trees, herbs, and vegetables (Caillee 1968:196-197, 202-203, 212, 224, 278, 282, 308).

Houses and courtyards served the needs of the dead as well as the living. Parks (Miller 1969:212) noted that the Mandingoes "frequently dig the grave in the floor of the deceased's hut, or in the shade of a favorite tree." Near the market town of Koolfie, Clapperton noted the Negro custom of burying the dead "in a round hole like a well, about six feet deep, sometimes in the house, sometimes in the threshold of the door, and sometimes in the woods . . .", while at Soccatoo, he learned that the Fellatas "always bury their dead behind the house which the deceased occupied while living" (Clapperton 1829:141-142; 213).

The primary accounts thus reveal that historically in West Africa, yards were used for work, for the raising of poultry, for gardening, for socializing, and sometimes as repositories for the dead. Such patterns are seen to have continued as West Africans were brought to the Caribbean and the American South in bondage.

The Caribbean

To understand slave yards in the Caribbean, descriptions by travelers and residents and commentary by modern scholars were surveyed. Most authors writing from the late-18th century through Emancipation based their observations on experiences in the British West Indies, particularly Jamaica and Barbados. Though varying in importance from island to island, the yards of enslaved men and women fulfilled several common needs. Following West African traditions, enslaved people used their yards to cook, to grow fruits and vegetables (often raising surplus for market), to perform domestic chores, and, less frequently, to bury their dead.

On mountainous islands like Jamaica, planters initially provided enslaved workers with grounds adjacent to their dwellings which they were encouraged to cultivate. As plantations grew and land was needed for additional cane cultivation, owners bribed, coerced, or otherwise persuaded them to give up this land in favor of provision grounds located on less desirable pieces of land some distance from the quarters (McDonald 1993:19-20). A two-tiered self-provisioning system emerged in which enslaved residents undertook relatively large scale agriculture at grounds some distance from their home and cultivated foodstuffs for domestic consumption in the yards immediately surrounding their dwellings. They sold surplus food raised at the provision grounds or in house yards at weekly markets, using the profits to buy additional food, livestock, and a range of material goods.

On Barbados, Antigua, and other relatively flat islands, planters chose to use all available land to raise cash crops and purchased most of the food provisions for their workforce (Mintz and Hall 1960:10). As a result, yards became the only locations where enslaved families could produce foodstuffs and raise small livestock. This land management policy resulted in a more intensive use of yard space and, consequently, a greater dependence on the planter for the necessities of life. West Indian historian Hilary Beckles argues, however, that, "All these slaves had was the little house spot, generally no more than 15 square yards, on which to base their autonomous production and marketing activity . . . and yet the vibrancy of their huckstering business was no less developed than that in Jamaica where slaves cultivated acres of land" (Beckles 1989:78). Indeed, visitors to Barbados noted enslaved women "travelling . . . for several miles to market with a few roots, or fruits, or canes, sometimes a fowl or a kid, or a pig [from] their little spots of ground . . ."(Dickson 1789:11).

Late 18th- and 19th-century accounts from both Jamaica and Barbados describe slave houses and their accompanying yards on several occasions, recording the practice of growing groves of fruit trees and tending plots of vegetables close to the house. Gardens contained herbs, edible plants, ornamentals, and plants used for preparing medicines and cosmetics, fulfilling household chores, or making household items (Pulsipher 1994:215). Enslaved residents also raised and penned small livestock in house yards (Beckford 1788:91, 1790:[1]229; McNeill 1788:3-4; Pinkard 1806:[2]116-117; Barclay 1826:315, 317; Bayley 1833:92-93; Kelly 1838; Phillippo 1843:217). Regarding Jamaica, Bryan Edwards noted, "The cottages of the Negroes usually compose a small village. . . . They are seldom placed with much regard to order, but being always intermingled with fruit-trees, particularly the banana, the avocado pear and the orange (the Negroes own planting and property) they sometimes exhibit a pleasing and picturesque appearance" (Edwards 1793:[2]163). A visitor to Barbados in 1806 remarked "At the negro yards it is common for the slaves to plant fruit and vegetables, and to raise stocks. Some of them keep a pig, some a goat, some Guinea fowls, ducks, chickens, pigeons, or the like; and at one of the huts of Spendlove [estate], we saw a pig, a goat, a young kid, some pigeons, and some chickens, all the property of an individual slave . . ." (Pinkard 1806:[1]368). A Jamaican account notes that enslaved people raised poultry, pigs, and goats in their yards, and kept larger livestock in the plantation pen (McNeill 1788:3-4). Enslaved Jamaicans constructed "inclosures of pales or sticks . . . placed near their houses to confine their stock at night," roofing them with sticks or thatch. Pens for hogs were positioned on hillsides to facilitate drainage, while chickens were placed in hanging baskets at night to safeguard them from rats (Columbian Magazine or Monthly Miscellany 1797; Barclay 1826:315, 317).

Enslaved West Indians also used their yards for cooking. On Jamaica they built small sheds or kitchens behind the house, and constructed outdoor barbecues "made of sticks and bark cordage raised on four posts" (Columbian Magazine or Monthly Miscellany 1797; Phillippo 1843:221). The practice of cooking in a detached kitchen continued into the 20th century (Gardner 1873:181; Livingstone 1899:51; Davenport 1961:435-437).

The West African tradition of burying family members in the house or yard appears to have continued to at least a limited extent in the Caribbean. A visitor to Jamaica in 1823 noted such a burial. "Adjoining to the house is usually a small spot of ground, laid out into a sort of garden and shaded by various fruit-trees. Here the family deposit their dead, to whose memory they invariably, if they can afford it, erect a rude tomb" (Stewart 1823:267). Such practices also persisted in Barbados into the late 18th century, although common burial grounds determined by plantation managers appear to have been more prevalent by this time (Council of Barbados 1789; Parry 1789:17; Handler and Lange 1978:174; Watters 1994).

Comparison of African and Caribbean yard use shows much continuity. Slavery in the Caribbean, however, forced men and women to change traditional African uses of yard spaces, altering both the arrangement and the scale of activities. While the strictures of institutionalized slavery probably dictated many of the transformations from African practices, environmental and technological factors also contributed to changing patterns of domestic activities. Enslaved Africans brought to the Americas encountered unfamiliar animal and plant life, learned new work patterns, and became accustomed to using new tools and to building in new ways. These new plants, work patterns, and tools became incorporated into and transformed traditional African uses of yards.

The American South

Like many of their West Indian contemporaries, Southern planters allotted to enslaved persons patches or provisioning grounds within the planta-tion on which they could cultivate a variety of crops (Vlach 1991:220). Philip Fithian reported on the actions of enslaved men and women in Westmoreland County, Virginia on a Sunday in the spring of 1774, noting that "in several parts of the plantation they are digging up their small Lots of ground allow'd by their Master for Potatoes, peas &c. . . ." Later that year, Fithian added that "Sundays they commonly spend in fishing making potatoes &c, building & patching their Quarters or rather Cabins" (Farish 1957:96, 202-203).

Provision grounds were widely documented in the 19th century throughout the Southeast (Ball 1837:128; Thomas Jefferson's Poplar Forest 1844-1854; Stowe 1853:9; Silva 1914; Rawick 1972:7, 38, 53, 57; Hundley 1973:340-355; Morgan 1982:571-573; McDonald 1993:51-52; Schlotterbeck 1995:173-174).

Enslaved African Americans also located smaller kitchen gardens close to their cabins. Edward Kimber, an Englishman who visited Maryland and Virginia in the 1740s, described the quarters he saw as "a Number of Huts . . . where the Negroes reside with their Wives and Families, and cultivate, at vacant Times, the little Spots allow'd them" (Kimber 1907:6). In urban areas, garden patches might be set aside for the use of enslaved workers within the larger estate garden. Such was the case at Druid Hill in Baltimore, where an 1801 plat shows a 36 x 82 ft. (11 x 25 m) vegetable patch "for servants" adjacent to a quarter and a hog pen (Sarudy 1998:54-55). In the rural antebellum South, Frederick Law Olmsted reported that the slave households he observed had an area set aside where residents "could always grow as many vegetables as they wanted" (Hawke 1971:36). Observing quarters in South Carolina, Olmsted noted that "in the rear of the yards were gardens—a half-acre to each family" (Hawke 1971:74).

Gardens were located close to the quarters, thus enslaved residents could work in them during breaks in the daily work routine or in the evenings. This location also meant that the aged, retired from field work, could tend the family's crop of vegetables and herbs as well (McDonald 1993:51). Enslaved women, as well as men, appear to have been active gardeners (Ware 1997:156-157).

Evidence from the post-Emancipation era indicates that gardens were designed to be ornamental as well as useful. In an early 20th-century interview of a freed slave from South Carolina, social reformer Mark Hicks noted: "Encircling her house are lilacs, althea, and flowering trees that soften the bleak outlines of unpainted out-buildings. A varied collection of old-fashioned plants and flowers crowd the neatly swept dooryard" (Ware 1997:157). Hicks went on to describe the house of two African-American sisters. "their front yard is full of flowers. Vegetables are at the side in the same inclosure with the flowers" (Rawick 1972:59) (Figure 1).

Figure 1. Uncle Daniel's Cabin, Bon Air, Virginia, 1888. Note the clumps of irises along the snake fence. (Courtesy of Valentine Museum, Richmond, Virginia.)

Women and men recalled their yards in first-hand accounts of their experience during slavery. "When farm work was not pressing, we got all of Saturday to clean up 'round de houses . . ." (Adeline Jackson [Westmacott 1992:18]). One woman who was freed from slavery in South Carolina noted that "All de people would make dey own gardens in dem days" (Agnes James [Westmacott 1992:18]), while a freed woman from Virginia recalled, "people used to raise goard fer dippers, an' de goards grew on vines in ev'ybody's garden" (Mrs. Patience Avery [Perdue 1976:161]). Former enslaved men and women also made note of socializing and playing in their yards. In relating a story, one freedman from Virginia began, "One day all de little chillun wuz in the yard playing—running 'roun. An de gal's husband wuz settin' near de do' wid de baby in his arms-rockin' away—looking in child's face an' at de chillun play' in de yard . . ." (Rev. Ishrael Massie [Perdue 1976:207]). Another recalled that on evenings spent in the yard, "we would spin on the old spinning wheel, quilt, make clothes, talk, tell jokes. . . . We would have candy pulls, from cooked molasses, and sing in the moonlight by the tune of an old banjo picker" (Mrs. Marriah Hines [Perdue 1976:141]).

Beyond gardening, socializing, and relaxing out-of-doors, enslaved African Americans living in the South used the spaces around their cabins for performing household chores such as cooking, laundering, butchering, and raising animals (Figure 2). Poultry-keeping appears to have been most common, but sometimes they kept

pigs as well. In Virginia, owners purchased eggs, chickens, ducks, and turkeys from the men and women they held in bondage (Morgan 1988:468; Vlach 1991:220; Stanton 1993:165-166; Thompson 1993:15-16; Schlotterbeck 1995:174; Heath 1999:50). Olmsted (1861:442) noted that "eggs constitute[d] a circulating medium" on one South Carolina plantation, observing that the spaces to the sides of quarters were enclosed with palings to contain chickens and pigs. William Howard Russell, describing Louisiana African-American dwellings in 1863, noted that "the negroes rear domestic birds of all kinds" and that "behind each hut are rude poultry hutches, which, with geese, turkeys and a few pigs form the perquisites of the slaves" (Russell 1863:371, 396). The marketing of surplus garden produce and livestock provided an important source of economic autonomy for the Louisiana enslaved community (McDonald 1993:50-54, 56). In the Upper South, it appears that gardens were less economically significant, although there is good evidence that enslaved men and women sold their produce to their owners, at market, and at local stores (Martin 1993:308-309; Schlotterbeck 1995:175-176; Heath 1997).

Ethnographic Studies of Houses and Yards

While documents preserve glimpses of slave yards, modern ethnographers can provide important information about contemporary practices and attitudes that may have historic roots. Anthropologist Sidney Mintz (1974:225-250) pioneered the study of yards in the West Indies during the 1950s, detailing the importance of the house-yard

Figure 2. Yard scene, Southern Pines, North Carolina, 1914. (Photo by E. C. Eddy, courtesy of Prints and Photographs Division, Library of Congress, Washington.)

pattern in understanding the Caribbean peasantry. In the house yard, he observed, "decisions are made, food is prepared and eaten, the household group—whatever its composition—sleeps and socializes, children are conceived and born, death is ceremonialized. . . . Together, house and yard form a nucleus within which the culture expresses itself, is perpetuated, changed and reintegrated" (Mintz 1974:231-232). Since that time, anthropologists, folklorists, geographers, and landscape architects have studied African-American yards in the Caribbean and in the American South (McDaniel 1982; Westmacott 1992; Gundaker 1993; Ware 1997).

Ethnographic studies have confirmed that many of the practices noted during the era of slavery continue in contemporary communities, including the use of yards for subsistence activities, such as gardening and livestock rearing, for household work, for storage, and for socializing and recreation (McDaniel 1982:168; Westmacott 1992; Ware 1997:159-170). Additionally, they suggest modern activities and attitudes about yard spaces that may have roots in the past. These include the use of yards for storage (McDaniel 1982:168), keeping the yard clean by sweeping, and the creation and maintenance of spiritually and socially meaningful yard ornamentation (Thompson 1990:164-167; Westmacott 1992:45-50; Gundaker 1993).

Today, African, Caribbean, and African-American yards serve as locations for spiritual and artistic expression (Thompson 1984:142-158; Gundaker 1993). Swept yards are common features of West and Central African domestic compounds. There, the practice of sweeping carries spiritual as well as social dimensions (Thompson 1990:164). Among the Bakongo of Central Africa, "sweeping is an ordinary ritual gesture for ridding a place of undesirable spirits" in a landscape populated by day with the ghosts of witches and others who have not been accepted into the villages of the dead, and by night with the ancestors (MacGaffey 1986:45-56).

This African practice of yard sweeping has continued into the 20th century among African Americans from rural Maryland to the hills of Jamaica (Davenport 1961:435-437; Welty 1971:156; McDaniel 1982:158-160, 213; Jones-Jackson 1987:8; Westmacott 1992:76, 80, 99, 111, 126). Sweeping is explained as a way to keep the yard free from insects and provide a comfortable area for social activities (Jones-Jackson 1987:8), but may preserve spiritual meaning as well.

Much like swept yards, bottle trees—comprised of bottles, containers, and a variety of other spiritually meaningful elements arranged on or imitating trees—serve aesthetic and protective roles. The trees protect houses and yards from evil spirits by "luring them inside the colored bottles, where they cannot get out again" (Welty 1971:156). The presence of these trees in the New World may be traced to the Kongo custom of placing branches capped with bottles or pots around the house, a practice first recorded in the late 18th century (Thompson 1990:165). Bottle trees persist in both the American South and the Caribbean (Thompson 1990:164-164).

Yards have given rise to other forms of aesthetic expression as well. Grey Gundaker has studied the "dressed yards" of modern African Americans, spaces characterized by the recycling of castoff objects into works of sculptural art symbolic to their creator and perhaps to his or her community. In Gundaker's words, these yards use "a flexible visual vocabulary that creolizes and revitalizes American, European and African traditions through everyday materials. . . . The makers of these special yards work to please themselves and to instruct visitors in appropriate behavior, sometimes in the broadest spiritual sense" (Gundaker 1993:59). The history of contemporary yard art remains a mystery. The tradition of shaping one's yard in an effort to create an aesthetically pleasing or spiritually meaningful space, however, can be glimpsed in historic African and Caribbean descriptions of bottle trees, in the inclusion of ornamental plants in slave gardens, and in the burial of the dead in slave yards.

Finally, it is important to note that as extensions of the house, yards are seen as private spaces. In her novel *To Kill a Mockingbird*, set in a small Depression-era Southern town, Harper Lee used Southern views of proper and improper behavior to construct a defense for Tom, a black man accused of rape. "He seemed to be a respectable Negro, and a respectable Negro would never go up into somebody's yard of his own volition" (Lee 1974:196). People "went inside the fence" by invitation only.

This brief survey of documentary and ethnographic data suggests both some continuities between yards in West Africa and in the New

World, as well as some distinct differences. Yards appear to function across time and space as workspaces and as economic units, providing families with fruits, vegetables, meat, and eggs that could be sold or consumed. The extent of yard cultivation and livestock rearing is unclear, however, as much of the evidence presented here is anecdotal, and focuses on the late 18th and 19th centuries. By its site-specific approach, archaeology can help to trace the economic role of yards backwards in time and space. Ethnographic evidence has suggested the social dimensions of yards as private places that create both social barriers and convey social and symbolic messages. Did people in the past have such control over their environs, or were yards shared work spaces available to all within the quarter? Were spaces defined by the owner, by individual slave families, or by some process of negotiation? Contemporary sources also suggest that yard uses were divided along gender and age lines. Can we see evidence of such divisions within the slave household? Finally, West and Central African spiritual beliefs, reflected in yard sweeping, in the progenitors of bottle trees, and in the use of house-yard spaces for burials, appear to have been transplanted to the New World. How widespread were these practices? Did they change over time? Were house-yard burial practices ever used in the American South? When burials themselves ceased to occur in the house-yard complex, did enslaved people adopt other symbols to communicate the spiritual dimensions of their domestic spaces, or did the meanings of their houses and yards change? While archaeologists cannot perhaps answer all of these questions, they have some powerful tools at their disposal to study the changing use of yard spaces through time and space.

The Archaeology of Yards

Unlike historical archaeologists in general, who have made the study of yards integral to their research (Gibb and King 1991; Beaudry 1993; Cummings 1994; Rovner 1994), archaeologists working on African-American sites have seldom widened their frame of reference beyond dwellings. For the most part, attention has focused on the analysis of artifactual and structural data in an effort to reconstruct sites and lifestyles. These analyses have often neglected yards as an important part of the environment in which people lived. Landscape archaeology has in recent years begun to focus attention on yards and gardens, seeing landscapes as expressions of the "relationships among people in their physical environment" (Gleason 1994:20). Even with explicit attention to these relationships, little attention has been paid to the landscapes formed and experienced by African Americans. This is perhaps best exemplified by Yentsch and Kratzer's (1994:198) attention to "great gardens," those belonging to persons with "wealth, power, prestige and knowledge," rather than to the gardens of "ordinary folk."

Archaeologists, however, have recently focused their attention on understanding yards often associated with African-American tenants on postbellum farms throughout the South. Randall Moir has developed a model of yard usage based on the study of sheet refuse distributions across domestic farms on rural sites (Moir 1987:229-237). The active yard, of one-half to two-thirds of an acre immediately around the farmhouse, incorporates an immediate active yard extending in a circle of up to 20 ft. (6 m) from the house, and an outer active yard, which contains storage sheds, smokehouses and other dependencies, and extends to a distance of approximately 60 ft. (18 m) from the dwelling. Beyond these inner yard spaces lies the peripheral yard, which, at some distance from the house, provides the setting for major outbuildings such as barns. Moir argues that these zones are gender specific, with women's activities tending to cluster in the inner active yard and men's most often undertaken in the outer active yard (Moir 1987:234-235). The recognition of artifact patterning which corresponds to this division of space has allowed others to use Moir's work as a research tool (Crass and Brooks 1995).

The applicability of this model to antebellum slave yards has not been tested. Indeed, yards have not yet received much attention from those studying the archaeological record of slavery. A few notable exceptions include the work of Douglas Armstrong in Jamaica and Garrett Fesler at the Utopia Quarter in Virginia. Armstrong, working at the Drax Hall plantation, drew on Mintz's model to design his excavation strategy for areas associated with the slave village and post-emancipation housing. By exploring areas outside of identified house remains, he uncovered evidence of cooking sheds and identified a slave yard where "significant activities" took place (Armstrong 1990:104, 109, 121). These discoveries underscored the importance of the yard and associated garden to the house-yard complex (Armstrong 1990:268-269).

At the Utopia Quarter, archaeologists discovered the remains of 11 buildings and associated yard features, including fence lines, ditches, trash pits, a well, and an adjoining burial ground dating from 1670 to 1780 (Fesler 1997b:4). During the early 18th century, the enslaved residents constructed three houses and a storehouse, arranged to form a square compound with a central courtyard. Fesler argues that this house-yard complex, occupied by newly enslaved West African men and women, carried contrasting social meanings. Designed to reinforce the owner's philosophy of the management of his enslaved population, the space was perceived by its inhabitants as a familiar echo of home, and ultimately helped to strengthen their cultural identity (Fesler 1997a). By extending his analysis to the house yard, or domestic compound level, Fesler arrived at a richer and more complex interpretation of the site.

Slave yards have also been sampled at the Andrew Jackson's Hermitage quarters in Tennessee, and at several quarters in Virginia, including those at Monticello, Rich Neck, and Utopia (Kelso, et al. 1984, 1985; Agbe-Davies 1994; Thomas, et al. 1995:14-22; Fesler 1997a, 1997b; McKee 1997).

Methodological Concerns

There have been few efforts within African-American archaeology to create a methodology or a framework for analysis useful to the investigation of yard spaces. Landscape archaeology has attempted to define the parameters of the investigation of space, but in general has not led investigators to focus on what went on within those spaces. Absent are tools for understanding functional, community, and individual uses of yards. More broadly, space serves to define class, religious beliefs, personal and group identity, and the relationships among different communities and individuals. Investigative and interpretive methods must recognize all of these potential uses if they are to serve as a means for understanding past cultures.

One of the main goals in looking at slave yards is to first understand the differential uses of space at domestic sites over time, and then to assess the meaning of such differences. A major component of this process is the need to understand patterns of activities or "activity systems." Expanding on the model introduced by Edward Hall (1966), Amos Rapoport (1993:13) has outlined three arenas in which activity systems can be observed in the environment: fixed-feature elements, defined as architectural components; semi-fixed feature elements or "furnishings;" and non-fixed-feature elements, defined as people and their behavior at a given point in time. While individual activities cannot usually be detected in the archaeological record, evidence of activity systems are preserved in Rapoport's fixed and semi-fixed elements. For the purposes of yard analysis, fixed elements include permanent yard features such as fences, sheds, pens, or trees. Semi-fixed feature elements, or yard furnishings, might include rain barrels, wood piles, benches, and other semi-permanent artifacts, as well as cooking pits, trash pits, or middens, whose locations may shift around the yard over time. Past people and behaviors can only be observed indirectly, thus it is essential to look at both fixed and semi-fixed feature elements to understand past activity systems. For the most part, and for obvious reasons, archaeologists have concentrated on the recovery of fixed elements (architectural remains and fences), which tend to be most visible archaeologically. Others have suggested that refuse disposal areas are rich sources of data (Fairbanks 1976, 1977; Otto 1980:4-5).

On plantation sites, where stratigraphic layers and shallow features often have been erased by plowing, semi-fixed elements are difficult to locate and understand. The work of King, Miller, Pogue, and Riordan on 17th-century sites in Maryland. however, has demonstrated that spatial relationships are discernible on plowed sites, allowing for reconstructions of houselot layouts and domestic use patterns over time (King and Miller 1987:37-59; King 1988:23-37; Pogue 1988:43-55; Riordan 1988; Miller 1994:73-81). Even middens, though mixed vertically, remain visible within the plowzone, preserving many of their depositional relationships. On sites of short occupation, plowzone data can yield important information about semi-fixed elements of the

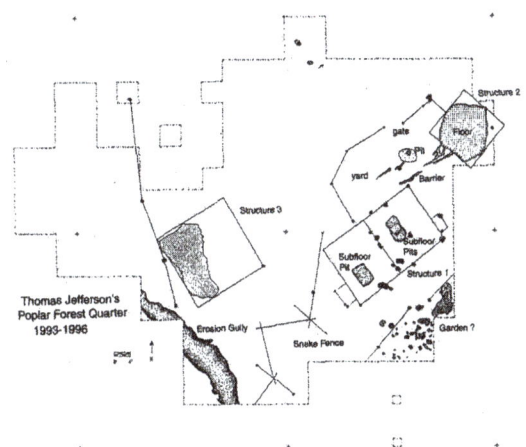

Figure 3. Map of Thomas Jefferson's Poplar Forest Quarter Site.

site. In short, ignoring the plowzone on African-American sites may mean throwing away most or all of the information concerning occupation of that site. An example of the combined use of feature and plowzone data to understand yard spaces is seen in the study of the Poplar Forest slave quarter.

The Poplar Forest Quarter Site

Between 1993 and 1996 archaeologists working at Poplar Forest, Thomas Jefferson's plantation in Bedford County, Virginia, discovered a complex of features associated with an early quarter. The site, known as the Quarter Site, dates ca. 1790-1812 (Figure 3). Although the quarter does not appear on any contemporary maps or letters, early 19th-century maps do provide some clues about the landscape of the property during this period. The site lay within the 45-acre "mansion house field" which contained the "mansion house" or overseer's house situated several hundred feet farther to the south and east. To the north, the maps locate a narrow stretch of land referred to as "the lane." Excavations undertaken from 1996 to 1998 explored an earlier quarter farther north within the lane.

By the summer of 1996, archaeologists had completed a block excavation measuring some 80 ft. (24 m) north-south by 100 ft. (30 m) east-west. Although the site was located on the side of a hill, its eastern half had been plowed in the 19th or early 20th century, while the western half,

downslope, consisted of occupation and destruction layers sealed by thick layers of wash. The hill ranged from 10% to 15% slope. Excavators removed all plowzone and cultural layers in 5 x 5 ft. (1.5 x 1.5 m) units and screened them through ¼ in. (6 mm) mesh to ensure high rates of artifact recovery. In addition, soil chemical samples were collected from plowzone and cultural layers at 10 ft. (3 m) intervals. Flotation samples were also collected from soils contained within features associated with structures.

Excavations unearthed the remains of three buildings, referred to in this discussion as Structures 1, 2, and 3. Structure 1, interpreted as a duplex cabin, measured approximately 15 x 25 ft. (4.5 x 7.6 m) and was divided into two equal sized rooms of 12.5 x 15 ft (3.8 x 4.5 m). Indicated only by the presence of postholes and quantities of daub, wood, and clay chimneys may have been located on the gable ends of the building, with a single fireplace heating each room. Three subfloor pits were contained within the building; one in the west room and two in the east.

Structure 2 was discovered by archaeologists, 13 ft. (4 m) northeast of the duplex cabin. This building measured approximately 13 ft. (4 m) square, and faced north, with a door opening along that wall. No evidence of a chimney survived. Large fragments of daub recovered from the fill within the building and from the adjoining yard suggest that the building was constructed of logs. Structure 2 may have been originally intended for use as a service room or storage space rather than a house. The lack of evidence for a chimney or subfloor pits are at odds with features of contemporary cabins. Numerous domestic artifacts found within the fill of the building and around the structure suggest that for part of its lifespan, the building served as a dwelling.

Structure 3 was located 14 ft. (4 m) northwest of Structure 1. It had been built on one of the steepest parts of the hillside, directly on top of a backfilled erosion gully. A posthole defined the location of the southeast corner. The building must have been raised on piers along its northern face to provide a level floor. Structure 3 measured 18.5 ft. (5.6 m) to a side. The presence of high levels of potassium and magnesium suggest that a chimney stood along the northeastern wall, while artifact concentrations suggest that the door faced north (Fischer 1996:19). Based on the number

TABLE 1
CERAMIC SHERD AND MINIMUM VESSEL COUNTS, QUARTER SITE MIDDENS

Ceramics	MIDDEN 1 Count	MNV	MIDDEN 2 Count	MNV	MIDDEN 3 Count	MNV
Black basalt	4	1	1	-	4	1
Bone china	1	1	-	-	-	-
Chinese porcelain	2	1	1	1	1	1
Creamware	300	11	29	1	217	12
Delft	-	-	-	1	1	-
Pearlware	202	16	28	1	210	12
Redware	42	10	8	-	49	11
Stoneware	34	6	6	1	14	3
TOTAL	585	46	73	4	496	41

and variety of domestic artifacts found in the crawl space beneath the building, along its western wall, and in a midden to the north, Structure 3 clearly served as a dwelling.

The excavation of this site was designed with the intent to recover as much information as possible about the size, orientation and use of associated yard spaces. The remains of five contemporary fences were uncovered at the site. The first fence enclosed a space beginning at the northwest wall of Structure 1 and extending to the northwest wall of Structure 2 (Figure 3). Small diameter posts set at approximately 10 ft. (3 m) intervals anchored panels of wooden pickets, forming the outside line of this fence. The line was interrupted by a 4.5 ft.(1.4 m) wide gate located midway between Structures 1 and 2.

This space was bounded to the south by a second barrier defined by a series of narrow trenches cutting through subsoil (Figure 3). Significant differences in artifact densities and soil chemical levels from one side of the trenches to the other indicate that some type of physical barrier divided this space (Fischer 1996:24).

The yard defined within these limits measured approximately 12 x 30 ft. (3.7 x 9 m). Soil chemical analysis provided clues for understanding the physical layout and use of the space within and adjacent to the yard. Four principal chemicals were investigated: phosphorus, calcium, potassium, and magnesium. Phosphorus is found in human and animal tissues and waste, and high levels can be associated with animal pens, trash dumps, or privies. Calcium is a component of bone and shell. In the acidic soils of central Virginia, these substances often decompose rapidly, leaving behind only their chemical signatures. High concentrations of calcium may mark the locations of middens or processing areas for meat. Potassium, found in wood and wood ash, can suggest the placement of hearths or ash deposits.

TABLE 2
GLASS SHERD AND MINIMUM VESSEL COUNTS, QUARTER SITE MIDDENS

Glass Type	MIDDEN 1 Count	MNV	MIDDEN 2 Count	MNV	MIDDEN 3 Count	MNV
Undecorated bottle						
Clear	15	1	6	-	9	2
Dk. green	268	13	29	1	166	13
Pattern molded bottle						
Blue-Aqua	6	-	4	-	9	1
Green-Aqua	1	-	-	-	1	-
Pharmaceutical	4	1	-	-	-	-
Tableware	5	1	-	-	1	1
TOTAL	299	16	39	1	186	17

Note: For vessels with counts but no minimum number assigned, the majority of sherds associated with this vessel were found elsewhere on the site

Some archaeologists studying soil chemicals have tentatively linked high magnesium levels in soil to activities associated with burning (Fischer 1996).

Elevated levels of phosphorus and calcium within the plowzone corresponded with areas of high artifact density and helped to confirm the location and formation of middens along the inner and outer edges of the yard fence. These middens may have contained refuse similar to the "heaps of . . . broken crockery, old shoes, rags, and feathers" reported by Russell to be "found near each hut" (Russell 1863 [1954:77]). Chemicals suggest that the enslaved residents may have deposited certain types of organic waste away from the larger middens where animal bones and household trash were dumped. A small concentration of artifacts and an elevated level of phosphorus was detected adjacent to the cabin, hinting at the location of a doorway along the north wall of the structure. For the most part, however, the yard between the structures contained lower densities of ceramics, bottle glass, and other domestic trash, suggesting that this area was considered a clean space.

Ceramic and glass (Tables 1 and 2) distributions from the area around Structure 1 were plotted to test the hypothesis that residents of the Quarter regularly swept the yard. Adams (1987:47) posited that yard sweeping should be detectable in the archaeological record by differences in sherd densities, with lesser densities in the swept areas, and greater densities in the outlying middens. He observed such a distribution, based on differential sherd weights, at the Mabry site at Kings Bay. At Poplar Forest, distributions were determined based on an analysis of size rather than weight. Sherds of both ceramics and bottle glass were divided into two size categories (those less than ½ in. [13 mm] diameter, and those greater than ½ in.), and the distribution of each was plotted. Over 80% of ceramic sherds and 56% of the bottle glass from the site were smaller than ½ in., thus results were inconclusive (Brooks 1996:2, 35-36). The fragmentary nature of the assemblage is probably a result of trampling during occupation of the site and post-occupation plowing. Analyses of distributions at sites benefiting from better preservation may, however, allow for the detection of this yard treatment.

The yard could have been entered directly from a door located on the northern wall of Structure 1. Non-residents could access the yard through the gate located along its northern boundary. The placement of the fence provides a spatial connection between at least the eastern half of that building and Structure 2, suggesting that the residents of these two housing units shared a common social bond. A letter between an overseer and Jefferson confirms that at least some extended enslaved families shared duplex cabins at Poplar Forest (University of Virginia 1814). Such family ties may be preserved in the evidence of a shared yard between dwellings at this quarter.

Historic maps suggest that the overseer's house (the "mansion house" referred to earlier) sat some distance south of the duplex cabin. It is interesting to note that residents of this cabin sited the enclosed yard on the north side of the dwelling. This plan allowed space, air, and light to work in, while at the same time effectively shielding residents working or socializing in the yard from the overseer's surveillance.

Evidence of a "worm" or "snake" fence was uncovered west of the Structure 1, separating that building from Structure 3 (Figure 3). Fences of this type sat on the surface of the ground, and could easily be disassembled and moved (Betts 1944:492-493). While many snake fences sat entirely on the surface, some were stabilized by opposing pairs of wooden stakes driven into the ground (Figure 1). Small diameter postholes, found in pairs separated by 10 ft. (3 m) intervals, provide evidence of such a fence treatment at the Quarter.

Four postholes located south of Structure 1 suggest the location of a fourth, gated fence (Figure 3). Limited access to this area precluded further excavations to define its limits. This section of the site was almost devoid of artifacts, but numerous irregular soil disturbances created by plants of varying sizes were discovered beneath the plowzone. Surrounding these planting features was soil rich in potassium and phosphorus, chemicals associated with burned wood and decaying organic matter. Such a chemical signature might be left by repeated applications of fertilizing agents such as wood ash and animal dung (Spurrier 1793:35, 41; Miller 1994; Fischer 1996:24-25). Together, these clues suggest that this space was cultivated. Whether it served as the site of the enslaved residents' vegetable patch or the edge of a garden associated with the overseer's house located further to the southeast is not known.

The analysis of macroplant remains recovered from subfloor pits and floor surfaces within each structure sheds light on plants consumed by the residents, some of which were possibly grown around the cabins. Archaeologists recovered fruit seeds and pits, including raspberry, cherry, peach, huckleberry, persimmon, and grape; vegetable remains including beans, sunflowers, and grains such as corn and wheat; and nut shells from walnuts and hickory trees. Besides harvesting nuts, the residents of the site may have used walnut bark as a dye for textiles. Weed seeds from goosefoot, smartweed, and pokeweed may represent the remains of plants that were consumed for food or for medicine, while a burned fragment of bedstraw may represent bedding material or may have been used medicinally (Raymer 1996:13-17).

Charred fragments of hickory were recovered from three of the postholes associated with Structure 1, suggesting its use as a construction material (Raymer 1996:18). Fragments of charcoal found in the fill of subfloor pits and associated with the floor surface in Structure 2 indicate that pine and oak constituted the primary fuel woods at the site, while smaller quantities of hickory and elm were also recovered (Raymer 1996:18).

A large part of the yard to the south and west of Structure 3 appears to have been roughly paved with local quartz cobbles. Additionally, numerous pieces of blacksmithing slag, material commonly used for paving, were found intermixed with the quartz cobbles. This surface may indicate a narrow, paved yard laid down to lessen the effects of erosion. The western edge of this yard is roughly defined by the site's fifth fence line, marked by the presence of four postholes set on 12 ft. (3.7 m) centers.

Most artifacts recovered from the site resulted from secondary deposition in one of three major middens associated with each of the structures (Tables 1 and 2). As such, they reflect residents' attitudes towards the appropriate disposal of trash rather than the location of individual activities such as dining, sewing, or socializing. An analysis, however, of the distribution patterns of specific

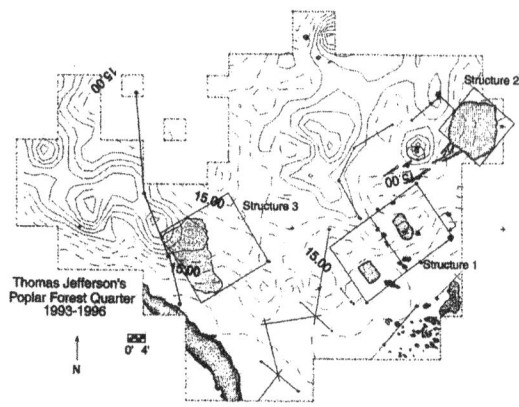

Figure 4. Distribution of ceramics recovered from the Thomas Jefferson's Poplar Forest Quarter Site.

artifact types within these middens and of the location of individual artifacts recovered from contexts other than the middens has offered some suggestions for yard use and raised some questions.

Midden 1 extended along the external line of the fence connecting Structures 1 and 2. Midden 2, a significantly smaller concentration of artifacts associated with Structure 2, appeared at the northeast corner of that building. Roughly half of that structure lay on land not owned by Poplar Forest, thus it was not possible to fully explore its associated yard. Based on crossmends between Structures 1 and 2 and the enclosed yard between them, it seems likely that trash from Structure 2 was deposited within Midden 1 as well.

The placement of Midden 3, associated with Structure 3, varied through time. The earliest phase of deposition overlay a backfilled erosion gully that cut the slope in this area. It is likely that historically a shallow depression marked the location of the gully as its backfill settled, and that trash generated by the residents of Structure 3 accumulated there. Over time, the depression was filled in, and the midden shifted to the south and east, drawing nearer to the northwest corner of the building.

Ceramic and glass distributions were plotted using SURFER, a commercially available software that can be used to create contour and isometric maps based on artifact densities (Figures 4 and 5). The main ceramic concentrations on the site were associated with Structures 1 and 3. The former is contained within the boundaries of Midden 1

Conclusions

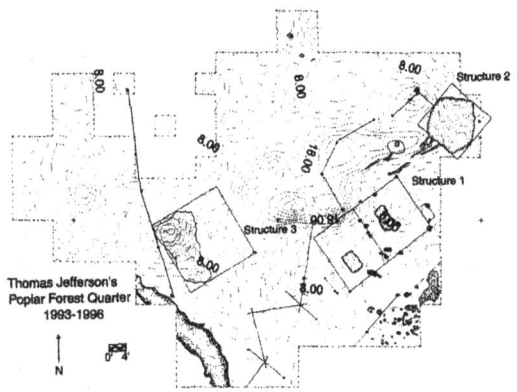

Figure 5. Distribution of glass recovered from the Thomas Jefferson's Poplar Forest Quarter Site.

and appears to indicate an intentional effort to keep ceramics and other forms of domestic refuse outside of the fenced yard (Brooks 1996:21). The latter, contained within Midden 3, runs downslope from Structure 3 in a northwesterly direction. By comparison, the distribution of green wine bottle glass runs parallel to the north wall line of Structure 1 and appears unaffected by the placement of the fence. Although the meaning of this glass distribution is far from clear, it is possible that it reflects glass usage as well as disposal. Perhaps some empty bottles were reused or stored within the yard and later broken in-situ, while other bottles joined ceramic waste and were disposed of outside of the fence.

Distribution patterns for other artifact types provide additional clues concerning the use of the yard. Most counts by type are too small to yield statistically significant findings; however they do suggest some interesting spatial relationships. Fragments of clay and stone tobacco pipes (n=66) clustered within each of the three cabins, the yard between Structures 1 and 2, and Midden 1, suggest that smoking and socializing took place both within and in close proximity to the cabins. Buttons (n=115), whose deposition archaeologically may reflect sewing, laundering, or accidental loss, clustered within each of the structures, in the northwest corner of the enclosed yard between Structures 1 and 2, in the middens, and along the line of the worm fence running southwest from Structure 1 (n=80). The association of buttons with fencelines may indicate the practice of hanging clothing on fences to air or to dry following laundering.

A survey of the historic, ethnographic and archaeological literature has provided some guidelines and provoked some important questions for those wishing to explore, through archaeology, the use and meaning of yard spaces shared by enslaved African Americans. For yards to contribute to our understanding of slavery, they must first be recognized as important sources of data. This brief survey has demonstrated that yard spaces have the potential to comment upon the economic, social, and spiritual lives of their occupants. Archaeologists must now seek methods of excavation and interpretation to fully realize this potential. Appropriate for the spatial and temporal contexts in which archaeologists work, research strategies must be designed which anticipate the recovery of features associated with gardens and small orchards, structures such as sheds, hen houses, pigsties, middens, and workspaces that provide information about the independent economic lives of residents. Equally important are attempts to recover subtle clues, preserved in the distributions of soil chemicals and artifacts, that allow yards to be seen as their creators saw them: spaces defined by clean swept surfaces and jumbled trash, by workbenches and fruit trees, through which people expressed a variety of messages to the living and the dead.

Many of these messages have been clouded through the passage of time and by subsequent disturbances to the site, often by plowing. Yet excavations at the Poplar Forest Quarter Site provide strong evidence that even in the face of sustained plowing and erosion, artifact distributions retain much of their horizontal integrity. Through a strategy which combined large area excavation with total plowzone recovery of artifacts and systematic soil sampling for chemical testing and flotation, the fixed remains of the yard's architecture and the artifactual and chemical signatures of its changing landscape were recovered.

Perhaps the most obvious problem with this approach is that it is extremely time-consuming and, consequently, costly. In the end, large areas of the "yard" remain undefined. What happened outside of the enclosures? Where are the conceptual boundaries of the house-yard complex, and how might they be found archaeologically? Clearly, standard shovel test intervals of 50 to 100 ft. (15 to 30 m) fail to provide firm site boundaries, or to distinguish accurately between one house yard and the next.

In spite of these problems, the study of yards at the Poplar Forest quarter provided important, and in some cases, unique insights into the lives of its occupants. The yards preserved evidence of communal activities and of time spent gardening, performing chores, and building and maintaining friendships. The yards also reflect messages sent by the African Americans to the plantation's white occupants. Yard spaces placed limits on the intrusions of outsiders into the quarter, limits which were mutually understood. They signaled a point of mediation across which black and white could meet, often through economic exchange, to define and maintain the delicate balance which was the plantation system.

Contained within the archaeological remains of African-American yards are the world views of those who created and used them. Archaeologists have much to learn by extending their perspective beyond the traditional limits to cover the broader landscape of sites occupied by enslaved people. As has been seen at Poplar Forest, there lie in yard scatters and fencelines expressions of individual identity and community structure waiting to be read and understood.

ACKNOWLEDGEMENTS

An earlier version of this paper was presented at the 1997 meeting of the Society for Historical Archaeology Conference on Historical and Underwater Archaeology, Corpus Christi, Texas. The authors would like to thank The Henry Luce Foundation for support of excavation and analysis of the Quarter Site; Thomas Jefferson's Poplar Forest for continuing support of archaeological research; Lisa Fischer for analysis and interpretation of soil chemical content; Alasdair Brooks and Heather Olson for artifact analysis; Leslie Raymer for macrobotanical analysis; Anna Agbe-Davies, Garrett Fesler, Maria Franklin, and Larry McKee for supplying unpublished data; and the reviewers, Leslie Stewart-Abernathy, Amy Young, and Sue Moore, for their helpful comments. Interpretations in this analysis are those of the authors alone.

REFERENCES

ADAMS, WILLIAM H. (EDITOR)
1987   Historical Archaeology of Plantations at Kings Bay, Camden County, Georgia. Report to Naval Submarine Base, U.S. Navy from Department of Anthropology, University of Florida, Gainesville.

AGBE-DAVIES, ANNA
1994   Preliminary Findings from the Rich Neck Slave Quarter Excavations. Paper presented at the Annual Meeting of the Council for Northeast Historical Archaeology, Williamsburg, VA.

ARMSTRONG, DOUGLAS V.
1990   The Old Village and the Great House: An Archaeological and Historical Examination of Drax Hall Plantation at St. Ann's Bay, Jamaica. University of Illinois Press, Urbana.

BALL, CHARLES
1837   Slavery in the United States: A Narrative of the Life and Adventures of Charles Ball, a Black Man. J. S. Taylor, New York, NY.

BARCLAY, ALEXANDER
1826   A Practical View of the Present State of Slavery in the West Indies. Smith Elder, & Co., London, England.

BAYLEY, F. W. N.
1833   Four Years Residence in the West Indies. William Kidd, London, England.

BEAUDRY, MARY C.
1993   Public Aesthetics versus Personal Experience: Worker Health and Well-Being in 19th-Century Lowell, Massachusetts. Historical Archaeology 27(2):90-105.

BECKFORD, WILLIAM
1788   Remarks upon the Situation of Negroes in Jamaica. London, England.
1790   A Descriptive Account of the Island of Jamaica. T. J. Egerton, London, England.

BECKLES, HILARY M.
1989   Natural Rebels, A Social History of Enslaved Black Women in Barbados. Rutgers University Press, New Brunswick, NJ.

BETTS, EDWIN M.
1944   Thomas Jefferson's Garden Book. American Philosophical Society, Philadelphia, PA.

BROOKS, ALASDAIR M.
1996   Analysis of Ceramics and Glass from the Quarter Site. Manuscript, Department of Archaeology, Thomas Jefferson's Poplar Forest, Forest, VA.

CAILLIE, RENE
1968   Travels through Central Africa to Timbuctoo and Across the great Desert, To Morocco, performed in the years 1824-1828, Vol. 1. Reprint of 1830 edition, Frank Cass, London, England.

CLAPPERTON, HUGH
1829   Journal of a Second Expedition into the Interior of Africa, from the Bight of Benin to Soccatoo. John Murray, London, England.

COLUMBIAN MAGAZINE OR MONTHLY MISCELLANY
1797   Characteristic traits of the Creolian and African
        Negroes in this Island, etc., etc. *Columbian
        Magazine or Monthly Miscellany*, April.

COUNCIL OF BARBADOS
1789   Replies to queries 6, 15, 22, 23, 24 and 25 of the
        Report of the Lords of the committee of Council
        . . . concerning the present state of the trade to
        Africa . . . and the effects and consequences of this
        trade . . . in Africa and in the West Indies, Part 3.
        Parliamentary Papers, 26. London, England.

CRASS, DAVID COLIN, AND MARK J. BROOKS (EDITORS)
1995   Cotton and Black Draught: Consumer Behavior
        on a Postbellum Farm. South Carolina Institute
        of Archaeology and Anthropology, University of
        South Carolina, *Savannah River Archaeological
        Research Papers 5*. Columbia.

CUMMINGS, LINDA SCOTT
1994   Diet and Prehistoric Landscape During the Nineteenth
        and Early Twentieth Centuries at Harpers Ferry,
        West Virginia: A View from the Old Master
        Armorer's Complex. *Historical Archaeology*
        28(4):94-105.

DAVENPORT, WILLIAM H.
1961   The Family System in Jamaica. *Social and Economic
        Studies* 10:420-454.

DEETZ, JAMES
1996   *In Small Things Forgotten: An Archaeology of
        Early American Life*. Anchor Books, New York,
        NY.

DICKSON, WILLIAM
1789   *Letters on Slavery*. J. Phillips, London, England.
        Reprinted 1970, Negro University Press, Westport,
        CT.

EDWARDS, BRYAN
1793   *The History, Civil and Commercial, of the British
        Colonies in the West Indies*. J. Stockdale, London,
        England.

FAIRBANKS, CHARLES
1976   Spaniards, Planters, Ships, and Slaves: Historical
        Archaeology on Florida and Georgia. *Archaeology*
        29:165-172.
1977   Backyard Archaeology as Research Strategy. *The
        Conference of Historic Site Archaeology Papers*,
        11. Columbia, SC.

FARISH, HUNTER DICKENSON (EDITOR)
1957   *Journal and Letters of Philip Vickers Fithian
        1773-1774: A Plantation Tutor of the Old Dominion*.
        University Press of Virginia, Charlottesville.

FESLER, GARRETT
1997a   Expressions of Power and Gender at an Early
        18th-Century African-American Chesapeake Slave

Quarter. Paper presented at The Society for
Historical Archaeology Conference on Historical and
Underwater Archaeology, Corpus Christi, TX.
1997b   Landscapes of Control and Autonomy: The
        Spatial Contestation of the Utopia Slave Quarter.
        Manuscript, Department of Archaeology, Thomas
        Jefferson's Poplar Forest, Forest, VA.

FISCHER, LISA
1996   Report on the Chemical Analysis of Soils at the
        Poplar Forest Quarter Site. Manuscript, Department
        of Archaeology, Thomas Jefferson's Poplar Forest,
        Forest, VA.

GARDNER, W. J.
1873   *A History of Jamaica*. F. Cass, London, England.

GIBB, JAMES G., AND JULIA A. KING
1991   Gender, Activity Areas, and Homelots in the 17th-
        Century Chesapeake Region. *Historical Archaeology*
        25(4):109-131.

GLEASON, KATHRYN L.
1994   To Bound and to Cultivate: An Introduction to
        the Archaeology of Gardens and Fields. In *The
        Archaeology of Garden and Field*, Naomi Miller
        and Kathryn Gleason, editors, pp. 1-24. University
        of Pennsylvania Press, Philadelphia.

GUNDAKER, GREY
1993   Tradition and Innovation in African-American
        Yards. *African Arts* 26:58-71.

HALL, EDWARD
1966   *The Hidden Dimension*. Doubleday, Garden City,
        NY.

HANDLER, JEROME S, AND FREDERICK W. LANGE
1978   *Plantation Slavery in Barbados: An Archaeological
        and Historical Investigation*. Harvard University
        Press, Cambridge, MA.

HAWKE, DAVID (EDITOR)
1971   *The Cotton Kingdom: A Selection*. Bobbs-Merrill,
        Indianapolis, IN.

HEATH, BARBARA J.
1997   Slavery and Consumerism: A Case Study from
        Central Virginia. *African-American Archaeology*
        19:1-8.
1999   *Hidden Lives: The Archaeology of Slave Life at
        Thomas Jefferson's Poplar Forest*. University
        Press of Virginia, Charlottesville.

HUNDLEY, DANIEL R.
1973   *Social Relations in Our Southern States*. Reprint of
        1860 edition, Arno Press, New York, NY.

JONES-JACKSON, PATRICIA
1987   *When Roots Die, Endangered Traditions on the Sea
        Islands*. University of Georgia Press, Athens.

KELLY, JAMES
1838   *Jamaica in 1831.* James Wilson, Belfast, Northern Ireland.

KELSO WILLIAM M., DOUGLAS W. SANFORD, DINAH CRADER JOHNSON, SONDY SANFORD, AND ANNA GRUBER
1984   A Report on the Archaeological Excavations at Monticello, Charlottesville, VA, 1982-1983. Manuscript, Thomas Jefferson Memorial Foundation, Charlottesville, VA.

KELSO, WILLIAM M., DOUGLAS W. SANFORD, ANNA GRUBER, DINAH CRADER JOHNSON, AND ANN MORGAN SMART
1985   Monticello Black History/Craftlife Archaeology Project 1984-85 Progress Report. Manuscript, Thomas Jefferson Memorial Foundation, Charlottesville, VA.

KIMBER, EDWARD
1907   Observations in Several Voyages and Travels in America. *William and Mary Quarterly*, 1st Series, 14:1-17, 15:215-225. Reprint of 1746 edition.

KING, JULIA A.
1988   A Comparative Midden Analysis of a Household and Inn in St. Mary's City, Maryland. *Historical Archaeology* 22(2):17-39.

KING, JULIA A., AND HENRY M. MILLER
1987   The View from the Midden: An Analysis of Midden Distribution and Composition at the van Sweringen Site, St. Mary's City, Maryland. *Historical Archaeology* 21(2):37-59.

LEE, HARPER
1974   *To Kill a Mockingbird.* Pan Books, London, England.

LIVINGSTONE, WILLIAM PRINGLE
1899   *Black Jamaica: A Study of Evolution.* S. Law, Marstan, London, England.

MACGAFFEY, WYATT
1986   *Religion and Society in Central Africa: The BaKongo of Lower Zaire.* University of Chicago Press, Chicago, IL.

MARTIN, ANN SMART
1993   *Buying into the World of Goods: Eighteenth-Century Consumerism and the Retail Trade from London to the Virginia Frontier.* Ph.D. dissertation, Department of History, College of William and Mary, Williamsburg, VA. University Microfilms International, Ann Arbor, MI.

McDANIEL, GEORGE W.
1982   *Hearth and Home: Preserving a People's Culture.* Temple University Press, Philadelphia, PA.

McDONALD, RODERICK A.
1993   *The Economy and Material Culture of Slaves, Goods and Chattels on the Sugar Plantations of Jamaica and Louisiana.* Louisiana State University Press, Baton Rouge.

McKEE, LARRY
1997   Summary Report on the 1994 Excavation at Alfred's Cabin. Manuscript, The Hermitage, Hermitage, TN.

McNEILL, HECTOR
1788   *Observations on the Treatment of Negroes in the Island of Jamaica.* G. G. J. and J. Robinson, London, England.

MILLER, NAOMI F.
1994   Fertilizer and the Indentification and Analysis of Cultivated Soil. In *The Archaeology of Garden and Field*, Naomi Miller and Kathryn Gleason, editors, pp. 25-43. University of Pennsylvania Press, Philadelphia.

MILLER, RONALD (EDITOR)
1969   *Mungo Park's Travels in Africa.* Dent, London, England.

MINTZ, SIDNEY
1974   *Caribbean Transformations.* Johns Hopkins University Press, Baltimore, MD.

MINTZ, SIDNEY, AND DOUGLAS HALL
1960   The Origins of the Jamaican Internal Marketing System. *Yale University Publications in Anthropology* 57. New Haven, CT.

MOIR, RANDALL W.
1987   Farmstead Proxemics and Intrasite Patterning. In Pioneer Settlers, Tenant Farmers and Communities: Objectives, Historical Background, and Excavations, Randall W. Moir and David H. Jurney, editors, Archaeology Research Program, Institute for the Study of Earth and Man, Southern Methodist University, *Richland Creek Technical Series* 4, Dallas, TX.

MORGAN, PHILIP
1982   Work and Culture: The Task System and the World of Lowcountry Blacks, 1700-1880. *William and Mary Quarterly*, 3rd Series, 39(4):563-599.
1988   Slave Life in Piedmont Virginia, 1720-1800. In *Colonial Chesapeake Society*, Lois Green Carr, Philip D. Morgan, and Jean B. Russo, editors, pp. 433-484. University Press of North Carolina, Chapel Hill.

OLMSTED, FREDERICK LAW
1861   *A Journey in the Seaboard Slave States, with Remarks on their Economy.* Mason Brothers, New York, NY.

OTTO, JOHN S.
1980   Race and Class on Antebellum Plantations. In *Archaeological Perspectives on Ethnicity in America*, Robert L. Schuyler, editor, pp. 3-13. Baywood, Farmingdale, NY.

PARRY, DAVID
    1789   Extract of a letter from Governor Parry to the Right
            Honourable Lord Sydney, 18 August 1788. *Par-
            liamentary Papers*, 26:13-24. London, England.

PERDUE, CHARLES L. (EDITOR)
    1976   *Weevils in the Wheat: Interviews with Virginia
            Ex-Slaves.* University Press of Virginia, Charlot-
            tesville.

PHILLIPPO, JAMES M.
    1843   *Jamaica: Its Past and Present State.* J. Snow,
            London, England.

PINKARD, GEORGE
    1806   *Notes on the West Indies.* Longman, Hurst, Rees,
            and Orme, London, England.

POGUE, DENNIS J.
    1988   Spatial Analysis of the King's Reach Plantation
            Homelot, ca. 1690-1715. *Historical Archaeology*
            22(2):40-56.

PULSIPHER, LYDIA MIHELIC
    1994   The Landscapes and Ideational Roles of Caribbean
            Slave Gardens. In *The Archaeology of Garden
            and Field*, Naomi Miller and Kathryn Gleason,
            editors, pp. 202-221. University of Pennsylvania
            Press, Philadelphia.

RAPOPORT, AMOS
    1993   Systems of Activities and Systems of Settings. In
            *Domestic Architecture and the Use of Space, an
            Interdisciplinary Cross-Cultural Study*, Susan Kent,
            editor, pp. 9-20. Cambridge University Press,
            Cambridge, England.

RAWICK, GEORGE (EDITOR)
    1972   *Kansas, Kentucky, Maryland, Ohio, Virginia and
            Tennessee Narratives.* Greenwood, Westport,
            CT.

RAYMER, LESLIE
    1996   Macroplant Remains from the Jefferson's Poplar
            Forest Slave Quarter: A Study in African-American
            Subsistence Practices. Report to Thomas Jefferson's
            Poplar Forest, Forest, VA, from New South Associ-
            ates.

RIORDAN, TIMOTHY B.
    1988   The Interpretation of 17th-Century Sites through
            Plow Zone Surface Collections: Examples from
            St. Mary's City, Maryland. *Historical Archaeology*
            22(2):2-16.

ROVNER, IRWIN
    1994   Floral History by the Back Door: A Test of
            Phytolith Analysis in Residential Yards at Harpers
            Ferry. *Historical Archaeology* 28(4):37-48.

RUSSELL, WILLIAM HOWARD
    1863   *My Diary North and South.* Bradbury and Evans,
            London, England. Reprinted 1954, Harper, New
            York, NY.

SARUDY, BARBARA WELLS
    1998   *Gardens and Gardening in the Chesapeake
            1700-1805.* Johns Hopkins University Press,
            Baltimore, MD.

SCHLOTTERBECK, JOHN T.
    1995   The Internal Economy of Slavery in Rural Piedmont
            Virginia. In *The Slaves' Economy: Independent
            Production by Slaves in the Americas*, Ira Berlin
            and Philip D. Morgan, editors, pp.170-181. Frank
            Cass, London, England.

SILVA, JAMES S.
    1914   *Early Reminiscences of an Old St. Marys Boy now
            in His 82nd year.* Southeast Georgian, Kingsland,
            GA.

SINGLETON, THERESA A.
    1992   Preface to *African-American Gardens and Yards in
            the Rural South*, by Richard Westmacott. University
            of Tennessee Press, Knoxville.

SINGLETON, THERESA A., AND MARK D. BOGRAD
    1993   The Archaeology of the African Diaspora in the
            Americas. *Guides to the Archaeological Literature
            of the Immigrant Experience in America*, 2. The
            Society for Historical Archaeology, California,
            PA.

SPURRIER, JOHN
    1793   *The Practical Farmer.* Brynberg and Andrews,
            Wilmington, DE.

STANTON, LUCIA
    1993   Those Who Labor for My Happiness. In *Jeffersonian
            Legacies*, Peter S. Onuf, editor, pp. 147-180.
            University Press of Virginia, Charlottesville.

STEWART, JOHN
    1823   *A View of the Past and Present State of the Island of
            Jamaica.* Oliver & Boyd, Edinburgh, Scotland.

STOWE, HARRIET BEECHER
    1853   *A Key to Uncle Tom's Cabin.* John P. Jewett,
            Boston, MA.

THOMAS, BRIAN W., LARRY MCKEE, AND JENNIFER
BARTLETT
    1995   Summary Report on the 1995 Hermitage Field
            Quarter Excavation. Manuscript, The Hermitage,
            Hermitage, TN.

THOMAS JEFFERSON'S POPLAR FOREST
    1844-   Hutter Farm Journal. Thomas Jefferson's Poplar
    1854   Forest, Forest, VA.

THOMPSON, MARY V.
1993   "Better . . . Fed than Negroes Generally Are?":
        Diet of the Mount Vernon Slaves. Manuscript,
        Mount Vernon Ladies' Association, Mount Vernon,
        VA.

THOMPSON, ROBERT FARRIS
1984   *Flash of the Spirit, African and Afro-American
        Art and Philosophy.* Vintage Press, New York,
        NY.
1990   Kongo Influences on African-American Artistic
        Culture. In *Africanisms in American Culture,*
        Joseph E. Holloway, editor, pp. 148-184. Indiana
        University Press, Bloomington.

UNIVERSITY OF VIRGINIA
1814   Letter from Jeremiah Goodman to Thomas Jefferson,
        30 December. University of Virginia Special
        Collections, Charlottesville.

UPTON, DELL
1985   White and Black Landscapes in Eighteenth-Century
        Virginia. *Places* 2(2):59-72.

VLACH, JOHN MICHAEL
1991   *By the Work of Their Hands: Studies in Afro-
        American Folklife.* University Press of Virginia,
        Charlottesville.

WARE, SUE ANNE
1997   The Sisterhood of Gardens: African-American
        Women's Gardens, from the Backwoods to the Cul-
        de-Sac. In *The Influence of Women on the Southern
        Landscape, Proceedings of the Tenth Conference
        on Restoring Southern Gardens and Landscapes*
        1995:154-171. Winston-Salem, NC.

WATTERS, DAVID R.
1994   Mortuary Patterns at the Harney Site Slave Cemetery,
        Montserrat, in Caribbean Perspective. *Historical
        Archaeology* 28(3):56-73.

WELTY, EUDORA
1971   *The Wide Net and Other Stories.* Harcourt, Brace,
        Jovanovich, New York, NY.

WESTMACOTT, RICHARD
1992   *African-American Gardens and Yards in the Rural
        South.* University of Tennessee Press, Knoxville.

YENTSCH, ANNE E., AND JUDSON M. KRATZER
1994   Techniques for Excavating and Analyzing Buried
        Eighteenth-Century Garden Landscapes. In *The
        Archaeology of Garden and Field,* Naomi Miller and
        Kathryn Gleason, editors, pp. 168-201. University
        of Pennsylvania Press, Philadelphia.

BARBARA J. HEATH
THOMAS JEFFERSON'S POPLAR FOREST
PO BOX 419
FOREST, VA 24551-0419

AMBER BENNETT
DEPARTMENT OF ANTHROPOLOGY
SWEET BRIAR COLLEGE
SWEET BRIAR, VA 24595-9999

EXCAVATION OF A SLAVE CABIN: GEORGIA, U.S.A.

ROBERT ASCHER
and
CHARLES H. FAIRBANKS

Soundtrack

If I could do it, I'd do no writing at all here. It would be photographs: the rest would be fragments of cloth, bits of cotton, lumps of earth, records of speech, pieces of wood and iron, phials of odors, plates of food and excrement. (Agee and Evans 1969:12)

Here is an interpretation of what was found in the ruins of a slave cabin. The ruins are on Cumberland Island, Georgia. The cabin was lived in between circa 1834 and 1865. We seek to discover and convey a sense of daily life as it might have been experienced by the people who lived in the cabin.

Until now, what slavery was like anywhere has been largely constructed from the writings of slave owning groups (Davis 1966:30). In the case of plantation slavery in Georgia, records and accounts of slave owning farmers often provide information (Flanders 1933). Another general source of information are the writings of men and women who once had

been slaves (Osofsky 1969). Third are materials from excavation. These differ from all writing in the matter of intent. We take it for granted that no one expected us to see or touch the things we unearthed.

Why excavate at a place lived in at a time for which written documents are abundant? With reference to earlier periods and other circumstances in American history, archaeologists have answered this question by saying that their endeavors were meant to supplement history (Deetz 1968:123; Harrington 1955:1122). This answer presumes that what happened is already known. Perhaps this presumption applies elsewhere; it does not fit here. For one thing, slaves broke the law when they read or wrote, and anyone who taught slaves to read or write also broke the law (for the law in Georgia, see King 1966; 182). Anyway, we reject the notion that writing is inherently superior to other objects as evidence for human activity.

In America, "historical archaeology" has focused on people (and their descendants) who came to these shores from Europe rather early (Noel-Hume 1969 a). There are relevant exceptions. One concerns the excavation of a small house in Andover, Massachusetts whose principal occupant was a woman called "Black Lucy." As a young person "Black Lucy" was a slave; when she moved into her house at the age of 58, she was free (Bullen and Bullen 1945). A similar case involves the excavation of a house in Concord, Massachusetts. For a while, this place was occupied by a man called "Casey." Like "Black Lucy," "Casey" lived the last portion of his life as a free person (Snow 1969). Recently, in the midst of Brooklyn, the remains of a freemen settlement came to light. Under the title "Project Weeksville," archaeological work on the settlement is underway (Hurley and Hurley 1969). We know of two excavations directly related to conditions under slavery. The first was undertaken by one of us (Fairbanks 1968) at Kingsley Plantation, Florida; the results of the second are presented here.

Our presentation includes a soundtrack and pictures. The soundtrack is composed from eye-witness accounts, slave narratives, and other sources. You are encouraged to sound out the words; the soundtrack selections are based on their auditory value and on their connection with the archaeological findings. The organization follows a modular plan; each module begins with a soundtrack and ends at the start of the next soundtrack. You are invited to reassemble the components to best suit yourself. Artifacts are three dimensional: they are visual and tactile and sometimes they smell and make noise. Word pictures and flat representations in photographs and drawings offer only limited help.

Soundtrack

The cotton crop was all they thought of. It was fuly admired, and the gentlemen returned with specimens to show his friends. I was ordered to carry water to wash his hands. (Jacobs 1961:143)

Someone able to read and free to travel in the American south in the middle of the nineteenth century might have consulted a published guide to Georgia. For instance, he might have chanced upon a book entitled: *Statistics Of The State Of Georgia: Including An Account Of Its Natural, Civil, And Ecclesiastical History; Together With A Particular Description Of Each County, Notices Of The Manners And Customs Of Its Aboriginal Tribes, And A Correct Map Of The State*

(White 1849). Under the entry Cumberland Island, the literate traveller would find that it was the most southerly of a string of islands just off the Georgian coast; it was three miles wide and eighteen miles long; the soil was good for growing cotton, corn, and potatoes; General Oglethorpe had named it, General Nathanial Green had owned land on it, and Admiral Cockburne had landed there and stayed for a short while during the War of 1812. Our hypothetical reader could hardly miss this sentence: "Population, 24th October 1846, thirteen white men, eight white boys, seven girls, eight women, negroes (sic) four hundred." (White 1849: 139-40)

The large number of blacks on Cumberland Island were there because cotton — with slave labor — was good business for the white population. Referring to the string of sea islands, one traveller wrote: "These make no great show on paper, but they are very important in commerce, as being the spots on which the finest kind of cotton is grown." (Hall 1829: 217) Indeed, sea island cotton with its long fibre or staple, at times brought more than twice the price of competing cottons (Bonner 1964:53). Around 1800 cotton fever seized all Georgia and through 1840 Georgia led the states in cotton production (King 1966:116). By 1830, the white opposition to slavery that had once existed in Georgia was gone (Scarborough 1933:185).

Soundtrack

First Voice:

I was immediately sent for, to be valued with the other property. Here again my feelings rose up in detestation of slavery. I had now a new conception of my degraded condition. Prior to this, I had become, if not insensible to my lot, at least partly so. (Douglas 1968:59)

Second Voice:

. . . Also grant sell and deliver unto the said party of the second part the fifty three following negro (sic) slaves to wit Matta, Bella, Suckey, Amaritta, Elick, Aimy, Frank, Dennis, Pessy, Camilla, Joe, Phebe, Molly, George, Abigail, Warren, Judy, Warren, Benter, Stass, Lynda, May, Dec, Quality, Prince, Seipio, Dye, Clarissy, Mary, Mingo, Simmon, Robbin, Dick, Stass, Dorothy, Nancy, Tom, Hetty, Judy, Primo, Lucy, Cuffy, Maria, Betsy, Lenor, Elick, Ozwell, Nelly, Ansel, Anny, Mary, Purity, and Peter together with the future issue and increase of the female slaves . . . (Camden County Superior Court 1831-1837: 192)

We think that some of the people just named lived in the excavated cabin. The names appear in a document dated April 2, 1834. In this document, the descendants of General Nathaniel Greene agreed to sell a cotton plantation called Rayfield. The size and location of the plantation are a fitting description for the place where we worked. The buyer, "the said party of the second part" mentioned in the document, was Robert Stafford.

Rayfield was one of two plantations owned by Stafford. His handling of these plantations is recalled in an article in *The Southeast Georgian* for September 25, 1914:

> The settlement south of this covers probably as much as one-third of the island and was owned by Mr. Robert Stafford. He had a large number of negro (sic) slaves whose labor was utilized in the cultivation of sea island cotton and sufficient food stuff for the plantations. This cotton was of a superior quality and I have been told that it commanded the high price of 75 cents a pound. The tract was divided into two plantations, each under separate management. This arrangement stimulated a rivalry as to which could produce the largest and best crops and was productive of good results. (Silva 1914)

This "early reminescence" was published when the writer was eighty-two years old. However, the pattern he describes conforms to the practice on other sea island plantations as observed by individuals who wrote in the 1830's (for example, Kemble 1863).

At Rayfield, slave quarters were arranged in two parallel rows of nine cabins each. The cabins may have been standing at the time of the sale; the details of the transaction offer little help on this point. Certainly more than fifty-three slaves could be housed in eighteen units, suggesting that additional slaves were brought in and more cabins were added after 1834. If the cabin we excavated was not standing in 1834, it was probably built soon thereafter because few of the datable excavated materials were manufactured later than 1830.

A passing remark appearing in a magazine in 1880 tells how Rayfield came to an end. "At the close of the war, it is related, Mr. Stafford, proprietor of the central portion of the island burned his negro (sic) houses to the ground, telling his people to go, as he had no more use for them nor they for him." (Ober 1880:243) The slave cabins at Rayfield are now reduced to slight rises in the ground containing mostly rubble from fallen chimneys.

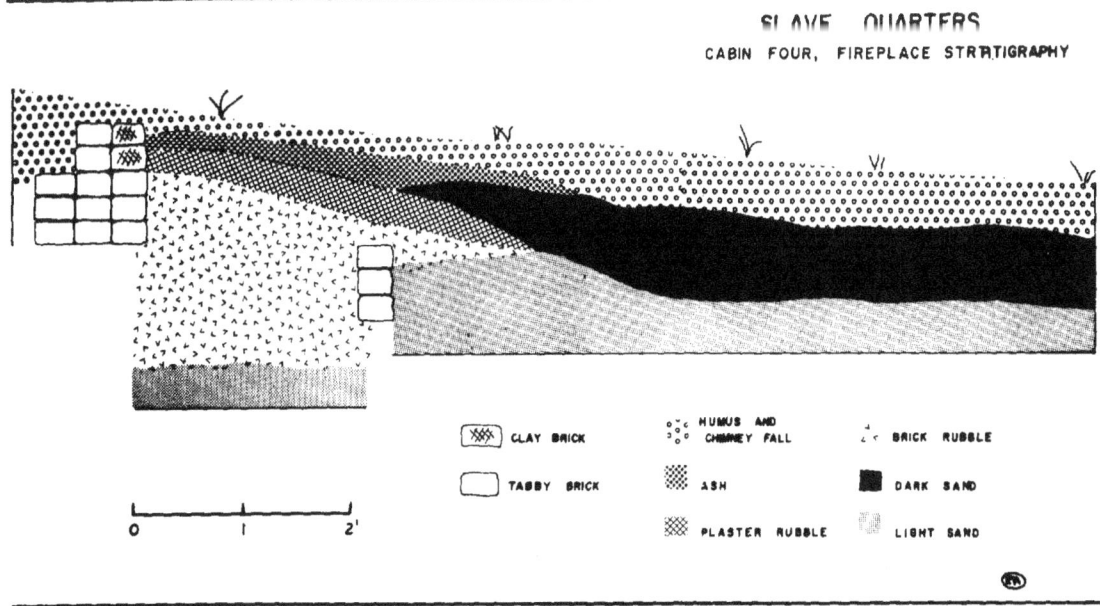

SLAVE QUARTERS
CABIN FOUR, FIREPLACE STRATIGRAPHY

CLAY BRICK	HUMUS AND CHIMNEY FALL	BRICK RUBBLE
TABBY BRICK	ASH	DARK SAND
	PLASTER RUBBLE	LIGHT SAND

FIGURE 1. *Stratigraphy of the excavated cabin in the area of the fireplace and chimney.*

Soundtrack

. . . I walked down the settlement toward the infirmary or hospital, calling in one or two houses along the row . . . two families (sometimes eight and ten in number) reside in one of these huts, which are mere wooden frames pinned, as it were, to the earth by a brick chimney outside, whose enormous aperture within pours down a flood of air, but little counteracted by the miserable spark of fire, which hardly sends an attenuated thread of lingering smoke up its huge throat. (Kemble 1863:30)

An outline history of the cabin is told in its stratigraphy and soils (Figure 1). It begins with a trench dug into the light colored sand for the placement of the fireplace. Incidentally, this disturbance turned over a few pottery sherds and a flint projectile left by Indians as many as nine centuries before. The lower portion of the fireplace was set; the trench was filled with brick rubble and topped with plaster; and the rest of the cabin was built around the central fireplace and chimney.

Life inside the cabin produced an ash layer that eventually spilled out of the fireplace and onto the floor where the sand turned a darker color through time and use (Figure 2). The fireplace and floor can be distinguished by chemical analysis as well as through color changes (Table 1).

Samples taken from the floor and fireplace show a systematic trend from lower to higher concentrations for all but one component. For the exception—organic matter—a lower reading is predictable on the basis of the destructive effects of burning. The history of life anywhere within the cabin as compared with the outside is also distinguishable at the chemical level. A soil sample taken from four inches below the ground, and twnety-four feet away from the chimney, gave markedly low concentrations for everything tested. Finally, the high concentrations of calcium in the floor and fireplace testify to the collapse of the chimney and with it, the cabin. When the chimney fell forward onto the fireplace and floor, it carried with it bricks and mor-

FIGURE 2. *Partially excavated fireplace as seen from the side. The humus and chimney fall have been excavated and the ash layer is exposed. (Marker in tenths of a foot.)*

Table 1

SOIL ANALYSIS*

	Outside Cabin	Cabin Floor	Cabin Fireplace
Organic Matter	0.9	4.3	3.5
pH	5.7	7.5	7.7
Manganese	4	32	38
Phosphorus	18	325	500
Potassium	20	70	250
Magnesium	70	300	1,025
Calcium	700	47,500	75,000

*Organic matter in % of weight: Manganese through Calcium in lbs./2 x 10^6 lbs.

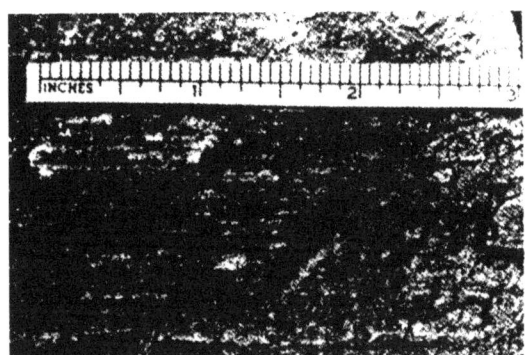

FIGURE 3. *Impressions from siding board in a block of tabby mortar from the chimney fall.*

tar made of tabby. Tabby is a combination of sand, lime, and oyster shell, in equal proportions by measure (Floyd 1937).

Other materials used to construct the cabin were mingled in its fallen ruins. Wood identified as southern yellow pine (genus *Pinus*, section *Australes*) may have been used for siding. A block of mortar from the chimney fall shows impressions where four inch boards

were held in position (Figure 3). Elsewhere in the cabin, the boards were nailed. The way nails were made changed during the second decade of the nineteenth century. These changes show up in the shear marks of a nail's cross-section and in the direction of the fibers of a nail's shank (Nelson 1963). After electrolytic cleaning, we microscopically examined 128 machine-cut nails, representing perhaps one-quarter of those used in the cabin's construction. Nine were made by a process already becoming absolete in 1820, and another twenty-six may fit this category; eighty-five were made after 1825 and eight more probably belong to this later period. This result eliminates any possibility of the cabin having been built before 1825. Three kinds of bricks were used; red clay ones lined the inside of the firebox, and another kind of clay brick filled the fireplace trench (Figure 4). But the majority of the bricks were made of tabby, a material already described.

A precariously leaning chimney remains (as of 1969) at one of the eighteen cabin sites in the slave quarter (Figure 5). Everything about it is consistent with the ruins of the

FIGURE 4. *Partially excavated fireplace seen from the front. The humus, chimney fall, ash, and plaster rubble were excavated exposing the brick rubble.*

FIGURE 5. *Leaning chimney at one of the cabins. The firebox is about 3 ft. wide.*

fallen chimney we excavated. It is therefore reasonable to use the leaning chimney to fill in our picture of the excavated cabin. Most importantly, plaster ridges toward the top of the leaning chimney give a clue about the cabin's dimensions. If we use the angle of the ridge as a guide, and extend a line from the midpoint of the chimney until it intersects a second line drawn six feet from the side wall of the fireplace and parallel to it, we reconstruct a cabin that is six feet high at the eaves and eighteen feet across. Lacking evidence to the contrary, we suggest that the excavated cabin was a square 18 x 18 feet (Figure 6). These dimensions are well within the range of other Georgian slave quarter cabins (Flanders 1933:152).

Soundtrack

He may have been twenty years old when stolen from Africa: left a wife and one child

there. Used to say he went home to Africa in the night and came back again in the morning: that is, he dreamed of home. (Thoreau 1949:285)

A bead is the smallest whole artifact recovered in the course of excavation (Figure 7). It measures only one-quarter of an inch in both length and diameter. If you hold it so as to look through the perforation, you can count six sides along the outer edge. With the exception of a white rim surrounding the perforation, the bead is blue, and is faceted. The manufacturing sequence, in part, went like this: a bulb of glass was rolled over marble; the result was rolled over half-molten blue glass; the glass was pressed into a mold to form facets (Sleen 1967:25). The nomenclature for beads requires that we describe this one as standard, hexagonal, blue, and drawn (Beck 1927).

We think it possible that this bead was carried from Africa to America by someone sold into slavery. The evidence is as follows. Slaves arrived in South Carolina as late as 1808 and the slave markets of this state often supplied slaves for Georgia (Stamp 1956:25; Curtin 1969:158). At about the same time, hundreds of thousands of beads were being produced in European glass factories. Wherever Europeans went, a variety of beads went with them as trade media. A bead meeting the specifications given above is frequently and specifically singled out in studies of African trade beads. It appears in Africa around the turn of the nineteenth century. In fact, the white rim, blue color, and hexagonal shape combination describe the "ambassador bead." The name comes from the belief that it was used as a "passport for bearers of messages between tribal chiefs" (Sleen 1969:40, Fig. 5, No. 12). A similar notion appears independently; this time the blue hexagonal is said to have played a role in native alliances that stretched from the west to the east coast of Africa (Laidler 1937:35-36). In still a third source, the blue hexagonal is connected with the purchase of slaves in the period beginning 1800 (Schofield 1938:353).

There are other ways to account for the presence of a bead in the slave cabin. For example, a European may have traded with an American Indian; the Indian, in turn, could have passed on the bead to a slave. Possibilities can be multiplied; more complex trade networks can be introduced. The first possibility is intriguing, direct, and simple.

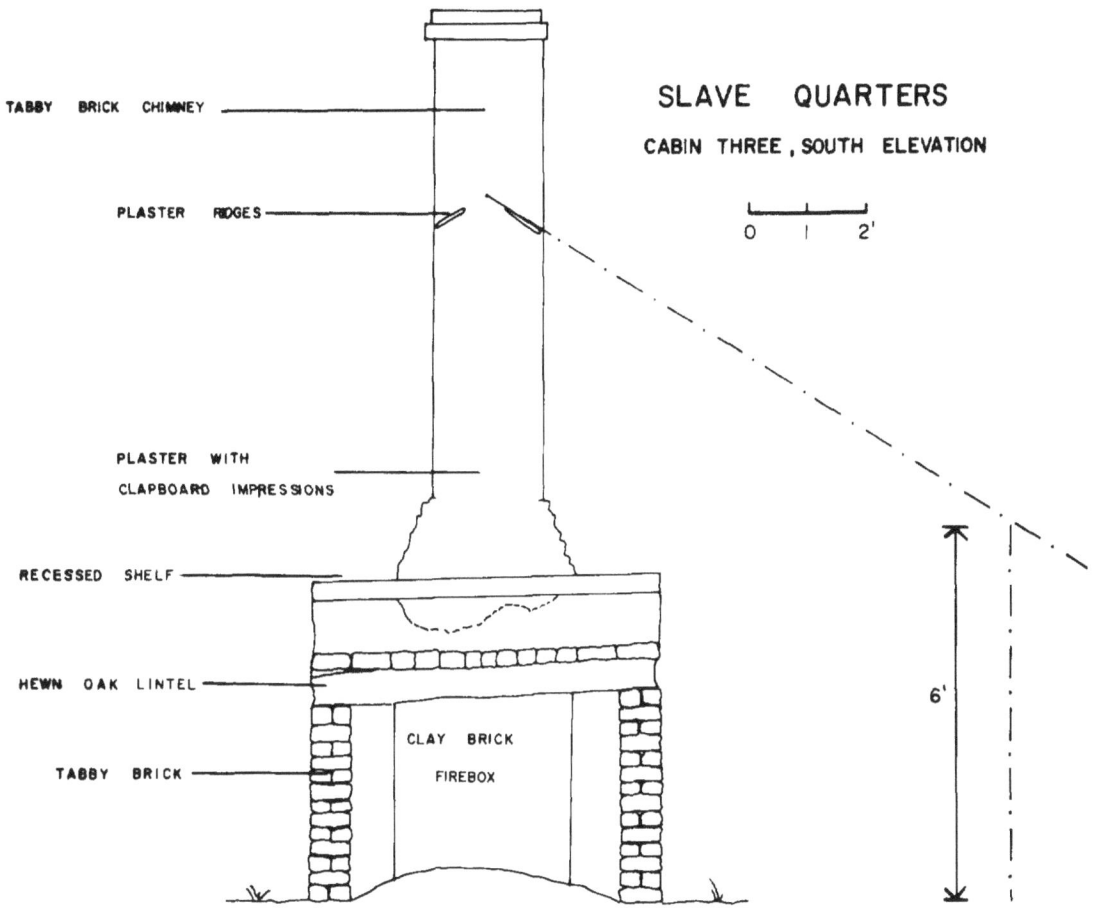

SLAVE QUARTERS

CABIN THREE, SOUTH ELEVATION

0   1   2'

TABBY BRICK CHIMNEY

PLASTER RIDGES

PLASTER WITH CLAPBOARD IMPRESSIONS

RECESSED SHELF

HEWN OAK LINTEL

TABBY BRICK

CLAY BRICK FIREBOX

6'

FIGURE 6. *Reconstruction of the dimensions of the excavated cabin using the leaning chimney as a guide.*

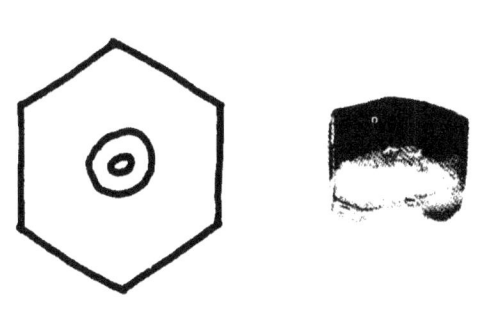

FIGURE 7. *Blue, hexagonal, faceted, bead. (Approximate real dimensions: .25, length and diameter.)*

Soundtrack

A water pail, a boiling pot, and a few gourds made up the furniture. When the corn had been ground in a hand-mill, and then boiled, the pot was swung from the fire and the children squatted around it, with oyster shells for spoons. (Smith 1882:8)

The space inside the cabin served as a combination kitchen, bedroom, and living room. Activities such as sleeping, eating, or just being, leave very different tangible remains. One expects to find more evidence for kitchen activities than for anything else people were doing. This expectation is born out in the excavated materials (Fig. 8).

For holding liquids: The people in the cabin had pieces of bottles, tumblers, cups and other kinds of containers. From slivers of glass, we can reconstruct parts of two dark green bottles (cf. McKearin 1941:428). Other

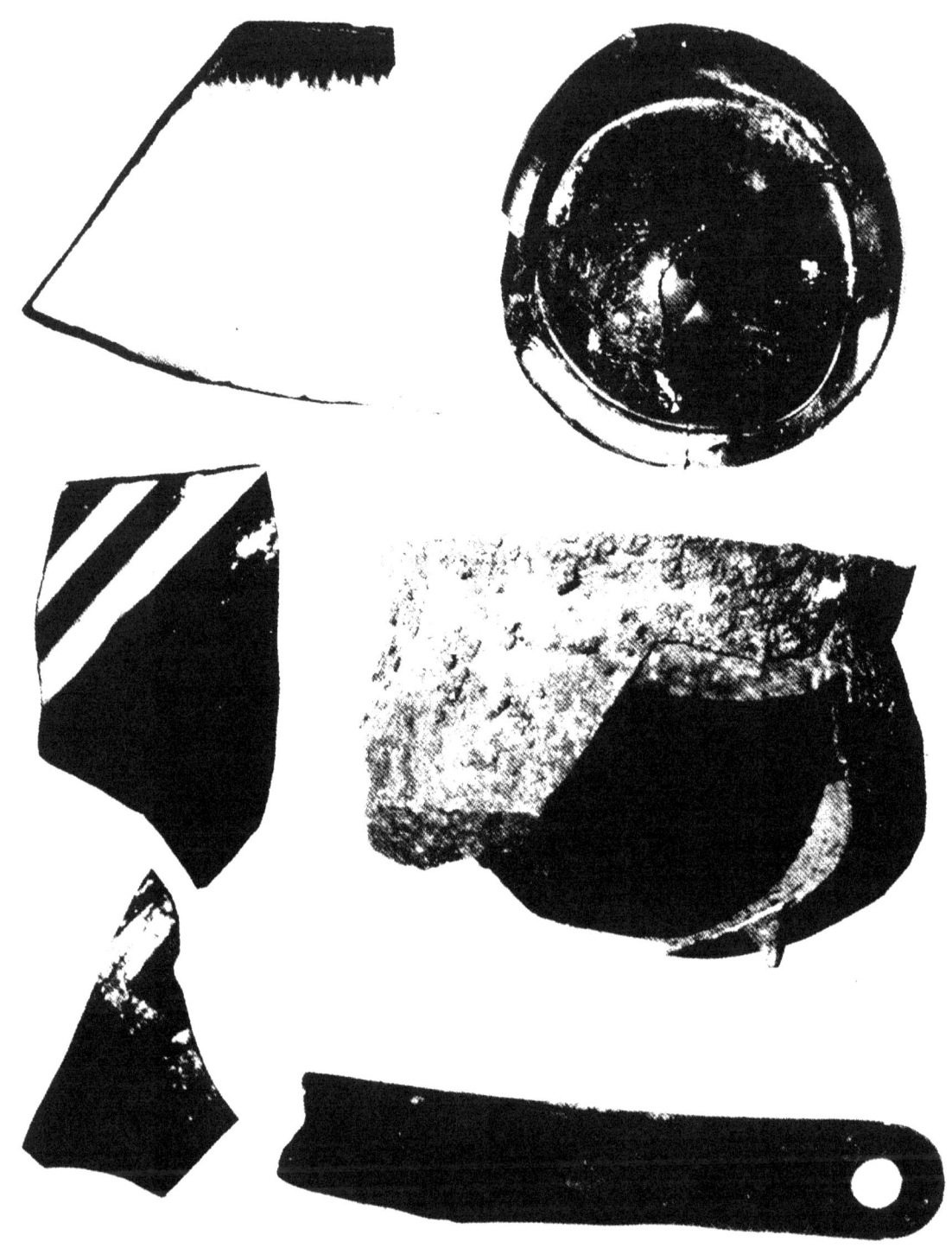

FIGURE 8. *Kitchen materials. Ceramics, left, top to bottom; shell-edged pearl ware, banded ware, stoneware. The base of a bottle is at the upper right, and a knifeblade handle is at the lower right. The cooking pot was excavated near another cabin, but a smaller section of an identical pot was recovered from the excavated cabin. (Approximate real dimensions: pearl ware, 2 in.; banded ware, 2 in.; stoneware, 1 in.; glass, 3 in.; pot, 10 in.; blade, 2.5 in.)*

class comes from common drinking vessels. Fragments of stoneware and similar pottery may be from jugs or pitchers (Watkins 1942: 134). The sherds of cups and other containers are semi-porcelain banded ware; they are decorated with mostly brown and black stripes on a pearlwhite band that interrupts a brown field (cf. Bemrose 1952:Pl. 26, 27; Nöel-Hume 1969 b:395). *For holding food:* Nearly half of the sherds come from three shell-edged, blue rimmed, pearlware plates (cf. Nöel-Hume 1969 b:393-394). The fragments are so small that taken together there are not enough pieces to add up to even a single plate. *For preparing food:* Bones taken from the floor and hearth show the marks left by a knife blade; and we recovered the handle segment of a knife. Among the many twisted bits of corroded metal, we can identify part of a boiling pot.

All the slivers of glass, pottery sherds, and bits of metal come from everyday things common in the first quarter of the nineteenth century. Much of it was imported. For example, the plates are the kind that were shipped to the U.S. from England in "vast quantities" through 1830 (Nöel-Hume 1969: 396). They have been found at places as diverse as townhouses in Virginia (Nöel-Hume 1969 b:392), ranch houses in New Mexico (Boyd 1956:240), at a trading post in South Dakota (Smith 1958:84), a log cabin in Tenessee (Morse and Morse 1964), and at the one time capital of the Cherokee Nation, New Echota, in Georgia (Fairbanks 1962:13). The glass and the stoneware may have been made in the United States.

If we had excavated the kitchen of a white middle class farmer in a house that collapsed in 1835, we would expect to find more of the same things in better condition. The kitchen hardware of the slave cabin ruin seems less out-of-place when one knows that the cabin was probably lived in through 1865. Further, all of the things from the slave cabin are broken up into small pieces. This can be accounted for in several ways: for example; the items could be from the discard pile of the slave owner and were already partially broken when taken to the cabin; they could be a selected sample where selection was based on being small enough to slip between the floor boards (if there were any); and, some of the items could have been left behind as useless when the people left.

Soundtrack

I can say, from ten years residence with Master Epps, that no slave of his is ever likely to suffer from the gout, superinduced by excessive high living. (Northup 1968:127)

People classify the food they eat in many ways. For example, a division into raw and cooked would be a meaningful starting place for most of us. From the point of view of the slave, a fundamental division was food distributed by the owner and food the slave supplied for himself. Corn was ubiquitious in the first category. If the corn ration were supplemented by meat, it would most likely be pig meat. In the second category, the range is wide in both content and amount, depending upon such particulars as opportunity, the environment, and individual tastes. This knowledge comes from fugitive slave narratives (Ball 1858:63, 120, 128, 195, 241; Bibb 1969:119; Douglas 1968:28; Jacobs 1861: 142; Northup 1968:127; Smith 1882:8; Steward 1857:14; Thompson 1856:17). With this knowledge, we abandon our usual categories and replace them with those meaningful to the people who interest us.

The people in the quarter probably carried much of their food refuse to a community deposit where it became mixed with other garbage. The refuse left inside the excavated cabin is clearly assignable to those who lived there. Most of the food remains belong to the "get-it-for-yourself" category. The one hundred and twenty-five bones divide about evenly into mammal, bird, and fish. Among these, there are catfish, chickens, and pigs. Several wild birds and small mammals are present, but the fragments are not the kind that permit naming the animals. The shells of oysters and clams were plentiful in the hearth and on the floor. We also recovered fish scales; perhaps they were from shad. The animals were young, old, and in-between, suggesting that their pursuer took whatever he could find.

Of the entire within-cabin assortment, we are reasonably sure that some form of pig was supplied by the slave owner. Let us assume that other foods in this category were vegetable. If so, these foods decayed beyond identifiable levels long ago. We recognize—but cannot identify—food debris in the chemistry of the soils (Table 1). In particular, organic matter is more vegetable than animal, but it is impossible to state how much of each is involved (Cornwall 1963:121). The high potassium concentration inside the cabin is also due in part to vegetable refuse (Cook and Heizer 1965:4). Then again, if vegetable refuse were recovered, we could not eliminate it having come from gardens planted and tended

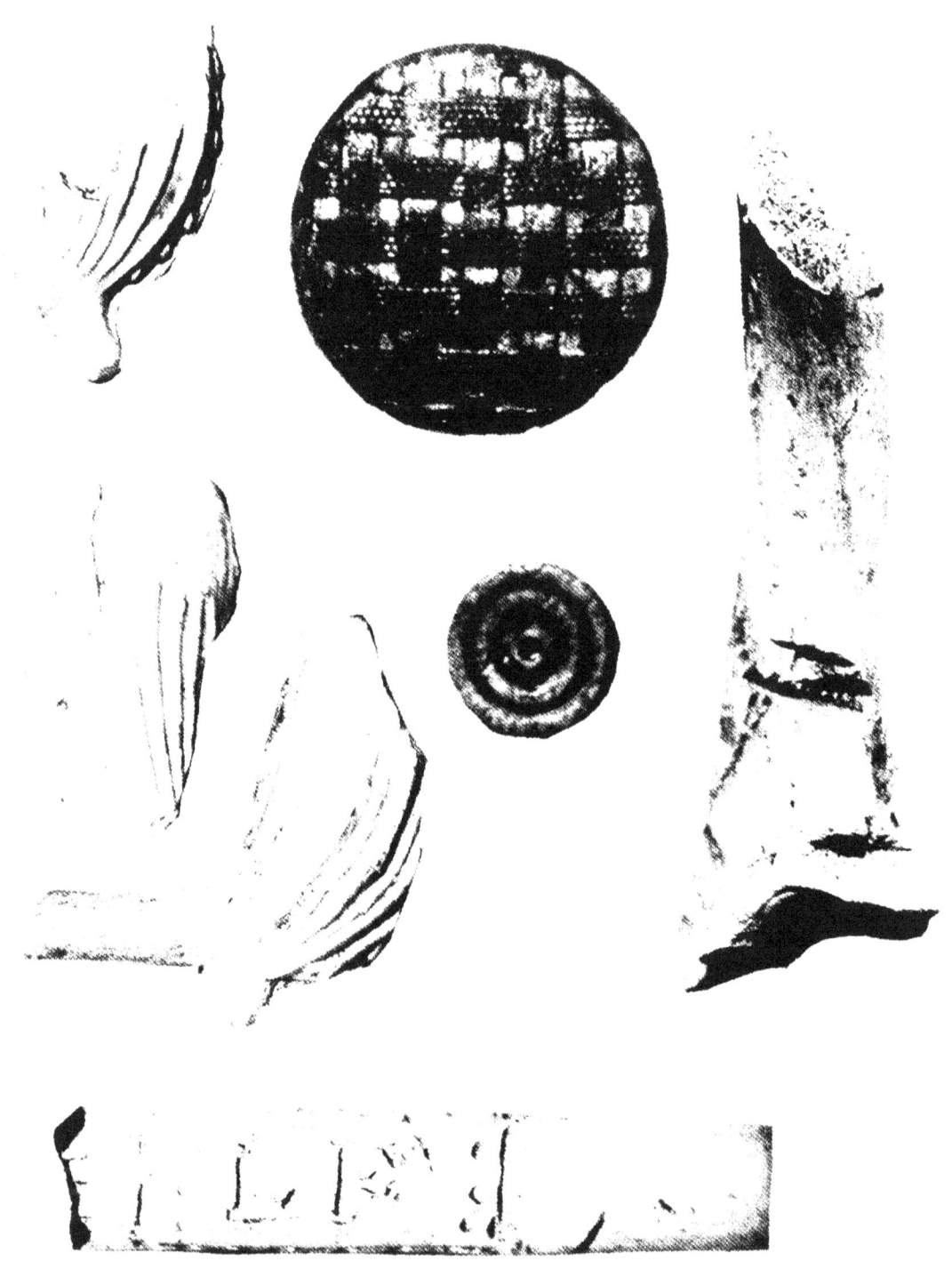

FIGURE 9. At the left, three pipe bowl fragments, and a section of a pipe stem with a manufacturers mark (LF) as shown. At the right, there is a metal button, a bone button, and the ilium of a pig with segments removed. (Approximate real dimensions: metal button, .5 in.; bone button, .25.; ilium, 7. in.; pipe stem, 1.5 in.; bowl fragments, 1 in. in diameter.)

by individuals. In sum, through excavation, we have learned that the people in one cabin managed to add considerable protein to their diet, apparently through their own efforts.

Soundtrack

For sale: Twenty acres of clay ground fit for making tobacco pipes, two negro (sic) slaves, utensils, and other conveniences to carry out that business. (Peterson 1963:3)

We sometimes feel closer to individuals when considering things associated with their personal habits and belongings. In this case, broken pipes and buttons may help to provide a sense of person. (Figure 9).

The shattered bowls and stems of clay pipes were strewn in the cabin floor. The clay pipe was the "cigarette of its day; . . . cheap, fragile, and expendable, it was made by the tens of thousands" (Peterson 1963:1). The decorations on the bowls do not indicate a fancy product but rather a stepped up manufacturing process. In particular, leaves and flutes were put on bowls to obsure the seams left by the pipe molds (Humphrey 1969:14). Earlier, the seams were trimmed by hand, sometimes, apparently, by slave labor. The stem fragments are mostly unadorned. The exceptions are the letters LF on two pieces of stem; this is the mark of L. Fiolet Company, St. Omer, France (Brown 1935:8). Pipes by Fiolet were on the shelves of a sundries store in Sacramento, California, when it burnt to the ground in 1852 (Humphrey 1969:17), and they turn up elsewhere in the west and midwest (Brown 1935:8; Wilson 1961:133). Presumabley, one or more of the people in the cabin liked tobacco. This is reinforced by our recovery of the distinctive bottom corner of a snuff bottle (cf. McKearin and McKearin 1941:143).

If pipe smoking and snuff bring to mind the image of a man, so do the buttons we recovered. Half of the dozen buttons are made out of bone, and they are the kind usually worn on trousers. Bone buttons can be made with a simple tool (Olsen 1963:553). It is reasonable to suppose that they were made in the slave quarter. It is faintly possible that someone in the cabin made them. The evidence suggesting this possibility is found in the ilium of a very large pig from which several sections of bone had been carefully cut and removed. The metal buttons are varied. A military button displays an eagle and the inscription "1 Rt." in an oval below the eagle. This was made in 1808 to be worn on an enlisted man's coat. Three other buttons have writing on the back: they say

"Best Quality," "Treble Gilt Standard;" and "Orange/Extra Fine/London." Buttons such as these were becoming "fashionable" for men's wear in England starting around 1830 (Jones 1924:13). We might speculate at length on the presence of quality buttons in the cabin. But the impression of masculinity noted above is already sufficiently speculative.

Soundtrack

I sat down and took my last dinner as the slave of my mistress, dividing the contents of my basket with my dog. After I had finished I tied my dog with a rope to a small tree; I set my gun against it, for I thought I should be better without the gun than with it . . . I now took to the forest keeping as nearly as I could, a north course all afternoon. (Ball 1858:309-310)

A chunk of lead, a gun flint, and three lead bullets were unearthed in the course of excavation (Figure 10). These led us to pose two questions: What kind of gun is involved? And, could the bullets have been made from the chunk of lead?

The gun flint tells us the kind of firing machanism; the three bullets bring us closer to a specific weapon. The largest of the three bullets has a maximum diameter of .638 in.; the two smaller ones are .370 and .337 in. (max. dia.). The large ball is the kind of ammunition that would be used with a .69 calibre, flint lock, smooth bore musket. This weapon was common for the times. The small bullets could be fired with this gun, but a second weapon may have been involved.

In the first half of the nineteenth century, a person who wanted ammunition made it with some lead and a bullet mold (Peterson 1967:307). It seems possible that the chunk of lead was the source from which the bullets were made. We investigated this possibility with analytic techniques.

As a first step, samples from close to the surfaces of the chunk and the bullets were submitted to neutron activation analysis (Sayre and Dodson 1957). Visual inspection of the graphed results were interpreted to mean that the two small bullets had probably come from the same source. We saw no relationship between these bullets and either the large bullet, or the chunk.

As a second step, we analysed the bullets and the chunk by spark source mass spectrometry (Roboz 1968). This time, samples taken from the interiors of the materials were tested for seventeen trace elements. For thirteen elements, the bullets and the chunk yielded

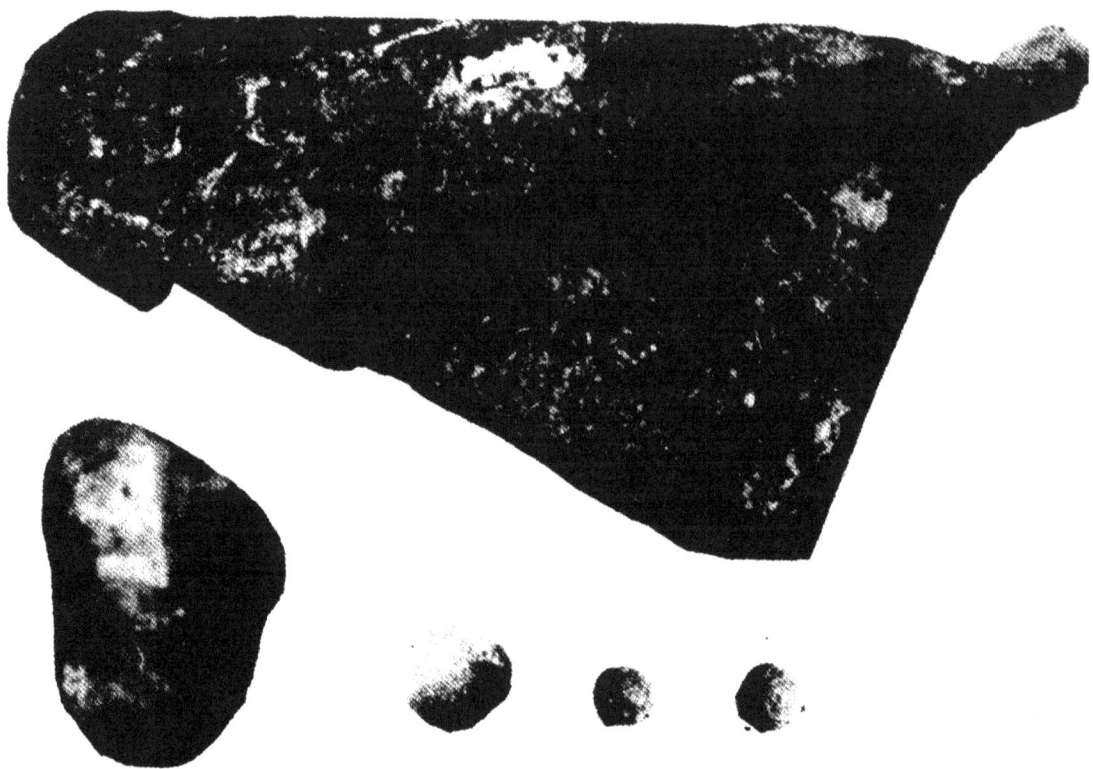

FIGURE 10. *Chunk of lead, gun flint, and bullets. (Approximate real dimensions: chunk, 4 in.; flint, 2 in.; bullets, see Table 2.)*

the same results: namely; Mg, P, S, Ti, 10-100 (parts per million atomic); elements C, Na, Si, Cl, Ca, Fe, Cu, As, 100-1,000; element K, 1,000-10,000. The results for the trace elements that differ are shown in Table 2. The similarities in the trace element concentrations are striking, especially considering the fact that no refined purification procedures were used in lead production in the early nineteenth century. The differences in oxygen and nitrogen are not diagnostic since they can arise from unavoidable contamination in the spectrometer, and the variations in aluminium and zinc are minor. Our second

question is answered: we think that the bullets are from the same source as the chunk, or from the chunk itself.

Soundtrack

History is forgotten. There is little record of the first Africans brought to this country. They were stripped of everything. A calculated cruelty was begun, designed to crush their spirit. After they were settled in the white man's land the malice continued. . . The practice of slavery stopped over a hundred years ago, but the minds of our citizens have never been freed. (Grier and Cobbs 1968:20)

Table 2

BULLET ANALYSIS*

Elements That Differ	.370	.638	.336	Chunk
Oxygen	1,000 − 10,000	100 − 1,000	1,000 − 10,000	100 − 1,000
Nitrogen	10 − 100	10 − 100	100 − 1,000	10 − 100
Aluminium	10 − 100	100 − 1,000	10 − 100	10 − 100
Zinc	−	10 − 100	10 − 100	−

*Numbers are part per million (PPM) atomic.

ACKNOWLEDGEMENTS

We thank the people of Cumberland Island, in particular, Mr. and Mrs. S. O. Candler, O. R. Ferguson, and C. C. Perkins, for their generosity and hospitality. We thank the field crew: M. Ascher, K. Deagan, C. Mc-Murray, J. Angley McMurray, and S. D. Smith. For important help with documents, we thank R. H. L. Wheeler and J. Graves. For assistance with the analysis of materials, we thank K. Anolik, R. H. Brill, J. D. Campbell, L. Corruccini, H. E. Evans, B. F. Kukachka, B. R. Lewis, G. H. Morrison, E. McMurry, G. W. Olsen, H. L. Peterson, J. R. Roth, S. Saraydar, and K. M. Wilson. In the initial stages, J. M. Corbett, J. C. Cotter, and C. E. Hatch, Jr. provided help. Grants from Cornell University and the Wenner-Gren Foundation to R. Ascher aided with the analytic and write-up phases of the work.

REFERENCES

AGEE, J. AND W. EVANS
1969 *Let Us Now Praise Famous Men*. Ballentine Books, New York, (Copyright, James Agee, 1939).

BALL, C.
1858 *Fifty Years in Chains or the Life of an American Slave*. H. Dayton, New York.

BECK, H. C.
1927 Classification and Nomenclature of Beads and Pendants. *Archaeologia*, Vol. 77, pp. 1-76.

BEMROSE, G.
1952 *Nineteenth Century English Pottery and Porcelain*. Faber and Faber, London.

BIBB, H.
1969 "Narrative of the Life and Adventures of Henry Bibb, An American Slave, Written by Himself." *Puttin' On Ole Massa*, G. Osofsky, editor. Harper and Row, New York, (Originally published in 1849).

BONNER, J. C.
1964 *A History of Georgia Agriculture 1732-1860*. University of Georgia Press, Athens.

BOYD, E.
1956 Non-Indian Ceramics in Southwestern Archaeology. *Antiques*, Vol. 69, pp. 239-241.

BROWN, R. D.
1935 *A Prehistoric Habitation Site On the St. Croix River. Minnesota Academy of Science, Proceedings*, Vol. 2, pp. 4-12.

BULLEN, A. K. AND R. P.
1945 Black Lucy's Garden. *Bulletin of the Massachusetts Archaeological Society*, Vol. 6, pp. 17-28.

CAMDEN COUNTY SUPERIOR COURT
1831-1937 Deed Book M., p. 192.

COOK, S. F. AND R. R. HEIZER
1965 *Studies on the Chemical Analysis of Archaeological Sites*. University of California Press, Berkeley and Los Angeles.

CORNWALL, I. M.
1963 "Soil, Stratification and Environment." *Science in Archaeology*, D. Brothwell and E. Higgs, editors. Basic Books, New York, pp. 113-122.

CURTIN, P. D.
1969 *The Atlantic Slave Trade*. University of Wisconsin Press, Madison.

DAVIS, D. B.
1966 *The Problem of Slavery in Western Culture*. Cornell University Press, Ithaca, New York.

DEETZ, J.
1968 "Late Man in North America: Archaeology of European Americans." *Anthropological Archaeology in the Americas*, pp. 121-130. The Anthropological Society of Washington, Washington, D.C.

DOUGLAS, F.
1968 *Narrative of the Life of An American Slave*. Signet Book Edition, New York, (Originally published in 1845).

FAIRBANKS, C. H.
1962 "European Ceramics from the Cherokee Capitol of New Echota." *Southwestern Archaeological Conference, Newsletter*. Vol. 9, pp. 10-16.

1968 Florida. *The Society for Historical Archaeology, Newsletter*. Vol. 1, p. 13.

FLANDERS, R. B.
1933 *Plantation Slavery in Georgia*. North Carolina Press, Chapel Hill.

FLOYD, M.
1937 "Revival of Tabby Building In the Nineteenth Century." *Georgia's Disputed Ruins*, M. E. Coulter, editor. University of North Carolina Press, Chapel Hill, pp. 73-87.

GRIER, W. H., AND P. M. COBBS
1968 *Black Rage*. Bantam Book, New York.

HALL, B.
1829 *Travels in North America in the Years 1827 and 1828*. Simpkin and Marshe, London.

HARRINGTON, J. C.
1955 Archaeology as an Auxiliary Science to American History. *American Ahthropologist*, Vol. 57, pp. 1121-1130.

HUMPHREY, R. V.
1969 "Clay Pipes From Old Sacramento." *Historical Archaeology*, Vol. 3, pp. 12-33.

HURLEY, J. AND W. T. HURLEY
1969 *Project Weeksville: Exhibit.* Namm Library, New York City Community College. Mineographed, 1 p.

JACOBS, H.
1861 *Incidents in the Life of a Slave Girl.* Published by the author, Boston.

JONES, W. V.
1924 *The Button Industry.* Isaac Pitman and Sons Ltd., London.

KEMBLE, F. A.
1863 *Journal of a Residence on a Georgian Plantation in 1838-1839.* Harper and Brothers, New York.

KING, S. B. JR.
1966 *Georgia Voices. A Documentary History to 1872.* University of Georgia Press, Athens.

LAIDLER, P. W.
1937 "Beads in Africa South of the Zambesi-II." *Rhodesia Scientific Association, Proceedings and Transactions*, Vol. 35, pp. 35-46.

MORSE, D. F., AND P. A.
1964 "The Brake Site: A Possible Early 19th Century Log Cabin in Stewart County, Tennessee." *Florida Anthropologist*, Vol. 17, pp. 165-176.

MCKEARIN, G. S. AND H. MCKEARIN
1941 *American Glass.* Crown Publishers, New York.

NELSON, L. H.
1963 "Nail Chronology as an Aid to Dating Old Buildings." *History News*, Vol. 19, pp. 25-27.

NOEL-HUME, I.
1969a *Historical Archaeology.* A. Knopf, New York.

1969b "Pearlware: forgotten milestone in English Ceramic History." *Antiques*, Vol. 95, pp. 390-397.

NORTHUP, S.
1968 *Twelve Years a Slave.* Louisiana State University Press, Baton Rouge, (Originally published in 1853).

OBER, F. A.
1880 Dungeness, General Green's Sea-Island Plantation. *Lippincott's Magazine*, Vol. 26, pp. 241-249.

OLSEN, S. J.
1963 "Dating Early Plain Buttons by their Form." *American Antiquity*, Vol. 28, pp. 551-554.

OSOFSKY, G.
1969 "The Significance of Slave Narratives, Introduction." *Puttin' On Ole Massa*, G. Osofsky, editor. Harper and Row, New York, pp. 9-44.

PETERSON, E. T.
1963 "Clay Pipes: A Footnote to Mackinac's History." *Mackinac History*, Leaflet No. 1, Mackinac Island State Park Commission, Michigan, pp. 1-8.

PETERSON, H. L.
1967 *Pagent of the Gun.* Doubleday, Garden City.

ROBOZ, J.
1968 *Introduction to Mass Spectrometry.* John Wiley and Sons, New York.

SAYRE, E. V. AND R. W. DODSON
1957 "Neutron Activation Study of Mediterranean Potsherds." *American Journal of Archaeology*, Vol. 61, pp. 35-41.

SCARBOROUGH, R.
1933 *The Opposition to Slavery in Georgia Prior to 1860.* G. Peabody College for Teachers, Nashville.

SCHOFIELD, J. F.
1938 "A Preliminary Study of the Prehistoric Beads of the Northern Transvaal and Natal." *Transactions of the Royal Society of Africa*, Vol. 26, pp. 341-371.

SILVA, J. S.
1914 "Early Reminescences of an Old St. Mary's Boy Now in This 82nd Year." *"The Southeast Georgian"*, Friday, September 25, 1914.

SLEEN, W. G. N. VAN DER
1967 *A Handbook of Beads.* Publication of the Journees Internationales de Verre, Liege, Belgium.

SMITH, G. H.
1968 *Big Bend Historic Sites.* Publications in Salvage Archaeology, No. 9. River Basin Surveys, Museum of Natural History, Smithsonian Institution, Lincoln, Nebraska.

SMITH, J. L.
1882 *Autobiography of James L. Smith.* Bulletin Co., Norwich.

Snow, C. T.
1969 *Excavations at Casey's House.* National Park Service, Minute Man National Park, Massachusetts. Mimeographed, 39 pp.

Stamp, K. M.
1956 *The Peculiar Institution.* Alfred A. Knopf, New York.

Steward, A.
1857 *Twenty-two Years a Slave and Forty Years a Freeman.* W. Alling, New York.

Thompson, J.
1856 *Life of John Thompson, A Fugitive Slave.* Published by the author, Worster.

Thoreau, H. D.
1949 *The Journal of Henry David Thoreau.* Editors, Bradford Torrey and Francis H. Allen, Houghton Mifflin Co., Boston. Vol. X, 1858.

Watkins, L. W.
1942 "The ABC's of American Pottery." *Antiques*, Vol. 42, pp. 134; 196.

White, G.
1849 *Statistics of State of Georgia.* W. T. Williams, Savannah.

Wilson, R. L.
1961 "Clay Pipes from Fort Laramie." *Annals of Wyoming*, Vol. 33, pp. 121-134.

RICHARD H. KIMMEL

Notes on the Cultural Origins and Functions of Sub-Floor Pits

ABSTRACT

A review of the current literature demonstrates that sub-floor and sub-surface "cellars" occur in many cultural, chronological, and functional contexts, and that many uses may produce pit features reminiscent of the hearth-front slave root cellars documented at Kingsmill Plantation. Recent site documentation at a 19th-century Virginia farmstead indicates that among some groups one original function might be as borrow for hearth fill or chimney mortar. Such pits might then be adapted for use as sub-floor storage. The review leads to several conclusions. First, the presence of a sub-floor pit should not be taken as prima facie evidence of root storage, storage of valuables, or of African-American occupation; instead, the assigning of ethnicity and site function must rely on a broad view of assemblage attributes. Second, the potential importance of sub-surface pits is such that Phase I testing strategies should add larger test units to the more typical shovel test research design. Third, problem-oriented research is needed to provide an objective basis for cultural and behavioral interpretations, and to identify the modifying influences of taphonomic factors on abandoned sub-floor pits.

Introduction

Since its publication in 1984, Kelso's *Kingsmill Plantations, 1619–1800* has taken its rightful place as one of the centerpiece studies in the field of historical archaeology. No one aspect of Kelso's research is more intriguing than his suggestion that sub-floor hearth-front storage pits "may be more Afro-American than English" (Kelso 1984:201) and that such features may be part of a pattern defining the "norm for slaves in general" (Kelso 1984:31). Kelso's (1984:114, 116–117, 201) interpretation of slave root cellars serving as places of concealment is based on supporting documentation and internally consistent 18th-century and early 19th-century archaeological data. His work has received indirect interpretive support from Sprinkle's (1991a, 1991b) discussion of the arti-

Historical Archaeology, 1993, 27(3):102–113.
Permission to reprint required.

facts making up the contents of Whitehall Plantation (Maryland) slave Charles Cox's mill house chest, and from Yentsch's (1991) brief commentary on similar pits among the Ibo. Furthermore, Kelso's work has served as an interpretive analogy for the excavations at nearby Carter's Grove (Epperson 1990).

This article suggests that while Kelso's (1984: 116–117, 201) interpretations are certainly well-substantiated, his findings should not be taken to mean that rectangular holes in front of hearths are sufficient to indicate African-American occupation. This is an interpretation which Kelso (1991, pers. comm.) did not intend, and one which has stimulated comment from other archaeologists (Mouer 1991; Sanford 1991) who have excavated pits in other ethnic and functional settings. Furthermore, the functions of such pits are variable both in terms of original functions and adaptive use.

In point of fact, there is probably not much danger of misinterpreting slave cabins and associated features when working on the well-documented, well-preserved plantation and town sites which characterize the more highly visible and nationally significant data base. But the reality is that many, perhaps most, historical archaeologists spend much of their time investigating much smaller, poorly documented sites within the confines of minimal Phase I testing schedules. At such sites, there is rarely a historic context which can be built on a corpus of family letters, tax and deed records, maps, floor plans, or local histories. Instead, if he or she is fortunate, the archaeologist first encounters scattered foundation stones amid a surviving assortment of ornamentals, overgrown wells, and a puzzling array of shallow depressions, twisted wire, road traces, and animal lots. Excavation or surficial feature recording is often limited to an intensification of shovel testing, hopefully sufficient for determining National Register eligibility or ineligibility. The documentation relating to such sites is often accomplished after the testing has taken place, and it often yields little more than a chain of title. Only rarely will there be family records or other documentation that provide anything truly meaningful in terms of interpreting the chronologically and functionally diverse archaeological record; rarer still is the opportunity to spend even a single season excavating, cataloging, and interpreting a single site. And, when documentation is available, it can be positively misleading (see, for example, the comments of Seasholes [1990:17–19] regarding the shortcomings of local histories and primary documentation, Reinhart [1991] regarding the proliferation of errors transferred through local historical traditions, and Reitz [1989] on the problems encountered when negative historical evidence is generalized to cultural behavior). Under these circumstances, it is not hard to see how, on finding a pit in front of a hearth, one might be tempted to assume African-American occupation.

Although one might consider this example extreme, at least one archaeologist (Epperson 1990: 34) has reinterpreted his findings in light of Kelso's work, changing a functional interpretation of features at Carter's Grove from tanning vats to slave storage pits. Epperson (1990:34) notes that "It was on [the] basis [of this reinterpretation] that the location was selected for the [slave] quarter exhibit." It should be noted that this reinterpretation is not under challenge in this article since Epperson (1990:34) states that it is consistent with the documentation and the archaeological record. Of importance here, however, is his discussion of the implications for the social modeling of plantation life which results from such interpretation:

> The embedded assumptions must be carefully considered of an interpretation which suggests that each pit was the private storage locker of a single individual or family, providing a means of concealment from other slaves as well as from the master. Although no evidence can be offered one way or the other on the archaeological analysis, such an interpretation risks imposition of the modern ideological construct of the autonomous, utilitarian, maximizing individual (Epperson 1990:34).

While Epperson's concern is with more advanced levels of inference, his theoretical problem is grounded in the methodological question of how the initial interpretation of pits as slave-constructed cellars used for concealment was made in the first place. Epperson's realization that alternative interpretations of features can have far reaching conse-

quences is more than a self-evident principle of historical archaeology: it is, instead, a central methodological reality of the discipline, and, for those who are faced with poorly documented sites and "laboriously achieved inferences" (DeBoer 1988:3), it is the primary reason why those varieties of materialist theory with high levels of etic organizational capability have gained so much popularity (e.g., Harris 1979; Kohl 1981; Orser 1988a:7–9, 1988b:316–318, 1989).

The Chronological, Cultural, and Functional Dimensions of Sub-Floor Pits

In his discussion of sub-floor storage, Kelso (1984:201) pointed out that the practice has a long history among the English. More recently, Mouer (1991:6) has also commented on the occurrence of English and Anglo-American butteries and cellars from the 17th-century occupations at Jordan's Journey and Curles Plantation, both located in Virginia's Chesapeake region. In addition, Pogue (1988:42; 1990:15) has reported numerous dairy and hearth-front root cellars from beneath both the hall-and-parlor house and the adjacent servant's quarter at the 1690–1715 King's Reach Plantation, Maryland. In Mecklenburg County, Virginia, Bracey (1977:139) presents the following brief account of a 1792 counterfeiting trial: "According to testimony presented at Stephen Mallett's trial in the Mecklenburg County Court, implements for making [Spanish milled dollars] were found hidden under the hearth in a shop on the Malletts' plantation near the Courthouse." Given the brevity of this report and its presentation in a local history, one wonders whether the hiding place may have actually been in front of rather than literally "under" the hearth. From further afield, Kehoe (1978) has excavated a total of five sub-floor storage pits from five of seven rooms associated with the 1768–1773 French Canadian occupation at "François' House," a trading outpost located on the Saskatchewan River in the province of Saskatchewan. These "cellars or storage pits" are up to 2 ft. deep, between 4 sq. ft. and 16 sq. ft. in plan, and are corner-braced and/or lined with clay or bark (Kehoe 1978:21, 64, Figures 5, 12). One pit shown by Kehoe (1978:64, Figure 12) clearly indicates that the pits were placed in a position paralleling the floor joists. Finally, DeBoer (1988) has presented an important ethnohistoric and archaeological review and commentary of sub-surface storage as a means of concealment among Native Americans. His findings indicate widespread use of hidden pit storage among semi-sedentary Plains and Eastern Woodlands groups or groups faced with "oppressive" political forces (DeBoer 1988:13–14, Table 1). DeBoer's article is significant both for raising important methodological considerations and for providing a comparative foundation for the type of African documentation suggested by Yentsch (1991).

Taken together, what these primarily 18th- and 19th-century examples suggest is that African-Americans, Euroamericans, and Native Americans were all likely to be aware of the use of sub-floor pits whether for storage or the more problematic function of concealment. Given the historically documented interaction among these groups, co-occupancy should be considered as a probable agent responsible for mutual reinforcement or creolization of what was undoubtedly an independently developed practice (cf. Sanford 1991:5).

In addition to these chronologically early examples, it is also clear that both African-American and Euroamerican occupations retain sub-surface, although not necessarily sub-floor, pits for storage and/or concealment well into the 20th century. In a clearly African-American context, Mouer (1991:5) reports that Chesapeake archaeologist Betsy Harker has found a "fine, late 19th-century tureen" in a sub-floor root cellar in use by suspected ex-slave Old Rhodie until her death in the early 1930s. Another African-American example is provided by Wheaton et al. (1990:99, 123, Figures 40, 55) in their investigation of the late 19th- to early 20th-century freedman town of James City near New Bern, North Carolina. Here the authors found eight rectangular pits associated with excavated house lots, noted the similarity in size of these features to the Kingsmill Plantation slave root cellars (Wheaton et al. 1990:123), but also noted that some of those at James City are believed

to be located outside of structures near the rear of the homelots or out in the yards (Wheaton et al. 1990:246). Also relevant to an urban context, Stewart-Abernathy (1986:8, Figure 2) has noted the varied uses of sub-surface pits in late 19th- and early 20th-century Washington, Arkansas, including root cellars, ice cellars, and flower pits. The use of "flower" pits for the winter storage of live plants recently has been documented for African-American gardens by Westmacott (1992) and has been mentioned by an informant for this study in early to mid-20th-century Euroamerican contexts in Michigan (Virginia Lee Marsh 1991, pers. comm.). Wheaton (1992, pers. comm.) has recently suggested that the house lot pits at James City (Wheaton et al. 1990:246) may have served as plant storage pits. McDaniel (1982:20, 154–155, 213) suggests that similar outdoor pits may be vegetable "kilns" for the year-round storage of "root vegetables such as parsnips and turnips." McDaniel's (1982:20) study also documents this root storage practice at an African-American occupied tenant farm for the period 1875–1900, and also for a 1918 Euroamerican tenant occupation at the St. Mary's County Cusic-Medley house:

> There was also a vegetable garden behind the house, and produce such as turnips was stored in a vegetable kiln. Nora Cusic described this as a circular hole in the ground about two feet deep in which vegetables were stored on a bed of straw and then covered with more straw and a mound of dirt (McDaniel 1982:154).

McDaniel (1982:155) cites this informant (Nora Cusic) in noting that such kilns were common among both Euroamerican and African-American families. Finally, Stine (1989:129) notes that in the late fall in Iredell County, North Carolina, for sweet potato storage:

> Occasionally, the farmers would construct an earthen potato house near the field. These were made by digging about a two-to-three foot hole, lining it with straw, and placing the sweet potatoes in it. The whole thing would be mounded over with dirt, leaving one small space to gain access by (Stine 1989:129).

Sub-floor pits have also been documented in a context associated with cottage industry. At the Barrow Farmstead in Forsyth County in the Piedmont of North Carolina, Wheaton et al. (1987:24) documented a continuously occupied farm dating from the late 18th century to the mid-1980s. The dominant occupation was by the Barrow family, the principal Euroamerican owners, with some tenant occupation (Wheaton et al. 1987:14–20, Table IV-1). One archaeological structure was a log cabin located adjacent to the surviving main house. This cabin, which had been torn down in the late 1930s, contained a sub-floor cellar in which the lower fill layers contained five shoes and a broken granite shoe last (Wheaton et al. 1987:29, 34–43, Figure IV-1). This assemblage supports the interpretation of the cellar at one time being associated with one of the senior Barrow women who is believed on the basis of a family informant to have been involved in shoe repair (Wheaton et al. 1987: 37). It is possible that the storage of shoes in a sub-surface pit would be useful for softening shoe leather prior to stitching. This possibility is based on an analogy with tobacco "ordering rooms" wherein natural moisture from excavated pits was used to soften cured tobacco (Matthewson and Moss 1917:38–39; Anthony and Drucker 1988:67; Abbott et al. 1991:258; Graham Hodge 1991, pers. comm.).

Sub-Floor Features as Borrow Pits

In addition to sub-floor pits being associated with a variety of storage functions, there is good reason to suspect that such pits may also be associated with the construction of hearths and chimneys. The recent discovery of a rectangular sub-floor pit measuring approximately 4 × 7 ft. by 11 in. deep under the standing mid-19th-century Nelson Harper Crowder (1848–1923) "Fruitland Farm" farmhouse, Mecklenburg County, Virginia (Figures 1, 2, 3), in a location near the foot of the chimney, is suggestive of the form and location of slave root cellars but in a chronological context post-dating the Civil War (Figures 4, 5). This pit was discovered during documentation of this privately owned, abandoned farmstead which initially came to the author's attention because it includes an existing pit icehouse and pond which will serve as an interpretive analogy for archaeological features at the nearby Corps of Engineers John H. Kerr Dam and Reservoir project area. The Nelson Harper Crowder family home consists of three structurally distinct components, one of which represents the earliest 30- × -18-ft. one and one-half story dwelling of the complex. Although documentation at this site is not yet completed and there has been no excavation of the pit (which appears to have only minimal erosional filling), neither informant interviews with two of the three surviving grandchildren of Nelson Crowder (Eleanor Marion [Crowder] Moore and Nelson Miles Crowder) nor a recently compiled family history (Cooper 1988) indicate that the site was ever occupied by slaves. Architectural characteristics and opportunistic surface collection also support a post-Civil War date for construction of the house, as does the fact that its owner was married in 1871 at the age of 24. Although informant interviews have not given any indication as to the original use of the sub-floor pit, it does not appear to have ever been used for concealment—there is no entry through the floor, the house is elevated over the pit on full stone foundation, the pit does not show evidence of being lined, and the pit is aligned perpendicular to and under several of the floor joists. One likely interpretation of this feature is that it was associated with construction and served as either a clay source for chinking during original construction of the chimney or as a source for hearth ballast. The interpretation of this pit as a source for hearth fill is compatible with the modern practice of earth-filled porches and foundations. The placement of this pit within rather than outside of the foundation would eliminate an inconvenient hole in the yard once the house was constructed.

The construction pit interpretation is also supported by Breeden's (1980) *Advice Among Masters: The Ideal in Slave Management in the Old South*, a compilation of 19th-century southern farm journal articles addressing various aspects of slave management (Ferguson 1992:58). Breeden (1980:121) cites an article that appeared in the November 1850 issue of *Southern Cultivator* that states: "Many persons, in building negro houses, in order to get clay convenient for filling the hearth and for mortar, dig a hole under the floor [this

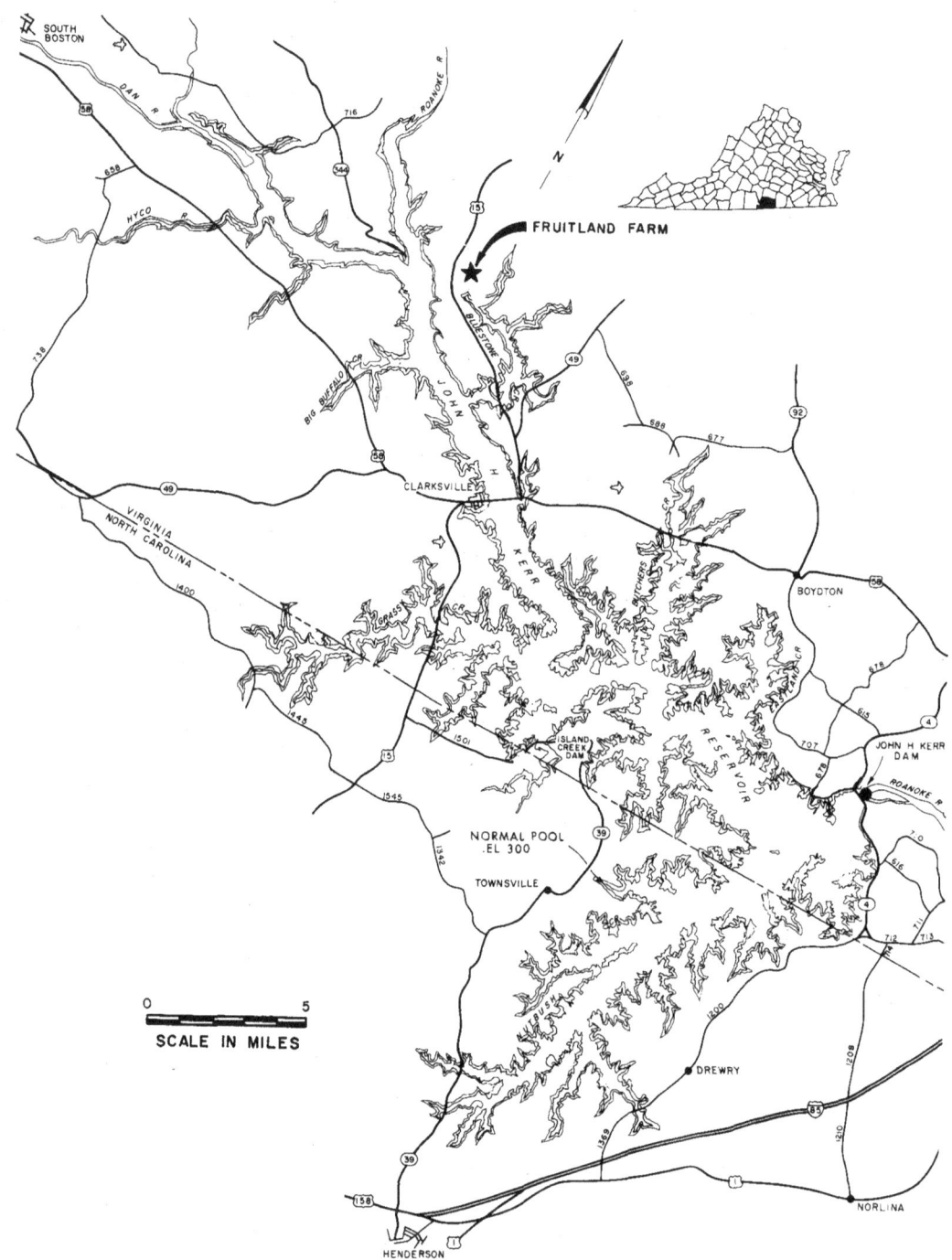

FIGURE 1. Location map, Nelson Harper Crowder "Fruitland Farm."

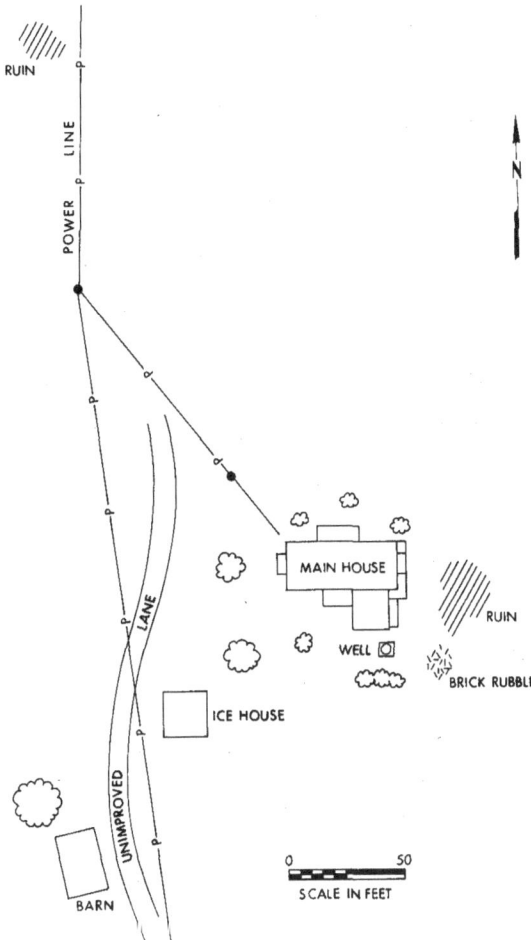

FIGURE 2. Fruitland Farm, plan of existing structures and ruins.

son 1992:58). Breeden's (1980:131) review also indicates that some plantation owners may have left the flooring of slave quarters loose so that cabins could be cleaned out underneath. In such situations, even the need for a trap door would be eliminated.

If the clay or construction pit inference is correct, then true root cellars and what should perhaps be called safe cellars (places for concealment of personal possessions) may not have been the initial function of all such sub-floor pits. Given Sprinkle's (1991a, 1991b) documentation that the kinds of highly valued goods might include perishable paper and clothing, it is reasonable to suggest that safe cellars generally would be lined in the manner described by Kelso (1984:31, 114, 117, 201) or that goods would be placed in insect-, rodent-, and moisture-proof secondary containers. Archaeologically excavated sub-floor pits which are unlined and empty, and even those containing mundane artifacts which could have fallen through the floor, may simply represent former clay pits used without substantial improvement as true root cellars.

Discussion

Given the well-documented "pan-cultural" nature of sub-floor pits (Sanford 1991:5), it is clear that even placement of such features near a hearth should not be taken as prima facie evidence of slave occupation. Only the archaeological verification of use as a safe cellar is evidence for this suspected African-American retention or adaptation, and this should be in conjunction with other culturally sensitive evidence, such as the architectural features at Yaughan and Curriboo Plantations, South Carolina, discussed by Wheaton et al. (1983:193, Appendix D); the stylistic tobacco pipe motifs noted by Emerson (1989) and more recently by Joseph (1991); the spoons, "lithics," and "ritual objects" reported by Klingelhofer (1987:114–117); or the incidental inclusion of valued possessions of the type suggested by Sprinkle's documentation (1991a, 1991b). Most importantly, one must heed Sanford's (1991:5) caution and shift the methodological focus from the identification of

practice, by the way, was to be discouraged since such pits might fill with household refuse and become a health hazard]." While this practice may not have always produced a uniform pit, it and the possible use of daub (Breeden 1980:124, 132, 134) are indicative of the use made of sub-floor soils. In cabins with wood and clay chimneys and log walls, there was undoubtedly a need for frequent maintenance of this type. In houses where an initial pit was excavated for construction purposes, only a little extra work would be required to adapt the pit to use as a root cellar or safe cellar (Fergu-

FIGURE 3. Perspective drawing based on floor plan projections and photos of the northern elevation of the "Fruitland Farm" domicile. The sub-floor pit is located near the far (eastern) chimney. No such feature is associated with the chimney serving the two-story section of the home. A later one and one-half story rear addition is attached to the eastern wing of the house.

ethnicity and pattern per se to the process of creolization in general. As Ferguson (1992:xli–xlv) has recently pointed out in his review of creolization, this process does not consist of a one-way stream of acculturative influences, but instead embodies both conscious and unconscious selection reflecting both practical needs and symbolic at-

tempts at incorporation and resistance. (See also the discussion by Epperson [1990:30] on the material manifestations of the interplay of contradictory elements of exclusionary and incorporative behavior among planters as opposed to denial and contestation among slaves.) Given the contact between Europeans, Africans, and Native Ameri-

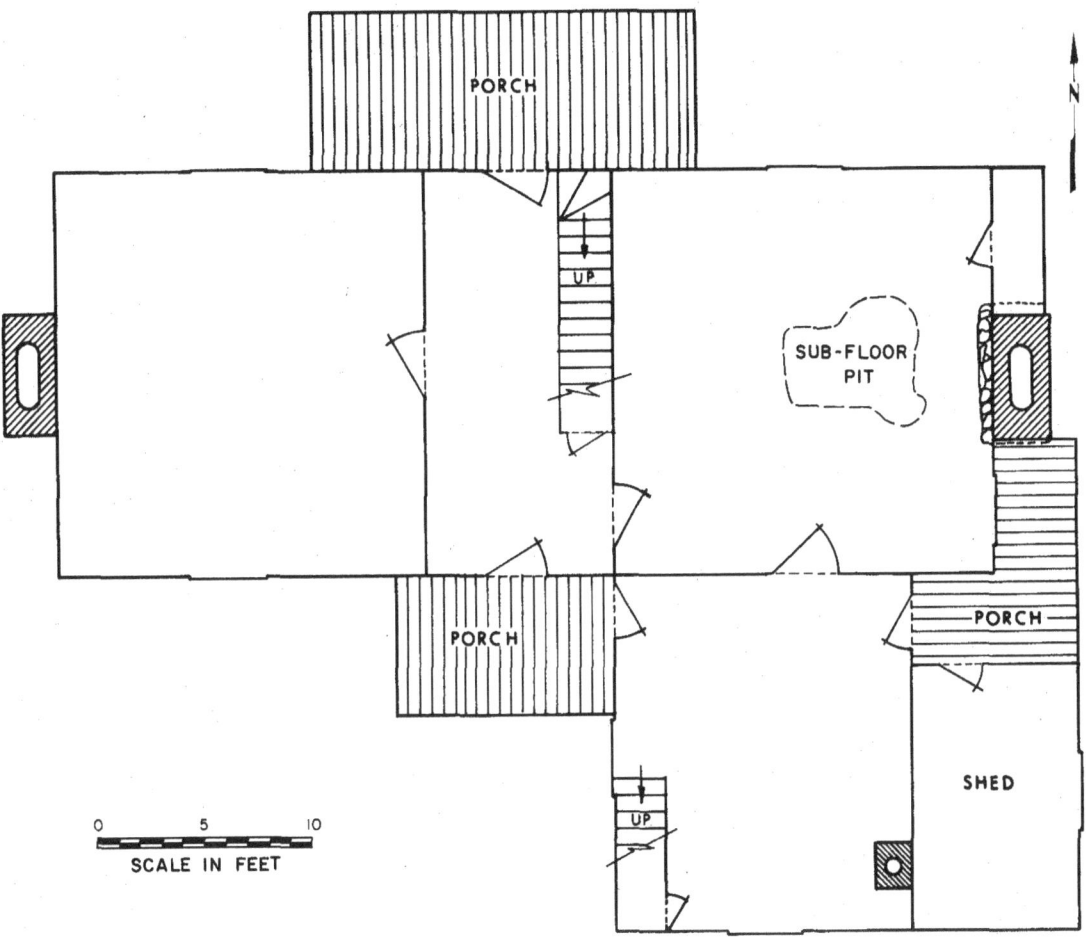

FIGURE 4. First-floor plan of Fruitland Farm showing the location of the sub-floor pit as triangulated from the northwestern and southwestern corners of the hearth foundation. The upper edges of the northeastern and southeastern corners of the pit are eroded and indistinct, probably due to wear from dogs (Miles Crowder 1992, pers. comm.).

cans, all with variable culture histories of their own, the potential pool of attributes contributing to creolization is likely to be much larger than currently realized.

A further implication of this review has been suggested by Linda France Stine (1992, pers. comm.) who believes that many small farmstead sites are found to be "insignificant" before a search for potentially fruitful sub-surface storage containers has been undertaken. Whereas the studies cited above indicate that sub-surface storage both inside and outside of structures is very common on 19th- and 20th-century sites, archaeologists should ensure that their sampling designs include test units of a size and shape likely to intersect pit edges rather than simply recover artifacts. Many rely heavily on small shovel tests to define site boundaries, and while definition of site boundaries may help delimit areas which are sensitive to encroachment, their value in determinations of significance is limited. What is called for is fuller use of larger contiguous units during early

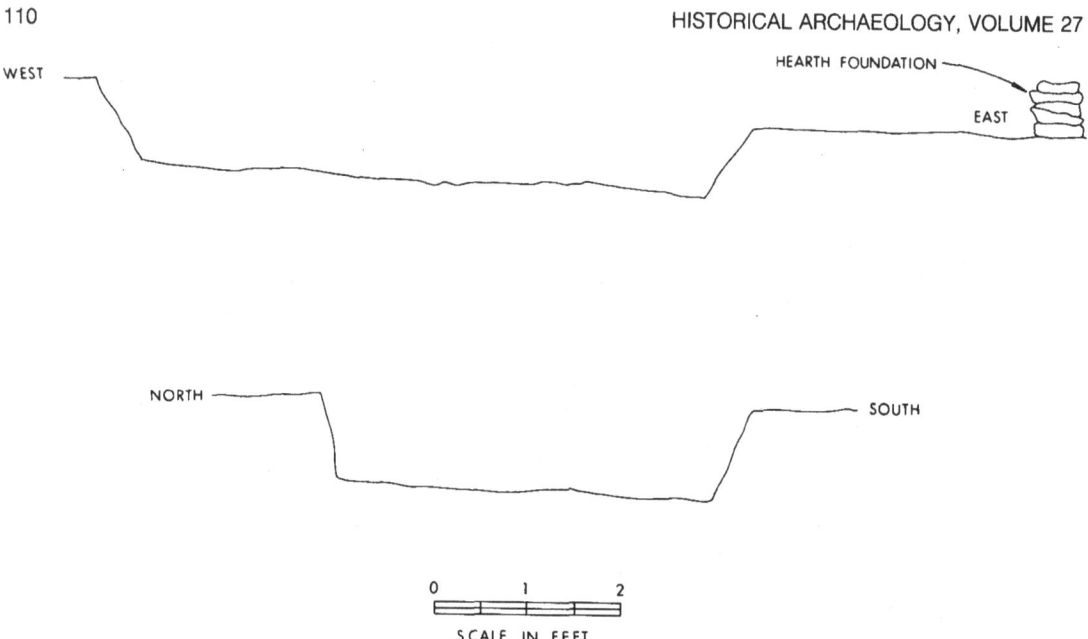

FIGURE 5. Approximate mid-line north–south and east–west profiles of the pit under the east wing of the Nelson Harper Crowder house.

phases of survey, and these units should be placed both within and outside of house foundations. Historical archaeologists are not alone in this need to reassess field methods. For example, Mathis (1991) has called for more liberal use of machine stripping during initial testing of coastal Woodland period sites. Mathis has found that the use of shovel tests and surface collection has focused attention on shell middens to the exclusion of nearby associated village occupation. His experience at the Broad Reach site is compelling: in an area where shovel testing indicated little cause for concern, he and his mostly volunteer labor force have recovered numerous verified or suspected structures, hundreds of associated features, and over 20 burials displaying an astonishing variety of interment practices. For those archaeologists regularly faced with allocating limited testing resources, broader areal testing is an option which deserves much wider application.

Other clues to former pits might be found among the typical surficial indicators associated with many 19th-century sites. These include specific vegetation types (Agorsah 1983:188) or the presence of animal burrows within overgrown excavations such as wells. It is common for old wells on abandoned sites in the John H. Kerr Reservoir vicinity to become heavily overgrown and selected as burrow entrances by burrowing mammals, and it is possible that other normally open features such as root cellars might be similarly used. Archaeologists would do well in the future to look for such indicators within old foundation lines and especially, of course, near hearths.

Taken together, the studies cited in this essay indicate the wide variety of cultural, functional, and chronological contexts of sub-surface pits. In order to accurately portray cultural practices in poorly documented settings, it is imperative that this variety be recognized, and that original functions and subsequent adaptations of pits be investigated (Schiffer 1977:21; Beaudry 1986:39). In this regard, two courses of future research are called for. The first should be the development of a taxonomy of pits based on archaeological and historical documentation that considers functional, formal, and adaptive variation within and between cultures. This approach would produce an expansive inventory of feature types for groups as culturally diverse as the Ibo of West Africa and the Euroamericans of the Virginia Piedmont. Such a taxonomy would serve as a heuristic device in defining or clarifying the appropriate limits of cross-cultural inferences. A second needed avenue of research is experimental, archaeological, and historical studies of the taphonomic processes acting on abandoned features. Such studies, conducted in a variety of climate and soil types, would provide a quantified basis for judging, for instance, length of exposure and original pit shape. While taxonomic and taphonomic studies such as these would not guarantee that every feature will be properly assigned to its actual function and period of use, they would provide an objective basis for comparison on which to build inferences and hypotheses. Without such studies, questions of cultural origins, independent invention, borrowing, functional and adaptive use, and a variety of behavioral implications cannot be realistically addressed in a context broader than individual sites.

ACKNOWLEDGMENTS

This article is based upon the author's ongoing research at the Nelson Harper Crowder family farm near Clarksville, Virginia. This work has benefited from volunteer effort, and I am indebted to Michael O. Hartley for his assistance and insights during recording of the Crowder farmhouse and icehouse. Special thanks is also due the current owners of the property, Karin and Kevin Kuhn, for their permission and patience in allowing me access to the homelot; and to Mrs. Eleanor Marion (Crowder) Moore, Bouldin McLean Crowder, and Nelson Miles Crowder for their kindness and insights on the Crowder family farms in the Clarksville, Virginia, vicinity; and to Mr. Graham Hodge of Henderson, North Carolina, for his descriptions of early to mid-20th-century tobacco farming. I wish to thank Leland G. Ferguson for introducing me to the work of James O. Breeden and for his comments on an early version of the text. I am also indebted to John H. Sprinkle, Jr., William Kelso, Tom Wheaton, Alice Kehoe, Doug Sanford, Linda France Stine, Dan Mouer, Tom Hargrove, Daniel Roberts, Linda Carnes-McNaughton, Richard Westmacott, and the anonymous reviewers for supplying important references and/or comments. At the Corps of Engineers in Wilmington, I wish to thank Jenny Owens, Hydrologic Technician, and Maxine Inman, Student Intern, for serving as field assistants; Betty Sue Westbrook, Librarian, for her tireless efforts in searching out repositories for papers and reports; and Joyce B. Benjamin, Cartographer, and Mike Penny, Landscape Architect, for a remarkable metamorphosis of rough field drawings into the finished figures. Thanks also go to the staff of the Resource Management Branch both at the Wilmington District Offices and John H. Kerr Dam and Reservoir, especially to John H. Feild and Mike Dodd. Finally, a continuing debt of gratitude goes to Christina E. Correale, former Chief of the Environmental Resources Branch, and Coleman Long, Acting Chief, for their encouragement and advocacy of professionalism.

REFERENCES

ABBOTT, LAWRENCE E., JR., C. SCOTT BUTLER, ASHLEY A. CHAPMAN, CHRISTOPHER T. ESPENSHADE, JEFFREY W. GARDNER, MARIAN D. ROBERTS, AND MATTHEW T. WILKERSON
1991   Inspection, Evaluation and Testing of Historic Sites Located at Falls Lake, Wake, Durham, and Granville Counties, North Carolina. Report prepared by Brockington and Associates, Atlanta, Georgia. Submitted to U.S. Army Corps of Engineers, Wilmington, North Carolina.

AGORSAH, EMMANUEL KOFI
1985   An Ethnoarchaeological Study of Settlement and Behavior Patterns of a West African Traditional Society: The Nchumuru of Banda-Wiae in Ghana. Unpublished Ph.D. dissertation, Department of Anthropology, University of California, Los Angeles.

ANTHONY, RONALD W., AND LESLIE M. DRUCKER
1988   Archaeological Survey, Site Relocation, and Site Testing within Seven Wildlife Subimpoundments, Falls Lake Project, Durham and Granville Counties, North Carolina. Report prepared by Carolina Archaeological Services, Columbia, South Carolina. Submitted to U.S. Army Corps of Engineers, Wilmington, North Carolina.

BEAUDRY, MARY C.
1986   The Archaeology of Historical Land Use in Massachusetts. *Historical Archaeology* 20(2):38–46.

BRACEY, SUSAN L.
1977   *Life by the Roaring Roanoke*. Whittet and Shepperson, Richmond, Virginia.

BREEDEN, JAMES O. (EDITOR)
1980   Advice Among Masters: The Ideal in Slave Manage-
        ment in the Old South. Greenwood Press, Westport,
        Connecticut.

COOPER, CYNTHIA B.
1988   The Godfrey Crowder Family of Mecklenburg
        County, Virginia, 1619–1988. Hugh and Cynthia
        Cooper, Lilburn, Georgia.

DEBOER, WARREN R.
1988   Subterranean Storage and the Organization of Sur-
        plus: The View from Eastern North America. South-
        eastern Archaeology 7(1):1–20.

EMERSON, MATTHEW C.
1989   Seventeenth-Century Chesapeake Tobacco Pipes:
        African Inspirations in a New World Art and Arti-
        fact. Paper presented at the Annual Meeting of the
        Society for Historical Archaeology Conference on
        Historical and Underwater Archaeology, Baltimore,
        Maryland.

EPPERSON, TERRENCE W.
1990   Race and the Disciplines of the Plantation. In His-
        torical Archaeology on Southern Plantations and
        Farms, edited by Charles E. Orser, Jr. Historical
        Archaeology 24(4):29–36.

FERGUSON, LELAND G.
1992   Uncommon Ground: Archaeology and Early African
        America, 1650–1800. Smithsonian Institution Press,
        Washington, D.C.

HARRIS, MARVIN
1979   Cultural Materialism: The Struggle for a Science of
        Culture. Random House, New York.

JOSEPH, J. W.
1991   Biblical Archaeology and the Dream: A Note from
        Springfield, Georgia. African American Archaeol-
        ogy No. 5:7–8. Theresa A. Singleton, Newsletter
        Editor. Smithsonian Institution, Washington, D.C.

KEHOE, ALICE B.
1978   François' House: An Early Fur Trade Post on the
        Saskatchewan River. Pastlog No. 2. Saskatchewan
        Culture and Youth, Regina.

KELSO, WILLIAM M.
1984   Kingsmill Plantations, 1619–1800: Archaeology of
        Country Life in Colonial Virginia. Academic Press,
        New York.

KLINGELHOFER, ERIC
1987   Aspects of Early Afro-American Material Culture:
        Artifacts from the Slave Quarters at Garrison Plan-
        tation, Maryland. Historical Archaeology 21(2):
        112–119.

KOHL, P. L.
1981   Materialist Approaches in Prehistory. Annual Review
        of Anthropology 10:89–119. Bernard J. Siegel, edi-
        tor. Annual Reviews, Palo Alto, California.

MATHIS, MARK A.
1991   Broad Reach: A Unique Site—Or, the Truth About
        What We've Missed. Paper presented at the 46th
        Annual Meeting of the Southeastern Archaeological
        Conference, Jackson, Mississippi.

MATTHEWSON, E. H., AND E. G. MOSS
1917   Tobacco Culture in North Carolina. Bulletin No.
        237. North Carolina Agricultural Experiment Sta-
        tion, State Department of Agriculture and the North
        Carolina State College of Agriculture and Engineer-
        ing, Division of Agronomy, Raleigh.

MCDANIEL, GEORGE W.
1982   Hearth and Home, Preserving a People's Culture.
        Temple University Press, Philadelphia, Pennsylva-
        nia.

MOUER, DAN
1991   "Root Cellars" Revisited. African American Ar-
        chaeology No. 5:5–6. Theresa A. Singleton, News-
        letter Editor. Smithsonian Institution, Washington,
        D.C.

ORSER, CHARLES, E., JR.
1988a   The Material Basis of the Postbellum Tenant Plan-
        tation: Historical Archaeology in the South Carolina
        Piedmont. University of Georgia Press, Athens.
1988b   Toward a Theory of Power for Historical Archaeol-
        ogy. In The Recovery of Meaning, edited by Mark P.
        Leone and Parker B. Potter, Jr., pp. 313–343.
        Smithsonian Institution Press, Washington, D.C.
1989   Critical Archaeology and Cultural Materialism. Pa-
        per presented at the Annual Meeting of the Society
        for Historical Archaeology Conference on Historical
        and Underwater Archaeology, Baltimore, Maryland.

POGUE, DENNIS J.
1988   Spatial Analysis of the King's Reach Plantation
        Homelot, ca. 1690–1715. Historical Archaeology
        22(2):40–56.
1990   King's Reach and 17th-Century Plantation Life. Jef-
        ferson Patterson Park and Museum Studies in Ar-
        chaeology No. 1. Maryland Historical and Cultural
        Publications, Annapolis.

REINHART, THEODORE R.
1991   Archaeology and Popular History: The Case of
        Hewick. Paper presented at the Annual Meeting of
        the Society for Historical Archaeology Conference
        on Historical and Underwater Archaeology, Rich-
        mond, Virginia.

REITZ, ELIZABETH J.
1989   Testing the Documents: A Case from Nineteenth-
        Century Charleston. Paper presented at the Annual
        Meeting of the Society for American Archaeology,
        Atlanta, Georgia.

SANFORD, DOUGLAS W.
1991   A Response to Anne Yentsch's Research Note on
        Below-Ground "Storage Cellars" Among the Ibo.

African American Archaeology No. 5:4–5. Theresa A. Singleton, Newsletter Editor. Smithsonian Institution, Washington, D.C.

SCHIFFER, MICHAEL B.
1977   Toward a Unified Science of the Cultural Past. In *Research Strategies in Historical Archaeology*, edited by Stanley South, pp. 13–40. Academic Press, New York.

SEASHOLES, NANCY S.
1990   History for Archaeologists: Interpretation Rather than Particularism. *The Society for Historical Archaeology Newsletter* 23(1):17–19. Norman Barka, Newsletter Editor. Williamsburg, Virginia.

SPRINKLE, JOHN H., JR.
1991a   Charles Cox's Mill Chest: A Documentary Example of Slave Material Culture. *African American Archaeology* 3:3.
1991b   The Contents of Charles Cox's Mill House Chest. *Historical Archaeology* 25(3):91–93.

STEWART-ABERNATHY, LESLIE C.
1986   Urban Farmsteads: Household Responsibilities in the City. *Historical Archaeology* 20(2):5–15.

STINE, LINDA FRANCE
1989   Raised Up in Hard Times: Factors Affecting Material Culture on Upland Piedmont Farmsteads, ca. 1900–1940s. Unpublished Ph.D. dissertation, Department of Anthropology, University of North Carolina, Chapel Hill.

WESTMACOTT, RICHARD
1992   African-American Gardens and Yards in the Rural South. University of Tennessee Press, Knoxville, in press.

WHEATON, THOMAS R., AMY FRIEDLANDER, AND PATRICK H. GARROW
1983   Yaughan and Curriboo Plantations: Studies in Afro-American Archaeology. Report prepared by Soil Systems, Inc., Marietta, Georgia. Submitted to the National Park Service, Southeast Regional Office, Atlanta, Georgia.

WHEATON, THOMAS R., MARY BETH REED, AND MARVIN A. BROWN
1987   Archaeological and Historical Investigations of the Barrow Farmstead, Forsyth County, North Carolina. Report prepared by Garrow and Associates, Inc., Atlanta, Georgia. Submitted to Waste Management of North America, Inc., Kernersville, North Carolina.

WHEATON, THOMAS R., MARY BETH REED, RITA FOLSE ELLIOTT, MARC S. FRANK, AND LESLIE E. RAYMER
1990   James City, North Carolina, Archeological and Historical Study of an African-American Urban Village. Report prepared by New South Associates, Inc., Stone Mountain, Georgia, and John Milner Associates, Inc., West Chester, Pennsylvania. Submitted to Bridge Pointe Development, Inc., New Bern, North Carolina.

YENTSCH, ANNE
1991   A Note on a 19th-Century Description of Below-Ground "Storage Cellars" Among the Ibo. *African American Archaeology* No. 4:3–4. Theresa A. Singleton, Newsletter Editor. Smithsonian Institution, Washington, D.C.

RICHARD H. KIMMEL
ENVIRONMENTAL RESOURCES BRANCH
U.S. ARMY CORPS OF ENGINEERS
P.O. BOX 1890
WILMINGTON, NORTH CAROLINA 28402

LESLEY M. DRUCKER

Socioeconomic Patterning at an Undocumented Late 18th Century Lowcountry Site: Spiers Landing, South Carolina

ABSTRACT

Data recovery at the Spiers Landing site (South Carolina 38BK160) was directed to the salvage of behavioral information from a construction-threatened, undocumented site which was ceramically datable to the turn of the late 18th/early 19th century. Research focused on the discovery of socioeconomic patterns associated with the occupation. Prehistoric components represented at the site included Archaic, Woodland and Mississippian periods. Analysis of faunal, floral, ceramic and structural remains associated with the historic component indicates that the site reflects a domestic occupation by low-status persons. Archival and documentary evidence strongly suggests that the site was a slave cabin on Fountainhead plantation, a part of property owned by Colonel Robert McKelvey. By 1850 the property as a whole was a small, multi-commodity production unit with a focus on subsistence-level agriculture and livestock raising. The Spiers Landing site is seen as an example of low-status occupation against which other small historic surface artifact scatters can be compared in order to develop a series of distributional patterns by which low-status Afro-American and Euro-American sites of the colonial and antebellum periods can be archaeologically defined.

From September through December 1978, Carolina Archaeological Services conducted field excavations and analysis under a federal mitigation program at the Spiers Landing site (38BK160) in Berkeley County, South Carolina (Figure 1). Funded by Interagency Archaeological Service-Atlanta (Heritage Conservation and Recreation Service Contract No. C-5767[78]), this work was undertaken to salvage archaeological data at a site facing construction impact from a federally funded Local Public Works project. Although the site had no directly documented historical

context, it was judged to contain potentially significant information concerning plantation dependency structures and low economic status behavior patterning, thereby qualifying it for eligibility to the National Register of Historic Places and for mitigation through data recovery procedures (36 CFR 800; 36 CFR 66).

The research performed at the site combined archaeological, ethnohistorical and statistical techniques, and data recovery was designed to produce artifactual, botanical, faunal and soil chemical information concerning the site's possible historical identity and socioeconomic character. The major research goals therefore were: 1) pattern discovery in the archaeological record and 2) comparison of the observed archaeological patterns with patterns that characterize the historically documented socioeconomic behavior of plantation workers. Comparative patterns and structural associations were drawn from Fairbanks (1974), Otto (1977) and South (1977a).

A detailed report on the site analysis has been published by Carolina Archaeological Services (Drucker and Anthony 1979), describing the complete data sets and evidence upon which the authors support the hypothesis that the Spiers Landing site reflects a slave occupation. The primary evidence presented below focuses on the combined use of artifact patterning, dietary analysis, ceramic analysis and archival research to arrive at an occupational interpretation in the absence of primary historical documentation.

The historic occupation identified at Spiers Landing was archaeologically defined on the basis of the posthole pattern of a structure, three large exterior refuse pits and one small refuse pit located within the posthole pattern (Figure 2). A fifth feature which could not be adequately investigated due to vandalism is thought to have represented a well. Features defining the historic component covered approximately one-third acre. Analysis of ceramics, bottles, buttons and pipe fragments yielded an occupation period ranging from

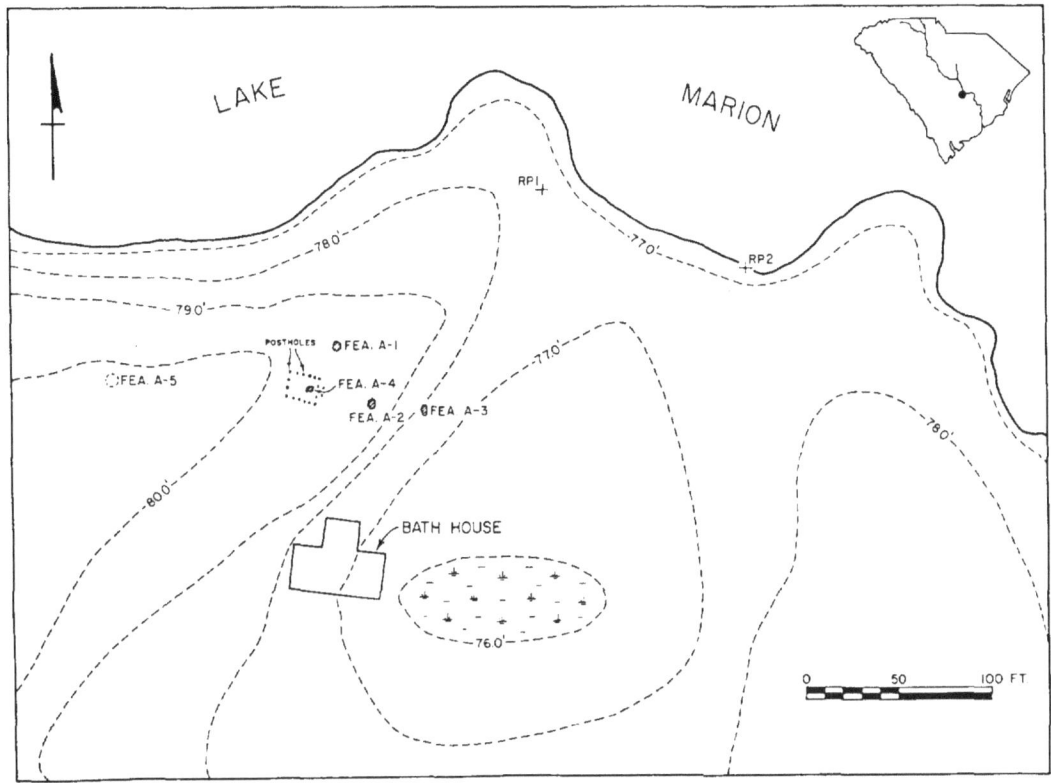

FIGURE 1. Spiers Landing project area in Coastal Plain South Carolina. The site lies approximately four miles south of the old Santee River channel on the present south shore of Lake Marion.

1780–1830 with a median occupation date of 1800.1 and a Mean Ceramic Date of 1798.4. Analysis of preserved post fragments, daub and brick ratios, a dripline feature and the relationship of the post alignments indicates that the occupants built a wooden structure which probably was supported largely by longleaf pine sills (Trinkley 1979) and sheathed by clapboard siding (Leland Ferguson, 1979, pers. comm.). All of the available evidence, both positive and negative, indicates that the structure had a mud and stick chimney; no footings or appreciable amounts of brick debris were present at the site, and the daub to brick ratio was relatively high. Mud and stick chimneys were not uncommon features in the lowcountry or upcountry during the 18th and 19th centuries,

and they have been documented in the nearby Cross community as late as 1940 (Anonymous 1941). The Spiers Landing structure also appears to have had an awning-type extension on the western side.

Household and farming debris included 970 glazed European sherds and 1,230 Colono-Ware sherds, the latter being a low-fired unglazed earthenware which was widely used by blacks during the plantation period (Baker 1972; Ferguson 1978; Lewis 1979; Anthony 1979). Debris from the living area appears to have been swept up from inside and around the dwelling and secondarily discarded in the three large exterior pits. Consideration of brick/daub ratios and of the size of the exterior pits in relation to the density of their contents has led to the hypothesis that these

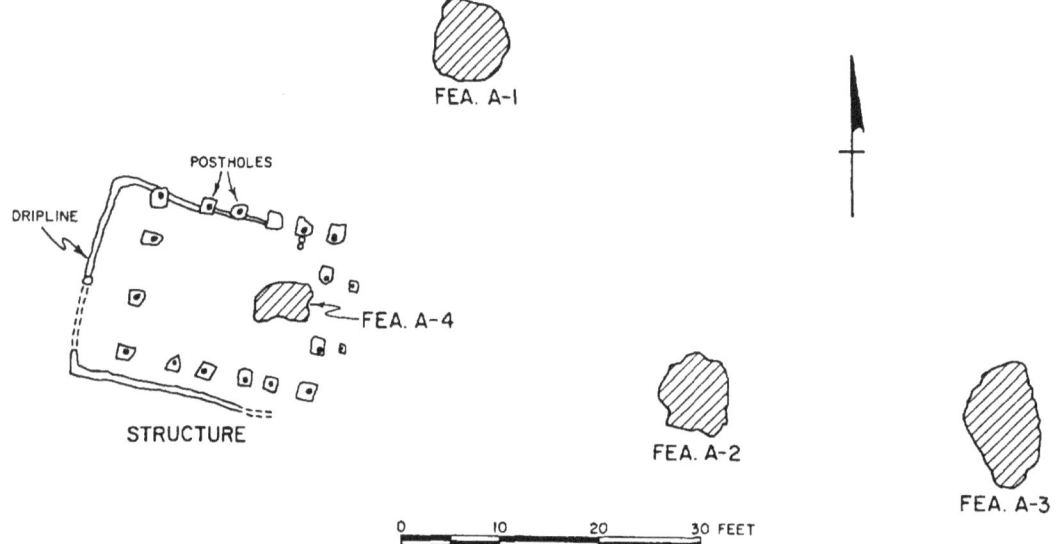

FIGURE 2. Site plan of Spiers Landing showing posthole pattern, pit features and dripline associated with the historic component.

pits were originally dug to extract clay for construction and repair of the house and chimney, and subsequently were used as garbage dumps by the inhabitants. A primary clay extraction function was suggested by the depth reached by the pits into large clay pockets in the surrounding sandy soil (up to ca. 5 feet) and by the low artifact density in each of the pits. The results of nitrogen, phosphorus and pH tests performed on refuse pit soil samples from inside and outside the structure suggest that the small interior refuse pit reflects specific hearth-related activities such as cooking and possibly candle- or soap-making. The latter hypothesis is based on an atypically and localized high pH value which reflects abnormally high alkalinity (Jeffcoat 1979).

Based on a ceramic *terminus post quem* and on experimental wattle-and-daub chimneys (Morrison 1978), it is hypothesized that the structure may have been built in the 1790s and occupied for three to six years.

Documentary records concerning the occupation itself are nonexistent; this is not surprising in view of the fact that the site was not associated with the "main house" dwellings which elderly community residents recall on the property. Land and census records pertaining to the Spiers property indicate that it was a part of the holdings of Colonel Robert McKelvey, Jr. or Colonel Robert McKelvey, Sr. during the late 18th and early 19th centuries. From 1790–1840 only one free person is listed in the McKelvey household census (1800) while the number of slaves residing on the property in that year was 30. This date is significant since the archaeological occupation can be assigned an estimated median date of 1800–1805. It is not known on which McKelvey property the free worker resided; if one assumes that all of the workers lived on Fountainhead plantation, there would be only one chance in seven, or 14% probability, that the Spiers Landing site represents a free worker occupation. Since it is highly unlikely that all McKelvey workers lived on a single plantation, probability statistics would support the contention that there is at least an 86% likelihood that the Spiers Landing site reflects a slave occupation. Again, if it is post-ulated that a maximum of five slaves lived in a single one-room dwelling (Atwater and Woods 1897:23–38; Genovese 1976:524), one could hypothesize that six wooden slave cabins and one wooden free worker cabin may have existed on one of the McKelvey properties in 1800.

Thus, although documentary details of the operation, structure and property history of Fountainhead plantation are very sparse and ambiguous, indirect evidence suggests initially that the Spiers Landing site may represent a slave cabin.

The Carolina Artifact Pattern was targeted as a potentially significant indicator of economic patterns which might be associated with low-status domestic occupation. The occupation pattern defined by South (1977a: 111, 119) reflects a mean and a range of urban-associated Euro-American artifact frequencies grouped into several functional classes, e.g., kitchen group, arms group, clothing group. A testable hypothesis for the Spiers Landing site was advanced which postulated that if the site reflected a domestic occupation, a variety of artifact classes (behaviors) should occur, i.e., the site should reflect multiple rather than specialized activities. Also, since the Carolina Artifact Pattern is derived from medium- and high-status Euro-

American occupations, a slave cabin should reflect statistically significant differences in mean artifact group percentages, particularly clothing, furniture, arms, personal and activities groups.

The entire range of artifact classes predicted by a generalized set of behaviors such as the Carolina Artifact Pattern was present at Spiers Landing, indicating a domestic occupation rather than a special activity (non-domestic) occupation. Statistically significant differences in individual artifact groups were confirmed in three groups: clothing, activities and kitchen (Tables 1 and 2). Non-significant differences were observed in arms, furniture and personal groups. The occurrence of large numbers of Colono-Ware sherds accounted for the difference observed in the kitchen group. Although the inclusion of Colono-Ware in the kitchen group rather than the activities group (South's original categorization) would be expected to affect the comparison of both groups, it was noted that statistically significant differences occurred in the activities group between the Carolina Artifact Pattern and the Spiers Landing assemblage even when omitting Colono-Ware from the entire analysis. It is therefore suggested that Colono-Ware may be a sensitive correlate of slave and/or free black occupations of the 17th and 18th centuries (Ferguson 1978).

TABLE 1
COMPARISON OF SPIERS LANDING WITH THE CAROLINA ARTIFACT PATTERN

Artifact Group	CAP Mean %[a]	% Range[a]	Pred. Range[a]	Spiers Landing	Frequency
Kitchen	63.1	51.8–69.2	47.5–78.0	73.7[b]	2275
Architecture	25.1	19.7–31.4	12.9–35.1	20.2	623
Furniture	.2	.1– .6	0 – .7	.1	2
Arms	.5	.1– 1.2	0 – 1.5	.2	6
Clothing	3.0	.6– 5.4	0 – 8.5	.8	24
Personal	.2	.1– .5	0 – .6	.1	2
Tobacco Pipes	5.8	1.8–13.9	0 –20.8	2.4	74
Activities	1.7	.9– 2.7	.1– 3.7	2.6	81
	N = 3087		$X^2 = 226.42$, d.f. = 7		$p < .01$

[a]All Carolina Artifact Pattern percentage figures as used by South (1977a).
[b]Rounded to nearest tenth

TABLE 2
ARTIFACT GROUP COMPARISONS FOR THE
CAROLINA ARTIFACT PATTERN

Artifact Group	Chi-Square Value	Rejection Level
Kitchen	52.20, d.f. = 4	$p < .01$
Architecture	9.14, d.f. = 4	$p < .10$
Clothing	62.65, d.f. = 4	$p < .01$
Tobacco Pipes	5.65, d.f. = 4	$p < .30$
Activities	23.47, d.f. = 4	$p < .01$

The overall difference between Spiers Landing and the Carolina Artifact Pattern is statistically significant ($p < .01$, d.f. = 7). However, individual mean percentage figures fall within the expanded predictive ranges for all artifact groups (South 1977a:119). The research and findings suggest that the archaeological study of refuse discard behavior may produce repetitive patterns which can be used to predict differences in subsistence and/or settlement behavior on plantation sites, and which may define a "plantation artifact pattern."

In seeking to establish possible functional contexts for the differences observed between the Carolina Artifact Pattern and the Spiers Landing assemblage, four major possibilities were considered: 1. That the site may represent a slave cabin, but that specific behaviors associated with the occupation set it apart from a predicted slave economic pattern (i.e., extremely low frequency of inorganic artifacts, absence of artifacts associated with arms, personal items, furniture and clothing); 2. That the site may represent a slave cabin and slave lifestyles differed from urban lifestyles more noticeably in some economic sectors than in others and predictably so, and/or in some geographic areas of the eastern seaboard, for instance Charleston vs. a small Piedmont village; 3. That the Spiers Landing site may represent the dwelling or workshop of a free worker; 4. That the site may represent a barn or shed (non-domestic unit).

The last explanation is not supported since a heavy domestic component is reflected at the site. The difficulties involved in recognizing free black and slave black occupations archaeologically are great (Explanation #3). Significant attempts are currently being made to begin to address this problem through the correlation of Colono-Wares and black slaves at documented slave sites (Leland Ferguson 1980, pers. comm.; Patrick Garrow 1980, pers. comm.). Explanation #3 is not supported by a significantly greater occurrence of any one or more artifact classes reflective of specialization, nor is it supported by census data, which report only one free worker on all of the McKelvey holdings at the turn of the 19th century. In fact, the records reflect an association between McKelvey and only one free person (unspecified racial designation) in 60 years, while from 23–42 slaves lived on the property during that time.

It therefore appears that the vast majority of workers associated with McKelvey property during the site occupation period were black slaves. Explanation #1 or #2 is therefore expected to identify the socioeconomic character of the Spiers Landing site.

Analysis of a household's food remains can be an important tool in defining economic status (Miller 1979). When combined with information from artifacts, faunal and botanical remains can contribute significantly to more dependable and valid site interpretations. Study of the identifiable faunal material from the Spiers Landing site (13% of the entire faunal sample) demonstrates that of an estimated 16 individuals represented, 50% are domestic species (cow and pig), and 50% are wild meat sources (white-tailed deer, raccoon, mudfish and unidentified bird).

Examination of the meat composition and treatment of food bones offers some clues to butchery and dietary practices of the site's inhabitants. Butchering of animals for the planter's table would be expected to show evidence of careful sawing and trimming of choice meat parts, usually hams, shoulders and loins (Hilliard 1969:4; Miller 1979:164, 168). Cut marks on poorer quality meat parts, such as skulls, neck, lower leg and hoof elements, could be expected to occur at slave quarters. Food bones from an overseer's cabin could be expected to reflect more high quality elements than low quality elements. Poor or low quality cuts of meat, by definition, imply poorer nutritional value, i.e., less protein, more gristle, connective tissue, and/or hoof.

Within the Spiers Landing sample, metapodial, hoof and cranial elements (poor quality elements) comprise 75% of the identifiable bone fragments, with high quality elements forming the remaining 25%. However, the majority of high quality meat elements are from wild resources, *not* from domesticated mammals. This suggests that the site's occupants gained a significant portion of their most nutritious means from hunting and fishing (Table 3).

From the condition of the recovered bone fragments, it was impossible to evaluate whether selective hunting or butchering was practiced. No saw marks were observed on the faunal material, but cut marks did occur. Butchering therefore appears to have been done with axes or cleavers. Spiral fracture on several long bones suggests also that the site's occupants utilized bone marrow from at least some of the food bones. It thus appears that animal butchery at the site produced predominantly inferior meat cuts for low-status consumption, supplemented by high quality wild meats.

Comparable assemblages of food remains are reported from slave cabins in Georgia and Florida (Ascher and Fairbanks 1971:11, 13; Fairbanks 1974:87–88) and from the Utopia site in Virginia (Miller 1979). Taken together, however, these sites reflect a greater variety of animal remains, and their distributions indicate that wild food resources contributed but a small percentage to the overall meat diet, a finding at variance with the Spiers Landing

TABLE 3
FAUNAL REMAINS FROM SPIERS LANDING

Provenience	MNI[a]	Taxa	Common Name
Fea. A-1	1	*Bos taurus*	Cow
(large exterior	1?	*Odocoileus virginianus*	White-tailed deer
refuse pit)	1?	*Procyon lotor*	Raccoon
	1	*Sus scrofa*	Pig
Fea. A-2	1?	*Bos taurus*	Cow
(large exterior	1?	*Odocoileus virginianus*	White-tailed deer
refuse pit)	1?	*Procyon lotor*	Raccoon
	1?	*Sus scrofa*	Pig
Fea. A-3	1	*Bos taurus*	Cow
(large exterior	1	*Sus scrofa*	Pig
refuse pit)			
Fea. A-4	1	*Bos taurus*	Cow
(small interior	1	*Procyon lotor*	Raccoon
refuse pit)	1	*Odocoileus virginianus*	White-tailed deer
	1	*Sus scrofa*	Pig
	1[b]	*Amia calva*	Mudfish
	1[b]	(Species unknown)	Bird

[a]Minimum Number of Individuals
[b]Several fragments of same individual represented

site, where at least 50% of the estimated number of individuals are wild resources. Regional differences in plantation structure and worker economies throughout the antebellum South will obviously require multi-disciplinary study in the future.

Plant food remains from the Spiers Landing site include small quantities of peach, corn, beans and wild foods such as acorns, hickory nuts, walnuts and grape seeds. Although all of the wild plant foods could have been collected in the site vicinity in the later summer through early fall, none are represented in sufficient quantity to suggest heavy dependence. Although not mainstays of the slave diet, such items were often useful in varying a monotonous diet and in providing sweetmeats (Hilliard 1972:182). Cultivated fruits, such as peaches, pears and apples, were also dried and used to make beverages. Fountainhead plantation contained eight peach orchards at the time of its purchase by the South Carolina Public Service Authority in 1939.

The southern black diet appears to have changed very little from the 17th to the 19th centuries and indeed continued its basic resource orientation into the early 20th century (Atwater and Woods 1897:8–15; Hilliard 1969:12–13; Wood 1974:120–121). Little is known about the dietary practices of overseers or free blacks, although several historical sources intimate that overseers ate and lived somewhat better than did the slaves (cf. Hilliard 1969, 1972; Blassingame 1972; Clifton 1978).

The slave diet can be characterized as follows (Miller 1979:160–161):

1. It was primarily vegetal; 2. It was high in carbohydrates, particularly corn; 3. The primary meat consumed was pork; 4. Butchering waste and old or diseased animals were occasionally eaten; 5. The diet was supplemented by wild animals, turtles, fish, birds and wild plant foods.

The faunal and botanical remains recovered from the Spiers Landing site, limited though they are quantitatively, are not at all inconsistent with historical characterizations of the slave subsistence economy. In the case of Spiers Landing, although little difference would be expected between free and non-free black worker diets, the historical census data, together with the ceramic pattern, tend to support a non-free black worker interpretation for this site. Detailed study of food remains at documented slave and free black worker sites in the South should provide invaluable information bearing on this interpretive problem.

A final test to which the "slave occupation" hypothesis was put during the site analysis was an attempt to determine the site's socioeconomic character through an analysis of ceramic types and forms. John S. Otto has hypothesized that early 19th century slaves on the Georgia coast often consumed their foods, largely liquid-based stews, from banded bowls, while the planter family ate their foods, largely meat cuts, from transfer-printed flatware (Otto 1977:101–105). His analysis of data from the Cannon's Point plantation (St. Simon's Island) led him to postulate that differences in ceramic needs would account for the differences in patterns of distribution of tableware shapes and types at plantation sites.

A comparison was made between Spiers Landing ceramics and Otto's distributions for a documented slave cabin and an overseer's house, on the basis of estimated Minimum Number of Individual vessels reconstructed from Spiers Landing. Most of the site's percentage distributions are much closer to that of Otto's documented slave cabin than they are to that of the overseer's house (Table 4). In addition, Otto's predicted "meat-based broth diet" contention is supported by the existence at Spiers Landing of a high percentage of serving bowls and a correspondingly low percentage of serving flatware. Further support for the proposition that dietary needs determined the ceramic shapes used by the site occupants is the observation that of an estimated 35 Colono-Ware vessels, 62.8% are unrestricted bowls. Inflected or straight-sided deeper vessels exhibit side and basal charring, suggesting use

TABLE 4
CERAMIC MORPHOLOGY COMPARISONS

	Canon's Point Slave Cabin[a]	Canon's Point Overseer's House[a]	Spiers Landing
Ceramic Types			
Banded, undecorated, blue/green-edged wares (sherds)	358 (66%)	127 (71%)	747 (77%)
Transfer-printed wares (sherds)	114 (21%)	25 (14%)	137 (14%)
Ceramic Shapes			
Serving bowls (vessels)	35 (44%)	19 (24%)	28 (50%)
Serving flatware (vessels)	39 (49%)	56 (72%)	17 (30%)
Tableware Shapes Grouped by Surface Decoration			
Banded serving bowls (vessels)	23 (29%)	13 (17%)	19 (30%)
Transfer-printed serving flatware (vessels)	15 (19%)	22 (28%)	3 (5%)

[a]St. Simon's Island, Georgia (Otto 1977:98–103).

as boiling kettles over an open fire (Drucker and Anthony 1979:66).

Ceramic shape and type distributions can also provide insight into the status of the Spiers Landing occupants (Ascher and Fairbanks 1971:11; Otto 1977). Otto's research has indicated that the percentages of shell-edged, transfer-printed and plain ceramics, as well as the percentages of bowl vs. flatware forms can be sensitive reflectors of social status differences on early 19th century plantations. Although differences were found to be much less pronounced ceramically between slaves and overseers than between slaves/overseers and planters, Otto predicts that blue and green edged sherd type frequencies may be a sensitive marker of slave status at small sites. More important for the present study is the hypothesis that ceramic *shape* could be a more sensitive indicator of social status than ceramic *type*.

Three specific hypotheses presented by Otto were tested against the Spiers Landing data. First, Otto (1977:107–108) predicted that banded, blue- and green-edged and undecorated sherds should be relatively common at both slave and overseer sites, comprising about 70% of the total sherd count. In contrast, transfer-printed sherds should be relatively rare, comprising less than 25% of the total sherds.

Of a total of 970 identifiable sherds of Euro-American produced wares from Spiers Landing, 77% (n = 747) are undecorated, banded and blue- and green-edged wares; only 14% (n = 137) are transfer-printed. These similarities to Otto's figures (Table 4) leads to a preliminary conclusion that the Spiers Landing site reflects a low-status plantation worker occupation. The percentage of blue- and green-edged sherds from the site unfortunately does not help to clarify a desirable distinction between possible overseer and slave occupation, as only 6% of the sample (n = 58) falls within this ceramic type, a percentage apparently consistent with Otto's overseer site and lower than his slave site. Since Otto has questioned the validity of relying too heavily on edged and banded sherd frequencies to distinguish overseer and slave sites, the Spiers Landing sample suggests a ceramic distinction which may compliment the correlation between edged sherd frequencies and slave status, and that is a high proportionate occurrence of Colono-Ware sherds. The assemblage reflects 56% Colono-Ware identification (n = 1,230).

This high Colono-Ware percentage distribution suggests that such a situation at antebellum sites may be a sensitive indicator of slave status. While there may be a socioeconomic tradition associated with Colono-Ware during the late 17th and 18th centuries which includes both blacks and poor whites, slave dwellings are probably more numerous in the South Carolina lowcountry than were poor white dwellings and were certainly more numerous than free black dwellings, which occurred largely in urban centers. For this reason, there exists a logical likelihood that the vast majority of sites containing appreciable quantities of Colono-Ware belong to slave occupations. This is not to say that free blacks and poor whites did not use Colono-Wares, perhaps more than Euro-American wares, due to their low cost. If, however, Colono-Wares were manufactured largely by blacks for utilitarian purposes, the majority of the users would have been slaves.

Otto's (1977:108) second hypothesis states that serving bowls should be relatively abundant at slave sites, making up over 40% of the total tableware shapes. As discussed above, 44% of the entire Spiers Landing sample of estimated whole vessels (n = 28) and 62.8% of the estimated Colono-Ware vessels (n = 22) are bowls. However, of tableware alone, 50% of the shapes are serving bowls (Table 4). A correspondingly low percentage (30%, n = 17) of flatware shapes occurs within the tableware category, while over 70% of Otto's overseer

assemblage is represented by flatware items. Although the low Spiers Landing percentage for flatware is also much lower than Otto's slave cabin percentage (49%), his relative distributions between slave and overseer sites support the contention that the Spiers Landing site probably reflects a slave occupation.

The third hypothesis (Otto 1977:108) states that banded bowl forms should be relatively common at slave sites, comprising about 30% of tableware forms, while banded bowls will be less common at overseer sites, comprising less than 20% of tableware forms. In contrast, transfer-printed flatware should comprise less than 20% of total tableware shapes at slave sites, while they should be more common at overseer sites (around 30%). Within the Spiers Landing sample, 30% (n = 19) of estimated tableware shapes are banded or polychrome decorated bowls; transfer-printed serving flatware comprises less than 6% (n = 3) of the estimated tableware shapes (Table 4). These data again support the hypothesis that Spiers Landing represents a slave occupation rather than a free worker occupation. It should also be noted that of the serving flatware, edged flatware at Spiers Landing comprises a much higher percentage than that of Otto's slave site or overseer site, although the percentage continues a trend suggested by Otto's slave cabin figures (Otto 1977:Table 5.5 and Table 5.6).

A final body of property history information was also brought to bear on the interpretation of the low-status occupation at the Spiers Landing site. A plat of the Spiers property which was made before the property was sold to the South Carolina Public Service Authority in 1939 located a slave cemetery in what is probably now an off-shore location in Lake Marion. Although no structures are depicted in the site area, the site would have been located approximately 295–394 feet southwest of the cemetery. Historical sources note that slave houses were often located in close proximity to their burial areas and to major plantation access roads (Handler and Lange 1978:173–184). No plats could be found showing whether or not a main house was located on the original plantation, or where the slave quarters or possible overseer's cabin may have been. However, the present dirt access road to the site appears to have been used as a major plantation road as late as the end of the 19th century and served as a property boundary at least as early as the mid-19th century; the site is located only about 249 feet east of this road. Although it is therefore only an unconfirmed location, the slave cemetery depicted on the 1939 plat may indicate the vicinity of the original location of one or more slave quarters or field cabins, of which the Spiers Landing site may represent the remnants.

Current study of 17th and 18th century slave quarters and other plantation dependencies promises to broaden our understanding of how the slave economy affected and was affected by the rice and cotton cultures of the South. Spatial contexts and artifact patterning at small historic sites will need to be carefully researched and compared against historical records in order to derive testable field models which will allow archaeologists to recognize such things as "slave sites," "free worker sites," and "tenant sites" within antebellum and postbellum contexts. Although this may appear to some to be a platitude, such study is a relatively new, untried and non-traditional topic for research in historical archaeology and is a concept more at home within the prehistorian's research kit.

The Spiers Landing project incorporated research approaches and methods designed to explore behavioral patterning at an undocumented, small historic site. This was done within the context and limitations of contract salvage requirements, but it has contributed important historical research data as a result of the Section 106 procedures of the National Historic Preservation Act (Public Law 89–665) and the Archeological and Historic Preservation Act (Public Law 93–291). Other recent research has sought to discover from documented sites the evolutionary trends which determined the culture history of the plantation South in its many regional expressions (Kelso 1979; Lewis 1979; Singleton 1979; Mullins 1979). All of these efforts will serve to increase our understanding of this aspect of American culture and will help us prepare guidelines on how better to preserve, conserve and protect the significant remains of that culture for the education and growth of future generations.

ACKNOWLEDGMENTS

Funding and administrative coordination for the Spiers Landing project was made available by Interagency Archeological Services-Atlanta (Heritage Conservation and Recreation Service), Berkeley County Federal/State Coordinator's Office, and the U.S. Economic Development Authority. Ms. Marlesa Gray, Dr. Stephanie H. Rodeffer, Mr. Stanley South and Dr. Leland G. Ferguson provided assistance during the analysis and provided constructive comment on the project draft report. I would also like to thank Ronald W. Anthony for the use of his data concerning the Colono-Wares recovered from the site. The editorial staff of Historical Archaeology also made valuable comments and suggestions during the drafting of this article. All of these people, while not responsible for the content, structure or possible factual errors contained in this article, contributed to the overall research quality which made the paper possible, and I thank them.

REFERENCES

ANONYMOUS
1941 Cross Cabin, Berkeley County (photograph). Historic American Buildings Survey, Division of Fine Arts. U.S. Government Printing Office, Washington.

ANTHONY, RONALD W.
1979 Descriptive Analysis and Replication of Historic Earthenware: Colono-Wares from the Spiers Landing Site, Berkeley County, South Carolina. *Conference on Historic Site Archaeology Papers 1978 (1979).* 13:253–268.

ASCHER, ROBERT AND CHARLES H. FAIRBANKS
1971 Excavation of a Slave Cabin: Georgia, U.S.A. *Historical Archaeology* V:3–17.

ATWATER, W. O. AND C. D. WOODS
1897 Food of the Negro in Alabama in 1895 and 1896. U.S. Department of Agriculture, Office of Experimental Stations, *Bulletin* 38.

BAKER, STEVEN G.
1972   Colono-Indian Pottery from Cambridge, South Carolina with Comments on the Historic Catawba Pottery Trade. *Institute of Archeology and Anthropology, University of South Carolina, Notebook* 4(1):3–30.

BLASSINGAME, JOHN W.
1972   *The Slave Community: Plantation Life in the Antebellum South.* Oxford University Press, New York.

CLIFTON, JAMES M. (EDITOR)
1978   *Life and Labor on Argyle Island: Letters and Documents of a Savannah River Rice Plantation, 1883–1867.* Beehive Press, Savannah.

DRUCKER, LESLEY M. AND RONALD W. ANTHONY
1979   *The Spiers Landing Site: Archaeological Investigations in Berkeley County, South Carolina.* U.S. Department of the Interior, Heritage Conservation and Recreation Service Contract C-5767(78).

FAIRBANKS, CHARLES H.
1974   The Kingsley Slave Cabins in Duval County, Florida, 1968. *Conference on Historic Site Archaeology Papers (1972)* 7(2):62–93.

FERGUSON, LELAND G.
1978   Looking for the "Afro" in Colono-Indian Pottery. *Conference on Historic Site Archaeology Papers 1977(1978)* 12:68–86.

GENOVESE, EUGENE D.
1976   *Roll, Jordan, Roll: the World the Slaves Made.* Random House (Vintage Books), New York.

HANDLER, JEROME S. AND FREDERICK W. LANGE
1978   *Plantation Slavery in Barbados.* Harvard University Press, Cambridge.

HILLIARD, SAM
1969   Hog Meat and Corpone: Food Habits in the Ante-bellum South. *American Philosophical Society Proceedings* 113(1):1–13.
1972   *Hog Meat and Hoecake: Food Supply in the Old South, 1840–1860.* Southern Illinois University, Carbondale.

JEFFCOAT, CAROL
1979   Soil Chemical Analysis of Samples from the Spiers Landing Site. Ms. on file, Carolina Archaeological Services, Columbia, South Carolina.

KELSO, WILLIAM M.
1979   *Houses of Cards and Castles: Virginia's Seventeenth Century Nomothetic Paradox.* Paper Presented at the 12th Annual Meeting of the Society for Historical Archaeology, Nashville.

LEWIS, KENNETH
1979   *An Archeological View of Limerick and Middleton Plantations.* Paper Presented at the Third Annual Symposium on Language and Culture in South Carolina, Columbia.

MILLER, HENRY M.
1979   Pettus and Utopia: A Comparison of the Faunal Remains from Two Late Seventeenth Century Virginia Households. *Conference on Historic Site Archaeology papers 1978 (1979)* 13:158–179.

MORRISON, A. H., II
1978   *An Experimental Wattle-and-Daub Chimney in St. Mary's City. Maryland.* Paper Presented at the 19th Annual Conference on Historic Site Archaeology, Winston-Salem.

MULLINS, SUE A.
1979   *The Southern Coastal Plantation: View from St. Simon's Island, Georgia.* Paper Presented at the 12th Annual Meeting of the Society for Historical Archaeology, Nashville.

OTTO, JOHN S.
1977   Artifacts and Status Differences—A Comparison of Ceramics from Planter, Overseer, and Slave Sites on an Antebellum Plantation. In *Research Strategies in Historical Archeology,* edited by Stanley South, pp. 91–118, Academic Press, New York.

SINGLETON, THERESA A.
1979   *Slaves and Ex-Slave Sites in Coastal Georgia.* Paper Presented at the 12th Annual Meeting of the Society for Historical Archaeology, Nashville.

SOUTH, STANLEY
1977a   *Method and Theory in Historical Archeology.* Academic Press, New York.
1977b   *Research Strategies in Historical Archaeology,* edited by Stanley South. Academic Press, New York.

TRINKLEY, MICHAEL B.
1979   Paleoethnobotanical Remains from Spiers Landing, 38BK160. Ms. on file, Carolina Archaeological Services, Columbia, South Carolina.

WOOD, PETER H.
1974   *Black Majority: Negroes in Colonial South Carolina from 1670 Through the Stono Rebellion.* W. W. Norton, New York.

LESLEY M. DRUCKER
CAROLINA ARCHAEOLOGICAL SERVICES
3932 HICKORY STREET
COLUMBIA, SOUTH CAROLINA 29205

WILLIAM HAMPTON ADAMS
SARAH JANE BOLING

Status and Ceramics for Planters and Slaves on Three Georgia Coastal Plantations

ABSTRACT

Previous work on Georgia plantations has provided useful data about life on the large plantations on barrier islands. More recent work on small to mid-sized plantations reveals that slaves' acquisition of ceramics may reflect more of their own decisions on what was purchased and what was used. Coarser ware frequencies indicate food preparation and storage in the slave quarters. Porcelain was often found in greater numbers in the slave quarters than in the plantation bighouse kitchen. Like earlier research, slaves at Kings Bay were found to have relatively more small bowls, but surprisingly they had relatively more plates as well. Comparison of slaves and planters using CC Index revealed that for several vessel forms the slaves had more expensive ceramics than their masters. This suggests that the slaves themselves viewed ceramics as status indicators and purchased them accordingly.

Introduction

The plantation is basically an agricultural factory using capital to manage labor to grow a product for the world market. Inherent in plantations is the creation of separate social and economic classes. While the degree of separation varied greatly through time and space, the presence of this dichotomy was inherent in the system. This article examines status as revealed by material culture on three plantations on the Georgia coast, and compares those plantations to ones elsewhere on that coast. The discussion centers upon the following research questions for different status groups (slave vs. planter; tenant vs. planter; small planter vs. middle planter; slaves of small planter vs. slaves of middle planter). The following analyses were run on these status groups for comparative purposes:

— Do these status groups differ in the ceramic wares used?
— Do these status groups differ in the ceramic vessel forms used?
— Do these status groups differ in the value of the ceramic tableware used?

These data were obtained from three nearly adjacent plantations on the mainland portion of the Georgia coast, in the southern-most county, Camden County. The plantations examined here were: Kings Bay Plantation (9CAM172; 1791-ca. 1850); Cherry Point Plantation (9CAM182, 1801-1806; 9CAM183, 1791-1823), and Harmony Hall Plantation (9CAM194; 1793-ca. 1832) (Figure 1).

While this article primarily focuses upon economic status, as revealed by goods produced for the mass market, economic status was related to social status in the antebellum South. The two are different, but interrelated. Furthermore, this is an etic analysis, from the perspective of a American society as a whole, and with an emphasis on manufactured items. This is not an emic analysis of social status within slave society where status was defined in ways which were not likely to leave traces in the archaeological record. Status among slaves was based upon occupations, as well as the ability to control the supernatural and fool their masters. Much slave material culture was made by them of perishable materials, so if one is to investigate relative status it is through the mass-produced materials bought by them or furnished to them.

Status in the Antebellum South

In the antebellum South, one's parents' statuses determined whether one was ascribed the status of being free or slave. While clearly linked to race, it was much more arbitrary than commonly believed for some planters were black or Native American (Adkins 1980; Olmsted 1856:636; Woodson 1968: 3–4). Status for slaves in the antebellum South was largely a legal condition, rather than one of race or skin color. However, their occupation and

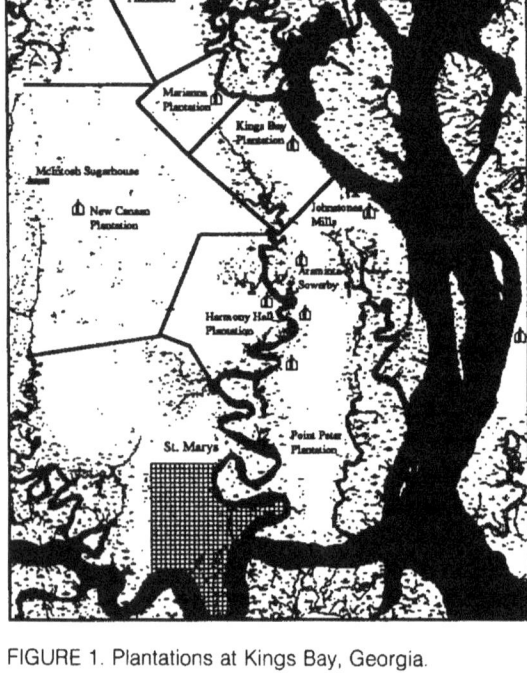

FIGURE 1. Plantations at Kings Bay, Georgia.

their fellow slaves alike (Frazier 1930:209; Hundley 1860:351–52; Kelso 1984:26; Orser 1987:126–28), because their acculturation was influenced through interacting with the planter's family and guests.

Slaves on task system plantations had a potentially different economic status than the slaves on gang system plantations because they provided more of their own subsistence needs and participated within the region's market economy selling their own produce and handcrafts; plantations with task systems permitted slaves to garden and raise chickens, eggs, and pigs, as well as making baskets, canoes, and other handcrafts for sale (Adams 1987:11–13; Adams et al. 1987:228–34; Morgan 1982, 1983). Such slaves were very much akin to peasants working on their landlord's manor or hacienda. Because of this participation, most of the material culture slaves possessed on a task system plantation were made by them or purchased using their own funds. Of course, on any plantation the slaves made much of what they possessed. One may hypothesize that the task labor plantation slaves could have had a higher amount of material goods through their own individual initiative.

Achieved status is that position in society obtained by an individual through his or her own achievements in life, like elected positions, and sometimes wealth and power or the lack of such. Status is relational; an individual's status is determined by reference to someone else's status. Each person has many different statuses, depending upon the circumstances of the moment and the people present (see Orser 1987:124–26 for discussion of this). One can be a father in one's own household, and a son in one's parents' household, wealthier than a beggar, and poorer than a merchant. The planters' relative economic status can be measured by the number of slaves owned, or acreage controlled. The planters' relative social status can be inferred by levels of interaction with their fellow planters and townspeople, as well as from the material culture indicating such interaction.

Three main classification schemes have been developed for the relative status of free whites in the South (Figure 2). David R. Hundley's (1860)

the status of their owners played an even greater role in their daily lives.

Slaves of planters with a higher status regarded their own status as being higher than that of slaves owned by poorer planters. ''They seemed to think that the greatness of their masters was transferable to themselves. It was considered bad enough to be a slave; but to be a poor man's slave was deemed a disgrace indeed'' (Rawick 1972:3). Many slaves considered their economic status to be superior to that of poor whites; as David Hundley (1860:256) has remarked these were the ''Poor White Trash, a name said to have originated with the slaves, who look upon themselves as much better off than all 'pó white folks' whatever.'' The slaves' social status on each plantation also depended upon their occupation. Field slaves had a lower social status than house slaves as viewed by the planter and

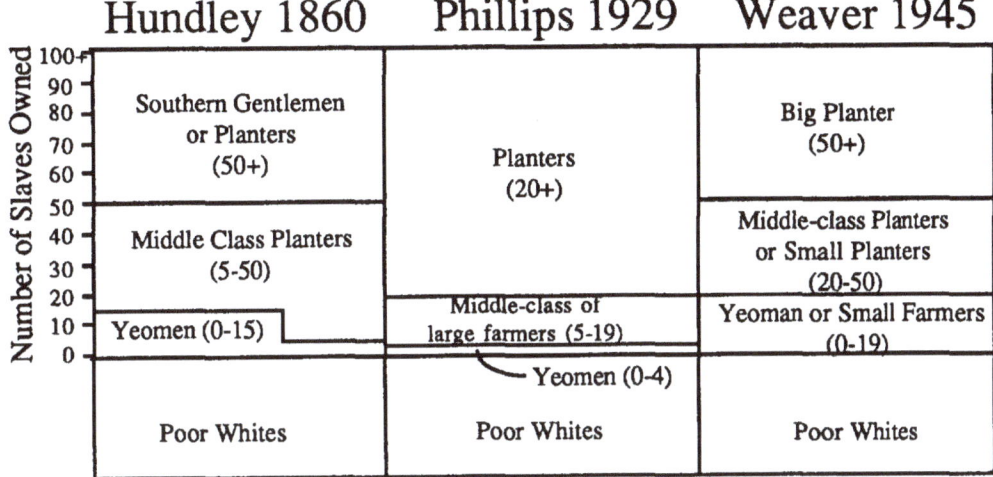

FIGURE 2. Comparison of social status of free whites on the basis of number of slaves owned.

classification centered upon slave ownership, with three classes of slave owners and a fourth class, Poor Whites, who owned no slaves. Ulrich B. Phillips (1929:339) thought a minimum of 20 slaves was needed to define a plantation, whereas owners of 5–19 slaves formed "a middle-class of large farmers and comfortable townsmen." Phillips admired Hundley's work and differs from it only by not distinguishing between middle class and upper class planters. Herbert Weaver (1945) objected to the above classifications because those were based solely upon slave ownership and did not take into consideration landownership. The problem in classifying slaveowners as planters, without considering their land as well, is that the two were not necessarily the same. "Quite frequently men without land owned large numbers of slaves whom they hired out to plantation owners; others were found to own extensive tracts of improved land but no slaves. The former were obviously not planters and the latter were probably middle-class farmers" (Weaver 1945:37).

Does Weaver's classification add anything to what Hundley or Phillips had done, or does it merely complicate it by adding a second variable? Weaver still based the definition of each class on the number of slaves owned. His Big Planter is the same, in terms of slaves, as Hundley's Southern Gentleman or Planter. He uses Phillips' dividing line of owning 20 slaves to distinguish planter from yeoman farmers. While he did not label these groups as upper, middle, and lower class, the distinction is implicit in his designating one group as middle-class planters. How does one classify a person with 150 slaves and only 100 acres who rented out his slaves or put them to work in a mill, or one with 5000 acres but only 10 slaves, using Weaver's classification? The economic control which can be brought to bear, not ownership, provides the relative economic status or worth. For example, at Waverly Plantation in Mississippi, George H. Young, owned 916 hectares (324 improved hectares) and 117 slaves in 1850, 1368 hectares (594 tillable) and 137 slaves in 1860, or ratios of 10.0 and 11.6 acres per slave (Adkins 1980:85–87). Young would be classified as a big planter on the basis of acreage and slave ownership, but he also rented other plantations and controlled twice as much land. Land control is as important as landownership as a socio-economic variable. Furthermore, to use acreage owned as the only criterion is misleading. How much of that land is forest or swamp? How much is in pasture or fields? While a census provides information on

TABLE 1
SLAVEHOLDERS IN THE UNITED STATES, 1850 (FROM DEBOW 1854:95)

	1	2–4	5–9	10–19	20–49	50–99	100–199	200–299	300–499	500–999	1000+	Total
Alabama	5204	7737	6572	5067	3524	957	216	16	2	—	—	29,295
Arkansas	1383	1951	1365	788	382	109	19	2	—	—	—	5,999
Columbia, D. of	760	539	136	39	2	1	—	—	—	—	—	1,477
Delaware	320	352	117	20	—	—	—	—	—	—	—	809
Florida	699	991	759	588	349	104	29	—	1	—	—	3,520
Georgia	6554	11716	7701	6490	5056	764	147	22	4	2	—	38,456
Kentucky	9244	13284	9579	5022	1198	53	5	—	—	—	—	38,385
Louisiana	4797	6072	4327	2652	1774	728	274	36	6	4	—	20,670
Maryland	4825	5331	3327	1822	655	72	7	—	1	—	—	16,040
Mississippi	3640	6228	5143	4015	2964	910	189	18	8	1	—	23,116
Missouri	5762	6878	4370	1810	345	19	—	1	—	—	—	19,185
North Carolina	1204	9668	8129	5898	2828	485	76	12	3	—	—	28,303
South Carolina	3492	6164	6311	4955	3200	990	382	69	29	2	2	25,596
Tennessee	7616	10582	8314	4852	2202	276	19	2	1	—	—	33,864
Texas	1935	2640	1585	1121	374	82	9	1	—	—	—	7,747
Virginia	11385	15550	13030	9456	4880	646	107	8	1	—	—	55,063
U.S. TOTAL	68,820	105,683	80,765	54,595	29,733	6,196	1,479	187	56	9	2	347,525
U.S%	19.80	30.41	23.24	15.71	8.56	1.78	0.42	0.05	0.02	<0.01	<0.01	100.0
Georgia %	17.04	30.47	20.03	16.87	13.15	1.99	0.38	0.06	0.01	<0.01	0.00	100.0

improved acreage, often this information is not available for a particular archaeological site.

While the above classifications can be used for mid-19th century plantations, using them for earlier plantations is riskier because the slave population was increasing during the 18th and early 19th centuries. And, of course, it is entirely useless after Emancipation, even though plantations continued to the present day. What is not clear from the literature is whether this increase meant more people could be slaveholders with time or if the increase was relative. Would a slaveholder with 30 slaves in 1780 be the equivalent of a slaveholder of 50 slaves in 1860? Furthermore, applying this classification to an individual plantation has problems, for a plantation may change classes through time with growth or from difficulties. Like most discussions of plantations, these classifications are ahistorical. Does a big planter who sells or emancipates his slaves lose status as a big planter?

Federal census-takers collected information on slaveholding within specific categories of slaveowners (Table 1; Figure 3). Whether these were emic categories or bureaucratic ones, they surely would have affected classification systems of later historians. The 1850 U.S. Census of Population summarized by DeBow (1854:95) revealed that Georgia slaveholders were in very similar proportions to the U.S. average, with 47.51% owning one to four slaves, 36.90% owning 5–19 slaves, 13.15% owning 20–49 slaves, and only 2.44% owning more than 50 slaves (Table 1; Figure 3). Thus, 84.41% of the *slaveholders* in Georgia in 1850 would be classified as small planters, 13.15% middle planters, and 2.44% large planters. Using these large planters to characterize plantation life is as valid as using millionaires to portray American life.

Figures for the county north of Kings Bay, Glynn County, during the 1820–1860 period also reveal that large and middle planters comprised only a small portion of the total population and of the slaveholders. Small planters comprised roughly 60–80% of the slaveholders, while slaveholders themselves were less than 15% of the white population (Otto 1979). The latter figure is somewhat misleading, however, for it does not show slave-

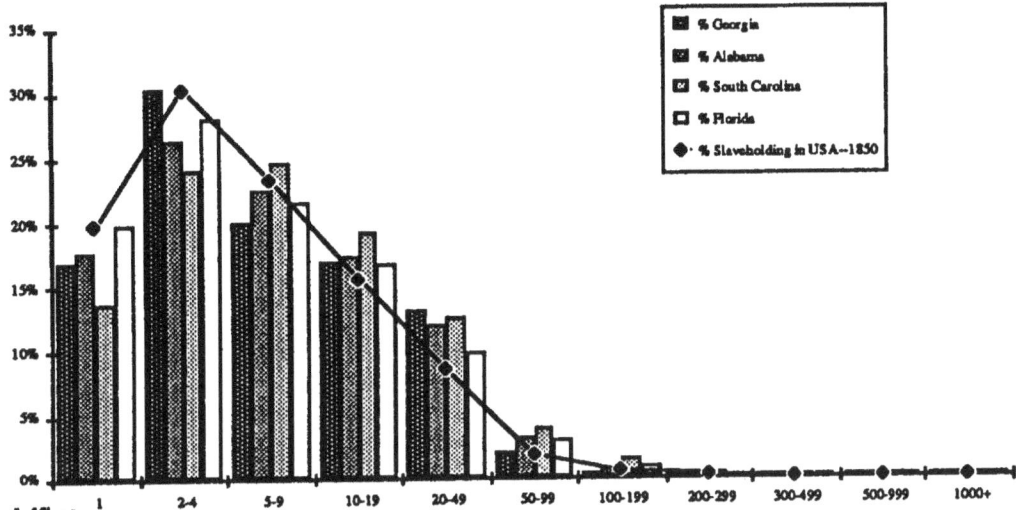

FIGURE 3. Slaveownership in the South, 1850.

holding by household, which would be a much higher percentage. In 1860, only a small number of free Southerners were involved directly with slavery, for most were small farmers or city dwellers who could not afford the expense of providing for slaves (Stampp 1956:29–30). For every plantation, there were many more small farms with no slaves at all.

Using the numbers of slaves owned as the determining factor in assigning status presents other problems. Knowing the total number of slaves on a plantation is not as useful as knowing the demography of that population. A plantation with about 50 slaves in a normal distribution of ages and sexes provides fewer full hands than one with about 30 young male slaves; in terms of economic output of the labor, the latter plantation would provide much more production for the short term. Yet to use the above classifications of Hundley and Weaver, one would be a big planter, while the latter plantation would be of a middle class planter. Furthermore, the labor system used determines the slave population to a great extent. For example, if two adjacent plantations having identical acreage cultivated and identical crops planted, were to use the different labor systems,

gang labor and task labor, the number of slaves required would differ. The plantation with task labor would have relatively more slaves, since each one would produce less than they would in a gang system; the planter can afford to have more slaves because he is providing proportionately less in weekly rations and the slaves are using their free time in gardening, raising meat, and hunting (Adams 1987:11–13; Morgan 1982, 1983; Reitz, Gibbs, and Rathbun 1985:165–166, 183–184). So if one uses the numbers of slaves owned by a planter as a status criterion, one should adjust for the labor system used.

More meaningful classifications need to be developed using other criteria. Clearly, a planter with more than 50 slaves was wealthy, even if his capital was invested only in slaves. Such individuals were upper class, economically (and probably socially as well). But based upon the investigation of one plantation with about 28 slaves—the Kings Bay Plantation—the Thomas King family would also have to regarded as upper class during the 1791–1819 period. The planter, Thomas King, served as an officer in the local militia, owned a town house as well as a plantation bighouse, and entertained at parties friends who were coming from Savannah and St. Augustine. He poured drinks from matched sets of decanters into gold inlaid goblets and decorated tumblers. His prominence would have been known outside the county, probably for much of the Georgia coast, since his parties were mentioned even in the Savannah paper.

By contrast, John King and son James King, who owned Cherry Point Plantation (1791–1823), had only eight slaves and, while locally prominent, were on a different economic and social level as Thomas King (not a relative). John and James King were small planters, while Thomas King was a middle planter, if we use slave ownership as the quantitative unit of measurement. If indeed Thomas King was wealthier, would this be revealed in the ceramic assemblages from these two planter's kitchens? Using the CC Index (Miller 1980) to compare these assemblages should (and does) reveal significant differences, as will be examined later here.

Status and Ware

Much of what we know about the planters' more mundane lives comes from archaeology and from studying probate inventories. Few descriptions of kitchens can be gleaned from historical sources, although what few do exist would offend most modern ideas of cleanliness. Fanny Kemble described her kitchen at Cannon's Point in 1838 as "a mere wooden outhouse, with no floor but bare earth" (Kemble 1863:26). Each kitchen at Kings Bay was dirt floored also and contained hundreds of broken ceramic vessels inside them and in the middens just outside.

Small plantations may have provided food storage and preparation in the planter's kitchens, whereas this was less feasible when one was feeding 28 slaves as Thomas King was faced with doing at the Kings Bay Plantation. Since coarse wares, tablewares, and food bone were all found at the small plantations' slave quarters we know some food preparation was done at the quarters.

Utilitarian vessels for storage and processing foods were made from coarse stoneware, coarse

redware, and yelloware. The higher frequency of coarser wares at the slave sites was evidence that food storage and processing was undertaken at the slave quarters. Refined stonewares included Westerwald from Germany and white saltglazed tableware from England. But few such vessels were found at Kings Bay, and those can be considered heirlooms. Coarser wares (yelloware, coarse redware, coarse stoneware) were used primarily for food storage and preparation.

The ceramic assemblage at the tenant site (the John King Site, 9CAM182, occupied by Woodford Mabry, 1801–1806), yielded only 7.3% of these coarser wares by vessel count (Tables 2 and 3); this may be a function of the short occupation which did not permit sufficient time to break enough vessels, or it may reflect less storage and food preparation at that site. Small planters at Harmony Hall Plantation and at Cherry Point Plantation had 8.4% coarser wares in their kitchen middens, compared to 6.4% at the middle planter's kitchen and yard at Kings Bay Plantation. Lumping planters together, the average for coarse wares was 7.6%, compared to the slave average of 15.7% (Table 3; Figure 4). The slave and planter site areas on small plantations were nearly identical in the amount of coarse wares, with 8.5% for slaves and 8.4% for planters. On the middle-sized plantation, the slaves' assemblage contained 22.8% coarse wares, compared with 6.4% of the planter's assemblage. Taken as a whole, the importance of coarse wares was essentially the same on all sites, except the Kings Bay Plantation slave quarters. This may reflect a different provisioning system on the middle-sized plantation, with the slaves there being responsible for their own food storage and preparation.

Porcelain was not a commonly recovered ware from the Kings Bay sites, as would be expected due to its cost. No porcelain was found at the John King Site (the tenant house), while the other sites had less than 7% of their ceramic assemblage in porcelain. Harmony Hall kitchen (9CAM194A) had the highest frequency of porcelain, 6.2%, while the slave quarters there (9CAM194B) had the next highest at 4.2%, followed by the Kings Bay Plantation slave quarters (9CAM172B),

TABLE 2
VESSELS BY WARE FOR SITES AT KINGS BAY

Site	John King Sawyer 182		James King Planter 183a		183c		Harmony Hall Planter 194a		Kings Bay Planter 172a		James King Slave 183 d		Harmony Hall Slave 194b		Kings Bay Slave 172b	
	N	%	N	%	N	%	N	%	N	%	N	%	N	%	N	%
Yelloware	0	0.0	4	3.7		1.3	3	1.6	5	1.4	1	2.9	0	0.0	13	8.5
Redware, coarse	0	0.0	3	2.8		2.6	4	2.1	6	1.7	2	5.9	2	1.7	12	7.8
Stoneware, coarse	3	7.3	1	0.9	1	6.0	6	3.1	11	3.0	3	8.8	5	4.2	10	6.5
Other earthenwares	0	0.0	0	0.0		0.0	1	0.5	1	0.3	0	0.0	0	0.0	0	0.0
Redware, refined	0	0.0	4	3.7		1.3	3	1.6	4	1.1	0	0.0	1	0.8	3	2.0
Stoneware, refined	0	0.0	3	2.8		1.3	2	1.0	1	0.3	1	2.9	0	0.0	0	0.0
Porcelain	0	0.0	2	1.8		0.9	12	6.2	9	2.5	0	0.0	5	4.2	6	3.9
Delft/Majolica	0	0.0	0	0.0		0.0	0	0.0	2	0.6	0	0.0	2	1.7	1	0.7
Creamware	18	43.9	26	23.9	35	14.0	37	19.3	62	17.1	6	17.6	7	5.9	31	20.3
Pearlware	20	48.8	66	60.6	175	72.8	124	64.6	259	71.6	21	61.8	97	81.5	77	50.3
Whiteware	0	0.0	0	0.0	0	0.0	0	0.0	2	0.6	0	0.0	0	0.0	0	0.0
Total	41	100.0	109	100.2	253	100.2	192	100.0	362	100.2	34	99.9	119	100.0	153	100.0

TABLE 3
VESSELS BY WARE AND STATUS AT KINGS BAY

	Sawyer		Small Planter		Middle Planter		Slave of Small Planter		Slave of Middle Planter		Kings Bay Planters		Kings Bay Slaves	
	N	%	N	%	N	%	N	%	N	%	N	%	N	%
Yelloware	0	0.0	10	1.9	5	1.4	1	0.7	13	8.5	15	1.7	14	4.6
Redware, coarse	0	0.0	13	2.4	6	1.7	4	2.6	12	7.8	19	2.1	16	5.2
Stoneware, coarse	3	7.3	21	3.9	11	3.0	8	5.2	10	6.5	32	3.6	18	5.9
Other earthenwares	0	0.0	1	0.2	1	0.3	0	0.0	0	0.0	2	0.2	0	0.0
Redware, refined	0	0.0	10	1.9	4	1.1	1	0.7	3	2.0	14	1.6	4	1.3
Stoneware, refined	0	0.0	8	1.5	1	0.3	1	0.7	0	0.0	9	1.0	1	0.3
Porcelain	0	0.0	16	3.0	9	2.5	5	3.3	6	3.9	25	2.8	11	3.6
Delft/Majolica	0	0.0	0	0.0	2	0.6	2	1.3	1	0.7	2	0.2	3	1.0
Creamware	18	43.9	96	17.9	62	17.1	13	8.5	31	20.3	158	17.6	44	14.4
Pearlware	20	48.8	361	67.4	259	71.6	118	77.1	77	50.3	620	69.0	195	63.7
Whiteware	0	0.0	0	0.0	2	0.6	0	0.0	0	0.0	2	0.2	0	0.0
Total	41	100.0	536	100.1	362	100.2	153	100.1	153	100.0	898	100.0	306	100.0

which at 3.9% was higher than the planter's kitchen at 2.5%. For porcelain, the planters do not differ significantly in their ceramic assemblages (3.0% vs. 2.5% for small vs. middle; Table 3). Slaves on the two small plantations had 3.3% of their ceramics as porcelain, compared to 3.9% for slaves on the middle plantation. The slaves' porcelain average was 3.6%, compared to the planter average of 2.8%. Due to porcelain's being more expensive, we would not expect it to be found frequently on slave sites, much less in higher quantities than at their masters'. Otto found at Cannon's Point, that porcelain was 1.1% on the slave site, 2.8% at the overseer's, and 1.4% at the planter's kitchen (Otto 1984:90). Perhaps the mistress of that bighouse simply wiped out or rinsed the tea service and that this resulted in less breakage of it there. Porcelains were most often found in tea service.

Pearlware gradually supplanted creamware as the vessel of choice for the table, so much so that by the early 1800s creamware was the cheapest tableware available (Miller 1980). The Kings Bay sites can be seriated (ordered) on the basis of the relative frequency of creamware and pearlware, with later sites having more pearlware. For example, the 1801–1806 John King Site had 48.8% pearlware, while the longer occupied and later sites like Harmony Hall had 64.6%. While the range of creamware:pearlware ratios is consider-

able between some of these sites, it is not part of this analysis. The ratio is thought to be mostly influenced by time, and we are considering distinct marks of status. On the basis of ware types, we found little meaningful difference between small and middle planter assemblages, or between their slaves' assemblages. Slave sites tended to have a few more coarse ware vessels than did the planters (or fewer refined wares for the table).

Status and Vessel Form

Vessel form has been suggested as indicating status on plantations (Otto 1977, 1984). If vessels were used for the purpose each was made, then the more vessel forms in a site, the greater the complexity of the meals partaken there. Researchers have observed that slave sites yielded a disproportionate amount of bowls and have inferred this has resulted from the cooking methods employed by the slave, particularly using pot-au-feu. The interpretation for Cannon's Point Plantation was that slaves ate from bowls, while at the planter's house people ate from plates, reflecting different methods of cooking there, stewing and roasting (Otto 1977:98, 1984:167). Others also found that slaves used bowls more (Booth 1971:33).

At Kings Bay, small bowls at the planters' kitchens ranged from 7.9% to 22.4% of the ce-

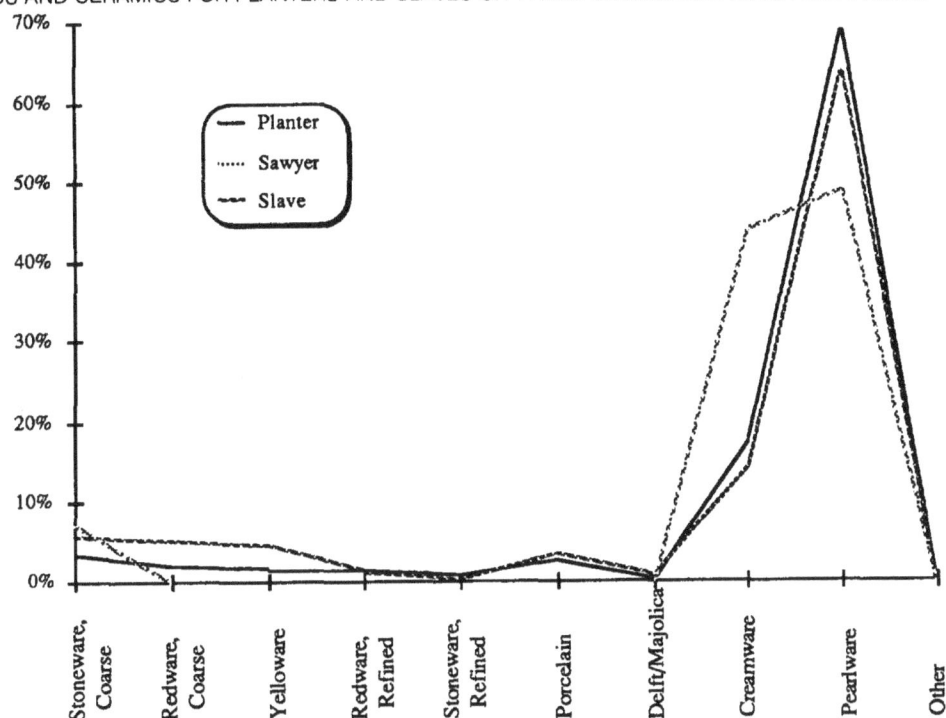

FIGURE 4. Vessels by ware for planters, sawyer, and slaves at Kings Bay.

ramic assemblage, while at the slave quarters there the small bowls ranged from 15.4% to 32.2%, consistently more than for the planters' kitchen (Table 4; Figures 5–8). If small bowls and large bowls are combined, the planters' kitchens totals ranged from 15.8% to 28.5%, while those at the slave quarters ranged from 24.1% to 35.8%. When we compare bowl frequency for planter and slave on the same plantation, the slave always has relatively more small bowls and fewer large bowls than the planter, but the range for slaves on one plantation overlaps that for planters on other plantations. Plates ranged from 23.2% to 37.6% at the planters' kitchens and from 24.8% to 40.4% at the slave quarters. Plates were more frequent at the Harmony Hall Plantation Slave Cabin and the Kings Bay Plantation Slave Quarters, compared to their planters. But for the Cherry Point Plantation, the slaves' plate frequency is less than that of the planter.

Oral histories of ex-slaves collected in the 1930s

indicated wooden implements and tableware were common in many areas of the South (Cade 1935: 300–301). Conversely, planters likely used pewter plates as well as ceramic ones (even though few pewter vessels were found in the Kings Bay sites). These are biases for which there can be no control. While it is true slave sites at Kings Bay did have relatively more small bowls (20.5% vs. 13.2%), they also had relatively more plates (31.2% vs. 30.7%) than the planters (Tables 4–6). The reason for this is that slaves had relatively few vessels other than plates and bowls, while the planter's assemblage contained a fuller complement of tableware vessels like cups, platters, teapots, and miscellaneous vessels. With the sites at Kings Bay we can now see that the variation between slave sites is much the same as the variation between planter sites, and that some slaves had higher frequencies of plates than the planters did.

Research suggests the tea ceremony in British-

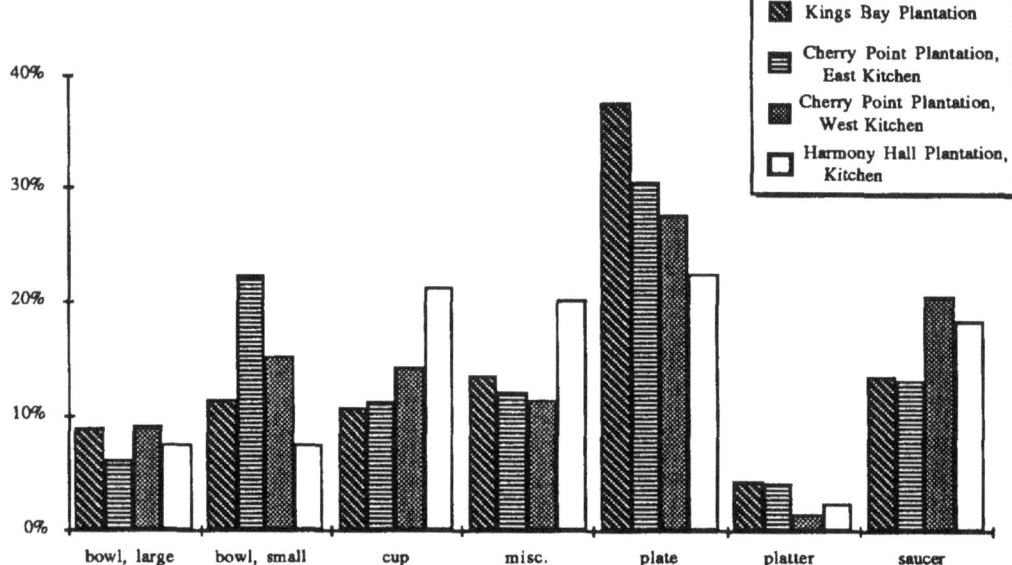

FIGURE 5. Vessel forms for the planters at Kings Bay.

American society had important status implications on a plantation, even though elsewhere after the Revolution its importance as a status indicator becomes less distinct (Roth 1961). On a plantation, however, the tea ceremony (not just tea drinking) should have been restricted to the planters and their guests; it would seem unlikely that slaves partook of it and hence the presence of tea service, especially porcelain, might have valid usage in defining status of site occupants. However, some archaeologists believe household servants may have become acculturated to the tea ceremony and acquired tea service for their personal use (K. Lewis 1985:58; Otto 1977:106, 1984:166). But we do not know whether the presence of tea pots and tea cups at a slave site implies the tea ceremony, or other uses. Otto noted that while the slaves and the overseer had teawares, these were not matched sets like the planter used (Otto 1984:166). Some of the slave sites at Kings Bay had more porcelain vessels for tea service than did the planter's assemblage. At Kings Bay, porcelain was not a common ware, only 1.8%, 0.9%, 6.2%, 2.5% at the four planter's

kitchens, and 0.0%, 4.2%, and 3.9% at the slave quarters (Table 2). This porcelain was almost always teaware, but matching vessels were found only at planter kitchens. At Kings Bay Plantation, the slave quarters had more porcelain than the planter's kitchen, not at all what would be expected on the basis of cost, for porcelain was more expensive than earthenwares (Miller 1980).

Comparing the Kings Bay vessels to other plantations on the Georgia coast is difficult because the level of analysis between reports differs considerably. Sue Mullins Moore in a study of status on the coastal plantation (Moore 1985:153) lumped all vessels into either holloware or flatware without defining either category or noting whether the data included pitchers, chamberpots, and other vessels associated with an assortment of activities in the bedroom, kitchen, dairy, and elsewhere. John S. Otto (1984) lumped cups, mugs, and other vessels into teaware, but did not explicitly define the category for Cannon's Point. Singleton (1980) did not distinguish between cups and bowls in her analysis of the material from Butler Island. Given the lack of any detailed analysis by previous

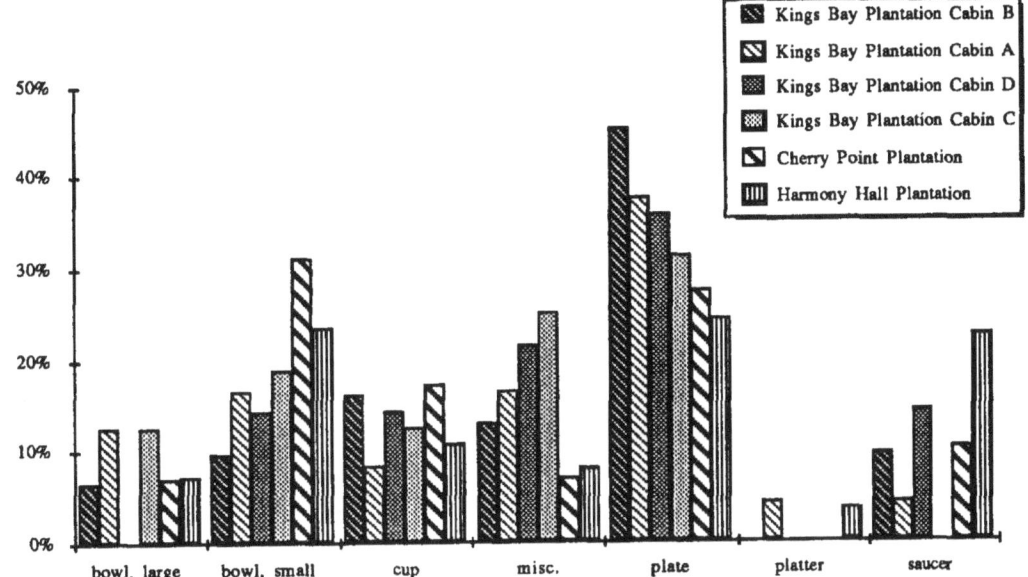

FIGURE 6. Vessel forms for the slaves at Kings Bay.

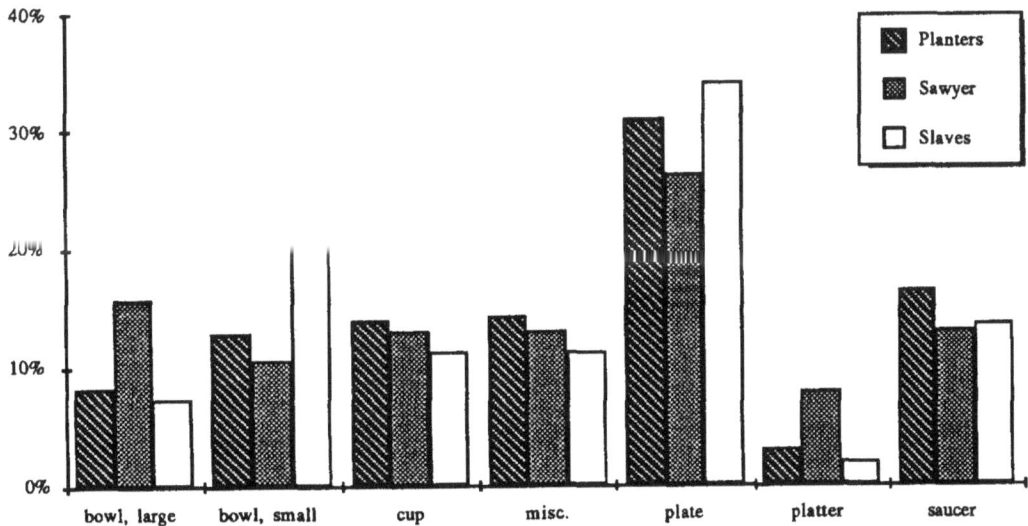

FIGURE 7. Vessel forms, comparing the planters, sawyer, and slaves at Kings Bay.

researchers, we can only compare using the simplistic dichotomy of flatware versus holloware.

For the following discussion, cups, teapots, miscellaneous vessels, and bowls will be subsumed into holloware, while saucers, plates, and platters will be lumped together as flatware. As one can easily see, functional groupings like vessels for serving food or liquids, for eating, for

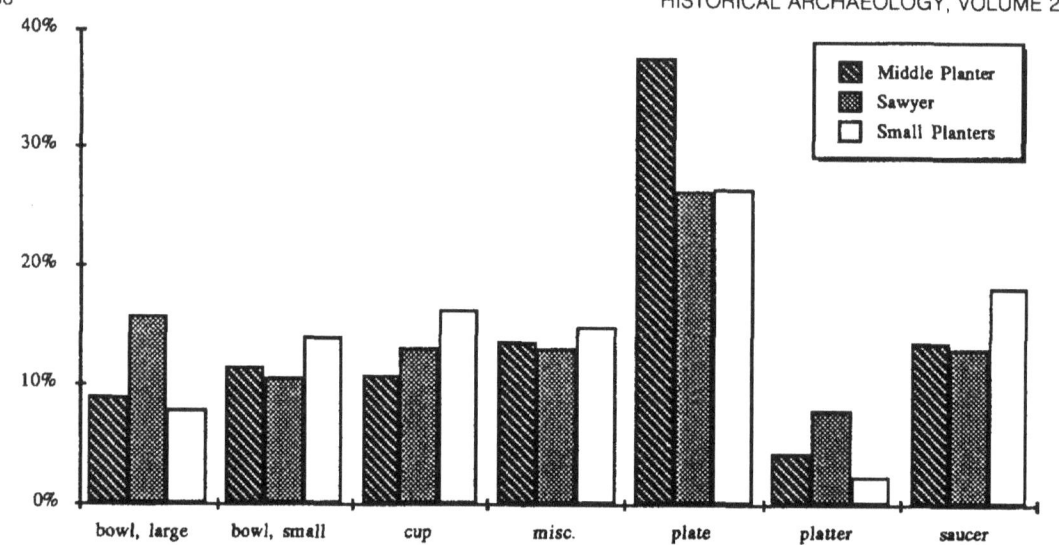

FIGURE 8. Vessel forms, comparing the middle planter, sawyer, and small planters at Kings Bay.

drinking, for storage, cross-cut these two arbitrary shapes of flat and hollow.

By ranking these sites on the frequency of flatwares in the tableware asemblage we derived three groupings. The group with the highest frequency of flatwares—roughly 55%—are planters' kitchens from the large planter at Cannon's Point Plantation, and the middle planters at Sinclair Plantation and at Kings Bay Plantation (Table 4). The second group, 45.1%–51.4% flatware, includes two slave cabins, the James King Site kitchens (Cherry Point Plantation), the overseer at the Cannon's Point Plantation, and the planter at Harmony Hall Plantation. The third group, 19.0%–39.3% flatware, includes the Pike's Bluff planter's assemblage and five slave cabin assemblages. Thus, we may conclude that this analysis, as simple as it is, does provide useful information regarding relative status.

Slaves had higher quantities of holloware, mostly bowls, while planters had more flatware. This generality simply confirms what Otto (1975) found at Cannon's Point more than a decade ago, but with a greater range of data we now see the situation is much more complicated. Indeed, some slave sites were found to have a higher flatware

frequency than some planter sites had. Thus, while there is a strong linear correlation between vessel form and status, with lower status sites having more holiowares, too many sites show exceptions to this trend for it to be any more than suggestive. In addition to this kind of analysis we must therefore turn to other methods to determine relative status.

Status and the CC Index

One way to analyze relative economic status is by assigning each vessel an index value, with plain creamware (CC, or cream colored ware) having an index of 1.0. The CC Index values were derived from potters' price fixing lists assembled by George Miller (1980); thus, vessels with a higher index were more expensive than ones with lower indices. Because the initial settlement of the Kings Bay sites began about 1791, the authors chose to use the 1796 price list whenever possible, or the next closest one when certain categories were not available. The price list chosen should be the one nearest to the date when the ceramics are assumed to have been purchased.

TABLE 4

PERCENTAGE OF CERTAIN VESSEL FORMS IN THE CERAMIC TABLEWARE ASSEMBLAGE FOR KINGS BAY SITES COMPARED TO OTHER PLANTATIONS ON THE GEORGIA COAST

Site	Area	Cup	Teapot	Misc.	Plate	Saucer	Platter	Large Bowl	Small Bowl
Kings Bay Plantation	Kitchen	10.5	1.0	12.7	37.6	13.1	4.2	9.2	11.6
James King Plantation	Kitchen, East	11.2	1.0	11.2	30.6	13.2	4.1	6.1	22.4
James King Plantation	Kitchen, West	14.5	3.4	7.2	28.0	20.7	1.4	9.2	15.5
Harmony Hall Plantation	Kitchen	22.6	4.2	12.1	23.2	19.5	2.4	7.9	7.9
John King	House	13.2	—	13.2	26.3	13.2	7.9	15.8	10.5
Kings Bay Plantation	Slave Cabins	10.6	0.9	16.4	40.4	6.7	1.0	8.7	15.4
Harmony Hall Plantation	Slave Cabin	11.0	1.8	4.6	24.8	22.9	3.7	7.3	23.8
James King Plantation	Slave Cabin	17.9	—	7.1	28.6	10.7	—	3.6	32.2

Site	Area	FLATWARE		TEAWARE		MISC.		BOWLS	
Cannon's Point Plantation[1]	Planter's Kitchen	55.3		34.0		5.7		4.9	
Cannon's Point Plantation[1]	Overseer	46.7		35.0		2.5		15.8	
Cannon's Point Plantation[1]	Slave Cabin	36.4		24.3		5.6		32.7	

Site	Area	FLATWARE	HOLLOWARE
Sinclair[3]	Planter	55.9	44.1
Cannon's Point Plantation[1]	Planter's Kitchen	55.3	44.7
Kings Bay Plantation	Planter's Yard and Kitchen	54.9	45.1
Harmony Hall Plantation	Slave Cabin	51.4	48.6
James King Plantation	Planter's West Kitchen	50.1	49.9
Kings Bay Plantation	Slave Cabins	48.1	51.9
James King Plantation	Planter's East Kitchen	47.9	52.1
John King	House	47.4	52.6
Cannon's Point Plantation[1]	Overseer	46.7	53.3
Harmony Hall Plantation	Planter's Kitchen	45.1	54.9
James King Plantation	Slave Cabin	39.3	60.7
Cannon's Point Plantation[1]	Slave Cabin	36.4	63.6
Pikes Bluff[3]	Planter	35.2	64.8
Sinclair[3]	Slave Cabin	28.6	71.4
Butler Island[2]	Slave Cabin	26.1	73.9
Jones[3]	Slave Cabin	19.0	81.0

[1]calculated from Otto 1984:180 and Table 3.14; Teaware was not defined by Otto, but presumably included teapots, cups, creamers, and saucers; Flatware was defined (Otto 1984:69) as plate, platter, soup plate. The figures here differ from those calculated by Moore (1985:153) for the Cannon's Point assemblages apparently because Moore used Otto's 1975 dissertation.
[2]from Singleton 1980: Table 8; cups and bowls were not distinguished
[3]from Moore 1985:153

The inhabitants of these sites bought their dishes between 1770 and 1834 (median date ranges from 1795 to 1820); it is impossible to tell what year, or at what price, any given vessel was purchased. Likewise, one cannot take into account birthday presents, inheritance, shipping delays, or estate sales. The authors used the price list from the earliest year a decorative type was mentioned in the lists, as long as it was between 1796 and 1834, to evaluate the whole range of decorative types. Porcelain and sponged wares appeared on the price lists so late that the former was left out of the calculations and the latter treated as dipped. All edgeware and transferprinted vessel prices were taken from the 1796 price lists, even when some patterns had not been manufactured until a later date, to avoid confusing the issue. Each tally of indices is made up of scores for different years. Analysis used 1.33 as CC Index for edged large serving bowls.

Ceramics were divided into gross types based on form as shown above: plates, platters, cups, saucers, small and large ($\geq6''$) bowls, teapots, chamberwares and other ceramic forms (Table 7). Over-

TABLE 5
TABLEWARE VESSEL FORMS FOR THE PLANTATIONS AT KINGS BAY.

vessel	CHERRY POINT PLANTATION				HARMONY HALL PLANTATION		KINGS BAY PLANTATION	
	WOODFORD MABRY 182	PLANTER KITCHEN 183a	PLANTER KITCHEN 183c	SLAVE CABIN 183d	PLANTER KITCHEN 194a	SLAVE CABIN 194b	PLANTER KITCHEN 172a	SLAVE CABIN 172b
bowl, large	6	6	19	1	13	8	28	9
bowl, small	4	22	32	9	13	26	36	17
cup	5	11	30	5	37	13	35	13
plate	10	30	58	8	40	26	111	45
platter	3	4	3	0	4	5	12	1
saucer	5	13	43	2	32	25	44	9
miscellaneous	5	12	24	3	26	8	40	20
Tableware Totals	38	98	209	28	165	111	306	114

TABLE 6
PLATE INDEX FOR TABLEWARE VESSEL FORMS FOR THE PLANTATIONS AT KINGS BAY.

vessel	CHERRY POINT PLANTATION				HARMONY HALL PLANTATION		KINGS BAY PLANTATION	
	WOODFORD MABRY 182	PLANTER KITCHEN 183a	PLANTER KITCHEN 183c	SLAVE CABIN 183d	PLANTER KITCHEN 194a	SLAVE CABIN 194b	PLANTER KITCHEN 172a	SLAVE CABIN 172b
bowl, large	.60	.20	.33	.12	.32	.31	.25	.20
bowl, small	.40	.73	.55	1.12	.32	1.00	.32	.38
cup	.50	.37	.52	.62	.92	.50	.32	.29
plate	1.00	1.00	1.00	1.00	1.00	1.00	1.00	1.00
platter	.30	.13	.05	.00	.10	.19	.11	.02
saucer	.50	.43	.74	.25	.80	.96	.40	.20
miscellaneous	.50	.40	.41	.38	.65	.31	.36	.44

glaze polychrome and plain blue painted pearlware received the same value, although overglaze painted wares may not have been in the potters' lists. Willow cups and saucers were classified with other blue transferprinted wares, porcelain was omitted, and blue or green scalloped edging on any vessel not plate or platter was classified as painted.

The results are quite surprising and indicate that while this method is useful, its application on slave sites must be done with caution. First, each plantation kitchen will be compared with its slave site. At the James King Site, the slaves had more expensive cups, the saucers and plates were of similar cost, but small and large bowls were considerably less expensive than the planter's assemblage (Figure 9). At Harmony Hall Plantation, the CC Index shows that the slaves' small bowls

were considerably less expensive, while the plates and platters were more expensive, and the cups and saucers considerably more expensive, than those of the planter there. Large bowls were about the same cost, for the ceramics *discarded at their site*. For the Kings Bay Plantation, the slaves also had somewhat less expensive small bowls, but at least one cabin had more expensive bowls than did the planter; otherwise the slaves had less expensive ceramics.

Comparison between slave sites at Kings Bay reveals that cups and saucers form one subset of the ceramic assemblage as do large and small bowls, because when the assemblage is ordered on the basis of cup CC Index values, the bowl values are inversely proportional. In other words, slave sites with expensive cups and saucers have inex-

TABLE 7
CC INDEX FOR VARIOUS SITES ARRANGED BY INDEX YEAR AND MEAN

SITE	AREA	LOCATION	DATE	INDEX	STATUS	N	CUPS	PLATES	BOWLS	MEAN	SOURCE
Diaz	Privy	Monterey, CA	ca. 1842–ca. 1858	1846	merchant	74	3.59	1.92	1.68	2.69	c
Walker Tavern	—	Detroit, MI	ca. 1834–ca. 1850	1846	tavern	35	2.31	2.44	2.32	2.37	b
Moses Tabbs	Context #1	St. Marys, MD	1800–1840	1846	tenant farmer	16	1.44	1.46	1.29	1.42	b
Green Mansion	—	Windsor, VT	1814–1870	1833	merchant	94	3.04	1.83	1.59	2.29	d
Black Lucy's Garden	—	Andover, MA	1815–1845	1833	freed slave	58	1.68	1.61	1.24	1.53	c
Cannon's Point	Kitchen	St. Simons, GA	1820–1850s	1824	big planter	166	2.50	2.79	1.22	2.61	d
Franklin Glass	House	Portage Co., OH	1824–1832	1824	glass worker	94	2.15	1.86	1.54	1.90	b
Franklin Glass	Factory	Portage Co., OH	1824–1832	1824	laborers	62	2.11	1.47	1.37	1.67	b
Skunk Hollow	B	NJ	—	1824	black laborer	64	1.53	1.51	1.18	1.43	e
Moses Tabbs	Context #2	St. Marys, MD	1840–1860	1824	tenant farmer	41	1.50	1.43	1.20	1.44	b
Jonathan Hale Cabin	—	Summit Co., OH	1810–ca. 1830	1824	farmer	45	1.45	1.23	1.36	1.34	b
Kings Bay Plantation	Kitchen	Camden Co., GA	1791–ca. 1840	1814	middle planter	274	1.94	1.87	1.60	1.81	f
Harmony Hall	Slave Cabin	Camden Co., GA	ca. 1793–ca. 1832	1814	slave	98	2.10	1.88	1.36	1.72	f
Cannon's Point	Slave Cabin	St. Simons, GA	1820s–1850s	1814	slave	80	1.71	2.07	1.27	1.68	c
Kings Bay	Planter average	Camden Co., GA	1791–1850	1814	planter	672	1.78	1.67	1.63	1.68	a
Kings Bay	Slave Average	Camden Co., GA	1791–1832	1814	slaves	208	1.95	1.62	1.61	1.66	f
Kings Bay Plantation	Slave Cabin C	Camden Co., GA	1791–ca. 1815	1814	slave	11	2.25	1.13	1.45	1.64	f
James King	West Kitchen	Camden Co., GA	ca. 1806–ca. 1823	1814	small planter	184	1.72	1.55	1.71	1.62	f
Harmony Hall	Kitchen	Camden Co., GA	ca. 1793–ca. 1832	1814	small planter	129	1.69	1.53	1.56	1.60	f
James King	Slave Cabin	Camden Co., GA	1791–ca. 1823	1814	slave	26	2.30	1.53	1.36	1.59	f
Kings Bay Plantation	Slave Cabin Avg.	Camden Co., GA	1791–ca. 1815	1814	slave	93	1.71	1.37	1.84	1.55	f
James King	East Kitchen	Camden Co., GA	1791–ca. 1806	1814	small planter	83	1.72	1.42	1.62	1.53	f
Kings Bay Plantation	Slave Cabin A	Camden Co., GA	1791–ca. 1815	1814	slave	34	1.33	1.44	1.57	1.47	f
Kings Bay Plantation	Slave Cabin B	Camden Co., GA	1791–ca. 1815	1814	slave	24	2.00	1.44	1.28	1.47	f
John Hamlin	House	Warren Co., NJ	1810–1856	1814	wealthy farmer	18	1.50	1.31	1.86	1.45	f
175 Water St.	Fea. 43	New York, NY	1795–1820	1814	merchants	58	1.80	1.19	1.29	1.33	a
175 Water St.	Fea. 49	New York, NY	1795–1820	1814	merchants	44	1.46	1.00	1.28	1.26	f

John Richardson	Privy/Cistern	Wilmington, DE	1810–ca. 1816?	1802	wealthy	21	3.40	1.93	2.53	2.31	a
					occupants						
Kings Bay Plantation	Kitchen	Camden Co., GA	1791–ca. 1840	1796	middle planter	274	2.22	2.08	1.81	2.03	f
Harmony Hall	Kitchen	Camden Co., GA	ca 1793–ca. 1832	1796	slave	—	2.30	2.11	1.60	1.95	f
Kings Bay	Planter average	Camden Co., GA	1791–1850	1796	planter	672	2.06	1.84	1.90	1.89	a
Kings Bay	Slave average	Camden Co., GA	1791–1832	1796	slaves	208	2.23	1.77	1.93	1.88	f
James King	West Kitchen	Camden Co., GA	ca. 1806–ca. 1823	1796	small planter	184	2.02	1.69	2.03	1.84	f
Harmony Hall	Kitchen	Camden Co., GA	ca 1793–ca. 1832	1796	small planter	129	1.94	1.68	1.77	1.77	f
James King	East Kitchen	Camden Co., GA	1791–ca. 1806	1796	small planter	83	2.02	1.52	2.00	1.74	f
James King	Slave Cabin	Camden Co., GA	1791–ca. 1823	1796	slave	26	2.60	1.61	1.43	1.74	f
Kings Bay Plantation	Slave Cabin C	Camden Co., GA	1791–ca. 1815	1796	slave	11	2.60	1.13	2.00	1.71	f
Thomas Hamlin	—	Warren Co., NJ	ca. 1790–1810	1796	farmer	74	1.67	1.19	2.14	1.68	a
Telco	Test Cut AX	New York, NY	ca. 1810	—	elite	33	1.65	2.02	1.39	1.68	a
Kings Bay Plantation	Slave Cabin A	Camden Co., GA	1791–ca. 1815	1796	slave	37	1.53	1.51	2.02	1.68	f
Kings Bay Plantation	Slave Cabin Avg.	Camden Co., GA	1791–ca. 1815	1796	slave	93	2.00	1.46	1.89	1.66	f
John King	House	Camden Co., GA	ca. 1801–ca. 1806	1796	sawyer	32	2.10	1.37	1.85	1.64	f
Kings Bay Plantation	Slave Cabin B	Camden Co., GA	1791–ca. 1815	1796	slave	24	2.33	1.54	1.57	1.64	f
Kings Bay Plantation	Slave Cabin D	Camden Co., GA	1791–ca. 1815	1796	slave	11	1.80	1.37	1.76	1.52	f
Barclays	Fea. 48	New York, NY	ca. 1800	1796	several	60	1.53	1.48	1.25	1.39	a

Sources: a Morin et al. 1986:6.43–45; Morin and Klein n.d.
          b Miller 1980
          c Felton and Schulz 1983:76–81
          d Spencer-Wood and Heberling 1984
          e Geismar 1982
          f Adams and Boling 1987

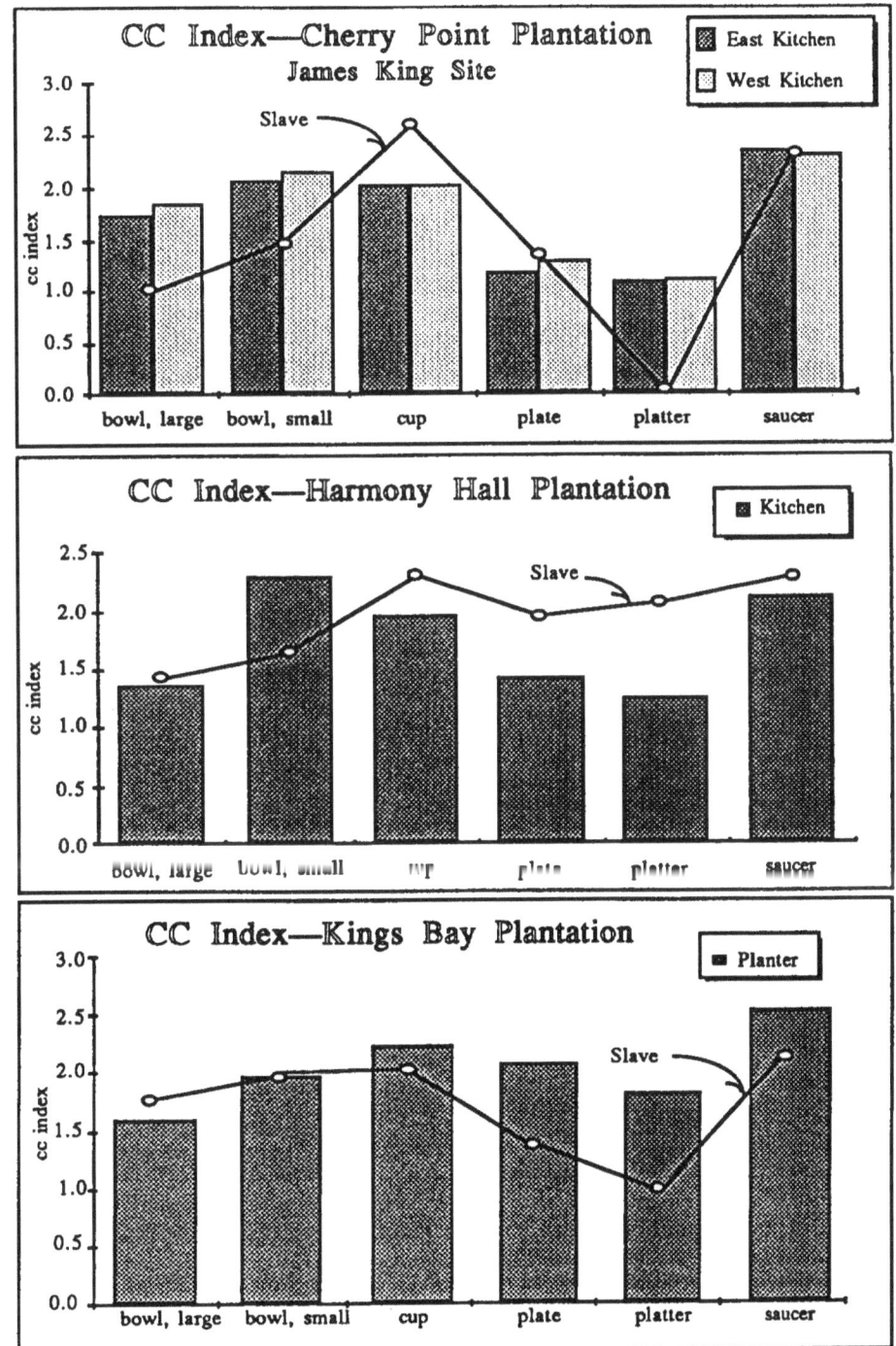

FIGURE 9. CC index for the planters and slaves on different plantations at Kings Bay.

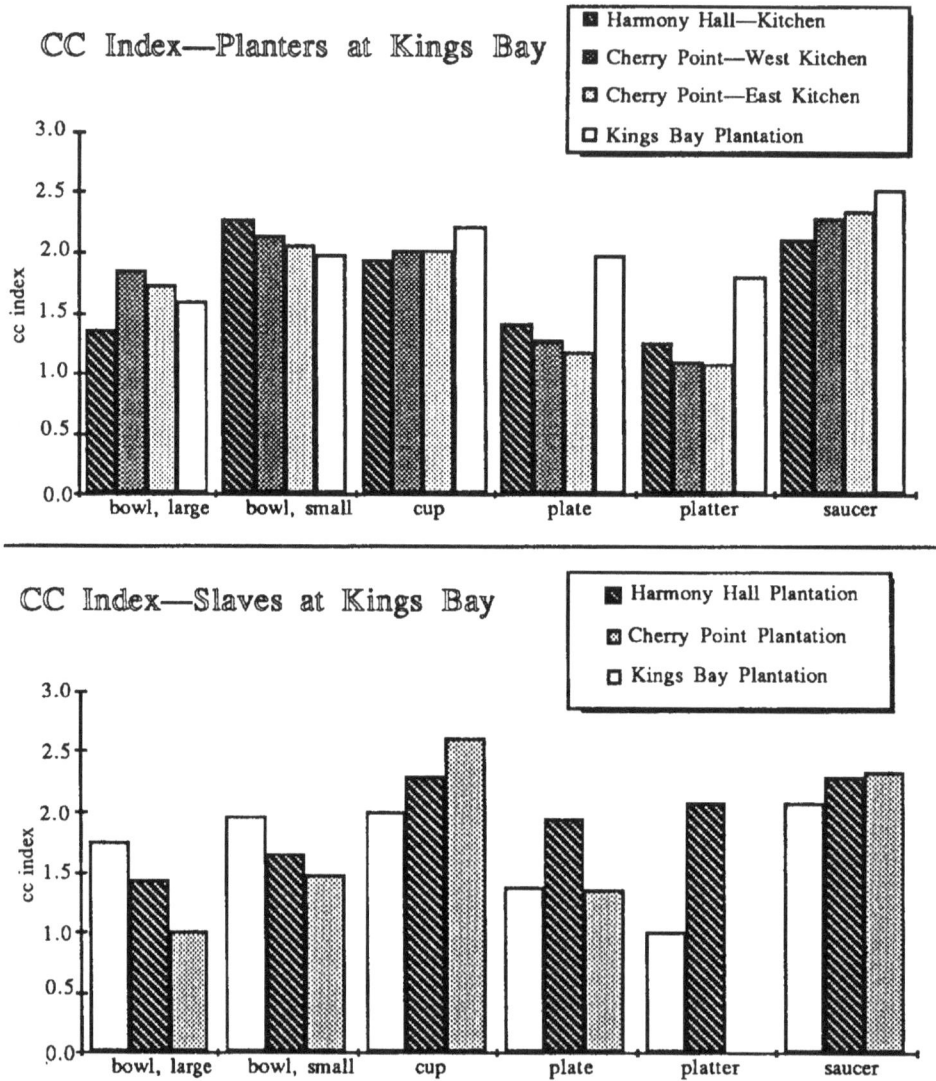

FIGURE 10. CC index for planters and for slaves at Kings Bay.

pensive bowls, while sites with inexpensive cups and saucers have more expensive bowls (Figure 10). The same is true in the planter households, but the differences are not as impressive. Since these are not dependent values, except in terms of capital expended on a given amount of ceramic vessels, this observation has some meaning. Why would planters and slaves alike have good tea service and cheap bowls or conversely cheaper tea service and more expensive bowls?

One would expect that the two kitchens at the James King Site (the east one is slightly earlier than the other) would have similar CC Index values, since they represent the same household.

Indeed, the two assemblages have very similar CC Indices, with the later kitchen having a slightly higher (1.84 vs. 1.74) value. If other evidence were available to support it, one would suggest a slightly higher economic status for James King, than for his parents (who built the first kitchen). Unfortunately, such supportive data do not exist for this site.

If the two kitchens at the James King Site are combined with the planter assemblage from the Harmony Hall Plantation to represent the small planter at Kings Bay, one can compare that with the CC Index for a middle planter, Thomas King at Kings Bay Plantation, a free white sawyer at the John King Site (Woodford Mabry), and their slaves. One would assume that order (based upon posited wealth) would be revealed in the ceramic assemblages of each. For the whites, this was true, but this was not the case if the slaves were included (Figure 11). The one middle planter had more expensive plates and saucers, the small planter had the most expensive small bowls and large bowls, and the slaves had the most expensive cups and platters. In every ceramic vessel form except bowls, the slave had more expensive vessels than the small planter and the sawyer. The middle planter generally had better ceramics than his neighboring small planters, bowls being the only exception. But this was tempered somewhat by the slaves having some even better ceramic vessels.

Grouping the planters together, to compare with the sawyer and slaves, yields essentially the same observations. Planter and renter had nearly the same price large bowls and cups, but in every other vessel the sawyer renter, Woodford Mabry at the John King Site, had much less expensive items (Figure 11). But the slaves had more expensive small bowls, cups, and platters. With the exception of large bowls, the slaves had more expensive ceramics than the white renter. (The identification of Woodford Mabry as white is based upon the paucity of free blacks in the county in 1800 and the fact that he rented the land from John King. He does not show up in the 1800 or 1810 censuses.)

The Thomas King ceramics do stand out for all but cups, large bowls, and small bowls. Thomas and Mary King's plates and platters were nearly half again as expensive as those of the other planters, but their cups and saucers were only somewhat more expensive. If glassware could be considered on a similar scale the entire dinner table of Thomas and Mary King would stand high over those of the smaller landowners, who had nothing near the splendor represented by gold-painted goblets, other fine stemware, and decanters. Likewise if porcelain tablewares could be calculated in the Thomas King and Harmony Hall tea equipages, well supplied with porcelain, would rise in apparent status. If miscellaneous tableware (teapots, vases, soup tureens) could be measured the small planters would cluster more closely, and Thomas King would again come out far above them.

Since this discussion treats ceramics as indicators of household finances, platters and serving dishes, which are nonessential, even luxury items, must be taken into account somehow. For convenience in this analysis, platters were given the index value of a 10″ plate of the same decorative category. However, a platter's price varied as much with size as it did with decoration. The price lists used have little chance of providing a ranking between archaeological assemblages, in which two or three broken rim fragments were classified as "platter," because the size of a platter must be known before its price can be attached, and determining if an oval platter was 10″ or 11″ from a small sherd is impossible. Also, the price difference between the two is comparatively large (Miller 1980:23–25). However, it hardly seems reasonable to exclude platters from this analysis, since they were such valuable items. A large creamware platter was more of of a luxury item than a transferprinted dinner plate—half again as expensive, and not as generally useful.

Therefore, a system of ranking sites by the value of serving dishes in the assemblage was necessary. In this case the results fit well with the other ceramic price patterns. Estimations, based on the dimensions of the few measurable platters, and how rim and base fragments of the others compared to them, were made of the size of each platter found on a site. Serving dishes of types listed on the Staffordshire Potters' price list for 1796, used by Miller, were counted from each site.

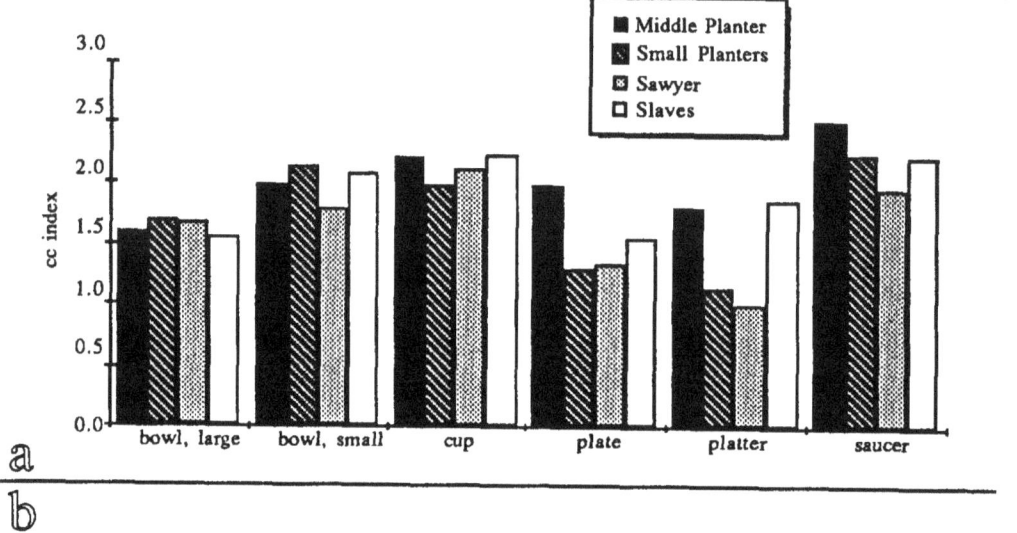

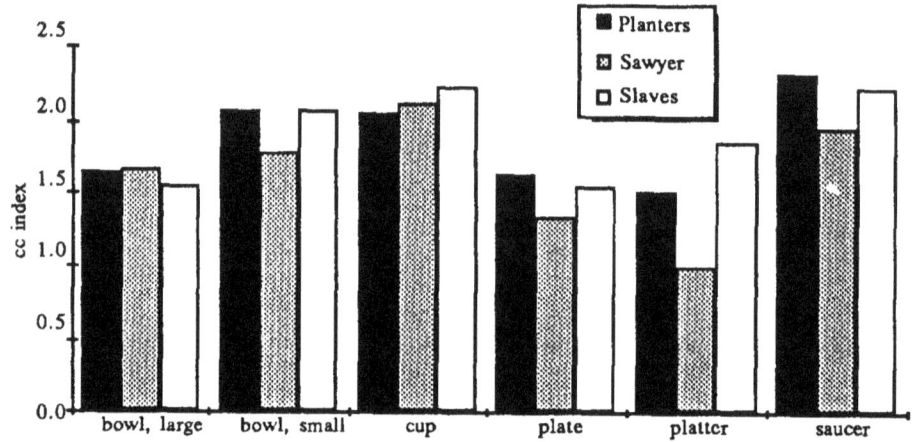

FIGURE 11. CC index by economic status at Kings Bay.

The price in English pence per dozen for each vessel was determined, and various weighting systems were tested to find one which made sense for Kings Bay.

The system which proved most useful for ranking sites by average value of platters also was least meaningful, in that it did not correct for the sample size (which in most cases was one to three vessels). That index gave a 12″ creamware platter, which seemed to be a good generic vessel, a value of 1.00 (in real terms, 48 pence/dozen). When all platters from all sites were run through this equation, the results were: Harmony Hall Slave, 3.75; Kings Bay Plantation Kitchen, 2.40; James King West Kitchen, 1.75; Harmony Hall Kitchen, 1.44; James King East Kitchen, 1.00; Woodford Mabry, 0.75, Kings Bay Plantation Slave, 0.62 (dividing the total 2.50 by the four cabins), and James King Slave 0.00, for there were no platters there.

This order, with one exception, is in keeping

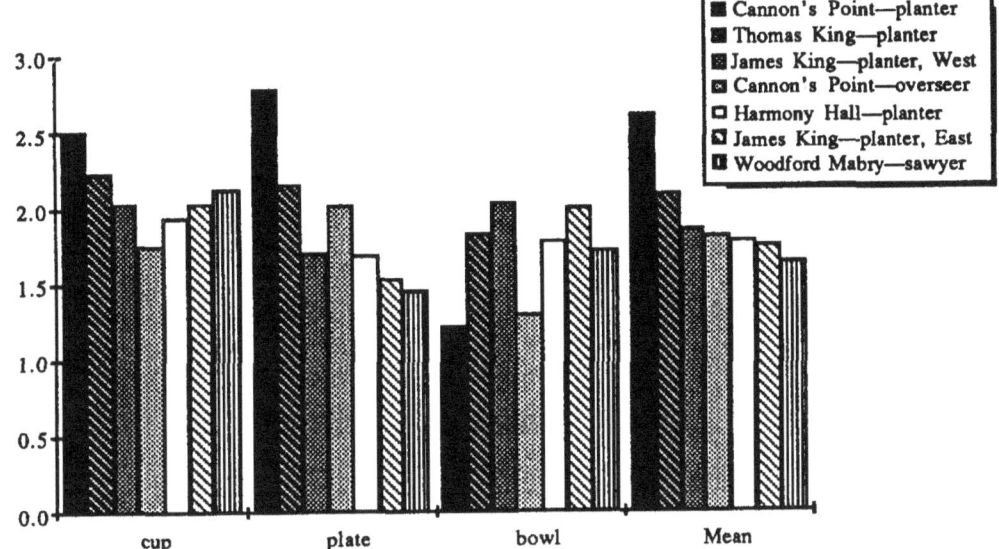

FIGURE 12. CC index for planters, overseer, and sawyer on the Georgia coast.

with the expected economic ranking of the occupants. The middle planter is first, the small planters next and close together, the sawyer close below them and the slaves, last; the Harmony Hall slave site does not fit into any appropriate pattern. One other approach which proved equally interesting was to add up the raw prices of all the platters and serving dishes for which prices were available, and rank the sites by this sum. In this case, the costliness of the Kings Bay Plantation ceramics was even more marked, and the anomalous Harmony Hall slave site became much more nearly equal to the small planter sites. It seemed to be the most vivid measure of conspicuous consumption possible.

The Harmony Hall Plantation slave quarters cannot, in fact, be compared well to any other site examined here in terms of average ceramic value, and another approach will be necessary to describe it. Its expensive platters distorted comparison of slaves and planters, in which a 40% lead in cost of platters appears in the slave column. Only one platter was recovered among the five other slave cabins excavated around the bay, and it was of the

most inexpensive variety. Plates, which are important in tableware in Kings Bay area slave quarters, come out the same in both social classes. Leaving aside platters as an unmanageable form to sample, one can see some of the cruder trends already mentioned reestablished as general. Specifically, cups and saucers are higher in average price among the slaves, large bowls are very close, and small bowls inexpensive, at a price between dipped and painted. The next detail to consider is, of course, how many of the different-priced wares each domestic site possessed.

Comparison of the Kings Bay sites with those at Cannon's Point Plantation reveals that the large planter there had far more expensive ceramics (Figure 12). One explanation for the high index values there may be that a later price list should have been used to calculate it—the 1814 and 1824 price lists were used, instead of the 1833 list (Spencer-Wood and Heberling 1984). While the Cannon's Point Plantation dates from 1791 to 1860 (and later), re-examination of the ceramics from those sites revealed no creamware and no other ceramics with dates definitely earlier than about

1830. The entire assemblage is much later than that from Kings Bay.

Following Cannon's Point Plantation in value, the Thomas King assemblage from Kings Bay Plantation was next, followed by the James King West Kitchen, the Cannon's Point Plantation Overseer, and the other sites at Kings Bay. Clearly, using the mean CC Index, the sites can be ordered in what we would surmise is a reasonable approximation of wealth, except that the Cannon's Point Plantation overseer should, it would seem, have been closer to the values for Woodford Mabry, the sawyer on Cherry Point Plantation. What this suggests is that the relative economic status of an overseer on a large plantation is roughly equal to that of a small planter. That overseer, though, had the lowest value of cups, perhaps suggesting that his household did not have a public position to maintain through entertaining guests on the premises.

Comparison of the Kings Bay sites with others outside the Southeast provides a way of ranking these sites (Figures 13, 14; Table 7). Selection of these sites was based upon the available published data (Felton and Schulz 1983:76–81; Geismar 1982; Morin et al. 1986:43–45; Morin and Klein n.d.; Miller 1980; Spencer-Wood and Heberling 1984). These were divided into three groups, those with a mean over 2.0, with a mean of between 1.5 and 2.0, and those with a mean below 1.5. Each of the individuals in the high grouping is known to have been a wealthy individual, upper class would not be an unreasonable label for these people (Table 5). The individuals with a mean less than 1.5 could be labelled lower class, for they are small farmers, tenant farmers, and tenement dwellers. The middle group, 1.5–2.0 is not necessarily what would be called middle class, and should not be labelled such. It is most interesting that each of the slave sites analyzed falls into this group, along with the small planters, factory worker, plantation overseer, and so forth.

A number of sites have been identified as having been occupied by blacks exclusively, for example, Black Lucy's Garden (Baker 1980) and Skunk Hollow (Geismar 1982). Comparing those sites to Cannon's Point and to the Kings Bay site averages revealed that in every vessel category, the slaves

had more expensive ceramics than the free blacks (Figure 15a). However, when the sites at Kings Bay are compared individually with the free black sites, the free black was found to have more expensive plates than half of the Kings Bay slave sites (Figure 15b). The general implication of this, bearing further investigation with a much larger sample of sites, is that free blacks may have had less disposable income, less access to expensive cast-offs, or chose to use their income in a different manner.

Using crude measures of income-disposal to determine status is a difficult process. Even when the subjects are still alive and willing to respond to questionnaires on what their, and their neighbor's, dishes mean to them, evaluating the household's status is even more complicated. For this reason, information about the Kings Bay inhabitants' dishes, beyond relative market price, is included here. Clear differences existed among the decorative quality of dishes on the various sites. By this we mean that a coherent taste, or devotion to ornament, of the family which had purchased the dishes emerged from the ceramic assemblages. The Harmony Hall planter household had a wide selection of fruit decorated early polychrome vessels, plenty of which represented partial sets. The household also owned a small selection of restrained blue transferprinted teawares and a miscellaneous collection of lathe decorated dipped bowls, plain creamware, and edged plates. The two James King kitchens were furnished with a heterogeneity of small-patterned printed, early polychrome painted, blue painted, overglaze painted, saltglazed, and creamwares. The Kings Bay Plantation kitchen had several sets of elaborate, large-pattern printed dishes, in tea and table sets, more variety in edged plates and dipped bowls than any other site, and a minimal assortment of unmatched painted dishes. Woodford Mabry set plain tablewares. The slaves had plain ceramics, like their masters did also, along with a few expensive decorated ones.

Conclusions

While the plantation bighouse has been studied in numerous circumstances as part of architectural

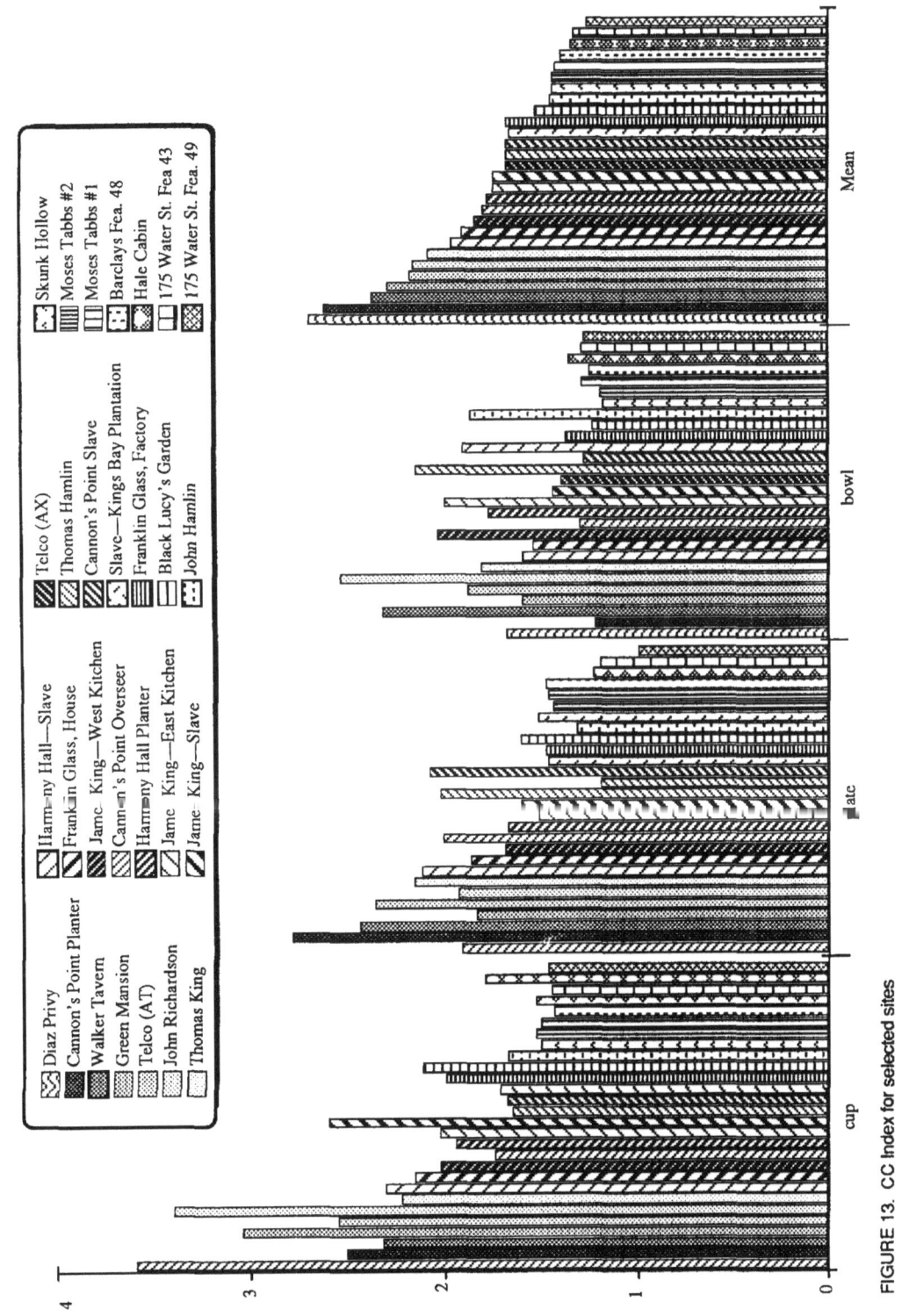

FIGURE 13. CC Index for selected sites

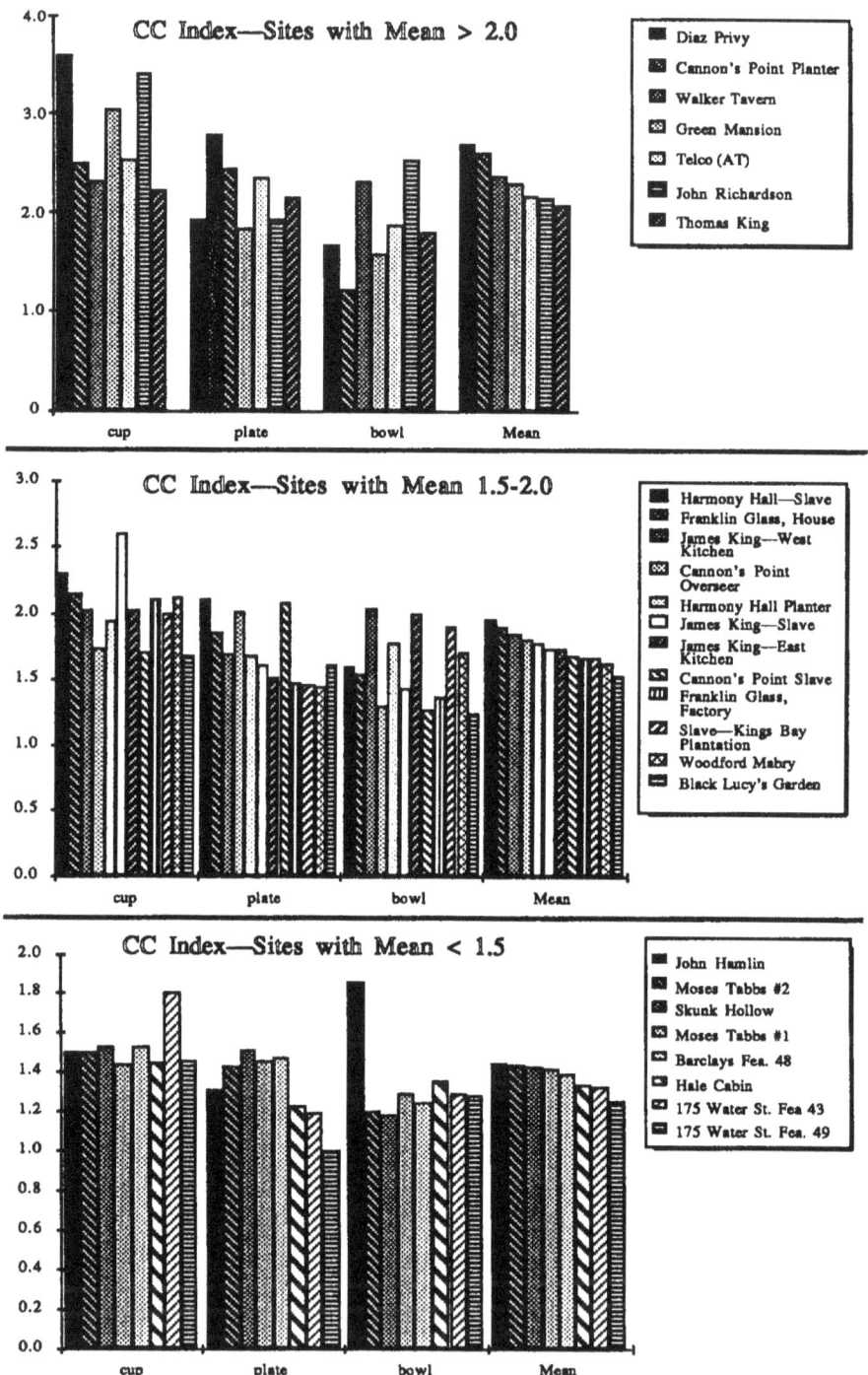

FIGURE 14. CC Index, comparing sites by mean range.

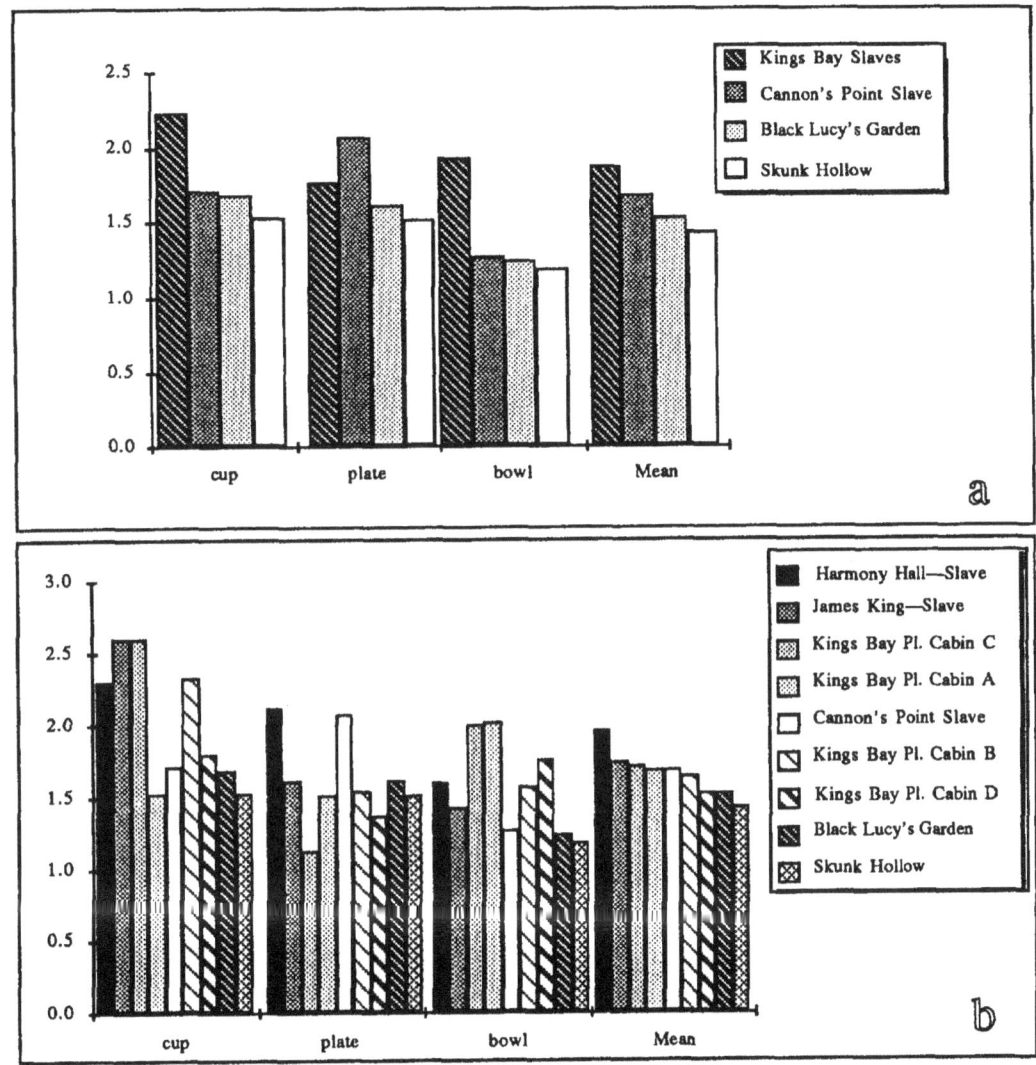

FIGURE 15. CC Index for sites with black occupants.

reconstruction, less work has been done on the material culture of the planter class. Otto found that the planter's wife at Cannon's Point set her table primarily with transferprinted plates, in sharp contrast to the banded bowls of the slave cabins (1984:151). Charles Orser (n.d.) in a re-analysis of the published data on Cannon's Point artifacts, found that ceramics were among the least sensitive indicators of status. William Kelso argued that it is in other material culture that we should be looking for status indicators. "As for other artifact patterns, matched sets of ceramics, monogrammed wine bottles, book clasps, jewelry, and coats of arms are indisputably all items that indicate wealth and high status far more strongly than whatever one can tentatively conjecture from masses of numbers of mugs or cups or bowls that happened to have been broken and thrown away" (Kelso

1984:205–206). The work at the various plantations at Kings Bay suggested that the wealthier planter had a greater variety of vessel forms for ceramics and glassware, rather than simply more expensive ones.

Status can be inferred from the artifacts, when we have sufficient sample size and a regional data base for comparison. Comparison by ceramic wares, for instance, revealed that slaves tended to have more coarse wares, that planters had more refined wares, or both possibilities together. Comparison by vessel form showed that while slaves did have many bowls, they also had many plates.

Using the CC Index was useful, because it showed that when one examines a larger variety of sites and distinguishes their ceramic assemblages by vessels, slaves might have more expensive vessels than their masters had for certain forms, and the slaves on these plantations had more expensive ceramics than many of the Northern white farmers and businessmen had on their table. Ceramics provide a good indicator of status, when approached as done here, but other indicators are also important, like the frequency of French gunflints, durable architecture, and reliance on different food species (Adams et al. 1987).

One important question not answered by this analysis was where the slaves acquired their ceramics and other material culture. The underlying assumption of nearly all previous research was that of a paternalistic system of the planter providing the ceramics and other material goods used by the slave. Whether these consisted of hand-me-downs from the planter's family or items purchased specifically for the slaves is an important distinction, but another alternative must be considered. The plantations at Kings Bay used the task system, which meant the slaves had the opportunity to earn outside income. The slaves may have purchased their own ceramics with money they themselves earned. Few, if any, of the ceramics from the slave quarters of the three plantations were hand-me-downs, for the matches between the planter and slave assemblages were in the commonest types of dishes and those assemblages showed no evidence of any substantial time lag. This means the ceramics were purchased and were used immediately:

perhaps the planter bought the ceramics solely for the slaves' usage, or the slaves bought them. Quite possibly the planter bought expensive transferprinted dishes for his slaves, even when plain creamware or pearlware would have sufficed. The slave assemblages ranged from 7.81% to 19.33% transferprinted wares, compared to 10.94% to 24.31% for the planter assemblages, with the means being 13.17% for slaves' vessels and 17.61% for the planters' vessels. Conversely, is it likely that the slaves would spend their income on more expensive items? Perhaps not, if one wishes to continue the paternalistic viewpoint of so many historians and historical archaeologists. But if one wishes to recognize that the slaves developed their own culture and some participated freely within the Southern market economy, archaeologists should reassess the evidence collected previously.

In the future, it is hoped that researchers will not eliminate slave data just because it does not fit their preconceived notion of slave access to material culture. Yet current studies of market access only tend to perpetuate this misunderstanding (e.g., Orser 1987:127; Spencer-Wood and Heberling 1987:70, 80). On gang labor system plantations most of the material culture was provided to the slave by the planter or made by slaves on the plantation, but on task labor system plantations the slave had the opportunity to participate directly within the market system. The degree of this participation has not been investigated adequately, but if the work of Morgan (1982, 1983) and the CC Index analysis here is any indication, that market participation was considerable. Indeed, on such plantations slaves may be better understood within the context of being peasants or serfs, regarding their economic status. Their legal status was still as chattel slave, of course, but their economic freedoms were much greater than most people realize.

ACKNOWLEDGMENTS

Archaeological research was conducted at Kings Bay with a contract (N00025-79C-0013) between the U.S. Navy and the University of Florida; the senior author served as Principal Investigator. We would like to thank Stephen Alexandrowicz, Susan Alexandrowicz, George L. Miller, and Timothy B. Riordan for their assistance in the ceramic analysis. This article was adapted from Chapters 12 and 13 of the site report (Boling and Adams 1987; Adams and Boling 1987). We would like to thank the anonymous reviewers of *Historical Archaeology* for their comments and suggestions.

REFERENCES

ADAMS, WILLIAM HAMPTON
  1987 Plantation Archaeology: An Overview. *In* Historical Archaeology of Plantations at Kings Bay, Camden County, Georgia, edited by W.H. Adams, pp. 9–22. *Reports of Investigations* 5. Department of Anthropology, University of Florida, Gainesville.

ADAMS, WILLIAM HAMPTON, WILLIAM R. ADAMS, CAROLYN ROCK, AND JANIS KEARNEY-WILLIAMS
  1987 Foodways on the Plantations at Kings Bay: Hunting, Fishing, and Raising Food. *In* Historical Archaeology of Plantations at Kings Bay, Camden County, Georgia, edited by W.H. Adams, pp. 225–76. *Reports of Investigations* 5. Department of Anthropology, University of Florida, Gainesville.

ADAMS, WILLIAM HAMPTON AND SARAH JANE BOLING
  1987 Material Culture and Status on the Plantations at Kings Bay. *In* Historical Archaeology of Plantations at Kings Bay, Camden County, Georgia, edited by W. H. Adams, pp. 293–310. *Reports of Investigations* 5. Department of Anthropology, University of Florida, Gainesville.

ADAMS, HOWARD G
  1980 The Antebellum Waverly Community. *Waverly Plantation: Ethnoarchaeology of a Tenant Farming Community*, edited by W.H. Adams, pp. 75–100. National Technical Information Service, Washington, D.C.

BAKER, VERNON G.
  1980 Archaeological Visibility of Afro-American Culture: An Example from Black Lucy's Garden, Andover, Massachusetts. *Archaeological Perspectives on Ethnicity in America*, edited by Robert L. Schuyler, pp. 29–37. Baywood, Farmingdale, New York.

BOLING, SARAH JANE, AND WILLIAM HAMPTON ADAMS
  1987 Foodways on the Plantations at Kings Bay: Putting Food on the Table. *In* Historical Archaeology of Plantations at Kings Bay, Camden County, Georgia, edited by W.H. Adams, pp. 277–92. *Reports of Investigations* 5. Department of Anthropology, University of Florida, Gainesville.

BOOTH, SALLY S.
  1971 *Hung, Strung, and Potted: A History of Eating in Colonial America*. Potter, New York.

CADE, J. B.
  1935 Out of the Mouths of Ex-Slaves. *Journal of Negro History* 20:294–337.

DeBow, J.D.B.
  1854 *Statistical View of the United States*. Beverley Tucker, Washington, D.C.

FELTON, DAVID L. AND PETER D. SCHULZ
  1983 The Diaz Collection: Material Culture and Social Change in Mid-Nineteenth-Century Monterey. *California Archeological Reports 23*. Cultural Resource Management Unit, Resource Protection Division, California Department of Parks and Recreation.

FRAZIER, E. FRANKLIN
  1930 The Negro Slave Family. *Journal of Negro History* 15(1):198–259.

GEISMAR, JOAN H.
  1982 *The Archaeology of Social Disintegration in Skunk Hollow, A Nineteenth Century Rural Black Community*. Academic Press, New York.

HUNDLEY, DAVID ROBINSON
  1860 *Social Relations in Our Southern States*. Henry B. Price, New York. [reprinted 1973, Arno Press]

KELSO, WILLIAM M.
  1984 *Kingsmill Plantations, 1619–1800: Archaeology of Country Life in Colonial Virginia*. Academic Press, New York.

KEMBLE, FRANCIS ANNE
  1863 *Journal of a Residence on a Georgian Plantation in 1838–1839*. Longman, Green, Longman, Roberts, & Green, London.

LEWIS, KENNETH E
  1985 Plantation Layout and Function in the South Carolina Lowcountry. *The Archaeology of Slavery and Plantation Life*, edited by Theresa Singleton, pp. 35–65. Academic Press, New York.

MILLER, GEORGE L.
  1980 Classification and Economic Scaling of 19th Century Ceramics. *Historical Archaeology* 14:1–41.

MOORE, SUE MULLINS
  1985 Social and Economic Status on the Coastal Plantation: An Archaeological Perspective. *The Archaeology of Slavery and Plantation Life*, edited by Theresa Singleton, pp. 141–60. Academic Press, New York.

MORGAN, PHILIP D.
  1982 Work and Culture: The Task System and the World of Low Country Blacks, 1700 to 1880. *William and Mary Quarterly* 39(Series 3):563–99.
  1983 The Ownership of Property by Slaves in the Mid-19th Century Low Country. *Journal of Southern History* 49(3):399–434.

MORIN, EDWARD M., TERRY H. KLEIN, AMY FRIED-
LANDER, MALLORY GORDON, AND META JANOWITZ
1986 *Hamlin Site (28WA532) Archaeological Data Recovery I-78, (103) Section Four Pohatcong Township,
Borough of Alpha, Warren County, New Jersey.*
Report prepared by Louis Berger & Associates, East
Orange, New Jersey, for the Federal Highway Administration and the New Jersey Department of Transportation.

MORIN, EDWARD M., AND TERRY H. KLEIN
n.d. The Hamlin Site, 1780 to 1856: A Study of Rural
Consumer Behavior. *Pennsylvania Archaeologist.* In
press.

OLMSTED, FREDERICK LAW
1856 *Journey in the Seaboard Slave States: With Remarks
on Their Economy.* Dix and Edwards, New York.

ORSER, CHARLES E., JR.
n.d. Archaeology and Antebellum Plantation Society in the
American South. Ms.
1987 Plantation Status and Consumer Choice: A Materialist
Framework for Historical Archaeology. *Consumer
Choice in Historical Archaeology,* edited by S.
Spencer-Wood, pp. 121–37. Plenum, New York.

OTTO, JOHN SOLOMON
1975 *Status Differences and the Archaeological Record: A
Comparison of Planter, Overseer, and Slave Sites
from Cannon's Point Plantation (1794–1861), St.
Simons Island, Georgia.* PhD dissertation, Department of Anthropology, University of Florida. University Microfilms, Ann Arbor.
1977 Artifacts and Status Differences—A Comparison of
Ceramics from Planter, Overseer, and Slave Sites on
an Antebellum Plantation. *Research Strategies in
Historical Archaeology,* edited by Stanley South, pp.
91–118. Academic, New York.
1979 Slavery in a Coastal Community—Glynn County
(1790–1861). *Georgia Historical Quarterly* 64(2):
461–68.
1984 *Cannon's Point Plantation, 1794–1860: Living Conditions and Status Patterns in the Old South.* Academic Press, New York.

PHILLIPS, ULRICH BONNELL
1929 *Life and Labor in the Old South.* Little, Brown,
Boston.

RAWICK, GEORGE P.
1972 The American Slave: A Composite Autobiography.
(Vol. 1. From Sundown to Sunup: The Making of the
Black Community.) *Contributions in Afro-American
and African Studies* 11. Greenwood Press, Westport,
Connecticut.

REITZ, ELIZABETH J., TYSON GIBBS, AND TED A.
RATHBUN
1985 Archaeological Evidence for Subsistence on Coastal
Plantations. *The Archaeology of Slavery and Planta-
tion Life,* edited by Theresa Singleton, pp. 163–91.
Academic Press, New York.

ROTH, RODRIS
1961 Tea Drinking in Eighteenth Century America: Its
Etiquette and Equipage. *United States National Museum Bulletin 225.* Washington, D.C.

SINGLETON, THERESA A.
1980 The Archaeology of Afro-American Slavery in
Coastal Georgia: A Regional Perspective of Slave
Household and Community Patterns. Unpublished
Ph.D. dissertation, Department of Anthropology,
University of Florida, Gainesville.

SPENCER-WOOD, SUZANNE M. AND SCOTT D. HEBER-
LING
1984 Ceramics and Socio-Economic Status of the Green
Family, Windsor, Vermont. *Northeast Historical Archaeology* 13:33–52.
1987 Consumer Choices in White Ceramics: A Comparison
of Eleven Early Nineteenth-Century Sites. *Consumer
Choice in Historical Archaeology,* edited by S.
Spencer-Wood, pp. 55–84. Plenum, New York.

STAMPP, KENNETH
1956 *The Peculiar Institution.* Vintage, New York.

WEAVER, HERBERT
1945 *Mississippi Farmers, 1850–1860.* Peter Smith, Glou-
cester, Massachusetts.

WOODSON, CARTER G. (EDITOR)
1968 *Free Negro Owners of Slaves in the United States in
1830, Together with Absentee Ownership of Slaves in
the United States in 1830* (reprint of 1924 ed.).
Negroe Universities Press, New York.

WILLIAM HAMPTON ADAMS
DEPARTMENT OF ANTHROPOLOGY
OREGON STATE UNIVERSITY
CORVALLIS, OREGON 97331

SARAH JANE BOLING
LIBRARY AND INFORMATION SCIENCE
SIMMONS COLLEGE
BOSTON, MASSACHUSETTS 02115

DAVID W. BABSON

The Archaeology of Racism and Ethnicity on Southern Plantations

Introduction

Ethnic studies have recently received great emphasis in American historical archaeology. Three groups have commonly been studied: blacks or African Americans, Hispanics, and Overseas Chinese (Staski n.d.). Each of these groups is seen as having an emic identity within the historic period being studied, an identity which is connected to the identity held by members of the present groups that descend from these historical ancestors (Staski n.d.). Indeed, a major reason why these three groups are studied is the desire of these present groups to understand their ancestors. Due to problems with biased or incomplete written records (Deetz 1977:7–8), archaeology is embraced as a method of inquiry, of building a bridge of understanding between these present groups and their forebears.

Such studies assume a continuity between the historical ethnic groups and their present descendants, so that, for instance, in the case of African Americans, a certain category or definition of ethnicity will be common between an 18th-century slave and a modern black person. To date, archaeology has attempted to describe this connection, first, by establishing the presence and vitality of past ethnic groups from the archaeological record—for example, Ferguson's identification of Colono ceramics as the products of black craftswomen (Ferguson 1980) and not of Native Americans, as had been thought previously (Noël Hume 1962a)—and second, by studying the "normative lives" of members of past groups. In the second instance, a narrative of everyday life is devised from which historical, social, or personal inferences can be drawn by the group's modern students.

Neither of these approaches is, in any way, wrong or misdirected. The social purpose they serve, especially in revealing the proud history of groups who have been unjustly discredited in the past or present, is vitally important. In this purpose, archaeology may serve well in creating a bond between present members of ethnic groups and their honored heritage as a way of fostering a strong, positive ethnic identity. Still, however, in simple procedural or technical terms, some problems may be encountered in fulfilling these most necessary functions.

One problem is that any study which proceeds simply on the basis of identifying ethnic markers, but stops at this basic level, will likely prove too simplistic to be of much value. Colono ceramics again provide an example. Recent research (Ferguson n.d.) reveals that these ceramics are not simply the product of enslaved African Americans, but rather of creole cultures created as adaptive responses to complex interactions between Africans, Native Americans, and Europeans, interactions which, furthermore, varied by the different geographical and cultural arenas in which they took place. Using Colono ceramics as a simple ethnic marker which equates with African Americans is an inaccurate oversimplification.

A more serious problem concerns the uncritical acceptance of a simple equation between past and present ethnic groups. A Gambian Muslim, kidnapped in Africa in the late 18th century, for example, is certainly the ancestor of a modern black family (Haley 1976). Important questions remain, however, such as: Was his experience, as an African, a Gambian, a Muslim, or as a slave in America, similar at all to the experience of a modern black American? Was this historical figure's own identity that of a black, an African, a Gambian, or a Muslim, a combination of these, or all of them in some succession? Certain broad similarities between this ancestor and his descendants may occur. The most unfortunate, perhaps, is the fact that each has experienced or will experience forms of oppression that are based in their ethnicity. Can these experiences be equated, and will each therefore have a similar ethnic identity? Archaeologists often assume that these questions have been answered and seldom design studies which incorporate these preliminary issues into a greater understanding of present and past ethnicity.

Simply accepting an "ethnic group" as a fact, as a goal to be identified and reached, makes for a stagnant study and tends to belittle and reify the groups in which archaeologists are interested. Stopping inquiry at the level of identifying an ethnic group, and then assuming that this group is historically equivalent to its modern descendants, prohibits any possibility of understanding this group's history, especially its growth and change in identity through time. An important component of this change must be how groups interacted with other identifiable, historically defined ethnic groups, particularly those which were antagonistic or oppressive toward the group under study. Such groups are themselves open to such studies, oriented toward delineating their membership, their interactions, and their alliances with or antagonisms against other groups. Above all, ethnic groups must be studied as fluid entities in a constant process of *interaction* with other groups, their allies, neutrals, or antagonists.

This research focus leads to the study of racism. This virulent ideology, enacted both in the past and in the present, can be an important determinant of ethnic interaction. It functions to allow one group to dominate another for its economic or social benefit.

Racism, however, also can help to define ethnic groups. Dominant, elite, or oppressor groups are defined by their members' acceptance of the ideology of racism, the perceived benefits it affords, and their often active ignorance of its heavy social costs. Subordinate or victimized groups are, of course, never unaware of the costs they pay as a result of attempts to impose this inimical ideology upon them. This understanding may also enable them to forge a stronger group, to understand themselves as an ethnic group in active resistance to their oppressors. This almost certainly happened to the people torn from so many different African societies, cultures, and ethnic groups, who were brought to America and became African Americans as they actively resisted the severe oppression of their new status as slaves.

It must be noted, however, that this way of constructing a new ethnic identity can proceed only under certain, perhaps incomplete, forms of racist ideology. If a variety of racism proceeds to its logical conclusion and becomes genocidal as it did in the Holocaust or during the destruction of Native American groups in the 19th century, victims' groups may not have a chance to form successfully, especially if their military efforts to resist their persecutors are not successful. Arrested racism, where the interests of the dominant group require them to preserve, at some minimal level, the lives of the oppressed group, may be the only form of racism that allows the creation of an enduring ethnic group, based on the resistance this group naturally undertakes to its oppression and oppressors. An example of this process may be seen in the interaction between enslaved Africans and their European owners on southeastern plantations, and in how these people, this ethnic group, became African Americans as they resisted the racism that was imposed upon them.

Defining American Racism

As a cultural element, racism may be best defined by its cultural function. In a most basic sense, racism is an intensification of "normal" ethnocentrism (Benedict 1934:8–9; Kroeber 1963: 106). It helps to create strong and apparently inviolable categories of "self" and "other," of "own group" and "foreigner" (Epperson 1988b). The dominant group reinforces this process by forcibly ascribing subhuman status to the group or groups it victimizes, the "others." Again, for all the groups involved, this process functions to increase the identity and solidarity of the group in the minds of its members.

"Race," as an intellectual construct, is employed to ascribe subhuman status to the subordinate group. This concept begins with physical and cultural differences (Jordan 1974:4–10), but by severing human connections between individuals, it creates categories of people (Harris 1964:54–56). These categories, sections cut from the human continuum, are then open to be exploited or benefited by the ideology of racism.

This exploitation, most particularly, economic exploitation, is the goal and purpose of racism. The forms this exploitation may take are many and various, and they can react with the form of racism employed, to define different forms of racism itself. Because it enables economic exploitation, however, an ideology of racism is particularly suited to a plantation economy since the exploitation of a large number of laborers is central to this economic form. A plantation economy cannot function without a strong class division between owners and the much larger group of producers (Orser 1988c:321–325). Racism, especially when it supports a grossly unequal economic relationship such as slavery, can provide this class division.

Racism functions most effectively when it selects human characteristics that are immediately obvious and largely inescapable, in cutting out sections from the human biological continuum (Harris 1964:54–56). This is almost certainly why skin color has been fastened on so strongly by American racism; it is obvious at a distance and generally permanent, unalterable within an individual's lifetime. Like clothing or other artifacts oriented to social display, skin color can define class or ethnic groups, and it can require certain social relationships between the groups so defined (Wobst 1977).

As an ideology, racism also functions to decrease understanding of and to cover the connections between human groups which this ideology attempts to sever. This is, of course, utterly without objective support or scientific merit, as proven by numerous anthropological studies undertaken in response to now-extinct racist theories (J. Ferguson 1984; Stein 1988) and common observation, for example, the observation that all so-called human "racial" groups interbreed successfully. Racism is, therefore, one of the common ideologies that are developed by modern, capitalist societies, one that masks reality in the service of economic or social gain (Leone 1982; Handsman 1985:5; Orser 1988c:315).

Resistance to racism is the common reaction of any group victimized by this pernicious ideology. This resistance can take a number of forms, ranging from armed rebellion or revolution (Genovese 1979) to establishment of a cultural or ethnic identity based in this resistance (Ferguson 1985, n.d.). In general, people who seek dominance through employment of racist ideology will also make quite sure that they possess an effective monopoly on violence within the society they are exploiting. Thus, armed rebellion or other noticeably militant forms of resistance are very chancy and only available at great cost to the individuals who pursue them. In such cases, establishment of a culture that resists racism and all the forms of dominance imposed upon its participants, is often the most effective way for the victims of racism to survive its imposition. This quest for survival, when successful, when racism does not proceed to actual genocide, can form effective ethnic groups that nurture and sustain their members.

The South Carolina Rice Coast

The rice plantations of coastal South Carolina, southern North Carolina, and northern Georgia (Clifton 1970:391) in the late 17th, 18th, and early 19th centuries provide an example of the employment of racism and its function in helping to create ethnic groups. This process began in the late 17th century when the area was first settled by Anglo-American planters from Barbados (Wood 1974: 13–34). These settlers brought with them the plantation economy, the *idea* of establishing an economy based on the exploitation of slave labor in support of their colony (Lees 1980:42–43), originally established for geopolitical and military reasons. The only real problem they faced was finding a crop suited to their geographical location, which could be grown profitably within this economy, so as to insure its success.

The plantation economy established in South Carolina in 1670 had two potential sources for supplying labor: people kidnapped from West Africa and Native Americans stolen from tribes existing on the coast and in the interior. For several reasons, Africans soon came to be preferred as slaves in South Carolina (Wood 1974:35–91). Of primary importance in this choice was that certain groups of West Africans were quite skilled in growing rice, a crop that sustained their native subsistence economies (Wood 1974:62; Littlefield 1981:86, 93–98). The enslavement of Africans thus not only provided a skilled labor force, but also the profitable crop for which the colonists had been searching. By A.D. 1700 the economy of South Carolina had come to be based on growing rice (Lees 1980:43–63). This rice was grown by the coercion of Africans and African methods and knowledge, a classic example of cultural imperialism and the exploitation of existing cultural differences (Caulfield 1974). Of course, with Europeans having so little input into this economy beyond its management and control, they needed an ideology to mask this obvious contradiction. Racism provided this mask by promoting the idea that the Africans who ran this economy were too stupid, too subhuman to manage either the plantations or their own lives without European assistance. The racist ideology was only intensified when the American Revolution and other social changes at the end of the 18th century (Deetz 1977) created another contradiction between the developing democratic ideals of the planters and their dependence upon the plantation economy, which utterly negated these ideals (Davis 1975: 299–306; Fields 1982:159–163).

That this ideology was based in logical inconsistency, even utter absurdity, did not prevent it from functioning to form and support the elite group which controlled plantation society along the rice coast. Absurdity, of course, is no barrier to belief, especially when adoption of that belief brings immediate economic and social benefits. As such, participation in this racist ideology probably provided a core belief for the rice planters, a way of defining themselves as a social class or group.

A more interesting effect, however, was the resistance that imposition of this racist ideology inspired in the group of Africans, later African Americans, who were exploited by the economy it supported. These people, of course, entirely rejected the tenets of the racist ideology. They were thus free to understand the basis of the plantation economy in which they were unwilling participants, to know that, of all its participants, they were the one group without which the economy could not function.

This knowledge gave them, perhaps more than other groups of enslaved African Americans, the ability to negotiate their position with their masters (Ferguson 1985) and to gain some relief from the oppression of slavery and racism. In this "breathing space" the slaves were able to create a vibrant, vital, and successful creole culture (Joyner 1984), which incorporated a number of elements that functioned to resist slavery and racism (Ferguson 1985). African elements in this culture—in cuisine, architecture, religion, and folklore (Joyner 1984; Ferguson 1985, n.d.)—helped to define it for its participants and to allow them to resist racist slavery. More important, however, is that in serving so vital a function for its participants, this culture created a group of African Americans, recognizable in history and archaeology, who are among the honored and successful ancestors of modern black Americans. As such, this was the culture of the demographic black majority of the rice coast (Wood 1974), and it was, most truly, the dominant culture in that area.

Observing Racism through Archaeology

An immediate problem in observing racism, or the groups it helped to define, by means of archaeology is that this observation must be indirect. With certain exceptions (Singleton 1984), explicitly racist artifacts, artifact patterns, features, or sites will not be found. In general, such inquiry into ideo-technic meaning in the archaeological record is always the most difficult level of meaning to recover (Binford 1962:219–220).

A potential solution to this dilemma is the realization that racism and specific racist ideologies provide a *context* for much of the European/other group or first world/third world (for example, European-American/African-American) interactions which have taken place since A.D. 1500 (Wolf 1982:3–23). Studies here must be oriented toward recovering mind, toward understanding the complete context behind an archaeological or historical observation (Leone 1982). The limits of archaeological inquiry—imposed by site-formation processes, sampling designs, research foci, or funding—may mean that many studies will necessarily be incomplete, but these studies will make continual (if slow) progress if this goal is adopted and understood.

With regard to racism, two major components of mind in the societies studied will be: (1) the imposition of racism, by and for the dominant elite, and (2) the resistance of racism, by and for the subordinate victims. These conflicted forms of mind may be approached by looking at artifacts, features, and sites as conveyors of information, as conduits for cultural processes of domination and resistance (Hodder 1979, 1985a). A recent example of such an approach was a study that viewed plantation geography, the distribution of archaeological sites across it, and the characteristics and functions of these sites as having meaning in a contest of domination and resistance between two planters and their slaves from A.D. 1790 to 1830 (Babson 1988). Another study establishes how freed slaves were able to reorganize a plantation's geography after the Civil War to help resist changed forms of economic domination which were developed after that conflict (Orser 1988c). Both of these studies show cultural communication taking place using cultural elements—in these cases, sites—which are recoverable by archaeology and best interpreted in the larger contexts that contained them.

On slave or tenant plantations, a specific problem arises. Archaeological observation of these societies is most likely to be direct observation of distinctions in economic class within the plantations or the larger societies (Orser 1987), and not directly of "racial" or ethnic distinctions. In many cases, this will not be a problem, because enough congruence exists between the ethnicity of slaves, overseers, or planters and their vastly different economic classes that these groups will be readily distinguishable in the archaeological record (Otto 1984:15).

In some cases, however, such as that of wealthy black freedmen, some of whom themselves owned slaves (Johnson and Roark 1984a), this congruence between archaeologically evident status and

ethnicity will not exist (Rosengarten et al. 1987: 161–162). The ethnicity of wealthy black freedmen may thus become invisible to archaeology, though probably not to history, since such people were often able to leave their own records (Johnson and Roark 1984b) or were anomalous enough to be noted in the records kept by more dominant groups (Rosengarten et al. 1987:47–92). This is, ultimately, the problem of observing a status which reflects an economic class whose members, by and large, though not always, are determined by an over-reaching ideology, in this case, racism. It is an example of the difficulties of indirect observation with which all archaeologists must cope, and which can only be controlled by a thorough understanding of the *specific* context in which an archaeological observation is made.

One area in which such questions of context may be pursued and the links between class and ethnicity may be tested is where ethnic identities changed within a particular society observed through archaeology. One good example of this is James Deetz's (1988) recent study of Flowerdew Hundred in Virginia. Here, as elsewhere in the Chesapeake area, plantation society began in the early 17th century by exploiting the labor of white indentured servants. These indentured servants were perhaps somewhat different in established ethnicity (Irish or Scots) or established social class (poor people or criminals) from their elite European-American masters, but they were not different in the soon-to-be-created social category of "race." The few Africans present in this early 17th-century society were also, by and large, indentured servants (Tate 1965: 2–3; Bennet 1982:34–35), and they were not as separated from their masters, or from the Europeans who were their fellows in servitude, as they would later be under racist slavery (Deetz 1988: 239). Later in the 17th century, this form of plantation society was replaced by one based in exploitation of Africans, and including the imposition of racist ideology (Jordan 1974:54; E. Morgan 1975). Deetz (1988) is able to trace this change through the introduction and use of different forms of Colono vessels, opening up a broad area for studies of shifts in ethnic and "racial" identity, the imposition and creation of these social categories, and of archaeological or other methods to observe these changes.

Changes in the ethnic identity of plantation producers were not confined to the development of plantation societies in North America. On the sugar plantations of Louisiana, changes in the ethnicity of plantation workers occurred after the Civil War. Due to a number of strikes and other disagreements between plantation owners and the black freedmen who were then working for wages on the sugar plantations (Cook and Watson 1985: 43–60), local planters began to replace black workers with Italian, Sicilian, and in a few cases, Chinese immigrants (Williams 1974; Scarpaci 1975). In one case, a Louisiana sugar planter partially replaced his plantation's black labor force with indentured Sicilian immigrants soon after he purchased his plantation in 1889. "He met [the Sicilians] on the dock in New Orleans, and [bought their indentures] as soon as they stepped off the boat" (Nancy Mascarella-Pate 1989, pers. comm.). On this plantation, two groups of quarters—one inhabited by African-American slaves and, later, African-American freedmen (quite probably the same people) and another group inhabited by these Sicilian immigrants—have been identified through archaeology (Babson 1989). Although this study could not progress beyond the locating and documenting of these two occupations, the suggestion remains that studies of ethnic shifts among laborers even on postbellum plantations may be pursued. These studies will be useful in answering questions about ethnic identity and class and status, and will help frame new questions concerned with comparing plantations which imposed "racial" differences between owners and producers and those with "only" ethnic differences between these strongly separated social classes.

Other more specific and technical problems will be encountered by archaeologists undertaking observations of ideology through ultimate context. One of these problems is that the study of racism will often first require the establishment of ethnic identities among the groups being studied, so that elite/subordinate groups may be identified and

their divisions along these ethnic lines may be studied. The specific problem of observing social or class status, which may or may not have a link to ethnicity, has already been explored (Otto 1984; Moore 1985; Orser 1988c). Other problems would include using fragmentary or biased documents, problems of historical distance (in that an ethnic identity may not now mean what it once meant), or again, the problem of establishing ethnic identity from archaeological "markers." In some cases, these problems may be partly resolved by assuming a racist relationship among ethnic groups from previous knowledge and then looking to see whether this relationship is reflected in the archaeological or historical records (Babson 1988:ix). Such an approach cannot be used, of course, in studies designed to determine the existence of such a relationship, because this exercise becomes a useless tautology.

Problems more directly accessible by archaeology involve middle-range theory (Raab and Goodyear 1984). Approaches to addressing these problems start with purely technical questions such as: What is the level of excavation minimally necessary on a site to allow studies of context, including racism? Should block excavations be used, or is testing and small-unit sampling adequate? What probabilistic sampling strategies are appropriate; which ones will produce sufficient and significant data? Are studies confined to single sites sufficient, or must a broader scope be employed? As historical sites are by definition complex and bountiful in their production of artifacts (Deetz 1978: 48–49), historical archaeologists must design studies aimed at deciding what amount of inquiry will be necessary to allow study of ideo-technic, contextual, and other over-arching topics, beyond the usual "more is better" rule. This caveat is especially important as these vital elements of research design are almost always largely determined by funding, time, or other nonarchaeological constraints, particularly in the cultural resources management studies that now produce most archaeological data (Orser 1984:7–8).

At the level beyond the individual site, historical archaeologists must address questions about data consistency and comparability. These questions include: What standards are necessary to compare data between sites? Must all sites compared have been excavated in the same way, to the same level of inquiry? Can a completely excavated site be compared to one only sampled, particularly by methods such as artifact pattern analysis (South 1977:82–139) that may tend to smooth over and obscure differences between artifact collections made according to different excavation strategies? The problem is that sampling differences, between sites and, therefore, their artifact collections, may cause differences in representation of the sites, and thus affect one's ability to determine and compare their cultures, contexts, and ideologies.

Analysis of artifacts can pose further difficulties. In historical archaeology, and particularly in cultural resources management, artifact analysis tends to proceed with reference to established typologies (e.g., Noël Hume 1969a; South 1977: 210–212), even though this approach is now sometimes questioned (Majewski and O'Brien 1987). Is it possible that conformity to these typologies can obscure the ideological context of artifacts, especially when the researcher's goal is the quick, mass identification of large numbers of artifacts? Again, the example of Colono ceramics—first regarded as Colono-*Indian* (Noël Hume 1962a), then Colono-*African* (Ferguson 1980), and now Colono-*creole* (Ferguson n.d.)—is instructive. Flexible work is needed here. As in the Colono ceramics example, much greater understanding, including sometimes that of cultural context, is derived by making mistakes, the correction of which demands revision of accepted, standard typologies.

As an example, one recent study points out how the above questions may be addressed. This study took place on the Levi Jordan Plantation, a sugar and cotton plantation on the gulf coast of Texas (Brown and Cooper 1989; Brown and Cooper, this volume). Thorough and complete, this project has yielded important information about an African-American community making the transition from slavery to tenancy, a transition between two different varieties of oppression. Also, this project has documented, from archaeology and perhaps for the first time ever, the definite presence of a traditional African healer in the community studied, an individual whose function within that community may have been to maintain traditions and to resist the racism that was imposed by and through the economic position of the community (Ferguson 1985). Further, this study has produced important insights into methods of inquiry (Brown and Cooper 1989:1–5). It demonstrates how established artifact typologies, oriented toward cultural function within the European-American societies from which the typologies were derived, can mask the very different functions these artifacts had in the African-American society being studied.

The Jordan Plantation project illustrates the overriding value of a thorough, relatively well-funded and well-organized study proceeding over several years' time. This last consideration is particularly important in that the evolution of the project through time has allowed reconsideration and refinement of research questions, producing greater understanding of the African-American community on that plantation. No less important, the project also benefited greatly from unusual site-formation processes within the slaves' and workers' quarters at Jordan Plantation, especially the abrupt and forced abandonment of the quarters and their contents in A.D. 1890 or 1891 (Brown and Cooper 1989:9–10). In this case an act of oppression, surely inspired at least in part by racism and representing a violent incident of ethnic interaction, led directly to the formation of an extraordinary archaeological record. Archaeologists would, no doubt, all be very happy if the time and funds were available to investigate each and every site as thoroughly as the Jordan Plantation site has been investigated. It would be foolish, however, to expect the extraordinary site-formation processes—an "African-American Pompeii"—which also aided studies there, on any but a very few sites. The challenge will come, then, in applying the directions and methods pointed out by Brown and Cooper at the Jordan Plantation to the "more usual" studies which will not be as well funded, which will not proceed over several years, and which will deal with ordinary, not extraordinary, plantation sites.

Finally, addressing the problem of the coincidence of social status, class, and ethnicity will also depend, in part, on the development of middle-range theory. With regard to plantation societies, a start has been made by developing methods to measure status within these societies (e.g., Otto 1984; Moore 1985; Garrow 1987). From this base, studies may be undertaken to test these archaeologically perceived statuses against those from other records, such as written or oral histories. Such studies should have particular utility in tackling the knotty problem of how statuses are determined within ethnic, status, or class groups. Many of the status distinctions used by archaeologists are derived from the recorded preferences of elite groups, and they may have had little or no meaning to the members of subordinate groups.

Middle-range theory is generally developed as a body of practice out of repeated experiences from a number of archaeological investigations (Raab and Goodyear 1984:265). Thus, no solutions or easy answers can be readily offered at this time. The goals noted above, however, should lend a direction to future work which in time will lead to the development and practice of this body of theory.

Conclusion

This essay began with a conundrum that archaeological studies of ethnicity in and of themselves are not sufficient to study the development of past ethnic groups. Studies oriented towards merely identifying or establishing a certain ethnic group in the past are like typologizing artifacts; they categorize much, describe more, and explain nothing. Studies of ethnic interaction are more useful in that they recognize that no ethnic group, past or present, existed in a vacuum, but that all such groups have always interacted with one another. Indeed, such interaction is a major hallmark of human culture.

Racism is here viewed as a variety of this ethnic interaction. It has particular relevance to historical archaeology because racism developed and became violently important during the period of European and capitalist expansion, from A.D. 1500

to the present, which is often viewed as the particular realm of study for American historical archaeology (Orser 1988c:315). Racism is especially important in studies focusing on southeastern plantations, as a particularly vicious and virulent form of racism was employed here to exploit the culture, knowledge, skills, and labor of enslaved Africans and their African-American descendants. Understanding the development and employment of racism is thus important in understanding how the African-American ethnic group developed and made its vital contributions to the nation's history.

In other situations, studying racism as an ideology, as a context for archaeological observation, should also have a role to play. For some immigrant groups—Irish, Italians, Sicilians, Greeks, Eastern Europeans, and Jews—ideologies approaching racism were sometimes employed, but the experience of these groups in the United States was not as severe; their oppression generally was not as great as it was for enslaved Africans. Asians, especially the Overseas Chinese, encountered a form of racism that functioned to exclude them almost completely from American society until recent events, such as the persecution of the Nisei during World War II and the Vietnamese immigration following the Vietnam War, began to break down strong stereotypes. Hispanics have also suffered from ideas approaching racism, especially from discrimination based in cultural and linguistic differences between the traditions of this group and what is often erroneously proposed as a North American cultural norm or standard. Native Americans suffered the most severe form of racism because, in many cases, this racism proceeded as far as genocide. This genocide was incomplete, and modern Native Americans are now using both their ancestral traditions and their understanding of their oppression to forge a new ethnic identity, to create, from their historical nations, an inclusive ethnic group of Native Americans. Archaeological and historical studies can be organized around all these general trends in ethnic interaction, these degrees and varieties of racism. Middle-range theory—or, better, theories—must be developed for each individual case and example.

In describing a line of inquiry that is at present

barely under way, much remains tentative and not yet known. As a preliminary measure, some problems in and directions for studies of ethnic interaction are identified. These directions, if somewhat arduous and challenging, will also be useful, illuminating, and fruitful. As always in archaeology, the future promises a better, more complete understanding of the past.

TERRENCE W. EPPERSON

Race and the Disciplines of the Plantation

Introduction

An interpretation or presentation of the construction of race in plantation society must ultimately grapple with two different, yet not entirely unrelated, forms of "discipline" (Foucault 1970, 1979). The first and most obvious connotation is that of labor discipline, the role racial ideology played in the assertion and exercise of control which was not immediately dependent upon physical coercion. The second connotation is the partitioning of knowledge and inquiry into discrete, bounded, and autonomous academic disciplines, a tendency which is particularly problematic since race itself is an ideological assertion of otherness, inferiority, and fragmentation.

These disparate forms of discipline can be examined by exploring two plantations in Virginia: that of Robert "King" Carter, the wealthiest man in the colony at the time of his death in 1732 (Wright 1940, 1970; Naisawald 1986), and that of one of his grandsons, Carter Burwell of Carter's Grove, who died in 1756. Carter's Grove, the site of a slave quarter recently (re)constructed as part of Colonial Williamsburg's interpretation of life in colonial America, also provides an opportunity to examine issues of public presentation.

"King" Carter and Plantation Discipline

Consideration of "King" Carter begins with a paradox. Although the planter's power and authority over slaves were ultimately predicated upon state-sanctioned violence, the actual application of that violence had limited efficacy. Witness, for example, Carter's interactions with Madagascar Jack, a slave with a penchant for absenting himself from his assigned plantation duties. Carter's diary

entry for 12 September 1722 reads: "At our court. Obtained an Order for cutting off Madagascar Jack's toes." The actual court order obtained by Carter warrants full quotation:

> On the motion of Robert Carter Esq. setting forth that Madagascar Jack a Negro slave belonging to him hath for some time past lain out hid & lurked in swamps and woods & other obscure places both here and in Maryland killing hogs & committing other injurys to his Majestys good subjects and that he hath with great Charge apprehended the said Negro[.] it is therefore ordered that the said Robert Carter have leave to cut off all the toes on one of the said Negros feet in order to the reclaiming him & terrifying others from the like practices (Lancaster County 1722).

Two days later Carter tersely noted in his diary, "Doctor Mann cutt [sic] off Madagascar fellow's toes," probably believing he had solved this particular labor problem (Carter 1722). However, Madagascar Jack reappeared five years later in one of Carter's letters to a general overseer:

> As for Madagascar jack I will by no means have him go to the new design [plantation]. I have many reasons against it. If he be gone order him down to your quarter and keep him to work there 'till you have further orders from me. . . . Ballazore is an incorrigeable [sic] rogue nothing less than dismembering will reclaim him. I would have you outlaw him and get an order of the court for taking off his toes. I have cured many a negro of running away by this means (Carter 1727).

Despite Carter's boast of having "cured many a negro of running away by this means," it is quite apparent that Madagascar Jack was still a disciplinary problem, if not a habitual runaway, half a decade after his toes had been amputated. Carter's frequent imposition of this punishment also demonstrates that, despite the court's stated intentions, this form of correction had only limited effectiveness in "terrifying others from the like practices" (Schwarz 1984, 1988).

In addition to physical punishment, Carter deployed a wide range of disciplines over his enslaved laborers, intervening in almost every aspect of their social life. In their totality, these disciplines were at least as important in the assertion of labor control as the threat or execution of physical punishment. For example, "King" Carter's proprietary attitude toward both the landscape and his laborers is indicated by a 1727 letter to a head overseer:

> I would have this plantation go by the name CARTERS RANGE and now I am about names I hope you will take care that the negros both men and women I sent you up last always go by the names we gave them for this reason I nam'd them here & by their names we can always know what sizes they are of & I am sure we repeated them so often to them that every one knew their names & would readly answer to them (Carter 1727).

Examination of the 733 slave names recorded in Carter's inventory reveals that the imposed names were almost entirely of English origin, a pattern he shared with his slave-holding neighbors (Carter 1732). During the height of the slave trade in Virginia's York and Lancaster counties only 3 percent of the recorded African-born youths retained or were given African names (Kulikoff 1986:325–326). Similarly, in Middlesex County, immediately across the Rappahannock River from Carter's home plantations, a study of slave names recorded between 1650 and 1750 found no significant evidence of "African roots or patterns" (Rutman and Rutman 1984a:296, 1984b:83–106). This pattern stands in stark contrast to Jamaica, where an analysis of the Worthy Park sugar estate revealed that in 1730 a quarter of the slaves had Akan day names, an additional 28 percent had recognizably African names, and the remainder had European names (Craton 1978:156–167).

All forms of domination are characterized by a fundamental contradiction between the exclusionary impulse represented by the need to create the "Other" as different and alien and the need to incorporate the "Other" into a single social and cultural system of domination (Pandian 1985; Sider 1987). Physical mutilation represented a particularly exclusionary aspect of domination through the literal, severe, and permanent marking of difference. On the other hand, a slaveowner's imposition of English names upon recently arrived Africans would seem to represent an incorporative aspect of domination, yet even here is a subtle marking of difference and inferiority. The lack of family names and the overwhelming use of familial diminutives simultaneously connoted attitudes of condescension, parental authority, and intimacy toward slaves.

The use of the name "Robin" provides insight into the complexities and nuances of name usage. In his correspondence and diary Robert "King" Carter generally addressed and referred to his son Robert, Jr., as Robin, an expression of parental authority and affection. The use of the diminutive form outside the immediate family, however, was an unmistakable expression of disdain, as indicated by Governor Nicholson's statement, "In contempt of him he is sometimes called King Carter & other times Robin Carter even to his face" (Stanard 1900:65). Carter owned only one slave named Robert but had 19 slaves named Robin and an additional father-son pair named Old Robin and Young Robin.

The tensions between exclusion and inclusion should also be apparent in the spatial discipline Carter exercised on his plantations, but the data are sparse and contradictory. In addition to the home plantation, Carter's land holdings consisted of some 47 independent plantations scattered over nine Northern Neck and northern Virginia counties. The quarters typically had one to two dozen slaves—one of whom was designated as the foreman—and a white overseer. On one hand, the relative autarky and spatial dispersion of the plantations indicates a measure of autonomy for the overseers and enslaved carpenters in siting and constructing plantation buildings. Carter's papers provide only one instance of instructions about siting buildings:

> If there would want a tobacco house [barn] at Cab Run for the crop, you had best set them [the carpenters] to do that first. You should contrive to set the house, where there is a large quantity of good land round; however contrive that it may stand so near to the Quarter to be of usefulness to it. I believe there wants a Negro Quarter there as much as anything (Carter 1731).

Conversely, Carter exercised considerable control over many details of building construction on the outlying quarters:

> When you write your next I expect you will let me know what is done at your new design[.] If I remember right I ordered your quarter and your overseers house to be lofted. It is very necessary not only for the warmth of the houses

but to lay the peoples corn up in. . . . I have already ordered very good cabbins to be made for my people that their beds may lye a foot and a half from the ground if this is not yet done pray let it be done out of hand (Carter 1727).

"King" Carter's "mansion dwelling" at Corotoman, completed in about 1725 and destroyed by a fire of unknown origin in 1729, was probably the finest Virginia plantation house of its day. Although relatively little is known about the landscape of the plantation nucleus or the housing of domestic slaves at Corotoman, the forecourt and arcaded piazza of the house recorded during recent archaeological excavations suggest a relatively formal and symmetrical landscape (Hudgins 1981, 1984, 1990; Hudgins and Guerrant 1981). A comparative archaeological analysis of Carter's home plantation and a sample of the outlying quarters would be especially helpful in understanding the contested definition and control of landscape and architectural space. Regardless of the form or extent of spatial disciplining exercised by Carter, intriguing indications exist that his slaves occasionally expressed their own trenchant architectural critiques, as given in a diary entry for 27 December 1827: "Sunday last I had news of the burning of my tobacco house at Park Quarter. 8 hogsheads tobacco [. . .] 17 hogsheads corn. The Negros not heard of" (Carter 1722).

Ideology, Space, and Reconstruction

In his will "King" Carter specified that a tract of land near Williamsburg formerly known as Merchant's Hundred should:

> go to my grandson Carter Burwell & to the heirs male issue of his body lawfully begotten . . . and my further will is that this estate in all times to come be called & to go by the name of Carter's Grove, provided alwaies & it is my will and meaning that the number of slaves that are now upon the said plantation shall always be kept up & that the mortalitys shall be still supply'd out of the profits of this estate (Carter 1732).

On 12 December 1751, Carter Burwell purchased a copy of William Salmon's (1734) *Palladio Londinensis, Or the London Art of Building* for 10 shillings, and by 1755 he had completed the Georgian mansion still known as Carter's Grove (Stephenson 1964; Whiffen 1984:64, 263–274; Reiff 1986:256–260). This plantation is also the site of a (re)constructed slave quarter and interpretive program on late 18th-century Chesapeake slavery recently initiated by Colonial Williamsburg (Brown 1988; Chappell 1988; Ellis 1988). Although located where archaeological investigations indicate the home farm quarter once stood (Noël Hume 1982, 1985), the Carter's Grove complex is not a literal reconstruction, but is rather a compilation based upon site-specific documentary and archaeological investigations, extensive comparative research, and the requirements and goals of Colonial Williamsburg's interpretative and educational programs. The Carter's Grove exhibit is both a visualization of a typical Chesapeake slave quarter and an interpretative resource, providing an opportunity to address issues of spatial definition, control, and contestation during the second half of the 18th century in addition to problems of interpretation and presentation in the late 20th century.

An essential point of departure is an examination of how elite architecture works as ideological discourse in both colonial and contemporary contexts (Cosgrove 1984). In this analysis, ideology is not seen as false consciousness opposed to objective truth, but rather as an instance of what architectural critic Demetri Porphyrios (1982, 1985) calls "naturalized rhetoric." Architectural ideology masks not because it is in error, but because it simultaneously articulates a specific system of domination and presents it as inevitable, eternal, and matter-of-fact common sense. The planters adopted classical Roman architectural motifs not as a specific historical metaphor, but rather as part of a generalized attempt to appropriate the ahistorical aura and authority of classical culture, making specific relations of domination appear timeless and inevitable.

Yet, this attempted aesthetic hegemony was not without contradiction or contestation. The conflicting inclusive and exclusive aspects of domination are especially apparent in and near the plantation nucleus. The incorporative impulse can be seen in planters' efforts to impose what might be called a "disciplinary grid" on the slave quarters, particularly within the plantation nucleus. Upton's (1982, 1985, 1990) analysis of slave dwellings dating from the second half of the 18th century indicates that the spacing, alignment, and even facade configuration were carefully controlled in an attempt partially to incorporate the quarters into the formal landscape space of the plantation, even when they were excluded from the direct gaze of the Big House. The inclusive aspect of domination was naturalized even further by the paternalistic attitude of planters who referred to their slaves as "my family," in essence asserting that slavery was a natural extension of the patriarch's authority (Morgan 1987).

Conversely, the importance of manipulating the landscape to exclude slaves from view—and hence consciousness—is apparent in this description of Gunston Hall, a northern Virginia plantation completed in 1756, one year after Carter's Grove:

> To the east [of the mansion] was a high paled yard, adjoining the house, into which opened an outer door from the private front, within, or connected with which yard, were the kitchen, well, poultry houses, and other domestic arrangements; and beyond it on the same side, were the corn house and granary, servants houses (in those days called negro quarters) hay yard and cattle pens, all of which were masked by rows of large cherry and mulberry trees. . . . The west side of the lawn or enclosed grounds was skirted by a wood, just far enough within which to be out of sight, was a little village called Log-Town, so called because most of the houses were built of hewn pine logs. Here lived several families of the slaves serving about the mansion house; among them were my father's body-servant James, a mulatto man and his family, and those of several negro carpenters (Rowland 1892).

Thus, the plantation landscape was characterized by a complex series of separations, disjunctions, and denials. It embodied contradictory attempts to control the slaves and simultaneously to render them invisible. A literal reconstruction of this landscape, even if it were possible, would not necessarily reveal the embedded power relationships. If it is accurate to reconstruct a slave quarter that is not visible from the mansion, then it should be done. Site visitors must also constantly be reminded, however, of what this disjuncture meant

in terms of domination and the possibilities for the relative autonomy and resistance of slaves. If archaeologists choose to reconstruct a disarticulated landscape, they must also portray some knowledge of the totality of the power relations which were—or are—denied by that spatial separation. The critical historian or archaeologist must analyze not only the manner in which elite architecture naturalizes and de-historicizes an historically created reality, but also the circumstances under which hegemonic spatial conceptions are contested.

Another issue relates to the political potential of oppositional aesthetic practice. Manfredo Tafuri (1980a, 1980b), grounded in the work of Louis Althusser, emphasizes the "semi-autonomy" of the levels and practices of social life and views politics as being radically disjointed from aesthetic practice. In his rather pessimistic view, political praxis is possible, but only on its own level, while aesthetic and architectural production can never be immediately political.

Somewhat more convincing is Fredric Jameson's (1981, 1985) analysis, particularly his essay "Architecture and the Critique of Ideology." Drawing upon the work of Antonio Gramsci, Jameson is concerned with identifying hegemonic and counter-hegemonic spatial conceptions and views architectural practice as immediately and directly political. His reading of Gramsci displaces the materialist/idealist dichotomy as well as the traditional base/superstructure concept. It is not "idealist" in the pejorative sense to suggest that counter-hegemony includes production and preservation of alternative "ideas" of space. These concepts have an "objective" existence and conditions of possibility as rigorous as any material artifact. The concrete existence of radically different conceptions of space, regardless of the extent to which they are actually realized in the built environment, maintains the possibility of counter-hegemonic values. Thus, in Jameson's view, the 18th-century slave who resists the aesthetic of the elite planter and the 20th-century museologist who strives to preserve and present alternative spatial conceptions within the closure of late capitalism are both engaged in political struggle (see Dowling 1984; Stone 1984).

FIGURE 3-1. The Carter's Grove reconstruction.

The Carter's Grove Reconstruction

Through deliberate design and serendipitous circumstance, the (re)constructed Carter's Grove quarter exhibit effectively conveys the contradictory inclusive and exclusive aspects of the formal plantation landscape as well as the partial contestation of this aesthetic by the folks in the quarter. As shown in the preliminary design scheme, the complex consists of a cluster of four buildings and associated yard features located some 800 ft. northwest of the mansion (Figure 3–1). The structure shown at the top of the graphic is a log corncrib which is generally locked and the key held by

the plantation owner or the slave foreman. To the right is the one-room, lofted log house of the slave foreman and his family whose status and authority are conveyed in several ways. The house is on a slight topographic rise and is the structure closest to the mansion. The yard has the highest quality, the most symmetrically rectilinear fenced enclosure in the quarter. It is the only instance where the interpretative program shows a single nuclear slave family living within one architectural space. The structure at the bottom of Figure 3–1 is a barracks-style log quarter with two end chimneys. The largest structure is a clapboard quarter with a center chimney.

The entire complex is partially screened from the gaze of the Carter's Grove mansion by the quarter's lower topographic position and a row of trees, effectively embodying the exclusionary aspect of the formal plantation space. However, the interpretative scheme notes that, at the insistence of the owner, the facade of the log quarter is rigidly symmetrical and is oriented toward the river at the same angle as the mansion. This symmetrical facade is also the first view the modern visitor has of the slave quarter complex as he or she walks the path from the visitor's center to the mansion. Although the quarter is visually screened from the mansion, the facade alignment and configuration incorporate it into the formal disciplinary grid of the plantation nucleus; thus, visitors are reminded of the very definite limits placed upon the cultural autonomy of those who lived in the slave quarter.

Yet this control was not absolute. In the rear of the log quarter an opening which had originally been designed by the planter as a window has been converted by the inhabitants of the quarter into a door. The position of this door within the rear facade is markedly asymmetrical, and it opens into a semi-enclosed area between the two large buildings. This area, which is presented as the primary social space of the quarter, is not visible from the path leading to the quarter and is even somewhat concealed from the resident foreman's gaze. This configuration effectively conveys the presence of both hegemonic and counter-hegemonic conceptions of space within the landscape. The rigidly symmetrical, alienated space of the formal plantation embodied in the mansion, its terraced garden, and the primary facade and orientation of the log quarter overwhelms, but does not totally obscure, the less formal and relatively invisible spatial configuration within the quarter. Although the separations encoded in the colonial landscape are reconstructed, the interpretation also helps visitors to bridge that disjuncture and begin to grasp the totality of the relations of domination within the plantation.

Despite the exhibit's success in the presentation of competing spatial conceptions within the plantation, several aspects of the program are potentially problematic. Although the interpretative pro-

gram is still very tenuous, certain issues can be posed for consideration as the exhibit develops. Massive archaeological investigations conducted during the early 1970s in the vicinity of the mansion revealed a series of rectangular pits (Noël Hume 1982:9–21). These were initally interpreted as tanning pits, but subsequent research, particularly at the nearby Kingsmill plantations (Kelso 1984), resulted in a reinterpretation of these features as storage areas beneath 18th-century slave dwellings (cf. Noël Hume 1978a:51, 1985:51). It was on this basis that the location was selected for the quarter exhibit, and the pits have been effectively incorporated into the reconstruction. The interpretative scenario indicates that at least some of these features were used for surreptitious storage of items taken without permission from the plantation stores. This presentation seems entirely appropriate and is supported by both archaeological and documentary evidence. It has the additional advantage of presenting a covert form of resistance which effectively supplemented the slaves' diet and material living standard.

However, the embedded assumptions must be carefully considered of an interpretation which suggests that each pit was the private storage locker of a single individual or family, providing a means of concealment from other slaves as well as from the master. Although no evidence can be offered one way or the other on the archaeological analysis, such an interpretation risks imposition of the modern ideological construct of the autonomous, utilitarian, maximizing individual (Handsman 1983; Patterson 1987). Furthermore, it is an individualism constituted by ownership, or "possessive individualism" (MacPherson 1964). Within the Lockean tradition, property ownership is equated with rationality and humanity; therefore, people such as wage earners who owned no property could be excluded from the franchise. For people who were themselves considered property, this constitution of individualism is particularly problematic. This example poses the fundamental issue: How do archaeologists present interpretations in terms which can be appreciated by an audience—whether fellow academicians or museum visitors—without universalizing their own ideological categories? Even though no answers can now be offered, the issue needs to be addressed explicitly.

A similar issue is posed by a small lean-to shed added to the large clapboard quarter. The preliminary interpretative scenario presents this addition as the residence of an elderly African-born man, probably a revered griot, a patriarch and keeper of the oral tradition. This scenario has several interpretative and didactic advantages. It indicates that social valuation within the quarter did not necessarily correspond with the hierarchy imposed by the master. In addition, it presents the possibility of discussing interaction between creole and African-born slaves and the partial survival of African cultural traditions (Kulikoff 1986). However, care should be taken not to suggest a dichotomy between acculturation and autonomy or that resistance to the horrors of slavery necessarily depended upon the literal survival of African cultural traditions (Nassaney 1986; Handsman 1987). This indicates a more general concern which plagues the New Social History: How does one convey and valorize the relative cultural autonomy and accomplishments of subaltern groups without glossing the context of domination which imposed very severe limits (Eley and Nield 1980; Fox-Genovese and Genovese 1983b)? Again, no ready answer can be provided, but it can be suggested that overemphasizing the autonomy of slave culture runs the risk of mystifying relations of power, of reifying the very separation planters asserted with the visual screening of their quarters.

Summary

In closing, the dual disciplines alluded to in the title can be reconsidered. Although slaveowner power was ultimately predicated upon the threat and occasional practice of physical violence, day-to-day domination depended upon the deployment of a wide spectrum of disciplines, ranging from the imposition of European-American names to food rationing and control of architectural and landscape space. Because these forms of control were less overt than physical punishment, the forms of re-

sistance they elicited were also relatively subtle. Critical archaeologists and historians must be sensitive to these less obvious forms of domination and resistance.

Just as slaves resisted the disciplines imposed by the masters, contemporary archaeologists should resist the disciplinary impulse of today. In the same way the disarticulated landscape of the plantation obscures relations of domination, the tendency toward disciplinary fragmentation limits researchers' ability to grasp and present the totality of power relations within both the plantation and society as a whole. The Carter's Grove exhibit is most effective when it transcends disciplinary boundaries such as historical archaeology, "academic" architectural history, and landscape architecture.

Interdisciplinary cooperation is not here advocated in the mundane and traditional sense, however, but as a fundamental critique of these divisions of labor and knowledge. When addressing the construction of race within what remains a largely racist society, this concern is paramount. Instead of a mere adjunct to existing disciplines, African-American archaeology and history must become integral to the fundamental critique of oppression and domination, both historically and in the present. Such a social and political commitment will not only improve the quality of current archaeological research and interpretations, but also help to bridge the gap between academic disciplines and the communities archaeologists purportedly study and serve.

In the process, archaeologists and historians should transcend the false dichotomy of "equality-versus-difference" and embrace the "double strategy" advocated by many feminist scholars, learning to fight inequality and injustice while preserving and fostering diversity (Spivak 1987: 134–153; Scott 1988; Smith 1988:132–151). In presentations, contemporary archaeologists must "de-naturalize" race, emphasizing that it is not a universal, natural, or inevitable aspect of the human condition, but rather a constructed category of domination, an assertion of "Otherness" and inferiority which can be apprehended historically and transcended through social practice (Fields

1982; Chappell 1988, 1989). At the same time archaeologists must also struggle to recognize and celebrate the unique African-American heritage without glossing the context of oppression within which this oppositional culture was, and continues to be, forged. These two goals—valorization of the African-American culture of resistance and the denaturalization of essentialist racial categories—are by no means antithetical, and are indeed vital if archaeologists are to help create a more humane social order. The Carter's Grove quarter exhibit, tentative and nascent though it may be, represents an important contribution toward both of these goals.

ACKNOWLEDGMENTS

Preliminary versions of this paper were presented at the 1988 American Society for Ethnohistory meeting in Williamsburg and at the conference "Digging the Afro-American Past: Archaeology and the Black Experience" at the University of Mississippi in May of 1989. At Williamsburg I had the pleasure of discussing these issues with Marley Brown III, Edward Chappell, and Rex Ellis. The Oxford conference was an engaging combination of scholarly research and social engagement, and I thank organizers Ronald Bailey and Theresa Singleton as well as Rachel Chapman, Nancy Muller, Mark Leone, Neil Silberman, and Charles Joyner for their comments and encouragement. I also wish to thank the Department of Architectural Research, Colonial Williamsburg Foundation, for permission to reproduce the preliminary design drawing of the Carter's Grove exhibit. This paper was written under the auspices of a pre-doctoral fellowship at the Carter G. Woodson Institute for Afro-American and African Studies at the University of Virginia. I have especially benefited from discussion with Doug Chambers, Julia McDonough, LouAnn Pearthree, Chris Taylor, Mariane Ferme, Michele Wagner, and Julie Weiss. Richard Handler discussed his own ethnographic research at Colonial Williamsburg (Handler and Saxton 1988). As always, my work is informed by ongoing discussions with Tom Patterson and Rus Handsman.

Melanie A. Cabak
Mark D. Groover

Bush Hill: Material Life
at a Working Plantation

ABSTRACT

Bush Hill plantation, located near Aiken, South Carolina, and Augusta, Georgia, along the middle Savannah River valley, was owned by four generations of the George Bush lineal family between ca. 1807 and 1920. Drawing upon the interpretive concept of the working plantation, perceptions regarding material conditions and the standard of living experienced by southern planters are explored in this essay. Economic records indicate that the George Bush family was among the top wealth-holding groups within the surrounding community. Although the planter family was affluent, the standard of living revealed archaeologically was economically conservative. The Bush family used inexpensive household items and did not acquire the luxury goods often thought to be archaeological hallmarks of genteel society, such as expensive dining sets or tea ware. Conversely, archaeological data revealed they were aggressive consumers, indicated by the sheer quantity of material discarded at the site. The example provided by Bush Hill underscores the complexity of planter households in the past and illustrates that the wealth held by former site residents is not always directly discernable in the archaeological record.

Introduction

Since the end of the 19th century, the southern plantation has endured as an emotionally charged symbol of America's contradictory and turbulent past. Shrouded in myth and misconception, plantations are often considered to be the setting that nurtured southern society during the 18th and 19th centuries. Consequently, romanticized portrayals of plantation life often extol opulence and material excess among planter elites. Such depictions likewise inadvertently de-emphasize the harsh institution of slavery that formed the basis of this economic system.

In fact, only a very small proportion of white males in the South were ever slaveholders. Among this small proportion of slave owners, an even smaller fraction of individuals were

large-scale planters. In contrast to the prevalent perception of rural affluence and excess among slaveholders, on the eve of the Civil War in the 1850s, the majority of slaveholders in the South owned 18% of rural landholdings, held 20 or fewer slaves, and practiced a standard of living comparable to many farming households. Even among medium- to large-scale planters, or those individuals that owned more than 20 slaves, material conditions were probably not drastically different from their non-slave-owning neighbors, for example, the dwellings they resided in, the range of household items they used, and the type of food they consumed (Gray 1933; Hilliard 1985; Doughty 1989: 343–344; Vlach 1993:7–8).

Based on period descriptions and primary records, scholars have noted the distinction between showplace and working plantations (Vlach 1993). Showplace plantations were owned by economic outliers and used by planter elites to entertain guests. An underlying function of showplace plantations, in addition to producing cash crops such as rice, cotton, and tobacco, was to flaunt wealth and power within a planter's social circle. Unfortunately, these residences are often depicted as the typical example of plantations in the popular media and especially at historical sites developed for tourism. In contrast, working plantations contained smaller planter residences, landholdings, and enslaved labor forces compared to showplace estates (Vlach 1993). This research reconstructs the material conditions and standard of living practiced by George Bush and his lineal family at Bush Hill. Bush Hill was a working plantation formerly located in Barnwell District, South Carolina, near the Savannah River.

The results of this study are archaeologically relevant because they aptly illustrate the complex and ambiguous relationship between economic practices and material life among southern slaveholders. The results likewise call into question the use of pat generalizations regarding the standard of living practiced by planters. For example, despite substantial wealth in the form of land and enslaved labor, during the 19th

Historical Archaeology, 2006, 40(4):51–83.
Permission to reprint required.
Accepted for publication 9 May 2005.

century the George Bush family practiced a relatively modest standard of living, as illustrated archaeologically by recovered household items and historically by information preserved in probate inventories. Although material life was influenced by a frugal economic orientation among the planter households at Bush Hill, increasing levels of material consumption and consumerism were revealed in the archaeological record, especially during the second half of the 19th century. Likewise, the planter household at the study site did not live extravagantly, but the two-story Carolina I-house in which George Bush and his lineal family resided for approximately 100 years probably denoted rural affluence.

Archaeological information for this study was obtained from data recovery excavations conducted at site 38AK660, the main house complex at Bush Hill. Located on the Savannah River Site in Aiken, South Carolina, a research facility operated by the United States Department of Energy (Figure 1), site 38AK660 was occupied between the early-19th century and early-20th century. The site is located in Barnwell County, South Carolina, formerly

called the Barnwell District during the 19th century. Site 38AK660 is also located within the larger study area encompassing the middle Savannah River valley. This geographic area has been the focus of ongoing archaeological studies by personnel with the Savannah River Archaeological Research Program (SRARP) since the 1970s. Archaeological site 38AK660 contains the remains of the planter's house at Bush Hill, the home place of George Bush and his descendants. During the 19th century, grain and livestock agriculture was practiced at Bush Hill. Only a very small amount of cotton was produced at the plantation during its operation. The archaeological site also contains an early Bush family cemetery near the main dwelling. The slave quarters at the plantation are located approximately 600 ft. north of the main dwelling. Personnel with the SRARP, a division of the South Carolina Institute of Archaeology and Anthropology, University of South Carolina, conducted block excavations at the planter's dwelling between June 1996 and December 1999. Excavations were conducted as a data recovery project prior to site destruction (Cabak 2004; Cabak and Groover 2004; Cabak et al. 2004).

Popular perceptions of plantations, the family history of George Bush, and a review of economic information related to Bush Hill plantation provide the economic context associated with the George Bush family revealed through historical records, which is then contrasted with the archaeologically defined standard of living that was practiced at the plantation. Material conditions, the standard of living within the planter household, and consumption trends are reconstructed through probate inventories and the archaeological record. Probate inventory analysis is used to determine the range of household furnishings used by the planter family, in comparison to members of the larger extended family and the surrounding community. Archaeological information related to architecture and foodways is used to reconstruct the standard of living practiced by the planter family. Lastly, using artifact density as an analysis variable, consumption levels at the planter's residence and the slave quarters are compared. Considered together, available information indicates the planter family at Bush Hill was economically frugal yet discarded a large amount of

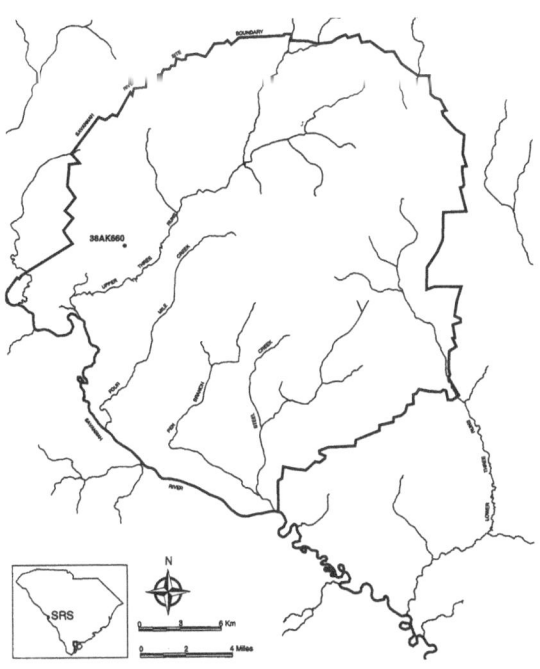

Figure 1. Location of Bush Hill plantation (38AK660) in South Carolina. (Drawing by George Wingard.)

inexpensive consumer items, especially during the second half of the 19th century.

Southern Myth: Popular Perceptions of Plantation Life

Historical archaeologists typically rely upon two main information sources to interpret the recent past, the archaeological record and primary historical documents. A less acknowledged, third information source is also often unconsciously drawn upon to mold our interpretations of the past, consisting of preconceptions, generalizations, assumptions, and informal hypotheses that archaeologists bring to a specific topic. At a minimum, the assumptions that can influence interpretations are often proven to be false, and new research questions or priorities are reformulated as the research process progresses. In other situations, assumptions about specific research topics can become accepted as valid generalizations about the past, taking on a life of their own, even though in fact they may be wrong or unknowingly distorted about a specific topic.

Archaeological study of plantations is one such area where contemporary assumptions about the past can potentially blur historical reality. Common wisdom suggests that plantations (for the most part) were characterized by monocrop agriculture, were owned by autocratic planters residing in large columned dwellings, and were operated by a large enslaved labor force. In actuality, there was a broad spectrum of different types of plantations, ranging from large stereotypical operations to smaller, more modest holdings (Gray 1933).

For example, most residents of the South in the 18th and 19th centuries worked the land they owned and were not slaveholders (Gray 1933; Vlach 1993:7). Despite this basic fact, avenues lined with live oaks leading to stately manor houses adorned with white Greek columns and surrounded by immaculately landscaped grounds and gardens embody the archetypal image of southern life, as portrayed in the popular 20th-century film *Gone With the Wind*. In contrast to this prevalent portrayal of southern plantation life, a Georgia newspaper editor wrote in 1857, "A log house half decayed with age, or a frame house without paint, and ... a yard without a shrub or a flower ... are too frequently the insignia of a planter's premises" (Vlach 1993:9).

This description, written by an actual observer with a critical eye during the era of slavery, differs markedly from the contemporary stereotypical image of the southern plantation. Research conducted by archaeologists and architectural historians likewise illustrates that the grand plantation perception is largely a contemporary historical myth and that large, manor-like dwellings were the exception rather than the rule on southern plantations. The homes of planters, often modest in size, were usually not elaborate structures. John Vlach (1993:7) summarizes this misconception, stating,

> ... in 1860, when plantation agriculture had reached its furthest extent, there were only 46,274 plantations in the entire South. Though this figure may seem large, it represents only 12 percent of all slaveholding families. The greatest proportion of these estates—some 20,789—were run with between twenty and thirty slaves and though considered small plantations, they were, in fact, only slightly larger than slaveholding farms and not much different in character. Only the plantations that were run with large numbers of slaves, a hundred or more, approached the manorial ideal. By this measure, there were in 1860 only about 2,300 truly large-scale plantations, and perhaps only half of those were developed to the state of elegance promoted by the widespread southern mythology. By the middle of the nineteenth century, less than 1 percent of all slaveholding families fit the plantation stereotype, a percentage that had remained constant since the middle of the eighteenth century.

By focusing upon the grandest, wealthiest, and most historically noteworthy examples, scholars, members of public historical societies, personnel at outdoor museums, and even archaeologists potentially perpetuate romanticized and unrealistic characterizations of southern planters, the plantations they owned, and the African American laborers that they enslaved. Admittedly, some planters indeed owned 100s of enslaved laborers, vast tracts of land, and resided in textbook examples of Palladian-influenced dwellings like Drayton Hall or Middleton Place in the South Carolina low country. Holding sway over feudal-like estates, appropriately called "showplace plantations" by Vlach (1993:4–5), this small group of planters often equipped their imposing residences with the latest furnishings fashionable in Europe. Historically prominent planters such as Henry Drayton in the low country or Henry Hammond in the upcountry of South Carolina are very extreme examples of the upper ranks of the planter class in the Old South. These individuals represent a very small proportion of slave owners.

As a means of archaeologically exploring the plantation myth, this research focuses on the other, more prevalent yet historically deemphasized type of operation—the working plantation that contained a smaller labor force and a modest planter residence. Bush Hill is a relevant example of a working plantation in South Carolina's middle Savannah River valley.

George Bush Family History

Bush family tradition states that ancestors of George Bush first migrated to North America from Bristol, England, in the early-17th century. According to surviving records, the Bush family first came to Orangeburg District, South Carolina, in 1762 from Craven Precinct, Johnston County, North Carolina. John Bush (George Bush's father) came with his brother Edward, his stepfather and mother Thomas and Mary Castellaw, his uncle Isaac Bush, Sr., along with other families such as the Roundtrees and Foremans that settled in the area (DeHuff 1967: 51). The Cracker Neck and Upper Three Runs Creek area along the Savannah River valley was sparsely populated in the 1760s, making the Bush family members some of the earliest settlers in the study area.

George Bush, John's third son, was born in 1784, possibly near Upper Three Runs Creek or Cracker Neck adjacent to the Savannah River. George Bush married Eleanor Sapp of nearby Burke County, Georgia, in 1807. According to family tradition, George Bush constructed their family home shortly after his marriage (Edwards 1977:148). George and Eleanor had 10 children, 5 sons and 5 daughters. Extant historical sources indicate most of their children appear to have married and stayed in the local community (SRARP n.d.). Martha and Catherine, the two youngest daughters, both died when they were young married women. Thomas and James, the second and fifth sons, may have left the area because little is known about what became of them. According to family papers, George and Eleanor Bush both died at their home, Bush Hill, and were buried in Bush Hill cemetery (SRARP n.d.).

At his death, land and enslaved African Americans were George's primary financial assets that were divided among his heirs. Documents indicate that he owned 64 slaves and more than 3,000 acres, which included Beech Island plantation, Bush Hill plantation, Cracker Neck plantation, and a plantation in Burke County, Georgia (Barnwell County 1845, 1859; SRARP n.d.). Although these plantations cannot be precisely plotted on a map, they do illustrate that George Bush's agricultural operations and landholdings were widely dispersed, rather than being concentrated on one large tract. The existence of these multiple plantations, especially the Georgia plantation, shows that George must have had help with the management of his plantations, perhaps from his adult children.

Surviving family documents indicate that Hansford D. Bush and George W. Bush, the third and fourth sons, were both owners of the land containing Bush Hill plantation. Hansford died in 1868 at the age of 44. Most of Hansford's property (1,161 acres) was sold to pay his debts, and the rest of his estate was divided among his heirs. It was at this time that George W. Bush, Hansford's brother, purchased Bush Hill plantation (SRARP n.d.).

George Washington Bush, born in 1815, was the second eldest son of George and Eleanor Bush. George W. Bush, at the time of his death in 1891, was the owner of Bush Hill plantation. The 1870 and 1880 industrial schedules of the U.S. Census provide insight into some of George's business activities (South Carolina Department of Archives and History [SCDAH] 1870b, 1880b). George owned several small industries related to agriculture, consisting of a cotton gin, thresher, sawmill, and blacksmith operation.

George W. Bush was 47 years old when he married 29-year-old Augusta J. Foster, from Augusta, Georgia, in 1862. Augusta J. and George W. Bush had at least seven children. George W. Bush died at Bush Hill in 1891 when he was 76 years old. He was buried in Bush Hill cemetery, along with his father, mother, and several of his siblings. Documents in his son Arthur's probate bundle indicate that George W. Bush died of heart disease (Aiken County 1954). The previous year he had conveyed all of his landholdings to his wife Augusta (Aiken County 1890). George's will basically conveyed all of his assets to his wife and children. His financial resources were divided equally among his immediate family members, and his wife served as the executrix. George requested that his estate remain intact until the youngest child (Arthur) came of age (SCDAH 1891).

Arthur R. Bush, born in 1875, was George and Augusta's only son to survive into adulthood. According to family genealogy, Arthur never married nor had children (Manning and Anderson 1949–1967). Unlike his father and grandfather, Arthur never appears to have purchased land. All of Arthur's land appears to have originated from his father's estate. During Arthur's years as a young adult, documents state that he was a productive farmer and politician.

In 1900, the population census indicates that Arthur resided with his sister and brother-in-law. Arthur R. Bush was elected to the South Carolina State Legislature for the 68th Assembly, 1909–1910 (Edgar 1974:491), but his term was cut short by mental illness. Arthur R. Bush was declared *non compos mentis* and was eventually committed to the South Carolina State Hospital in 1910.

The application that declared Arthur *non compos mentis* provides insight into his life (Aiken County 1954). He was described in the application as an unmarried 32-year old, a member of the Christian church, and a planter. His disposition was cheerful and frank, and prior to his illness he was industrious. He suffered from recurring episodes or bouts of mental illness that began gradually and occurred irregularly (every 10 to 15 days). Over time, the episodes became more prevalent. The cause of the condition was not known, and Arthur was not capable of working while he was ill. He remained in the hospital until his death in June 1952. In 1951, Atomic Energy Commission acquired the property containing Bush Hill plantation to create the Savannah River Plant.

Bush Hill Economic Contexts

The economic context for the study site and surrounding community was reconstructed from archival data pertaining to landholding trends, slaveholdings, and agricultural production. Economic information pertaining to landholdings, slaveholdings, and annual agricultural production among a sample of rural households was examined to define basic economic groups in the study area. Mark Groover (1998, 2003a)

previously developed these analysis methods for dissertation research. By defining economic or wealth groups, the study site can be placed within a quantitative interpretive framework. The relative economic position of the study subjects can be determined in relation to their neighbors. By establishing the economic characteristics of the study household, trends relating to material culture can be more effectively identified and explored.

Relative socioeconomic class is first defined via archival information for the George Bush family and is reconstructed by comparing household level information for the George Bush family to several analytical levels or categories, consisting of the extended family, the community, the district/county, the region, and state. The community category was created by selecting approximately 30 cases from the agricultural censuses that were listed immediately adjacent to the Bush households. The Barnwell District/County comparative information as well as regional and state information was abstracted from the censuses for specific census years. An average for each of the above analysis categories (study household, community, district/county, region, and state) was calculated from census information. After economic contexts are defined for the Bush family, the character and quality of the material culture recovered from the site can then be contrasted against this documentary information.

Slaveholdings

Demographic trends associated with the slave population at Bush Hill from 1790 to 1860 were defined. Slave population records were used to reconstruct demographic trends at the study site and in the surrounding community (SCDAH 1790, 1800, 1810, 1820, 1830, 1840; 1850b; 1860b; U.S. Department of State 1841; U.S. Bureau of Census [USBC] 1853; U.S. Department of Interior [USDI] 1864). The adjacent community analysis variable was defined by selecting 15 census cases above the study subject and 15 cases below the study subject in a specific census year. The local regional context refers to slaveholders within the surrounding district of the study site. Slaveholding data indicate that George Bush and George W. Bush had a much larger slave population than the

TABLE 1
SLAVEHOLDING TRENDS IN THE STUDY AREA, 1790–1860

Census Year	Local Region	Community	Extended Family	John Bush	George Bush	George W. Bush
1790	1	1	9	15	–	–
1800	4	1	7	24	–	–
1810	3	2	12	15	9	–
1820	4	4	21	–	30	–
1830	4	12	21	–	43	–
1840	6	9	19	–	53	–
1850	6	15	28	–	53	11
1860	7	8	29	–	–	46
Average	4	7	18	18	38	29

average household in the surrounding community, in Barnwell District (later renamed Barnwell County and subdivided to form Aiken County), and within their extended family.

At the community and regional levels, the average slaveholding household owned approximately one slave in 1790. This number increased to seven slaves by 1860 (Table 1). Most households in the region owned very few if any slaves. Conversely, based on the average number of slaves per household, the descendants of John and Mary Bush had a fairly large slave population for the study area. George Bush's slaveholdings started with 9 slaves when his household was young and peaked at 53 slaves by the time he was 55 years old. He actually owned 64 slaves at his death in 1857, but Table 1 only contains decennial census data. The slaveholdings of his son, George W. Bush, increased rapidly after he started his own household in 1850. George W. Bush's slave population grew over 300 percent between 1850 and 1860, from 11 to 46 individuals. The growth of the slave population occurred through purchase and inheritance. The larger slave population among the Bush family enabled them to maintain greater agricultural production than most households in Barnwell District, resulting in greater wealth accumulation. Accumulated wealth, in turn, helped financially sustain the family through the remainder of the 19th century and into the early-20th century.

To further emphasize the above-average slaveholding trends among the Bush family, community-level samples of slaveholders sur-

rounding Bush Hill plantation were examined for the population census years of 1800, 1820, and 1850 (SCDAH 1800, 1820; USBC 1853). A sample of slaveholders was obtained from the population census for each census year. Approximately 30 census entries were selected adjacent to the entries for John Bush and George Bush to define a community average. A mean average was then taken for each census year sample, and the standard deviation was added to the average to define interval groups. Results of this comparison indicated that the proportion of slaveholders in the surrounding community more than doubled between 1800 and 1850 (Figure 2). Slaveholders comprised 30% of residents in the study community in 1800, 45% in 1820, and 75% in 1850.

As illustrated in Figure 3, four main slaveholding groups existed in the Bush Hill community in 1800. Overall, the distribution shows that most slave owners owned only one slave, and a small group of slaveholders owned more than one slave. Average-level slaveholders correspond to Group 1 in the study sample and comprise 70% of the planters in the local community. At the upper end of the range, Group 5 held five slaves in 1800 and comprised 10% of the sample. John Bush, the father of George Bush, was an extreme outlier in the surrounding community sample and owned 24 slaves.

In 1820, an interesting trend developed among slaveholders that persisted during the remainder of the antebellum period in the study area. A bimodal distribution develops by 1820 in which approximately 94% of the planters own

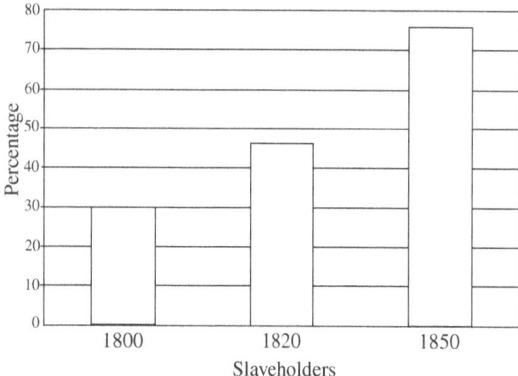

Figure 2. Distribution of slaveholders in study community in 1800, 1820, and 1850. (Drawing by George Wingard.)

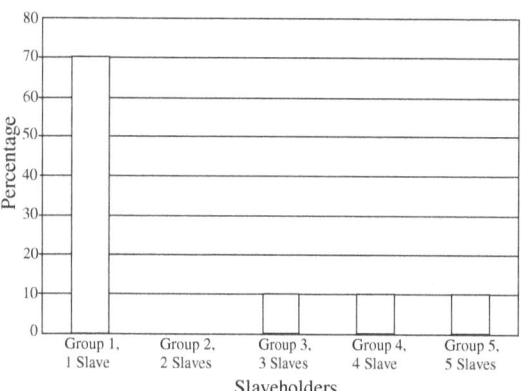

Figure 3. Distribution of slaves held by economic groups in 1800. (Drawing by George Wingard.)

approximately 20 or fewer slaves (Figure 4). The remaining 6% of planters were outliers who owned 20 or more slaves, and in some instances owned approximately 40 to 50 slaves. In 1820, George Bush, the son of John Bush and resident of site 38AK660, owned 22 slaves and was a member of slaveholding Group 4.

The bimodal distribution among slaveholders first observed in 1820 becomes even more pronounced by 1850 (Figure 5). By this time, the average slaveholder, corresponding to Group 1, owned 15 slaves and comprises 58% of the slaveholding population. Group 4, composed of outliers, represents 10% of the slaveholding population yet owns between 52 and 69 slaves. Owning 53 slaves, George W. Bush in 1850 was a member of Group 4 and an outlier in the local planter community. Only three other planters in the local community were members of Group 4 in 1850.

Considered together, the larger slaveholdings identified through archival analysis enabled the George Bush family, as well as his extended family, to maintain greater levels of agricultural output than other households. At the same time, Bush Hill plantation would have required more food to support slaves and livestock.

Landholdings

In 1850, George Bush's acreage exceeded the average landholdings of the Bush extended family by 25% (USBC 1853) (Table 2). George also had at least three times more land than

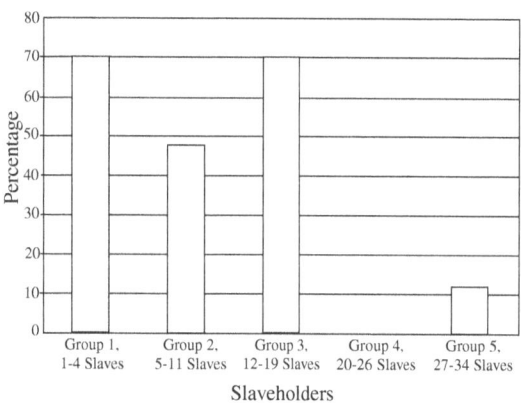

Figure 4. Distribution of slaves held by economic groups in 1820. (Drawing by George Wingard.)

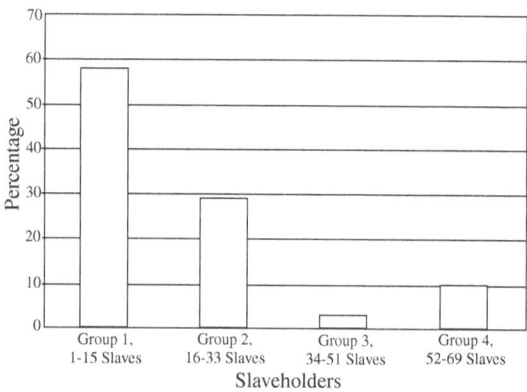

Figure 5. Distribution of slaves held by economic groups in 1850. (Drawing by George Wingard.)

TABLE 2
LANDHOLDING TRENDS WITHIN THE GEORGE BUSH FAMILY:
TOTAL ACREAGE (PERCENTAGE IMPROVED)

Household Level	1850	1860	1870	1880
George Bush	3,000 (36%)	–	–	–
George W. Bush	1,050 (43%)	2,860 (33%)	500 (67%)	2,700 (8%)
Hansford D. Bush	200 (90%)	1,000 (38%)	–	–
Bush family average	2,228 (32%)	1,886 (19%)	424 (34%)	988 (21%)
Community average	882 (33%)	788 (30%)	264 (63%)	176 (46%)
Region average	742 (28%)	726 (17%)	414 (34%)	176 (23%)
State average	541 (28%)	570 (24%)	233 (33%)	143 (44%)

the average household in the community, local region/district, and state. The same analysis methods used to analyze slaveholding trends help illustrate landholding trends within the Bush family. Approximately 30 cases were examined from the 1850 agricultural census (USBC 1853). The cases were neighboring households in the Bush Hill area. Based upon the analysis variable of improved acreage, five landholding groups were defined within the sample from the 1850 agricultural census (Figure 6). The average amount of improved acreage was 267 acres, corresponding to Group 1 that comprised 73% of landholders. Similar to slaveholdings by 1820, the amount of improved acreage in 1850 also exhibited a skewed distribution. Landholding groups 2 and 3, considered together, cultivated between

268 to 703 acres and represented 24% of the sample. In contrast, planters in Group 5, cultivating between 922 and 1,139 acres, comprised 3% of the community. George Bush was a member of Group 5, with 1,000 improved acres. In the agricultural sample, there was only one other planter, Stephen Newman (George's son's father-in-law) who cultivated 1,000 acres. Paralleling slaveholdings, George Bush was also an economic outlier based upon the variable of cultivated land.

The acreage of George Bush's sons, Hansford D. and George W., also increased after their father's death in 1857. This increased acreage undoubtedly partially reflects the land they inherited from their father's estate. George W. Bush's acreage exceeded the average landholdings in his extended family by almost one-third, and he owned at least three times more acreage than the average households at all other analysis levels in 1860. Landholdings decline across all analysis categories in 1870, probably due to readjustment in landownership after the Civil War. Despite this drop in acreage, there are no real estate records indicating that George W. Bush conveyed five-sixths of his landholdings to other individuals between 1860 and 1870, so the decline in landownership in the study family is puzzling. George W. Bush's acreage rebounds to its pre-Civil War level by 1880, and again, no surviving local documents record these transactions between 1870 and 1880. In 1880, his landholdings substantially exceed the landholdings of the other households in the analysis categories. The small landholding size at the community, regional, and state levels in

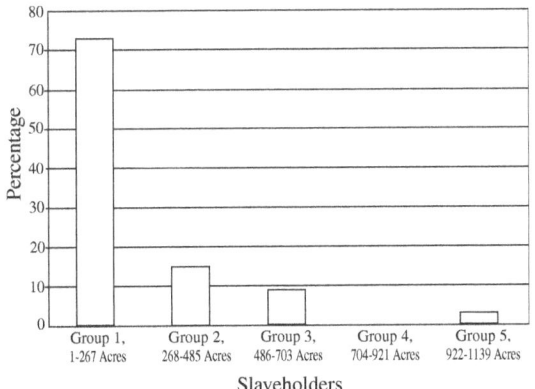

Figure 6. Distribution of improved acres owned by economic groups in 1850. (Drawing by George Wingard.)

1880 was probably due to the emergence of small farms and farm tenancy after the Civil War. In general, the large landholdings of George Bush and George W. Bush, along with their sizeable labor force before the Civil War, would have enabled them to produce more agricultural output than other households.

Agricultural Production

Agricultural production associated with the George Bush, George W. Bush, and Hansford D. Bush households is compared to production levels among the extended family, community, region (district/county), and state residents to reconstruct the economic activities that occurred at Bush Hill plantation. Agricultural comparisons are used to determine if the study households participated in the same economic activities as other households at the extended family, community, and regional levels. Further, comparing the different contexts helps determine if the study households (and their enslaved labor force) produced above average, average, or below average amounts of agricultural commodities.

The results of archival analysis indicate that agriculture at Bush Hill mainly centered upon grain and livestock production. Contrary to prevalent assumptions, mono- crop agriculture, such as cotton production, did not occur to any great extent at Bush Hill. Although beyond the topic of the present research, diversified agriculture was the main form of agriculture at Bush Hill, reminiscent of the 18th-century frontier in the South that often focused upon corn and livestock. Consequently, it is likely that an initial form of diversified farming became entrenched in the study area comprising Barnwell District and the surrounding middle Savannah River valley. Over time, grain farming originating in the frontier period developed into large-scale commercial agriculture among some planters.

Paralleling the slaveholding trends discussed previously, results of archival analysis indicate that the study households within the Bush family were outliers regarding the amount of agricultural products raised at Bush Hill. Their production levels often exceeded the other comparative levels in many crop categories. Trends affiliated with agricultural production were reconstructed from information in the U.S. Census of Agriculture Annual Reports (U.S. Department of State 1841; USBC 1853; USDI 1864, 1872, and 1883) and from the original agricultural census schedule forms for community and household-level contexts (SCDAH 1850a, 1860a, 1870a, and 1880a).

Historical studies indicate that early settlers in the South quickly established herds of swine (Hilliard 1984). Pork was a dietary mainstay in southern households. Everyone kept hogs, and pork was often served at every meal. Pork was also typically an important part of slave rations (Hilliard 1984:45; Taylor 1989:614). It is not surprising that large swine herds were raised in the study area as well as in the state. George Bush, Sr.'s, and George W. Bush's swine herds exceeded the household average for the extended family, community, regional, and state levels prior to the Civil War (Table 3).

TABLE 3
NUMBER OF HEADS OF SWINE IN STUDY SAMPLE

Household Level	1850	1860	1870	1880
George Bush	100	–	–	–
George W. Bush	100	90	20	15
Hansford D. Bush	60	100	–	–
Bush family average	73	81	17	31
Community average	67	43	9	17
Region average	44	24	16	10
State average	36	34	8	7

After the Civil War, George W. Bush's swine herds were similar in size to the average household in the surrounding community and extended family. The number of hogs that he owned, however, was still almost two times higher than the household average at the state level. This information may suggest that most households in the region raised more hogs than they consumed. The prominent drop in the number of swine certainly reflects the absence of slave labor, since planters typically provided slaves with pork rations.

The importance of cattle increased through time in the South. Cattle were raised primarily for cash and food. During the antebellum period, George Bush had a large cattle herd (n=30) as did his extended family—larger than the region and state analysis categories (Table 4). George Bush was probably keeping his large cattle herd for cash. This herd was considerably larger than would have been needed for food by the two-person household that occupied the site at this time. Further, beef was not typically a slave ration, since it was usually not smoked.

The value of the livestock in the George Bush household was about four times greater than the value for the average household in the surrounding community, region, and state (Table 5). In 1850, his sons' livestock holdings were more valuable than other household herds in the surrounding community, region, and state but fairly equal to that of other Bush family households. These dollar values suggest that the George Bush family may have been raising livestock commercially for profit. Raising livestock would have been a lucrative activity at Bush Hill plantation given the large landholding size and large labor force that could have managed the livestock during the antebellum period.

Regarding crops, Nicholas Hardeman (1989: 34) states, "Corn was, without serious rival, the universal plant of the South." Given corn's multitude of uses on the southern farm and plantation, it is not surprising that the study households produced it in large amounts. Prior to the Civil War, George Bush and his sons were producing considerably more Indian corn than the amounts produced by the average household in the community, region, or state. The amount

TABLE 4
NUMBER OF HEADS OF CATTLE IN STUDY SAMPLE

Household Level	1850	1860	1870	1880
Milk cows				
George Bush	20	–	–	–
George W. Bush	10	15	6	8
Hansford D. Bush	5	5	–	–
Bush family average	9	9	4	3
Community average	8	5	2	2
Region average	7	3	3	2
State average	6	6	2	2
Other cattle				
George Bush	30	–	–	–
George W. Bush	15	25	7	27
Hansford D. Bush	0	15	–	–
Bush family average	27	27	8	8
Community average	21	15	3	3
Region average	15	7	4	3
State average	19	11	3	2

TABLE 5
DOLLAR VALUE OF LIVESTOCK IN STUDY SAMPLE

Household Level	1850	1860	1870	1880
George Bush	$2,000	–	–	–
George W. Bush	$800	$3,210	$2,170	$1,000
Hansford D. Bush	$700	$1,680	–	–
Bush family average	$820	$1,948	$802	$385
Community average	$493	$997	$283	$127
Region average	$441	$1,031	$368	$148
State average	$503	$841	$240	$130

produced by the study households was even considerably larger than the average produced by the extended family (Table 6). The study households produced large amounts of Indian corn because of the large size of the economic household, including the planter's family and enslaved laborers. Corn was also probably used to feed livestock at the plantation.

By 1870, the amount of corn that was produced among all comparative contexts declined. Corn production fell among the George W. Bush household, the extended family, the surrounding community, the district, and the state. After the Civil War, former slave-owning households were providing feed to smaller livestock herds and no longer had slave populations to feed. The number of bushels of corn produced by George W. Bush declined by more than 75% after the Civil War (1870), reflecting the role of corn in the diet of enslaved African Americans and for livestock herds. Despite the reduction in corn production, George W. was still growing more

corn than other households. The higher production of corn at the plantation would have been at least partially related to the fact that his household size and livestock herd were still slightly larger than the other comparative categories.

After the invention of Eli Whitney's cotton gin in 1793, cotton became a staple crop in the interior of South Carolina. Planters and small farmers focused almost exclusively on cotton (Kovacik and Winberry 1987). Robert Mills (1972) noted in 1826 that many planters in Barnwell District were not exceptions to this trend, and they focused exclusively on cotton. George Bush, Sr., and his son George W. Bush produced very little cotton in the mid-19th century, despite their considerable slave population (Table 7). George Sr.'s cotton production equaled that of the surrounding community, even though he owned more acreage and a larger slave population than most other planters in the community. In fact in 1846, George W. Bush commented at the May meeting of the ABC

TABLE 6
BUSHELS OF INDIAN CORN IN STUDY SAMPLE

Household Level	1850	1860	1870	1880
George Bush	2,000	–	–	–
George W. Bush	2,500	2,500	600	900
Hansford D. Bush	1,000	1,500	–	–
Bush family average	1,701	1,750	409	462
Community average	923	911	245	194
Region average	539	363	287	145
State average	54	529	147	125

TABLE 7
NUMBER OF COTTON BALES (400 POUND) IN STUDY SAMPLE

Household Level	1850	1860	1870	1880
George Bush	19	–	–	–
George W. Bush	0	78	17	15
Hansford D. Bush	14	36	–	–
Bush family average	33	56	9	11
Community average	19	16	6	7
Region average	7	8	9	6
State average	10	12	4	6

Farmer's Club that he was "not accustomed to the cultivation of cotton" (Beech Island Farmers' Club 1846–1883:7). By 1860, however, George Bush's sons had noticeably increased their cotton production—exceeding community, regional, and state levels. In fact, the winter after George Bush's death, 75 bales of cotton were listed as part of his estate in one court document (Barnwell County 1858). George apparently became interested in producing cotton during the last years of his life. Conversely, his sons may have managed their ailing father's agricultural production during his last year of life and decided to raise cotton.

Despite being substantially below the antebellum production levels, George W. Bush continued to exceed the agricultural production averages of other households during the postbellum period. The reduction of cotton production by all households in the comparative categories was due to the abolition of slavery and the related smaller size of farms and tenant plantations in the middle Savannah River valley.

Material Life at Bush Hill Plantation

The concept of material life is drawn from the scholarship of French social historian Fernand Braudel. An inclusive concept, the idea of material life focuses upon economic practices that individuals and households engaged in during the past and considers how these economic activities influenced daily life and material consumption (Braudel 1974). In his exhaustive research, Braudel explored the origins of many aspects of material culture and daily life, such as dress, diet, and household furnishings (Braudel 1981). It is assumed here that there is a relationship, although not always direct, between economic activities that households engaged in and their living conditions.

Two main information sources are used to explore material conditions at Bush Hill, consisting of primary records and the archaeological record. Probate inventories are analyzed to reconstruct the standard of living practiced at Bush Hill in comparison to other households in the study region. The probate inventory of George Bush is first compared to samples of probate inventories associated with his extended family and other community members. This effort serves to define general material trends among the study family and larger community.

Archaeological information is used to illustrate the type of dwelling that the planter household occupied. Artifacts from the site excavations are used to identify the foodways practiced by the planter's family. Recovered artifacts are also used to reconstruct the standard of living experienced by the Bush household members and identify the extent of consumerism that they practiced. Ironically, members of the George Bush family were aggressive consumers and discarded a substantial amount of items in the rear yard of their house lot. The material that was used and discarded daily was inexpensive. Consequently, affluence and access to consumer goods are denoted archaeologically at the George Bush dwelling by the amount or sheer quantity, not the quality, of items discarded. Artifact density at the planter's residence and the slave quarters is compared to illustrate the extent of consumption differences among the residents of Bush Hill.

Standard of Living

Archival records related to financial activities demonstrate that George Bush was a member of one of the top economic groups in the study area, at least by the time of his death in 1857. This economic position would have enabled his household to enjoy a high standard of living compared to other households. George Bush's probate inventory provides valuable information regarding the personal possessions actually used by his household. To place this information in a broader perspective, the probate inventories for other households in the surrounding community were also analyzed. This information allowed the comparison of George Bush's standard of living to that of his extended family and community, helping to determine if George was living above or below the local standard of living based on the monetary value of items listed in inventories. Wealth groups were also defined from the probate inventory information. The wealth groups were based upon an average probate monetary value within a sample and the distance from the average, based upon the standard deviation for the average. The methods used for the analysis of the inventory sample are discussed in the first part of this section. The results of inventory analysis are then subsequently presented.

A total of 35 probate inventories was examined for this study. The probate analysis methods, developed by Groover (1991, 1998, 2003a), consist of selecting a sample of cases and conducting functional analysis of items enumerated in probate entries based on their monetary value. Analysis methods were developed by combining a modified form of Charles Orser's Millwood functional typology with probate analysis methods developed by Gloria Main (1982) in her research on household material culture in colonial Maryland. Main divided personal wealth into three analysis groups: (1) consumption goods, (2) capital, and (3) financial assets. In addition to the consumption goods and groupings provided by Main, the functional typology developed by Orser (1988) was also merged with Main's categories to make the probate data comparable with artifact data. Consumption goods comprise the items placed in the foodways, clothing, household/structural, and personal categories, except for the monetary subcategory. Capital includes all items placed in the labor category.

Financial assets consist of the monetary subcategory (Tables 8 and 9).

Probate records used for analysis were selected from the Barnwell County estate inventory maintained at the South Carolina archives. Two factors guided the selection of the individual probates that were examined: (1) the year of the appraisal and (2) the name of the individual. The probate inventories were chosen from those available—not all survived the passage of time, and some were never filed.

George Bush died in September 1857, and his probate inventory was recorded in March 1858. To have comparable data, probate inventories recorded between 1850 and 1865 were sampled. This date range was large enough to assemble at least 30 examples. All inventories used in this study were also recorded within seven to eight years of George Bush's death. It was expected that the short time span of the sample would insure comparability for the value of the items listed in the inventories.

The probate sample also included three of George Bush's relatives, an older brother and two younger cousins. The inventories of these three men were combined to create a Bush family average. Thirty-five cases were included in the inventory analysis. George Bush's inventory value was $44,939.45. The 35-case sample of probate inventories, representing members of the surrounding study community, ranged in value from $154.63 to $142,987.70. The average probate inventory value was $19,497.24.

George Bush Household

The total value of George Bush's probate inventory was $44,939.45. In addition, George's estate would have also included his substantial landholdings (he owned 3,000 acres in 1850) and the improvements on his land (including dwellings, slave cabins, and outbuildings). Based on the estate value, George Bush was a member of Wealth Group 3.

From the probate inventory, it appears that his dwelling was sparsely furnished. For example, the main living area (comprising one or possibly two rooms, perhaps a dining room and sitting room) contained 3 dining tables, chairs, a bureau, a lounge, and a sideboard. A looking glass and Yankee clock were accessories listed in these rooms. A bedroom with two beds and

TABLE 8
EXAMPLES OF PROBATE ITEMS PLACED WITHIN EACH SUBCATEGORY

Foodways

    Procurement

        Guns

    Preparation

        Cookware

        Grindstones

        Ovens

    Service

        Flatware

        Glassware

        Ceramics

    Storage

        Dairy furniture

        Containers

        Jars

Clothing

    Fasteners

        Clothes

    Manufacture

        Sewing machines

        Sewing table

Household/Structural

    Architectural/Construction

        Nails

        Shingles

    Furnishings/Accessories

        Andirons, firedogs, fenders

        Bath tub

        Candles, candlesticks, lamps

        Carpets

        Clock

        Closet contents

        Furniture

        Household tools (wash pots/tubs, tables, buckets)

        Linen

        Mirrors

        Pictures

        Smoothing irons

        Window shades

Personal

    Medicinal

        Equipment and supplies

    Cosmetic

        Shaving tools

    Recreational

        Piano

    Decorative

        Watches

    Others

        Books

        Lock

        Maps

        Riding gear

        Personal transportation[1]

        Umbrellas

    Safes

    Monetary

        Cash on hand

        Notes owed the estate

Labor

    Slaves

    Agricultural

        Wagons/Carts

        Crops

        Livestock

        Lumber

        Stored provisions

        Bees

        Fertilizers

        Tools[2]

    Industrial

        Boats

        Craft supplies (hides, iron)

    Craft tools[3]

        Farm supplies (ropes, bags)

        Plantation tools

        Tools

        Scales and measures

        Grindstones

[1]Buggies, carriages, gigs, rockaways, and barouches.
[2]Crop saws, cutter saws, hoes, axes, shovels, forks, corn shellers, gins, ploughs and gears, grindstones, and cradles.
[3]Blacksmith tools, shoemaking tools, carpentry tools, spinning wheels, and looms.

TABLE 9
CATEGORIES* USED FOR PROBATE INVENTORY ANALYSIS

Consumption goods	Capital
Apparel	Bonded labor
Jewelry	Livestock
Watches	Agricultural tools
Clocks	Agricultural equipment
Silver plate	Craft tools
Books	New goods
Musical instruments	Boats
Pictures	Crops
Flower pots	Stored provisions
Window curtains	Labor artifact category
Hangings	
Table linens	
Furniture	Financial Assets
Bedding	Debts receivable
Cooking/Dining utensils	Book debts
Riding gear	Domestic bills
Ammunition	Bills of exchange
Militia	Money
Foodways artifact category	Foreign coins
Clothing artifact category	Bullion
Household/Structural artifact category	Paper money
Personal artifact category	Monetary artifact subcategory

* Developed by Main (1982) and Orser (1988)

one dressing table and a third bedroom with three beds, two dressing tables, two trunks, and two chests followed the room with the dining tables in the probate inventory.

George's inventory listed very few personal items. The few personal items consisted of a gun, saddle and saddlebags, and a buggy and harness. No kitchen furniture was listed, and the only kitchen-related items in the inventory consisted of lots of pot ware, jars, a bucket, crockery, and broken glassware.

Information enumerated in George Bush's probate inventory indicates his assets mainly consisted of capital for agriculture, such as slaves, livestock, and crops, or monetary resources either in the form of cash or notes due the estate. The probate inventory contains numerous goods or capital that would be hard to identify spe-

cifically from archaeological data such as books, beds, chairs, dressing tables, trunks, accounts receivable to the estate, livestock, and crops. Several of the items could possibly be identified from artifacts such as the looking glass, clock, glassware, crockery, pot ware, jars, water bucket, gun, ploughs, and tools.

The contents of George Bush's inventory were also compared to members of his extended family and other Barnwell District residents to better understand the relative standard of living practiced by the planter at Bush Hill as compared to other family and community members.

George Bush's Extended Family

To determine the relative standard of living practiced by George Bush, his probate inventory was compared to members of his extended family who died during the same general time period. George's probate inventory value was worth one-third more ($44,939.45) than the average value for his extended family ($36,154.19). The members of his extended family used for this comparison consisted of an older brother and two younger second cousins.

Based on the appraised value of personal property, George and his extended family were members of Wealth Group 3. The values of the functional categories between George and his extended family are compared in Table 10. In comparison to other family members, George had a high personal category. When the subcategories are examined, it is clear that the differences between his probate inventory and that of the members of his extended family's

result from the higher dollar value of George's monetary subcategory rather than consumption goods. A notable difference between George and his extended family is that the value of George's slave labor was higher than his relatives' enslaved labor force, but the values of his agricultural tools and equipment, produce, and livestock were low in comparison.

Finally, comparing the probate inventory data by Main's three groupings re-emphasizes the fact that George Bush spent little on consumption goods, especially compared to his extended family (Table 11). While his estate value is more than $8,000 higher than the family average, the value of his consumption goods is approximately 25% of the extended family's' average for consumption goods. In comparison to the total estate value, no one expended a

TABLE 10
PERSONAL ESTATE OF GEORGE BUSH AND THE BUSH EXTENDED FAMILY

| | George Bush | | Bush Family | |
Functional Subcategory	Category	Subcategory	Category	Subcategory
Foodways	$15.25	–	$21.67	–
Procurement	–	$5.00	–	$1.00
Preparation	–	$6.00	–	$10.33
Service	–	$2.25	–	$10.00
Storage	–	$2.00	–	$0.33
Clothing	$0.00	–	$33.33	–
Manufacture	–	$0.00	–	$33.33
Household/Structural	$69.75	–	$339.93	–
Architectural/Construction	–	0.00	–	$0.33
Furnishings/Accessories	–	$69.75	–	$339.60
Personal	$7,030.13	–	$5,076.79	–
Monetary	–	$6,983.88	–	$4,961.79
Other	–	$46.25	–	$81.67
Recreational	–	0.00	–	$33.33
Labor	$37,824.32	–	$30,678.80	–
Slaves	–	$35,375.00	–	$25,017.17
Agricultural	–	$2,416.12	–	$5,648.63
Industrial	–	$33.20	–	$13.00
Unidentified	$0.00	$0.00	–	$3.67
	$3.67	–	–	–
Total Estate Value	$44,939.45	$44,939.45	$36,154.19	$36,154.19

TABLE 11
PERSONAL ESTATE OF GEORGE BUSH AND HIS EXTENDED FAMILY*

Functional Subcategory	George Bush		Bush Family	
All assets				
Consumption	$131.25	(0%)	$509.93	(1%)
Capital	$37,824.32	(84%)	$30,678.80	(85%)
Financial assets	$6,983.88	(16%)	$4,961.79	(14%)
Unidentified	$0.00	(0%)	$3.67	(0%)
Total estate value	$44,939.45		$36,154.19	
Excluding Financial Assets				
Consumption	$131.25	(0%)	$509.83	(2%)
Capital	$37,824.32	(100%)	$30,678.80	(98%)
Unidentified	$0.00	(0%)	$3.67	(0%)
Total Estate Value	$37,955.57		$31,192.30	

* Grouped by analysis categories developed by Main (1982)

large proportion of their income on consumption goods, even when financial assets are excluded from the probate tabulations.

George Bush Community

George Bush's probate total was almost $45,000, while the adjusted community average was approximately $16,000. This information indicates that George could have afforded a substantially higher standard of living than the surrounding community. The items listed in his probate inventory suggest that he chose not to spend money on household furnishings but spent, rather, on resources related to agriculture and the means of production, such as enslaved laborers and land.

Figure 7 illustrates the different wealth groups defined from probate analysis. The vertical scale in the figure refers to percentage rather than the actual number of cases. Proportionally, Wealth Group 1 comprises almost two-thirds of the population yet held only 22% of the personal wealth ca. 1857. Members of Wealth Group 1 were primarily small slaveholders (n=20) or nonslaveholders (n=3). Interestingly, Wealth Group 4, representing only 6% of the population, held 31% of the personal wealth. This 35-case sample suggests that around one-third

of the free population held 80% of the personal wealth in the area while the other two-thirds of the population held only 20% of the personal wealth. George Bush's financial resources placed him in Wealth Group 3 and among the top 20% of wealth holders.

Table 12 presents the probate data tabulated according to the Millwood typology. The household and labor categories, the only categories consistently represented in the probate inventories, increase in expected ways. The functional categories with higher wealth values are consistently associated with the higher wealth groups.

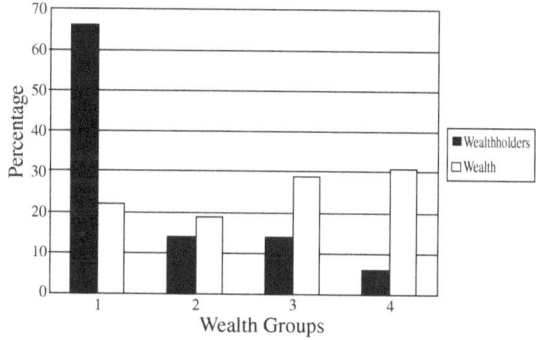

Figure 7. Wealth groups plotted by total probate inventory value. (Drawing by George Wingard.)

TABLE 12
FUNCTIONAL DISTRIBUTION OF THE PERSONAL ESTATE OF GEORGE BUSH
COMPARED TO FOUR WEALTHHOLDING GROUPS

	Foodways	Clothing	Household	Personal	Labor	UID
George Bush	$15	$0	$70	$7,030	$37,824	$0
WG 1	$24	$3	$111	$715	$5,545	$28
WG 2	$49	$1	$226	$2,200	$23,297	$1
WG 3	$45	$0	$512	$1,932	$36,637	$3
WG 4	$149	$50	$321	$19,062	$84,961	$8

WG=wealth group; UID=unidentified

The correspondence between the wealth groups and the functional categories suggests that using functionally based analysis methods is a useful way of analyzing wealth-holding trends preserved in probate inventories.

Interestingly, the personal category substantially increases with wealth-holding groups. As expected, upper wealth groups were expending higher levels of money on personal items than lower groups. Conversely, the clothing category is a weak measure of wealth because these items were rarely included in the inventories. The functional distribution of wealth defined from probate analysis also illustrates that food preparation, service, and storage items (artifact types that are usually central elements of archaeological analysis) generally increased in value in expected ways but overall were not appraised for large amounts of money in most of the probate inventories. George Bush's household possessions appear to be most similar in value to those of Wealth Group 1, while his labor-related possessions appear to be similar to Wealth Group 3. Consequently, analysis results indicate that George Bush practiced a standard of living very similar to most of the community members surrounding Bush Hill. Conversely, in the area of agricultural production, Bush was an outlier. This observation illustrates that the relationship between wealth and the household standard of living is usually complex and often not direct. The George Bush family appears to have lived modestly yet owned a large agricultural operation. Consequently, in this example the George Bush family may have conveyed social status via the means of agricultural production rather than through conspicuous consumption of consumer goods.

The wealth group information assembled from probate inventory analysis was then tabulated according to Main's three financial categories, consisting of consumption, capital, and financial assets (Table 13). This comparison revealed several important trends. First, the total value of George's consumption goods ($131) was considerably lower than that of the average for his wealth group ($938). In fact, the value of his consumption goods is even slightly less than the value of consumption goods for Wealth Group 1, the lowest economic group defined. Examining the probate inventories of the people in Wealth Group 1 further demonstrates that George's expenditures were similar. This information suggests that the interior of George's home was furnished in a similar manner to the homes of the lowest economic group, rather than being furnished in a manner similar to the homes of his economic peer group.

It should also be noted that gift giving prior to death can also skew the items listed in probate inventories. Before death, heads of households often gave away much of their household furnishings to immediate family members. For example, among families not encumbered by debt, a father or mother might give away most household furnishings and personal possessions to grown sons and daughters. This practice would bias the items listed in an inventory and create an estate value much lower than its original worth prior to gift giving.

TABLE 13
SUBDIVIDED WEALTH GROUPS

	Consumption		Capital		Financial Assets		Total[1]
All Assets							
George Bush	$131	(0%)	$37,824.32	(84%)	$6,984	(16%)	$44,939
WG 1	$218	(3%)	$5,545	(86%)	$634	(10%)	$6,426
WG 2	$596	(2%)	$23,297	(90%)	$1,880	(7%)	$25,774
WG 3	$938	(2%)	$36,637	(90%)	$1,551	(4%)	$39,128
WG 4	$1,230	(1%)	$84,961	(81%)	$18,852	(18%)	$105,049
Excluding Financial Assets							
George Bush	$131	(0%)	$37,824.32	(100%)			$37,955
WG 1	$218	(4%)	$5,545	(96%)			$5,763
WG 2	$596	(2%)	$23,297	(98%)			$23,893
WG 3	$938	(3%)	$36,637	(98%)			$37,575
WG 4	$1,230	(1%)	$84,961	(99%)			$86,191

WG=wealth group; subdivided by analysis categories developed by Main (1982)

[1]Totals include unidentified items even though there is no column showing these resources.

Capital represents the main component of wealth held by households. The capital category comprised between 81% and 94% of financial resources in the study sample. In the capital group, George's inventory items were of similar value to those of his wealth group peers. Lower income groups had a slightly smaller proportion of wealth invested in capital than higher wealth groups.

Planter's Dwelling at Bush Hill

When archaeological site 38AK660 was first discovered, it contained a large rectangular mound of brick rubble measuring 20 by 50 ft. Excavation of the brick mound revealed the foundation remnants of the planter's house at Bush Hill. The dwelling contained two brick chimneys that were single-hearth, exterior, gable-end chimneys. The chimney bases were similar in thickness; they were both two brick courses wide along the two short sides of the box, and the back long wall of the chimney was 2-1/2 brick courses wide. The chimney bases were also similar in size (53 x 73 in. and 56 x 71 in.).

All of the brick architectural elements at the site were constructed in English bond, which was prevalent in the United States during the 18th and 19th centuries (Morrison 1952:101–104). The pattern consists of brick courses with alternating rows of headers and stretchers (Figure 8).

The distribution of features and artifacts provided important information about the size of the planter's dwelling at Bush Hill (Figures 9 and 10). The dwelling contained five brick piers on each side of the structure's length. The piers were all aligned with each other and

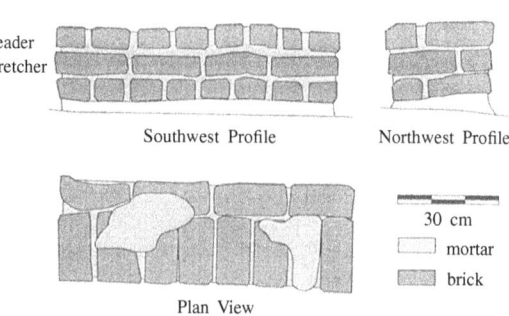

Figure 8. Example of English bond masonry pattern, Feature 5. (Drawing by George Wingard.)

Figure 9. Excavation block at Bush Hill. (Photo by SRARP staff.)

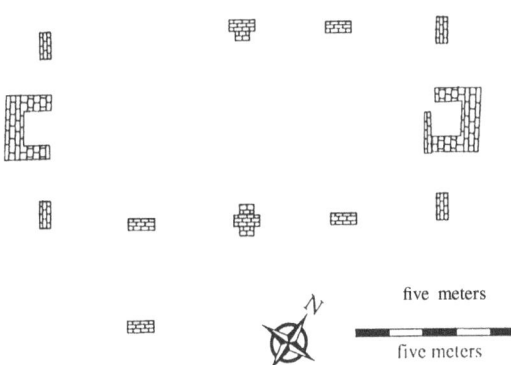

five meters

five meters

Figure 10. Plan of excavation block at Bush Hill showing the location of brick piers and chimney bases associated with the planter's house. (Drawing by George Wingard.)

outlined a rectangular floor plan. The floor plan was 20 by 43 ft., giving a total of 860 sq. ft.

Carefully dismantling the chimney falls during excavation provided important information about the height of the house. The west chimney fall contained architectural artifacts that indicated the house contained two stories. These important structural artifacts were iron fireplace lintels. Fireplace lintels are metal, horizontally placed bars that span the top opening of the fireplace directly below the mantle. Lintels provide structural support for the fireplace. Iron fireplace lintels were encountered in the west chimney rubble in two locations. The first set was found in the chimney fall near the base of the chimney. The second set was located a considerable distance from the ground floor firebox, yet belonged to the same chimney fall, indicating the structure

contained a second floor with gable chimneys. A second story, measuring the same size as the first floor, would have increased the overall dwelling size to 1,720 sq. ft.

The limited excavations conducted on the north side of the dwelling were intended to determine if the house contained an addition or porch on this side, presumably the front of the structure. Consequently, five trenches were excavated perpendicular to each of the house piers. No evidence of an addition or porch was found on the north face of the dwelling.

An additional feature composed of articulated bricks was aligned with the long axis of the brick piers on the south side of the dwelling. This feature was located 10 ft. from the southern side of the dwelling. This brick feature may have been a brick support for a porch or an addition. No other supports were found along the long axis of the dwelling that aligned with this feature. It was aligned with another brick pier located directly to the northwest, along the northern width of the dwelling. The bricks in this feature were not mortared. If it possessed companion piers in the past, they may have been removed after the dwelling was abandoned.

The presence of a porch or addition at the dwelling is not surprising since Virginia McAlester and Lee McAlester (1984:86) suggest that a full-width, shed-roofed front porch was popular on southern dwellings by the late-18th century. Based on features and the artifact distribution, it appears that the probable full-width porch was located on the rear of the dwelling. Typically, the back of a dwelling contained a rear addition rather than a porch. If the porch ran the entire length of the dwelling, as McAlester and McAlester's (1984) research indicates was typical, then the porch would have measured 10 by 43 ft. or 430 sq. ft. The dwelling may have also had a front porch, but no evidence of a front porch was recovered from the site.

Regarding the architectural style and floor plan of the dwelling at Bush Hill, archaeological information indicates that the dwelling at site 38AK660 was an I-house, a popular dwelling style between the late-18th and early-20th centuries. I-houses were typically one room deep, two rooms wide, and two stories high (Figure 11). This house style usually had a gable roof with its main entrance on a long axis of the dwelling. The structures varied regarding

Figure 11. An I-house on the Savannah River Site (AEC Tract J-920) ca. 1950. (Photo courtesy of SRS Archives.)

the placement of porches, sheds, pavilion rooms, central hall, and chimneys (McAlester and McAlester 1984; Kniffen 1990a and 1990b).

This architectural style is considered to be a vernacular or folk architectural form derived from British origins. The name "I-house" was coined by geographer Fred Kniffen (1990a: 53–54) who found this style was distributed throughout the "I" states of Indiana, Illinois, and Iowa. Kniffen came to regard it as one of the most widely distributed folk dwelling styles. The I-house was an architectural plan that was popular nationwide, but it is a particularly common folk dwelling in the Eastern and Midwestern states. In the South, I-houses first appear in the 18th century but were not common until the 1820s. McAlester and McAlester's (1984:82) research indicates that many of the colonists in the coastal areas of the South built linear plan houses, usually I-houses or hall-and-parlor dwellings.

The I-house has been called the "farmer's mansion" and was a rural symbol of prosperity, respectability, and social status in the 19th century (Southern 1978; Swaim 1978; Kniffen 1990a and 1990b). According to art historians "the essence of the I-House was its facade. With rare exception, it was built facing a roadway regardless of solar orientation. And its four rooms could not have been arranged to create a larger looking structure" (Swaim 1978: 38). McAlester and McAlester (1984:96) note that I-houses were common in the post-railroad south, "but these were usually the more preten-

tious houses of affluent local gentry. For this reason, many of these later southern I-houses have added stylistic detailing to make them appear fashionable." For example, they were customized by adding patterns of colored bricks in the chimneys (Lane 1984).

Geographers and folklorists have observed regional preference for placements of additions that served to expand and customize domestic space. For example, the I-house possessed a distinctive style in South Carolina and is called the Carolina I-house. This variant had two standard additions consisting of a one-story gallery, added to the front, and a one-story shed appended to the rear of the dwelling. The Carolina I-house typically had two large exterior chimneys located on the gable ends. The central hallway is also a typical feature and provided needed ventilation during the summer months. This architectural plan was well suited for warm climates, which might partially explain its prevalence in the Carolinas.

Although the I-house was commonly built throughout the South, it is important to determine if this was a common local dwelling style. In 1951, the Atomic Energy Commission acquired approximately 200,000 acres from residents in Aiken, Allendale, and Barnwell counties to form a nuclear research plant, today known as the Savannah River Site (SRS). When the government purchased the properties, the appraisers measured, described, assessed, and photographed all the structures located on the individual property tracts. The SRS archives contain information pertaining to improvements on the land that the government acquired.

A study of these records was conducted as part of a larger research project focusing on the topic of rural modernization among farmsteads in 1951 (Cabak and Inkrot 1997; Cabak et al. 1999). Dwelling styles prevalent in the region were reconstructed from a systematic search and analysis of records. The property records associated with 112 farmsteads were examined in detail and only 2% (n=2) of the rural dwellings contained two stories. Both of the two-story examples in the sample were I-houses. Government photographs indicate the structures were probably Carolina I-houses since they had front galleries and rear additions. The I-house on land tract J-920 (Figure 11) was 2,052 sq. ft. The house rested on brick piers and had a metal roof. Archaeological evidence indicates that this house was probably constructed in the mid- to late-19th century. The other I-house in the modernization study was located on land tract O-1426 and measured 2,097 sq. ft., contained a metal roof, and also rested on brick piers.

In summary, a review of relevant local historical records indicates that the I-house was the main type of two-story dwelling style found in the Aiken Plateau. The same trend probably applies for much of the middle Savannah River valley. Further, a very small proportion of affluent residents in the study area used this dwelling style. Archaeological information from Bush Hill plantation indicates that the dwelling was 20 by 43 ft. with a porch or addition that probably was full width (10 × 43 ft.), which corresponds to the typical dimensions and size of an I-house. Carolina I-houses often had exterior gable-end fireplaces and additions, paralleling archaeological data recovered from Bush Hill plantation. Available information indicates the planter's dwelling at Bush Hill was probably an I-house (Figure 12).

Foodways at Bush Hill

Kitchen artifacts and faunal remains illustrate the foodways practiced by the planter family at Bush Hill. The general types of food consumed by the residents were determined from faunal remains. Kitchen items from the site revealed foodways characteristics of the study households

Figure 12. Conjectural sketch of the planter's dwelling at Bush Hill. (Drawing by George Wingard.)

and also provided information pertaining to consumerism within the Bush family.

Diet and Faunal Remains

Domesticated animals comprised a larger proportion of the site residents' diet than wild game. Cow, pig, chicken, and sheep or goat remains were recovered from both midden and features. The recovered skeletal elements also indicate that onsite butchering and consumption of these animals occurred at the plantation.

Although most of the domestic mammal remains are teeth (due to poor preservation of faunal material), several skeletal elements were also recovered. These remains allowed for an assessment of the various cuts or portions of meat that were consumed at the site (following Schulz and Gust 1983; Szuter 1996). In addition to cow, chicken, and pig remains found in all contexts, sheep or goat remains were present only in the later deposits (post 1850). The species composition and meat cut information suggests a slight increase in the quality of meat consumed by the main house residents over time. The addition of mutton, even in small amounts, also implies that a slightly greater use of domestic meat sources occurred during the later period. In addition, the pork and beef cuts from the second half of the site's occupation are of a higher quality than the cuts that were eaten during the first half of the site's occupation.

Economics and Table Service at Bush Hill Plantation

Dining and Serving Utensils

Thirty-four dining utensils were recovered from Bush Hill plantation. The sample represents a range of utensil types and quality. The assemblage contained at least 6 knives (in addition to several pocket knives), 4 forks, 13 spoons, and 11 handle/bolster fragments. The forks consisted of three two-tined forks and one three-tined fork.

One of the spoons is a complete example of a coin-silver teaspoon, which was found in the chimney rubble at the site. The spoon was engraved with a monogram and contained a maker's mark. The initials are probably ESB and refer to George's wife, Eleanor Sapp Bush

(Figures 13 and 14). The remaining 12 spoons were all rusted. Two teaspoons and three serving spoons were identified among the spoon sample. Five spoon handles were also recovered, and two of the handles had a decorative pattern on the end of the spoon. According to the 1909 Sears catalog, these spoons were decorated with the shell and bead pattern (Feinman 1979).

The households at site 38AK660 probably had several sets of dining utensils. A full range of utensils was found in addition to two types of spoons and forks. The higher quality silverware, such as the coin-silver spoon, may have been used for special or formal occasions. Silver teaspoons are rarely recovered archaeologically. They were usually curated by a family and passed down the family line as heirlooms. For example, a Bush family descendent has similarly styled spoons that lack a monogram. According to Katherine Hubbard (the great granddaughter of George W. Bush), her spoons belonged to Augusta Jane Foster Bush (George

W. Bush's wife). The other utensils, represented by the rusted flatware, were probably intended for utilitarian purposes and were often lost, broken, and frequently replaced.

Porcelain

Porcelain was an expensive ceramic that also functioned as a status symbol between the 16th and 19th centuries. Interestingly, the George Bush family used very little porcelain in their daily lives. Porcelain comprised a mere 3% of the entire ceramic assemblage from the site. Eleven percent of the total porcelain sample occurred in the earliest deposits at the site. The porcelain that was used by the site residents was usually plain porcelain rather than decorated tea ware. Reflecting frugal consumer practices among the Bush family, plain porcelain was less expensive than decorated porcelain tea ware and tableware.

Refined Earthenware

Archaeologists often rank ceramics by cost to gain insight into the assumed relationship between socioeconomic class and ceramic use (Miller 1980, 1991; Earl et al. 1993). For the analysis of refined earthenware, sherd counts were placed in four economic tiers that represent a slight simplification of Miller's (1980:3–4) scaling method. Amy Earl and colleagues' (1993:535–536) expansion of the system for 20th-century ceramics was also incorporated into the analysis methods. Miller's system is based on the skill needed to produce and decorate ceramics and, hence, their cost to the consumer. Tier 1 in this system consists of the least-expensive undecorated ceramics. Tier 2 consists of decorated ceramics that required minimal artistic skill and labor to produce and are only slightly more expensive than undecorated ceramics. At Bush Hill plantation these are ceramics with molded decorations; shell-edged wares; and banded, sponged, and slip-decorated wares. The third, moderate-priced tier contains wares with painted patterns and decalcomania. The fourth and most expensive group contains transfer-printed, flow blue, and luster wares. These tiers were used to establish the general cost of ceramics used by the George Bush household.

Figure 13. Detail of engraved coin-silver spoon found at Bush Hill plantation. (Photo by SRARP staff.)

Example of 1820's "B"

Example of 1820's "D"

Figure 14. Line drawing of engraving on coin-silver spoon. (Drawing by George Wingard.)

Table 14 illustrates several trends emerge when the refined earthenware sample is divided by relative cost. Foremost, the George Bush family primarily purchased inexpensive, minimally or undecorated wares; however, expensive transfer-printed vessels were the most commonly purchased ceramic within the decorated ceramic category. One important trend noted in the analysis is that the distribution of decorated ceramics is skewed or biased when the sample is quantified by sherd count. This bias is due to the fact that some ceramic decoration techniques, such as transfer-printing, completely cover the vessel and consequently produce an inflated sherd count in comparison to edge-decorated vessels, such as molded and shell-edged flatware. Usually, these ceramics were only decorated on the vessel rims. Consequently, most of the sherds from edge-decorated vessels would be placed in the undecorated category. George Miller and Robert Hunter's (1990) observation that "A shelf full of shell edged plates just looks like a collection of frames with the subjects missing," aptly emphasizes this point. Consequently, it

was hoped that analysis using rim sherds as the distinguishing attribute might adjust for this bias, since all of the decorated vessels usually had decorated rims.

The previously discussed distribution in Table 14 is substantially altered when only rim sherds are used as the main analysis attribute, and decorated body sherds are excluded. The plain molded sherds shift to being the most prevalent decorated type, followed by shell-edge flatware. Interestingly, transfer-printed ceramics, although the same in proportion, become the third most-common decorative type when only rim sherds are counted. The undecorated wares, still the most common category, dramatically decline in count. To determine if purchasing patterns changed during the 19th century, the relative cost of ceramics recovered stratigraphically was examined. Most excavation units were excavated in five 10-cm arbitrary levels (designated levels A, B, C, D, and E). Decorated ceramics in levels A and B (mainly dating to the late-19th and early-20th centuries) were compared to the ceramics found in levels C, D, and E (dating to the first half of the 19th

TABLE 14
CERAMIC DECORATIVE TYPES BY WARE

Decoration	All Sherds		Rim Sherds	
	Number	Percentage	Number	Percentage
Tier 1				
Undecorated	3,135	66%	476	41%
Tier 2				
Dipped	91	2%	20	2%
Gilded	10	<1%	7	1%
Molded	388	8%	250	21%
Shell-edged	203	4%	203	17%
Sponged	42	1%	21	2%
Tier 3				
Decalcomania	66	1%	16	1%
Painted	191	4%	33	3%
Tier 4				
Flow blue	15	<1%	7	1%
Luster	5	<1%	–	–
Transfer-printed	597	13%	149	13%
Total	4,768	100%	1,182	101%

century). Very few differences in the temporal occurrence of decorated ceramics were noted between earlier and later spatial/stratigraphic contexts (Table 15).

TABLE 15
DISTRIBUTION OF CERAMICS
AT BUSH HILL PLANTATION

Tier	Late Period	Early Period
Tier 1	43%	41%
Tier 2	41%	39%
Tier 3	4%	4%
Tier 4	12%	16%
Total	100%	100%

The assemblage is clearly dominated by the least expensive, undecorated wares. Forty-one percent of the assemblage is composed of undecorated rim sherds. The decorated wares used by the George Bush household consist primarily of inexpensive ceramics in Tier 2. These ceramics consist of gilded, banded, sponged, shell-edged, and molded wares.

Further consideration of ceramics provides insight into the dining table that was set at Bush Hill plantation. From the late-18th to the late-19th centuries, three types of ceramics dominated the market, consisting of plain, shell-edged, and transfer-printed vessels. Plain, cream colored ware dominated the market until the War of 1812. After this date, shell edged was the most common decorated tableware until about 1830, when transfer-printed forms became very popular.

Bush Hill plantation contained very little creamware, since its production date range predates the site occupation in ca. 1810. As stated above, however, undecorated whiteware dominates the assemblage.

The artifact assemblage from Bush Hill plantation contains 203 shell-edge sherds. Only a few examples of the earliest rococo style shell-edge earthenware were identified in this assemblage since its period of use predates the site occupation (Table 16). Numerous examples of even-scalloped and impressed shell-edged flatware were found at the site. These decorative techniques were popular in the first third of the 19th century. Numerous examples of unscalloped, impressed shell-edged sherds that were produced in the mid-19th century were also identified. Although declining in number, the site also contained examples of the poorly decorated shell-edged wares common in the late-19th century. The prevalence of shell-edged flatware demonstrates that the planters at Bush Hill set their table with these wares during the height of shell-edge's popularity in the first third of the 19th century. The persistence of the later styles indicates that the Bush family continued to use these inexpensive wares throughout the 19th century, even after they had declined in popularity.

Although the Bush household consistently purchased inexpensive shell-edged plates throughout

TABLE 16
SHELL-EDGED EARTHENWARE BY DECORATIVE TYPE

Type	Number	Percentage
Asymmetrical scalloped edge/impressed lines	3	1%
Symmetrical scalloped edge/impressed lines	51	25%
Symmetrical scalloped edge/painted lines	16	8%
Embossed edge	18	9%
Unscalloped edge/impressed lines	33	16%
Unscalloped edge/painted lines	10	5%
Other edge	40	20%
Unidentified	32	16%
Total	203	100%

the 19th century, they also used a substantial amount of more fashionable and expensive transfer-printed ceramics. The Bush family purchased numerous transfer-printed vessels in a range of colors and forms. Examples of blue, black, brown, red, mulberry, and purple transfer-printed vessels were recovered from the site.

The transfer-printed sherds indicate that the George Bush household purchased some matching quantities of expensive plates. It appears unlikely from archaeological evidence, however, that the site residents used complete dinner sets composed of several different matching vessel types, such as dinner plates, soup plates, salad plates, dessert plates, a tureen and ladle, and matching tea ware. Further, there appears to have been a lack of pattern duplication among the blue transfer-printed plates, which comprised a large proportion of the printed sherds and identified minimum vessel counts from the site. The lack of duplicated patterns among the blue transfer-printed sherds implies that the residents probably used a hodge-podge of flatware that was decorated in different blue transfer-printed patterns. The color was similar among these expensive vessels, but the patterns did not match. This observation, if accurate, parallels the conservative, down-to-earth consumer practices of the site residents as identified in other material domains. The site residents purchased transfer-printed plates in matching colors but were not concerned with matching patterns.

Local ceramic availability may have also influenced the lack of pattern duplication in the blue-printed sample. It is probably unlikely that local merchants in the first half of the 19th century stocked large supplies of matching flatware constituting "sets" in the contemporary sense. Rather, local rural stores were probably stocked with lots or shipments of assorted wares ranging in price and vessel form. Bush Hill is located less than 20 mi. from Augusta, Georgia, a major city during the 1800s, suggesting that elaborate sets of matching dinnerware were locally available.

Regardless of potential market access via Augusta, archaeological finds indicate that over time the site residents of Bush Hill periodically purchased different quantities of assorted transfer-printed patterns from local merchants. Further, the site residents apparently never felt compelled to purchase or special order a complete matching set of ceramics. Interestingly, this same type of assorted ceramic use has likewise been documented at numerous slave sites (Otto 1975, 1984; Michie 1987, 1990).

Refined earthenware provides insight into the consumer habits of the George Bush family. It appears that the family was thrifty when it came to ceramic purchases, as illustrated by the prevalence of undecorated, molded, and shell-edged forms. Conversely, they were also aware of and participated in current popular culture and fashion trends, as demonstrated by the use of expensive transfer-printed vessels.

Consumerism and Artifact Density

Analysis of probate inventory information and artifacts recovered from site excavations at Bush Hill suggests that members of the George Bush family were frugal but active consumers. For example, qualitative data indicates the house was modestly furnished and household members used inexpensive consumer goods, such as shell-edge ceramics and undecorated tableware. Although the residents of site 38AK660 did not purchase expensive items, the sheer amount of material that they used and discarded in the house lot midden is informative and reveals the extent of consumption that occurred within the household. From this perspective, consumption itself, regardless of material quality, can be a useful indicator of affluence.

Material consumption at Bush Hill was measured through artifact density, which was calculated from items recovered from shovel test pits excavated during initial site survey and testing. The shovel test pits (30 × 30 cm) were located in a formal site excavation grid, and test pits were excavated at 10 m intervals. To calculate artifact density, the total number of historic artifacts recovered from the shovel test pits was divided by the total number of positive shovel test pits. The resulting quotient indicates the average number of artifacts at the site per positive shovel test pit. The average number of artifacts per positive shovel test pit is regarded to be an expedient general measure of consumption at a site (Groover 2003b).

To better understand the extent of consumerism at Bush Hill, the artifact density from the slave quarters at the plantation was also calculated. The Bush Hill quarters are located approximately 100 yards north of the main house. Christine Crabtree (2003) conducted site testing at the quarters for thesis research in the Department of Anthropology, University of South Carolina.

The extent of consumerism at the planter's residence is aptly illustrated by shovel test pit information. The artifact density at the planter's house averaged 19.62 artifacts per positive shovel test pit. In stark contrast, the artifact density at the slave quarters averaged 2.7 artifacts per positive shovel test pit. Put another way, during the occupation of the plantation, the planter family was discarding approximately 10 times the amount of material as enslaved African Americans discarded at Bush Hill. The consumption differences between the two groups can be effectively illustrated using artifact density maps. As Figure 15 illustrates, artifact density at the planter's residence consists of a very prominent artifact spike. In contrast, artifact discard at the slave quarters is barely perceptible in comparison to the extent of consumption at the planter's residence.

An additional way of expediently defining consumption patterns is to compare the basic number of objects discarded at the planter's house during the first and second half of the

residence's occupation period. For this comparison, material from levels in the excavation units was dated and sorted into a pre-1870 period and a post-1870 period. As Table 17 shows, the results of this comparison indicate that most of the material at the site was discarded during the second half of the 19th century. Considered together, artifacts from shovel test pits and excavation units indicate that the Bush family was economical regarding the quality of household items that they used, yet they discarded a large amount of artifacts in the house lot during the late-19th century.

Conclusion

A case study of Bush Hill, a prosperous working plantation in Aiken County, South Carolina, allows the critical evaluation of stereotypes regarding material life among planters on southern plantations. Further, at the site level, archaeological investigations at Bush Hill examined the relationship between wealth and material culture within a lineal planter family.

This study explored the so-called plantation myth at Bush Hill. The land encompassing Bush Hill plantation was owned by four generations of the same family. Specifically, these owners

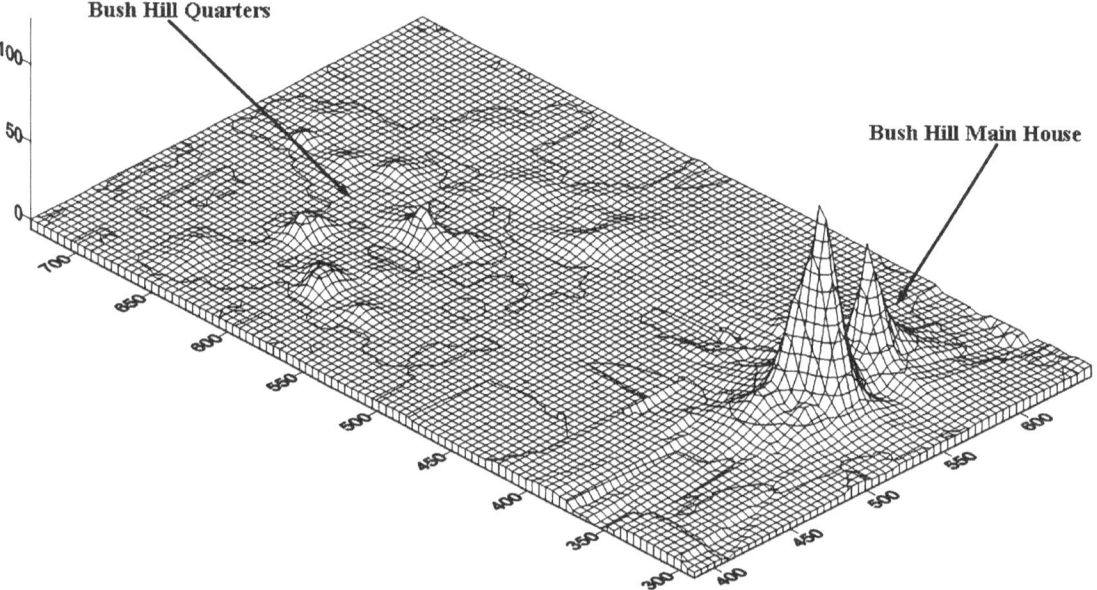

Figure 15. Spatial distribution of artifacts at the planter's dwelling and the slave quarters at Bush Hill. (Drawing by George Wingard.)

TABLE 17
DISTRIBUTION OF ARTIFACTS SORTED BY LEVELS AND TEMPORAL AREAS

Level	Pre-1870 Area		Post-1870 Area		Both Areas	
	No.	Average[1]	No.	Average	No.	Average
A	1,677	25	40,575	148	42,252	125
B	2,512	38	37,801	138	40,313	119
C[2]	1,367	21	14,755	105	16,122	78
D	119	7	1,404	27	1,523	22
E[3]	10	10			10	10
Unit[4]	5,685	86	95,250	344	100,935	295

[1]This is the average number of artifacts per level, for artifact bearing levels only. [2]Levels C and D were not always a full 10 cm level as each unit was only excavated until sterile soil was encountered. [3]Level E was only excavated in one unit. [4]The artifact total for the Post-1870 and Both Areas is higher than the total of the levels as some artifacts could not be specifically placed within a level (i.e., artifacts that originated from profile, excavation errors, and surface finds) but could be associated with an excavation unit.

consisted of the family patriarch, John Bush, who arrived in the study area in the 1760s and his son, grandsons, and great grandson. John Bush's son George and his wife Eleanor were the original residents of Bush Hill plantation. After their deaths, the plantation was passed along to their son and grandson until the federal government condemned the land in 1951.

Surviving historical records revealed that Bush Hill was clearly a working plantation that in many respects resembled a prosperous farm. Ironically family-level landholding trends, slave-holding trends, and agricultural production, indicate that the George Bush lineal household that occupied the excavated residence was wealthy from the early-19th to the early-20th centuries. While Bush Hill plantation never approached the size of large-scale plantations, measured by slaveholdings and landholdings, as discussed by Vlach (1993), it nevertheless was one of the larger and more successful plantations in the surrounding community. Despite considerable wealth, material life and the standard of living practiced at the planter's house were not extravagant or excessive, especially compared to popular perceptions of plantation life.

Extant archaeological evidence indicates that George Bush lived in a two-story dwelling that measured 20 by 43 ft. and probably contained a full-width porch or addition. The house was elevated above the ground with brick piers and contained two gable-end fireplaces. The dwelling had numerous glass windows, which were replaced on several occasions, and a wooden shingle roof. By the early-20th century, the house may have had screen doors and running water. This dwelling, although not manor-like, would have denoted rural affluence and success among 19th-century planters and farmers. Stylistically, the planter's dwelling at Bush Hill was probably a Carolina I-house.

A review of existing photographs from the local study area indicates that Carolina I-houses were typical among successful planters. However, the local study area encompassing Barnwell District and the larger middle Savannah River valley did contain at least one showplace plantation, Henry Hammond's Redcliffe. Hammond, a very wealthy individual and extreme economic outlier, built Redcliffe to flaunt "the wealth, taste, and refinement he acquired in his years as plantation master" (Faust 1982:335). The dwelling that Hammond built was not a typical plantation house for the area, and even Hammond owned a modest dwelling on his working plantation. Earlier archaeological studies in South Carolina (Michie

1987, 1990) have also shown that most planters, regardless of wealth, appear to have lived in vernacular style dwellings, which were often small in size. In most cases, however, it appears that dwelling size usually correlates with wealth.

The material culture used and discarded within the planter households at Bush Hill illustrates that household members were aware of and participated in popular consumer trends, as indicated by transfer-printed ceramic dishes and a coin-silver spoon. It appears that the George Bush household could set a reasonably fashionable dinner table, although most of the transfer-printed ceramics were mismatched. Despite the presence of fashionable consumer goods, mundane and inexpensive items, such as undecorated or minimally decorated tableware, inexpensive glassware, and utilitarian goods, dominate the artifact assemblage. Although the Bush family was apparently cost conscious of manufactured goods, the site residents nonetheless were fairly aggressive consumers, as indicated by artifact density. From this perspective, the sheer quantity of discarded material alone, regardless of cost or quality, can be viewed as an indicator of affluence.

Most of the mundane yet abundant refuse deposited in the planter's house lot at Bush Hill appears to have been discarded during the second half of site occupation. This occupation interval, associated with the George W. Bush and Arthur R. Bush ownership of the plantation during the postbellum period, also corresponds to a period of increasing industrialization and consumerism in the United States. The material dating to this period can be divided between essential utilitarian items and items that were nonessential goods, such as luxury items, decorative goods, or leisure-time consumer products. Paralleling national trends, a greater amount of financial resources appears to have been expended toward maintaining a more comfortable standard of living for the site occupants at Bush Hill during the second half of the 19th century compared to the first half of the century. Considered in its entirety, the artifact assemblage from the dwelling suggests the residents for the most part were frugal consumers, although they did discard a large amount of inexpensive consumer items by the late-19th century. The artifact assemblage paralleled and enhanced the findings from probate

inventory analysis indicating that George Bush was a frugal consumer. Surviving information indicates that George maintained a comfortable but not extravagant standard of living throughout his life and not just during the time before his death.

Despite substantial economic resources, the planter family at Bush Hill was composed of relatively frugal consumers. If members of the Bush family were wealthy but frugal, then how did they choose to expend their surplus financial resources? The answer to this question reveals much about the economic priorities of the George Bush family. Extant information indicates that throughout the 19th century, financial resources were mainly used to purchase land and slaves. For example, in 1858, slaves comprised 79% of George Bush's personal estate, which does not include his real estate (around 3,000 acres and improvements). George Bush's financial resources were distributed to his children when they married, came of age, or after his death. George's grown children used these economic gifts to start their own plantations or supplement the plantations already owned by their spouses. George W. Bush's share of his father's estate and the landholdings that he acquired during his career as a planter were never sold. Rather, these resources were passed on to his children after his death. The land and slaves given to Bush family members provided the necessary means of production to engage in plantation agriculture. These conveyances also illustrate the economic basis of social reproduction and how the planter class maintained itself over time within extended kin networks.

Interestingly, similar economic strategies have been noted among other rural families throughout North America (Salamon 1992; Groover 1998, 2003a). In fact, a predominantly held view among social scientists and historians of rural life is that many agricultural families maintained landholdings through time by reverently viewing their land as a sacred trust held for future generations (Peasall 1959; Bryant 1981). Consequently, among successful farm and plantation families over time, most of the agricultural profits were often reinvested into production or used to purchase more land. South Carolina architectural historian Mills Lane (1984) aptly noted, "The vast majority of people lived in modest comfort but without much display, for even rich farmers put their money in land and slaves." The land purchased from long-term profits was then eventually parceled out to family members as financial gifts or inheritance. The main purpose of this economic strategy was social reproduction, the long-term maintenance of the lineal family through intergenerational wealth transfer and the transfer of the means of production in the form of land and slaves to younger family members. At Bush Hill, this economic strategy succeeded in sustaining members of the George Bush family for approximately 125 years.

Acknowledgments

This essay is based upon a long-term field project conducted by personnel with the Savannah River Archaeological Research Program. The Savannah River Operations Office, United States Department of Energy, supported archaeological investigations at Bush Hill plantation. Investigations at the archaeological site were conducted under contract number DE-FC09-98SR18931. SRARP personnel and numerous volunteers assisted in the site excavations and artifact analysis. George Wingard drafted the figures in this essay. The authors thank all of the individuals that participated in the archaeological research conducted at Bush Hill. The authors also thank Glenn Ferris for his editorial guidance and the comments provided by the anonymous reviewers of the manuscript.

References

AIKEN COUNTY
    1890 Aiken County Deed Book T:148. Aiken County Registrar of Mesne Conveyance Office, Aiken County Office Complex, Aiken, SC.
    1954 Estate Records of Arthur R. Bush. Bundle 153, Package 17. Microfilm, Aiken County Probate Judge's Office, Aiken County Court House, Aiken, SC.

BARNWELL COUNTY
    1845 Barnwell County Deed Book BB:155. Barnwell County Clerk of Court's Office, Barnwell Court House, Barnwell, SC.
    1858 Estate Documents of George Bush. Probate Bundle 134, Package 6. Barnwell County Probate Judge's Office, Barnwell Court House, Barnwell, SC.

    1859 Barnwell County Deed Book LL:485. Barnwell County Clerk of Court's Office, Barnwell Court House, Barnwell, SC.

BEECH ISLAND FARMERS' CLUB
    1846–1883   Beech Island Farmers' Club Minutes. Savannah River Archaeological Research Program, South Carolina Institute of Archaeology and Anthropology, University of South Carolina, Columbia.

BRAUDEL, FERNAND
    1974 *Capitalism and Material Life, 1400–1800*. Harper and Row, New York, NY.
    1981 *The Structures of Everyday Life: The Limits of the Possible*. Harper and Row, New York, NY.

BRYANT, F. CARLENE
    1981 *We're All Kin: A Cultural Study of a Mountain Neighborhood*. University of Tennessee Press, Knoxville.

CABAK, MELANIE A.
    2004 Plantations without Pillars: Archaeology, Wealth, and Material Life at Bush Hill. Vol. 3, Appendixes. *Savannah River Archaeological Research Papers*, No. 11. Occasional Papers of the Savannah River Archaeological Research Program, South Carolina Institute of Archaeology and Anthropology, University of South Carolina, Columbia.

CABAK, MELANIE A., AND MARK D. GROOVER
    2004 Plantations without Pillars: Archaeology, Wealth, and Material Life at Bush Hill. Vol. 1, Context and Interpretation. *Savannah River Archaeological Research Papers*, No. 11. Occasional Papers of the Savannah River Archaeological Research Program, South Carolina Institute of Archaeology and Anthropology, University of South Carolina, Columbia.

CABAK, MELANIE A., MARK D. GROOVER, AND MARY M. INKROT
    1999 Rural Modernization during the Recent Past: Farmstead Archaeology on the Aiken Plateau. *Historical Archaeology* 35(4):19–43.

CABAK, MELANIE A., MARK D. GROOVER, AND ELIZABETH M. SCOTT
    2004 Plantations without Pillars: Archaeology, Wealth, and Material Life at Bush Hill. Vol. 2, Technical Description of Excavations, Features, and Artifacts. *Savannah River Archaeological Research Papers*, No. 11. Occasional Papers of the Savannah River Archaeological Research Program, South Carolina Institute of Archaeology and Anthropology, University of South Carolina, Columbia.

CABAK, MELANIE A., AND MARY M. INKROT
1997 Old Farm, New Farm: An Archaeology of Rural Modernization in the Aiken Plateau, 1875–1950. *Savannah River Archaeological Research Papers*, No. 9. Occasional Papers of the Savannah River Archaeological Research Program, South Carolina Institute of Archaeology and Anthropology, University of South Carolina, Columbia.

CRABTREE, CHRISTINE N.
2003 Antebellum Slave Life on the Aiken Plateau. Master's thesis, Department of Anthropology, University of South Carolina, Columbia.

DeHUFF, ELIZABETH WILLIS
1967 The Bush Family as Descended from John and Mary Bryan Bush of North Carolina. Manuscript, South Caroliniana Library, University of South Carolina, Columbia.

DOUGHTY, ROBIN W.
1989 Land Use. In *Encyclopedia of Southern Culture*, Charles Reagan Wilson and William Ferris, editors, pp. 343–344. University of North Carolina Press, Chapel Hill.

EARL, AMY C., PATRICK L. O'NEILL, DENNIS WILLIAMS, CHRISTOPHER LINTZ, W. NICHOLAS TRIERWEILER, J. MICHAEL QUIGG, GUS HAMBLETT, ABBY C. TREECE, AND DAN SCURLOCK
1993 Cultural Resource Investigations in the O. H. Ivie Reservoir, Concho, Coleman, and Runnels Counties, Texas. Vol. 5, Historical Resources. Report to Colorado River Municipal Water District, Big Spring, TX, from Mariah Associates, Inc., Austin, TX.

EDGAR, WALTER B.
1974 *Biographical Directory of the South Carolina House of Representatives, Volume 1*. University of South Carolina Press, Columbia.

EDWARDS, KATHARINE BUSH
1977 Bush Hill Cemetery. *South Carolina Historical Magazine* 78:148–149.

FAUST, DREW GILPIN
1982 *James Henry Hammond and the Old South: A Design for Mastery*. Louisiana State University Press, Baton Rouge.

FEINMAN, JEFFREY (EDITOR)
1979 *Sears, Roebuck and Co. Incorporated: 1909 Catalog*. Ventura Books, New York, NY.

GRAY, LEWIS C.
1933 *A History of Agriculture in the Southern United States to 1860*. Carnegie Institution, Washington, DC.

GROOVER, MARK D.
1991 Of Mindset and Material Culture: An Archaeological View of Continuity and Change in the Eighteenth-Century South Carolina Backcountry. Master's thesis, Department of Anthropology, University of South Carolina, Columbia.
1998 *The Gibbs Farmstead: An Archaeological Study of Rural Economy and Material Life in Southern Appalachia, 1790–1920*. Doctoral dissertation, Department of Anthropology, University of Tennessee, Knoxville. University Microfilms International, Ann Arbor, MI.
2003a *An Archaeological Study of Rural Capitalism and Material Life: The Gibbs Farmstead in Southern Appalachia, 1790–1920*. Kluwer Academic/Plenum, New York, NY.
2003b Identifying Consumption Differences between Social Groups. *North American Archaeologist* 24(3): 245–257.

HARDEMAN, NICHOLAS P.
1989 Corn. In *Encyclopedia of Southern Culture*, Charles Reagan Wilson and William Ferris, editors, pp. 33–34. University of North Carolina Press, Chapel Hill.

HILLIARD, SAMUEL B.
1984 *Hogmeat and Hoecake: Food Supply in the Old South, 1840–1860*. Southern Illinois University Press, Carbondale.
1985 *Atlas of Antebellum Southern Agriculture*. Louisiana State University Press, Baton Rouge.

KNIFFEN, FRED B.
1990a Folk Housing: Key to Diffusion. *Geoscience and Man, Cultural Diffusion and Landscapes* 27:49–68.
1990b The Study of Folk Architecture. *Geoscience and Man, Cultural Diffusion and Landscapes* 27:35–48.

KOVACIK, CHARLES F., AND JOHN J. WINBERRY
1987 *South Carolina: A Geography*. Westview Press, Boulder, CO.

LANE, MILLS
1984 *Architecture of the Old South: South Carolina*. Beehive Press, Savannah, GA.

MAIN, GLORIA L.
1982 *Tobacco Colony: Life in Early Maryland, 1650–1720*. Princeton University Press, Princeton, NJ.

MANNING, WILLIAM H., AND EDNA ANDERSON
1949–1967 Barnwell County Records South Carolina, Volumes 1–15. Manuscript Division, South Caroliniana Library, University of South Carolina, Columbia.

McALESTER, VIRGINIA, AND LEE McALESTER
1984 *A Field Guide to American Houses*. Alfred A. Knopf, New York, NY.

MICHIE JAMES L.
    1987   Richmond Hill and Wachesaw: An Archaeological
           Study of Two Rice Plantations on the Waccamaw
           River, Georgetown County, South Carolina. *South
           Carolina Institute of Archaeology and Anthropology,
           Research Manuscript*, No. 203, University of South
           Carolina, Columbia.
    1990   *Richmond Hill Plantation, 1810–1868: The Discovery
           of Antebellum Life on a Waccamaw Rice Plantation.*
           Reprint Co., Spartanburg, SC.

MILLER, GEORGE L.
    1980   Classification and Economic Scaling of Nineteenth-
           Century Ceramics. *Historical Archaeology* 14:1–40.
    1991   A Revised Set of CC Index Values for Classification
           and Economic Scaling of English Ceramics from 1787
           to 1880. *Historical Archaeology* 25(1):1–25.

MILLER, GEORGE L., AND ROBERT R. HUNTER, JR.
    1990   English Shell-Edged Earthenware: Alias Leeds Ware,
           Alias Feather Edge. In *Proceedings of the Thirty-Fifth
           Annual Wedgwood International Seminar*, pp. 107–136.
           Birmingham, AL.

MILLS, ROBERT
    1972   *Statistics of South Carolina.* Reprint Co., Spartanburg,
           SC.

MORRISON, HUGH
    1952   *Early American Architecture from the First Colonial
           Settlements to the National Period.* Oxford University
           Press, New York, NY.

ORSER, CHARLES E. JR.
    1988   *The Material Basis of the Postbellum Plantation:
           Historical Archaeology in the South Carolina Piedmont.*
           University of Georgia Press, Athens.

OTTO, JOHN S.
    1975   *Status Differences and the Archaeological Record: A
           Comparison of Planter, Overseer, and Slave Sites from
           Cannon's Point Plantation (1794–1861), St. Simons
           Island, Georgia.* Doctoral dissertation, Department
           of Anthropology, University of Florida, Gainesville.
           University Microfilms International, Ann Arbor, MI.
    1984   *Cannon's Point Plantation (1794–1860): Living
           Conditions and Status Patterns in the Old South.*
           Academic Press, New York, NY.

PEASALL, MARY
    1959   *Little Smoky Ridge: The Natural History of a Southern
           Appalachian Neighborhood.* University of Alabama
           Press, Birmingham.

SALAMON, SONYA
    1992   *Prairie Patrimony: Family, Farming, and Community
           in the Midwest.* University of North Carolina Press,
           Chapel Hill.

SAVANNAH RIVER ARCHAEOLOGICAL RESEARCH PROGRAM
(SRARP)
    n.d.   Bush Family Documents. Savannah River
           Archaeological Research Program, South Carolina
           Institute of Archaeology and Anthropology, University
           of South Carolina, Columbia.

SCHULZ, PETER D., AND SHERRI M. GUST
    1983   Faunal Remains and Social Status in Nineteenth-
           Century Sacramento. *Historical Archaeology* 17(1):
           44–53.

SOUTH CAROLINA DEPARTMENT OF ARCHIVES AND HISTORY
(SCDAH)
    1790   Manuscript Census, Population. Microfilm, South
           Carolina Department of Archives and History,
           Columbia.
    1800   Manuscript Census, Population. Microfilm, South
           Carolina Department of Archives and History,
           Columbia.
    1810   Manuscript Census, Population. Microfilm, South
           Carolina Department of Archives and History,
           Columbia.
    1820   Manuscript Census, Population. Microfilm, South
           Carolina Department of Archives and History,
           Columbia.
    1830   Manuscript Census, Population. Microfilm, South
           Carolina Department of Archives and History,
           Columbia.
    1840   Manuscript Census, Population. Microfilm, South
           Carolina Department of Archives and History,
           Columbia.
    1850a Manuscript Census, Agricultural. Microfilm, South
           Carolina Department of Archives and History,
           Columbia.
    1850b Manuscript Census, Population. Microfilm, South
           Carolina Department of Archives and History,
           Columbia.
    1860a Manuscript Census, Agricultural. Microfilm, South
           Carolina Department of Archives and History,
           Columbia.
    1860b Manuscript Census, Population. Microfilm, South
           Carolina Department of Archives and History,
           Columbia.
    1870a Manuscript Census, Agricultural. Microfilm, South
           Carolina Department of Archives and History,
           Columbia.
    1870b Manuscript Census, Industrial. Microfilm, South
           Carolina Department of Archives and History,
           Columbia.
    1880a Manuscript Census, Agricultural. Microfilm, South
           Carolina Department of Archives and History,
           Columbia.
    1880b Manuscript Census, Industrial. Microfilm, South
           Carolina Department of Archives and History,
           Columbia.
    1891   Estate Documents of George W. Bush. Aiken
           County, South Carolina Probate, Box 9, Number 20,
           Columbia.

SOUTHERN, MICHAEL
1978   The I-House as a Carrier of Style in Three Counties of
       the Northeastern Piedmont. Towards Preservation of
       Place: In Celebration of the North Carolina Vernacular
       Landscape, Doug Swaim, editor, pp. 70–83. *The Student
       Publication of the School of Design*, Vol. 26, North
       Carolina State University, Raleigh.

SWAIM, DOUG
1978   North Carolina Folk Housing. Towards Preservation of
       Place: In Celebration of the North Carolina Vernacular
       Landscape, Doug Swaim, editor, pp. 28–45. *The Student
       Publication of the School of Design*, Vol. 26, North
       Carolina State University, Raleigh.

SZUTER, CHRISTINE R.
1996   A Faunal Analysis of Home Butchering and Meat
       Consumption at the Hubbell Trading Post, Ganado,
       Arizona. In *Images of the Recent Past: Readings in
       Historical Archaeology*, Charles E. Orser, Jr., editor,
       pp. 333–354. AltaMira Press, Walnut Creek, CA.

TAYLOR, JOE GRAY
1989   Foodways. In *Encyclopedia of Southern Culture*,
       Charles Reagan Wilson and William Ferris, editors,
       pp. 613–616. University of North Carolina Press,
       Chapel Hill.

UNITED STATES BUREAU OF CENSUS (USBC)
1853   *Seventh Census of the United States: 1850, Schedule 4,
       Production of Agriculture*. U.S. Bureau of the Census,
       Washington, DC.

UNITED STATES DEPARTMENT OF INTERIOR (USDI)
1864   *Of the United States in 1860, Compiled From the
       Original Returns of the Eighth Census*. U.S. Department
       of the Interior, Washington, DC.

1872   *The Statistics of the Wealth and Industry of the United
       States*. U.S. Department of the Interior, Washington,
       DC.

1883   *Report of the Production of Agriculture as Returned
       at the Tenth Census*. U.S. Department of the Interior,
       Washington, DC.

UNITED STATES DEPARTMENT OF STATE
1841   *Of the Enumeration of the Inhabitants and Statistics
       of the United States, as Obtained at the Department of
       State, from the Returns of the Sixth Census, by Counties
       and Principal Towns, Exhibiting the Population, Wealth,
       and Resources of the Country*. U.S. Department of
       State, Washington, DC.

VLACH, JOHN M.
1993   *Back of the Big House: The Architecture of Plantation
       Slavery*. University of North Carolina Press, Chapel
       Hill.

MELANIE A. CABAK
SOUTH CAROLINA INSTITUTE OF ARCHAEOLOGY AND
ANTHROPOLOGY
SAVANNAH RIVER ARCHAEOLOGICAL RESEARCH
PROGRAM
UNIVERSITY OF SOUTH CAROLINA
PO BOX 400
NEW ELLENTON, SC 29809-0400

MARK D. GROOVER
DEPARTMENT OF ANTHROPOLOGY
BALL STATE UNIVERSITY
200 W. UNIVERSITY AVE.
MUNCIE, IN 47306-0435

Tanya M. Peres

Foodways, Economic Status, and the Antebellum Upland South in Central Kentucky

ABSTRACT

Regional cuisines or foodways have been a topic of interest to both historians and archaeologists for at least the past 30 years. Scholars recognize a regional foodway in the antebellum Upland South that is part of the larger "Upland South" cultural tradition. The agricultural and archaeological data on subsistence in the antebellum Upland South have been woven into an idealized set of subsistence practices that revolved around agricultural practices. The examination of four contemporaneous faunal assemblages representative of different societal classes living in 19th-century Kentucky shows that this generalized version of Upland South foodways does not hold true across economic classes. Instead, a closer look reveals that many people living on Kentucky's antebellum farmsteads struggled regularly for food security and that the idealized version of a shared "Upland South foodway" was restricted to the wealthy planter class that had ready access to the market economy.

Introduction

The earliest recorded historical archaeology in Kentucky was conducted in 1936, when William S. Webb and William D. Funkhouser recorded evidence of saltpeter mining in Menifee County rockshelter sites (McBride and McBride 1990b). Many of the subsequent investigations of Kentucky's historic sites in the 1960s and 1970s were conducted to aid the reconstruction of large plantations and urban residences, Civil War fortifications, and at least one mill site (McBride and McBride 1990b, 1993). Investigations such as these were common in historical archaeology during this time, causing the discipline to be viewed by some as a handmaiden to history (Harrington 1955; Noël Hume 1969; Faulkner 2003). In the late 1970s, the recording of historic sites increased, in conjunction with cultural resource management projects; however, many of these sites went unexcavated, with the exception of a few sites associated with individuals of the upper class of society. These excavations were largely descriptive, with few exceptions, and added to the database of historic sites, artifacts, and features of Kentucky.

Investigations of historic period sites in Kentucky have steadily grown in volume and complexity since the late 1960s, and by the mid-1980s, several full-scale excavations of sites from this time period were undertaken by archaeologists housed in government agencies (i.e., Kentucky Transportation Cabinet and Kentucky Archaeology Survey), universities (i.e., University of Kentucky and University of Louisville), and private cultural resource management firms (McBride and McBride 1990b). Analytically, a shift occurred from description of artifacts (late 1970s), to "synthetic and methodological studies," to "detailed problem-oriented research designs" (McBride and McBride 1990b:560). Research topics included settlement patterns, spatial organization, household formation, ethnicity, economic development, subsistence strategies, and social and economic status differences (McBride and McBride 1990b:560). Early analyses of faunal remains from historic sites in Kentucky date to the early and mid-1980s and focus on the collection of basic data (for example, Fay 1980; Walters 1985). Emphases were placed on species lists, minimum numbers of individuals, edible meat weights, and some taphonomic factors pertaining to sample formation.

The increased emphasis in historical archaeology placed on the study of foodways in general during the past three decades is evidenced by more systematic, comprehensive, and sophisticated zooarchaeological analyses performed on Kentucky sites during the 1990s and into the current decade. Sites like the William Whitely House (Linebaugh and Loughlin 2003), Vardeman House (Madsen et al. 2005; Peres 2005), Duckworth Farm (Peres 2003a), Cowan Farmstead (Peres 2003b; Huser and Lynch 2005), Armstrong Farmstead (Barber 2003), McConnell Homestead (Day and Clay 2000), Locust Grove (Young 1995b, 1997; Lev-Tov 2004), and Logan's Fort (Davenport 2000), among others,

Historical Archaeology, 2008, 42(4):88–104.
Permission to reprint required.
Accepted for publication 15 August 2007.

have allowed zooarchaeologists the opportunity to ask and answer questions pertaining to consumer choice, temporal and socioeconomic variations in diet, farmstead economies, regional foodways, and ethnicity.

While some thematic topics have gained the attention of Kentucky's historical archaeologists, Kim McBride and Stephen McBride (1990a, 1990b) emphasize the lack of attention to the topic of rural slavery in the antebellum period (1820–1861). This is not surprising, given that archaeology conducted pre-1990 at most historic sites in the commonwealth was concerned with large urban residences and even larger plantations. An exception is the multiyear excavation conducted at the Locust Grove plantation near Louisville, Kentucky, by the University of Louisville's Department of Anthropology. The multiyear excavations produced information about the slaves who lived at the site during the antebellum period (Young 1995a, 1995b, 1997; Young et al. 1995, 1998). The data from the three slave houses and corresponding pit cellars yielded important information on subsistence strategies practiced by the slaves at Locust Grove (Young 1995b, 1997; Lev-Tov 2004).

Regional cuisines or foodways have been a topic of interest to historians and archaeologists alike (Hilliard 1969, 1972, 1988; Owens 1976; Reitz and Honerkamp 1983; Brown and Mussell 1984; Berlin and Morgan 1991, 1993; Young 1993; Lev-Tov 1994; Singleton 1995; Patterson 1998; Poe 1999, 2001; Scott 2001; Hodgetts 2006; Reitz et al. 2006). The focus of defining regional cuisines within an archaeological framework is useful because it allows for the recognition of patterns and trends; however, a large database from the circumscribed region in question is needed to draw broad definitive conclusions on dietary patterning. Few would argue against the unique foodways that are part of the American South. In the antebellum period of Kentucky, scholars recognize a regional foodway that is part of the larger Upland South cultural tradition.

Historians and geographers (Bidwell and Falconer 1925; Power 1953; Hilliard 1969, 1972, 1988; Mitchell 1972, 1978; Mason 1984) have traditionally viewed Upland South foodways as an expression of values and farming practices shared by those living in Kentucky and Tennessee in the 19th century and based this on

historic documents of agricultural production for the region. In contrast, archaeologists have tended to view Upland South foodways as shared but differentiated among socioeconomic classes and even ethnic groups, based on cuts of meat as interpreted from faunal assemblages (Walters 1985; Young 1993; McKelway 2000; Allgood and Kirkwood 2002). As often happens with archaeologists' views of the past, the foodways have been woven into an idealized or romanticized view of what life was like for people living in the past (Perkins 1991; Stothers and Tucker 2002; Cabak and Groover 2006). Upon further examination, however, this generalized version of Upland South foodways does not hold true across economic classes that were represented in Kentucky during the 19th century. Instead, a closer look reveals that many people living on Kentucky's antebellum farmsteads struggled regularly for food security and that the idealized version of a shared Upland South foodway was restricted to the wealthy planter class that had ready access to the market economy.

The Upland South Cultural Tradition

The term "Upland South" has been used to signify a geographic and physiographic region, a "highland way of life" (Jordan-Bychkov 2003:5), an agricultural complex, and a cultural tradition (Owsley 1949; Kniffen 1965; Mitchell 1972, 1978; Newton 1974; McCorvie 1987; O'Brien and Majewski 1989; McBride and McBride 1990b; Jordan-Bychkov 2003). Robert Mitchell (1978) and Terry Jordan-Bychkov (2003) describe the diffusion of different components of the Upland South cultural tradition from the primary "hearth areas" of the lower Delaware River Valley, the Chesapeake Tidewater, and the Carolina Low Country into the interior of the eastern United States and its eventual emergence in Kentucky and Tennessee. The expression of this tradition in Kentucky and Tennessee was distinct from that in the Lower South—an area known for the production of export crops such as cotton, rice, and sugar as well as corn, cattle, and mules. Additionally, the Lower South's farming practices centered on vast plantations worked by large populations of enslaved laborers, in contrast to the Upland South where fewer slaves were needed (Mitchell 1972; McKelway 2000). Farmsteads and plantations that fit into the Upland South definition include those that were located in areas where mono-cropping was not environmentally feasible. Henry McKelway (2000:27) states that, archaeologically, Upland South plantations are found in specific physiographic regions, located to the north and west of the Coastal Plain, specifically, the Piedmont Plateau, Blue Ridge, Ridge and Valley, Appalachian Plateau, Interior Low Plateau, Ouachita Plateau, and Ozark Plateau.

The social and agrarian components of this tradition are the result of the fusion of elements from the primary hearth areas: the lower Delaware River Valley, where corn, wheat, and livestock were emphasized; and the Chesapeake region, where tobacco, hemp, and slavery were dominant. These ideals and preferences rapidly spread from western Virginia to central Kentucky after 1780 (Mitchell 1972:741, 1978:81) but also flourished in the Carolinas, Tennessee, northern Georgia, and Alabama and eventually spread into southeastern Illinois (Mitchell 1972; McCorvie 1987). By 1860, states situated in the Upland South region—Maryland, Virginia, North Carolina, Tennessee, Missouri, and Kentucky— led as the top producers of tobacco, hemp, and flax in the U.S. and were the "second-level producers" of corn, wheat, beef cattle, and hogs (Mitchell 1972:740). The antebellum expression of the unique Upland South culture in Kentucky included the diversified agricultural production of crops such as tobacco, hemp, flax, barley, rye, wheat, corn and the raising of pigs and cattle (Mitchell 1972, 1978). Generally, landholdings by individual Upland South planters were not as big as some of the plantations located in the Lower South (McKelway 2000). As in the Lower South, however, two classes of people existed in the agricultural Upper South: "direct producers, with the general status of 'slaves,' and owners with the general status of 'planters'" (Orser 1987:126). The need for copious amounts of labor, whether enslaved or hired, was not as prevalent in the Upper South as compared to the Lower South, due in part to the size of the farms, the crops under cultivation, and differences in environmental settings (McKelway 2000).

Documentary and archaeological research have shown that pigs, cattle, and other domestic livestock were important to antebellum farmstead economies in Kentucky and the surrounding region. One historic account of the livestock kept on Judge Adam Beatty's plantation in Mason County (situated due north of Bath County, along the present-day Kentucky-Ohio border) notes that, "large, stout horses and mules are mostly used for the farm work; the cows for milk, and the cattle for fattening, are principally a high cross of the Durham, the swine a greater or less intermixture of Irish Grazier or Berkshire; and the sheep of pure or mixed Merino blood" (Schwab 1973:302). The relative importance of domestic stock (especially pigs) versus wild species in the Upland South diet has been previously examined from site-specific contexts, and that importance is not disputed here (Walters 1985; McCorvie 1987; Young 1993; Lev-Tov 1994, 2004; Young 1997; Patterson 1998; McKee 1999; Day and Clay 2000; Tuma 2000; Allgood and Kirkwood 2002; Peres 2002, 2003a, 2003b, 2005; Groover 2003, 2005).

The research presented here compares the idealized Upland South foodways to the zooarchaeological records of four mid-19th-century farmsteads to better understand the role economic status played in the dietary reality of central Kentuckians. The study of these four sites together is able to provide a new and important contribution to the understanding of Upland South foodways because, unlike the material analyzed in previous studies, the sites examined here all fall within a restricted date range, and they represent at least three different economic classes of society in Central Kentucky. Furthermore, the author examined all of the faunal assemblages over a three-year period, making the data analyzed fully comparable from a methodological standpoint. The ultimate goal is to show that the foodways traditionally associated with the Upland South cultural tradition are largely idealized and do not reflect the daily food insecurities that different classes of this society faced.

Archaeology of Four Upland South Farmsteads in Central Kentucky

The zooarchaeological data from four contemporaneous sites are compared to assess the degree to which different economic classes in antebellum Central Kentucky participated in the Upland South foodways. The assemblages included here were recovered from sites dating from 1817 to

1870 and represent enslaved peoples as well as free planters from middling and wealthy economic classes.

Slaves Owned by Middling to Wealthy Planters: Duckworth Farm

The major component at the Duckworth Farm site (15BH212), located in Bath County, Kentucky, represents a domestic occupation that spanned approximately 75 years (ca. 1775–1850) (Peres 2003a) (Figure 1). The faunal remains discussed here belong largely to the period from 1817 to 1850 when the Duckworth family owned the property. Historic documents record that the Duckworths, a middling to wealthy family, owned properties in the nearby town of Sharpsburg in addition to the family farm. They raised wheat and "Indian corn," on the farm as well as horses, mules, cows and cattle, sheep, and hogs. They also owned slaves (Peres 2003a). Archaeobotanical analyses indicate that some of the plants that were being grown on the property included corn, peaches, gourds, and barley (Rossen 2003). The area excavated

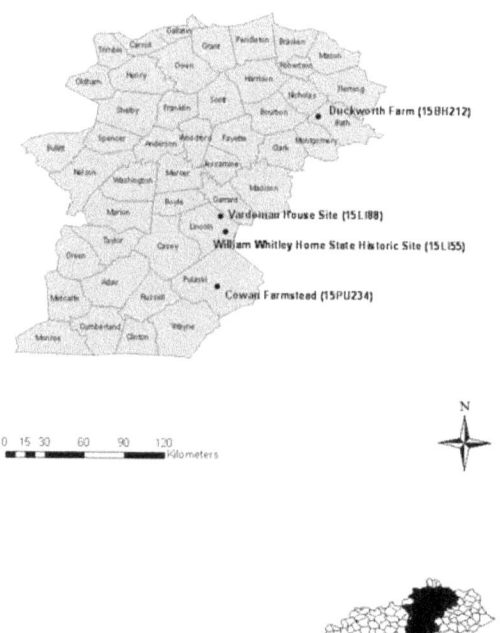

FIGURE 1. Location of Antebellum Upland South sites discussed in the text, central Kentucky. (Map by Lacey Fleming, 2007.)

included two root cellars, the only remaining evidence of slave houses at the site (Peres 2003a). The faunal assemblage recovered from these two root cellars was large (n=5,104), owing to the remarkable preservation of the root cellar features.

Middling Class Planters: Cowan Farmstead

The Cowan Farmstead (15PU234) in Pulaski County, Kentucky, yielded deposits that date to the early- to mid-19th century (Figure 1). During the early historic period of Kentucky, Pulaski County was one of the most sparsely settled areas of the frontier; hence major transportation routes connecting the rural county to more urban areas were slow to develop (Torma et al. 1985:1; Huser and Lynch 2005). The Cumberland River was the main transportation route until 1877 when the railroad established a line through the county (Tibbals 1952; Huser and Lynch 2005).

The major component at the Cowan Farmstead is the 19th-century rural domestic occupation by Robert Cowan, his wife Elinore, and their 10 children. By 1829 this single-family farm totaled 244 acres, which were later divided between Robert's heirs according to his will (Henderson 1989; Huser and Lynch 2005). The Cowan family lived on the farm from as early as 1826 until after the death of Robert Cowan in 1845, and the contents of the residence and farm were divided in 1856 (Huser and Lynch 2005). According to the estate sale record of Robert and Elinore Cowan, the family raised cows, horses, pigs, sheep, oats, flax, wheat, and corn on the farm. The few faunal remains recovered from the excavated features, including a pit cellar, two fire pits, robbers' trench, two trash pits, robbed wall trench, privy shaft, and two features of unknown function, were combined to increase sample size. These deposits all date to the Cowan occupation of the property. The composite faunal assemblage totaled 966 specimens (Peres 2003b).

Slave-Owning Wealthy Planters: Vardeman House

The Vardeman House Site in Lincoln County, Kentucky, was owned and occupied by several generations of the Vardeman family (Figure 1). John Vardeman, Jr., a member of Daniel Boone's company that blazed the Wilderness Trail into Kentucky, had acquired the land ca. 1781 from his son-in-law, William Menifee (Sussenbach 2000; Milton-Ping and Madsen 2005). Morgan Vardeman, who acquired the property from his father, John, was the head of household on record from 1803 until his death in 1844 (Milton-Ping and Madsen 2005). After his death, Morgan's son Jeremiah lived on the property until it was sold, sometime between 1851 and 1853, to Ephraim Pennington (Morgan's brother-in-law, Jeremiah's uncle, who occupied the William Whitley house during this period; see below). The dataset included here is from Morgan Vardeman's occupation of the site. Historic documents indicate that Morgan was a wealthy landowner and the local magistrate. He had numerous relatives living in Lincoln and adjoining counties (Madsen et al. 2005). In Morgan's will he refers to his landholdings as his "plantation," and it is clear from the numerous deed transactions recorded at the time that Morgan acquired more than 400 acres of land in Lincoln County during his lifetime (Milton-Ping and Madsen 2005:53). Census records indicate there were at least 5 slaves living on the Vardeman property in 1820, increased to 10 by 1840 (Milton-Ping and Madsen 2005). Additionally, historic documents indicate hogs (n=50), cattle (n=20), sheep (n 50), and horses (n=8) were being raised on the Vardeman farm (Milton-Ping and Madsen 2005). Available historic documents make little mention of crops being grown on the farm, although in Morgan Vardeman's will, several fields of corn were sold to Ephraim Pennington (Madsen et al. 2005:Appendix B).

The faunal remains included in this analysis were recovered from six trash pit features. The associated mean ceramic dates for these features, ranging from 1824 to 1828.5 (x=1825.92), place them in contemporaneous association with one another. The total number of faunal remains recovered from these six features consists of 1,912 specimens (Peres 2005). The lengthy review of the Vardeman House Site is given here to underscore the fact that the Vardemans were relatively wealthy and had long-standing ties to the community.

Slave-Owning Wealthy Planters: William Whitley State Historic Site

The William Whitley State Historic Site (15LI55) in Lincoln County, Kentucky, was the state's first brick home, built in 1794 by William and Esther Whitley (O'Malley 2000; Linebaugh and Loughlin 2003) (Figure 1). The Whitleys had a circular clay racetrack for horse racing built in the 1790s, which increased the reputation of the home as a fall gathering place and earned it the nickname "Sportsman's Hill" (Kentucky Department of Parks 2005). William Whitley was killed in 1813, leaving his property to his wife Esther (Linebaugh and Loughlin 2003:13). The property was sold in 1824 to David Shanks who in turn sold it to Ephraim Pennington (Morgan Vardeman's brother-in-law) in 1827 (Lincoln County Deed Books 1827a, 1827b; Linebaugh and Loughlin 2003:13). Recent archaeological investigations have been focused on the period from 1827 to 1919 when the site was occupied by Ephraim Pennington and his family (Linebaugh and Loughlin 2003). Pennington was a farmer and a magistrate. Information in the 1840 census indicates that he and his wife (Bettie Vardeman) and their five children were living on the property. In addition, Pennington had 15 male and 17 female slaves, quite a few for a Kentucky landowner at that time (O'Malley 2000). Ten years later, Ephraim was living with his second wife, Jane, their infant son, and three of Ephraim's sons from his first marriage. His real estate value was in excess of $21,720, and he owned 16 male and 17 female slaves (O'Malley 2000). In 1860, his real estate value was $29,200, and his personal value was $19,115—very high values compared to his neighbors. Forty slaves lived on his property, 21 males and 19 females (although 14 of these were fugitives from the state at the time of the census) (U. S. Bureau of the Census 1860; O'Malley 2000).

The lengthy treatment of the Penningtons is included here to stress the relative wealth of this early Kentucky family. The zooarchaeological assemblage included in this study was recovered from an intact sheet midden dating from the 1830s that was found near the house. The faunal assemblage consists of 1,119 specimens.

Patterns of Subsistence and Economic Status in the Upland South

Faunal remains can be useful in answering questions about status-related behaviors and choices, but there are clear limitations when assigning status based on identified faunal remains (Reitz 1986, 1987; Lyman 1987). The use of the term "status" can be problematic if not defined clearly. The terms "social status," "socioeconomic status," and "class differentiation" are often used interchangeably, although they do not always mean the same thing (Otto 1980; Schulz and Gust 1983; Lyman 1987; O'Brien and Majewski 1989). A person's socioeconomic status may be defined by income level, thus controlling consumer choices, but social status may have no direct correlation to income level. In the present study, a person's status is defined as economic standing within a community. To relate status to consumer choice as reflected in the zooarchaeological record is dependent upon a number of variables. These variables include but are not limited to ethnicity, cost of product/service, access to resources/goods, time period, environment, and site function (Reitz and Scarry 1985; Reitz 1987:105–107; Scott 2001; Lev-Tov 2004). Many of these variables are interrelated and, if looked at individually, may produce data patterns that are similar to those produced by other variables, or as Elizabeth Reitz (1987:105) states, "ethnicity may become confused with a culture of poverty."

It is imperative that status interpretations be based on multiple lines of evidence, including documentary sources, architectural remains, and material culture in addition to faunal evidence (Reitz 1987; Spencer-Wood 1987; O'Brien and Majewski 1989). The use of a single-line of evidence, instead of multiple lines, may result in misleading interpretations of diet and subsistence at a site (McKee 1987; Crabtree 1990). Faunal remains and historical documents taken alone may not reflect the original diet or deposit, and other factors that operate directly on zooarchaeological assemblages such as taphonomy, disposal, and recovery of the remains must be taken into consideration. If not, archaeologists risk the misinterpretation of deposits based on what Justin Lev-Tov (2004:304) terms "ethnic

faunal indices," when in reality the deposits may be reflective of economic status and access to resources, regardless of ethnic identity.

Status and ethnic determinations for the sites discussed here were based on multiple lines of evidence, including historical documentation, assemblage provenience, and material culture status markers. It is outside the scope of this paper to review the data for each of the four sites; for that, the reader is referred to works by Nancy O'Malley (1999), Donald Linebaugh and Michael Loughlin (2003), Tanya Peres (2003a), William Huser and David Lynch (2005), and Andrew Madsen and colleagues (2005). The goal of this research is to understand how food choices in the antebellum Upland South were affected by economic status and access to resources, regardless of ethnic identity.

One of the main traits of the "idealized" diet practiced in the Upland South is an emphasis on the consumption of pigs to the near exclusion of other domestic and wild animals. A number of studies have demonstrated that pork is a fundamental part of the Upland South diet (Breitburg 1976, 1983; Price 1985; Martin 1986; McCorvie 1987; Lev-Tov 1994, 2004; Day and Clay 2000; Peres 2002, 2003a, 2003b, 2005; Groover 2003, 2005). The intersite comparison presented here addresses the general diet at each site in terms of diversity and richness of taxa exploited, the composition of the diet in terms of wild and domestic animals, the importance of the hallmark Upland South dietary indicator (pig) at each of the sites, the application of Upland South consumption patterns to different classes of the Upland South society (wealthy planter, middling planter, slave), and the social and archaeological implications of the observed foodways.

The first component of the analysis is the diversity of species within each assemblage and among assemblages. Assemblage diversity was addressed in two ways. First, diversity of each assemblage is calculated based on the number of different taxa represented. The present analysis compares the species diversity of the four assemblages, using only the vertebrate taxa. The most diverse assemblage is that from the Duckworth Farm with 20 taxa represented. The Vardeman House and the Cowan Farmstead both had 12 taxa represented, and the William Whitley House is the least diverse, having 8 taxa represented. These numbers may be due to sample size but also may be due to other causes such as cultural and economic factors in play at the time of use and deposition, differential deposition, length of occupation of the site, and taphonomic factors.

A second approach to sample diversity is one that looks at the number of taxa that are expected for a particular sample size, thus allowing researchers to control for the potential bias of sample size. It is reasonable to assume that larger assemblages (in terms of NISP) tend to contain a richer composition of taxa than smaller assemblages (Reitz 1987; Rhode 1988; Kintigh 1989; Baxter 2001). It should not be assumed that larger assemblages with more taxa are more diverse than smaller assemblages with fewer taxa, as richness and equitability may be functions of sample size. To overcome the possibility that sample sizes are biasing interpretations of diversity within the four assemblages included here, the statistical program DIVERS was employed (Kintigh 1984, 1989, 1991). The DIVERS program compares the diversities of different assemblages to themselves, based on the expectations for diversity, given the sample sizes. The assemblages then are compared not to each other but, rather, to the expected diversity for a sample of a given size (Kintigh 1984). This allows zooarchaeologists to bypass the issue of sample-size differences completely. The actual values are then plotted against sample size with a 90% confidence interval that is based on the expected values (VanDerwarker 2006). Values that plot above the confidence interval are more

diverse than expected, while values that plot below the confidence interval are less diverse than expected (VanDerwarker 2006).

Discrete taxa were entered into Kintigh's DIVERS program, and the results for diversity are plotted in Figure 2 and evenness in Figure 3. The center line of the plot indicates the expected richness or evenness, while the lines above and below the center indicate the 90% confidence interval for the expected values. The faunal assemblage from the Cowan Farmstead is within the 90% confidence interval, meaning that, given the sample size, the diversity values for this assemblage are what can be expected (Figure 2). In contrast, the other three sites show diversity values that are less rich than would be expected, given the sample size. The Duckworth Farm assemblage falls just below the confidence interval, while the William Whitely House and Vardeman House assemblages fall well below the confidence interval.

The evenness values calculated by the DIVERS program show that the Duckworth Farm faunal assemblage is more evenly distributed than expected, falling above the 90% confidence interval (Figure 3). The Cowan Farmstead faunal assemblage is the only sample that falls within the 90% confidence interval of the expected range of values. Both the William Whitely House and Vardeman House faunal assemblages fall below the 90% confidence interval for the expected evenness figures, thus these samples are skewed towards specific taxa. The results of the DIVERS analyses strongly suggest that the Vardemans and Penningtons (of the William

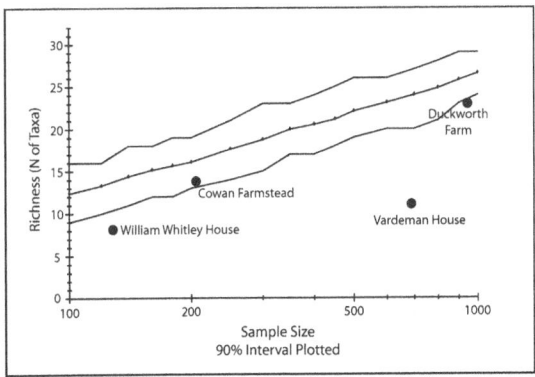

FIGURE 2. DIVERS richness plot of faunal assemblages, by site. (Graph by Amber M. VanDerwarker, 2006.)

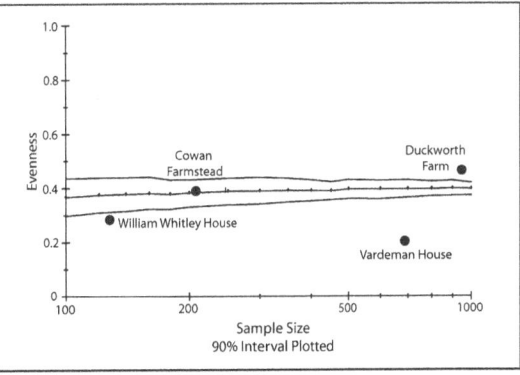

FIGURE 3. DIVERS evenness plot of faunal assemblages, by site. (Graph by Amber M. VanDerwarker, 2006.)

Whitely House) exploited fewer types of animals than did the occupants of the Cowan Farmstead and Duckworth Farm.

In addition to diversity and evenness of taxa, the four assemblages are composed of a variety of both wild and domesticated animals (Table 1); the second issue addressed is species use. Using NISP values for identified taxa (identified to genus or species), divided into either wild or domesticated, the percentage

TABLE 1
TAXA IDENTIFIED FROM SITES DISCUSSED IN THE TEXT

Taxon	Common Name	Vardeman House		William Whitely		Duckworth Farm		Cowan Farmstead	
		NISP	MNI	NISP	MNI	NISP	MNI	NISP	MNI
Domesticated Taxa									
Canis familiaris	domestic dog	2	1	0	0	0	0	0	0
cf. *Felis domesticus*	domestic cat	0	0	0	0	3	2	0	0
Equidae	horse, mule, zebra	0	0	0	0	0	0	1	1
Equus caballus	horse	6	1	0	0	1	1	0	0
Sus scrofa	pig	588	9	96	2	532	41	128	2
cf. *Sus scrofa*	pig	3	0	0	0	0	0	0	0
cf. Bovidae	sheep, goat, bison, cows	0	0	0	0	1	1	0	0
Bovidae	sheep, goat, bison, cattle	2	0	5	1	0	0	0	0
Ovis/Capra sp.	sheep/goat	0	0	0	0	2	2	1	1
Bos taurus	domestic cattle	29	1	7	1	12	8	1	1
Gallus gallus	domestic chicken	0	0	10	1	149	16	36	2
Wild Taxa									
Didelphis virginiana	opossum	0	0	2	1	34	3	0	0
Talpidae	moles	0	0	0	0	5	3	0	0
Parascalops breweri	hairy-tailed mole	0	0	0	0	2	1	0	0
Mustelidae	weasels, minks, skunks, otters	0	0	0	0	3	2	0	0
Mustela sp.	mink	0	0	0	0	1	1	0	0
cf. *Ursus americanus*	black bear	0	0	0	0	1	1	0	0
Cervidae	elk, deer	0	0	0	0	3	0	1	0
Cervus canadensis	eastern elk, wapiti	0	0	0	0	3	1	1	1
cf. *Odocoileus virginianus*	white-tailed deer	0	0	0	0	0	0	2	0
Odocoileus virginianus	white-tailed deer	5	1	2	1	28	2	16	2
Rodentia	rodents	2	0	0	0	0	0	1	1
Marmota monax	woodchuck	0	0	1	1	0	0	0	0
Sciuridae	chipmunks, squirrels, muskrats	0	0	0	0	2	0	0	0
cf. *Tamias* sp.	chipmunk	0	0	0	0	2	1	0	0
Sciurus sp.	squirrel	1	0	0	0	47	7	0	0
cf. *S. carolinensis and niger*	gray and fox squirrel	0	0	0	0	2	1	0	0
Sciurus carolinensis	gray squirrel	14	2	0	0	23	11	0	0
Sciurus niger	fox squirrel	11	1	0	0	98	8	0	0
Cricetidae	rats and voles	0	0	0	0	2	2	0	0
Sylvilagus sp.	rabbit	0	0	1	1	16	4	0	0
Sylvilagus floridanus	eastern cottontail	0	0	8	1	2	1	6	1
Phasianidae	bobwhites	9	2	0	0	0	0	0	0
Turdus migratorius	American robin	0	0	0	0	0	0	4	1
Amphibia	amphibians	0	0	0	0	1	1	5	1
Ranidae/Bufonidae	frogs/toads	0	0	0	0	17	3	0	0
Osteichthyes	bony fishes	0	0	4	1	3	1	7	1
Ictaluridae	freshwater catfish	0	0	0	0	1	1	0	0

TABLE 1 (CONTINUED)
TAXA IDENTIFIED FROM SITES DISCUSSED IN THE TEXT

Taxon	Common Name	Vardeman House		William Whitely		Duckworth Farm		Cowan Farmstead	
		NISP	MNI	NISP	MNI	NISP	MNI	NISP	MNI
Wild Taxa (Continued									
Aplodinotus grunniens	freshwater drum	0	0	0	0	0	0	4	2
Micropterus salmoides	freshwater bass	0	0	2	1	0	0	0	0
Bivalvia	bivalves	6	1	4	3	47	12	17	0
cf. *Villosa taeniata*	painted creekshell	0	0	0	0	0	0	5	2
Gastropoda	gastropods	6	1	1	1	6	3	3	0
Anguispira alternata	flamed tiger snail	0	0	0	0	6	3	0	0
Anguispira cumberlandia	Cumberland tiger snail	0	0	0	0	4	3	0	0
Helix sp.	garden snail	1	1	0	0	0	0	0	0
Mesodon thyroidus	white-lip globe	0	0	0	0	0	0	2	2
Stenotrema sp.	slitmouth snail	0	0	0	0	8	5	1	1
Stenotrema stenotrema	inland slitmouth	0	0	0	0	2	2	0	0
Mollusca	mollusks	25	0	2	0	2	0	0	0
Indeterminate Domesticated/Wild Taxa									
Vertebrata	vertebrates	117	0	3	0	258	0	8	0
Mammalia	mammals	938	0	760	0	2,933	21	497	0
Canis sp.	dog, wolf, coyote	1	0	0	0	0	0	0	0
Artiodactyla	"even-toed" ungulates	0	0	2	0	0	0	0	0
Aves	birds	99	0	209	1	809	16	216	0
Anatidae	ducks, geese	14	0	0	0	12	3	0	0
Branta canadensis	Canada goose	21	3	0	0	1	1	0	0
cf. *Branta canadensis*	Canada goose	2	0	0	0	0	0	0	0
Meleagris gallopavo	turkey	2	1	0	0	17	3	2	2
TOTALS		1,912	25	1,119	17	5,104	199	966	24

of wild vs. domesticated taxa are compared. Identified taxa are those specimens that are identifiable to genus or species. The more general categories that subsume both wild and domestic taxa as well as geese and turkey were not included in either category since it is unclear if these are domesticated or wild forms. The Duckworth Farm slave assemblage has the highest wild to domesticated ratio of the four sites (Table 2). The wild taxa portion of the Cowan Farmstead assemblage is lower than the Duckworth Farm assemblage but is higher than the William Whitley midden assemblage. The Vardeman House assemblage is comprised predominantly of domestic animals with a very low percentage of wild taxa represented. The slaves at the Duckworth Farm appear to have used the most wild taxa out of all the groups represented in this study. The Vardemans, the wealthiest group in this study, were using the least amount of wild taxa and the highest amount of domestic taxa.

The third issue addressed in this analysis is the occurrence of pork at each of these sites. Settlers on the western frontier are traditionally thought to have relied on whatever locally available foods they could hunt to survive (Hilliard 1972). This traditional theory has not been borne out in historic documents or the archaeological record of the antebellum Upland South. In fact, settlers relied on the high productivity of the domestic swine that they brought with them into the region (Hilliard 1988). Indeed, according to Sam Hilliard (1969, 1972), Kentucky and Tennessee were the highest pork-producing states from 1840 to 1860, based on census records. This is not to say that local wild animals were not eaten, for they certainly were. By whom

TABLE 2
PERCENT NISP OF WILD VS. DOMESTICATED
TAXA IDENTIFIED AT EACH SITE

	Vardeman House	William Whitely	Duckworth Farm	Cowan Farmstead
Wild Taxa	4.66%	12.40%	27.81%	19.62%
Domestic Taxa	91.69%	87.60%	70.18%	79.43%

TABLE 3
PERCENT NISP OF PIG (SUS SCROFA)
FROM IDENTIFIABLE PORTIONS OF FAUNAL
ASSEMBLAGES

	Vardeman House	William Whitely	Duckworth Farm	Cowan Farmstead
Pig (Sus scrofa)	55.76%	71.82%	54.68%	53.00%
Remainder of identifiable assemblage[a]	44.24%	28.18%	45.32%	47.00%

[a]Identifiable assemblage refers to those taxa identified to genus or species level.

and to what degree they were eaten, however, is unclear.

In the Duckworth Farm faunal assemblage, pig is represented by 54.68% of the identified faunal assemblage (Table 3). Cows, sheep/goat, and chickens are represented as well. In addition, there were numerous eggshell fragments present in the assemblage; they could not, however, be identified to a specific bird species. As can be seen in tables 1 and 2, many of the wild taxa are more abundant in this assemblage than the domesticated species.

The Cowan Farmstead faunal assemblage contained the lowest percentage of pig in any of the comparative assemblages but not in a significantly lower amount than the majority of the other assemblages. The other domesticated mammals in this assemblage are all represented by one specimen each and include the horse, sheep/goat, and cow.

The William Whitley faunal assemblage included the highest occurrence of pig. Other domestic animals identified include cow and chicken. There were also numerous eggshell fragments present in the assemblage; they could not, however, be identified to a specific bird species. The extremely low number of cow remains recovered from the intact sheet midden may be evidence that cows were used for their secondary resources, such as dairy products and labor, or raised to sell at market.

Pig is one of two domestic animals identified in the Vardeman House assemblage; the other is cow. The Vardeman House faunal assemblage shows a heavy reliance on domestic mammals, particularly pigs. One can conclude that the Vardemans were subsisting mainly on pork, using few wild taxa to augment their diet. Beef seemed to have played a very small role in their diet, even though cattle were being raised at the Vardeman House site. The faunal assemblage is similar in domestic livestock composition to

the others described here but does exhibit some differences, such as the lack of specifically identified chicken remains (although these may be included in Galliformes and are listed in the estate sale of bill).

Discussion

The comparison of these four historic faunal assemblages supports the view that pork was very important in the Upland South cultural tradition practiced in Kentucky in the 19th century. It appears, however, that the only constant in the Upland South diet is the widespread consumption of pork. The variation in diet among the four Central Kentucky sites compared here shows that use of domesticated animals as the foundation of the Upland South diet was variable. Dietary practices were restricted by access to resources and economic status. Animals that could be hunted, trapped, or fished were important to those economic classes that were faced with food shortages when the availability of domestic livestock was limited due to restricted access (i.e., accessible markets, money, food rations).

Differential access to food was surely a factor for some economic classes in the Upland South. Detailed discussions of slaves, subsistence, and risk theory are available elsewhere (McKee 1988, 1999; Berlin and Morgan 1991, 1993; Young 1997; McKelway 2000; Lev-Tov 2004), so only a summary will be offered here. The diets of enslaved groups in the Upland South were dependent on a number of factors, which have been incorporated into what Larry McKee (1988:28) calls a "subsistence triangle." These factors include (1) provision/rations provided by the masters, (2) self-production of produce and livestock, (3) hunting/fishing/gathering, and (4) theft of food from the master's coffers. The archaeological correlates of some of these factors likely overlap, as for the case of self-production of crops and livestock vs. theft. Some of these factors may not leave a strong signature at all (i.e., provisioning of salt pork, cornmeal, molasses). Generally the strongest case can be made for hunting and fishing by enslaved persons, as evidenced in faunal assemblages (i.e., diversity of wild taxa). One must be cautioned against making assumptions about economic or social status based solely on the presence of a variety of wild taxa from farmstead faunal assemblages. The presence of wild taxa should not be the only line of evidence considered when determining ethnicity of a site or assemblage.

A diet consisting of domestic animals, especially pork, augmented by wild taxa, was followed by the slaves at the Duckworth Farm. This supports the hypothesis that the slaves there followed a modified Upland South diet, in which wild animals were regularly used to supplement the diet. The domestic animal portion of the slave diet may have been rationed by the master, bought, expropriated from the master, or raised by the slaves themselves. If they were raising the animals themselves, this suggests that they may have had to be self-reliant in providing their own food. In the absence of documentary evidence to support or refute the degree of self-reliance of these individuals, and regardless of what provisions (or lack of) were provided by the Duckworth family, the analysis of the faunal assemblage suggests that the slaves at this site had to hunt to meet their dietary needs, not an uncommon practice in Kentucky and Tennessee. This phenomenon has been illustrated at other sites (Young 1997; McKelway 2000; Lev-Tov 2004). Additionally, the high diversity of taxa represented at this site attests to this practice. The diet followed by the slaves at the Duckworth Farm is one based in Upland South realities (i.e., the major crops and livestock produced in the region) but deviates from the idealized notion of Upland South foodways. Food insecurity would have been common for those groups that had limited access to markets and domestic livestock, as was the case for most slaves. The dietary remains analyzed from the root cellars attributed

to the slaves living at the Duckworth Farm were likely influenced equally by economic status and limited access to resources.

Also interesting are the data from the Cowan Farmstead. The Cowan family is not considered to have been of low economic status; rather, this was a middling, landowning, planter family living in a very rural, sparsely populated area of central Kentucky. The family's access to markets would have been limited due to the absence of substantial trade routes in Pulaski County at that time. Given the low population density and isolation of the area, among other factors, it is likely the Cowans hunted wild animals in addition to slaughtering some of the domestic animals they raised, either by necessity or choice. The DIVERS analysis of the assemblage recovered from this site shows that the Cowans had a varied diet, in that one or a few taxa were not favored to the exclusion of all others. The importance of hunting wild animals for even middling planter families living in the Upland South during the 19th century is underscored at this site. The faunal assemblage suggests that the inhabitants of the Cowan Farmstead followed the Upland South diet to the extent that they could. The location of the farmstead in Pulaski County suggests that it may have been relatively isolated until the late-19th century when the Cincinnati & Southern Railway built a line through the county (Tate 1992:748). This isolation may have resulted in residents of the county subsisting on what livestock they could raise and animals they could hunt and catch locally.

The analysis of the Cowan Farmstead faunal assemblage is most similar to the assemblage from the Duckworth Farm, suggesting that access to resources, regardless of economic standing, is the highest-ranking factor in the diet followed by individuals living in the early- to mid-19th-century Upland South. For those individuals who were both impoverished and living in rural isolated areas, the daily subsistence struggle would surely have been even more pronounced. It should be noted that while everyday diet composition for these two groups may have been similar, food was likely prepared in ways that had different meanings for each group. Additionally, these faunal assemblages almost certainly reflect the everyday diet and not any special meals, foods, or seasonings that people from different economic classes may have had.

The diets interpreted from the Vardeman House and William Whitley House sites are the most similar in this analysis. What is most interesting about the Vardeman House faunal assemblage is the low variety of domesticated species the wealthy inhabitants here seemed to have consumed. According to the available documentary evidence, at least six different animals (horses, pigs, cows, mules, sheep, and chickens) were being raised at the farmstead, yet only two of these (pig and cow) are definitively represented in the archaeofaunal record. Given the added value of horses, cows, mules, sheep, and chickens, it is likely that some of these animals were eaten on an infrequent basis, if at all. The secondary resources these animals can provide in the form of traction (horses, mules, cows), transportation (horses, mules), dairy products (cows), wool (sheep), eggs (chicken), and economic profit (horses for racing, and breeding; horses, cow, mules, sheep, and eggs for sale or trade) will always be underrepresented in archaeofaunal assemblages.

The faunal assemblage recovered from the Pennington occupation of the William Whitley House suggests a fairly restricted diet, one that closely follows the idealized Upland South foodways. The Penningtons subsisted mainly on pork and chicken, supplementing these with very few wild animals. This may speak to the Penningtons relatively higher socioeconomic status as compared to the other assemblages included in this analysis. Given the high economic status and physical location of the Vardeman and Pennington families, access to markets would have been fairly stable and regular, which is evident in the material culture recovered from excavations at these sites (Linebaugh and Loughlin 2003; Madsen et al. 2005). In addition, the Vardemans and Penningtons were part of a larger extended kin group, and this undoubtedly affected the food available to these two families. To what extent, however, is unclear at this time.

Conclusions

In summary, the faunal assemblages recovered from four contemporaneous sites in Central Kentucky analyzed here can nuance understanding of the foodways idealized as part of the Upland South cultural tradition. Previous research has shown that pig, cattle, and other domestic livestock were important to antebellum farmstead economies in Kentucky. It should be noted, however, that the importance of domestic animals in Upland South foodways has been overstated. All evidence points to pig as the most important faunal resource for this region during the 19th century. The research here does not dispute this. The research presented here does suggest, however, that some economic classes were faced with food insecurity and thus hunted wild animals to fill the dietary gap. The faunal assemblages from both impoverished slaves and middling planters show that limited access to resources, whether due to social standing (slaves) or isolation from markets and necessary transportation routes (regardless of economic situation), was the main factor in dietary choices during this time. Based on the faunal assemblages from these two sites, it appears that the slaves at the Duckworth Farm and the Cowan family of Pulaski County had similar diets. These two groups also had the most limited access to resources. Concomitantly, the Vardemans and Penningtons, two related kin groups of high economic status, had the most restricted diet (in terms of species diversity) and would have had the most access to resources via family relationships, wealth, and markets. The traditionally held notion that people living in the Upland South during the 19th century followed a circumscribed set of foodways has been shown to have been an overdrawn ideal that does not match the practice of those groups with poor market access, whether due to low social and economic standing or to living in isolated rural areas.

Acknowledgments

The Kentucky Transportation Cabinet provided the funding for the analysis of samples from the William Whitley House, Duckworth Farm, and Vardeman House. HMB Professional Engineers, Inc., of Frankfort, Kentucky, under contract with the Somerset-Pulaski County Airport Board, provided funding for the analysis of the Cowan Farmstead faunal sample. I am most grateful to Amber VanDerwarker for preparing the DIVERS figures for this study. Lacey Fleming provided her GIS skills for Figure 1. An earlier version of this paper was presented at the 60th Annual Meeting of the Southeastern Archaeological Conference November 6–9, 2002, Charlotte, North Carolina. Elizabeth Colantoni, Amber VanDerwarker, Amy Lambeck Young, Shannon Hodge, and two anonymous reviewers provided valuable comments on earlier drafts of this paper. Their comments greatly enhanced the quality of this paper and provided encouragement to look at the data in new ways; any omissions or errors, however, are the full responsibility of the author.

References

ALLGOOD, JESSICA, AND J. TRACE KIRKWOOD
    2002 The Armstrong Farmstead (15FA185): Spatial Patterning, Social Relations, and Consumer Behavior at a Nineteenth-Century Central Bluegrass Farmstead. Paper presented at the Symposium on Ohio Valley Historical and Urban Archaeology, Transylvania University, Lexington, KY.

BARBER, JENNIFER
    2003 Phase II and III Archaeological Excavations at the Armstrong Farmstead (15FA185) Fayette County, Kentucky (Item No. 7-163.00). Report to Kentucky Transportation Cabinet, Frankfort, from Cultural Resource Analysts, Inc., Lexington, KY.

BAXTER, M. J.
    2001 Methodological Issues in the Study of Assemblage Diversity. *American Antiquity* 6(4):715–725.

BERLIN, IRA, AND PHILIP D. MORGAN
    1991 Introduction. In *The Slaves' Economy: Independent Production by Slaves in the Americas*, Ira Berlin and Philip D. Morgan, editors, pp. 1–27. Frank Cass & Co, Portland, OR.
    1993 Labor and the Shaping of Slave Life in the Americas. In *Cultivation and Culture: Labor and the Shaping of Slave Life in the Americas*, Ira Berlin and Philip D. Morgan, editors, pp. 1–45. University Press of Virginia, Charlottesville.

BIDWELL, PERCY W., AND JOHN I. FALCONER
    1925 *History of Agriculture in the Northern United States, 1620–1860*. Carnegie Institution of Washington, Washington, DC.

BREITBURG, EMMANUEL
    1976 Faunal Remains from the First Hermitage. In *An Archaeological and Historical Assessment of the First Hermitage*, Samuel D. Smith, editor, pp. 249–269. Archaeology Research Series No. 2. Tennessee Division of Archaeology and the Ladies Hermitage Association, Nashville.
    1983 An Analysis of Faunal Remains from Wynnewood State Historic Site, Sumner County, Tennessee, and Its Implications to Tennessee Plantation Site Archaeology in the Central Basin. *Tennessee Anthropologist* 8(2):182–199.

BROWN, LINDA KELLER, AND KAY MUSSELL (EDITORS)
    1984 *Ethnic and Regional Foodways in the United States: The Performance of Group Identity*. University of Tennessee Press, Knoxville.

CABAK, MELANIE A., AND MARK D. GROOVER
    2006 Bush Hill: Material Life at a Working Plantation. *Historical Archaeology* 40(4):51–83.

CRABTREE, PAMELA
    1990 Zooarchaeology and Complex Societies: Some Uses of Faunal Analysis for the Study of Trade, Social Status, and Ethnicity. In *Archaeological Methods and Theory*, Vol. 2, Michael B. Schiffer, editor, pp. 155–205. University of Arizona Press, Tucson.

DAVENPORT, CHRISTOPHER
    2000 Faunal Remains. In Archaeological Investigations at Logan's Fort, Lincoln County, Kentucky, by Kim A. McBride and W. Stephen McBride, pp. 80–94. Research Report No. 3. Kentucky Archaeological Survey, Lexington.

DAY, GRANT L., AND R. BERLE CLAY
    2000 A Phase III Excavation of the McConnell Homestead Site (15BB75) Bourbon County, Kentucky. Contract Publication Series 00-117. Manuscript, Cultural Resource Analysts, Inc., Lexington, KY.

FAULKNER, CHARLES
    2003 Foreword. In *An Archaeological Study of Rural Capitalism and Material Life: The Gibbs Farmstead in Southern Appalachia, 1790–1920*, by Mark D. Groover, pp. vii–x. Kluwer Academic/Plenum Publishers, New York, NY.

FAY, ROBERT P.
    1980 The Vertebrate Faunal Remains from Liberty Hall, Frankfort, Kentucky. Manuscript, Kentucky Heritage Council, Frankfort.

GROOVER, MARK D.
    2003 *An Archaeological Study of Rural Capitalism and Material Life: The Gibbs Farmstead in Southern Appalachia, 1790–1920*. Kluwer Academic/Plenum Publishers, New York, NY.
    2005 The Gibbs Farmstead: Household Archaeology in an Internal Periphery. *International Journal of Historical Archaeology* 9(4):229–289.

HARRINGTON, J. C.
    1955 Archaeology as an Auxiliary Science to American History. *American Anthropologist* 57(6):1121–1130.

HENDERSON, A. GWYNN
    1989 Cultural Resource Assessment of Proposed Additions to the Somerset-Pulaski County Airport. Archaeological Report, No. 212. Program for Cultural Resource Assessment, University of Kentucky, Lexington.

HILLIARD, SAM B.

1969   Pork and the Ante-Bellum South: The Geography of Self-Sufficiency. *Annals of the Association of American Geographers* 59(3):461–480.

1972   *Hog Meat and Hoecake: Food Supply in the Old South, 1840–1860.* Southern Illinois University Press, Carbondale.

1988   Hog Meat and Cornpone: Foodways in the Antebellum South. In *Material Life in America, 1600–1800,* Robert Blair St. George, editor, pp. 311–322. Northeastern University Press, Boston, MA.

HODGETTS, LISA M.

2006   Feast or Famine? Seventeenth-Century English Colonial Diet at Ferryland, Newfoundland. *Historical Archaeology* 40(4):125–138.

HUSER, WILLIAM A., JR., AND DAVID P. LYNCH

2005   Phase II Archaeological Testing of Three Sites at the Somerset Airport, Pulaski County, Kentucky. Report to Somerset-Pulaski County Airport Board, Somerset, from HMB Professional Engineers, Inc., Frankfort, KY.

JORDAN-BYCHKOV, TERRY G.

2003   *The Upland South: The Making of an American Folk Region and Landscape.* Center for American Places, Harrisonburg, VA.

KENTUCKY DEPARTMENT OF PARKS

2005   William Whitley House State Historic Site, Kentucky Department of Parks, Kentucky Commerce Cabinet, Franklin <http://parks.ky.gov/statehistoricsites/ww/details.htm>. Accessed 9 April 2007.

KINTIGH, KEITH W.

1984   Measuring Archaeological Diversity by Comparison with Simulated Assemblages. *American Antiquity* 49(1):44–54.

1989   Sample Size, Significance, and Measures of Diversity. In *Quantifying Diversity in Archaeology,* Robert D. Leonard and George T. Jones, editors, pp. 25–36. CUP, New York, NY.

1991   *Tools for Quantitative Archaeology.* Self published, Tempe, AZ.

KNIFFEN, FRED B.

1965   Folk Housing: Key to Diffusion. *Annals of the American Association of Geographers* 55(4):549–577.

LEV-TOV, JUSTIN S. E.

1994   Continuity and Change in Upland South Subsistence Practices: The Gibbs House Site in Knox County, Tennessee. Master's Thesis, Department of Anthropology, University of Tennessee, Knoxville.

2004   Implications of Risk Theory for Understanding Nineteenth-Century Slave Diets in the Southern United States. In *Behaviour behind Bones: The Zooarchaeology of Ritual, Religion, Status, and Identity,* Sharyn Jones O'Day, Wim Van Neer, and Anton Ervynck, editors, pp. 304–317. Proceedings of the 9th Conference of the International Council of Archaeozoology, No.1. Oxbow Books, London, England, UK.

LINCOLN COUNTY DEED BOOKS

1827a   Deed Book M:253–254, Lincoln County Deed Books, Lincoln County Courthouse, Stanford, KY.

1827b   Deed Book S:185, Lincoln County Deed Books, Lincoln County Courthouse, Stanford, KY.

LINEBAUGH, DONALD W., AND MICHAEL L. LOUGHLIN

2003   Additional Archaeological Investigations at the William Whitley State Historic Site, Lincoln County, Kentucky. Technical Report No. 470. Program for Archaeological Research, University of Kentucky, Lexington.

LYMAN, R. LEE

1987   On Zooarchaeological Measures of Socioeconomic Position and Cost-Efficient Meat Purchases. *Historical Archaeology* 21(1):58–66.

MADSEN, ANDREW D., JAY BARIL, KATIE BECRAFT, STEVE CULLER, DANIEL DAVIS, A. GWYNN HENDERSON, DONALD W. LINEBAUGH, MICHAEL L. LOUGHLIN, REBECCA MADSEN, MELISSA MILTON-PUNG, TANYA M. PERES, JACK ROSSEN, ERIC SCHLARB, MARCIE VENTER, AND PATRICK WALLACE

2005   A Phase III Archaeological Data Recovery of the Antebellum Vardeman House Site (15LI88), Lincoln County, Kentucky. Technical Report No. 464. Program for Archaeological Research, University of Kentucky, Lexington.

MARTIN, TERRENCE J.

1986   Analysis of the Arbuckle's Fort, West Virginia, Faunal Remains. Manuscript, Kentucky Archaeological Survey, Lexington.

MASON, ROGER D.

1984   *Euro-American Pioneer Settlement Systems in the Central Salt River Valley of Northeast Missouri.* Publications in Archaeology, No. 2. University of Missouri, Columbia.

McBRIDE, KIM A., AND W. STEPHEN McBRIDE

1990a   Historic Period Culture History. In *The Archaeology of Kentucky: Past Accomplishments and Future Directions, Vol. 2,* David Pollack, editor, pp. 583–747. Kentucky Heritage Council, Frankfort.

1990b   Historic Period: Previous Archaeological Research. In *The Archaeology of Kentucky: Past Accomplishments and Future Directions, Vol. 2.,* David Pollack, editor, pp. 559–582, Kentucky Heritage Council, Frankfort.

1993   From Colonization to the Twentieth Century. In *Kentucky Archaeology,* R. Barry Lewis, editor, pp. 183–211. Univeristy Press of Kentucky, Lexington.

McCORVIE, MARY R.

1987   *The Davis, Baldridge, and Huggins Sites: Three Nineteenth-Century Upland South Farmsteads in Perry County, Illinois.* Preservation Series, No. 4. American Resources Group, Carbondale, IL.

McKee, Larry
  1987 Delineating Ethnicity from the Garbage of Early
      Virginians: Faunal Remains from the Kingsmill
      Plantation Slave Quarter. *American Archaeology*
      6(1):31–39.
  1988 *Plantation Food Supply in Nineteenth-Century*
      Tidewater Virginia. Doctoral dissertation, Department
      of Anthropology, University of California, Berkeley.
      University Microfilms International, Ann Arbor,
      MI.
  1999 Food Supply and Plantation Social Order: An
      Archaeological Perspective. In *"I Too, Am America":*
      Archaeological Studies of African American Life,
      Theresa A. Singleton, editor, pp. 218–239. University
      Press of Virginia, Charlottesville.

McKelway, Henry S., with contributions by Gary D.
Crites, Lance K. Greene, and Amy L. Young
  2000 *Slaves and Master in the Upland South: Data*
      Recovery at the Mabry Site (40KN86), Knox County,
      Tennessee. Publications in Archaeology, No. 6.
      Tennessee Department of Transportation, Office of
      Environmental Planning and Permits, Nashville.

Milton-Ping, Melissa, and Andrew D. Madsen
  2005 Prehistoric and Historic Contexts. In A Phase III
      Archaeological Data Recovery of the Antebellum
      Vardeman House Site (15LI88), Lincoln County,
      Kentucky, by Andrew D. Madsen, Jay Baril, Katie
      Becraft, Steve Culler, Daniel Davis, A. Gwynn
      Henderson, Donald W. Linebaugh, Michael L.
      Loughlin, Rebecca Madsen, Melissa Milton-Pung,
      Tanya M. Peres, Jack Rossen, Eric Schlarb, Marcie
      Venter, and Patrick Wallace, pp. 29–60. Technical
      Report No. 464. Program for Archaeological Research,
      University of Kentucky, Lexington.

Mitchell, Robert D.
  1972 Agricultural Reorganization: Origin and Diffusion
      in the Upper South before 1860. In *International*
      Geography, Vol. 12, W. Peter Adams and Frederick
      M. Helleiner, editors, pp. 740–742. University of
      Toronto Press, Toronto, Ontario, Canada.
  1978 The Formation of Early American Cultural Regions: An
      Interpretation. In *European Settlement and Development*
      in North America: Essays on Geographical Change in
      Honour and Memory of Andrew Hill Clark, James R.
      Gibson, editor, pp. 66–90. University of Toronto Press,
      Toronto, Ontario, Canada.

Newton, Milton B.
  1974 Cultural Preadptation and the Upland South.
      Geoscience and Man 5:143–154.

Noël Hume, Ivor
  1969 *Artifacts of Colonial America*. Vintage Books, New
      York, NY.

O'Brien, Michael J., and Teresita Majewski
  1989 Wealth and Status in the Upper South Socioeconomic
      System of Northeastern Missouri. *Historical*
      Archaeology 23(2):60–95.

O'Malley, Nancy
  1999 Archaeological Investigations of Site 15LI55 at the
      William Whitley State Historic Site, Lincoln County,
      Kentucky (TPWW0010). Technical Report No. 427.
      Program for Archaeological Research, University of
      Kentucky, Lexington.

Orser, Charles E., Jr.
  1987 Plantation Status and Consumer Choice: A Materialist
      Framework for Historical Archaeology. In *Consumer*
      Choice in Historical Archaeology, Suzanne M.
      Spencer-Wood, editor, pp. 121–137. Plenum Press,
      New York, NY.

Otto, John Solomon
  1980 Race and Class on Antebellum Plantations. In
      Archaeological Perspectives on Ethnicity in America,
      Robert L. Schuyler, editor, pp. 3–13. Baywood
      Publishing Company, Farmingdale, NY.

Owens, Leslie H.
  1976 *This Species of Property: Slave Life and Culture in*
      the Old South. Oxford University Press, Oxford,
      England, UK.

Owsley, Frank L.
  1949 *Plain Folk of the Old South*. Louisiana State University
      Press, Baton Rouge.

Patterson, Judith A.
  1998 Dietary Patterning at an Upland South Plantation:
      The Ramsey House Site (40KN120), Knox County,
      Tennessee. Master's Thesis, Department of
      Anthropology, University of Tennessee, Knoxville.

Peres, Tanya M.
  2002 Analysis of the Faunal Assemblage from the William
      Whitley House (15LI55), Kentucky. Manuscript,
      Program for Archaeological Research, University of
      Kentucky, Lexington.
  2003a A Phase II Archaeological Evaluation of Site 5BH212,
      Associated with the KY11 Project, Bath County,
      Kentucky. Technical Report No. 462. Program for
      Archaeological Research, University of Kentucky,
      Lexington.
  2003b Zooarchaeological Remains from the Cowan
      Farmstead (15PU234), Pulaski County, Kentucky.
      Technical Report No. 506. Program for Archaeological
      Research, University of Kentucky, Lexington.
  2005 Zooarchaeological Remains from the Vardeman
      House. In A Phase III Archaeological Data Recovery
      of the Antebellum Vardeman House Site (15LI88),
      Lincoln County, Kentucky, by Madsen, Andrew D.,
      Jay Baril, Katie Becraft, Steve Culler, Daniel Davis,
      A. Gwynn Henderson, Donald W. Linebaugh, Michael
      L. Loughlin, Rebecca Madsen, Melissa Milton-Pung,
      Tanya M. Peres, Jack Rossen, Eric Schlarb, Marcie
      Venter, and Patrick Wallace, pp. 389–424. Technical
      Report No. 464. Program for Archaeological Research,
      University of Kentucky, Lexington.

PERKINS, ELIZABETH A.
1991 The Consumer Frontier: Household Consumption in Early Kentucky. *The Journal of American History* 78(2):486–510.

POE, TRACY N.
1999 The Origins of Soul Food in Black Urban Identity: Chicago, 1915–1947. *American Studies International* 37(1):4–34.
2001 The Labour and Leisure of Food Production as a Mode of Ethnic Identity Building among Italians in Chicago, 1890–1940. *Rethinking History* 5(1):131–148.

POWER, RICHARD LYLE
1953 *Planting Corn Belt Culture: The Impress of the Upland Southerner and Yankee in the Old Northwest.* Indiana Historical Society, Indianapolis.

PRICE, CYNTHIA R.
1985 Patterns of Cultural Behavior and Intra-Site Distributions of Faunal Remains at the Widow Harris Site. *Historical Archaeology* 19(2):40–56.

REITZ, ELIZABETH J.
1986 Urban/Rural Contrasts in Vertebrate Fauna from the Southern Atlantic Coastal Plain. *Historical Archaeology* 20(2):47–58.
1987 Vertebrate Fauna and Socioeconomic Status. In *Consumer Choice in Historical Archaeology*, Suzanne M. Spencer-Wood, editor, pp.101–119. Plenum Press, New York, NY.

REITZ, ELIZABETH J., AND NICHOLAS HONERKAMP
1983 British Colonial Subsistence Strategy on the Southeastern Coastal Plain. *Historical Archaeology* 17(2):4–26.

REITZ, ELIZABETH J., BARBARA L. RUFF, AND MARTHA A. ZIERDEN
2006 Pigs in Charleston, South Carolina: Using Specimen Counts to Consider Status. *Historical Archaeology* 40(4):104–124.

REITZ, ELIZABETH J., AND MARGARET C. SCARRY
1985 *Reconstructing Historic Subsistence with an Example from Sixteenth Century Spanish Florida.* The Society for Historical Archaeology, Special Publications Series, No. 3. California, PA.

RHODE, DAVID
1988 Measurement of Archaeological Diversity and the Sample-Size Effect. *American Antiquity* 53(4):708–716.

ROSSEN, JACK
2003 Appendix C: Archaeobotanical Report. Botanical Remains from Features 10, 11, and 12 at Site 15BH212, Bath County, Kentucky. In *A Phase II Archaeological Evaluation of Site 5BH212, Associated with the KY11 Project, Bath County, Kentucky*, by Tanya M. Peres, pp. C.1–13. Technical Report No. 462. Program for Archaeological Research, University of Kentucky, Lexington.

SCHULZ, PETER D., AND SHERRI M. GUST
1983 Faunal Remains and Social Status in Nineteenth-Century Sacramento. *Historical Archaeology* 17(1):44–53.

SCHWAB, EUGENE L.
1973 *Travels in the Old South.* University of Kentucky Press, Lexington.

SCOTT, ELIZABETH M.
2001 Food and Social Relations at Nina Plantation. *American Anthropologist* 103(3):671–691.

SINGLETON, THERESA
1995 The Archaeology of Slavery in North America. *Annual Review of Anthropology* 24:119–140.

SPENCER-WOOD, SUZANNE M.
1987 Introduction. In *Consumer Choice in Historical Archaeology*, Suzanne M. Spencer-Wood, editor, pp. 1–24. Plenum Press, New York, NY.

STOTHERS, DAVID M., AND PATRICK M. TUCKER
2002 The Dunlap Farmstead: A Market-Dependent Farm in the Early History of the Maumee Valley of Ohio. *Archaeology of Eastern North America* 30:155–188.

SUSSENBACH, TOM
2000 Phase II Archaeological Investigations at the Vardeman Homeplace Site (15LI88) in the Proposed Cedar Creek Lake Impoundment Area, Lincoln County, Kentucky. Report of Investigation, No. 57. Sterling Archaeological Consultants, Inc., Winchester, KY.

TATE, ROGER D.
1992 Pulaski County. In *The Kentucky Encyclopedia*, J. E. Kleber, editor, pp. 747–749. University Press of Kentucky, Lexington.

TIBBALS, ALMA OWENS
1952 *A History of Pulaski County Kentucky.* Grace Owens, Bagdad, KY.

TORMA, CAROLYN, CAMILLE WELLS, AND THOMASON AND ASSOCIATES
1985 *Architectural and Historical Sites of Pulaski County.* Kentucky Heritage Council, Frankfort.

TUMA, MICHAEL W.
2000 Faunal Analysis for Site 15BB75. In *A Phase III Excavation of the McConnell Homestead Site (15BB75) Bourbon County, Kentucky*, Grant L. Day and R. Berle Clay, editors, pp. 10.83–10.133. Contract Publication Series 00-117. Manuscript, Cultural Resource Analysts, Inc., Lexington, KY.

UNITED STATES BUREAU OF THE CENSUS
1860 *United States Census of Agriculture: 1860.* U.S. Department of Commerce, Washington, DC.

VANDERWARKER, AMBER M.
2006 *Farming, Hunting, and Fishing in the Olmec World.* University of Texas Press, Austin.

WALTERS, MATTHEW
    1985 Faunal Remains at Waveland (15FA177), Fayette
          County, Kentucky. *Proceedings of the Symposium
          on Ohio Valley Urban and Historic Archaeology*
          3:145–150.

YOUNG, AMY LAMBECK
    1995a Archaeology at Locust Grove Plantation, Jefferson
          County, Kentucky. In *Current Archaeological
          Research in Kentucky: Vol. 3*, John F. Doershuk,
          Christopher A. Bergman, and David Pollack,
          editors, pp. 279–296. Kentucky Heritage Council,
          Frankfort.
    1995b Risk and Material Conditions of African American
          Slaves at Locust Grove: An Archaeological
          Perspective. Doctoral dissertation, Department of
          Anthropology, University of Tennessee, Knoxville.
    1997 Cellars and African-American Slave Sites: New Data
          from an Upland South Plantation. *Midcontinental
          Journal of Archaeology* 22(1):95–115.

YOUNG, AMY LAMBECK, SUSAN C. ANDREWS, AND PHILIP
J. CARR
    1995 Ceramics and Slave Lifeways at Locust Grove
          Plantation. In *Historical Archaeology in Kentucky*,
          Kim A. McBride, W. Stephen McBride, and David
          Pollack, editors, pp. 253–264. Kentucky Heritage
          Council, Frankfort.

YOUNG, AMY LAMBECK, PHILIP J. CARR, AND JOSEPH E.
GRANGER
    1998 How Historical Archaeology Works: A Case Study of
          Slave Houses at Locust Grove. *The Register of the
          Kentucky Historical Society* 96(2):167–194.

YOUNG, AMY LYNNE
    1993 Slave Subsistence at the Upper South Mabry Site,
          East Tennessee: Regional Variability in Plantation
          Diet of the Southeastern United States. Master's
          thesis, Department of Anthropology, University of
          Tennessee, Knoxville.

TANYA M. PERES
DEPARTMENT OF SOCIOLOGY AND ANTHROPOLOGY
MIDDLE TENNESSEE STATE UNIVERSITY
TODD HALL, ROOM 342
MTSU PO BOX 10
MURFREESBORO, TN 37132

RESEARCH NOTES AND COMMENTS

ERIC KLINGELHOFER

Aspects of Early Afro-American Material Culture: Artifacts from The Slave Quarters at Garrison Plantation, Maryland.

ABSTRACT

The 1964–65 excavation of the slave quarters at Garrison Plantation near Baltimore, Maryland, yielded groups of objects that display certain 'Africanisms.' The groups of objects are proposed elements of early Afro-American material culture and are compared to items from similar sites in the mid-Atlantic region.

Introduction

Investigators into past Afro-American culture have been faced with the prospect that little survived the rigors of the African internment compounds, the deadly Atlantic crossing, and the American slave markets. Plantation life further discouraged African customs, beliefs, and even skills as the transported slaves and their descendants were granted identity and status based solely upon a capacity to produce—either more crops or goods, or more slaves (for bibliographies of slave life, see Gyrisco and Salwen 1980; Olson 1983).

These considerations have led scholars of Afro-American history and culture to search for evidence of African traditions that survived the deculturation caused by American slavery. Such elusive 'Africanisms' are often controversial and prone to subjective interpretation (Bastide 1971; Garret 1966; Vlach 1978; Thompson 1983; Jones 1985). Archaeology can contribute much to addressing this problem, as repeated investigations of Black settlement sites should reveal patterns to the elements of their material culture, and these pat-

terns can be compared chronologically and geographically (Kelso 1984; Lange and Handler 1985; Wheaton and Garrow 1985). Adding to the growing number of sites yielding evidence of slave life, excavations at the Garrison Plantation near Baltimore, Maryland, yielded several examples of artifact types that appear to be significant components of early Afro-American material culture.

In 1964 and 1965, members of the Archaeological Society of Maryland led by John Sprinkle undertook archaeological excavations at Garrison Farm in northwestern Baltimore County, Maryland. A stone building 100 feet from the farmhouse had been identified as that built about 1696 for a garrison of Maryland Rangers by a Captain Oldham and is thus the oldest surviving building in this part of Maryland (Forman 1982: 109). The 'fort' was planned for demolition, as part of a housing subdivision. To recover evidence of the Ranger garrison, archaeological fieldwork took place on weekends and involved volunteer excavators with little archaeological experience. Most of the effort went into digging out two nearby 19th century refuse pits, but the excavators did find poorly preserved early floor surfaces within the building, where the stratigraphy had been severely damaged by rat holes and tunnels and by its use as a slaughterhouse in the late 19th century. The Baltimore County Historical Trust eventually prevailed upon the developer to spare the building, and it stands today stabilized and intact but surrounded by split-levels on a tiny plot of land. Unfortunately, while most of the objects retrieved during the excavation have been kept in storage, nearly all the excavation records have been lost.

The Garrison Plantation slave quarters were created by the landowner, Robert Carnan, from an obsolete military structure. Around the year 1800, he altered it, raising the walls to add a second storey 'half floor' (Forman 1963). In the 1798 federal tax returns (M.H.S. 1798), there were 22 slaves on the Garrison estate, a fairly large slave population for a landholding on Maryland's upper Western Shore but smaller than the large plantation centers and separate 'quarter' holdings typical of the Tidewater area from the Patuxent valley to the James valley (Kulikoff 1978: 251–52). The

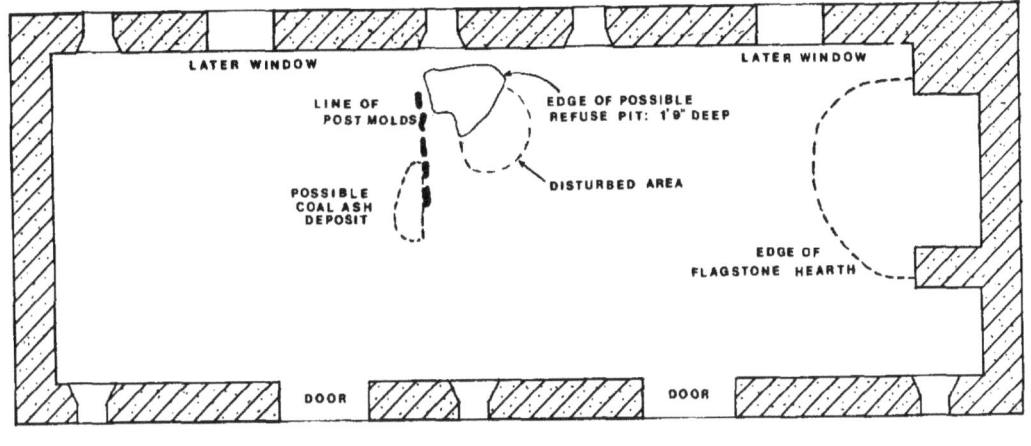

GARRISON PLANTATION, MARYLAND

SLAVE QUARTERS (FORT GARRISON) WITH SLAVE PERIOD FEATURES

0   5   10 FEET

Figure 1. Plan of Garrison Plantation slave quarters, based upon a preliminary site plan, 1965.

excavated stone "Negroe Quarter" measured 48 × 18 feet, with an internal division of vertical posts that made two equal-size rooms, each of which had one door on the south wall (see Figure 1). The eastern room was dominated by an 8 foot wide fireplace, before which lay a well-paved surface. This working kitchen for the original garrison was retained during the slave period. The kitchen room also contained a poorly preserved feature by its north wall (measuring approximately 3 feet broad) which the excavators thought might have been a refuse pit but which more likely had served as a root cellar.

The nature of the excavation and the state of its records do not permit a reliable analysis of the recovered artifacts, (we do not even know what percentage of the interior was excavated). This certainly hinders the already difficult process of identifying elements of the slave culture. Indeed, one could argue that much of the Black material culture under slavery was not overly different from that of free Blacks and poor Whites—the share-croppers and farm laborers. Avery Craven suggested this 50 years ago (Craven 1930). More recently, John S. Otto has concluded, from his work at Cannon's Point Plantation, Georgia, that

"despite racial, legal and symbolic differences, [Blacks and poor Whites] often experienced a basically similar material existance" (Otto 1984: 121).

Yet, it must be acknowledged that even those objects in the personal possession of American slaves were largely predetermined by the fact of slavery. The plantation masters, consciously or unconsciously, had a sense of what was appropriate for their slaves, for example, permitting one style of dress or one type of building (Georgia Writers' Project 1940: 179). Therefore the dwellings, diet, and possessions that formed the basis of the slaves' material culture were to a great degree determined by notions of 18th and 19th-century landowners. Early Afro-American culture developed within the limitations of what activities were permitted and what objects were obtainable. At the Garrison Plantation slave quarters, three groups of objects—of unexceptional materials—had characteristics atypical of early American material culture. Their discovery within a recorded slave structure permits one logical conclusion: they represent elements of the American slave culture. Moreover, the same groups appear in artifact collections of other mid-Atlantic slave sites.

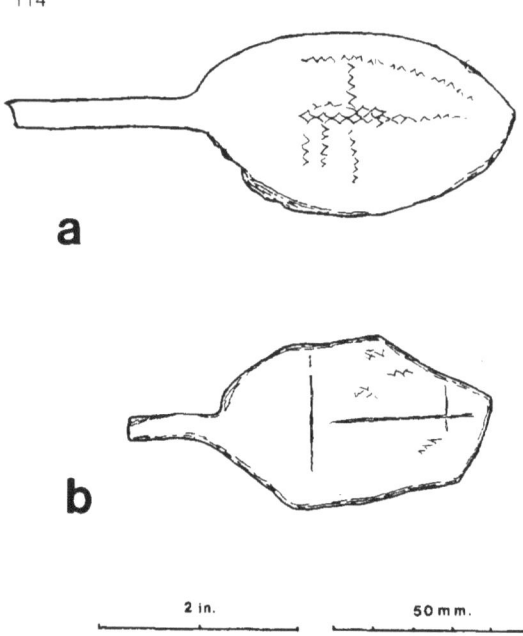

a

b

Figure 3. Spoon bowl 'a', surface condition fair to poor, with pitting and corrosed edges. Shows little sign of wear.

2 in.   50 mm.

Figure 2. Pewter spoons with vestiges of incised decoration: a, bowl 45 × 80 mm., geometric pattern of 'herringbone' lines; b, bowl 40 × 70 mm., incised axial and perpendicular lines, with slight remains of 'herring-bone' markings.

Material Culture

Decorated Spoons

The Garrison excavators found two pewter spoons plus some of the pewter 'sprue', or waste material, that had been trimmed away from molded spoons. The bowls of both spoons retain traces of inscribed geometric designs, remarkably similar to the spoon bowls and handles decorated today by Maroon tribes (descendants of escaped slaves) in Guyanna, South America (Price and Price 1978: 38,39) (see Figures 2,3,4,5). At least 15 such pewter spoons were found among the slave quarters at Kingsmill Plantation (with one complete example from Kingsmill, KM359b, on loan to the Smithsonian Institution). The designs on these spoons are decorative, perhaps symbolic, but their rouletting and infill patterns are not like the monogram or merchant-mark signs that probably denoted ownership of spoons found on contemporary military sites. A spoon with a stamped monogram is on display at Valley Forge, Pennsylvania; an example with an incised personal mark is reproduced in the Fort Stanwix, New York, excavation report (Hanson and Hsu 1975: 145–46). The presence of the two Garrison decorated spoons, and their possible manufacture on the site, extends the range of 'Maroon' decorated spoons to northern Maryland.

Lithic Industry

The Garrison slave quarters yielded evidence of a 'lithic industry' that reworked European manufactured goods into utensils and tools for a lower level of technological production. The base of a pressed glass tumbler was carefully chipped into a sharp scraping edge (see Figure 6), similar to a scraper made of an 18th century wine bottle from a James River site (44JC160) recently excavated by the College of William and Mary. A similar item reworked from an English gunflint came from Kingsmill (KM379A), and at least one piece of mirror glass there appears to have been reworked to form a sharp cutting edge (KM356B). The plantation site of Oxon Hill, Maryland, is also yielding worked glass objects (William Henry 1986, pers. comm.). A small piece of English flint from outside the slave quarter (J16-1), presumably from a late 18th- early 19th century gunflint, also appears to have been worked into a little scraping

Figure 4. Spoon bowl 'b', surface condition very poor. Shows signs of heavy wear, apparently both right and left handed use.

tool, if it did not serve in some way as a tinderbox component. Such scrapers in a prehistoric context are attributed to the preparation of hides, basketry fibers, and gourd vessels, but these historic examples of 'lithic technology' are not related to a Native American cultural tradition—the sites in Virginia and in Maryland postdate the elimination of the Indian as significant factor in the Tidewater and Piedmont areas of the mid-Atlantic region (Porter 1980).

'Ritual' Objects

Archaeologists tend to classify unidentified items according to their contexts: on prehistoric sites, as ritual objects; on historic sites, as gaming pieces. Without a doubt, most items found at a slave site can be readily recognized as part of the Western historical tradition. At the same time, certain early Afro-American activities and accompanying objects were never described in writing and others were perhaps never even observed by Whites. The Black world was, after all, generally restricted to what took place in slave cabins between sundown and sunup (Genovese 1974). This time and place was the cradle of Afro-American culture, and during the early evolution of that culture, there must have been many instances of specific survivals from Africa (and perhaps newly created beliefs and activities as well) that were

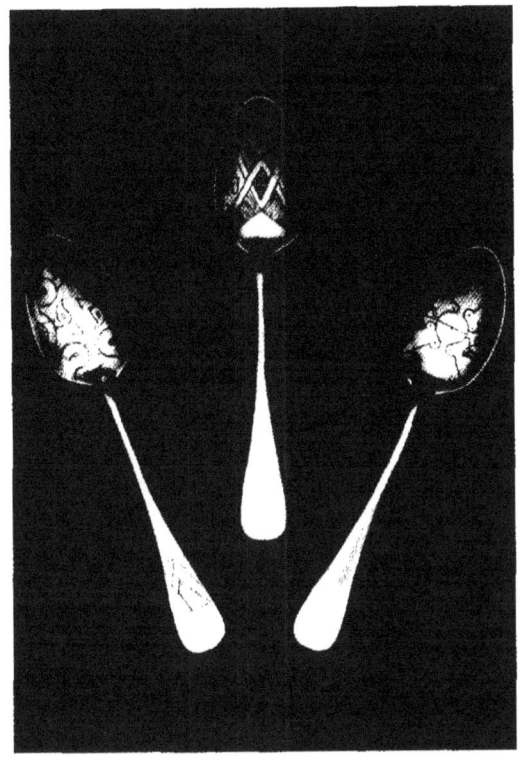

Figure 5. Suriname Maroon decorated spoons, examples made in 1961 by members of the Djuke tribe. Reproduced from *Afro-American Arts of the Suriname Rain Forest*, with permission of the authors, Sally and Richard Price, and the U.C.L.A. Museum of Cultural History.

soon discarded or blended into the heterogeneous cultural identity that Black Americans created for themselves. Indeed it was in Maryland that colonial authorities complained about the presence and effective use of ''Negro Drums'' that called slaves together for illicit gatherings and rituals (Menard 1978: 37).

The Garrison site yielded objects that might be discounted as oddities or gaming pieces, perhaps even children's items. Nevertheless, the appearance at other slave sites of one or two unusual or unexplained objects suggests that the place of ritual in slave material culture cannot be discounted. Among this group, there are objects that have unusual colors or properties, or are regularly shaped (spherical, ovoid) with one or more side

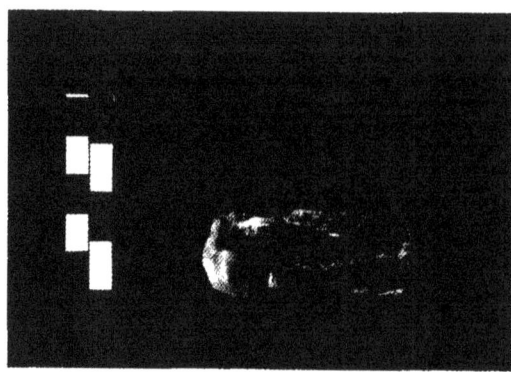

Figure 6. Fragment of tumbler base, reworked as scraper. Length 60 mm.

deliberately flattened. A large natural crystal was recovered from a slave site at Monticello (E.R.# 968 C2). Excavators from College of William and Mary found a 3 inch diameter spherical quartzite stone with three of the six possible perpendicular faces flattened at a probable slave site near the Chicahominy River (44 JC 298).

Three Garrison Plantation items had been deliberately shaped (see Figure 7). The most impressive was a polygonal-sided glass stopper, of a flattened ovoid form, from a cut-and-pressed glass decanter. Its stem had been broken off, resulting in a crude but functional base. There was also a potsherd, of red earthenware with a thick black glaze on one side, which had the form of an isosceles heptagon (or perhaps a truncated octagon). Nearly the same size as the stopper, it had been shaped so that only one side could keep the object upright when on edge. Similar in size to both of the above was a cut and shaped piece of wood (apparently pine), also an isosceles heptagon. It too could be supported on edge at only one place. The similarity of size and shape strongly suggests that the wood and ceramic objects were created in imitation of the glass piece.

From the currently limited knowledge of Black slave culture—as opposed to plantation routine and economics—all three polygonal objects could have served as gaming pieces as markers for a 'board' game, and indeed they resemble recently excavated polygonally-shaped sherds from London, ca.

1700, identified as counters or markers (Thompson, Grew, and Shofield 1984). Alternatively, the apparent 'base' edges of the Garrison items suggest that they stood upright, perhaps as targets to be knocked over. However, the fact that these objects are decidedly larger than the typical gaming piece, the care in their creation, the notable choice of a different material for each, and the rarity of such items compared to the ubiquitous clay and stone marbles, prohibits one from dismissing the possibility that these items served another purpose. Certain African religious practices did survive for a time under slavery: legends, funeral customs, medicinal charms, and even the practice of making small clay figurines (Puckett 1968; Otto 1984: 86,87). Yet until more is known about Negro pagan religions, or games that slaves brought with them or devised in American bondage, the identity of these objects cannot be determined. The three polygonal artifacts from Garrison Plantation slave quarters, therefore, may plausibly be considered possible charms or ritual objects, testaments to the time when Blacks had been cut off from their traditional African religions, but had not yet been permitted or encouraged to embrace Christianity.*

*Another possible 'ritual' object was a smooth, dark stone, of local metabasalt. Its natural oval shape may have been enhanced, as it bore signs of having been polished. The central section of one of its long edges had been flattened so that it too could stand on edge. The site yielded some prehistoric material, and this stone might have served an Indian industrial use as a rubber or polisher, though its small size (5 × 2 inches) makes the flattened surface an unpromising whetstone. It could equally be related to the three other unexplained items that had a single side for standing upright, and a comparison to documented Afro-American ritual stones (Bastide 1971: 107; Puckett 1968: 197, 292) cannot be ignored.

Conclusions

At Garrison Plantation, slave archaeology revealed three distinctive elements of material cul-

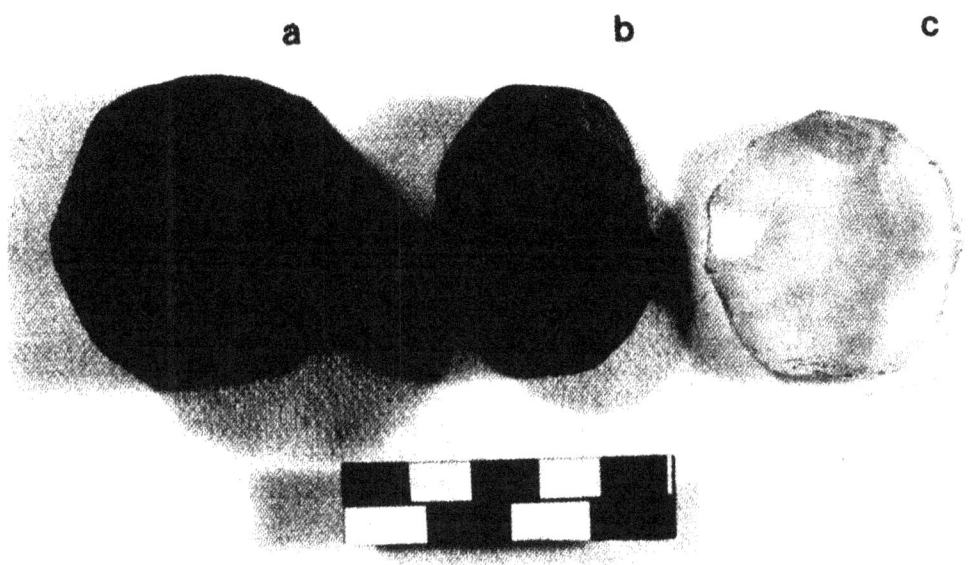

Figure 7. Polygonal objects of possible ritual use: a, wood, 48 × 31 mm. high; b, black-glazed earthenware, 43 × 33 mm. high; c, glass decanter stopper top, 41 × 27 mm. max. width.

ture that are absent in the European and colonial traditions. Moreover, the three elements appear on other Tidewater slave sites, though they have not yet been reported further south (Fairbanks 1984; Otto 1984; Armstrong 1985). There was a ready access to a skill generally long abandoned in Europe—lithic industry—by which items of European manufacture were re-fashioned to serve different functions for Black needs. There appeared, too, traces of an artistic mode that is not part of the White world, the application of incised geometric decorations to metal spoons. This particular decorative art is still practiced in tribal communities of African descendants in South America. Both skills must be seriously considered denominative elements of early Afro-American culture. And finally, it was observed—though not understood— in certain carefully chosen and shaped objects, that a slave ritual may have existed.

For Allan Kulikoff (1978: 255), the "skimpy surviving evidence" suggested that the Maryland and Virginia Tidewater slaves added "values and beliefs of their West African ancestors" to certain adopted aspects of White colonial society and created a new culture different from both. The growing archaeological record of slave life in Maryland and Virginia substantiates this view, as the Garrison Plantation slaves had a material culture perhaps typically both 'African' and 'American.'

ACKNOWLEDGEMENT

This paper is based upon the report (Klingelhofer 1985) of the research project No. P.20.5501 of The Johns Hopkins University, conducted by its Department of History and funded by the Baltimore County Community Block Grants Office. The report accompanied an inventory of artifacts associated with the slavery period of the Fort Garrison stone building, site 18BA27. The bulk of the finds are held by the Division of Archaeology, Maryland Geological Survey, and the artifacts associated with the slave period of occupation have been deposited at the Banneker-Douglass Museum, administered by the Maryland Commission on Afro-American History and Culture.

Thanks must go to Professor John Russell-Wood, to Professor Philip Curtin, and to Drs. Richard and Sally Price and the UCLA Museum of Cultural History to use the photograph of the Suriname spoons. I want to also thank John McGrain of the Baltimore County Landmarks Preservation Commission, John Sprinkle, who excavated Fort Garrison, and especially William Henry who redrew the site plan, Richard Hall, the research assistant, and Alexandra Klingelhofer, the contracting conservator. At the Maryland Geological Survey, Tyler Bastian, State Archaeologist, and his associates Joseph McNamarra and Lois Brown extended every courtesy and assistance. I am pleased to acknowledge the contribution made by other archaeologists who graciously spared time during their excavation season to discuss slave archaeology and the Garrison Plantation artifacts: Carter Hudgins, Ivor and Audrey Noël Hume, Bill Kelso, Alain Outlaw, Ted Rheinhart, Marley Brown, and all their associates with whom I examined finds lists and storage boxes.

REFERENCES

ARMSTRONG, DOUGLAS V.
1985 An Afro-Jamaican Slave Settlement: Archaeological Investigations at Drax Hall. In *The Archaeology of Slavery and Plantation Life*, edited by Theresa A. Singleton, pp. 261–87. Academic Press, Orlando.

ASHER, ROBERT AND CHARLES FAIRBANKS
1971 Excavation of a Slave Cabin: Georgia, U.S.A. *Historical Archaeology* 5: 3–17.

BASTIDE, ROGER
1971 *African Civilization in the New World*. Harper & Row, New York. Translated from *Les Amériques Noires*. Edition Payot, Paris, 1967.

CRAVEN, AVERY O.
1930 Poor Whites and Negroes in the Antebellum South. *Journal of Negro History* 15: 14–25.

FAIRBANKS, CHARLES H.
1984 The Plantation Archaeology of the Southeastern Coast. *Historical Archaeology* 18: 1–14.

FORMAN, H. CHANDLEE
1963 Report on the Inspection of Fort Garrison, MS report

in the State Historic Site Survey form, Maryland Historical Trust.
1982 *Manor and Plantation Houses of Maryland*. Bodine and Ass., Baltimore. Original edition, 1934.

GARRETT, ROMEO B.
1966 African Survivals in American Culture. *Journal of Negro History* 51: 239–49.

GENOVESE, EUGENE D.
1974 *Roll, Jordan, Roll: The World the Slaves Made*. Random House, New York.

GEORGIA WRITERS' PROJECT
1940 *Drums and Shadows*. University of Georgia Press, Athens.

GYRISCO, GEOFFREY M. AND BERT SALWEN
1980 Archaeology of Black American Culture: An Annotated Bibliography. In *Archaeological Perspectives on Ethnicity in America*, edited by Robert Schuyler, pp. 77–85. Baywood Publishing Co., Farmingdale, N.Y.

HANSON, LEE AND DICK PING HSU
1975 *Casemates and Cannonballs: Archaeological Investigations at Fort Stanwix, Rome, New York*. U.S. National Park Service Publications in Archaeology 14.

JONES, STEVEN, L.
1985 The Afro-American Tradition in Vernacular Architecture. In *The Archaeology of Slavery and Plantation Life*, edited by Theresa A. Singleton, pp. 195–213. Academic Press, Orlando.

KELSO, WILLIAM M.
1984 *Kingsmill Plantations, 1619–1800: An Archaeology of Country Life in Colonial Virginia*. Academic Press, Orlando.

KLINGELHOFER, ERIC
1985 Afro-American Material Culture at Garrison Plantation. MS report on file with The Maryland Commission on Afro-American History and Culture, and the Archaeology Division, Maryland Archaeological Survey.

KULIKOFF, ALAN
1978 The Origins of Afro-American Society in Tidewater Maryland and Virginia, *William and Mary Quarterly* 3rd series 35, pp.226–59.

LANGE, FREDERICK W. AND HANDLER, JEROME S.
1985 The ethnohistorical Approach to Slavery. In *The Archaeology of Slavery and Plantation Life*, edited by Theresa A. Singleton, pp. 15–32. Academic Press, Orlando.

MENARD, RUSSELL R.
1975 The Maryland Slave Population, 1658–1730: A Demographic Profile of Blacks in Four Counties. *William and Mary Quarterly*, 3rd series, 32, pp.29–54.

M.H.S.
1798 Maryland Historical Society, Film Roll No. 606: *1798 Direct Federal Assessment, Soldiers Delight Hundred.* Entries Nos. 3169, 3347, 3665.

OLSON, JAMES S.
1983 *Slave Life in America. A Historiography and Selected Bibliography.* University Press of America, New York.

OTTO, JOHN SOLOMON
1984 *Cannon's Point Plantation, 1794–1860.* Academic Press, Orlando.

PORTER, FRANK W, III
1980 Behind the Frontier: Indian Survivals in Maryland. *Maryland Historical Magazine* 75: 42–54.

PRICE, SALLY AND RICHARD PRICE
1980 *Afro-American Arts of the Suriname Rain Forest.* University of California Press, Berkeley.

PUCKETT, NEWBELL N.
1968 *Folk Beliefs of the Southern Negro.* Negro Universities Press, New York. Reprint of 1926, Chapel Hill.

THOMPSON, ALAN, FRANCES GREW AND JOHN SCHOFIELD
1984 Excavations at Aldgate, 1974. *Post-Medieval Archaeology* 18, pp. 1–148.

THOMPSON, ROBERT FARRIS
1983 *Flash of the Spirit: African and Afro-American Art and Philosophy.* Random House, New York.

VLACH, JOHN MICHAEL
1978 *The Afro-American Tradition in Decorative Arts.* Cleveland Museum of Arts, Cleveland.

WHEATON, THOMAS J. AND GARROW, PATRICK H.
1985 Acculturation and the Archaeological Record in the Carolina Lowcountry. In *The Archaeology of Slavery and Plantation Life,* edited by Theresa A. Singleton, pp.239–59. Academic Press, Orlando.

ERIC KLINGELHOFER
ASSISTANT PROFESSOR
DEPARTMENT OF HISTORY
MERCER UNIVERSITY
MACON, GEORGIA 31207

LAURIE A. WILKIE

Glass-Knapping at a Louisiana Plantation: African-American Tools?

ABSTRACT

During the analysis of glass artifacts recovered from undisturbed archaeological contexts at Oakley Plantation, West Feliciana Parish, Louisiana (16WF34), a number of glass sherds were found to have retouching and edge damage consistent with wear found on utilized lithics. Of these, 35 sherds were determined to exhibit significant evidence of use as tools. These tools were recovered from four African-American assemblages dating from the 1840s through the 1930s. This paper discusses the analysis of these tools, whether variations among the tools are representative of distinct types, a review of the occurrence of similar tools at other sites, and whether the tools can be considered to be of uniquely African-American origin.

Introduction

During archaeological excavations in 1991 and 1992, 35 utilized glass sherds were recovered from assemblages dating from the 1840s to the 1930s at Oakley Plantation, West Feliciana, Louisiana (Table 1). These investigations were conducted as a follow-up to an earlier surface survey by Holland and Orser (1984), and further explored several features identified by them. In each instance of glass tool occurrence at the site, strong oral historical or documentary evidence associates the archaeological assemblages with African-American occupants.

Oakley Plantation was founded in 1796 as a cotton plantation in Feliciana Parish of Spanish West Florida. At its economic peak in the 1840s, the plantation comprised over 3,000 acres of land and over 200 slaves (Wilkie 1994). The plantation remained in the ownership of the same family and was continuously farmed by African Americans until the 1940s. In 1947, 100 acres of the plantation, including the planter's house and plantation yard area, were sold to the State of Louisiana for preservation and interpretation as the Audubon State Commemorative Area.

Historical Archaeology, 1996, 30(4):37–49.
Permission to reprint required.

Three loci excavated during the 1991 and 1992 field seasons provided the archaeological materials for this study (Figure 1). These areas were defined as features in the Holland and Orser (1984) surface collection, and to maintain continuity for management purposes, feature numbers used by Holland and Orser were retained. Each of Holland and Orser's (1984) features—better thought of as loci—represented clusters of archaeological features associated with two house areas. The loci investigated included a cabin and yard area which were occupied throughout the antebellum and postbellum periods (Features 5, 29) and a house built by 1920 and occupied until 1949 by Sam Scott and his wife Nettie Scott (Feature 30). Specific details of excavations at each of these areas are given in the following discussion.

Mean Artifact Dates, a variation on South's Mean Ceramic Date method, which incorporates datable artifacts such as metals and glass in addition to ceramics, were used to date the assemblages. The author has found that manufacturing date ranges on artifacts such as glass, plastic, and rubber can provide tighter chronological control for late 19th- and early 20th-century sites than ceramics alone. For a detailed discussion of individual features and strata, see Wilkie (1994) and Wilkie and Farnsworth (1992, 1993).

TABLE 1
NUMBER OF TOOLS RECOVERED FROM EACH
AFRICAN-AMERICAN
ASSEMBLAGE AT OAKLEY

Assemblage	Mean Artifact Date (MAD)	Number of Tools Found
Features 5 and 29 (Antebellum)	1842–1843	5
Feature 5 (Silvia Freeman family)	1897	22
Feature 5 (Delphine and Eliza Freeman family)	1923	8
Feature 30 (Samuel and Nettie Scott)	1938.5	0

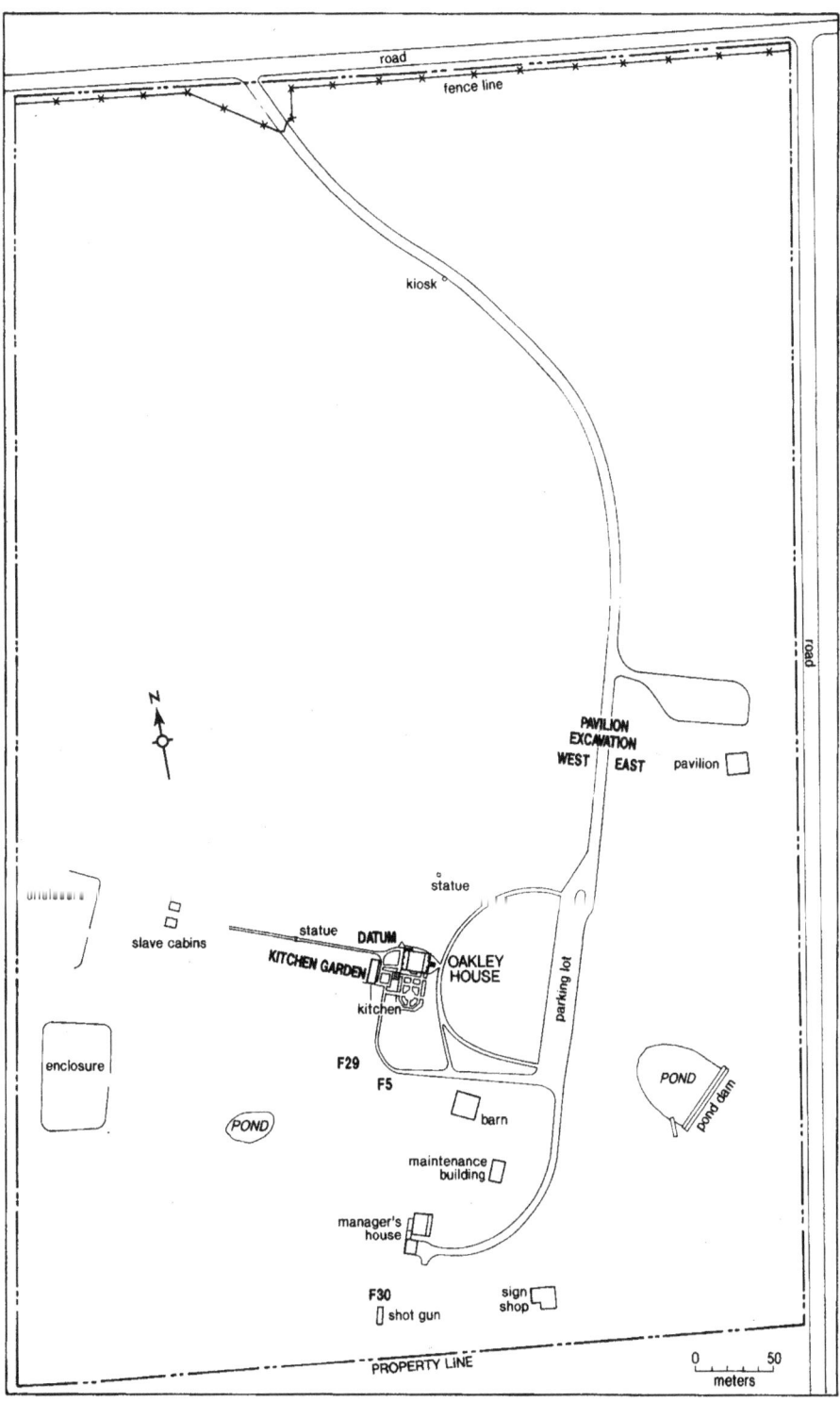

FIGURE 1. Archaeological Features at Oakley Plantation associated with African Americans.

Feature 5

The area designated Feature 5 was described by Holland and Orser (1984) as a possible house site. In 1991 the area was tested with four 1-m units and three shovel test pits. The brick foundation of a pier and beam house were identified in association with mid- to late 19th- and early 20th-century materials.

Further testing was undertaken in 1992 to determine the preservation of the structural remains and the extent of the yard area deposits. A 7-x-9-m excavation grid (Grid A) of 1-m units was laid out and oriented along the brick foundations found in 1991 to insure that as far as possible, excavation units outside versus under the structure would be distinct. Both a second 3-m square grid (Grid B) was laid out to the west of Grid A and three additional 1-m units were placed to the south of Grid A to examine further a major artifactual concentration found in 1991.

During the course of excavation, a number of archaeological features were encountered at this locus, including three shallow trash pits, 25 postholes representing the extent of the house, a brick-mining pit, and three trenches. Each of these components was excavated separately, and color, diameter, shape, and depth recorded. This information was important in establishing the chronology of, and associations between, archaeological features at this locus.

Large quantities of material cultural remains were recovered from undisturbed contexts immediately around and under the house, and in the western yard area of the house. Materials recovered from stratigraphic levels and archaeological features determined to be of the same age through their *termini post quem* have been treated as single assemblages. In this way, three assemblages representing activities related to three occupations of the house were identified archaeologically.

Antebellum materials were recovered in the southwestern area of Grid A from a dark grayish-brown mottled clay overlying the sterile clay level and from two small trash pits and provided a Mean Artifact Date (MAD) of 1842.5 (Wilkie

1994:178). Above this level was a yellowish-brown to dark yellowish-brown mottled loam which contained artifacts dating to the end of the 19th century. Additional materials from this time period were recovered from postholes and another small pit. Materials from this level provided a MAD of 1897 (Wilkie 1994:180–181). A brownish-yellow loam overlying the 19th-century strata contained early 20th-century materials which provided a MAD of 1923 (Wilkie 1994:182–183).

Historical Context for Feature 5

The construction of the cabin at Feature 5, based upon its architectural style and archaeological remains, probably took place in the 1840s (Wilkie 1994). Given the proximity of the cabin to the planter residence, the antebellum materials recovered from Feature 5 are most probably associated with an enslaved family that worked in the great house.

Henry Cummings and John Hulbert, former tenants of Oakley, both described this feature during interviews as corresponding to the location of the "cook's house" which was lived in by the African-American Freeman family (Cummings 1991; Hulbert 1992). Most clearly, they remembered a woman named Delphine Freeman working in that capacity during the 1920s and 1930s but thought that her mother had also been a cook. Delphine Freeman had inherited the position from her mother, Silvia Freeman (Wilkie 1994:199–201).

Silvia Freeman and her family worked as domestic servants for the Matthews family through the late 19th and early 20th centuries. The late 19th-century materials from Feature 5 are most likely associated with their occupation of the cabin. Silvia Freeman's employment began sometime in or prior to 1886, when William Wilson and Isabelle Matthews owned the plantation. After Isabelle Matthews's death, Silvia Freeman and her family continued to work as domestics for Lucy and Ida Matthews.

The earliest documentary evidence available for Silvia Freeman is found on her marriage license. On 5 June 1875, Lewis Freeman paid

$50.00 for a license to marry Sylvia [sic] Hill. The date of their actual marriage was not recorded by the parish (West Feliciana Parish Records 1875). Lewis Freeman's family is known to have lived in this ward and parish as early as 1870, but Silvia Hill does not appear in the 1870 West Feliciana census (U.S. Bureau of the Census [USBC] 1870). In 1880, the census shows Silvia Freeman living with Lewis Freeman and their two sons, Joseph and John, at Oakley. Lewis Freeman's occupation was listed as "planter" and Silvia Freeman's as "farming" (USBC 1880).

The earliest reference to Silvia Freeman working in the house as the cook is an 1886 ledger entry in the Oakley Collection. No mention of Lewis Freeman is made in the ledger; however, Silvia Freeman's youngest child was born in 1889 and bears the last name Freeman, suggesting that Lewis Freeman had passed away no earlier than 1888. By 1900, Silvia Freeman is listed as a widow in the manuscript census (USBC 1900).

Silvia Freeman appears to have passed away between 1900 and 1910; she does not appear in the 1910 census. By 1910, Eliza Freeman, presumably "Lizzie" in the 1900 census, and Delphine Freeman were both still living at Oakley. Eliza was working as a servant and Delphine as a cook (USBC 1910).

The Freeman daughters appear in the 1920 census as well; Eliza is listed as "Louisa" Freeman, and still employed as the Matthews house servant (USBC 1920). Henry Cummings (1991) remembers Eliza and Delphine Freeman living together at the plantation through the 1930s but had no clear recollection of their daughters. The 20th-century materials recovered from Feature 5 are most probably related to the Freeman sisters' occupation.

Feature 29

Feature 29 was not previously identified by Holland and Orser (1984). During the 1991 surface collections, a concentration of mid-19th-century artifacts was found eroding at a tree base located to the northwest of, and in close

proximity to, Feature 5. A 1-m unit was subsequently excavated to a depth of 40 cm below the surface at this locus. Large quantities of household refuse dating to the 19th century were recovered (Wilkie and Farnsworth 1992). Two additional 1-m units were excavated in 1992 to define further the deposit. Both 1992 units were excavated to depths of 40 cm below the surface and contained concentrations of antebellum household materials. No evidence of architectural remains was found at this loci. Intact, antebellum deposits including pearlwares, shell-edged whitewares, and green-glazed redwares, were recovered, concentrated between 20 and 30 cm deep. These materials place the MAD of this locus at 1843 (Wilkie 1994:185), comfortably within the antebellum period and very close to the 1842.5 date for the antebellum materials recovered at Feature 5.

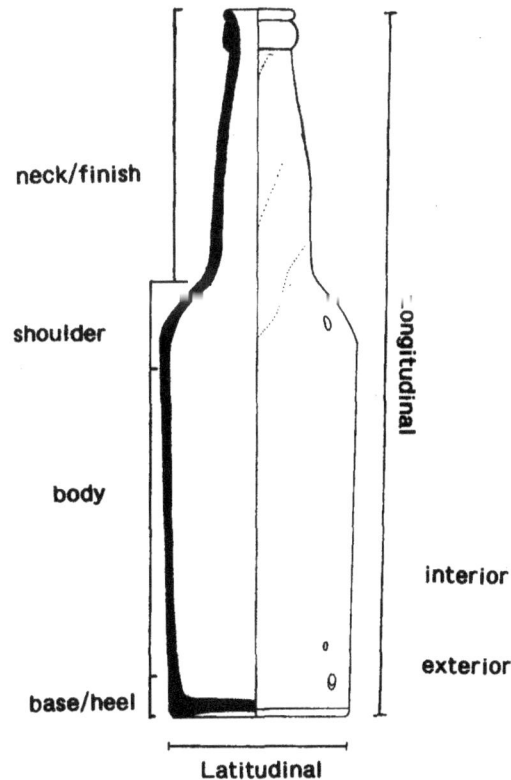

FIGURE 2. Terms used to describe bottle anatomy and sherd orientation during analysis.

TABLE 2
CONTINGENCY TABLE: RETOUCH VERSUS ANGLE EDGE

Edge Angle	Retouched	Not Retouched
Less than 35°	0	11
Greater than 35°	24	0
Total	24	11

Although it has not been possible to determine which enslaved family may have been associated with the antebellum deposits at Features 5 and 29, the spatial and chronological proximity of these deposits suggests that the two groups of artifacts may both represent the activities of the same enslaved African-American family. Accordingly, glass tools from the antebellum period deposits at Features 5 and 29 were analyzed as a single group.

Feature 30

Feature 30 is the location of the only standing tenant house remaining in the park, and excavations in this area were directed in relationship to this architectural feature. During testing in September 1991, a 5-m grid was excavated north of the house to test the extent of a midden deposit first identified in the summer of 1991. These units contained large quantities of glass, plastic, ceramic, and metal artifacts dating between the 1920s and the 1940s, all concentrated in a soft, black oily midden soil that was 15 cm thick close to the building, and thinning to only a couple of cm thick at the west and north edges of the grid. The back room of the house served as the kitchen, thus likely explaining the large concentration of artifactual materials behind it. The MAD for this feature is 1938.95 (Wilkie 1994:187).

This house is known to have been built about 1920 by African-American Sam Scott. Henry Cummings (1991) remembered Sam, also called

Sammy, living in the house with his wife, and for a time, his father. Sam and his wife had no children. John Hulbert (1992), the Scotts' nephew, was also able to provide information about the family. According to Hulbert (1992) and Cummings (1991), the Scotts were the only family to live in this house; therefore, the assemblage recovered here must be associated with them. While no glass tools were recovered from this assemblage, this feature was the only one at Oakley Plantation to produce steel razor blades. The possible impact of razor blades on glass-knapping traditions will be discussed below.

Description of the Glass Tools

In analyzing the 35 glass tools—nearly all made from fragments of glass bottles or jars, it was necessary to define descriptive terms that both reflected the nature of the raw materials used to construct the tools as well as those attributes of the tools which were functionally meaningful. To achieve this end, a standardized set of descriptive terms was used during analysis to describe the portion of the original bottle being utilized, the orientation of the sherd in the original vessel, and the interior and exterior of the bottle. The description of bottle components is drawn from Jones and Sullivan (1985:77, Figure 52) and is comprised of finish, neck-finish, shoulder, body, heel, and base.

In lithic analysis, flake tools typically are described and measured relative to the bulb of percussion (Keeley 1980; Vaughan 1985). Since glass sherds lack such a percussion bulb, it is necessary to use other means to describe them. The form and use of bottle sherds as tools is in part dictated by the original shape of the vessel. To describe the orientation of the utilized edge relative to the sherd's original position in the bottle, the circumference of the bottle is called the latitudinal plane, and the vertical aspect of the bottle is called the longitudinal plane. Therefore, utilized edges that would have been parallel to the base or finish of the intact bottle are referred to as longitudinal edges, and those that would have been perpendicular to the base and finish are referred to as latitudinal edges (Figure 2).

Other variables considered as potentially important attributes include the presence/absence of retouching, the angle of the utilized edge, the shape of the utilized edge, the distribution of use wear along the utilized edge, and placement of the contact edge or leading aspect (Keeley 1980:21) relative to the interior or exterior of the original vessel. To determine whether different attributes were meaningfully linked, contingency tables were constructed to determine if there were meaningful relationships between attributes and, therefore, typological differences between the tools (Sackett 1989).

This level of analysis formed the foundation for microwear analysis and for identifying relationships between use and morphology. Through this analysis, meaningful relationships were established between retouching, edge angle, and sherd orientation. In addition, some patterns related to the portion of the bottle utilized, and the nature of the tools has been established.

Correlating Attributes

Visual observation indicated that the tools fell into two rough groups, including those that had no retouching (n = 11) and those that were unifacially retouched (n = 24). To determine whether retouching may have served a functional purpose, a contingency table was constructed comparing the presence of retouch and the angle of the utilized tool edge. A general relationship has been established by lithic researchers be-

TABLE 3
CONTINGENCY TABLE: RETOUCH VERSUS LONGITUDINAL/LATITUDINAL UTILIZATION

Utilization	Retouched	Not Retouched
Latitudinal Edge	0	11
Longitudinal Edge	24	0
Total	24	11

TABLE 4
CONTINGENCY TABLE: EDGE ANGLE AND ASSEMBLAGE OF RETOUCHED TOOLS[a]

	Assemblage		
Edge Angle	Antebellum	Silvia Freeman	Delphine and Eliza Freeman
40°	0	1	0
50°	0	3	6
60°	1	6	2
70°	0	5	2
80°	1	0	0
Total	2	15	7

[a] Retouched tools listed in Table 3 comprise these tools.

tween angle edge and use. For instance, whittling activities are usually associated with acute angles, whereas planing is usually associated with more obtuse edge angles (Keeley 1980:16–17). These criteria were compared, since edge angles had been observed to cluster below 35 degrees and above 45 degrees. The contingency table relating these two variables demonstrated that all of the tools with retouch had edge angles of greater than 35 degrees, while all tools lacking retouch had edge angles smaller than 35 degrees (Table 2). When a second contingency table was constructed relating longitudinal/latitudinal edge utilization with presence/absence of retouching, a correlation was found. All tools with retouching, a total of 24, were utilized on the latitudinal edge of the sherd, while all of the unretouched sherds were utilized on their longitudinal edge (Table 3). A comparison of edge angle by assemblage demonstrated that 60 degrees was the most common edge angle, with Silvia Freeman's assemblage demonstrating the greatest variation (Table 4).

Glass bottles/jars served as the raw material for all but two of the tools, with wine bottles being the most commonly used. The other two tools were made from tumbler sherds. Additional comparisons were made to determine whether certain components of the bottles were preferred for retouched versus unretouched tools. Components of the bottles used for tools fell into the categories heel and base, neck and finish, shoulder, and body. Both heel and base and neck and finish are combined because tools were derived from both of these elements, as compared to body and shoulder sherds, which did not contain portions of any other bottle part. This analysis demonstrated that body sherds were most often used for tools. Base and heel sherds were only used to manufacture retouched tools (Table 5), but were by no means the exclusive choice for these tools.

Given the variety of bottle parts represented, several tables were then constructed to compare the distribution of bottle parts being utilized. Within each of the assemblages, body sherds were the most common. Shoulder sherds, used for both retouched and unretouched tools, were only associated with the assemblage of Silvia Freeman (Table 6). Whether the selection of the shoulder sherds represented a personal preference or a functional decision may be clarified when microwear analysis is conducted.

Visual observation suggested that the shape of the contact edge, in addition to edge angle, may be an important attribute for the retouched tools. Retouched tools were found to have concave-or convex-shaped contact edges. Comparison of the shape of the contact edge with bottle part (Table

TABLE 6
CONTINGENCY TABLE: ASSEMBLAGE VERSUS
BOTTLE ANATOMY

Bottle Part	Antebellum	Silvia Freeman	Delphine Freeman
Heel and Base	1	1	2
Neck and Finish	1	2	1
Shoulder	0	4	0
Body	3	15	5
Total	5	22	8

7) demonstrated that convex edges were almost exclusively associated with body sherds. Analysis of edge angle with the shape of the contact edge (Table 8) demonstrated that convex contact edges were associated with edge angles of 50–70 degrees, while concave contact edges were associated with a broader range of edge angles (40–80°).

Other correlations failed to reveal meaningful trends. A comparison of edge angles with bottle parts found no correlations. An ambiguous correlation is related to the orientation of leading edges. The majority of the recovered tools utilized the exterior wall of the bottle as its leading or contact edge. However, five examples of interior wall contact edges were included in the assemblage of Silvia Freeman (Table 9). The use of interior versus exterior walls may represent a personal preference, as this decision affects how one grips the tools.

Exploring Potential Functions

Several conclusions can be drawn from the above analysis. First, there are clear correlations between the presence/absence of retouch, edge angle and utilized sherd edge, suggesting the presence of at least two tool types. The first type can be defined primarily as retouched, the second type as unretouched (Figure 3).

All retouched sherds are worked on a latitudinal edge and have an edge angle of greater than

TABLE 5
CONTINGENCY TABLE: RETOUCH AND BOTTLE
ANATOMY

Bottle Part	Retouched	Not Retouched
Heel and Base	4	0
Neck and Finish	1	3
Shoulder	3	1
Body	16	7
Total	24	11

35 degrees. The steep edge angle that these tools possess suggest that they functioned as scrapers. The reason for the selection of the latitudinal edge for working may be related to comfort in gripping the finished tool or may reflect differences in ease of knapping along the edges. Given that these tools are retouched, their production required a certain degree of knapping ability and investment of time. They appear, therefore, to be intentionally produced tools.

Convex and concave contact surfaces were noted among the retouched tools; however, it is unclear whether these are meaningful attributes. Concave edges had a broader range of edge angles and bottle body sherds associated with them than did the convex edges. Further exploration of these issues through microwear analysis and comparison with other assemblages is necessary further to define the significance, if any, of these differences.

Bottle bases and heels were used exclusively for retouched tools. Bottle body sherds were the

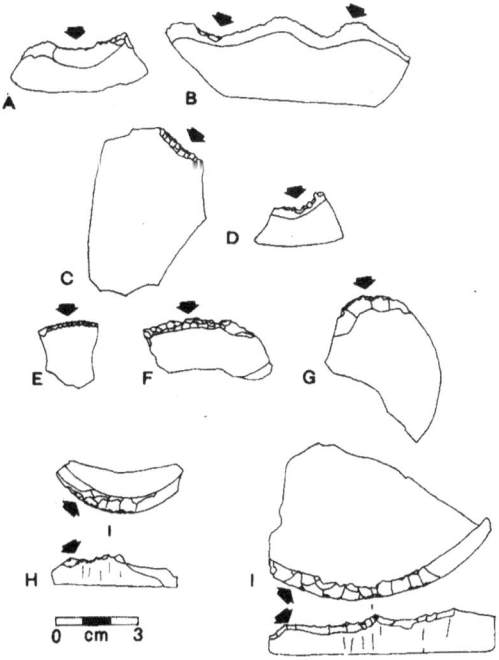

FIGURE 3. Examples of retouched and unretouched tools from Oakley Plantation: A–B, unretouched tools; C–I, retouched tools. Arrows indicate utilized edges.

most common (24 of the 35 tools). Shoulder sherds (n = 4) were only utilized by Silvia Freeman's family. Likewise, Silvia Freeman's assemblage is the only one to include contact edges on the bottle interior. Without an additional level of analysis, such as microwear, or the comparison of these tools with similar examples from other sites, it is not possible to determine which patterns reflect the preferences of the tool knappers/users or represent functional differences.

All of the unretouched sherds exhibit edge wear damage—scarring, pitting, and chipping—on their longitudinal or utilized edges, and all have edge angles of less than 35 degrees. Longitudinal edges are potentially longer and straighter than are latitudinal edges, suggesting that such tools may have been used for cutting rather than scraping. Since longitudinal tools lack retouching, it is not clear whether they were intentionally produced or if glass sherds from broken bottles were selected to be used as expedient tools when necessary. They may, in fact, represent tools of convenience rather than forethought.

Examination of the unretouched tools demonstrates that the wear damage on eight of the 11 was irregularly distributed along the length of both surfaces. This form of wear is typically associated with longitudinal motions, such as sawing or cutting (Vaughan 1985:20). The remaining three examples exhibit dense scarring on both edge surfaces. The motion associated with this distribution is less clear, for such wear has been found associated with both transverse and longitudinal motions (Vaughan 1985:20–21). However, the general pattern suggests that these tools were likely to have been used for cutting rather than scraping.

Putting the Tools in Context

Oral history and an evaluation of other cutting tools recovered from the African-American assemblages at Oakley can provide some insight into tool use. Mintz and Price (1976:48) have documented the use of broken bottles by Africans during the middle passage to shave tradi-

TABLE 7
CONTINGENCY TABLE: CONTACT EDGE SHAPE
VERSUS
BOTTLE PART ANATOMY, RETOUCHED TOOLS[a]

Bottle Part	Contact Edge Shape	
	Convex	Concave
Base and Heel	0	4
Shoulder	1	2
Body	10	6
Neck Finish	0	1
Total	11	13

[a]Table 3 comprises this same sample.

tional designs in their hair. The practice of using broken glass as a razor was common in the Bahamas until the 1930s (Ferguson 1995).

In Louisiana, John Hulbert (1992), a former tenant of Oakley, remembers glass tools used on the plantation to smooth axe and hoe handles in the 1930s. He indicated that making such tools was not a skill he possessed, stating that some people on the plantation knew how to break glass in a certain way to make a tool. He compared the use of these tools to the way a razor blade was used for the same purpose. His description suggests that the production of these tools was a specialized skill not shared by the entire tenant population.

John Hulbert's comment that only a few people had the skill to create these tools suggests that by the 1930s, when he was a child, this glass tool tradition may have been becoming less common. The Scott assemblage, Feature 30, contains none of these artifacts but does contain an artifact type not found in the other assemblages: razor blades. Razor blades are a versatile tool that can be used for cutting as well as scraping, depending upon the angle at which they are held. This metal tool can perform the tasks of the glass tools and maintains a functional edge for a longer period of time.

To determine whether there may be a relationship between the appearance of razor blades and the disappearance of glass tools in the Scott assemblage, a review of Oakley Plantation commissary ledgers from the 1890s to 1920 was conducted. These ledgers did not include any purchases of razor blades (Matthews 1889–1891, 1890–1901a, 1890–1901b, 1890–1901c; Matthews and Matthews 1902–1920a, 1902–1920b). The ledgers are nearly complete through the 1890s, and less complete for the remainder of this time period. However, enough of the records are available to demonstrate that razor blades, if available during this time period, were not commonly purchased. Archaeologically, the only other evidence of cutting tools recovered were two broken pairs of scissors from Silvia Freeman's assemblage.

The lack of razor blades in Oakley's commissary records may be related to the cost of purchasing these items. Razor blades, or blades for safety razors, were relatively expensive when first introduced. The 1897 Sears, Roebuck catalog ran the following advertisement for the Star Safety Razor:

An invention which obviates all danger of cutting the face. It is especially adapted to old and young, and is indispensable to travelers, miners and persons camping out. Blades of best steel and fully concave, which can be easily removed and placed in handle for strapping (Israel 1968:112).

The Star Safety Razor sold for $1.50, and extra blades for $1.00. Similarly, straight blade prices started at $.60, and single-bladed pocket knives at $.25, although both items were most commonly available in the $1.50 price range (Israel 1968:112). In 1891, Silvia Freeman was earning $4.00 a month, and had been working at that salary for at least two years (Matthews 1889–1891). The purchase of a knife or razor would therefore represent a significant portion of her monthly income.

No safety razors are listed in the 1900 Sears, Roebuck catalog (DBI Books 1970). By 1908, 10 safety razor blade replacements could be purchased through Sears, Roebuck and Company for a price of $.50 (Schroeder 1971:775). Straight razors were still the razor most commonly available through the catalog, with the cheapest option costing $.96 (Schroeder 1971:773). Prices for pocket knives are not available in this edition of the catalog. The 1927 Sears, Roebuck Catalog advertised 10-packs of razor blades for as low as $.54 (Mirkin 1970:529). Straight razors could be purchased for no less than $1.25 (Mirkin 1970:529), while pocket knives ranged in price from $.79 to $1.89 (Mirkin 1970:510).

The cost of razor blades dropped relative to straight razors and pocket knives between the 1890s and the 1930s. It is possible that the availability of this cheap, commercially-made alternative eventually rendered glass-knapping obsolete. It is also possible that the Scotts, as an individual family, simply did not possess the knapping skills or chose not to participate in this practice. An understanding of glass tools in a broader regional and chronological context is necessary before such conclusions confidently can be drawn.

Razor blades are commonly used today by African Americans in rural Louisiana for cutting, scraping, and whittling (Bibens 1994). If kept in the proximity of the house, razor blades can be

TABLE 8
CONTINGENCY TABLE: CONTACT EDGE SHAPE
AND
EDGE ANGLE, RETOUCHED TOOLS[a]

Edge Angle	Contact Edge Shape	
	Convex	Concave
40°	0	1
50°	3	3
60°	5	4
70°	3	4
80°	0	1
Total	11	13

[a] Table 3 comprises this same sample.

TABLE 9
CONTINGENCY TABLE: LEADING EDGE FACE
AND ASSEMBLAGE

Assemblage	Leading Edge Face	
	Interior Edge	Exterior Edge
Antebellum	0	5
Silvia Freeman	5	17
Delphine and Eliza Freeman	0	8
Total	5	30

easily stored and used. Pocket knives are certainly a safer portable option. While not the focus of this paper, it is interesting to note that preliminary analysis by the author of artifacts from a late 19th- to early 20th-century trash pit at Crawford Park, 1MB99, an African-American midwife's house site in Mobile, Alabama, has also identified glass tools. All of the tools from that site are retouched and, given the outcome of the Oakley analysis, were probably used as scrapers. While no glass knives have been identified as yet, two pocket knives have been recovered. Again, razor blades may be present at the Scott house instead of glass tools because they may have represented a functional substitution of one artifact type for another.

Glass Tools: A Distinctive African-American Trait?

Intentionally worked glass artifacts are not a new phenomenon and have been recovered from both Native American and other African-American archaeological sites. This discussion will focus upon examples recovered from plantation contexts. Two antebellum and two postbellum planter assemblages were recovered from Oakley Plantation. Neither glass tools nor razor blades were recovered from any of the planter contexts, and Native Americans have not been clearly associated with the sites where these particular tool types were recovered.

TABLE 10
ARCHAEOLOGICAL SITES WHERE WORKED GLASS HAS BEEN
RECOVERED FROM NON-NATIVE AMERICAN CONTEXTS

Site	State	Site Type	Date	Ethnic Affiliation
Oakley Plantation[a]	Louisiana	Plantation	1840s–1940s	African American
Riverlake Plantation[b]	Louisiana	Plantation	1840s–1990s	African American
St. Rose Plantation[c]	Louisiana	Plantation	1790–1810	African American and Euroamerican
Bennett House[d]	Louisiana	Plantation	1840–1860	African American and Euroamerican
Crawford Park[e]	Alabama	Urban house	1890–1910	African American
Garrison Plantation[f]	Maryland	Plantation	early 19th c.	African American
Monticello[g]	Virginia	Plantation	18th–19th c.	African American
Levi-Jordan Plantation[h]	Texas	Plantation	?	African American and Euroamerican

[a]Wilkie (1994)
[b]Site currently under study by the author
[c]Wilkie and Tannert (1994)
[d]Port Hudson State Commemorative Area Archaeological Collections, Louisiana
[e]Site currently under study by the author
[f]Klingelhofer (1987)
[g]Patten (1992)
[h]Anonymous SHA manuscript reviewer (1995, pers. comm.)

In Maryland, Klingelhofer (1987:114–115) found an intentionally chipped tumbler at Garrison Plantation, and reported that similar artifacts had been recovered in Virginia. Patten (1992:6) reports the recovery of chipped glass from Monticello, as well as from other Virginia tidewater sites. The author has identified isolated examples of glass tools from the Bennett House and St. Rose Plantation, both in Louisiana. As noted earlier, significant numbers of these tools are currently under analysis by the author from Crawford Park, and from Riverlake Plantation, Pointe Coupee Parish, Louisiana. Excavations at Riverlake Plantation were focused on the African-American quarters buildings, which have been continuously occupied from the 1840s until the 1990s. Analysis of these materials is ongoing, but the glass tools from these sites will be compared with those from Oakley to determine if broader regional patterns are visible. Of the sites known to the author to contain glass tools, the vast majority come from contexts that are either clearly African American or from contexts which may have been used jointly by African Americans and Euroamericans (Table 10). Such tools have been recovered from both rural and urban settings. At this point, however, published reference to glass tools recovered from strictly Euroamerican contexts has not been found.

What is not clear, however, is whether glass tools are more likely to be recognized in African-American assemblages by archaeologists aware of their presence in other African-American sites. It is important that non-African-American contexts for such tools be explored so that it can be determined whether their production and use is tied to a distinct ethnic heritage or whether they were broadly used by many ethnic groups. The association of such tools with predominately female contexts at both Oakley Plantation and Crawford Park also suggests that glass flake tools, like prehistoric lithics (Gero 1991), deserve further attention for their potential engendered meanings.

Conclusion

Thirty-five utilized glass sherds from African-American contexts have been recovered from Oakley Plantation, West Feliciana Parish, Louisiana. Attribute analysis of these glass sherds has demonstrated that the sherds easily divide into two major groups which seem to be functionally significant, one group of unretouched sherds serving as knives, and the other group of retouched sherds serving as scrapers. Additional differentiations may be identifiable in conjunction with microwear analysis.

The tools were recovered from three different African-American assemblages at Oakley Plantation dating 1840–1930. No glass tools were recovered from the latest African-American assemblage, dating 1920–1940. It is unclear if the absence of tools from this context represents the abandonment of the tradition by this time period or simply represents the nonparticipation of this family. It is suggested that cheaper, commercially manufactured cutting tools such as razor blades may have replaced glass tools at this time.

In closing, the tools discussed in this paper were drawn from strictly African-American contexts. It is unclear at this juncture whether these tools are distinctly African American in nature or if they have only been recognized in African-American contexts. The majority of glass tools reported in the literature have been recovered from rural settings, and it may be that closer examination of glass from Euroamerican rural contexts will reveal the presence of similar practices.

ACKNOWLEDGMENTS

The author would like to thank the Louisiana State Division of Archaeology and the National Park Service for funding archaeological research at Oakley Plantation. Additional assistance was provided by the University of California, Los Angeles, Friends of Archaeology, and students from UCLA and Louisiana State University, who participated in field schools at the site. Finally, I would like to thank Paul Farnsworth, Christopher R. DeCorse, Daniel G. Roberts, and two anonymous reviewers for their comments on this manuscript.

REFERENCES

BIBENS, DAVID
    1994 Interview at Riverlake Plantation. Notes on file, Department of Geography and Anthropology, Louisiana State University, Baton Rouge.

CUMMINGS, HENRY
    1991 Videotaped Interview at Oakley Plantation. On file, Department of Geography and Anthropology, Louisiana State University, Baton Rouge.

DBI BOOKS
    1970 *Sears, Roebuck and Co. Consumer Guide, Fall, 1900.* DBI Books, Northfield, IL.

FERGUSON, "PAPA D"
    1995 Oral History Interview, Crooked Island Bahamas. Notes on file, Department of Anthropology, University of California, Berkeley.

GERO, JOAN M.
    1991 Genderlithics: Women's Roles in Stone Tool Production. In *Engendering Archaeology: Women and Prehistory,* edited by Joan M. Gero and Margaret W. Conkey, pp.163–193. Blackwell, Cambridge.

HOLLAND, CLAUDIA C., AND CHARLES E. ORSER, JR.
    1984 A Preliminary Archaeological Investigation of Oakley Plantation, Audubon State Commemorative Area, West Feliciana Parish, Louisiana. Report on file, State Division of Archaeology, Baton Rouge, Louisiana.

HULBERT, JOHN
    1992 Interview in Baton Rouge. Notes on file, Department of Geography and Anthropology, Louisiana State University, Baton Rouge.

ISRAEL, FRED L.
    1968 *1897 Sears, Roebuck Catalogue.* Chelsea House, NY.

JONES, OLIVE, AND CATHERINE SULLIVAN
    1985 *The Parks Canada Glass Glossary.* Government Publishing Centre, Québec.

KEELEY, LAWRENCE
    1980 *Experimental Determination of Stone Tool Uses.* University of Chicago Press, Chicago, IL.

KLINGELHOFER, ERIC
    1987 Aspects of Early Afro-American Material Culture:
          Artifacts from the Slave Quarters at Garrison
          Plantation, Maryland. *Historical Archaeology*
          21(2):112–119.

MATTHEWS, ISABELLE
    1889– Plantation Ledger Kept by Isabelle Matthews. Oakley
    1891   Collection. Audubon State Commemorative Area, St.
           Francisville, LA.
    1890– Store Receipts. Oakley Collection. Audubon State
    1901a Commemorative Area, St. Francisville, LA.
    1890– Store Receipts, James Pirrie Bowman Papers.
    1901b Louisiana and Lower Mississippi Valley Collections.
           Hill Memorial Library, Louisiana State University,
           Baton Rouge.
    1890– Store Receipts, Turnball-Slocum Papers. Louisiana
    1901c and Lower Mississippi Valley Collections. Hill Memorial
           Library, Louisiana State University, Baton Rouge.

MATTHEWS, LUCY, AND IDA MATTHEWS
    1902– Store Receipts. Oakley Collection. Audubon State
    1920a Commemorative Area, St. Francisville, LA.
    1902– Store Receipts, Turnball-Slocum Papers. Louisiana
    1920b and Lower Mississippi Valley Collections. Hill Memorial
           Library, Louisiana State University, Baton Rouge.

MINTZ, SIDNEY, AND RICHARD PRICE
    1976 *The Birth of African-American Culture.* Beacon Press,
          NY.

MIRKIN, ALAN (EDITOR)
    1970 *1927 Edition of the Sears, Roebuck Catalogue.* Bounty,
          NY.

PATTEN, DRAKE
    1992 Mankala and Minkisi: Possible Evidence of African-
          American Folk Beliefs and Practices. *African-
          American Archaeology* 6:5–7.

SACKETT, JAMES R.
    1989 Statistics, Attributes, and the Dynamics of Burin
          Typology. In Alternative Approaches to Lithic
          Analysis, edited by Donald O. Henry and George H.
          Odell. *Archaeological Papers of the American
          Anthropological Association* 1:51–82.

SCHROEDER, JOSEPH J.
    1971 *1908 Sears, Roebuck Catalogue.* DBI Books,
          Northfield, IL.

UNITED STATES BUREAU OF THE CENSUS (USBC)
    1870 Population Census, West Feliciana Parish, Louisiana.
          U.S. Government Printing Office, Washington, DC.
    1880 Population Census, West Feliciana Parish, Louisiana.
          U.S. Government Printing Office, Washington, DC.
    1900 Population Census, West Feliciana Parish, Louisiana.
          U.S. Government Printing Office, Washington, DC.
    1910 Population Census, West Feliciana Parish, Louisiana.
          U.S. Government Printing Office, Washington, DC.
    1920 Population Census, West Feliciana Parish, Louisiana.
          U.S. Government Printing Office, Washington, DC.

VAUGHAN, PATRICK C.
    1985 *Use-Wear Analysis of Flaked Stone Tools.* University
          of Arizona Press, Tucson.

WEST FELICIANA PARISH RECORDS
    1875 Marriage License of Lewis Freeman and Silvia Hill.
          Marriage Book C, No. 161. Recorded 5 June 1875.
          West Feliciana Parish, LA.

WILKIE, LAURIE A.
    1994 *"Never Leave Me Alone": An Archaeological Study
          of African-American Ethnicity, Race Relations and
          Community at Oakley Plantation.* Ph.D. dissertation,
          Archaeology Program, University of California, Los
          Angeles. University Microfilms International, Ann
          Arbor, MI.

WILKIE, LAURIE A., AND PAUL FARNSWORTH
    1992 National Register Testing at Oakley Plantation
          (16WF34), West Feliciana Parish, Louisiana, 1991.
          Report on file, State Division of Archaeology, Baton
          Rouge, LA.
    1993 National Register Testing at Oakley Plantation
          (16WF34), West Feliciana Parish, Louisiana, 1992.
          Report on file, State Division of Archaeology, Baton
          Rouge, LA.

WILKIE, LAURIE A., AND STEPHANIE TANNERT
    1994 An Archaeological and Historical Investigation of
          Site 16SC77 Discovered During Construction of State
          Project No. 700-19-0001 F.A.P. No. HES-373-1(004),
          St. Rose-Destrehan Highway Route LA 48, St. Charles
          Parish. Report on file, State Division of Archaeology,
          Baton Rouge, LA.

LAURIE A. WILKIE
DEPARTMENT OF ANTHROPOLOGY
UNIVERSITY OF CALIFORNIA
BERKELEY, CALIFORNIA 94720-3710

AARON E. RUSSELL

Material Culture and African-American Spirituality at the Hermitage

ABSTRACT

In this article, artifacts excavated from 19th-century Afri-can-American contexts at the Hermitage plantation near Nashville, Tennessee, are examined in light of their possible use in religious ritual, traditional healing, and other behav-iors related to spirituality. While specific spiritual behaviors cannot be determined from the Hermitage archaeological and documentary record, the presence of a distinct African-American belief system at the Hermitage is suggested through comparison of selected artifacts from the Hermitage assem-blage with various historical, folkloric, and archaeological sources. This belief system and its associated behaviors may have aided African Americans in achieving limited social and economic autonomy within the system of plantation slavery.

Introduction

In recent years, many historical archaeologists involved with the study of plantation slavery have attempted to address questions of African-American ideology in their analyses. Within this area of inquiry, a central focus of archaeologists has been the reconstruction of African-American religious ritual, along with other behaviors re-lated to spirituality (Orser 1994:33). Several scholars have attempted to identify syncretisms between the African-American archaeological record and traditional West African religious practice (Brown and Cooper 1990; Cabak 1990; Ferguson 1992:109–120; Patten 1992; Adams 1994; Brown 1994; Orser 1994; Young 1994; Jones 1995; Wilkie 1995). The ideological mo-tivation for these studies, following such schol-ars as Melville Herskovitz (1958[1941]) and Robert Farris Thompson (1983), has largely been to demonstrate the African descent of African-American culture, in opposition to the idea that traditional African cultures and worldviews were completely destroyed by the rigors of the middle passage and subsequent generations of slavery (Frazier 1957:3–21).

While these culture-historical questions are a necessary starting point for any study of African-American religion, scholars must begin to ask questions of their data that are more pointedly concerned with process and function in African-American culture: Why were particular ideas and behaviors retained from traditional West African cultures? What functions, if any, did they serve in enslaved African-American communities? How were these traditional beliefs transformed by processes of innovation, oppression, and creolization? These are some of the questions that must be addressed if the study of the reli-gious and spiritual practices of enslaved African Americans is to have much relevance to students of African-American culture and anthropology.

The archaeological study of African-American spiritual behaviors has proceeded on several dis-tinct levels of understanding. Initially, certain types of artifacts found in African-American con-texts were thought of as possibly being associ-ated with ritual behaviors. Leland Ferguson's (1992:1–32, 109–116) study of traditional Afri-can-American folk pots (colonoware), which pre-sents evidence of religious and medicinal uses for these pots, is a classic example of this type of study. Other archaeologists have concerned themselves with the roles played by beads, metal charms, and Christian religious paraphernalia in African-American spiritual life (Smith 1987; Cabak 1990; Singleton 1991; Orser 1994; McKee 1995; Wilkie 1995; Stine et al. 1996). In addition, some attention has been paid to possible ritual uses of such "ephemera" as pre-historic lithic artifacts, modified potsherds, quartz crystals, smooth stones, and seashells (Klingelhofer 1987; Jones 1995; Wilkie 1995) which had previously been ignored by archaeolo-gists whose main concerns lay in the reconstruc-tion of diet and other physical conditions of enslaved life.

In addition, some researchers have attempted to identify archaeological contexts and assem-blages that represent religious behavior on the part of enslaved African Americans. The best-known example of this approach is Brown and Cooper's (1990; Brown 1994) research at the

Historical Archaeology, 1997, 31(2), 63–80.
Permission to reprint required.

Levi Jordan plantation in east Texas. In this study, the authors attempted to define "activity areas" within the slave (later tenant) quarter that represented the primary occupations of the individual inhabitants. Among the occupations of the Jordan slaves and tenants so identified were those of African craftsman, political leader, and healer/magician. The healer/magician's cabin was distinguished by the presence of a "tool kit," recovered from a restricted area of the dwelling, consisting of:

> Several cast iron kettle bases; cubes of white chalk; bird skulls; an animal's paw; two sealed tubes made of bullet casings; ocean shells; small dolls; an extraordinary (for this site) number of nails, spikes, knife blades, and "fake" knife blades; small water rolled pebbles; two chipped stone scraping tools; several patent medicine bottles; and a thermometer (Brown 1994:109).

In the context in which they were discovered, this group of somewhat mundane artifacts was thought to be analogous to traditional "tool kits" employed by West African, Afro-Caribbean, and creole healer/magicians in curing rituals (Brown 1994:109–110). A similar discovery was made by archaeologists excavating an early 19th-century deposit beneath the Charles Carroll house in Annapolis, Maryland. Here, archaeologists discovered a group of 12 quartz crystals, along with a smooth black stone and a faceted glass bead. These objects appear to have been placed intentionally together, and were covered with an inverted pearlware bowl which had an asterisk-like design on its interior base (Logan 1992; Jones 1995). Lynn Diekman Jones (1995) states that this group of artifacts is similar to several *minkisi* (charms) employed by the Bakongo, a cultural group originating in the Congo-Angolan region of Africa. In addition, George Logan (1992) cites this group of artifacts as producing the "breakthrough" to the interpretation that African Americans lived and worked in the area of the Carroll house in which the objects were found.

The archaeological assemblages at the Levi Jordan plantation and at the Carroll house are particularly important to the study of African-American religion, as they are highly suggestive of the survival of African worldviews and religious knowledge during slavery. *Minkisi*, for example, are conceived of by the Bakongo as alive, each *nkisi* containing medicines which both embody and direct the spirit which dwells within it (Thompson 1983:117–118). The creation and use of *minkisi*, in addition to achieving particular ends, reflects a general conception of life, death, and the structure of the cosmos. This knowledge is codified in the Bakongo cosmogram, *Yowa* (Figure 1), in which

> God is imagined at the top, the dead at the bottom, and water in between. The four disks at the points of the cross stand for the four movements of the sun, and the circumference of the cross the certainty of reincarnation: the especially righteous Kongo person will never be destroyed but will come back in the name or body of progeny, or in the form of an everlasting pool, waterfall, stone, or mountain (Thompson 1983:109).

The amply documented presence of symbols similar in appearance, meaning, and function to this cosmogram, as well as objects similar to *minkisi*, in the New World (Thompson 1983:108–131) lends further weight to published interpretations of the archaeological record at the Levi Jordan plantation and Carroll house. In addition, this evidence strongly supports the idea that the belief systems reflected in the archaeological record of plantation slavery were not simply random amalgamations of Euroamerican "mental heirlooms," as suggested by Puckett (1968[1926]:2–3), but rather were coherent bod-

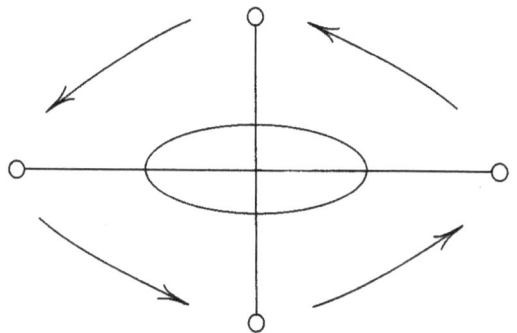

FIGURE 1. Bakongo Cosmogram *Yowa* (from Thompson [1983]).

ies of knowledge with clearly recognizable African roots.

At the same time, however, African-American culture must be viewed as the result of an intense process of creolization between Africans of varying cultural backgrounds, their African-American descendants, Native Americans, and Euroamericans (Mintz and Price 1992; Ferguson 1992). This process, combined with the relative isolation imposed upon communities of enslaved African Americans resulted in considerable local cultural variation. This variation, together with a paucity of documentary evidence, presents difficulties in determining the precise nature of the beliefs and practices reflected by the archaeological record in all but the clearest of archaeological contexts.

Another major stumbling block in studying artifacts with apparent spiritual and religious associations is that many objects documented as having served a role in African-American and West African spiritual behaviors are quite commonplace, becoming spiritually charged by specific ritual (MacGaffey 1991; Wilkie 1994:142). Many potential ritual objects can also be interpreted as having had utilitarian and/or domestic functions. For this reason, the findings at the Carroll house and at the Levi Jordan plantation, while spectacularly relevant to the study of African-American religion, cannot be considered a "Rosetta stone" for interpreting similar artifacts recovered from other African-American contexts, as has been suggested by art historian Robert Farris Thompson (Adams 1994).

The Hermitage

The remainder of this article consists of a discussion of various artifacts which are possibly connected to spiritual behaviors on the part of enslaved African Americans. The artifacts selected for inclusion in this study were excavated from contexts associated with the African-American antebellum occupation at the Hermitage, the 19th-century plantation home of Andrew Jackson, near Nashville, Tennessee. The material comes from five former African-American households at the Hermitage (Figure 2), selected both for their

intact antebellum deposits as well as for their varied locations on the plantation landscape. Two of the dwellings, known as the Triplex Middle (the central unit of a three-unit brick structure) (McKee et al. 1994) and the Yard Cabin (probably a log dwelling), are adjacent to the Hermitage mansion and were probably occupied by enslaved African Americans who worked in and around the mansion. A third structure, the South Cabin, was located approximately 165 m northeast of the mansion (Smith 1976:93–112). Cabin 3, one of a group of brick duplex dwellings about half a kilometer north of the mansion, likely housed enslaved African Americans occupied with agricultural tasks (McKee

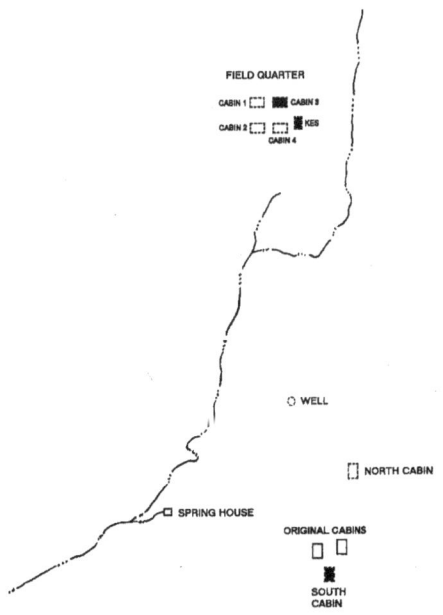

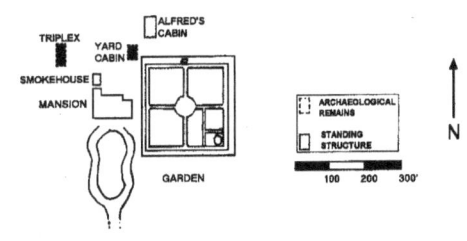

FIGURE 2. Map of the Hermitage property.

1993; Thomas et al. 1995). The main period of occupation for the dwellings mentioned above falls between 1821, when the Jackson family moved from their initial log dwellings to the present Hermitage mansion, and 1857–1858, when the Jacksons moved off the property. In addition to these dwellings, this study discusses the remains of a log structure known as KES, located near Cabin 3 in the Hermitage field quarter. This cabin was probably occupied by enslaved African Americans during the first decades of the 19th century, prior to the construction of the Hermitage mansion and brick field quarter (McKee 1993).

While all of the contexts examined are quite rich in artifacts, the generally mixed and disturbed nature of the deposits makes it difficult to define specific activity areas within the dwellings. The entire assemblage from each dwelling, consisting of artifacts recovered from 19th-century midden deposits and from features such as root cellars within the dwellings, will therefore constitute the basic unit of analysis for comparing the various sites at the Hermitage. Due to these archaeological limitations, concrete interpretations of "spiritual" behaviors on the part of African Americans at the Hermitage cannot be made at the present time. In addition, the lack of historical documentation concerning the spiritual beliefs and practices of enslaved African Americans, along with difficulties in constructing analogies with African-American folklore and African ethnographic material (Mintz and Price 1992:52–60; Thomas 1995a), may make such assertions generally unwarranted. Certain artifacts from the Hermitage, however, such as three small brass fist-shaped charms, a pierced coinlike medallion, and a distinctive assemblage of glass beads seem to indicate the presence of an active system of beliefs among African Americans at the Hermitage (McKee 1995). The data available will also be used to point out similarities between the material cultures of enslaved African Americans living and working on various areas of the Hermitage property, as well as the apparent selectivity shown by these people in acquiring various types of material objects. Finally,

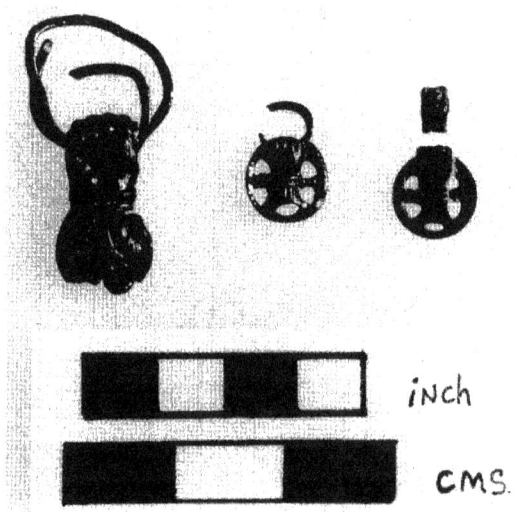

FIGURE 3. Hand-shaped copper alloy charms from the Hermitage.

some interpretation will be made of the apparent persistence of certain aspects of culture related to the spiritual realm throughout slavery, and the functions that these beliefs and behaviors may have served for the enslaved African-American community.

Material Culture

Categories of material culture may shed light on the lives of enslaved African Americans at the Hermitage. Hand charms, lucky bones, pierced coins, glass beads, "x" marbles, prehistoric stone tools, odd smooth stones, and modified ceramic sherds are treated further below.

Hand Charms

Three tiny copper alloy charms, each in the shape of a human fist (Figure 3), were recovered from African-American contexts at the Hermitage (Smith 1976; Singleton 1991:161; McKee 1993; Orser 1994:39–40). Two of these were recovered from Cabin 3, at the site's field quarter, while one was recovered from the South Cabin. Among other small objects probably used for personal adornment by African Americans at the

Hermitage, these are particularly evocative of meanings beyond the purely decorative. The word *hand* occurs frequently in African-American folklore as a generic term for any small—not necessarily hand-shaped—good-luck or protection charm (Puckett 1968[1926]), and this usage may relate to the significance that these objects had for enslaved African Americans at the Hermitage. Samuel Smith (1987:9) has pointed out the similarity between these charms and the Islamic "Hand of Fatima," used to ward off the evil eye. In addition, Larry McKee (1995) has noted a similarity with Latin American *figas* (hand-shaped charms) and *milagros* (votive items), which are thought to confer luck, fertility, and protection from supernatural forces. This physical similarity with *figas* and *milagros* suggests the possibility that these artifacts were brought to the Hermitage by African Americans acquired by Andrew Jackson in Florida (McKee 1993). References dating to the 1930s exist documenting African-American use of hand-shaped charms, including a reference to one stamped from metal (Hyatt 1970[1935]:583–585). Charms of this sort appear to have been used to ensure personal luck and protection from harm. Interestingly, Anne Yentsch (1994:32–33) has recovered an almost identical amulet from an enslaved African-American context in Annapolis, Maryland. This amulet and those recovered from the Hermitage are the only artifacts of this type reported in the archaeological literature. Larry McKee, director of archaeology at the Hermitage, is currently preparing an article describing the specific archaeological contexts and metallurgical composition of the Hermitage artifacts.

In the summer of 1995, the author brought photographs of the Hermitage "fist charms" along on a vacation to New Orleans, with the hopes that similar objects might be found for sale, and that information could be gathered concerning current and past uses of such objects. Although attempts to identify the Hermitage hand charm were unsuccessful, two different types of hand-shaped charms were encountered and purchased during a tour of the various voodoo and *botanica* shops in the city: a wooden

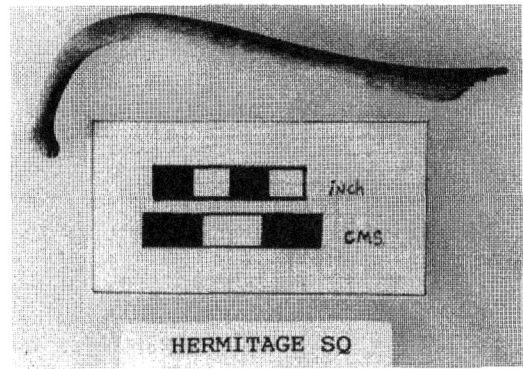

FIGURE 4. Raccoon penis bone from Cabin 3 root cellar.

"mojo hand" in the form of a human fist; and a "lucky hand root," a tiny plant resembling a human hand. Instructions for the use of these charms echoed Frederick Douglass's (1986[1845, 1982]:111) description of his, admittedly skeptical, use of a "certain root" as a protection charm. The specific meanings that the Hermitage hand charms held for their owners, along with the belief systems that they were a part of, are, of course, not made completely clear by these examples. These examples may, however, represent the continuity of a significant symbol in African-American culture, although questions concerning its specific origin remain unanswered.

Lucky Bones

Although folkloric anecdotes concerning the use of animal bones as charms by African Americans are quite common (Puckett 1968[1926]:256–259; Hyatt 1970:74–76), culturally modified bones—apart from such commercial items as buttons, combs, and knife handles—do not appear with any frequency in the archaeological record at the Hermitage. One possible exception is a raccoon penis bone recovered from a root cellar in the Cabin 3 West dwelling (Figure 4). A similar bone was recovered from an African-American context at Mount Vernon (Pogue and White 1991:44–46). The Mount Vernon bone has an incised line encircling its distal end, and was possibly used as a pendant. The Hermitage example is broken off in the area where the Mount Vernon bone is incised. Baskets of drilled raccoon penis bones, strung on leather thongs, are seen for sale in New Orleans "voodoo" shops for use as personal charms. Although these commercial examples exist in radically different contexts from the archaeological examples mentioned above, they suggest a continuing folk tradition concerning the use of these bones.

Highly problematic in terms of archaeology is the possibility that animal bones used as charms may not have been visibly modified in any way. Hyatt's (1970[1935]:74–76) documentation of the traditional "black cat bone" charm repeatedly highlights the circumstances of the bone's collection, rather than subsequent modification. The specially collected bone may be used without further alteration as an ingredient in a charm bag, or simply carried in a pocket.

Pierced Coins

Another example of an item of material culture repeatedly connected through folklore and archaeology with African Americans is the pierced silver coin. These coins have been widely documented by folklorists as having been

used for good luck, protection from "conjuration" and as a general "cure-all" (Puckett 1968[1926]:314–315, 391). Pierced silver coins are often recovered from archaeological contexts associated with enslaved African Americans. These archaeological finds have been correlated with folklore, and with historical accounts of their use as adornments and charms by African Americans (Patten 1992:6; Orser 1994:41; Singleton 1995:131). Two items of this type have been recovered archaeologically at the Hermitage. One is a pierced (white metal?) medallion, recovered from the middle unit of the Triplex, in the mansion backyard (Figure 5). Another, a drilled dime dating between 1828 and 1836 (the hole is drilled through the date), was recovered from a 20th-century utility trench crossing the Yard Cabin site during excavations in the summer of 1996 (Larry McKee 1997, pers. comm.). The hole is drilled so that, when suspended, an image of an eagle on one side of the coin hangs right-side up. Unfortunately, this coin's uncertain context makes it impossible to associate it definitely with the 19th-century occupants of the Yard Cabin, although its date suggests that it was likely part of the 19th-century midden deposit at the site before the utility trench was dug.

Similarly to bones, coins have been used as charms without any modification, such as particular "lucky" coins carried in the shoe or in a pocket. Although usage of this type is practically impossible to determine archaeologically, particularly archaic or unusual coins such as a cut silver Spanish coin, dating to 1726, recovered from the yard of an enslaved African-American dwelling near the Hermitage mansion, as well as a cut coin dating to 1789 from Cabin 3, suggest that some African Americans at the Hermitage may have valued coins as keepsakes (McKee 1993:22).

Glass Beads

Glass beads, items commonly recovered from plantation excavations, have come under scrutiny from historical archaeologists as possibly having had meanings beyond the purely decorative for

FIGURE 5. Pierced (white metal?) medallion (45.89 mm diameter), recovered from the middle unit of the Triplex.

enslaved African Americans. A variety of researchers have argued that African Americans' uses of beads represent continuity between West African and African-American culture (Cabak 1990; Singleton 1991:164; Stine et al. 1996), indicate the presence of African-American women on sites (Smith 1977:159–161; Otto 1984:175), and indicate status differences within communities of enslaved African Americans (Otto 1984:72–74). European traders, in fact, exploited the pre-existing African preferences for certain types of beads in order to gain economic access to West Africa (Cabak 1990). It is likely, then, that enslaved African-Americans' uses of glass beads represent some degree of cultural continuity with West Africa, even if only through the continued preference for a specific category of material culture.

The assemblages of glass beads recovered from the various Hermitage dwellings selected for this study are illustrated by Table 1. Overall, the glass bead assemblage at the Hermitage is dominated by beads of hexagonal, drawn construction, making up 59 percent of all glass beads examined for this study, or 38 of a total of 64 beads. These beads are divided in color between blue, colorless, and black, with blue predominating (20 out of 37 beads, or 54% of this category). Blue beads of this type were recovered from all of the contexts examined here, except from the dwelling site near the mansion known as the Yard Cabin. Here, the entire collection of beads consists of just two green, globular, mandrel-wound beads. In addition to the glass beads, two bone beads were recovered from these dwellings, along with several naturally and artificially perforated sections of fossil crinoid stems that may have served as beads.

Although sample sizes are small, the residents of all of the slave dwellings examined, except for those at the Yard Cabin, appear to have had equal access to glass beads. This supports Brian Thomas's (1995b) thesis of a high degree of cooperation and reciprocity among enslaved African Americans at the Hermitage. The assemblages of beads recovered at these households—again, with one exception—are also quite similar to one another, which may indicate consensus among enslaved African Americans at the Hermitage as to which sorts of beads were desirable. The assemblage suggests that African Americans at the Hermitage had fairly open access to beads. No archaeological or documentary evidence reveals the exact method of acquisition, i.e., whether it was through direct purchase, barter within African-American trade net-

TABLE 1
GLASS BEADS FROM HERMITAGE SITES

Types	Triplex Middle	Cabin 3 East	Cabin 3 West	South Cabin	KES	Yard Cabin	Total
Blue hexagonal	3	10	3	3	2	0	21
Black hexagonal	1	0	2	4	0	0	7
Colorless hexagonal	3	0	0	5	1	0	9
Brown hexagonal	0	0	0	1	0	0	1
Colorless tube	0	0	0	1	0	0	1
Dark globular/spheroid	2	2	0	0	0	0	4
Blue globular/spheroid	0	0	2	0	1	0	3
Colorless globular/spheroid	0	0	5	0	1	0	6
Green globular/spheroid	0	0	0	0	0	2	2
Amber globular/spheroid	0	0	0	1	5	0	6
Turquoise toroid	0	0	1	0	0	0	1
Colorless faceted	0	0	2	0	0	0	2
Dark faceted spheroid	0	0	0	1	0	0	1
Total	9	12	15	16	10	2	64

works, direct or indirect distribution from the mansion household, or through other means.

Thomas (1995b:117–118) suggests that the notable lack of beads recovered from the Hermitage Yard Cabin may indicate accommodation on the part of house enslaved African Americans to white modes of dress. While this may have been true for the residents of the Yard Cabin, the bead assemblage at the Triplex middle, equally near the mansion, was more substantial. This suggests that both house and field enslaved African Americans at the Hermitage had access to and used beads. The notable lack of beads from the Yard Cabin may also indicate a lack of women and children, more often associated with African-American bead use than men, at this dwelling.

A cursory examination of beads excavated from historical Cherokee sites and Euroamerican trading sites in eastern Tennessee suggests that glass beads traded to Native American populations slightly before and during the initial occupation of the Hermitage were predominantly of different types than those acquired by enslaved African Americans at the Hermitage. At the Tellico Blockhouse site, a trading fort, spherical red beads with green cores make up 60.7 percent of the total bead assemblage (65 of 107 beads), while blue beads make up 2.8 percent of the assemblage (3 of 107 beads) (Polhemus 1977:212–213). In addition, no blue beads were recorded among the trade goods shipped from Philadelphia to the Tellico Blockhouse between 1797 and 1807, or listed in a 1798 inventory (Polhemus 1977:323). Of the 72,772 beads recovered in six field seasons from the historical Overhill Cherokee site of Chota-Tenase, lamp black and white are the predominant colors, and 80.4 percent of the total sample are seed beads (Schroedl 1986:427–436). In addition, "preliminary analysis of beads from Tomotley and Mialoquo suggests that black and white are the predominant colors at these Cherokee sites" (Schroedl 1986:427–436). Although the mechanisms of bead acquisition by enslaved African Americans are unclear, the distinction between the bead assemblage at the Hermitage and those in demand by nearly contemporaneous Native

American populations in the Upper South may indicate that enslaved African Americans were able to exercise some degree of personal choice in bead selection. In addition, Stine, Cabak, and Groover (1996:50–52, 55–57) note that, while blue beads are consistently predominant in archaeological African-American bead assemblages throughout the southern United States, Native American bead assemblages are quite variable and suggest that consumer choice played a role in the composition of each.

There are several possible African antecedents for the use of beads by African Americans at the Hermitage. Beads of all kinds are currently used throughout West Africa for decorative, medicinal, religious, and economic purposes (Thompson 1983:43, 93–95; Fisher 1984:90–103; Blier 1995; Stine et al. 1996:53–54). Melanie Cabak (1990) and Theresa Singleton (1991:164) state that blue beads are sewn on clothing by Muslims to ward off the "evil eye." Caesar Apentiik (1995, pers. comm.), a Ghanaian archaeologist working on the Hermitage excavation crew during the 1995 field season, reports that small beads similar to the blue and colorless hexagonal beads recovered at the Hermitage are currently used throughout Ghana by children, who wear them as a form of preventative medicine, a usage also described by Stine, Cabak, and Groover (1996:54) as widespread in West Africa. At the African Burial Ground in New York City, two child burials dating to the colonial era, one with waistbeads and another with a beaded necklace, were found, suggesting that this usage of beads persisted in the New World (La Roche 1994a:131–132, 1994b:14).

In addition, Apentiik stated that strings of beads are currently worn on the waists of some married Ghanaian women in order to ensure fertility. The use of waistbeads has considerable historical depth in Africa, and the beads themselves "have ontological, spiritual, metaphysical, and historical meaning" (La Roche 1994b:14). Native folklore suggests that enslaved African Americans on St. Eustatius, in the Dutch West Indies, used blue faceted beads in this manner, indicating the possibility that this practice was accepted by some Africans brought to the New

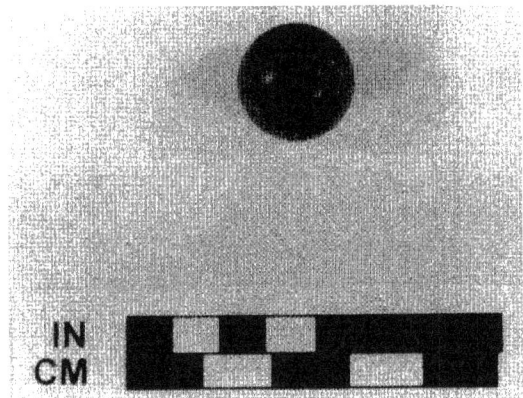

FIGURE 6. Stone marble with incised "x" from the South Cabin.

World (Smith 1987:7–8). A more direct indicator of the survival of this practice in the New World is burial 340 at the African Burial Ground, that of a woman aged between 28 and 35, with "a strand of primarily blue waist beads found *in situ*" (La Roche 1994a:4). In addition, burial 340 exhibited dental modification, suggesting to researchers that she was born in Africa (La Roche 1994a:3; Stine et al. 1996:62).

Although it is difficult to assign specific meanings to the beads recovered at the Hermitage, the very presence and distinctiveness of the bead assemblage may indicate some degree of cultural autonomy on the part of enslaved African Americans at the Hermitage. The beads themselves appear to be more similar to beads traded to African markets by Europeans (Karklins 1985:7–39), and to those recovered from other African-American sites in the Southeast (Stine et al. 1996:50–52) than to those traded to nearby Native American groups in the Southeast. Even if bead choice and distribution at the Hermitage was entirely in the hands of the Jacksons, the particular beads selected may represent the continuation of a previous trade "negotiation" between Europeans and Africans. If the beads were acquired independently in local markets or from traders, their presence indicates the participation of enslaved African Americans in the local economy, as well as their choice to expend limited economic resources on beads. Although the specific function of the beads re-

covered at the Hermitage is unknown, their presence is an important piece of evidence of the limited, negotiated cultural and economic autonomy of enslaved African Americans at the Hermitage.

"X" Marbles

Among the large variety of stone, glass, and ceramic marbles recovered from African-American contexts at the Hermitage are three small limestone marbles that have "x" marks incised on their surfaces (Figure 6). These might simply be marks of ownership. On the other hand, the "cross in a circle" motif is evocative of the Kongo cosmogram (Figure 1). This motif has been noted on items of African-American manufacture, such as colonoware bowls (Ferguson 1992:110–116), and inscribed on objects of Euroamerican manufacture found in African-American contexts, such as spoons (Klingelhofer 1987:114–115; Young 1994). Two of the copper hand charms recovered at the Hermitage (Figure 3) can also be seen as an example of this motif (Thomas 1995b:121). Newbell Puckett (1968[1926]:319), in his collection of African-American folk beliefs, describes the use of the cross symbol in "conjuration," giving a game of marbles as an example of this use. In this example, the "x" is inscribed on the ground in order to give one's opponent bad luck in the game. Significantly, an almost identical "x"-incised marble was recovered from the Gowen farmstead, located about 5 mi. from the Hermitage (Weaver et al. 1993:280), possibly indicating shared beliefs and significant contact between enslaved African Americans living at the Hermitage and the African-American community at this nearby farm. Similar marbles have also been unearthed at a Kentucky plantation by Amy Young (1994). Further investigation of gaming practices in the rural South would perhaps be useful concerning questions raised here. These marbles may provide an example of how beliefs are spread through the informal education that children receive during play with one another and through instruction from adult caregivers.

Prehistoric Stone Tools

Prehistoric Native American stone artifacts were found in all African-American contexts at the Hermitage. These objects include a number of whole and fragmentary chert projectile points (Figure 7), a large amount of debitage, several ground stone tools, and a very small amount of prehistoric ceramic. The recovery of prehistoric artifacts in African-American contexts at the Hermitage raises the possibility that enslaved African Americans were actively collecting and using them for some purpose. An alternative explanation for this lies in the fact that the Hermitage property has been the site of human activity for thousands of years. The occurrence of prehistoric artifacts in African-American contexts cannot, for this reason, be solely attributed to the actions of historic period residents. Conversely, the abundance of prehistoric artifacts present in the fields and gardens at the Hermitage provided ample opportunity for their active collection and possible use by these people.

As a partial test of the idea that African Americans at the Hermitage actively collected and curated prehistoric stone tools, the ratios of chert flakes to stone tools were calculated for the cabin interior and feature fill for each of the dwellings examined (Figure 8). These ratios were then compared with the flake/tool ratio from excavation in the mansion garden, which is extraordinarily rich in prehistoric flakes and tools, and may have been the site of a considerable amount of prehistoric lithic production. It was predicted that if historic site occupants actively collected stone tools (and did not collect flakes), the ratio of flakes to tools would be lower in historic deposits. Unfortunately, the

FIGURE 7. Prehistoric artifacts from the West unit of Cabin 3.

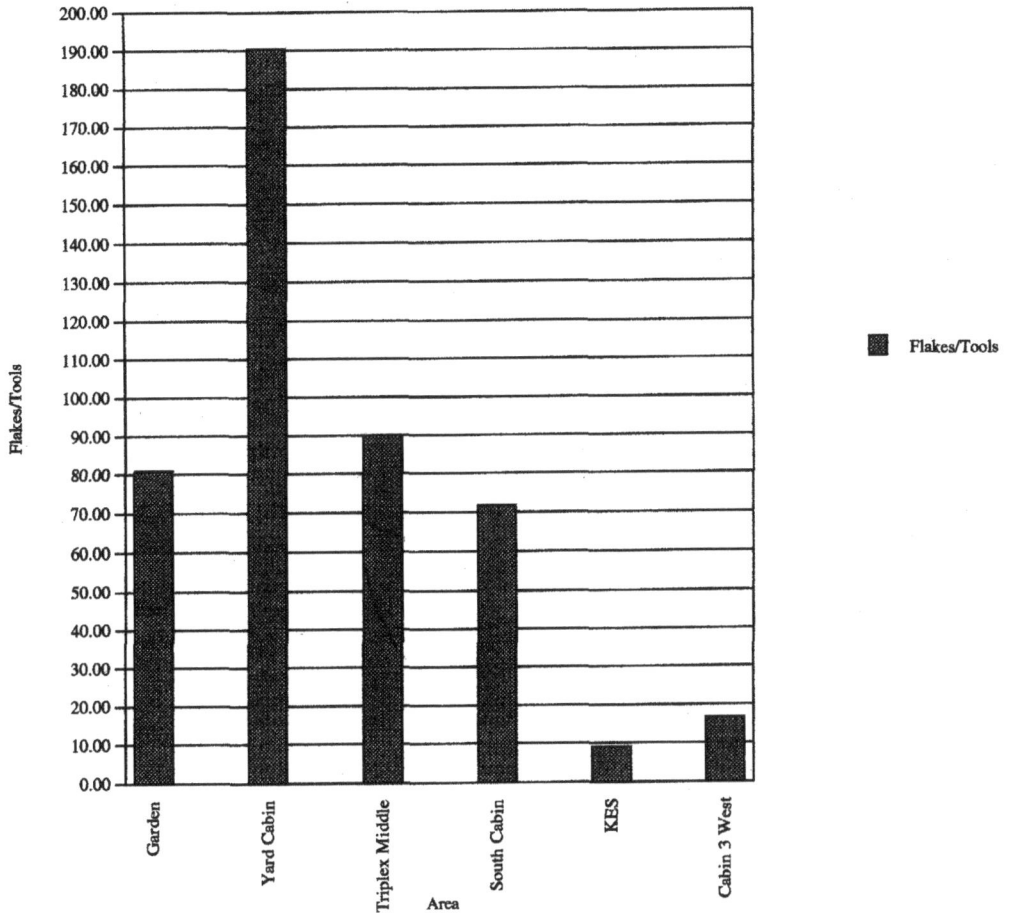

FIGURE 8. Graph showing ratios of chert flakes to flaked tools from the Hermitage Garden, and from historic midden deposits and feature fill at the Yard Cabin, Triplex Middle, South Cabin, KES, and Cabin 3 West sites.

results of this experiment were somewhat inconclusive. The flake/tool ratio decreases relative to the distance from the Yard Cabin (adjacent to the mansion garden), and may reflect prehistoric site use patterns rather than historic activity.

No distinct prehistoric middens or features have been encountered at the Hermitage, and it is probable that such prehistoric remains have been thoroughly mixed with later historic deposits through bioturbation—extensive rodent disturbance is evident at most Hermitage slave dwelling sites, or through cultural activities such as plowing. Although more research into the

Hermitage's prehistoric occupation must be done in order to properly address these questions, this does not preclude the possibility that some African Americans at the Hermitage collected stone tools.

Prehistoric artifacts are commonly recovered from African-American contexts throughout the Southeast, and several theories have been advanced to explain their presence. Puckett (1968[1926]:315) suggests that these objects were instrumental in the production of charms, either by virtue of their own intrinsic talismanic value, or in the ritual production of sparks with a steel strike-a-light. In my survey of New Orleans voodoo shops, I saw chert projectile points being sold in one shop as being "essential for your mojo bag."

A more direct explanation may be that the primary use of these objects was as utilitarian fire-starters, ready-made from high quality chert and easily collected by African Americans working in the fields at the Hermitage. Several of the points recovered do, in fact, show evidence of reuse as spark-strikers (Figure 9). These points show evidence of bashing along their edges, and a sample will be subjected to microwear analysis to look for more specific evidence of association with steel. Even if, however, it can be shown that these artifacts were used with strike-a-lights, we cannot determine the specific intentions of the striker beyond the creation of sparks. In addition, it is possible

that these artifacts simply represent the collections of children and other curiosity seekers.

Odd Smooth Stones

At each of the sites examined here, small chert nodules were recovered (Figure 10). Most of these artifacts are likely prehistoric hammerstones and small grinders, although some may have been collected and used by African Americans. Examples can be cited of African Americans using stones in conjuration, and similar worn, smooth stones were excavated at the Garrison plantation in Maryland (Klingelhofer 1987:116) and at Poplar Forest in Virginia, as well as at other African-American sites (Patten 1992). The function of these stones at the Hermitage, however, cannot readily be ascertained. In addition, a number of small, smooth pebbles

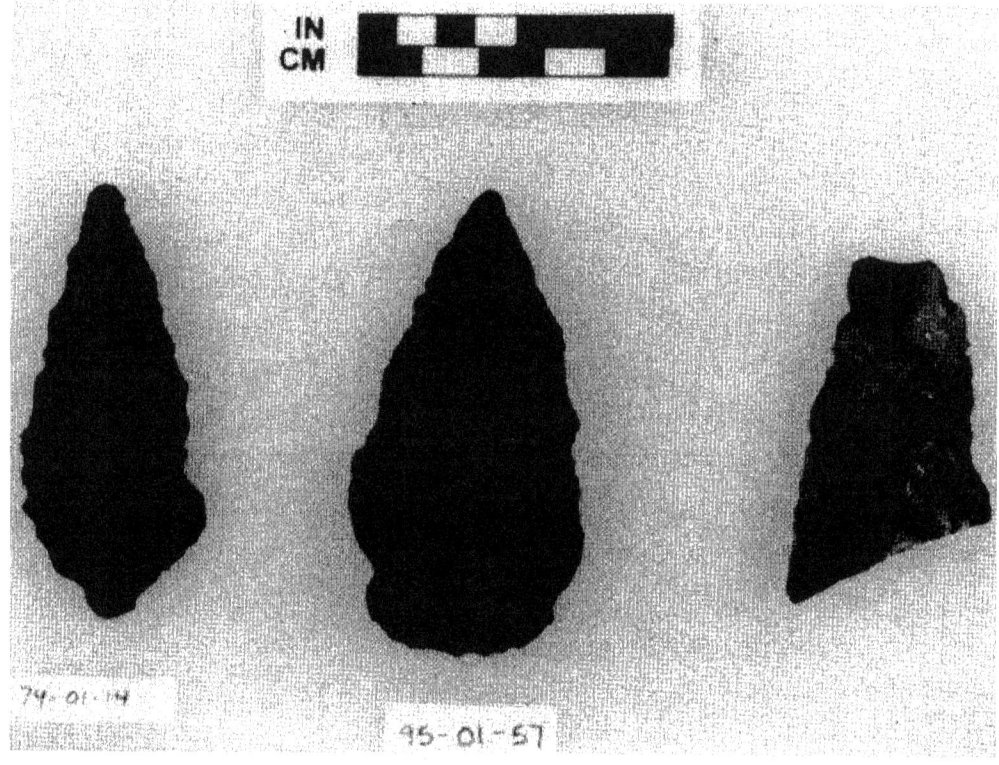

FIGURE 9. Prehistoric projectile points from Hermitage sites, with edge-wear possibly indicating reuse as spark strikers.

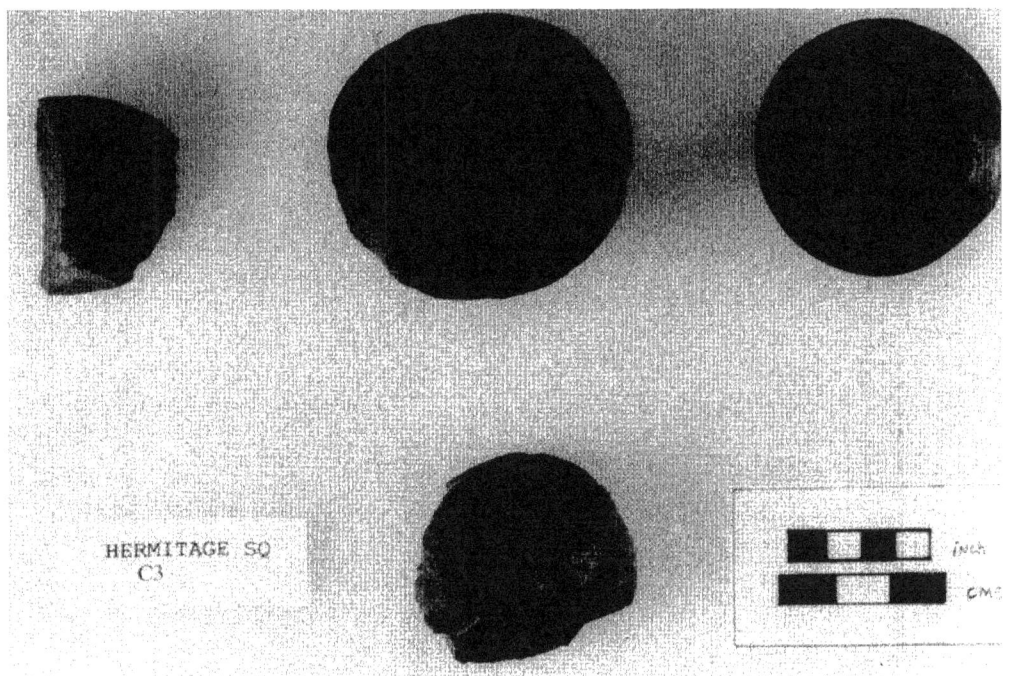

FIGURE 10. Round, smooth stones from the West unit of Cabin 3.

were recovered from the South Cabin area. While these pebbles appear to be of an ideal size to be used as gaming pieces, they may have been used for some other purpose, such as graveling a pathway.

Modified Ceramic Sherds

Several small ceramic sherds that appear to have been worked into "gaming pieces" were recovered at the Hermitage (Figure 11). Objects similar to these have also been recovered from African-American contexts in other regions, including Jamaica and Maryland (Klingelhofer 1987:115–117; Armstrong 1990:137–138). While these sherds are definitely worked, the functions that they served cannot easily be established. They do, however, look like checkers and may have been used as gaming pieces or counters.

In addition to these "gaming pieces," a number of much smaller, smoothly worn ceramic sherds were also recovered at the Hermitage. These artifacts, while relatively few in number, were recovered from all contexts examined for this paper. They are all approximately 5–10 mm in diameter and roughly triangular in shape. Artifacts of this type have been found at a number of sites throughout the Southeast and Middle Atlantic states (Wilkie 1994:271–273; Daniel Allen 1995, pers. comm.). These objects have been variously described as possible chicken or turkey gizzard stones (Smith 1976) and as "intentionally water worn" for possible use in charm bags, in divination rituals, or as gaming pieces (Wilkie 1994:271–273).

A sample of these sherds was shown to Emmanuel Breitberg, a faunal expert at the Tennessee Division of Archaeology. Breitberg (1995, pers. comm.) stated that the sherds appeared to have been worn by tumbling, possibly in a stream or in the gizzard of a bird, and that the sherds were of a size suitable for ingestion by domestic fowl. The types of ceramics that have been found to be worn in this manner are those that are relatively hard-bodied yet tend to break into large numbers of small sherds. Coarse earthenwares would be ground to dust in a very short time by gizzard action, while thick, hard-bodied stonewares tend to break into pieces too large to be ingested.

The use of potsherds as gizzard stones by domestic fowl helps to explain the rarity of these artifacts as well as their presence on a number of sites. As gravel consumed by domestic fowl is generally ground to dust and excreted within a day or so, the consumption and destruction of inedible grit by these birds occurs daily (Schorger 1966:94).

The only stones to survive this process would be either those excreted by the bird before being ground to dust, or those recovered from dead animals. Interestingly, I have received reports of an intentional turkey burial containing small whiteware sherds in the gizzard area (Leslie Stewart-Abernathy 1995, pers. comm.), as well as of "old blue dishes" being broken up and fed to hens (Camehl 1946[1916]:xvii). Gravel is not generally found in the gizzards of slaughtered domestic fowl, as the birds are not fed for 24 hours before slaughtering (Emmanuel Breitberg 1995, pers. comm.). It is, however, not known

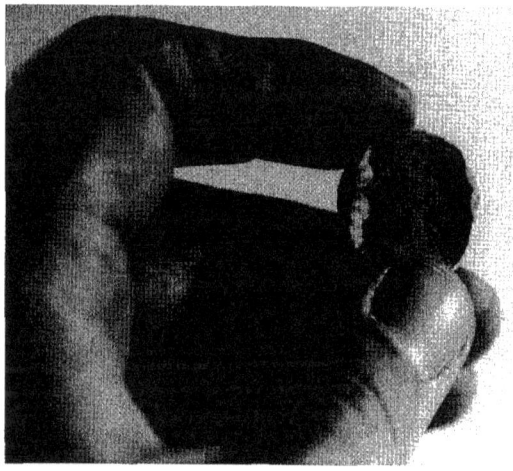

FIGURE 11. Reworked transfer-printed ceramic sherd from Cabin 2, in the Hermitage Field Quarter.

whether this practice was common at 19th-century farming operations such as the Hermitage.

The two best hypotheses to account for the presence of these sherds are intentional selection and alteration by enslaved African Americans, or the use of potsherds as gizzard stones by domestic fowl. The available information seems to favor the latter of these explanations. In addition, no reference to the use of potsherds or gizzard stones in African-American gaming or ritual has come to light during research.

Conclusion

Archaeological research at the Hermitage has not as yet provided the data necessary to delineate specific ritual behaviors on the part of the Hermitage's enslaved African-American population. However, the presence of items such as the brass "fist charms" and the distinctive bead assemblage are suggestive of both an active system of beliefs associated with specific items of material culture and the success of strategies employed by enslaved African Americans to acquire these items. Although the documentary record at the Hermitage is completely silent with regard to these objects, it is highly probable that the Jacksons were not actively engaged in providing beads and charms to their slaves. The presence of these objects, therefore, is an important piece of evidence of the limited economic autonomy that enslaved African Americans were able to negotiate with a planter-dominated society that was at turns indifferent to or directly opposed to slave participation in the marketplace economy. Several historical essays detailing the market-related activities of enslaved African Americans in the United States and Caribbean can be found in *Cultivation and Culture* (Berlin and Morgan 1993), and together provide a good overview of this complex subject.

As the archaeological study of questions related to African-American religion and ideology moves beyond the simple documentation of African "survivals," it is important to assess the significance that these beliefs and behaviors held in the African-American community. Wilkie (1995) notes the predominance of charms related to marriage, love, and family life. She suggests that the persistence of these beliefs reflected African-American attempts to maintain stable families and communities in the face of the strongly disruptive influence of slavery. Wilkie argues that the spiritual realm provided an autonomous sphere, compatible with African-American worldview, which allowed enslaved African Americans to exercise control over their own communities (Wilkie 1995). This, in turn, argues against the widespread perception that status in enslaved African-American communities was conferred mainly through relationships with the Euroamerican plantation household. Rather, it can be argued, following Mintz and Price, that "the institutions created by the slaves to deal with what are at once the most ordinary and most important aspects of life took on their characteristic shape *within* the parameters of the masters' monopoly of power, but *separate from* the masters' institutions" (Mintz and Price 1992:39).

Maria Franklin, in her assessment of Colonial Williamsburg's reconstruction of the Carter's Grove slave quarter, takes a similar standpoint when she argues that "of primary importance to enslaved blacks would have been their community in the quarters. It was a place where they could be themselves and where the creolized African-American culture was created" (Franklin 1995:149).

It has also been argued by Kenneth Brown (1994) that African-American practitioners of traditional medicine and ritual held an important place in the internal plantation economy. Status was ascribed to these individuals by traditionally-minded African Americans, and these healers played an important role in the African-American community from which they stood to benefit economically. This takes the argument for the autonomy of enslaved African-American communities one step further, by indicating the persistence and economic importance of a profession which was wholly unrelated to plantation production, and which was generally discouraged and even repressed by the white planter class.

In addition to their influence within the enslaved African-American community, respect for traditional African-American healer/magicians may have extended beyond the immediate plantation community, and even into the surrounding Euroamerican community. Although plantation owners generally decried the presence of "superstition" and "ignorance" among their enslaved, these wealthy, generally well-educated individuals were probably not representative of the bulk of the poorer white population who owned few if any slaves and formed the majority of the Euroamerican population in the antebellum upper South. These poorer whites, who generally shared with enslaved African Americans a broad sympathy with the spiritual realm, may have generally acknowledged the power of traditional African-American healers and "conjurers." In addition, the position of some enslaved African Americans as primary caregivers to members of the Euroamerican plantation elite, along with local reputations earned by successful traditional healers, may have convinced some slaveholders of the efficacy of these methods.

The hypothesis that whites, in addition to African Americans, sought treatment from traditional African-American healers is given further weight by an 1831 Tennessee law forbidding slaveholders from allowing their enslaved "to go about the country under the pretext of practicing medicine or healing the sick" (Public Acts of Tennessee 1831:122, 123). The presence of this law would seem to indicate that such a problem was perceived by the state legislature. It is perhaps significant that slaveholders themselves are mentioned by this law as possibly permitting enslaved African Americans to practice medicine.

Traditional medicine, practiced by both whites and African Americans, may have been viewed as a healthier alternative to established "scientific" medical treatment, which often involved the administration of strong toxins to sick persons. Leaky bottles of a 19th-century cure-all known as "calomel" (mercurous chloride) excavated at the Hermitage South Cabin in 1974 prompted archaeologist Samuel Smith (1977:156–158) to advise caution when excavating 19th-century medicine bottles.

In conclusion, although archaeology at the Hermitage has not uncovered contexts that can be linked to specific ritual behaviors, the overall artifact assemblage suggests that African Americans at the Hermitage actively participated in a shared pattern of beliefs that was distinct in many ways from the dominant planter ideology. In making this assertion, this study has tried to avoid the promulgation of archaeological "folklore." Although some of the analogies presented in this paper may be poorly founded, they are offered merely as suggestions to promote further research into this area of African-American history. There is really very little doubt that certain broad classes of African-American spiritual artifacts, such as charm bags prepared by skilled practitioners, have antecedents in a number of West African cultures (MacGaffey 1991; Jones 1995). It is important, however, to move beyond constructing genealogies of African-American belief systems and begin to question the functions that these beliefs and practices served in enslaved African-American communities. In addition, future research should be aimed at achieving a better understanding of the religions and cosmologies which underlay these practices.

Archaeological study of these questions will require particularly close attention to archaeological context, along with a willingness on the part of scholars to move artifact analysis beyond simple functional categories. It is important to recognize that enslaved African Americans participated in a shared system of beliefs that served important functions within their communities, and that successful strategies were employed by these men and women to practice and maintain these traditions in defiance of slaveholders. Ironically, the very ephemerality which characterizes these expressions of a functioning African-American belief system makes them quite difficult to observe archaeologically.

ACKNOWLEDGMENTS

My thanks to Larry McKee, director of archaeology at the Hermitage, and to Brian Thomas, research archaeologist at the Hermitage, for reading and commenting on an earlier draft of this article, as well as an initial version presented at The Society for Historical Archaeology Conference on Historical and Underwater Archaeology in 1996. Larry and Brian also generously provided access to the Hermitage artifact collection and photographic library during the preparation of this article, and gave a large amount of their own time in helping me see this project to completion. In addition, I acknowledge the support of the Ladies' Hermitage Association for my work, as well as the ongoing study of the Hermitage slave community of which it is a part.

REFERENCES

ADAMS, ERIC
    1994 Religion and Freedom: Artifacts Indicate that African Culture Persisted Even in Slavery. *African-American Archaeology* (11):1–2.

ARMSTRONG, DOUGLAS
    1990 The Old Village and the Great House: An Archaeological and Historical Examination of Drax Hall Plantation, St. Anne's Bay, Jamaica. University of Illinois Press, Urbana and Chicago.

BERLIN, IRA, AND PHILIP D. MORGAN (EDITORS)
    1993 *Cultivation and Culture: Labor and the Shaping of Slave Life in the Americas.* University Press of Virginia, Charlottesville.

BLIER, SUZANNE PRESTON
    1995 *African Vodun: Art, Psychology and Power.* University of Chicago Press, Chicago.

BROWN, KENNETH L.
    1994 Material Culture and Community Structure: The Slave and Tenant Community at Levi Jordan's Plantation. In *Working Toward Freedom: Slave Society and Domestic Economy in the American South*, edited by L. E. Hudson, pp. 95–118. University of Rochester Press, Rochester, NY.

BROWN, KENNETH L., AND DOREEN C. COOPER
    1990 Structural Continuity in an African-American Slave and Tenant Community. *Historical Archaeology* 24(4):95–118.

CABAK, MELANIE A.
    1990 Searching for the Meaning of Blue Beads to Afro-American Slaves. Manuscript on file, The Ladies' Hermitage Association, Hermitage, TN.

CAMEHL, ADA WALKER
    1946 *The Blue China Book: Early American Scenes and History Pictured in the Pottery of the Time.* Reprint of 1916 edition. Tudor Publishing, NY.

DOUGLASS, FREDERICK
    1986 *Narrative of the Life of Frederick Douglass, an American Slave.* Reprint of 1982, 1845 editions. Penguin, NY.

FERGUSON, LELAND
1992   *Uncommon Ground: Archaeology and Early African America, 1650–1800*. Smithsonian Institution Press, Washington, DC.

FISHER, ANGELA
1984   *Africa Adorned*. Harry N. Abrams, NY.

FRANKLIN, MARIA
1995   Rethinking the Carter's Grove Slave Quarter Reconstruction: A Proposal. *Kroeber Anthropological Society Papers* 79:147–162.

FRAZIER, E. FRANKLIN
1957   *The Negro in the United States*. Revised edition. Macmillan, NY.

HERSKOVITZ, MELVILLE J.
1958   *The Myth of the Negro Past*. Reprint of 1941 edition. Beacon Press, Boston, MA.

HYATT, HARRY MIDDLETON
1970   *Hoodoo—Conjuration—Witchcraft—Rootwork*, Vol. 1. Reprint of 1935 edition. Western Publishing, Hannibal, MO.

JONES, LYNN DIEKMAN
1995   The Material Culture of Slavery from an Annapolis Household. Paper presented at the Annual Meeting of The Society for Historical Archaeology Conference on Historical and Underwater Archaeology, Washington, DC.

KARKLINS, KARLIS
1985   *Glass Beads*. Parks Canada, Ottawa, ON.

KLINGELHOFER, ERIC
1987   Aspects of Early Afro-American Material Culture: Artifacts from the Slave Quarters at Garrison Plantation, Maryland. *Historical Archaeology* 21(2):112–119.

LA ROCHE, CHERYL J.
1994a Glass Beads Excavated from the African Burial Ground, New York City: Conservation, Analysis, and Interpretation. Unpublished M.A. thesis, Department of Museum Studies, State University of New York—F.I.T., New York, NY.
1994b Beads from the African Burial Ground, New York City: A Preliminary Assessment. *Beads: Journal of the Society of Bead Researchers* 6:3–20.

LOGAN, GEORGE C.
1992   *Archaeology at Charles Carroll's House and Garden and of His African-American Slaves*. Charles Carroll House of Annapolis, Baltimore, MD.

MACGAFFEY, WYATT
1991   *Art and Healing of the Bakongo Commented by Themselves: Minkisi from the Laman Collection*. Folkens Museum-Etnografiska, Stockholm.

MCKEE, LARRY
1993   Summary Report of the 1991 Field Quarter Excavation. *Tennessee Anthropological Association Newsletter* 18(1).
1995   The Earth Is Their Witness. *The Sciences* (March/April):36–41.

MCKEE, LARRY, BRIAN THOMAS, AND JENNIFER BARTLETT
1994   Summary Report on the Hermitage Mansion Yard Area. Manuscript on file, The Ladies' Hermitage Association, Hermitage, TN.

MINTZ, SIDNEY W., AND RICHARD PRICE
1992   *The Birth of African-American Culture: An Anthropological Perspective*. Originally published in 1976 as *An Anthropological Approach to the Afro-American Past*. Beacon Press, Boston, MA.

ORSER, CHARLES E.
1994   The Archaeology of African-American Slave Religion in the Antebellum South. *Cambridge Archaeological Journal* 4(1):33–45.

OTTO, JOHN SOLOMON
1984   *Cannon's Point Plantation, 1794–1860: Living Conditions and Status Patterns in the Old South*. Academic Press, Orlando, FL.

PATTEN, DRAKE
1992   *Mankala* and *Minkisi*: Possible Evidence of African-American Folk Beliefs and Practices. *African-American Archaeology* (6):5–7.

POGUE, DENNIS J., AND ESTHER C. WHITE
1991   *Summary Report on the "House for Families" Slave Quarter Site (44 Fx 762/40–47), Mount Vernon Plantation, Mount Vernon, Virginia*. Mount Vernon Ladies' Association, Archaeology Department, Mount Vernon, VA.

POLHEMUS, RICHARD
1977   *Tellico Blockhouse Site*. Tennessee Valley Authority, Chattanooga, TN.

PUBLIC ACTS OF TENNESSEE
1831   *Public Acts of the State of Tennessee passed by the General Assembly*. Jean and Alexander Heard Library, Law Library, Vanderbilt University Law School, Nashville, TN.

PUCKETT, NEWBELL NILES
    1968   *Folk Beliefs of the Southern Negro.* Reprint of 1926
            edition. Patterson Smith, Montclair, NJ.

SCHORGER, A. W.
    1966   *The Wild Turkey: Its History and Domestication.*
            University of Oklahoma Press, Norman.

SCHROEDL, GERALD F.
    1986   *Overhill Cherokee Archaeology at Chota-Tenasee.*
            Tennessee Valley Authority, Chattanooga.

SINGLETON, THERESA A.
    1991   The Archaeology of Slave Life. In *Before Freedom
            Came: African-American Life in the Antebellum South,*
            edited by J. D. C. Campbell and K. S. Rice. University
            Press of Virginia, Charlottesville.
    1995   The Archaeology of Slavery in North America. *Annual
            Review of Anthropology* (24):119–140.

SMITH, SAMUEL D.
    1977   Plantation Archaeology at the Hermitage: Some
            Suggested Patterns. *Tennessee Anthropologist*
            2(2):152–163.
    1976   *An Archaeological and Historical Assessment of the
            First Hermitage.* Division of Archaeology, Tennessee
            Department of Conservation, Nashville.
    1987   Archaeology of Slavery: Some Tennessee Examples.
            Paper presented at the Afro-American Local History
            Sixth Annual Conference, Nashville, TN.

STINE, LINDA FRANCE, MELANIE A. CABAK, AND MARK D.
GROOVER
    1996   Blue Beads as African-American Cultural Symbols.
            Historical Archaeology 30(3):49–75.

THOMAS, BRIAN WILLIAM
    1995a   Source Criticism and the Interpretation of African-
            American Sites. *Southeastern Archaeology* 14(2).
    1995b   *Community Among Enslaved African-Americans on
            the Hermitage Plantation.* Ph.D. dissertation,
            Department of Anthropology, State University of
            New York at Binghamton, Binghamton. University
            Microfilms International, Ann Arbor, MI.

THOMAS, BRIAN WILLIAM, LARRY MCKEE, AND JENNIFER
BARTLETT
    1995   Summary Report on the 1995 Hermitage Field Quarter
            Excavation. Manuscript on file, The Ladies' Hermitage
            Association, Hermitage, TN.

THOMPSON, ROBERT FARRIS
    1983   *Flash of the Spirit: African and Afro-American Art
            and Philosophy.* Random House, NY.

WEAVER, GUY G., JEFFREY L. HOLLAND, PATRICK H.
GARROW, AND MARTIN B. REINBOLD
    1993   *The Gowen Farmstead: Archaeological Data Recovery
            at Site 40DV401 (Area D), Davidson County,
            Tennessee.* Garrow and Associates, Memphis TN.

WILKIE, LAURIE
    1994   *"Never Leave Me Alone": An Archaeological Study
            of African-American Ethnicity, Race Relations and
            Community at Oakley Plantation.* Ph.D. Dissertation,
            Department of Anthropology, University of California
            at Los Angeles, Los Angeles. University Microfilms
            International, Ann Arbor, MI.
    1995   Magic and Empowerment on the Plantation: An
            Archaeological Consideration of African-American
            World View. *Southeastern Archaeology* 14(2):136–
            148.

YENTSCH, ANNE ELIZABETH
    1994   *A Chesapeake Family and Their Slaves: A Study in
            Historical Archaeology.* Cambridge University Press,
            Cambridge, England.

YOUNG, AMY L.
    1994   Change and Continuity in African-Derived Religious
            Practices on an Upland South Plantation. Paper
            presented at the Southeastern Archaeology Conference,
            Lexington, KY.

AARON E. RUSSELL
DEPARTMENT OF ANTHROPOLOGY
WAKE FOREST UNIVERSITY
BOX 7807
WINSTON-SALEM, NC 27109

CHARLES E. ORSER, JR.

On Plantations and Patterns

ABSTRACT

South's pattern concept has acquired prominence in archaeological research since its explanation in the late 1970s. Nowhere has this prominence been greater than in plantation archaeology. Unfortunately, the pattern concept is inappropriate for the analysis of plantation remains because its scope is too large and its perspective is mainly synchronic.

Introduction

In the recent history of historical archaeology, few methods of analysis have been evaluated and adopted more than has Stanley South's pattern concept. Although the majority of such studies were prepared in the late 1970s and early 1980s, just after South's (1977, 1978) presentation of the concept, many such studies are still being conducted. Pattern studies have become particularly important in the analysis of southern plantations. A Slave Artifact Pattern, a Carolina Slave Artifact Pattern, a Plantation Artifact Pattern, and a Tenant Artifact Pattern have been proposed and tested in the South (Brockington et al. 1985; Drucker 1981; Garrow 1982; Lewis 1985: Moore 1981, 1985; Singleton 1980; Trinkley and Caballero 1983; Wheaton and Garrow 1985; Wheaton, Friedlander, and Garrow 1983; Zierden and Calhoun 1983).

When taken as a whole, these studies present a unified image of southern plantations for the archaeological community at large. Unfortunately, this image is a false one, not because the archaeologists involved are poorly trained or ideologically driven, but because the pattern concept itself is inappropriate for the analysis of plantation phenomena. This inadequacy stems, not from the construction of the patterns as such (Warfel 1982; Stevenson 1983), but from the epistemological foundation of the concept itself. Because analysis cannot be conducted apart from theory (Gibbon

1984:45; Kemeny 1959:89), a possible conclusion is that those who accept South's analytical methods also accept, although tacitly, his underlying theory. Thus, although South has not conducted plantation research, much plantation archaeology is forged in his theoretical image. This theory deserves careful scrutiny because of its prevalence.

The purpose of this paper is to evaluate critically the theoretical foundation of South's pattern concept and to suggest why it cannot be used in the archaeological study of plantations. This examination suggests that the pattern concept must be removed from further plantation analysis.

South's concept is flawed for two important reasons. First, the eclectically constructed concept does not provide an effective scale of analysis (after Marquardt and Crumley 1987:2) that is suited to the complexities of plantation organization; and second, the concept provides no mechanism for investigating historical change. Even though its foundation is explicitly evolutionary (that is, diachronic), the pattern concept permits only synchronic, functional analysis. Plantations were distinct, complex, historical, and spatial entities that, by their very nature, embodied change.

The Scale and Eclectic Foundation of the Pattern Concept

The essence of South's (1977, 1978) two major expositions on the pattern concept incorporate a call for more quantification in historical archaeology. For South, quantification permits the identification of patterned variability in artifact collections. South maintains that an emphasis on patterns allows historical archaeologists to transcend their reliance on historical documents and leads to true theory building in historical archaeology. In a practical sense, these patterns lead archaeologists away from preparing wholly descriptive reports and toward a wider appreciation of cultural processes (South 1977:31–43, 125; also see South 1974:5–6, 315–16, 1978, 1979:235, 1988a:35, 1988b). Toward this goal, South (1977: 83–164) illustrates the "Carolina Artifact Pattern'' and the ''Frontier Artifact Pattern'' using data from nine sites in the eastern United States.

South (1977:86–88) also argues that individual households—represented as discrete archaeological sites with domestic components—exist within a larger cultural system that imposes uniformity on them. This uniformity, expected to be reflected in the material cultural remains left by these households, should be expressed as ratios of occurrence of various artifact groups; in other words, the artifact patterns. South's underlying assumption is that a per capita rate of artifact disposal occurs around occupation sites in a manner consistent with the behavioral uniformity imposed on the inhabitants of those sites. The search for such regularity is largely the subject of *Method and Theory in Historical Archaeology* (South 1977).

By the early 1960s, the concept of patterns of culture was considered to be a ''byword'' in American anthropology (Lesser 1961:43), and the word ''pattern'' itself had acquired many meanings. In explaining the theoretical basis, or perhaps anthropological justification, of his pattern concept in the light of the term's widespread usage, South (1977:84) states that the patterns he looks for in archaeological deposits are analogous to Kroeber's (1919:259) ''great pulsations'' and Steward's (1955:88) ''regularities.''

Among those anthropologists who use the pattern concept, Kroeber is perhaps the most circumspect. He recognizes four kinds of patterns: universal, systemic, whole-cultural, and style type (Kroeber 1948:320).

The universal pattern was first proposed by Wissler (1923) to refer to a scheme that could be applied to all cultures. Subsumed under this universal pattern are speech, material traits, art, knowledge, religion, society, property, government, and war. Each of these subjects is further subdivided; material traits, for example, includes food, shelter, dress, tools, weapons, and industries. This kind of pattern, analogous to the contents of a book, is fairly meaningless to Kroeber because its logical conclusion is the descriptive ethnography. In other words, because all cultures have speech, material traits, art, and so forth, ''the universal pattern consists merely of the series of

these common demonstrators expectably represented in any culture'' (Kroeber 1948:312). Thus, the universal pattern merely represents a plan for the convenient ordering of cultural elements and, therefore, is not theoretically rigorous.

The systemic pattern consists of a complex of cultural material that continues to persist by demonstrating its utility. These patterns exhibit what Radcliffe-Brown (1952:43) might call ''functional consistency'' if they were not limited to only one aspect of culture, such as the alphabet or plow cultivation. The significance of these systemic patterns ''becomes more evident on a historical view'' (Kroeber 1948:313). As such, they are ''blocks and pieces of culture'' that have a common origin and are arranged ''in a common pattern persistent enough to be recognizable for a long time, even after direct historical record of the community of origin has been lost'' (Kroeber 1948:321).

Whole-cultural patterns relate to entire cultures, and Kroeber (1948:316) speaks of ''an Italian, a French, [and] a British pattern.'' Kroeber argues that discrete cultures produce whole-cultural patterns by their distinctive customs. In order to delineate these patterns, one must view them in a manner ''akin to recognition of style in art'' (Kroeber 1948:318). Although lacking the same psychocultural element, this pattern is similar to that espoused by Benedict (1934:48), who states that what ''has happened in the great art-styles happens also in cultures as a whole.'' Kroeber (1948:326) uses a number of historical examples to argue that ''whole-cultures'' grow in a succession of ''unpredictable swells or waves'' that tend ''to come intermittently, in pulses or irregular rhythms.'' This rise and fall of whole cultures is also termed the ''life histories of civilizations'' (Kroeber 1966:18–27).

Kroeber's style pattern represents a particular method of accomplishing a task, or ''a way of achieving definiteness and effectiveness in human relations by choosing or evolving one line of procedure out of several possible ones, and sticking to it'' (Kroeber 1948:329). The use of particular styles does not occur indefinitely; styles are acquired, used, and once exhausted, fall into disuse as new styles are produced. Kroeber (1948: 331) also equates these patterns with art styles and says that style patterns can be associated with whole-cultural patterns. Examples of style patterns are represented in Kroeber's celebrated studies of European women's dress fashions (Kroeber 1919; Richardson and Kroeber 1940; for an interesting and more recent study, see Turnbaugh 1979).

In concluding their study of dress fashions, Richardson and Kroeber (1940:150) stress that such investigations "may serve as a precedent for the more exact definition of other stylistic patterns in the same or other civilizations." South (1977: 32) takes their advice seriously and asserts that these fashion studies are "particularly relevant to those archaeologists excavating sites of the historic period." To South, such studies demonstrate both the pure investigative value of the nomothetic approach and the presence of patterns in the past. South (1977:84) asserts that his patterns are similar to Kroeber's (1919:259) "great pulsations." Thus, Kroeber's studies of stylistic and whole-cultural patterning in dress fashions become the theoretical basis for South's pattern concept, and his great pulsations become the model for the patterns themselves.

In addition to the explicit reliance on Kroeber, South (1977:84) also attaches Steward's notion of "regularities" to his idea of artifact patterns. In fact, South (1977:5) states that Steward's regularities serve as a "fundamental inspiration" for the nomological goals of the New Archaeology. The concept of regularity, like "pattern," has had longevity in American anthropology (Lesser 1939; Lowie 1936).

For Steward, "regularities" are similarities of form and content that occur "cross-culturally in historically separate areas," whereas "uniformities" are similarities that occur within areas (Steward 1955:88). Regularities are considered to be causally related and are discovered using a comparative method in areas that are not historically related. Steward's plan is to use these causal relationships diachronically in multilinear evolution, an idea once referred to as "parallelism" (Lowie 1929:88). Because Steward's (1955:4, 14–15) assumption is that "certain basic types of

culture may develop in similar ways under similar conditions," he sees multilinear evolution as a methodology "distinctive in searching for parallels of limited occurrence." Thus, Steward's methodology focuses on discrete cultural entities whose similarities can be empirically verified as sequential, parallel lines of development.

The perspectives of Kroeber and Steward are expanded by South to include a psychological element. Here, South's ideas are more consistent with those of Bronislaw Malinowski, and careful examination shows that South's concept of culture is consistent with that expressed in Malinowski's biocultural functionalism.

South's view of culture does not receive explicit, detailed examination in *Method and Theory in Historical Archaeology*, his major work of theory. However, some idea of his view can be gained by examining his brief statements about the British Colonial Tea Ceremony illustrated in his Figure 4 (South 1977:39–43). This figure, showing the "relativity of cultural systems to the orbit of archaeological science," is an astronomical heuristic device intended to illustrate the positivist way in which archaeologists can formulate hypotheses to be used in building theories for archaeological science.

The main significance of South's Figure 4 rests in the "Causal Constellation." This constellation is composed of the following sequence: "man" → "biological need: survival" → "dynamics: cultural process" → "cultural mechanism: economic subsistence base" → "related human behavior: food procurement and consumption" → "social-psychological need and function: relaxation, social intercourse, communication, status reinforcement, ego building, and sexual interaction." These elements are represented as planets linked sequentially, or "causally," by unidirectional arrows. Accordingly, the "social-psychological need and function" leads to the "British Colonial Culture (Lifeways): Tea Ceremony." This Tea Ceremony, part of the British whole-cultural pattern, is represented today in archaeological deposits by broken and discarded pieces of tea sets. The historical record, constituting a "Historical Satellite" to the larger "Systemic Orbit," suggests that the Tea

TABLE 1
SOUTH'S (1977) "CAUSAL CONSTELLATION" AND MALINOWSKI'S (1939, 1944a)
THEORY OF CULTURE

	South	
Cultural Mechanism	Related Behavior	Social-psychological Need and Function
Economic subsistence base	Food procurement and consumption	Sexual interaction Status reinforcement Ego building Relaxation Communication Social intercourse
	Malinowski	
Basic Needs	Direct Response	Associated Cultural System
Nutrition	Commissariat	Economics
Reproduction	Kinship	
Bodily comforts	Shelter, Dress	Social control
Safety	Protection	
Relaxation	Play	Education
Movement	Activities	
Growth	Communication	Political organization
	Training	

Ceremony was "an upper class status symbol in eighteenth century colonial America."

The framework presented in South's Figure 4 bears a remarkable similarity to one used by Malinowski (Table 1). Malinowski (1939, 1944a) postulates that culture is adaptive and that humans (and their cultures) survive by using cultural responses to meet certain basic biological needs. The needs are individual but the responses are collective; people band together in various organizational forms to meet their basic needs as individuals. Hence, for Malinowski, the central aspect of culture is the need → activity → purpose → function cycle (Voget 1975:515).

The similarities between Malinowski's needs and South's "Causal Constellation" for the Tea Ceremony are clear (Table 2). Not only are many of South's terms exactly those of Malinowski, South's concept of "social-psychological need and function" indicates that the Tea Ceremony is individualistic. In South's scheme, the need for the Tea Ceremony (the activity) creates its function: to provide relaxation, social intercourse, communication, status reinforcement, ego building, and interaction

between the sexes. Thus, Malinowski's need → function cycle is not only maintained, South's Tea Ceremony meets at least three of Malinowski's basic human needs: food consumption, relaxation, and communication. The other "social-psychological" needs satisfied by the Tea Ceremony are "derived needs," cultural ways in which humans further ensure their survival and comfort (Malinowski 1944a:120). The Tea Ceremony serves the needs of individuals through the collective actions of members of the British Colonial Culture.

South's theory of culture, then, like Malinowski's, presupposes personal satisfaction. In Malinowski's (1939:944) terms, the Tea Ceremony represents the "cultural satisfaction of the individual impulses." Thus, South adopts Malinowski's behaviorist perspective in his acceptance of the "social-psychological need and function" of the Tea Ceremony.

It should now be clear that South's pattern concept is built on a foundation drawn from diverse theorists. From Kroeber, South takes the concept of systemic and whole-cultural patterns and great pulsations; from Steward, South takes

TABLE 2
COMPARISON OF TERMS USED BY SOUTH AND MALINOWSKI

South	Malinowski
Economic subsistence base	Economics
Food procurement and consumption	Nutrition, Commissariat
Sexual interaction	Reproduction
Relaxation	Relaxation
Communication	Communication

the notion of regularities; and from Malinowski, South takes the idea of the collective satisfaction of individual social-psychological needs and functions. In more recent essays, South (1988a, 1988b) adds ideas from the world-system theorists and even Karl Marx. Although it does not figure into the pattern concept in any clear way, it might be added that South draws inspiration from White (South 1977:xix).

South's adoption of a number of distinct theories is a form of scholastic eclecticism. Eclectics have no commitment to any theoretical orientation and are at liberty to change position as the situation seems to warrant (Harris 1980:287–314). However, rather than constituting academic versatility and open-mindedness, eclecticism and the conscious choosing of theoretical principles provides a "scattershot" approach that fails to offer unified interpretations (Price 1980:155). Eclecticism ensures that no strong theoretical link holds diverse research together. While it cannot be argued that South has not been consistent in his approach, his pattern concept is nonetheless built upon a shaky eclectic foundation. The problem posed by South's eclecticism is compounded by his consistent advocacy of a non-eclectic position: cultural evolutionism. In other words, even though South has advocated cultural evolutionism for many years, his application, at least as far as the pattern concept is concerned, is actually eclectic. This eclecticism seriously compromises the validity of his cultural evolutionary framework.

The Temporal Failings of the Pattern Concept

Long before South devised the pattern concept, he had committed himself to the diachronic anal-

ysis of past human activities by way of an overt cultural evolutionism. In an essay entitled "Evolutionary Theory in Archaeology," South (1955) argues that evolutionary theory is inherent in archaeological research even though many archaeologists do not realize it. In a well-constructed argument, South shows how the ideas of some archaeologists are consistent with those of classical evolutionists E. B. Tylor and Lewis H. Morgan. For example, in examining the "developmental stages" of Willey and Phillips (1955), and particularly their disclaimer that these stages do not represent an evolutionary sequence, South (1955: 24–25) illustrates the almost word-for-word agreement between them and Morgan (1877). Even the developmental stages outlined by Willey and Phillips—Early Lithic, Archaic, Preformative, Formative, Classic, and Postclassic—bear strong similarity to Morgan's now-famous elaboration of Tylor's evolutionary stages—Lower, Middle, and Upper Savagery, Lower, Middle, and Upper Barbarism, and Civilization. South's (1955:26) conclusion is if "archaeologists are going to use evolutionary stages, and operate under basic evolutionary assumptions, why not say so?"

After an examination of Steward's (1955) multilinear evolution and a statement that Steward is "perhaps the most outstanding anthropologist in America today who uses the evolutionary approach," South (1955:30) concludes that "archaeologists should not apologize when they find their monographs are influenced by evolutionary theory." For South, archaeologists may wish to substitute other terms for evolution, such as the "historical-developmental" stages of Willey and Phillips (1955), but they at least should be explicit in their use of evolutionary theory.

South's call for an explicit cultural evolutionism in archaeology is again voiced, this time specifically for historical archaeology, in his "Evolution and Horizon as Revealed in Ceramic Analysis in Historical Archaeology" (1972). Although this paper has received widespread attention because of the "Mean Ceramic Dating Formula," what is important here is South's (1972:73) statement that the paper, and by extension the formula itself, "is anchored in the assumption that evolution of form is basic to the culture process and is the foundation'' of archaeological reasoning.

South's interest in cultural evolutionism is explicitly expressed in *Method and Theory in Historical Archaeology*. South (1977:xix) acknowledges his intellectual debt to Leslie White, and argues much as he did in the 1955 essay, but with greater reliance on Steward. However, South's eclecticism carries over into his view of cultural evolution because, even though the book is ostensibly an evolutionary manifesto for historical archaeology, his pattern concept is decidedly non-temporal in character. On the one hand, South seems to accept by association Kroeber's (1946:1) view that evolution is a historical process studied by historians and that White's ''evolutionistic approach'' is ''plainly historical.'' As is well known, Kroeber (1917) maintains that cultural progress occurs majestically as part of the superorganic, in terms of the macrodynamics of its own laws, ''an existence, an order, and a causality'' of its own (Kroeber 1919:263). Thus, Kroeber (1960:3) is comfortable referring to himself as ''a historian of sorts.'' On the other hand, South's agreement with Malinowski's framework suggests that his thoughts on historical change actually may be quite different from Kroeber's. Although it can never be said that Malinowski contributed to the development of diachronic or evolutionary theory, he was not against it (Lowie 1946: 227). In fact, Malinowski even argues for evolutionary (that is, diachronic) anthropology— ''the functional view obviously does not dispose of a sound and limited evolutionary concept of culture''—and notes the importance of evolutionary stages in anthropological research even though he rejects the nonempirical stages of nineteenth-century evolutionists as ''fantastic evolutionary schemes'' (Malinowski 1927:41, 1944a:41, 176, 1944b:194,238). However, Malinowski believes that evolutionary studies have a place in anthropological research only after a solid functional analysis has been completed. Thus, it would seem, again by association, that South also accepts Malinowski's view that functional, synchronic studies must precede diachronic interpretations. For South, however, these synchronic studies must be phrased in the evolutionary terms of Steward and Kroeber.

This viewpoint is implied by South's (1977:327) stated agenda: (1) to reveal patterns in artifact collections that (2) can be used ''to gain insight into behavior patterns'' (3) for the purposes of framing behavioral laws that will (4) provide an understanding of ''the processes at work within, and between, cultural systems'' (clearly Steward's uniformities and regularities, respectively). Significantly, South (1977:327) states that as historical archaeologists ''delineate *change and dynamics between systems* [i.e., regularities] we can begin to understand something about cultural evolution'' (emphasis added). At least two conclusions can be drawn from this summary statement. First, that South may not consider himself far enough along to ''understand something about cultural evolution''; and second, that regardless of his admiration of the cultural evolutionists, his pattern concept begins, as Malinowski would have it, at the level of synchronic, functional analysis.

This interpretation is given added weight by South's statements about the hypothetical British family in colonial America. South (1977:86–87) argues that the average British family brought to the New World ''a basic set of behavioral modes, attitudes, and associated artifacts that would not vary regardless of whether their ship landed in Charleston, Savannah, or Philadelphia.'' South maintains that the uniformity imposed on these people by their cultural system would create patterns within the archaeological deposits. As such, ''a middle class laborer in Charleston would contribute his per capita, per year procurement-use-breakage-discard record in a ratio similar to his counterpart in Savannah or Philadelphia'' (South 1977:87, 1978:228). This ''basic set'' of attitudes, beliefs, and ideas of the British family, with its attendant ''associated artifacts'' that produce the patterns, clearly represents a whole-cultural pattern. Environmental adaptation does not figure into the structure of the artifact patterns, even though South does profess an overt interest in Steward's regularities.

Thus, the scope of South's patterns is clearly on the whole-cultural level. His failure to relate his artifact patterns to any sort of diachronic sequence—even the ''pulses or irregular rhythms'' of Kroeberian history—makes the patterns lose all temporal meaning. While some might consider South's approach "a step that American historical archaeology had to take" (Cordell 1981:452), the step has no clear direction. The Carolina Artifact Pattern, based on sites ranging in date from about the 1720s to the early 1820s (South 1977:92), is synchronic and aleatory.

The internal contradictions, overt eclecticism, and synchronic perspective in South's theoretical foundation are partially to blame for the lack of success historical archaeologists have had during the past ten years applying his analytical methods. The rest of the blame must fall at the feet of uncreative archaeologists who uncritically employ South's patterns as if they were a calculus for unadulterated truth.

That South's pattern concept has been used by so many historical archaeologists in a synchronic manner is ample evidence that the concept can be used quite independently of any diachronic interest. This usage, in addition to the scope of the pattern concept, has greatly hampered historical archaeology in general and plantation archaeology in particular.

Plantations and Patterns

Archaeologists who have used South's pattern concept in the analysis of plantations have been particularly trapped by its whole-cultural focus and synchronic view. This trap appears most evident in their interpretations. When the patterns between two or more sites are similar, these archaeologists reason that the past owners of the artifacts were members of the same whole culture; when the patterns are different, they reason that the differences are functional. This dual interpretation was explicitly made by Singleton (1980) in her pioneering study of slavery in coastal Georgia. For her, the similarities between the patterns at the different sites studied reflect the "general patterns in coastal slave lifeways," but the differences relate "to functional characteristics of specific plantations" (Singleton 1980:212). In other words, the difference between the artifact patterns have some-

thing to do with how each plantation was used, but the similarities relate to the cultural tradition of the plantation's inhabitants. Others have faced the same interpretive problem. When comparing the artifact pattern from Spiers Landing, South Carolina, with South's Carolina Artifact Pattern, Drucker (1981:62) sought to understand the differences in the patterns by attempting "to establish possible functional contexts" for them. Similarly, in their examination of the Campfield Settlement in South Carolina, Zierden and Calhoun (1983:44) see the similarities between its artifact pattern and those from other sites as an example of Singleton's Slave Artifact Pattern. These authors all invoke the whole-culture argument by stating, as do Zierden and Calhoun (1983:44), that this pattern exists "regardless of the geographical or temporal affiliation" of the assemblages. Clearly, these authors all make tacit use of the whole-cultural pattern in their interpretations.

In making these kinds of interpretations, plantation archaeologists overlook the complexity of plantation life, and minimize the social relations that existed on them. Although the main groups of plantation inhabitants were from distinct whole cultures (African and Euro-American), their interaction was not necessarily whole cultural. Rather, these complicated plantation relations can be conceptualized as social fields.

Developed in British social anthropology, the social field concept was used by American anthropologist Alexander Lesser to show that peoples living in groups maintain a number of social interactions that are both internal and external to that group. The social aggregates formed should not be viewed as isolated, or "separated by some kind of wall, from others, but as inextricably involved with other aggregates, near and far, in weblike, netlike connections" (Lesser 1961:42). Social fields, therefore, are historically created social interactions that transcend the more artificially created concepts of "culture" and "society" (Lesser 1961:42). The social field approach disassembles artificially perceived human organizational units, such as whole cultures, and emphasizes social interaction. This approach has been recently championed by Wolf (1984), who uses the idea in his masterful study of European expansion throughout the world (Wolf 1982).

Coupled with this idea of social fields is the mode of production, a concept derived from Marxian historical materialism. Although the concept is decidedly complex, because Marx used the concept in at least three slightly different ways (Cohen 1978:79–84; Copans and Seddon 1978:38–39; Himmelweit 1983; Hindess and Hirst 1975:9), the mode of production concept has interpretive power when defined simply as "an historically occurring set of social relations through which social labor is deployed to wrest energy from nature by means of tools, skills, organization, and knowledge" (Wolf 1981:46, 1982:75).

The foundation of the mode of production concept is the idea that humans interact with and transform nature through labor (Wolf 1981:45). This labor process is one wherein humans initiate, control, and regulate nature in order to serve their basic needs (Marx 1967: I,177). This production distinguishes humans from all other animals.

Human production consists of two irreducible elements: the forces of production and the relations of production. The productive forces establish and reproduce a society's articulation with nature and include the means of production (raw materials and tools) and labor-power (the physical and mental power necessary to produce the needs of society), while the productive relations establish and reproduce the structure of the relations in that society and include control of production, political control, exchange, and so on (Laibman 1984:261; Marquardt 1985:85–86). The techniques of production and the availability of the finished products help define the forces of production; the social regulation of the productive process and the allocation of labor, surplus, and wealth help define the relations of production (Little 1986:43). In truth, production exists on at least three levels, economic, political, and ideological. Things, power, and thoughts and ideas are produced in each, respectively, but none can exist independently (Nowak 1983; Orser 1987).

Minimally, production involves two groups of people: those who produce and those who consume. Economic production involves the interaction of direct producers (those who use the means of production) and owners (those who own the means of production). The people in each group constitute a distinct social class because of their common relationship to the productive process. These classes have been termed "fundamental classes" because the producing class uses its labor to produce a surplus that is employed by the owning class to cement further their superordinate position in society (Resnick and Wolff 1982:2–3).

Although plantation slaves helped create their world within the plantations of their bondage (Blassingame 1979; Genovese 1974; Rawick 1972), it would be oversimplistic to state that they did so in isolation of the prevailing plantation social fields, or relations of production. On the contrary, slaves (and other plantation inhabitants, including postbellum tenant farmers) lived and worked within an intricate network of social fields. Without masters there could be no slaves, and without landlords there could be no tenants. With the end of slavery came the end of master-slave relations and the beginning of landlord-tenant relations. Both sets of relations were historical creations.

A plantation, whether antebellum or postbellum, was created and maintained to increase the wealth of its owner (Orser 1988a). Plantations were economic institutions first and foremost. Although distinct whole cultures were clearly involved in the creation and operation of plantations, plantation laborers (slaves and tenants) were at plantations to work. Thus, the two historically created, fundamental classes on plantations were owners (planters and later landlords) and producers (slaves and later tenants).

The social relations on antebellum plantations existed within a slave mode of production, wherein planters exerted control over their slaves both economically (in terms of production) and politically (in terms of denying them access to positions of self-reliance and power). Thus, in a purely structural sense, slaves were both producers of labor and consumers of oppression. As southern sugar, rice, and cotton became major money crops within national and international markets, planters became involved not only in crop production, but also in the production of surplus labor as well (Marx 1967: I,236). Planters used the fruits of this surplus labor in their "quest for luxury" (Nowak 1983:75), given expression by their conspicuous consumption of material goods that symbolized wealth and power.

On the other hand, slaves held a certain power over their owners because the owners relied on their labor. The quest for luxury could not occur in the plantation world without slaves. As a result, slaves demonstrated their power by malingering, feigning ignorance, sabotage, running away, and open rebellion (Aptheker 1964, 1968; Genovese 1974:587–660, 1979). Because slaves knew that their labor would be appropriated by their masters or by those to whom their master had temporarily loaned them, they found themselves in a difficult position. If they did not work in a manner consistent with their owner's standards, they could be punished with whipping, disfigurement, job demotion, or sale; if they did work in a manner consistent with their owner's standards they could be rewarded with money, extra clothing, and trips to town (Blassingame 1979:292; Breeden 1980: 257–65). However, conforming to the owner's work standards often meant suffering a loss of prestige within the slave community (Blassingame 1976).

When the United States entered its "revolutionary period" following the Civil War (Marx and Engels 1937:277) a tenant mode of production gradually replaced the experimental modes established shortly after 1865 (Orser 1986, 1988b: 54–55). The tenant mode of production engendered a different set of social fields than did the slave mode of production, even though in many cases the same individuals were involved in both. The classes maintained the same relative relationship as before the war (owners and direct producers), but the social fields were new. The relations between plantation owners (landlords) and plantation laborers (freed men and women tenant farmers) resulted in the development and growth of widespread sharecropping, debt peonage, and summary dismissal from the plantation, all of which were impossible in the slave mode of production (Fields 1982, 1983). Tenants found themselves in situations similar in magnitude, but different in content, from those of slavery. Rather than being faced with bondage, former members of the slave mode of production were faced with terrorism, poor educational opportunities, usurious rates of credit, discrimination, and racism. In response, tenants fled into large cities or formed short-lived tenant farmer unions and staged occasional strikes (Grubbs 1971; Schwartz 1976).

This brief summary suggests that the life of a plantation, in both antebellum and postbellum times, was composed of a complex network of interconnected social fields that existed in specific time and space. These historical social formations created and structured the plantation.

Conclusion

The application of South's pattern concept to plantations oversimplifies these important social relations by substituting a less exact and impressionistic synchronic, whole-cultural pattern analysis. Although one might reasonably argue that some measure of synchronic analysis is inherent in all archaeological research, given the inanimate nature of the primary data, South's pattern concept provides overwhelmingly for synchronic study. When he fails to introduce any semblance of cultural change among his hypothetical middle-class laborers, he condemns them to a synchronous existence in a world devoid of change. Thus, in Lesser's (1961) terms, this laborer maintains no "weblike, netlike connections" with surrounding Native Americans, Afro-Americans, and other European colonists, but is rather only part of an "isolated, closed social unit." In other words, by adopting the view that colonization is merely a geographically extended expression of Kroeber's whole-cultural pattern, South does not elucidate the social relations of colonial life in North America. His analytical units do not account for the association between social relations and material items, but merely the relations between the inert items themselves as secondary reflections of whole-cultural, pulsating stylistic behavior. Ironically, then, his patterns do exactly what Boas' historical particularism did: provide a mass of interesting data that in the long run will not contribute to any unified theme (Harris 1968:314). As long as archaeologists continue to devise specific "patterns" for particular sites, or kinds of sites, an unconnected catalog of worldwide patterns will result. Although South (1988a, 1988b) argues that this was not his original intention, this has been the practical legacy of his pattern concept.

When plantation archaeologists devise whole-cultural patterns they similarly ignore the complexities of plantations and, through the construction of regional or subregional artifact patterns, ignore plantation social relations. Given the economic orientation of plantations, one primary social network revolved around occupation (Olson 1983; Orser 1988a). This important organizing principle of modes of plantation production cannot be understood with a whole-culture approach.

In place of South's whole-culture pattern concept, archaeologists must adopt a different perspective. This perspective should be constructed around the following precepts (Larrain 1986:121–22):

1. Society is not merely a collection of individuals, but a set of relations;
2. To understand social relations, one must first of all examine the way in which individuals transform nature during the process of production;
3. Society and production must be studied as historical forms; and
4. A clue to the historical analysis of society appears in the mode of production concept.

Thus, what is really important in the study of plantations is not whether slaves were members of whole cultures, but how they were incorporated into, worked within, and struggled against the slave mode of production. This is not to say that studies of slave communities or the retention of African traits by slaves are insignificant, but only that these studies do not necessarily inform plantation issues, even though in some case they in fact may do so. That all slaves were members of a whole-culture is a given. It must be kept in mind, however, that black slave masters and plantation owners were members of the same whole-culture

as their slaves, but that their collective position in the mode of production was vastly different. The interesting questions, then, concern the social relations these black masters had with their slaves, not whether they produced artifact patterns that reflect their whole cultures. Historical research suggests that black master-black slave relations were not based on whole-cultural characteristics, but that black masters held slaves "to exploit them, to profit from them, just as white slaveholders did" (Johnson and Roark 1984:141). These relations were clearly based on the slave mode of production. Using different terms, the same statements can be made about postbellum plantation tenant farmers.

Using historical records and archaeological evidence, historical archaeologists can devise concepts and ideas about the changing nature of plantation relations in historical terms without relying on South's vague evolutionary statements or on his whole-cultural patterns. Once these relations are understood, artifact classes can be created that directly address their attendant modes of production (for a postbellum example, see Orser 1988b). These empirical representations will not be universal; they will not be represented in every case by the relative proportions of "kitchen," "architecture," and "clothing" artifacts, for, to paraphrase Kroeber's (1948:311–12) criticism of Wissler's universal pattern, all peoples in North America had kitchen, architecture, and clothing objects. The key is not to determine the proportions of the same items at all sites; the key is to understand how these artifacts were used in class formation, class struggle, alienation, and social change within the dominant mode of production.

ACKNOWLEDGMENTS

I am grateful for the insightful comments and useful ideas offered by William Adams, David Babson, Philip L. Kohl, Mark Leone, William Marquardt, Michael O'Brien, and Stanley South. Their careful comments on an earlier draft significantly improved my presentation and forced me to rethink certain positions. I also appreciate the assistance of and careful reading by my wife, Janice. The ideas expressed are mine alone and I take full responsibility for them.

REFERENCES

APTHEKER, HERBERT
1964 Negro Slave Revolts in the United States, 1526–1860. In *Essays in the History of the American Negro*, by Herbert Aptheker, pp. 1–70. International Press, New York.
1968 Slave Guerrilla Warfare. In *To Be Free: Studies in American Negro History*, by Herbert Aptheker, pp. 11–30. International Press, New York.

BENEDICT, RUTH
1934 *Patterns of Culture*. Houghton Mifflin, Boston.

BLASSINGAME, JOHN W.
1976 Status and Social Structure in the Slave Community: Evidence from New Sources. In *Perspectives and Irony in American Slavery*, edited by Harry P. Owens, pp. 137–51. University Press of Mississippi, Jackson.
1979 *The Slave Community: Plantation Life in the Antebellum South*. Revised and enlarged ed. Oxford University Press, New York.

BREEDEN, JAMES O. (EDITOR)
1980 *Advice Among Masters: The Ideal in Slave Management in the Old South*. Greenwood, Westport, CT.

BROCKINGTON, PAUL, MICHAEL SCARDAVILLE, PATRICK H. GARROW, DAVID SINGER, LINDA FRANCE, AND CHERYL HOLT
1985 *Rural Settlement in the Charleston Bay Area: Eighteenth and Nineteenth Century Sites in the Mark Clark Expressway Corridor*. South Carolina Department of Highways and Public Transportation, Columbia.

COHEN, G. A.
1978 *Karl Marx's Theory of History: A Defense*. Princeton University Press, Princeton.

COPANS, JEAN AND DAVID SEDDON
1978 Marxism and Anthropology: A Preliminary Survey. In: *Relations of Production: Marxist Approaches to Economic Anthropology*, edited by David Seddon, pp. 1–46. Frank Cass and Company, London.

CORDELL, LINDA S.
1981 Academic Press Publications in Archaeology. *American Antiquity* 46:446–54.

DRUCKER, LESLEY M.
1981 Socioeconomic Patterning of an Undocumented Late 18th Century Lowcountry Site: Spiers Landing, South Carolina. *Historical Archaeology* 15(2):58–68.

FIELDS, BARBARA J.
1982 Ideology and Race in American History. In *Region, Race, and Reconstruction: Essays in Honor of C. Vann Woodward*, edited by J. Morgan Kousser and James M. McPherson, pp. 143–177. Oxford University Press, New York.
1983 The Nineteenth-Century American South: History and Theory. *Plantation Society in the Americas* 2:7–27.

GARROW, PATRICK H. (EDITOR)
1982 *Archaeological Investigations of the Washington, D.C., Civic Center Site*. Department of Housing and Community Development, Washington, D.C.

GENOVESE, EUGENE D.
1974 *Roll, Jordan, Roll: The World the Slaves Made*. Pantheon, New York.
1979 *From Rebellion to Revolution: Afro-American Slave Revolts in the Making of the Modern World*. Louisiana State University Press, Baton Rouge.

GIBBON, GUY
1984 *Anthropological Archaeology*. Columbia University Press, New York.

GRUBBS, DONALD H.
1971 *Cry from the Cotton: The Southern Tenant Farmers' Union and the New Deal*. University of North Carolina Press, Chapel Hill.

HARRIS, MARVIN
1968 *The Rise of Anthropological Theory: A History of Theories of Culture*. Thomas Y. Crowell, New York.
1980 *Cultural Materialism: The Struggle for a Science of Culture*. Vintage Books, New York.

HIMMELWEIT, SUSAN
1983 Mode of Production. In: *A Dictionary of Marxist Thought*, edited by Tom Bottomore, pp. 335–37. Harvard University Press, Cambridge.

HINDESS, BARRY AND PAUL Q. HIRST
1975 *Pre-Capitalist Modes of Production*. Routledge and Kegan Paul, London.

JOHNSON, MICHAEL P. AND JAMES L. ROARK
1984 *Black Masters: A Free Family of Color in the Old South*. W. W. Norton, New York.

KEMENY, JOHN G.
1959 *A Philosopher Looks at Science*. D. Van Nostrand Company, Princeton, NJ.

KROEBER, A. L.
1917 The Superorganic. *American Anthropologist* 19:163–213.
1919 On the Principle of Order in Civilization as Exemplified by Changes in Fashion. *American Anthropologist* 21:235–63.
1946 History and Evolution. *Southwestern Journal of Anthropology* 2:1–15.
1948 *Anthropology*. Harcourt, Brace, and Company, New York.
1960 Evolution, History, and Culture. In: *Evolution After Darwin, Volume II, The Evolution of Man: Man, Culture, and Society*, edited by Sol Tax, pp. 1–16. University of Chicago Press, Chicago.
1966 *An Anthropologist Looks at History*. Edited by Theodora Kroeber. University of California Press, Berkeley.

LAIBMAN, DAVID
  1984 Modes of Production and Theories of Transition. *Science and Society* 48:257–94.

LARRAIN, JORGE
  1986 *A Reconstruction of Historical Materialism.* Allen and Unwin, London.

LESSER, ALEXANDER
  1939 Research Procedure and the Laws of Culture. *Philosophy of Science* 6:345–55.
  1961 Social Fields and the Evolution of Society. *Southwestern Journal of Anthropology* 17:40–48.

LEWIS, LYNNE G.
  1985 The Planter Class: The Archaeological Record at Drayton Hall. In *The Archaeology of Slavery and Plantation Life*, edited by Theresa A. Singleton, pp. 121–40. Academic Press, Orlando.

LITTLE, DANIEL
  1986 *The Scientific Marx.* University of Minnesota Press, Minneapolis.

LOWIE, ROBERT H.
  1929 *Culture and Ethnology.* Peter Smith, New York.
  1936 Cultural Anthropology: A Science. *American Journal of Sociology* 42:301–20.
  1946 Evolution in Cultural Anthropology: A Reply to Leslie White. *American Anthropologist* 48:223–33.

MALINOWSKI, BRONISLAW
  1927 The Life of Culture. In: *Culture: The Diffusion Controversy* by G. Elliott Smith, Bronislaw Malinowski, Herbert J. Spinden, and Alexander Goldenweiser, pp. 26–46. W. W. Norton, New York.
  1939 The Group and the Individual in Functional Analysis. *The American Journal of Sociology* 44:938–64.
  1944a *A Scientific Theory of Culture and Other Essays.* University of North Carolina Press, Chapel Hill.
  1944b *Freedom and Civilization.* Roy Publishers, New York.

MARQUARDT, WILLIAM H.
  1985 Complexity and Scale in the Study of Fisher-Gatherer-Hunters: An Example from the Eastern United States. In: *Prehistoric Hunter-Gatherers: The Emergence of Cultural Complexity*, edited by T. Douglas Price and James A. Brown, pp. 59–98. Academic Press, Orlando.

MARQUARDT, WILLIAM H. AND CAROLE L. CRUMLEY
  1987 Theoretical Issues in the Analysis of Spatial Patterning. In: *Regional Dynamics: Burgundian Landscapes in Historical Perspectives*, edited by Carole L. Crumley and William H. Marquardt, pp. 1–18. Academic Press, San Diego.

MARX, KARL
  1967 *Capital: A Critique of Political Economy.* 3 vols. International Publishers, New York.

MARX, KARL AND FREDERICK ENGELS
  1937 *The Civil War in the United States.* Edited by Richard Enmale. International Publishers, New York.

MOORE, SUE MULLINS
  1981 *An Antebellum Barrier Island Plantation: In Search of an Archaeological Pattern.* Ph. D. dissertation, University of Florida. University Microfilms, Ann Arbor.
  1985 Social and Economic Status on the Coastal Plantation: An Archaeological Perspective. In *The Archaeology of Slavery and Plantation Life*, edited by Theresa A. Singleton, pp. 141–60. Academic Press, Orlando.

MORGAN, LEWIS H.
  1877 *Ancient Society.* Henry Holt and Company, New York.

NOWAK, LESZEK
  1983 *Property and Power: Towards a Non-Marxian Historical Materialism.* D. Reidel Publishing Company, Dordrecht, Holland.

OLSON, JOHN FREDERIC
  1983 *The Occupational Structure of Plantation Slave Labor in the Late Antebellum Era.* Ph.D. dissertation, University of Rochester. University Microfilms, Ann Arbor.

ORSER, CHARLES E., JR.
  1986 The Archaeological Recognition of the Squad System on Postbellum Cotton Plantations. *Southeastern Archaeology* 5:11–20.
  1987 Plantation Status and Consumer Choice: A Materialist Framework for Historical Archaeology. In: *Consumer Choice in Historical Archaeology*, edited by Suzanne M. Spencer-Wood, pp. 121–37. Plenum Press, New York.
  1988a The Archaeological Analysis of Plantation Society: Replacing Status and Caste with Economics and Power. *American Antiquity*, 53:735–751.
  1988b *The Material Basis of the Postbellum Tenant Plantation: Historical Archaeology in the South Carolina Piedmont.* University of Georgia Press, Athens.

PRICE, BARBARA J.
  1980 The Truth is Not in Accounts but in Account Books: On the Epistemological Status of History. In *Beyond the Myths of Culture: Essays in Cultural Materialism*, edited by Eric B. Ross, pp. 155–80. Academic Press, New York.

RADCLIFFE-BROWN, A. R.
  1952 *Structure and Function in Primitive Society: Essays and Addresses.* The Free Press of Glencoe, New York.

RAWICK, GEORGE P.
  1972 *From Sundown to Sunup: The Making of the Black Community.* Greenwood, Westport, CT.

RESNICK, STEPHEN AND RICHARD D. WOLFF
  1982 Classes in Marxian Theory. *The Review of Radical Political Economics* 13(4):1–18.

RICHARDSON, JANE AND A. L. KROEBER
    1940 Three Centuries of Women's Dress Fashions: A Quan-
          titative Analysis. *University of California Publica-
          tions in Anthropological Records* 5(2):111–53.

SCHWARTZ, MICHAEL
    1976 *Radical Protest and Social Structure: The Southern
          Farmer's Alliance and Cotton Tenancy, 1880–1890.*
          Academic Press, New York.

SINGLETON, THERESA A.
    1980 *The Archaeology of Afro-American Slavery in Coastal
          Georgia: A Regional Perception of Slave Household
          and Community Patterns.* Ph. D. dissertation, Univer-
          sity of Florida. University Microfilms, Ann Arbor.

SOUTH, STANLEY
    1955 Evolutionary Theory in Archaeology. *Southern Indian
          Studies* 7:10–32.
    1972 Evolution and Horizon as Revealed in Ceramic Anal-
          ysis in Historical Archaeology. *The Conference on
          Historic Site Archaeology Papers* 6:71–116.
    1974 *Palmetto Parapets: Exploratory Archaeology at Fort
          Moultrie, South Carolina, 38CH50.* Anthropological
          Studies 1, Institute of Archaeology and Anthropol-
          ogy, University of South Carolina, Columbia.
    1977 *Method and Theory in Historical Archaeology.* Aca-
          demic Press, New York.
    1978 Pattern Recognition in Historical Archaeology. *Amer-
          ican Antiquity* 43:223–30.
    1979 Historic Site Content, Structure, and Function. *Amer-
          ican Antiquity* 44:213–37.
    1988a Santa Elena: Threshold of Conquest. In *The Recovery
          of Meaning: Historical Archaeology in the Eastern
          United States,* edited by Mark P. Leone and Parker B.
          Potter, Jr., pp. 27–71. Smithsonian Institution Press,
          Washington.
    1988b Whither Pattern? *Historical Archaeology* 22(1):25–
          28.

STEVENSON, MARC G.
    1983 Pattern in Pattern Recognition? *The Conference on
          Historic Site Archaeology Papers* 15:57–70.

STEWARD, JULIAN H.
    1955 *Theory of Culture Change: The Methodology of Mul-
          tilinear Evolution.* University of Illinois Press, Ur-
          bana.

TRINKLEY, MICHAEL AND OLGA M. CABALLERO
    1983 *An Archaeological and Historical Evaluation of the
          I-85 Northern Alternative, Spartanburg County,
          South Carolina.* South Carolina Department of High-
          ways and Public Transportation, Columbia.

TURNBAUGH, SARAH PEABODY
    1979 The Seriation of Fashion. *Home Economics Research
          Journal* 7:241–48.

VOGET, FRED W.
    1975 *A History of Ethnology.* Holt, Rinehart, and Winston,
          New York.

WARFEL, STEPHEN G.
    1982 A Critical Analysis and Test of Stanley South's
          Artifact Patterns. *The Conference on Historic Site
          Archaeology Papers* 14:137–90.

WHEATON, THOMAS R., AMY FRIEDLANDER, AND
PATRICK H. GARROW
    1983 *Yaughan and Curriboo Plantations: Studies in Afro-
          American Archaeology.* Archaeological Services
          Branch, National Park Service, Atlanta.

WHEATON, THOMAS R. AND PATRICK H. GARROW
    1985 Acculturation and the Archaeological Record in the
          Carolina Lowcountry. In *The Archaeology of Slavery
          and Plantation Life,* edited by Theresa A. Singleton,
          pp. 239–59. Academic Press, Orlando.

WILLEY, GORDON R. AND PHILIP PHILLIPS
    1955 Method and Theory in American Archaeology II:
          Historical-Developmental Interpretation. *American
          Antiquity* 57:723–819.

WISSLER, CLARK
    1923 *Man and Culture.* Thomas Y. Crowell, New York.

WOLF, ERIC R.
    1981 The Mills of Inequality: A Marxian Approach. In:
          *Social Inequality: Comparative and Developmental
          Approaches,* edited by Gerald D. Berreman, pp.
          41–57. Academic Press, New York.
    1982 *Europe and the People Without History.* University of
          California Press, Berkeley.
    1984 Culture: Panacea or Problem? *American Antiquity*
          49:393–400.

ZIERDEN, MARTHA AND JEANNE CALHOUN
    1983 *An Archaeological Assessment of the Greenfield Bor-
          row Pit, Georgetown County.* Archaeological Contri-
          butions 4, The Charleston Museum, Charleston,
          South Carolina.

CHARLES E. ORSER, JR.
MIDWESTERN ARCHAEOLOGICAL RESEARCH CENTER
ILLINOIS STATE UNIVERSITY
NORMAL, ILLINOIS 61761

JEAN E. HOWSON

Social Relations and Material Culture: A Critique of the Archaeology of Plantation Slavery

Introduction

The archaeology of southern plantations promises to provide new data about slave life. This is most welcome, but like all sets of data—whether historical, anthropological, or archaeological, archaeological data require analysis and interpretation before becoming important or even useful. It is well to pause periodically and assess the links between methods of analysis and the theories which shape archaeological interpretations.

The way archaeologists think about the relationship of material remains to slave societies will—and should—shift in response to changing ideas about slave culture and about culture change in general. Plantation archaeology is currently undergoing a shift: (1) like historians, archaeologists are coming to view the culture of slaves as a key to understanding social structure and its transformation in the plantation South; (2) the meaning of the African heritage is being explored critically; (3) material culture studies are beginning to help in addressing questions about meaningful cultural categories and social change; and (4) a social action approach is replacing a status model of plantation social relations. All of these reflect, perhaps belatedly, the development of social theory in which culture is viewed in terms of a dynamic relationship between structure and practice, and symbols are analyzed in contexts of action. A critical approach to the relevant theoretical issues hopefully will be part of the new direction in which plantation archaeology is beginning to move.

This brief examination of the archaeology of plantation slavery reviews some of the dangers into which archaeologists have already fallen and offers

suggestions for enhancing the theoretical underpinnings of archaeological work. First, a look at the use of cultural markers points up the need for a more sophisticated approach to the issue of culture change. Next is an exploration of the ways in which interpretations of material culture can be enriched through a more dynamic understanding of context. Finally, the usefulness of status definitions for modeling plantation social relations is assessed. To begin, a discussion of the relation between historical archaeology and the discipline of history brings out a curious fact: most archaeologists' notions about the purpose of history have hindered the participation of historical archaeology in some of the most interesting debates in the historiography of American slavery, centering on the meaning of slave culture.

History and Historical Archaeology: The Search for Africa in Slave Culture and the Problem of Acculturation

As historians of slavery have turned their attention to questions of culture, providing an important bridge to anthropological archaeology, archaeologists must be aware of historiographic issues and develop a critical approach to the broader arguments. Critical reading of the work of historians over the past 15 years (e.g., Genovese 1974; Gutman 1976; Mintz and Price 1976; Levine 1977; Blassingame 1979; Joyner 1984; Sobel 1987; Stuckey 1987; Fox-Genovese 1988) points out both how fruitful the cultural approach to history can be and the variation in orientation possible within the culturalist framework. Archaeologists for the most part still tend to turn to history for "the facts," confining their historiographic critique to a discussion of how "good" the documents are for specific purposes. History is often seen as a set of givens which provide background for archaeological research; at best, documentary research provides a complementary body of data which can promote constructive feedback between the disciplines (Deetz 1988:363; Salwen 1988; Schuyler 1988). But the historiography of slavery surely stands as one of the outstanding examples of how complex theoretical issues underlie scholarly historical research (e.g., Fox-Genovese and Genovese 1983a:136–171). History is not an established sequence of events, nor is it an existing explanatory structure just waiting to be filled in with more data, some documentary, some archaeological. Many archaeologists—especially those in public archaeology—applaud the interdisciplinary approach of historical archaeology, but what they are really extolling is the benefit they derive from having trained historians on the job to supply the facts about people, places, and things. If "the gap between history and anthropology appears to be closing in plantation archaeology" (Orser 1984: 3), it is more a by-product of the fact that people trained in anthropology are being forced to draw on historical research methods than a move toward interdisciplinary theory-building.

Turning to a concrete example, a potentially wasteful direction for archaeological research may be avoided by adopting a more sophisticated approach to the place of African roots in slave society. Just as social anthropologists went through a period of searching for tangible remnants of true African culture—or "survivals" or "retentions"—in African-Caribbean and African-American culture (Herskovits 1941; Mintz and Price 1976), historical archaeologists were for a time concerned with finding a visibly African style in the material remains they unearthed. Because archaeologists did not find many clear stylistic markers, they have had to be more subtle in their analyses in order to *make* materially visible the African component in the material remains of slaves. The focus recently among many researchers has been on finding an African-American "pattern" in the material record (e.g., Singleton 1980; Wheaton et al. 1983; Armstrong 1985), but others still seek tangible evidence of stylistic continuity. Leland Ferguson's (1989) study of pottery marks and Matthew Emerson's (1988) work on clay pipes are perhaps the best examples of the latter approach and demonstrate that African stylistic elements could survive in material culture as submerged indicators of belief systems or in a syncretic alliance with European style.

What is not always explicitly recognized by archaeologists is that the study of "Africanisms" is a politically significant and highly charged issue; for a brief review see Watson (1978). Important debates in linguistics, folklore, art and architecture, family and kinship studies, sociology, economics, and every other field relating to black America have centered on the question of cultural roots. But while it is beyond doubt that African culture did survive in many important ways under slavery and played an immense role in the forging of a new and viable society among slaves, sorting this sense of an African tradition out from the equally important constraints of slavery is no simple matter. For one thing, the very diversity of African societies from which slaves came needs to be taken into account from the start (Posnansky 1989). This diversity had a profound affect on the cultural transformation that took place in the plantation societies of the Western hemisphere.

A seminal essay argues that, given the diversity of African cultures and the process of adaptation necessary in the New World setting, archaeologists need to look for continuities at the level of underlying assumptions and structure:

> Those deep-level cultural principles, assumptions and understandings which were shared by the Africans in any New World Colony—who tended to be a tribally heterogeneous aggregate of individuals—would have represented a limited though crucial resource. For they could have served as a catalyst in the processes by which individuals from diverse societies forged new institutions, and could have provided certain frameworks within which new forms could have developed (Mintz and Price 1976:7).

The notion of transformational principles which lay beneath the "creolization" process has proven useful to historians, as well:

> Changes in other aspects of culture were akin to the transformation in [Gullah] language. Implicit but pervasive grammatical principles of culture lay behind the transformation of slave folklife in all its various manifestations. It is axiomatic that any people must build their response to the challenges and demands of a new environment out of the materials at hand. But those materials are put together in the manner they perceive to be most appropriate to the situation. The response may be in itself innovative—the creation of a new language, a new house-type, or new folktales—but the perception of appropriateness is cultural. Traditional notions of appropriateness in work and worship,

in feeling, thinking, and living—notions . . . influence the cultural choices forced by new conditions (Joyner 1984: 237).

Care should be taken in such an approach, however, not to imply a uniform understanding of "appropriateness" among African Americans. Culture is not a uniform thing in the first place, and the diversity of African origins meant that variation was a particularly essential aspect of culture in slave societies. The relation between *variation* and *change* has been central in analyses of creole language, and the extension of a creolization model to all of culture should incorporate a concept of variation as a locus of change (Drummond 1980; Le-Page and Tabouret-Keller 1985). Mintz and Price (1976:7) themselves are actually cautious about just how much weight can be given to a shared cultural "grammar" given a context of rapid change, stating that, "The probable importance of such generalized principles notwithstanding, the Africans in any New World colony in fact became a community and began to share a culture only insofar as, and as fast as, they themselves created them."

Although others would consider them overly cautious about tangible African "survivals" (e.g., Braithwaite 1971; Sobel 1987), Mintz and Price are certainly correct in pointing out that *traits do not equal culture,* and that even the act of reconstituting African cultural forms in the New World plantation setting implied creative transformation. Herbert Gutman (1976:260), who was influenced by Mintz, also argues in his study of the black family that African-American beliefs, even given African roots, had to be sustained by cultural forms and institutional arrangements which developed over time within slavery. But the "problem" of slave culture remains: The building of an African-American community with its own culture involved the development of traditions of practice within a day-to-day existence conditioned unavoidably by the fact of enslavement itself. Eugene Genovese (1974) thus chooses a model of class conflict and focuses on the role of the master-slave relationship in the development of black culture under slavery. All of these authors recognize the political significance of slave culture.

Given the foregoing, plantation archaeologists address some fairly central social and historical issues whenever they explore issues of "Africanism" and "acculturation." Simplistic notions of culture change will not work when applied to material culture any more than to belief systems or social structure. Reliance on cultural markers—specific material traits which archaeologists can discern—in reconstructing so-called "acculturation" sequences not only is dangerous in terms of over-simplifying the role of "Africanisms," but also is naive about the role of material culture. Material evidence about slave life on the plantations should be analyzed within a theoretical framework in which *both* change and continuity, at various times and in various contexts, embodied the process of cultural and political struggle of African Americans.

The study of slave-produced ceramics provides a good example of the "cultural marker" approach. A great deal has been said about these artifacts (Ferguson 1978; Lees and Kimery-Lees 1979; Anthony 1979; Deetz 1988), and no review is attempted here; however, a study published by Wheaton, Friedlander, and Garrow (1983)—see also Friedlander (1985) and Wheaton and Garrow (1985)—on South Carolina plantation sites points out the complexities in the interpretation of "Africanisms" and their relation to "acculturation." These authors are sensitive to the fact that slaves' material culture was restricted by slaveholders, and they have chosen to study foodways because this intimate aspect of slave life is less likely to reflect direct coercion from above. They present "a chain of data . . . which tends to link Colono with colonowares in other regions of the east coast, and to the Caribbean Islands and possibly to Africa" and conclude that "Colono and colonoware may be the most African 'Africanism' to appear on slave sites and as such the single most useful artifact for studying slave acculturation" (Wheaton et al. 1983:335). (As an aside, Wheaton, Friedlander, and Garrow mis-cite Handler and Lange as stating "that as Barbadian slaves became more acculturated the African attributes in their pottery disappeared" [Wheaton et al. 1983:335]. No such sequence was revealed for Barbados, nor is "acculturation" mentioned. Rather, and importantly, Handler and Lange [1978:144] discuss specific historical, geographic, and "industrial" factors which affected the slave manufacture of ceramics.)

The acculturation model posits a gradual process of adapting to European-American ways with concurrent loss of African traits. The hypothesis of these researchers (Wheaton et al. 1983) is that the observed decrease in Colono ceramics was due not simply to availability of European wares but to the changing attitude of slaves toward those items—in other words, the cultural identity of slaves was being transformed. But the development of their argument involves a specific historical sequence:

> [The] data . . . showed a clear increase in the nonlocal ceramics and a decrease in Colono from 1740 to 1825. . . . Reasons for this trend were hypothesized to have been an increase in the slave population, a resident owner at Yaughan, and intensification of agricultural activity which caused greater regimentation to be imposed on the slaves and allowed them less free time to pursue individual craft activities. Perhaps the most important reason for this trend was acculturation of the slaves themselves (Wheaton et al. 1983:343).

The "most important" reason for the decline of Colono ceramics may never be known. Significantly, these authors have chosen to see the decline in terms of cultural change rather than as a function of the trans-Atlantic trade and economic conditions in the Old South (see Lees and Kimery-Lees 1979). But by abstracting this change from the context of power within which it occurred, they have obscured rather than clarified the nature of the process. Acculturation is an inaccurate, passive model for a dynamic process: the creation of a community and shared culture among slaves in the context of their struggle against an oppressive system, a system with styles of domination and resistance shaped by specific relations of production. The whole concept of acculturation rests on an inadequate definition of culture, one which emphasizes complexes of traits rather than peoples' ongoing interpretation, evaluation, and creative response, the strategies and symbolic revaluing that form the basis of cultural process. The acculturation model was developed in the context of the anthropological study of Native American groups,

and some of the best criticism of the model comes from Americanists; see especially Fowler (1987).

Wheaton, Friedlander, and Garrow adopt an interdisciplinary approach at the outset of their research (Friedlander 1985:217). The ahistorical model which they develop is not a function of any lack of historical information, which is amply provided, but rather the result of the kinds of a priori assumptions about culture change which most archaeologists adopt. Their argument rests on the idea that slave-owner interaction is a *demographic* issue (Friedlander 1985), that somehow the degree of contact between the two is the crux of the matter and has determined the course of culture change. This position is a troubling notion akin to the idea that social structure in itself determines the meaningful content of social action. The approach corresponds to the mistaken archaeological notion that the meaning of things somehow can be construed directly from frequency distributions (Wheaton and Garrow 1985:253). As these authors are no doubt aware, the forces behind culture change were not demographic but had to do with the kinds of social interaction—among slaves and between slaves and free whites—that developed in slave societies.

Others also are aware that master-slave relations played a part in determining African cultural continuity:

> Despite the apparent persistence of certain African architectural traits, most planters openly discouraged African style huts on their plantations. . . . Thus, the more intimate expressions of tidewater slave life—which were either overlooked by plantation whites *or were hidden from their view*—often contained vestiges of the African cultural past: these included cookery, speech, stories, sorcery, basketry, quilting, the carving of figurines and walking sticks, and dance forms . . . intangible words, behaviors, or artifacts that were fashioned from perishable wood and fiber [emphasis added] (Otto 1984:43,87).

Like Wheaton, Friedlander, and Garrow, Otto recognizes that power was exercised over slaves in terms of cultural style. What kind of power was this, and how did it operate? *Why* did slaves have to hide their cultural expression? Otto addresses this question for workplace contexts:

> The plantation whites were most concerned that slaves acquire the appropriate standards of speech and behavior

that would allow them to perform their agricultural, skilled, and service roles. In the work context, there was much interaction between blacks and white supervisors, and the domestic servants, in particular, were under the close scrutiny of whites. Therefore, the slave operating cultures in the white-dominated work contexts would have shown conformity to white American standards (Otto 1984:86).

The "more intimate" lives of slaves, it can be argued, also were subject to pressure from above, all the more reason for slaves to hide as much as they could. That pressure stemmed from the masters' fear, from their understanding that cultural expressions are not harmless, and from their ideology of paternalism. As Genovese (1974) has so well understood, paternalism was an invasive policy. The problem of cultural hegemony and the debate over the "paternalistic compromise" needs to be addressed in examining the significance of African style—if only because Genovese has brought Gramsci's concept to bear on slave studies and created heated controversy in so doing (see criticisms by Anderson 1976; Wilson 1976; Johnson 1978:91). But in each specific case the question remains as to whether, how, and to what extent pressures on slave culture penetrated and were resisted—surely a pertinent question in the study of material culture.

Historical archaeologists have a tendency to confuse behavior with culture. Particularly disturbing are comments such as J. W. Joseph's (1989:64) suggestion that "more diligent supervision may have inspired more rapid acculturation" on the part of slaves housed along orderly streets. "Acculturation" is not an appropriate or accurate way to describe slave response to "diligent supervision." Culture change is rarely a simple response to coercion; behavior can be coerced, not culture. Cultural continuity is not simply the residue surviving in the interstices of imposed change. Change and continuity characterize all cultural systems and can be evaluated only insofar as archaeologists understand specific historical contexts and the social relations that obtained in those contexts. It is the political content of cultural style that is lost when archaeologists adopt an acculturation model.

The search for African style misses a crucial point about the nature of slavery, having to do with relations between classes, not with forms of culture contact or the contact of cultural forms. What has been called "acculturation" was a question of power in the broadest sense. Thus, resistance, rather than mere conservatism or continuity, may be the relevant context within which to view expressions of separate cultural style on the part of slaves. Perhaps "separatism" is a better concept than "persistence" or "continuity," because it does not exclude transformations, is interactive, and has more political force than "boundary maintenance." At the same time, culture change within the slave community which can be "demonstrated" archaeologically or otherwise is not necessarily an indicator of acculturation, except insofar as the material idiom of the political battle had shifted.

Wheaton, Friedlander, and Garrow (1983) are not alone in neglecting the political aspects of culture change, and the conceptual muddiness inherent in an acculturation model has not cleared. The model continues to lead to rather unfortunate interpretations and has been misapplied in an approach which sees change as bidirectional. In a recent example, Joseph (1989) has written an otherwise useful article which picks up on the contrast between plantations studied in South Carolina and Georgia first pointed out by Theresa Singleton (1985a:7). Differences in agricultural region, research design, and excavation strategy can account for some of the variations in "artifact pattern" that have been discerned, but time period is also shown to determine which pattern applies. Joseph suggests this reflects real culture change between the 18th and 19th centuries. Instead of seeing this change as one way, he argues that slaves and masters alike "acculturated" on the plantations. Other archaeologists probably will be attracted to a bidirectional model, even though it represents an incorrect use of the term acculturation and is a potential way of sidestepping the important issues. (Acculturation, in its classic formulation, meant the gradual loss of indigenous culture traits and assimilation to white European-American culture [see Linton 1940; Spicer 1961]. Archaeologists subsequently adapted the concept for use in classifying material culture in terms of degrees of acculturation. The model is unidirectional in any case.)

Joseph (1989:64–65) suggests that whites realized "by the 19th century" that slaves were humans, became concerned with slave health when the slave trade was cut off, came to view their chattels differently, and thus were "acculturated." There can be little doubt that masters recognized the humanity of their slaves all along, and it also seems clear that the strongest racist ideologies developed alongside 19th-century paternalist policies, while mutual cultural exchange was particularly marked in the 18th century (Sobel 1987). The argument that acculturation on the part of masters "fostered an improved, and also more Anglo American, material culture for 19th-century slaves" (Joseph 1989:65) cannot stand close scrutiny. An argument for the changing perceptions of slaveholders, however, can in fact be made, not on the basis of their recognition of slaves' humanity and the need for a self-reproducing labor force, but on entirely different grounds: Slaves had so staunchly fought for and defended their customary rights, and through slaves' efforts, the patterns of material exchanges between them and their masters had become so entrenched, that the perceptions of the masters came to include many "taken-for-granteds" brought about through this interaction. Whether this is labeled a "paternalistic compromise"—after Genovese (1979)—or not, at its core is the struggle between slaves and masters, *not* a shift between cultural models.

Attitudes toward time and work rhythms are another good example of the dialectic within which slave culture affected slaveowners' relations with their labor force—and hence the whole character of the southern economy—as well as vice versa (Genovese 1974:283–324; Joyner 1984:41–89; Sobel 1987:21–67). While plantation owners forced slaves to do specific kinds of harsh labor necessary to keep profits up, slaves took advantage of agricultural, season-, and crop-oriented rhythms, as well as community forms of labor, to create distinctive work patterns. This in turn reinforced the essentially rural and preindustrial character of a system highly resistant—in terms of culture as well as economics—to the type of change associated with capitalist production.

In rejecting the idea of slaves as passively acculturated, archaeologists must not merely rely on a simplistic argument that acculturation was a two-way street; the nature of the relationship between the two groups involved must remain central. In contact situations both cultures change, but surely New World slavery is a special case of "contact." The plantation clearly provided a special environment for intimate contact between bearers of African and white European-American culture, but at the same time it was the locus of profound class antagonisms between enslaved and free. Recent historical treatments reflect this dualism, and archaeologists can benefit from insights gained through different approaches. Mechal Sobel presents the Virginia masters' and slaves' "world they made together" as a product of cultural interaction, and often convergence, over the course of the 18th century. If Sobel seems to overlook too much of the political content of cultural interaction, she nevertheless provides an important addition to the history of plantation life and the necessary historical foundation for studies of the 19th century when "the social and emotional distance between whites and blacks grew" (Sobel 1987: 240). From Joyner's (1984) point of view, the distinctive life of the quarters underpinned a viable creolized slave culture which can be studied as a coherent whole on its own terms. To understand how slaves used the cultural space which they carved out for themselves is crucially important, but Joyner downplays the political, contested aspects of culture and the class-consciousness behind cultural distinctiveness. Focusing on the 19th century, Elizabeth Fox-Genovese (1988) sees the plantation "household" as a context for surface intimacy between mistresses and slaves, underlain by deep divisions and racist oppression. Like Genovese (1979), Fox-Genovese sees class and cultural identity as inextricably intertwined and conflict as the motor force behind social and cultural change on the plantations.

Archaeologists may find one of these approaches more appropriate to their data than the others, depending on the important variables of time and place, but change within the dominant class culture and within slave culture cannot be subsumed within a model of mutual acculturation. The imposed conjunction of class and race tended to over-determine all social relations, and the struggles within which African-American culture developed must be placed with this context of unequal interaction. At the same time, the fundamentally separatist aspect of slave culture is not obviated because slaves eventually lived in, used, wore, and ate European material goods. All cultures change as people actively create and respond to historical realities. What archaeologists should want to know is how the institution of slavery and the African heritage alike shaped the process by which African Americans made their world.

In sum, when historical archaeologists set out to "build a case for acculturation" (Wheaton and Garrow 1985:243), it is not clear whether they view it as an active *response* to oppression or as a *by-product* of culture contact. In any case, neither approach to culture change in the slave community is appropriate. These authors insist that material culture can be an index of change, but their notion of change is far too simplistic:

> The acculturation of the Afro-American slaves from an Afro-Caribbean (or West African, or Afro-Caribbean-American Colonial) cultural model within Yaughan and Curriboo plantations to a more Euro-American cultural model can be demonstrated through a study of architectural evidence, recovered artifacts, and subsistence data (Wheaton and Garrow 1985:243).

People do not shift from Cultural Model A to Cultural Model B, and if "acculturation" is to be used by plantation archaeologists in this way, the term should be discarded. Moreover, it would be difficult for material culture to "demonstrate" any such shift, for material things are imbedded in multiple contexts of behavior and meaning.

The Contexts of Material Culture

From the point of view of archaeology, material culture is at least quadruply imbedded—its past

involved contexts of production, distribution (including procurement, acquisition, exchange), use, and discard. Archaeologists working at plantation slave sites have too often erred in focusing on only one or at most two of these contexts. The interpretation of cultural remains depends upon the ability not only to reconstruct individual contexts, but to discern multiple and often ambiguous ones. Furthermore, archaeologists need to consider relationships between the relevant contexts for particular classes of artifacts.

A concentration on either distribution context or use context characterizes much plantation archaeology, including both Handler and Lange's (1978) study of a Barbadian cemetery and Otto's (1984) work at Cannon's Point Plantation. These researchers have advanced the interpretation of material remains, and their analyses make it abundantly clear that information about social life potentially can be gleaned from archaeological data. Their work also points to a next step in the analysis of material culture, however, which relates distribution to use in attempting to derive meaning. If the treatment of one specific artifact, clay pipes, is examined, the problem can be highlighted.

As an illustration of their ethnohistorical approach, Handler and Lange discuss their research into the reward/incentive system on the plantation. Documents were reexamined for information on artifacts recovered archaeologically, including clay pipes. Pipes and tobacco were among the material items used as "rewards" to slaves, and Handler and Lange

> began to suspect that the occurrence of particular artifacts . . . with interments may have been a manifestation of plantation rewards or incentives. As a result, the notes were more intensively reexamined, the presence of a reward-incentive system was established to a degree not previously understood, and the function of various archaeological materials as remnants of the system was inferred (Handler and Lange 1978:218).

If, however, the use context of clay tobacco pipes on slave plantations is examined, the interpretation can be richer and more pertinent to the study of slave life. As noted by archaeologists, pipe smoking was a very important "recreation" among slaves (Handler and Lange 1978; Otto 1984:91). The use of tobacco marked their leisure hours, their Sundays off, "their" time as opposed to their master's time (Genovese 1974:556; Joyner 1984:127–140). Smoking could also be a social activity, and social life within the quarter was the crucible of slaves' resistance, central to their survival and humanity. This means that even if the white owners on Barbados thought that the reward/incentive system created compliance, obedience, and status hierarchy among slaves—as well as social distance between slaves and paternalistic masters, the material and behavioral results of that system also may have furthered the social and cultural distinctiveness of slaves and made more obvious the existence of an alternative society to that envisioned by planters.

So when Handler and Lange find burials containing clay pipes, are they seeing evidence of a system meant to foster obedience through status-striving, or are they actually seeing evidence for a system of values among slaves that resulted in people being buried with the items that they enjoyed in daily life among their fellows and that represented membership in a community? It should be obvious that both are represented; the ambiguity is real. Lange and Handler (1985:26) in fact do suggest that the pipes buried with some Newton slaves had symbolic significance. The question is, from what social contexts did that significance derive? Many archaeologists have limited their interpretations by choosing to focus on factors of distribution, such as the common categories "imported" versus "local," and to neglect use context. Care should be taken not to assign social meaning to material remains without taking into account the ambiguous contexts which produced that meaning, because:

> Material symbols can be used covertly to disrupt established relations of dominance. . . . The 'power' of material symbols . . . resides also in the ambiguous meanings of material items. Unlike spoken language, the meanings of material symbols can remain undiscussed and implicit. Their meanings can be reinterpreted and manipulated covertly (Hodder 1983:10).

Otto's (1984:168–169) analysis of plantation material culture sets slaves' clay pipes against the cigars which were used by white owners and over-seers, a material pattern related to one kind of status difference between blacks and whites. This difference is said to reflect the "white dominance" pattern, a material reflection of the fact that whites of any bracket held higher racial-legal status than slaves. Otto focuses on the use context of pipes to derive this pattern but points out that slaves *acquired* these goods through purchase or trade in garden produce or livestock (Otto 1984: 71–80). (The subject of slaves' "internal economy" has received a great deal of recent attention among historians of the plantation South, though its importance has long been recognized in the Caribbean [Mintz and Hall 1960; McDonald 1981; Morgan 1982, 1983].) Distribution context is therefore at least as relevant as use context in this case. The ability of slaves to purchase and trade for "luxury" items places such goods firmly within a separate category. The pipes can hardly be said to "reflect" slaves' given subordinate status when they are the result of a clear bid for a degree of autonomy and an independent livelihood. Once again the struggle between slaves and owners, not their structural position, must be centralized. It can be argued that the internal economy was just another aspect of the slaves' exploitation to the extent that they were merely providing their own subsistence. The meaning of the system for its participants, however, could never have been determined solely through such an objective analysis. As Otto (1984:79–80) notes, planters fought to restrict slaves' trading activity; evidence that this was an area of contention should draw attention to the possible implications for the meaning of material goods at slave sites.

It would probably be possible to incorporate an analysis of acquisition context within Otto's formulation of status patterning since the boundary between slaves and whites was maintained, the line of "white dominance" drawn from above. But in identifying such a "pattern" it is necessary to focus on the *contrast* between the smoking habits of slaves and whites, thus obscuring the internal meaning of pipe smoking within slave culture. Likewise, overseers' material culture had an internal social meaning: The smoking habits of overseers would be more similar to planters than to slaves because it is the planters with whom they wished to identify socially, not because they were legally dominant over blacks. Here again, material culture theorists have urged caution against over-simplifying the processes of cultural categorization of the material world. Hodder (1983:9) notes that "the meaning of an object resides not merely in its contrast to others within a set. Meaning also de-rives from the associations and use of an object, which itself becomes, through the associations, the node of a network of references and implications. There is an interplay between structure and content," and Miller (1987:129) states, "The physicality of the artifact lends itself to the work of praxis—that is, cultural construction through ac-tion rather than just conceptualization." In other words, material objects are more than just a lan-guage of distinction between social groups. The contrast between cigars and clay pipes has to do with the meaningful contexts of their acquisition and use, not just with the structural relationship between whites and slaves. Just as the context of pipe acquisition was the struggle for a measure of autonomy, the social context of pipe smoking among slaves was the internal life of the slave quarter. The abstraction of a pattern has in this case meant the reduction of meaning.

If archaeologists have tended to isolate either use or distribution context, they have also failed to look for relationships between contexts. The study of slave diet illustrates this problem. It has been suggested that "one of the most promising areas of study" in regard to understanding "the archaeo-logical nature of plantation slavery in concrete, material terms" is the study of slave diet (Orser 1984:4). Many have shared this optimism, as an examination of the sections on diet in most studies of plantation sites demonstrates—see, however, a review of the evidence by Reitz (1987). But ar-chaeologists should also be interested in viewing food in less "concrete" and "material" terms.

Twenty years ago, Robert Ascher and Charles Fairbanks stated:

> People classify the food they eat in many ways. . . . From the point of view of the slave, a fundamental division was food distributed by the owner and food the slave supplied for himself. . . . With this knowledge, we abandon our usual categories and replace them with those meaningful to the people who interest us (Ascher and Fairbanks 1971:11).

Accepting this position, historical archaeologists classify food remains accordingly. This classifica-tion by production and procurement/acquisition contexts is an appropriate one, and analyses of diet that follow from it are equally so. But analysis of context should not stop here. It should be possible, with historical research, to relate use context—that is, consumption—to these other contexts when an-alyzing archaeological remains. Did consumption of slave-raised stock and produce or slave-collected wild foods take place at different times and on different social occasions than that of planter-provided fare? And what about stolen food? Were consumption patterns related solely to supply and the dictates of hunger and nutrition, or did the preparation, serving, and consumption of food have additional cultural significance in part *derived from* its means of acquisition?

A pattern is emerging regarding the co-option by slaves of items associated with or produced by their masters, to be given new meaning and new context within their own society. Much more research is required, perhaps, concerning the adoption by sub-ordinate classes of the cultural property of elites. This forms a part of the larger problem of culture change and the role of material culture in that pro-cess. The problem is particularly relevant in situ-ations of culture contact, colonialism, and slavery. It can be argued that what has recently been labeled "recontextualization" (D. Miller 1987) in fact has long been the central interpretive issue addressed by all American historical archaeology.

The role of material goods in maintaining and articulating social categories and relations—with consumption serving to establish, mark, or trans-form people's perceptions of themselves especially in relation to others—has been explored in detail (Douglas and Isherwood 1979), to which has been added a cross-cultural perspective (Appadurai 1986) which may be more attuned to the realities of slave society. The crossing of a cultural bound-ary between slaves and slaveholders by commod-ities may involve very shallow sets of shared val-ues (Appadurai 1986:14) yet result in considerable overlap in material goods. Moreover, it seems possible that different values nonetheless might be deliberately expressed through very similar, even identical, things, especially if one group perceives a commodity as having been diverted and hence its value enhanced or transformed. The flouting of implicit sumptuary laws on the part of slaves caused continual annoyance to white southerners, for instance. The supposed preference of slaves for stolen meat was, if anything, an example of this conscious revaluing. Arjun Appadurai (1986:26), in referring to theft as a form of commodity-diversion, illuminates its political implications. It does seem obvious that "theft" by slaves of their masters' goods was a political act. The pertinent question becomes, then, in what ways did the "paths" of commodities—in Appadurai's sense—determine their meanings to consumers?

What all of this means is that archaeologists must contextualize their data more fully. Hodder (1987) has conceived the method of "contextual analysis" as threefold: (1) to examine functional-environmental context; (2) to analyze material things structurally-semiotically, as in reading a text; and (3) to examine particular situations to derive historical meaning. The first task traditionally has been most archaeologists' strong suit, and the second has been enjoying primacy among structuralist-oriented researchers. The third task is most basic if archaeologists wish to incorporate a view of culture as constituted through praxis, a view too often lacking in historical archaeologists' treatment of slave material culture. Marshall Sahlins (1976:22) has contrasted "praxis theory"— which holds that "the specific construction of culture is the product of a concrete activity which transcends the system to appropriate the novelty and actuality of the material world—with structuralism, in which the focus is on the system itself. Writing on material culture, Christopher Tilley (1983) uses the "notion of praxis as mediation between activity and consciousness" to argue that material things, as foci of social action, embody ideational systems. The assignment of artifacts to particular classes within overall distribution patterns cannot continue based on partial understandings of context. The derivation of meaningful patterns can only rest on meaningful and thickly conceived historical and anthropological interpretations.

Status Patterning

Handler and Lange (1978:226) note that a central problem in the study of plantation sites is that the sources of material goods were available to free whites, free nonwhites, and slaves, and that patterns of lateral cycling through "purchase, trade, exchange, or gift giving would have tended to blur absolute artifactual distinctions between the nonslave and slave segments" of a population. Otto (1984) has taken as his starting point the elucidation of a pattern that at first simply appears "blurred." By holding status constant, he can look at how variously defined status differences produced patterning in the archaeological remains. Classes of artifacts were found to reflect one of three patterns: (1) "white dominance," based on racial/legal status (housing construction, housing amenities, liquor bottles, pipes, and glass beads); (2) "hierarchical," based on social/occupational status (housing living space, ceramic shape and form); and (3) "wealth-poverty," based on economic status (wild food, domestic food, and ceramic decorative type). The classification depends upon whether each item is most similarly distributed between overseers and planters versus slaves (white dominance), overseers and slaves versus planters (wealth-poverty), or graded between the three (hierarchical).

Otto's work has been criticized for oversimplifying plantation social organization in terms of planter/overseer/slave, when in fact social distance between overseers and planters varied greatly (Orser 1984:5–6). The importance of Otto's work, however, is not in showing how to recognize these three groups archaeologically (Drucker 1981), but in demonstrating that different kinds of status may be manifested materially by different kinds of remains; in other words, that status and its material correlates are too complex to be inferred directly. Nevertheless, archaeologists persist in applying a status model, concentrating on explaining deviations from Otto's original formulation. There is less need for a continued refinement of the artifact assignments (e.g., Adams and Boling 1989) than for an examination of the underlying reason for inconsistencies, namely the limitations of the model itself.

The problem Otto faces—along with many others—stems from conceiving of society in terms of differing levels of status in the first place, rather than in terms of social relations (Orser 1988a). Slaves had lower status than their owners because they were owned—clearly the power relations are primary, and status is simply a static way of describing the product of social action.

Dominance is not a status term, it is a relation, one in which the dominant group always has an effect on the dominated, and in which the autonomy of the dominated is restricted in order to be consistent with the interests of the dominant group. The response of one group to domination by another takes certain forms. What archaeologists should study is how domination operates and how responses to it are enacted, which means that differences in material remains should be examined in terms of their function within a context of social action, rather than as status markers. Furthermore, material culture must be understood not as merely reflecting social relations, but as participating actively in their creation, operation, and maintenance. Regardless of the nature and degree of elite penetration of slaves' cultural identity, the material contexts of daily life certainly played a role. The resistance of slaves was largely acted out daily in the assertion of a degree of cultural autonomy, which necessarily had to make use of material "givens" and their manipulation. Again, the work of Douglas and Isherwood, Hodder, Daniel Miller, and Appadurai on material culture can be useful for historical archaeologists.

Through co-opting items of material culture, slaves created material contexts for the internal social life of their community. Clay pipes suggest that Otto's pattern of "white dominance" in material remains was at best ambiguous. Beads and liquor bottles fall into the same category of "white dominance," but these objects, too—regardless of their distribution among slaves, overseers, and owners, speak to slaves' private and/or communal lives, not to the structure of subordination.

What about the "wealth-poverty" and "hierarchical" patterns? The first is problematical because Otto fails to consider fully the relationship between planters and specific overseers—some of whom were planters' sons—at Cannon's Point. Once again, social relations have been overlooked in the desire to establish status. If overseers look "poor" in terms of food and ceramic patterns, it may be because they actually participated in the domestic life of the great house to a greater extent than assumed by Otto. But the fact remains that many poor overseers lived on southern plantations. This situation does not mean, however, that the relevant contrast is between poor slaves and overseers on the one hand and wealthy planters on the other. Ideologically speaking, poor whites were participants in the same social caste as wealthy ones, whereas slaves were a separate caste. To consider slaves and poor whites as members of the same economic class is to overlook the caste aspect of slavery. Put another way, it is to see class as fully definable in terms of its economic determinants, without its social and ideological correlates.

In a critique of the analyses of both Otto (1984) and Sue Mullins Moore (1985), Charles Orser (1988a) argues that their caste model of plantation society links race and class but gives race primacy. He prefers to focus on the power the class of slaveowners held over their slaves, a power that included control over material items slaves possessed. Orser is right to bring economics and power more prominently into the archaeological analysis of plantation social relations, but these factors cannot "replace" caste and status. The imposed conjunction of race and class is precisely what gave planter hegemony its strongest tool.

"Hierarchy" is equally problematical. To use the concept of hierarchy is to assume the existence—either actual or ideal—of a continuous series of social statuses. No such continuous series—either actual or ideal—existed in southern society. The series was discontinuous at the point where some groups of people owned others and at the point where racial lines were drawn. Orser (1988a) rightly calls attention to the occupational ranking system on plantations, but his argument that "occupation can be looked upon by archaeologists as the most important social characteristic" within the plantation hierarchy (Orser 1988a:741) is disquieting; occupation may have been the *second* most important criterion of social rank, but surely the slave/free dichotomy came first. This is part of a wider issue which continues to have relevance today, the question of cultural evaluation of social situations. Groups and individuals *interpret* their inequality differently: Where some see occupation and wealth as the primary determinants of status, others see discrimination and racism as key, reflecting real differences in experience as well as "objective" analysis. This is a good example of how structural relations are subject to varying interpretation as well as ideological manipulation. Diane Austin (1984) analyzes the ideology of education in Jamaica as the modern outgrowth of an earlier ideology of occupational ranking that had its roots in the slave plantation. She argues that this dominant-class ideology is refuted by the poor, who interpret inequality in terms of discrimination.

Given the fact that legal and racist barriers do exist in societies such as the plantation South under slavery, the expression of hierarchy in material culture nevertheless may serve a very real social end. The pretense of a status hierarchy can function in society toward fostering the acceptance of inequality. Slaves were clearly not simply on the bottom rung of some social ladder. The interest of the elite was to create an illusion of such a social order to promote a sense of "naturalness" in inequality, which they possibly accomplished partially through overt material signs.

If Otto's classification of material remains relating to housing is examined, an interesting "pattern of patterns" can be discerned. In terms of how well built the structures are and the amenities they contain, "white dominance" is indicated. But in terms of sheer space, hierarchy is represented. Bernard Herman (1984:276) also notes that in the South dwelling size was not necessarily correlated with quality, comfort, or expense of furnishings and concludes somehow that this situation contradicts Genovese's (1974) contention that planter he-

gemony was expressed in housing. What may be expressed is the creation of an environment—the material context of life on the plantation—in which external signs illustrate and promote the false and artificial concept of social hierarchy, only to be belied by the evidence for actual quality of life.

Whether or not planters were attempting to express and create the cultural hegemony of their class—based on the idea of a patriarchal order—in this way becomes an historical question. Of particular interest to some historical archaeologists is the role of material culture in relation to ideology, used here in the sense of the establishment of taken-for-granteds which serve to obscure power relations (Leone 1982). At first glance, a Marxist definition of ideology may seem inappropriate for slave societies. After all, here is a case where dominance and coercion were overt, where status was assigned by law, and where the need for promoting a false consciousness on the part of the oppressed was surely obviated by their legal enslavement. The question of motivation is complicated: Planters needed an ethical justification for the basic inequality on which they depended and may have sought it in the "natural order," while conscious misdirection of observers' perceptions of plantation life may have motivated others. These "internal" and "external" factors motivating plantation planning need to be explored through research into the historical records relating to plantation housing. It is hardly necessary to point out here that the use of material symbols by planters to establish a naturalness in the patriarchal order does not at all mean that slaves were "taken in." Slaves knew all too intimately what occurred within planters' and overseers' houses. Likewise, poor whites, especially plantation dependents, may have been well aware of the political nature of their subordination and may have seen it as anything but natural. It is a grave mistake to assume that what planters told themselves about plantation life ever convinced anyone else who had to experience it.

Other archaeologists have looked at status patterning in the material record in their attempts to apply or add to Otto's formulation. William Adams and Sarah Boling (1989:94), for example, point out that slaves on three coastal plantations in

Georgia had higher priced ceramic wares in some forms than their owners. They argue that the task system allowed these slaves time to earn income of their own. Given that many of their material goods were obtained through purchase, Adams and Boling conclude that these slaves were using ceramics, much as did whites, as status markers within their *own* community. But this interpretation begs the question: *Why* would these items have held status value for slaves? If such goods were indeed high-status possessions for slaves, their meaning derives at least as much from their context of acquisition as from their association with white European-American culture. Care must be exercised when interpreting material goods in the same way for slaves as for plantation whites precisely because slaves did *not* "participate freely within the Southern market economy" (Adams and Boling 1989:94). To conclude that "on [task-labor] plantations slaves may be better understood within the context of being peasants or serfs, regarding their economic status" (Adams and Boling 1989:94) is to overlook a host of economic, political, social, and cultural realities for the sake of retaining status-markers as analytical tools. Historical archaeologists need to examine historically how slaves' interpretations, reinterpretations, and contested interpretations of material things were worked out.

Conclusions

Otto has done historical archaeologists an important service. He has shown that status cannot possibly be inferred directly from material remains. He and many others nonetheless have retained this concept, simply assigning independent status definitions to various data as they seem to fit. The analytical weakness of a concept of status has been demonstrated, but plantation archaeologists do not seem to realize the implications, choosing instead to refine the heuristic device in order to apply it more closely without noticing that this approach only takes the discipline further from society conceived as a whole. Human social relations are not reducible to sets of status variables,

any more than historical change is reducible to models of acculturation.

What is needed is a contextual description of material culture that is conscious of both plantation class relations and historical processes of culture change—an ambitious goal. The study of slave culture can liberate historians—and slaves—as historical actors from the bare analysis of exploitation and oppression. On the other hand, a focus on the class structure of plantation society and the master-slave relationship, always keeping in view the issue of power and the political fact of enslavement, prevents researchers from *neglecting* the bare realities of exploitation and oppression. This essay has attempted to show that given an adequate conception of culture and social action, contexts of both power/resistance and cultural separatism are relevant to the interpretation of material remains at slave sites. The exercise of power affects the material idiom of cultural expression and the political interpretation of material symbols. Cultural separatism allows meanings to be articulated and contested by individuals and groups within the black community, but also constitutes a form of resistance to slaveholder power. Throughout, archaeologists need to recall that meaning is generally negotiable and that material things are susceptible to various or contested meanings through contexts of action. As Sahlins (1985:ix) notes, "If culture is as anthropologists claim a meaningful order, still, in action meanings are always at risk."

Artifacts, then, do not work well either as cultural markers or as status markers. Their distributions do not "map" culture change or social relations in a direct way. An interpretive step must be taken in the archaeological study of slave culture and plantation society, a step which should incorporate: (1) an analysis of whether material change reflects the structure of power relations or social strategies and cultural recontextualization within that structure; (2) an understanding of how material things come to have meaning through specific and historically definable contexts of action; and (3) an exploration of how manipulation of material symbols helps to create and maintain particular interpretations of social reality. Culture itself must be defined in a way that reflects the acknowledgment of contested interpretations of symbols and experience. A more sophisticated understanding of culture in turn will allow archaeologists to approach the historical issues from a new perspective, with new means for using material culture to address key questions.

Acknowledgments

This essay is a substantially revised version of a paper delivered at the 1987 Northeastern Anthropological Association meeting, Amherst. I would like to thank Randall White for his helpful comments on the original essay. The present version benefitted substantially from the careful reading and suggestions of Marjorie Ingle and Diana Wall. Charles Orser also commented on an early draft, and I thank him for his help in preparing the final version for publication. I cannot fully measure the late Bert Salwen's influence on the development of the ideas that have gone into this paper. Even though the opinions expressed are my own, I do hope that the result at least reflects his commitment to interdisciplinary research goals.

J. W. JOSEPH

White Columns and Black Hands: Class and Classification in the Plantation Ideology of the Georgia and South Carolina Lowcountry

ABSTRACT

Social relations on the plantations of the South Carolina and Georgia Lowcountry were structured by a series of classifications which in turn expressed and codified plantation ideology. Racism, paternalism, and emergent capitalism have all been demonstrated through archaeological investigations as major constellations within this ideological universe. The expression of these social and ideological relations occurred symbolically within the plantations, as evidenced by settlement systems, architecture, and material remains. This ideology was also expressed in the documentary record in the ways in which planters classified their slaves and other social groups. This article considers the archaeology of ideology among the plantations of the Georgia and South Carolina Lowcountry as expressed through symbolization and classification and examines the evolution of plantation ideology from the 17th century to the end of the Antebellum era. It suggests that the social and ideological structure shifted from one based on racial classification to one dependent on labor specialization and social stratification, in response to changes in the Lowcountry's plantation economy.

Introduction

Understanding *The Mind of the South* (Cash 1941) has been the Holy Grail of southern history since the first recognition of the South as a distinctive region. The various efforts to expose the southern mind, however, have invariably been confronted with the multiplicity and duplicity of their quarry. Southern ideology catered to the prevailing winds of an 18th- and 19th-century social hurricane; at various times "southernness" was defined in response to a variety of referents. Among planters the ideology of class was domi-

Historical Archaeology, 1993, 27(3):57–73.
Permission to reprint required.

nant; among whites race replaced class consciousness; between races paternalism was revered; white southern men placed white southern women on a pedestal of virtue and rallied to the cry of honor, while black southern women pulled around them the worn fabric of family and huddled in its shelter against the hypocrisy of white southern men. Ultimately, the South claimed coalition in opposition to the North and found, wagered, and redeemed southern identity within the ideology of regionalism. The South was consistently comprised and defined on the basis of "us" and "them": whites versus blacks; rich versus poor; men versus women; southerners versus northerners. The South was inevitably a class culture, yet one whose definition of class was transient, far-reaching, and fluid. More than class, the South was a culture of classification.

The archaeological ability to probe the southern mind has focused upon the most prominent of southern class distinctions: racial and social status. This article reviews the archaeology of plantation ideology and finds within it an avenue which offers further potential toward understanding the plantation ideology of the Lowcountry of Georgia and South Carolina. The plantation South defined itself in relation to its component parts as well as outward opposition. Ultimately it presented an ideology of class and classification whose symbolic representation achieved its greatest expression in the material record. This article considers the archaeology of Lowcountry plantation ideology by first reviewing the results of previous studies, and then embellishing upon these observations to develop a theory of ideological classification. This theory is then applied to the documentary and material record of Lowcountry plantations, an application which suggests substantive historic shifts in the minds of the plantations of the Georgia and South Carolina Lowcountry.

The Plantation's Periphery: The Archaeology of Race

Axiomatic to the understanding of the South in relation to either itself or the world at large was its unique dependence upon and perception of racial dominance. Other New World colonies would flourish from interracial relations, yet in the South alone were race and social class inextricably linked, and the exploitation of one race by another as brutally followed in the pursuit of financial gain. The origins and transfer of such racial bias are discussed below, but it is important to recall that southerners sought to settle and recreate English society in the lowland swamps of the Carolinas and Georgia. Southerners would not adapt to the New World as an uncensored society, as to some degree did the French and Spanish, but rather maintained the rituals and rigor of English culture beneath the pines and palmettos of the southern coast (Ferguson 1977). Historical evidence suggests that race relations may not have been as rigid and reprehensible during the early period of colonization as they later would become; southerners' hunger for black labor would eventually engulf their coastal society and place the preservation of white supremacy as paramount over human justice and social concern. For whatever circumstances, the origins of southern ideology were clearly cemented in the ideology of race, and it is racism which forms the foundation of current understanding of the southern mind.

While all of plantation archaeology is, fundamentally, the archaeology of racism, the most persuasive treatment of racism within plantation ideology is provided by David Babson (1987, 1988; see also Lees 1980) from research at the Tanner Road slave settlement of Limerick Plantation. Babson's definition of racism emphasizes the Marxian characteristics of social classification, drawing from Orser (1987), Benedict (1934), Wobst (1977), and others. Babson (1987:43) views racism as serving "to hierarchically organize a society dependent on the coercion of unfree labor, and to legitimate and justify this society against changes in its larger ideology which espoused greater individual freedom." Racist coercion was accomplished by infusing "racial or ethnic characteristics (in this case, the lightness or darkness of skin color) with social meaning, meant to define social groups and organize relations between them" (Babson 1987:43).

Babson's perception of racism at Limerick Plan-

tation derives from two factors: geographic location and social control. Babson (1987, 1988) notes that the Tanner Road settlement was located on the periphery of Limerick Plantation, a sort of limbo in which Babson claims blacks attempted to negotiate their relationship to whites. Drawing from broader plantation settlement analyses (Ferguson and Babson 1986), he observes that such peripheral occupations by slaves were characteristic of the Colonial period of Lowcountry slavery, but would gradually be replaced during the Federal era. Babson notes that at Tanner Road greater control and recognition of these peripheral settlements is evidenced by the recording of the settlement's location on plantation plats. For him, such recognition implies that planters were beginning to extend greater control over their dominion slaves, delimiting the boundaries of the plantation, and in turn limiting the boundaries of negotiation.

Babson further recognizes control in the gradual replacement of slave-made African-American Colonowares with European industrial ceramics. Following Ferguson (1985), Babson views Colonoware as a marker of African-American identity and resistance to slavery, and thus considers these changes in material possessions as reflective of a negotiation of cultural meaning. For Babson (1987, 1988), this negotiation concerns dominance and control. The gradual erosion of slaves' ability to negotiate their position within the plantation society, both in terms of residential privacy and material possessions, is considered by Babson to signify a physical and ideological loss of African-American semi-independence fostered in turn by the cessation of the slave trade. Within his discussion, such change is presented as neither the intensification nor relaxation of racism, but rather recognizes changes in racist ideology in response to other stimuli. Among these, the most critical is perceived as a gradual shift within European and American ideology which placed greater emphasis on individual freedom (Davis 1975; Fields 1982). As such a perception ran counter to the ideology of racism, Babson suggests that planters responded by seizing those limited individual freedoms which slaves enjoyed, in defiance of individual independence. His work thus sheds light on transitions within Lowcountry plantation ideology, although it should be noted that the social changes which he addresses have also been presented in socioeconomic, rather than ideological, terms (Lees 1980; Zierden and Calhoun 1983; Joseph 1989). While the integration of his model with others discussing change among the Lowcountry plantations has not yet been advanced, Babson's emphasis on racism as the foundation for plantation ideology provides a meaningful contrast and corollary to the archaeology of status and social structure.

The Big House and the Manor Grounds: Settlement, Architecture, and Social Control

As Babson notes, plantation ideology was defined in part through settlement patterning. Planters inevitably secured their position both on the plantation and beyond as evidenced by their command and control; command and control which were often most visibly expressed through the plantation's architecture and landscape. Archaeologists have recently refocused their attention on social power and have emphasized the political, economic, and ideological mastery of the planter elite as critical elements of a plantation ideology, while recognizing that power was always the object of contention, and that incessant give-and-take occurred between planters and their overseers, planters and their wives, planters and their slaves (Orser 1989). Indeed, the history of some plantations brings into question just who held the reins of power, and a subtle thread runs throughout the plantation text which suggests that slaves may have had a greater hand in their destiny than planters would have willingly acknowledged (Faust 1982). However, whether in the presence or absence of real control, the image of control overshadowed its substance. Plantation architecture and the plantation landscape appear to have been carefully constructed as an altar to the planter's perceived omnipotent relation to the world.

In a series of reports and articles, Lewis (1979, 1985) and others (Lewis and Hardesty 1979; Lewis and Haskell 1980; Ferguson and Babson 1986; Babson 1987; Wheaton 1989) have focused on the organization and settlement of Lowcountry plantations as an indicator of plantation ideology. Lewis emphasizes the Georgian characteristics of plantation settlement in expositions upon a view of plantation ideology which stress order, hierarchy, and symmetry. Within this landscape ideology, the main house dominated the visual perception, both in size and appearance, and was flanked by its dependencies, both architectural and social. Slave dwellings were rarely immediately associated with the planter's home, and instead were placed in subservient positions, either behind the main house or along its flank, sometimes in association with the livestock pens. As presented by Lewis, such settlement dynamics served to illustrate the social dominance of planters, particularly in relation to their slaves.

Power and control as expressed through landscape ideology have also been discussed by Wheaton (1989) in an examination of Drayton Hall's orangerie. This structure, a Colonial greenhouse, was situated along the Ashley River, in a setting somewhat distant from the main house settlement, but which, Wheaton notes, would have been highly visible to river traffic. As waterways served as the interstates of their day, Wheaton argues that such position was intended as a notice to the passersby. Reviewing the role of orangeries on plantations of the Lowcountry and beyond, Wheaton echoes the observations of Yentsch (1990) and others (Yentsch et al. 1987) that such structures were intended to display their owners' ability to control nature. Greenhouses, in essence, defied nature, allowing plants to grow in winter which otherwise would have died, and provided for the cultivation of exotic vegetation. Their use on the one hand provided an enthusiastic response to the scientific curiosity of the Enlightenment, as well as a practical effort to identify and propagate new plant species which might be of financial benefit to the plantation. Yet greenhouses, as with formal landscaping, also served to demonstrate the planter's ability to control nature. Within an agrarian society, such ability would have served to reify the planter's social and political status, an observation apparently not lost on either planters or their contemporaries.

Dwellings, Sherds, and Bones: The Archaeology and Ideology of Ethnic and Social Status

Perhaps one of the most perceptive appraisals of plantation social structure and ideology was provided by John Otto (1975, 1977, 1980, 1984) in a series of publications emanating from his landmark studies of Cannon's Point Plantation. While Otto's research nominally sought to explain and assess status differences in the archaeological record, his study of the archaeological correlates of status emphasized the duplicity of class and social classification and thus provides important insights to the plantation ideology of the Lowcountry.

Otto's work at Cannon's Point benefited from the presence of architectural and archaeological remains associated with individuals from three social classes: planter, overseer, and slave. Indeed, it is the presence of the materials associated with the socially intermediate overseer occupation which provide the greatest insight to the classification and social structure of Cannon's Point. Otto observed that the material record supported two distinct sets of social associations. Buildings, in their construction and location, served to emphasize what Otto termed "ethnic status." White planter and overseer dwellings were comparable in construction materials, permanency, square footage per occupant, and location, and would have outwardly indicated a racial coalition and the segregation of the white plantation occupants in opposition to black slaves. In its outward appearance, Otto argued that architecture served symbolically to emphasize race as the foundation of the plantation's social structure. However, the material detritus of these occupations—the pottery, glass, personal items, and faunal remains associated with planter, overseer, and slave sites—supported a socioeconomic status model, in which planters were distinct and opposed to both overseers and slaves by the quality, quantity, and nature of their material possessions (Otto 1975:360–362). While Otto was primarily concerned with the archaeological ability to detect status, his interpretations of the ways in which social class was manipulated and symbolically presented signalled to plantation archaeology the elu-

sive nature of southern class structure, and the range of classifications presented by southern ideology.

Ourselves and the Others: Classification as an Ideological System

As outlined above, the plantation South found and expressed its identity through a hierarchical social structure in which the role of each social tier was defined by its object of comparison. Because of this dependence on social structure, archaeologists and historians alike have focused on class as the basis of plantation culture, and in consequence the archaeology of the Lowcountry has mostly devoted itself to the study of status, in its ethnic, social, and economic expressions. This review of prior archaeological thrusts at defining southern plantation ideology suggests that while the plantation South attempted to maintain a hierarchical social structure, the basis of this hierarchy was far more fluid than the traditionally recognized social categories of planter, overseer, and slave. As noted at the outset of this article, social structure was defined in reference to a number of critical oppositions, and different structural oppositions could be simultaneously maintained which in turn supported and obscured the foundation of the social hierarchy. It should also be recognized that the plantation social structure was far more elastic than traditionally assumed (cf. Moore 1985; Rosengarten 1986; Adams 1987). Planters were not always rich, and rich planters chose to expend their financial resources differently. Slaves played a role in the Lowcountry economy through their participation in the task labor system, and task labor in turn yielded historically notable differences in the social and economic positions of the various members of the slave society (Morgan 1982, 1983; Joseph 1987; Adams and Boling 1989). Slaves may also have shared to some degree in the financial successes of their planters (Moore 1981, 1985; Joseph 1986), placing the plantation as a whole as a unit of study in opposition to other plantations. The ways in which the social structure of the plantation were expressed served to maintain the social hierarchy, while the economic successes and failures of all members of the plantation culture provided some movement within, if not between, social categories. While the social structure and ideology of the plantation South is thus less readily explained than might previously have been thought, the key to understanding the ideological basis of this structure appears to rest in classification.

Classification has long been recognized as perhaps the most fundamental of cultural systems, and this recognition has in turn influenced the development of anthropological theory regarding both cultural ideology and social structure. Indeed, social anthropologists from Evans-Pritchard (1940) on have identified classification as the single most critical mental aspect of a culture, and have noted the necessity for ethnographers to master classification in order to understand the intricacies of the society under study (Needham 1963). The definition of kin, the boundaries between the real and supernatural worlds, the hierarchy and relations of social groups—all of these are classifications which must be understood before the operation of a foreign culture can be grasped. Clearly, classification is crucial to the ideational and social structural operation of a culture. Yet despite the historical importance of classification to the development of the cultural mind, anthropological interest in classification has been geared more toward the elaboration of specific cultural systems, and not toward an understanding of the overreaching role of classification within cultural ideology.

One of the earliest and still most influential anthropological approaches to cultural classification was published by Emile Durkheim and Marcel Mauss in 1903. *Primitive Classification* established the importance of classification to the understanding of social organization. Durkheim and Mauss (1963[1902]:81–83) recorded several aspects of cultural classification which bear relevance to the current consideration. Among these was their depiction of classification as a hierarchical system which structured ideological thought. In their words "classifications are thus intended, above all, to connect ideas, to unify knowledge; as such, they may be said without inexactitude to be

scientific, and to constitute a first philosophy of nature" (Durkheim and Mauss 1963[1902]:81). Durkheim and Mauss recognized classification in a Linneaean sense; classification represented each culture's attempt to structure and define the social and natural world, and to order and understand the objects recognized within such a system of classification. Their opinion that classification served to connect ideas and unify knowledge clearly demonstrates a recognition of classification as an ideological system. However, their perception of cultural classification as "scientific" in nature does not bear scrutiny. As is discussed below, classification served to justify and preserve the dominant social structure by placing such dominance within a hierarchical formulation of the natural and social worlds. In this respect, classification does not represent an objective ordering of the universe, but rather a set of subjectively constructed categories designed to support the social order.

Durkheim and Mauss were at least partially cognizant of this fact and broke from the natural sciences view of classification in their contention that order and classification was not observably inherent in nature, but rather represented a social and cultural construct. While their argument that the individual was incapable of recognizing and classifying without social instruction has since been countered, their formulation of classification as a cultural, rather than individual, system remains intact. Rather than viewing the natural world as the object of classification's attention, Durkheim and Mauss argued that classification was based in the social world and extended to the natural as a means of integration and control. They recorded that the "first logical categories were social categories; the first classes of things were classes of men, into which these things were integrated" (Durkheim and Mauss 1963[1902]:82).

This basic definition of classification is followed in the discussion of Lowcountry ideology presented below. Classification is considered as an ideological system which represents each culture's basis for ordering and understanding the social and natural worlds. At the origin of this structure is social classification and the ways in which social categories within and beyond the culture are defined and represented. This social structure is likely to find extension to the natural world, such that the entire classificatory system will be integrated in support of the presentation of social categories as fundamental, objective, and natural truths. As such, classification is likely to be hierarchical in nature, and dominance and control exerted in the social world are likely to be reflected in the construction of a natural hierarchy.

The understanding of cultural classification is thus based on the recognition of social categories and of social/natural hierarchy. At its most fundamental level, classification is bilateral in nature; an object (or individual) is defined not only by what it is, but also in opposition to what it is not. Classificatory systems are also elaborated and expanded in part in response to the importance of an object type to a given culture. Each culture may have a variety of definitions and categories for natural or cultural items, the extent of which quantify the importance of these objects to the culture at hand. The Eskimos' numerous classifications for snow or contemporary America's plethora of categories of automobiles are indices of the ways in which each culture views and structures its world, and the proliferation of categories within a particular type provides a gauge to the significance of that type to the culture as a whole. Classification thus forms the basis of cultural ideology in what it recognizes, in what it counterposes, in its degree of elaboration, but also in what it ignores.

The review of plantation ideology presented here suggests that dismissal and the failure to recognize objective "types" presents the most powerful application of a classificatory ideology. A perhaps now classic example of dismissal and inelaboration exists in the Cold War confrontation between Capitalism and Communism, or the struggle between the free and the unfree world as it was also portrayed. The importance of this dialectic to the understanding of capitalist political ideology derives from the direct polar opposition of these defined political extremes, an opposition which dismisses numerous recognized intermediary political and economic philosophies in an effort to emphasize cultural and ideological difference. At this level, the relationship of classificatory ideology to

classic structuralism cannot be ignored, as both theories are based on bilateral opposition. However, while structuralism's oppositions are perceived as buried and subconscious, classificatory ideology recognizes that the structure of cultural ideology is at least presented as explicit on the surface of its meaning. The oppositions are recognized; what is obscured is the existence of intermediary categories which would weaken bilateral tension.

Classificatory ideology also functions in some respects within classic Marxian formations of ideological structure. Here it is critical to recognize that each culture creates and employs its own system of classification, and that separate systems operating in the same historical context may define material items, social roles, human behavior, and explicit ideology through different classificatory structures. Hence the meaning of an object is dynamic and dependent upon the cultural context in which it is defined. The recognition of this disagreement in cultural classification has been noted by historians of the plantation South, many of whom have recognized that planters' and slaves' definition and interpretation of religious precepts varied greatly, to the extent that neither recognized nor fully understood the other's perspective definition (Joyner 1984). More recently, an archaeological recognition of the African-American definitions of certain material goods, as opposed to their commonly associated European classifications, has illustrated the ways in which many common 19th-century material items may have been reused in African-American rituals, and thus culturally redefined (Brown and Cooper 1990). Since classification is constructed by each culture as a means of justifying its social structure, it is not surprising that classification masks or misidentifies those elements of a society which threaten the dominant structure.

The values of the application of a theory of classificatory ideology to historical archaeology are three-fold. First, as stated above, the ideological structure of any culture should be found in its definition and classification of social categories. For the historic period, many of these social classifications were explicitly stated, and thus can be recovered through the examination of the contemporary written record. Second, since social classification was frequently integrated and justified through the divisions of the natural world, it follows that such social and natural structure would be symbolically expressed. Material culture thus offers perhaps the most accurate record of the expressed social structure. Finally, historical archaeologists work incessantly at classification through the analysis and study of historic artifacts. While many of the categories which archaeologists apply to these artifacts are derived from their modern—as opposed to historic—contexts, this constant attention with the ways in which material items were defined and presented offers a unique perception of the historical structuring of the material world. As an effort to demonstrate the linkage between social and natural structure, the written record of historic classification, the material residue of the expression of this social structure, and its meaning to historical ideology, a classificatory approach is applied to the ideology of the Lowcountry's plantations, below.

Linnaeus and the Great Chain of Being

The ideology transferred across the Atlantic to the Lowcountry featured a potent dialogue between theology and emergent scientific thought, and the give-and-take between these two poles would largely structure the debate concerning slavery through the end of the Revolution. Classification was explicit within this ideological system. On the one hand, the *Systema Naturae*, presented by Carl Linnaeus (1806 [1735]) offered a scientific classification of the world which recognized *Homo sapiens* as a natural creature within the Primate Order of the Mammalian family. While the Linnaean system presented an overall unspoken hierarchy, humans were given no special prominence over other members of the primate family, nor were divisions recognized among people, and in this respect Linnaeus provided a truly objective view of the human condition. Such a view was countered and co-opted by a cultural classification which made use of theology and pseudo-science to

justify social categories, a co-option in keeping with classificatory ideology theory. As Winthrop Jordan (1974) has documented, the fulcrum of this classification system was the Great Chain of Being. The Great Chain of Being had its origins in Classical Greece but witnessed its most expansive development in 17th- and 18th-century Europe. The Chain was a hierarchical structure which extended from the simplest living creature into the supernatural. Within this hierarchy, *Homo sapiens* was composed of both heavenly and earthly forces, suspended between angel and beast. Such a system provided for both a classification of the natural world and for a spiritual quality in people, and also left open the prospect that the various forms of human beings might place differently upon this sliding scale.

The discovery of Africans, in combination with the encounter of a variety of other human "types" which occurred during the Age of Exploration, placed a premium on the definition and relation of these various human forms. Through the work of physical anthropologists and anatomists such as Peter Camper and Josiah Nott (1844), biologists such as Sir William Petty, and others, there soon developed a system of classification in which blacks were presented as a lower stage of human development (Jordan 1974:102–130; Stocking 1982:42–68). Camper's measurement of "facial angle" yielded a reported gradation from apes, to Negroes, and then to Europeans (Camper in Jordan 1974:103). Petty, a founder of the Royal Society, was among the first to comment upon the variation among human types and summarized the sentiments of the day:

> I say that the Europeans do not onely differ from the . . . Africans in Collour, which is as much as white differs from black, but also in their Haire . . . in the shape of their Noses, Lipps, and cheek bones, as also in the outline of their faces and the Mould of their skulls. They differ also in their Naturall Manners, and in the internall Qualities of their Minds (Petty in Jordan 1974:102).

As Jordan (1974:5–9, 100–105) notes, the perception of Africans as inferior humans was dependent upon several factors: skin color (English ideological thought associated whiteness with purity and blackness with sin prior to the African voyage and thus carried this association into the relations between Europeans and Africans), climate (the hot and humid jungles of Africa were viewed in opposition to the cold but cultivated environs of northern Europe in a climatological association of temperature and human behavior), and a misconstrued association between apes and Africans brought back by English voyagers. As Jordan (1974) observes, it is important to recognize the co-discovery of apes and Africans by the Europeans. Early accounts referenced the physical coupling of blacks and apes, and such reports, in combination with the human-like appearance of the apes, served not only to justify the Great Chain of Being but also to position blacks at the bottom of the human scale and in close association with the top flight of the animal world, the ape. The symbolic and ideological basis for classifying blacks in opposition to whites thus pre-existed the African discovery: "What Englishmen did not at first fully realize was that Africans were potentially subjects for a special kind of subordination which was to arise as adventurous Englishmen sought to possess for themselves and their children one of the most bountiful dominions of the earth" (Jordan 1974:25). Historian Drew Faust's (1981:12) recognition of planters' manipulation of social and natural categories echoes the response of classificatory ideology: "Nature produced individuals strikingly unequal in both qualities and circumstances. 'Scientific' truths demonstrated through empirical study prescribed a hierarchically structured society reproducing nature's orderly differentiations." Classification did not dictate slavery, but it provided the ideological and social structure within which slavery could occur.

Mulatto, Quadroon, Black, and White: Race and Classification in the Colonial Lowcountry

The documentary basis of social classification within the Colonial period in the Lowcountry not surprisingly supports race as the most fundamental element within the emergent social structure. As touched upon above, the climatological philosophy of human nature was evident with regard to plant-

ers' views of Africans. The geographic (and to a lesser degree tribal-cultural) origin of slaves was emphasized in notices of sales and auctions, and planters frequently communicated their own assessments of the relative merits of Gold Coast or Calabar slaves for the climate and labor conditions of the Lowcountry (Littlefield 1981; Smith 1985). Such discussion and review was partially racial in nature, as the pros and cons of slaves from various parts of Africa were discussed in terms of human aptitude and physical conditioning, a sort of sliding scale within the greater scale of the Great Chain.

Skin color was remarked upon as one calibration of this scale. Planters preferred darker skinned Africans to those of lighter hues, associating blackness with the physical ability to labor and survive the conditions of the Lowcountry. Such preference was also in keeping with the social opposition which justified slavery; blackness and an animal nature were linked which in turn explained a slave's hardiness and justified slavery. As contact between the races increased, miscegenation complicated the racial question. Lowcountry planters nominally recognized the mulatto as intermediate between black and white, yet such recognition was rarely verbalized and carried with it no social benefit, as existed in the English colonies of the Caribbean and India and with the French and Spanish colonies. It is worth noting both that the Spanish developed an extensive listing of terms indicative of the percentages of a person's racial admixture—achieving a total of 64 classifications in the extreme—and that the English and French colonies of the Caribbean employed a three-tiered social structure in which mulattos were able to enjoy greater social freedom and status than blacks (Genovese 1969:106). Yet Lowcountry planters spoke mainly in terms of blacks and whites, occasionally of mulattos, seldom of quadroons or mestizos, and maintained a two-tiered social status structure in which anyone with any percentage of negro biological heritage was considered a black, and where nearly all blacks were slaves. Such denial of intermediary classes emphasizes the position of race within the plantations' social and ideological structure.

Thus within the classification system of the Colonial Lowcountry, the social adaptation of the

Great Chain of Being, racial distinctions are considered as forming the basis of the proscribed social structure. Blacks were depicted as a lower form of humanity, more directly associated with the animal world, uncivilized and pagan, and socially and racially distinct from whites. For whites, especially those who held the reigns of power within this social structure, the associations with civilization, a higher spiritual quality, and power and control all appear to have represented critical social signifiers. Not surprisingly, the archaeological record of the Lowcountry's plantations indicates a physical effort symbolically to represent such associations.

The plantation archaeology of the Lowcountry has documented a distinctive African-American material culture which was dominant throughout the Colonial era but withered rapidly following the Revolution. This heritage has been best documented in two material realms: ceramic production/use and architecture. Lowcountry archaeologists have focused on slaves' manufacture and use of Colonowares as one of the more significant attributes of African-American culture in the Lowcountry (Ferguson 1978, 1985; Lees and Kimery-Lees 1979; Wheaton et al. 1983; Wheaton and Garrow 1985; Anthony 1986; Garrow and Wheaton 1989). Colonowares—slave-made, hand-coiled, open-fired coarse earthenwares—represent one of the most visible aspects of African-American culture during the Colonial period. Architecturally, excavations at Yaughan and Curriboo plantations (Wheaton et al. 1983) have revealed the presence of wall trench-mud walled and post-wattle and daub constructions within the Colonial slave villages, architectural traditions which are reflective of a West African building heritage (Vlach 1978).

The significance of these material expressions as presented here lies not in their suggestion of an African heritage but in their ability visually and symbolically to segregate black slaves from white planters as socially, culturally, and racially distinct. The use of mud-walled and wattle-and-daub dwellings and coarse earthenware Colonoware vessels is symbolically reflective of the classification system presented above, as these material possessions would have signalled to other Europeans that blacks were less civilized and more closely associated with nature (an association measured here by the degree to which natural materials were modified to form cultural artifacts). Similarly, the positioning of slave settlements on the plantation's periphery physically disassociated blacks from whites. Conversely, the construction of brick manors featuring Greek and Roman classical design elements, the demonstration of the control of nature through landscaping and as expressed through the construction of buildings like greenhouses, and the setting of tables with European refined stonewares and earthenwares and Chinese porcelains employing a range of decorative design elements counter-signalled that whites, at least those near the top of the social structure, possessed greater social and racial qualifications than blacks. The construction by some planters of small churches on their properties, and the donations and prominent pews of many in Charleston's, Beaufort's, and Savannah's most affluent cathedrals, also served to signify their spiritual superiority. Thus this material culture symbolically expressed the classification ideology and social structure espoused by the plantation elite. It should not be forgotten that this expression in no way negated the significance of Colonowares or mud-walled houses to African-American slaves, whose own classification system was likely to have emphasized cultural autonomy in the face of racial repression. Unfortunately, the classificatory system of Colonial slaves is far more difficult to extract from the documentary record.

As noted above, many of these material attributes faded rapidly from the plantation landscape near the close of the 18th century. Lowcountry plantation archaeologists have spilled considerable ink in a dialogue concerning these changes in plantation material culture and the meaning of such change. African-American independence and resistance (Ferguson 1985; Babson 1988), acculturation (Wheaton et al. 1983; Joseph 1989), socioeconomic change and adaptation (Singleton 1985), technological innovation (Zierden and Calhoun 1983), and social power (Howson 1990) have all been presented as the mechanisms guiding and driving this social transformation. This article recognizes all of these aspects in the evolution of Lowcountry plantations, but views the primary catalysts toward such change as being the technological reorganization of Lowcountry plantations to exploit the potential of tidal rice agriculture and the subsequent reordering of plantation social structure and ideology to respond to this new infrastructure.

Half Hand, Full Hand, Carpenter, Smith: Labor Management in Lowcountry Classification

Toward the end of the 18th century and throughout the first half of the 19th, planters wrote about and referred to their slaves with a different system of classification. Race was no longer the predominant concern; labor skills and ability became the most common of slave categorizations. As Morgan (1986:97) notes, "the increasing size of the plantations reflected other changing economic realities. One of the most significant components of the slaves' economic world was their opportunity to do specialized work." His review of slave inventories indicates that by 1770 nearly 18 percent of Lowcountry adult male slaves were exempt from fieldwork on the basis of their possession of some special skill. While similar statistics have not yet been compiled for the Lowcountry, Marks' (1987) research from St. Marys County, Maryland, shows a steady increase in the percentage of skilled male slaves to all slaves through the 1830s. While neither Marks nor Morgan recognize the influence of classification on plantation inventories, it should be noted that the increases discussed above may also reflect changes in classification as well as actual increases in the number of skilled slaves. Morgan (1986:101) lists 51 separate skill classifications among the Lowcountry inventories which he reviewed, including bakers, blacksmiths, boatmen, bricklayers, carpenters, cooks, coopers, drivers, seamstresses, shoemakers, and washerwomen. The recording of slaves by specialization represents in part economic adaptation and the maturation of the plantation society as well as the realignment of plantation ideology; skilled slaves were of greater value, and hence planters obviously found reassurance in their enumeration of the skilled slaves in their possession.

Far more prevalent than the inventory of slave skills was a second system of classification which underscores the planters' obsession with the division of labor. Beginning in the late 1700s, planters began to classify their slaves in reference to an index which established the quantity of work a healthy adult male slave was expected to accomplish in a day. This index was referred to as a "hand." Throughout the slave inventories, sale advertisements, and day-books this system of classification was heavily relied upon. Slaves' labor capacity was indexed to the hand system: children old enough to work in the fields might be denoted as quarter hands in the slave inventories; adults with infirmities or whose age limited their abilities would be likely for classification as half hands; healthy adults would be expected to perform to full hand specifications. The hand index provided a measurement for a number of different Lowcountry plantation tasks, so that planters knew how many acres could be hoed, or how many feet of rice ditching should be dug, by a full hand. In turn, plantation jobs were measured in the number of hands which they required. A planter might refer to the repair of a rice pond dike as a job for two and a half hands, not as an indication that he expected two and a half individuals to accomplish this task, but that he thought the job would require two and a half days for a full hand, or five days for a half hand (Morgan 1982, 1983; Anthony 1989).

This effort to classify and quantify labor was also expressed on Lowcountry plantations through task labor. Task labor, the dominant labor system employed on Lowcountry rice plantations, established a number of units which represented the amount of work a full hand was expected to accomplish within a day. Once these tasks were completed, the slave's obligations for the day were fulfilled. The combination of hand classification and task labor provided one of the most management-efficient expressions of the plantation economy, establishing a system in which work was measured, quotas assigned, and rewards provided for the prompt fulfillment of labor obligations. This system was dramatically different from the labor relations employed elsewhere in the plantation economy, and from the social structure of the Colonial era.

The basis of this ideological shift is uncertain, but it is considered to lie largely in response to the economic and social changes produced by the adoption of tidal rice agriculture and in turn by the influence of the Industrial Revolution. Tidal rice agriculture employed the tidal surge to flood and drain rice ponds and provided significant financial returns to planters who could afford the labor to construct dikes and gates and thus transform the Lowcountry's swamps into agricultural factories. Tidal rice agriculture by its very nature subdivided the plantation landscape and provided units of measurement for agricultural production. It also established the basis for a more stable and permanent settlement, since rice ponds were self-fertilizing and hence could be used over extended periods of time. The Industrial Revolution brought about two significant changes in 19th-century labor: labor specialization and labor quantification. The second has historically been largely ignored, but refers to the emergence of an assembly-line mentality in which a worker's productivity was predetermined and measured. In the factories this was accomplished by the assembly line, in which each worker responded to the speed of the operative machinery. On tidal rice plantations this same effect was achieved by the classification of hands and the grading of tasks in hand units. While the notion of a transfer of industrial philosophy to the plantations of the Lowcountry requires far greater research and consideration, it nonetheless appears that industrial philosophy as applied to tidal rice agriculture influenced the development of a new plantation ideology which emphasized labor management.

The integration of this system of classification and social structure into the natural world is also not as readily recognized as with the Colonial plantation ideology. It appears likely that this transformation was supported by the spread and acceptance of the Linnaean system and by subsequent theories of nature. By the late 1700s and early 1800s Linnaean classification was very much a part of the Lowcountry, as witnessed by the work of William Bartram, the LeContes, and other naturalists at classifying the flora and fauna of the region. Linnaean classification emphasized the distinctive characteristics of each species as separating one from other members of the genus. In turn, Spencerian theory and particularly the concept of the "survival of the fittest" (Spencer 1890 [1850]) and the later theory of Darwinian adaptation (Darwin 1964[1859]) represent the most widely recognized works of a general trend toward identifying species adaptation within the natural sciences. Substituting skills for natural qualities, these natural classifications could have supported a social world in which people were segregated based upon their abilities and socially assigned on the basis of their adaptive work environment.

While planters' classifications stressed labor qualities in the 19th century, this situation should not be mistaken as evidence that racism had withdrawn from the landscape. Rather, the ideological need to express and support racial segregation was lessened by a series of laws passed across the South which placed severe restrictions on slaves' actions while at the same time securing the institution of slavery and its association with blacks. Such legislation was enacted in South Carolina as early as the 1740s in response to the Stono Rebellion, and the title of the bill which placed these limitations on Lowcountry slaves clearly reflects its racial bias. This bill was known simply as the Negro Act, and it served to maintain the association between blacks and slavery to the extent that it prohibited masters from manumitting their slaves, transferring that right and responsibility to the legislature (Wood 1974:323–324). With the linkage between race and slavery cleared established by the law, planters were less motivated ideologically and symbolically to display their racial superiority than they had been in the absence of such legal justification.

"Let Our Fields Be Factories": Nineteenth-Century Plantation Ideology

The social structure of industrialization maintained a status hierarchy, although one which recognized labor specialization and the hierarchy of supervisory roles. This ideology also emphasized order and organization, employing a strategy in which resources were orderly distributed to provide for the uninterrupted flow from raw material to finished good. The transformations in Lowcountry plantations, alluded to above, mirror in many respects this emergent ideological structure. In terms of settlement, slave villages were pulled in from the periphery and established nearer the main house complex on Lowcountry plantations of the 19th century. These villages were referred to as "quarters" or "settlements" on plantation plats, and appear to have represented labor units on many plantations. Ten structures was a common number of houses to be found in a slave village, and these would have housed from 30 to 60 plus slaves. Plantations with more than 60 or 70 slaves were likely to have possessed additional quarters, and these were most often established in proximity to agricultural fields in which the slaves were employed (Singleton 1985; Anderson and Joseph 1988). On some plantations special settlements were established where intransigent slaves were sent; Pierce Butler's Settlement Four apparently housed the least cooperative of the Butler slaves and was situated the furthest from the main house complex and in the most hostile natural environment (Scott 1984; Bell 1987).

These settlements were organized as "streets," parallel rows of houses with an even spacing. Planters emphasized the benefits of streets by stressing the facility which they provided to supervision (Breeden 1980). Along these streets, 19th-century Lowcountry slave housing was normally of frame construction, with tabby and occasionally brick also employed as construction materials. Slave cabins were raised off the ground and placed on wood or brick piers; piered construction made these cabins cooler in the summer and also more cleanly, and increased planter supervision by eliminating subfloor hiding places. By this time planters and southern agricultural journals expressed greater concern with the health of slaves (Breeden 1980). In most respects these dwellings were barren and rudimentary, although a slave might expend income gained through the task labor system on plate-glass windows (Joseph 1986). It was customary for the slave driver to occupy the first house upon entering the village (Anthony 1976), a symbolic reflection of his superior social status within the slave society.

The material culture of slavery changed also. Colonoware was no longer made on a broad scale; slaves ate from English and American industrial ceramics purchased and distributed by planters. These ceramics were usually of the most inexpensive forms; planters reserved for their own tables transfer-printed wares and porcelain. The slave diet provided by planters was also rudimentary, and was supplemented by wild fish and game (Reitz et al. 1985). As with other items provided by planters, a considerable gap separated the quality and quantity of slave and planter assemblages.

All of these observations intermesh with the ideological structure expressed above. Plantation settlement reflected an efficient distribution of resources across the landscape: slave villages were dispersed as labor units and placed adjacent to rice fields; the planter's home, barns, livestock pens, and other buildings housing non-human resources were clustered and centrally located (Prunty 1955). Domestic architecture was indicative of this social scale. Slave dwellings were not nearly as different from planters' homes in construction as they had been in the Colonial era, and while they would not be mistaken for a planter's residence, the materials and construction of these buildings were common to both, suggesting that social scale was the intended signifier, not race. Within the village a status hierarchy based on labor skills was recognized in the relative position of occupants and possibly in materials and ornamentation as well. Finally, the material possessions of slaves reflected their relative social position within the plantation, a status also made malleable by slaves' ability to earn income through the task labor economy. In these respects, a social structure based on labor skills and socioeconomic status appears to have replaced race as the determinant of 19th-century Lowcountry plantation social organization and ideology.

"No African Hut": Conclusions

The ideology of Lowcountry plantations expressed above, the ideology of classification, suggests a shift in the Lowcountry mind-set from a classification based on race to one which emphasized labor skills and socioeconomic stratification. This ideological transition occurred during the second half of the 18th century, and is considered to be the product, and not the producer, of the particular history of the Lowcountry. Specifically, two aspects of the history of this region are regarded as fundamental to the nature of the plantation economy in the Lowcountry and in turn of its ideology. The dramatic influx of African slaves in the early decades of the European settlement, the corresponding "black majority" (Wood 1974), and the relatively isolated and forbidding landscape which formed the rural hinterland provided the basis for a plantation economy composed of isolated and semi-isolated settlements occupied predominantly by African slaves. This settlement and social structure in turn substantially provided for the non-European appearance of the African settlements within these early plantations. The introduction of tidal rice agriculture in the latter decades of the 18th century rewrote the Lowcountry's settlement and social structure. Tidal rice provided the basis for a more stable, complex, and elaborate plantation settlement, which the income generated by this crop helped to secure. Much of the material expression of the Lowcountry's plantations can thus be understood with regard to these demographic and socioeconomic forces; much, but not all.

The shift in plantation settlement which accompanied the introduction of tidal rice agriculture can explain the locations of slave settlements, but not the corresponding change in their organization and appearance. It has been argued that on Colonial plantations racial difference—and indeed, racial superiority—was symbolically represented by the appearance of slave and owner housing and in the material assemblages associated with masters and slaves. While the shift to tidal rice agriculture brought about a more compact and more stable settlement, such social differences could still have been maintained architecturally and materially. They were not. Instead, planters apparently sought to minimize cultural differences while emphasizing the social hierarchy. House form, settlement patterning, and material culture were all changed, at the planters' insistence. Ben Sullivan, a former

slave of Thomas Cooper on St. Sullivans Island, Georgia, recalled that:

> Ole man Okra an ole man Gibson an ole Israel, dey's African an dey belong tuh James Couper an das how I knows em. . . . Ole man Okra he say he wahn a place lak he hab in Africa so he buil im a hut. I membuh it well. It wuz bout twelve by foeteen feet an it hab dut flo an he buil duh side lak basket weave wid clay plastuh on it. It hab a flat rof wut he make from bush an palmettuh an it hab one doe an no winduhs. Bu Massuh make im pull it down. He say he ain wahn no African hut on he place (*Drums and Shadows* 1940:179–180).

With the shift to tidal rice agriculture, European-American planters stopped emphasizing the differences between Africans and Europeans, to the point that the material evidences of such cultural variation disappeared. This dramatic change in material culture cannot be explained simply in terms of changing socioeconomics or acculturation. Rather, it reflects a fundamental difference in the ways in which planters thought. It is suggested here that their new way of thinking reflected the "industrialization" of the plantation economy brought about by the shift to tidal rice agriculture, and that this change, and the ideological structure which proceeded it, are legible in the archaeological record.

The theory of classificatory ideology presented herein was developed in response to the particular circumstances of Lowcountry plantation archaeology. It remains to be seen whether its application is unique or universal. It is suggested, however, that classification offers a rare access into the minds of other cultures, and one with particular relevance to historical archaeology. Historical archaeology is inherently associated with the classification of material culture. By extending systems of classification away from the archaeological and toward the historic, and by understanding the ways in which material items could have been used to symbolize social structure, it may be possible to work from the ground up and to reconstruct historic ideologies and classifications which are not represented in the documentary record. It is a difficult process to attempt to step back into the minds of historic cultures. The study of classification offers one possible path, and thus the potential for historical archaeology to move away from What happened? and When? to the more important Why?

ACKNOWLEDGMENTS

The theory of classificatory ideology presented herein has been influenced by and partially developed in response to the writings of John Otto and Winthrop Jordan, and to graduate coursework at the University of Pennsylvania with professors Sandra Barnes, Drew Faust, Henry Glassie, and Robert Schuyler. Their scholarship and teachings are gratefully acknowledged. I would particularly like to thank Dr. Schuyler for his efforts at exposing the range of theoretical approaches applicable to historical archaeology, and for encouraging theory building in historical archaeology. An earlier version was presented in a symposium synthesizing and comparing Lowcountry and Chesapeake plantation archeology at the 1991 SHACHUA annual meeting in Richmond. I would like to thank Julia King, co-chair of that symposium, as well as all of the symposium's participants: Natalie Adams, Rick Afleck, Ed Chappell, Terry Epperson, Julie Ernstein, Leland Ferguson, Bill Kelso, Lynne Lewis, Patricia McGuire, George McDaniel, Sue Moore, Vanessa Patrick, Eric Poplin, Doug Sanford, Theresa Singleton, and Tom Wheaton for promoting a synthetic and comparative understanding of plantation archaeology. I would also like to acknowledge the influence of the work in plantation archaeology and history being carried out by Bill Adams, Ron Anthony, David Babson, Lesley Drucker, Dee Dee Joyce, Charles Joyner, Ken Lewis, Charles Orser, Mary Beth Reed, and Martha Zierden. Finally, I am grateful for the comments provided by *Historical Archaeology*'s anonymous reviewers, and accept full responsibility for any errors or omissions which might appear within these pages.

REFERENCES

ADAMS, WILLIAM H. (EDITOR)
1987   Historical Archaeology of Plantations at Kings Bay, Camden County, Georgia. *Reports of Investigations* No. 5. Department of Anthropology, University of Florida, Gainesville.

ADAMS, WILLIAM H., AND SARAH J. BOLING
1989   Status and Ceramics for Planters and Slaves on Three Georgia Coastal Plantations. *Historical Archaeology* 23(1):69–96.

ANDERSON, DAVID G., AND J. W. JOSEPH
1988   *Prehistory and History Along the Upper Savannah River: Technical Synthesis of Cultural Resource Investigations, Richard B. Russell Multiple Resource Area.* Russell Papers 1988. Interagency Archeological Services, National Park Service, Atlanta, Georgia.

ANTHONY, CARL
1976   The Big House and the Slave Quarters, Part I: Prelude to New World Architecture. *Landscape* 21(1): 8–19.

ANTHONY, RONALD W.
1986   Colono Wares. In *Home Upriver: Rural Life on Daniel's Island, Berkeley County, South Carolina*, by Martha A. Zierden, Lesley M. Drucker, and Jeanne Calhoun, pp. 7-22–7-50. Report prepared by Carolina Archaeological Services/Charleston Museum Joint Venture, Columbia. Submitted to the South Carolina Department of Highways and Public Transportation, Columbia.
1989   Cultural Diversity at Mid to Late 18th-Century Lowcountry Plantation Slave Settlements. Unpublished M.A. thesis, Department of Anthropology, University of South Carolina, Columbia.

BABSON, DAVID W.
1987   Plantation Ideology and the Archaeology of Racism: Evidence from the Tanner Road Site (38BK416), Berkeley County, South Carolina. *South Carolina Antiquities* 19(1&2):35–47.
1988   The Tanner Road Settlement: The Archaeology of Racism on Limerick Plantation. *Volumes in Historical Archaeology IV, Conference on Historic Sites Archaeology.* South Carolina Institute of Archaeology and Anthropology, University of South Carolina, Columbia.

BELL, MALCOLM, JR.
1987   *Major Butler's Legacy: Five Generations of a Slaveholding Family.* University of Georgia Press, Athens.

BENEDICT, RUTH
1934   *Patterns of Culture.* Houghton Mifflin, Boston.

BREEDEN, JAMES O. (EDITOR)
1980   *Advice Among Masters: The Ideal in Slave Management in the Old South.* Greenwood Press, Westport, Connecticut.

BROWN, KENNETH L., AND DOREEN C. COOPER
1990   Structural Continuity in an African-American Slave and Tenant Community. In Historical Archaeology on Southern Plantations and Farms, edited by Charles E. Orser, Jr. *Historical Archaeology* 24(4): 7–19.

CASH, W. J.
1941   *The Mind of the South.* Alfred A. Knopf, New York.

DARWIN, CHARLES
1964   *On the Origin of Species.* Reprint of 1859 edition. Harvard University Press, Cambridge, Massachusetts.

DAVIS, DAVID BRION
1975   *The Problem of Slavery in the Age of the Revolution.* Cornell University Press, Ithaca, New York.

DRUMS AND SHADOWS
1940   *Drums and Shadows: Survival Studies Among the Georgia Coastal Negroes.* Savannah Unit, Georgia Writer's Project, Works Project Administration. Brown Thrasher Books. University of Georgia Press, Athens.

DURKHEIM, EMILE, AND MARCEL MAUSS
1963   *Primitive Classification.* Reprint of 1902 publication (*Année Sociologique* 6:1–72). University of Chicago Press, Chicago, Illinois.

EVANS-PRITCHARD, E. E.
1940   *The Nuer.* Clarendon Press, New York.

FAUST, DREW GILPIN
1981   Introduction. In *The Ideology of Slavery: Proslavery Thought in the Antebellum South, 1830–1860*, edited by Drew Gilpin Faust, pp.1–20. Louisiana State University Press, Baton Rouge.
1982   *James Henry Hammond and the Old South: A Design for Mastery.* Louisiana State University Press, Baton Rouge.

FERGUSON, LELAND G.
1977   An Archeological-Historical Analysis of Fort Watson: December 1780–April 1781. In *Research Strategies in Historical Archeology*, edited by Stanley A. South, pp. 41–71. Academic Press, New York.
1978   Looking for the "Afro" in Colono-Indian Pottery. *Conference on Historic Sites Archaeology Papers, 1977* 12:68–86.
1985   Struggling with Pots in Colonial South Carolina. Paper presented at the 18th Annual Meeting of the Society for Historical Archaeology, Boston, Massachusetts.

FERGUSON, LELAND G., AND DAVID W. BABSON
1986   Survey of Plantation Sites Along the East Branch of the Cooper River: A Model for Predicting Archeological Site Location. Report prepared by Department of Anthropology, University of South Carolina, Columbia. Submitted to the South Carolina Department of Archives and History, Columbia.

FIELDS, BARBARA J.
1982   Ideology and Race in American History. In *Religion, Race and Reconstruction: Essays in Honor of C. Vann Woodward*, edited by J. M. Kousser and J. M. McPherson, pp. 143–177. Oxford University Press, New York.

GARROW, PATRICK H., AND
THOMAS R. WHEATON, JR.
1989   Colonoware Ceramics: The Evidence from Yaughan and Curriboo Plantations. In Studies in South Carolina Archaeology: Essays in Honor of Robert L. Stephenson. *Anthropological Studies* No. 9:175–184. South Carolina Institute of Archaeology and Anthropology, University of South Carolina, Columbia.

GENOVESE, EUGENE D.
1969   *The World the Slaveholders Made.* Vintage Books, New York.

HOWSON, JEAN E.
1990   Social Relations and Material Culture: A Critique of the Archaeology of Plantation Society. In Historical Archaeology on Southern Plantations and Farms, edited by Charles E. Orser, Jr. *Historical Archaeology* 24(4):78–91.

JORDAN, WINTHROP D.
1974   *The Whiteman's Burden: Historical Origins of Racism in the United States.* Oxford University Press, New York.

JOSEPH, J. W.
1986   CRM: Vogtle-Effingham-Thalmann 500 KV Electric Transmission Line: GP-LI-01: Data Recovery. Report prepared by Garrow & Associates, Inc., Atlanta, Georgia. Submitted to the Georgia Power Company, Atlanta.
1987   Highway 17 Revisited: The Archaeology of Task Labor. *South Carolina Antiquities* 19(1–2):29–34.
1989   Pattern and Process in the Plantation Archaeology of the Lowcountry of Georgia and South Carolina. *Historical Archaeology* 23(1):55–68.

JOYNER, CHARLES
1984   *Down by the Riverside: A South Carolina Slave Community.* University of Chicago Press, Urbana.

LEES, WILLIAM B.
1980   Limerick, Old and In the Way: Archaeological Investigations at Limerick Plantation. *Anthropological Studies* No. 5. South Carolina Institute of Archaeology and Anthropology, University of South Carolina, Columbia.

LEES, WILLIAM B., AND KATHRYN M. KIMERY-LEES
1979   The Function of Colono-Indian Ceramics: Insights from Limerick Plantation, South Carolina. *Historical Archaeology* 13:1–13.

LEWIS, KENNETH E.
1979   Hampton: Initial Archaeological Investigations at an Eighteenth-Century Rice Plantation in the Santee Delta, South Carolina. *Research Manuscript Series* No. 151. South Carolina Institute of Archaeology and Anthropology, University of South Carolina, Columbia.
1985   Plantation Layout and Function in the South Carolina Lowcountry. In *The Archaeology of Slavery and Plantation Life*, edited by Theresa A. Singleton, pp. 35–65. Academic Press, Orlando.

LEWIS, KENNETH E., AND DONALD L. HARDESTY
1979 Middleton Place: Initial Archaeological Investigations at an Ashley River Rice Plantation. *Research Manuscript Series* No. 148. South Carolina Institute of Archaeology and Anthropology, University of South Carolina, Columbia.

LEWIS, KENNETH E., AND HELEN W. HASKELL
1980 Hampton II: Further Archaeological Investigations at a Santee River Rice Plantation. *Research Manuscript Series* No. 161. South Carolina Institute of Archaeology and Anthropology, University of South Carolina, Columbia.

LINNAEUS, CARL VON
1806 *Systema Naturae: A General System of Nature, Through the Three Grand Kingdoms of Animals, Vegetables, and Minerals: Systematically Divided Into Their Several Classes, Orders, Genera, Species, and Varieties, With Their Habitations, Manners, Economy, Structure and Peculiarities.* Reprint of 1735 edition. Lackington, Allen & Co, London.

LITTLEFIELD, DANIEL C.
1981 *Rice and Slaves: Ethnicity and the Slave Trade in Colonial South Carolina.* Louisiana State University Press, Baton Rouge.

MARKS, BAYLEY E.
1987 Skilled Blacks in Antebellum St. Mary's County, Maryland. *Journal of Southern History* 53(4):537–564.

MOORE, SUE MULLINS
1981 The Antebellum Barrier Island Plantation: In Search of an Archeological Pattern. Unpublished Ph.D. dissertation, University of Florida, Gainesville.
1985 Social and Economic Status on the Coastal Plantation: An Archaeological Perspective. In *The Archaeology of Slavery and Plantation Life*, edited by Theresa A. Singleton, pp. 141–160. Academic Press, Orlando.

MORGAN, PHILIP D.
1982 Work and Culture: The Task System and the World of the Lowcountry Blacks, 1700 to 1880. *William and Mary Quarterly* 39(4):563–599.
1983 The Ownership of Property by Slaves in the Mid-Nineteenth-Century Low Country. *Journal of Southern History* 49(3):397–420.
1986 Black Society in the Lowcountry, 1760–1810. In *Slavery and Freedom in the Age of the American Revolution*, edited by Ira Berlin and Ronald Hoffman, pp. 83–142. University of Illinois Press, Chicago.

NEEDHAM, RODNEY (TRANSLATOR)
1963 Introduction. In *Primitive Classification*, by Emile Durkheim and Marcel Mauss, pp. vii–xviii. University of Chicago Press, Chicago.

NOTT, JOSIAH C.
1844 *Two Lectures on the Natural History of the Caucasian and Negro Races.* Dade and Thompson, Mobile, Alabama.

ORSER, CHARLES E., JR.
1987 Plantation Status and Consumer Choice: A Materialist Framework for Historical Archeology. In *Socio-Economic Status and Consumer Choice: Perspectives in Historical Archaeology*, edited by Suzanne Spencer-Wood, pp. 121–137. Plenum Press, New York.
1989 On Plantations and Patterns. *Historical Archaeology* 29(2):28–40.

OTTO, JOHN SOLOMON
1975 Status Differences and the Archeological Record: A Comparison of Planter, Overseer, and Slave Sites from Cannon's Point Plantation (1794–1861), St. Simons Island, Georgia. Unpublished Ph.D. dissertation, University of Florida, Gainesville.
1977 Artifacts and Status Differences—A Comparison of Ceramics from Planter, Overseer, and Slave Sites on an Antebellum Plantation. In *Research Strategies in Historical Archaeology*, edited by Stanley A. South, pp. 91–118. Academic Press, New York.
1980 Race and Class on Antebellum Plantations. In *Archaeological Perspectives on Ethnicity in America: Afro-American and Asian American Culture History*, edited by Robert L. Schuyler, pp. 3–13. Baywood, Farmingdale, New York.
1984 *Cannon's Point Plantation, 1794–1860: Living Conditions and Status Patterns in the Old South.* Academic Press, Orlando.

PRUNTY, MERLE, JR.
1955 The Renaissance of the Southern Plantation. *Geographical Review* 45:459–491.

REITZ, ELIZABETH J., TYSON GIBBS, AND TED A. RATHBUN
1985 Archaeological Evidence for Subsistence on Coastal Plantations. In *The Archaeology of Slavery and Plantation Life*, edited by Theresa A. Singleton, pp. 163–191. Academic Press, Orlando.

ROSENGARTEN, THEODORE
1986 *Tombee: Portrait of a Cotton Planter.* William Morrow, New York.

SCOTT, JOHN S. (EDITOR)
1984 *Journal of a Residence on a Georgian Plantation in 1838–1839*, by Frances Anne Kemble. University of Georgia Press, Athens.

SINGLETON, THERESA A.
1985 Archaeological Implications for Changing Labor Conditions. In *The Archaeology of Slavery and Plantation Life*, edited by Theresa A. Singleton, pp. 291–307. Academic Press, Orlando.

SMITH, JULIA FLOYD
1985   *Slavery and Rice Culture in Low Country Georgia, 1750–1860.* University of Tennessee Press, Knoxville.

SPENCER, HERBERT
1890   *Social Statistics: Or, the Conditions Essential to Human Happiness Specified, and the First of Them Developed.* Reprint of 1850 edition. D. Appleton, New York.

STOCKING, GEORGE W.
1982   *Race, Culture, and Evolution: Essays in the History of Anthropology.* University of Chicago Press, Chicago.

VLACH, JOHN M.
1978   *The Afro-American Tradition in the Decorative Arts.* Cleveland Art Museum, Cleveland, Ohio.

WHEATON, THOMAS R., JR.
1989   Drayton Hall: Archeological Testing of the Orangerie. *Technical Report* No. 11. Report submitted to the National Trust for Historic Preservation. New South Associates, Stone Mountain, Georgia.

WHEATON, THOMAS R., JR., AMY FRIEDLANDER, AND PATRICK H. GARROW
1983   *Yaughan and Curriboo Plantations: Studies in Afro-American Archaeology.* Soil Systems, Marietta, Georgia.

WHEATON, THOMAS R., JR., AND PATRICK H. GARROW
1985   Acculturation and the Archaeological Record in the Carolina Lowcountry. In *The Archaeology of Slavery and Plantation Life*, edited by Theresa A. Singleton, pp. 239–259. Academic Press, Orlando, Florida.

WOBST, H. MARTIN
1977   Stylistic Behavior and Information Exchange. In Papers for the Director: Research Essays in Honor of James B. Griffin, edited by C. E. Cleland. *Anthropological Papers* No. 61:317–342. Museum of Anthropology, University of Michigan, Ann Arbor.

WOOD, PETER H.
1974   *Black Majority: Negroes in Colonial South Carolina from 1670 through the Stono Rebellion.* W. W. Norton, New York.

YENTSCH, ANNE
1990   The Calvert Orangery in Annapolis, Maryland: A Horticultural Symbol of Power and Prestige in an Early Eighteenth-Century Community. In *Earth Patterns: Archaeology of Early American and Ancient Gardens and Landscapes*, edited by William Kelso and Rachel Most, pp. 169–187. University of Virginia Press, Charlottesville.

YENTSCH, ANNE, NAOMI F. MILLER, BARBARA PACA, AND DELORES PIPERNO
1987   Archaeologically Defining the Earlier Garden Landscapes at Morven: Preliminary Results. *Northeast Historical Archaeology* 16:1–29.

ZIERDEN, MARTHA A., AND JEANNE A. CALHOUN
1983   An Archaeological Assessment of the Greenfield Borrow Pit, Georgetown County, South Carolina. *Charleston Museum Contributions* 4. Charleston, South Carolina.

J. W. JOSEPH
NEW SOUTH ASSOCIATES
4889 LEWIS ROAD
STONE MOUNTAIN, GEORGIA 30083

JAMES G. GIBB

Necessary but Insufficient: Plantation Archaeology Reports and Community Action

ABSTRACT

From broken pots, rusted fishhooks, and scraps of bone, archaeologists bring to light aspects of African-American life on antebellum plantations. But it is a dim light, shared by a few through technical reports and scholarly journal articles. This paper examines the distillation of information and ideas from technical reports into publications written specifically for nonarchaeologists. Historical and genealogical society journals, museum newsletters, and church bulletins provide venues through which archaeologists can convey not just what they are doing, but what they have learned. That knowledge has value in the political arena.

Introduction

Site tours effectively introduce the public to archaeology. Guides describe for visitors what the archaeologists are looking for and why, and they show artifacts and the remains of historic buildings, tangible links to an otherwise intangible past. The archaeologists, however, have little opportunity to share with visitors what they have learned from excavating the site. After all, the archaeological team is still collecting the data and has had little or no time to analyze and interpret. By the time the team completes its analyses and sets down its interpretations in a technical report, the excavations are long closed. The public walks away with some knowledge of how archaeologists work and, perhaps, preliminary interpretations that remain to be substantiated and documented for ready reference. Ideas that might serve important social ends and foster public discussion remain buried in limited distribution technical reports or in physically and intellectually inaccessible professional journals. Buried, that is, unless the archaeologist takes the next step: publication for general audiences.

Although largely methodological in scope, drawing on the author's experience in writing for a variety of audiences, this paper also examines the relationship between writer and audience, and particularly between the historical archaeologist as writer and the community for which the archaeologist writes. The second section provides a method for public writing. By no means a primer in writing, this section suggests and illustrates techniques useful for sharing archaeological and historical ideas with nonarchaeologists. The third section presents and critiques a brief article on an antebellum plantation intended for a general audience. The article demonstrates how a small amount of archaeological and archival data can be used to write about African-American experiences on antebellum plantations.

The Archaeologist at Home

Numerous writers in recent years have pointed out that scholars do not exist in a social vacuum (e.g., Eiseley 1958; Hodder 1992; Potter 1994). Scholars live and work within social contexts, their backgrounds and social positions affecting their interests and interpretations of data (McGuire 1992). Such observations place scholars in a global context, emphasizing intellectual milieu (Eiseley 1958) or class, in the Marxian sense (e.g., McGuire 1992; Potter 1994). This paper emphasizes the local context—the township, village, parish, or county—in which the historical archaeologist lives, works, and participates (cf. Shanks and McGuire 1996).

Intruder or Community Participant?

Consider the following dialogue between an archaeologist and a trustee of a historical society. The archaeologist has just written a letter to the society's board of trustees regarding one of its policies:

Board Member: I got your letter. You know it has caused some trouble.
Archaeologist: Yea, I thought it might. But I think this is an important issue that the board needs to address.
Board Member: Sure it needs to be addressed, but it will take time to change.

Historical Archaeology, 1997, 31(3):51-64.
Permission to reprint required.

Archaeologist: The board has had 20 years to change its policy.

Board Member: You have to remember, *this is their culture.*

Archaeologist: [Aside] Am I an outsider in my own community?

The details of this dialogue need not concern the reader. Suffice it to say that it occurred essentially as related, and that the board member is a humanities scholar, well-respected socially and professionally.

The board member's last statement raises important questions that every social scientist must consider: what is my relationship and what are my responsibilities to the community that I am studying and about which I write? For historical archaeologists, the questions gain greater specificity: what is my relationship as a scholar to the community that I study, write about, live and raise my children in, and pay taxes to support? Should I refrain from offering opinions in matters of which I am knowledgeable as a result of my professional work, or am I morally and professionally obligated to speak out? Do I have a role in my community as a historical archaeologist?

For historical archaeologists, the issue differs from that confronted by many ethnographers working in societies other than their own. The site or sites under study generally are situated in the same village, city, parish, county, province, or state in which the archaeologist lives, and will continue to live long after completion of the research. Regardless of the cultural background of the site's occupants, their actions, values, and choices contributed to the development of the community of which the archaeologist has become a part. In short, historical archaeologists can study the development of prevailing conditions and attitudes in the community from which they derive some of their own social identity. The separation between *their* history and *my/our* history, if ever distinct, becomes very hazy, the historical archaeologist occupying the statuses of client and service provider simultaneously.

Clearly, this ambiguity can be abused, the scholar using knowledge acquired with the aid of community resources to advance personal interests and views. That knowledge, however, must become public before it is of any social value, and it would be very naive to assume that individuals with opposing interests necessarily acquiesce to the archaeologist's authority, or necessarily recognize the archaeologist as an authority. Publishing, therefore, becomes both ethical and necessary: use of public resources, including nonrenewable archaeological resources, demands some kind of return, and the resulting insights have little value outside of the public arena.

The rules of publishing have changed since the 1970s. Prior to the rapid growth of cultural resources management programs, archaeological research involved little in the way of public support—the New Deal programs of the 1930s excepted—and occurred largely out of view. Publication was, and remains, an important means of advancement in the academy, a route to improved salaries, tenure, and prestige. In the 1990s, archaeology not only consumes far more in public resources, it also is difficult to hide as crews work along highway shoulders and in the midst of urban parking lots. Television programs such as *Archeology* play an important role in introducing ever-widening audiences to archaeology, creating a constituency for the discipline that is both local and national, and far larger than any scholarly audience. Many practitioners, now working in cultural resources management firms, museums, and government agencies, can get along very nicely without publishing anything in scholarly journals. The reward system developed in the academy bears little relevance in the business world; clients, neighborhood groups, and government agencies are replacing university provosts, deans, and department chairs as those who must be pleased. The rules have changed, and so have the responsibilities.

Reflection and Responsibility

Archaeologists occupy a privileged position vis-à-vis access to historical data and time and training devoted to the interpretation of those data. This privileged position—having the training and resources with which to gain unique insights into the history of one's community—comes with certain responsibilities. Potter (1991:95) defines social responsibility as "having a full awareness of the contexts and consequences of the work one does, the conclusions one reaches, and the modes of expression one chooses . . . using the most sophisticated means available to mean what is said and to say what is meant, to an acknowledged audience." The archaeologist acts responsibly by reflecting on the needs and interests of a particular audience, and his or her role in helping to meet those needs (Potter 1991:100; cf. McKee [1994:3] on intellectual autonomy). Potter suggests four approaches to reflection in plantation archaeology:

1. Archaeologists should attempt to understand objects and events in terms of their native meanings (Potter 1991:101). Attention to native meanings potentially can gain a large and supportive constituency, particularly when that constituency includes millions of African Americans who want to learn about their ancestors and not necessarily about English ceramics. Plantation archaeology that examines slavery from the perspective of the planter will lose both African-American audiences, whose interests largely are in the slave's perspective, and Euroamerican audiences for whom slavery is a sensitive issue not willingly engaged. An archaeology of African-American life and antebellum plantation society should measure the quality of life of enslaved and free Africans in their own terms, evoking their fears, frustrations, glimpses of hope, sense of accomplishment, and identity. Focusing on African-American attitudes and strategies overcomes some of the limitations imposed by a relatively uniform material culture, or, objects produced on an industrial scale for nameless masses of consumers, without turning plantation excavations into searches for "Africanisms." More importantly, a concern for strategy brings a local focus to plantation archaeology, recognizing and analyzing variability and rejecting stereotypes.

2. The specific conditions of slavery, and patterns identified archaeologically, must be placed in larger social and historical contexts (Potter 1991:102). Archaeologists, for example, can interpret trends in ceramic acquisition as evidence of increased economic freedom (e.g., Adams and Boling 1989). Whether such a trend can be documented for one plantation or for plantations throughout a region, economic freedom must be understood within the larger context of plantation society, itself a part of a larger world economy. Potter (1991) argues that a claim of increased economic freedom, even if supportable within very narrowly defined limits, betrays a lack of reflection. The costs of a slave's ability to purchase crockery must be taken into account, and the slave owner's motivation for permitting such freedoms must be examined in terms of the actors' larger objectives. Decontextualizing specific behavioral patterns and events precludes understanding of the past and, potentially, produces ill-founded ideas subject to misuse in the political arena.

3. On a related point, Potter (1991:102) states that aspects of slave life should not be separated from the fact of slavery. In other words, all aspects of slave life should be seen in terms of their role in the maintenance or rejection of slavery. For example, the use of firearms for hunting by some slaves—allowed by the slave owner—suggests an ability to improve the quality and variety of their diet. Lead shot, spent gunflints, and a worn garden hoe found in slave house trash deposits could indicate a diet rich in fresh meat and vegetables, produced and subject to the control of the slaves, an observation testable with faunal and botanical data. Considered in the context of reduced prices offered for plantation staples, economic independence becomes more apparent than real. Evidence of hunting, fishing, and gardening could point to greater hardship as slaves were forced to spend more of their free time producing their own subsistence, freeing slave owners of their responsibility to adequately feed, clothe, and house their slaves. Placing the artifact analysis within a larger historical context leads to a richer story and a greater understanding of slavery and plantation society in an expanding global economy. Rich

historical contexts, derived through archaeological and archival data analyses, lead to dynamic, rather than static, views of African-American life on antebellum plantations (Gibb and Davis 1989).

4. Potter's fourth suggested approach to reflection enjoins the archaeologist to take control over how data, and by extension the ideas derived from those data, are presented to the public (Potter 1991:103). Working with *Archaeology in Annapolis*, a joint program of the University of Maryland and Historic Annapolis, Inc., Potter has been a leading proponent of on-site public historical interpretation (Potter 1994). Potter's argument, and the principle tenet of *Archaeology in Annapolis*, is that archaeologists must recognize archaeology as a political act and develop research questions that take this fact into account. Archaeology should lead the public to question the validity and legitimacy of widely held beliefs.

Archaeology in Annapolis personnel actively engage site visitors in dialogues about past and present. But, as pointed out in the introduction to this paper, site visitors cannot question the validity or relevance of a project's results because those results are not finalized until long after the completion of fieldwork. As long as archaeologists confine their public outreach programs to site tours, the politics of the past and of archaeology remain largely in the background. The rudiments of archaeological technique and general background information on the site busy the guide, and the novelty of the experience can overwhelm the visitor. Most visitors will find ideas about the past difficult to grasp and retain as they shift their weight from one foot to the other, strain to hear the guide over the noise of passing traffic, or anxiously count heads to make sure that they have as many children as they started with. Even blatantly unconventional ideas may dissipate unless given physical form as exhibits or publications.

Pamphlets and guidebooks, developed for use at particular archaeological sites, serve as inter-

pretive tools, post-visit reference works, and promotional literature (McManus 1995). These publications, and follow-up articles in local periodicals, can bring ethical and historical questions to the fore (e.g., Logan 1992). With texts in hand, seated in comfortable chairs out of the sun, wind, or rain, people can contemplate what their archaeologists have said and done. They have time to consider whether or not a cemetery or a battlefield should be excavated, or whether a team of Euroamerican archaeologists should be digging an African-American dwelling site. They might realize that the archaeologists' interpretations, possibly paid for with public funds, undermine cherished beliefs or claim to uncover evidence of past and ongoing oppression. Such material is easily shared, or submitted in evidence in debates over public support for archaeology. Archaeological findings, committed to print in nontechnical, locally available publications can contribute to community debates about important issues, including the future of publicly funded archaeological research and historic preservation. Such printed matter also bears the name or names of those responsible for its publication.

Authorship implies perspective and individual responsibility; Davis and Gibb (1988) provide a discussion of authorship and museum exhibits. Publishing ideas locally, in an intellectually accessible style—readable and comprehensible, invites response and that response may not be positive or measured. Public criticism can be caustic and, sometimes, warranted. It also indicates success, measurable in terms of letters to newspaper editors and by follow-up or spinoff stories by other writers. Whether or not readers accept what archaeologists say is irrelevant: if they begin to think historically, we have succeeded. If any of my stories ever lead to public debate, even controversy, so much the better. I am willing to apologize for factual or interpretive errors, as long as I have worked conscientiously and acted responsibly. Potter's four approaches to reflective, responsible writing provide a good beginning for making those determinations. No amount of reflection, however, will bring scholarship to general audiences. Commitment to publishing in local venues and clear, interesting prose are essential.

Method in Popular Writing

Bookstores and libraries offer large selections of treatises on writing aimed at students, aspiring professional writers, and professional writers avoiding the act of writing (Becker and Richards 1986). Two bits of advice appear in virtually every one of these books: know your subject and know your audience. Historical archaeologists know their subject well and, as long as they write for one another, they know their audience well. As pointed out above, however, data and interpretations presented to fellow professionals may have little influence in larger social arenas. Socially and politically relevant archaeology shares archaeological information and ideas with nonarchaeologists, and that entails identification of audiences and means of reaching those audiences.

Identifying Audience and Venue

American consumers are familiar with the phrase "one size fits all," and at least some regard such claims with skepticism. One sock size does not fit all, nor does one style of writing meet all needs or reach all audiences. Some of the papers in this volume, for example, address issues not ordinarily encountered in the pages of *Historical Archaeology*. Hence, they differ in some respects from the kinds of scholarly papers ordinarily published in this journal. The audience is the same, but the needs are different. For example, insisting that interpretation derives from a socially positioned observer requires the active voice and judicious use of first person pronouns, though editorial guidelines discourage the latter. To do otherwise casts doubt on the author's sincerity and understanding of the subject, since a text written in the third person and passive voice suggests authority that transcends the author and defies attribution. Similarly, an article in a local history journal on the kinds of crockery purchased by the

community's founding families should not have the descriptive and statistical detail needed by other historical archaeologists working in the same area.

How can archaeologists identify other audiences and venues other than scholarly journals? Let us reverse the order of the questions since the existence of a venue implies a specific audience. Identifying the kinds of publications available in a community could require as little as a visit to the public library or historical society and an examination of the various publications on their shelves or in their vertical files. Statewide museum associations maintain lists of their member institutions, including addresses, principal officers, and the nature and periodicity of their publications. Many community organizations—including churches, youth groups, garden clubs, and business associations—publish newsletters that can accommodate brief historical articles of relevance to the organization's mission. Local newspapers also may accept for publication articles by nonstaff writers (e.g., Gibb 1993a, 1994). I have found that most newsletter and journal editors are pleased to receive submissions, provided the author first asks about appropriate subject matter and length. Outside submissions relieve the editor of having to solicit material or write copy, and such pieces can broaden the appeal of the publication. Well-executed, informative line drawings, produced at a scale appropriate to the physical format of the publication, and an interesting photograph or two also make welcome additions.

Nonprofessional editors tend to accept manuscripts for publication with minimal or no editing, seeking approval from the author for any changes. Professional editors, meeting publication deadlines, are more inclined to make changes—often for the better, but not necessarily so—and print the article without asking for the author's approval. Sure, loss of editorial control could lead to problems (I have not had any of note), but consider a common, alternative means of sharing archaeology with the public. Archaeologists notify print and broadcast journalists of an excavation, its purpose, and preliminary findings. A journalist visits the site or laboratory, interviews the principal investigator and possibly several assistants and volunteers, and writes a story. If the archaeologist is lucky, the journalist will call again to verify facts. Hopefully, the final story will be positive, interesting, and substantially correct. Given the very ephemeral nature of news stories, minor errors can be overlooked—nobody but the journalist and the archaeologists involved are likely to notice or remember. The archaeologist surrenders all control to the journalist and relies on that individual's intelligence, experience, and integrity to tell the story accurately and well. Calling for local news coverage, although a valuable approach for reaching the public, surrenders control over one's presentation of data.

Trained journalists can tell an archaeological story well. With a little practice and attention to detail, archaeologists can tell their own story as well, if not better, with greater accuracy, precision, broader social and historical context, reflection, and genuine passion. The trick is to lay aside those writing techniques that may be appropriate in academic or legal compliance contexts and adopt those best suited for journalism (Gibb 1993b). A few recommendations will suffice: 1) use the narrative, rather than analytical, form; 2) "people" your story, preferably with the site occupants and with professional archaeologists, site visitors, local historians, politicians, and museum curators; 3) favor Anglo-Saxon words over borrowed words, and clear phrases over contorted academic constructions (Becker and Richards 1986:26–42); and 4) reject the passive voice and contrived third person.

Analytic writing and statistical analysis have value for scholarly audiences concerned with subject, method, and scientific proof; but a narrative approach is more suitable for nonsocial scientists. In a narrative, the author stresses relationships, usually chronological, between events rather than a particular research problem with its attendant methodology and analysis. Individual people initiate, and respond to, events. Their actions reverberate to the present, environmentally, culturally, and genetically. As the literal or cultural ancestors of the current community they provide a point of interest and as living,

breathing people—metaphorically speaking—they enliven the narrative. Just how lively depends on the writer's use of clear phrasing and active verbs.

Ironically, anthropological writers—those with a professed interest in cultural change—often write in the passive voice, the author camouflaged behind third person pronouns relating states rather than strategies and processes. Active verbs vitalize sentences and force the author to identify the actors behind the action. (For example, the passive voice is uninteresting, and it is often unclear who did what or why.) Unnecessary qualifiers and complex words, and convoluted or jargonistic phrases also hide the action and actors, depriving the narrative of clarity and, in some cases, meaning. Words should work semantically, not ceremonially (Becker and Richards 1986:31): they should challenge, not obfuscate.

Of the four recommendations, all but the first can improve both scientific and popular writing. Analytical writing poses research problems and methods for addressing those problems, describes and analyzes data, and interprets the results. Note the progression: problem, method, analysis, and interpretation. This is the scientific method. Although inappropriate for most public writing, scientific method should underlie popular writing; namely, popular writing should focus on the product and not the process of scientific method. Focusing on product requires application of the method: research, analysis, and interpretation precede popular writing. In archaeology, as in any science, the technical report comes first. But, a technical report cannot substitute for a popular account of the research. A popular account is not a technical report written with fewer words, nor does popular writing simply summarize scientific findings. Popular writing identifies an audience, selects a venue suitable for reaching that audience, and relates an interesting storyline that can be told within the physical limitations of the venue. The approach should be narrative, not analytical. After all, the public's principal interest is in what we have learned, and not necessarily in how we have learned. The ideas have value in public discourse, not the methods for collecting and analyzing data.

Finding Africans on Antebellum Plantations

The following text is an example of what can be written for a general audience with a minimal amount of archaeological and archival data. The story concerns Riversdale, an early 19th-century plantation in Prince Georges County, Maryland (Figure 1). Slave labor built the 1803 mansion for a Belgian émigré family, the Stiers, and for the Calvert family, descendants of the lords Baltimore, proprietors of the Maryland colony. I have written this story with a particular venue in mind: *Passports to the Past*, a newsletter published by the History Division of the Maryland-National Capital Parks and Planning Commission (M-NCPPC), sponsors of the research (Gibb and Weiskotten 1996). *Passports* presents articles on historical research and cultural events related to the organization's mission. (The article also is suitable for *The Riversdale Letter*, a quarterly newsletter of the Riversdale Historical Society, Inc., and could be printed in both publications.)

The M-NCPPC distributes the newsletter free of charge at its various parks and historic sites, as well as through a mailing list. While the nature of the readership is largely unknown, it likely includes a culturally and occupationally diverse audience in the Washington–Baltimore area, with a demonstrated interest in history (expressed by their having visited a historic site administered by the commission). My purposes in writing this article for *Passports* are twofold: to inform this diverse, self-selected audience of archaeological findings at Riversdale and to remind them that enslaved Africans built, main-

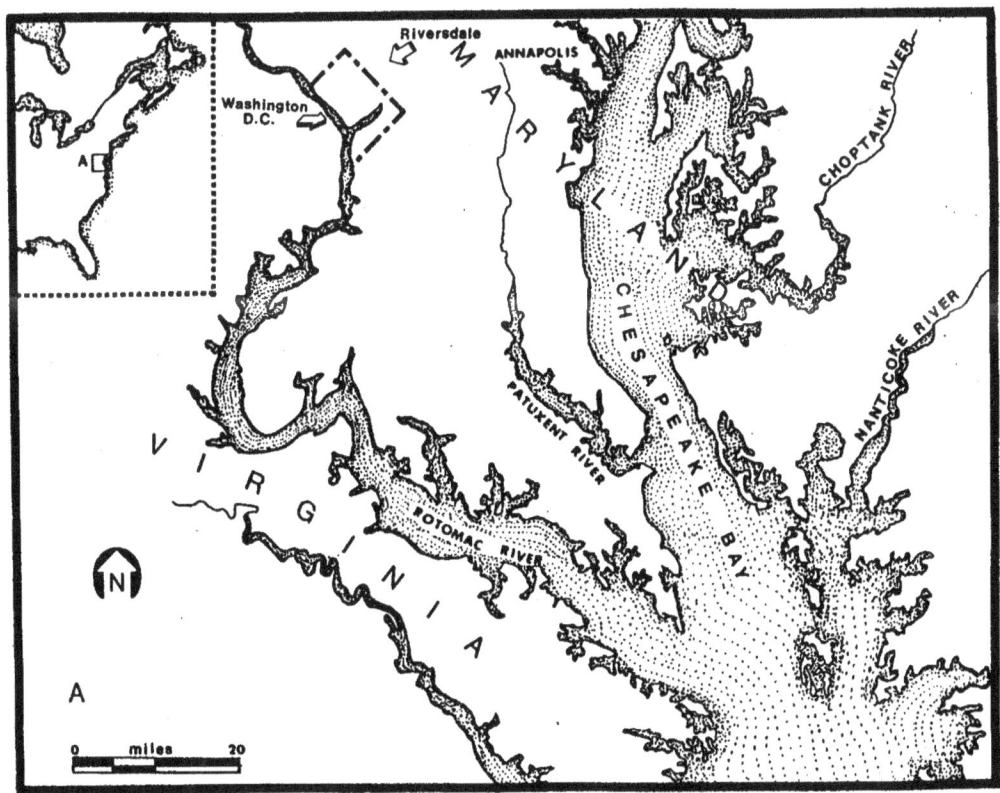

FIGURE 1. Location of Riversdale Mansion in Prince Georges County, Maryland.

tained, and occupied the home of Maryland's politically powerful, Anglo-American Calvert family. The mansion and grounds stand as a testament to the power and aesthetic discernment of the Calverts, but they also represent the skills, pride, fortitude, oppression, and exploitation of African America.

Building Riversdale

Frederick Law Olmsted dismounted from his horse in front of Riversdale Mansion on 14 December 1852 (Figure 2). His fame as America's preeminent landscape architect—designer of Central Park in New York City and Woodley Park in Washington, DC—lay years in the future. In 1852 he was a largely unknown journalist charged with touring the southern states and reporting on the conditions of slavery for a moderate antislavery newspaper in New York City. He brought with him an outlook on slavery not shared by his first host, Charles Calvert, and the stage upon which they met belied the beliefs of both.

Olmsted's visit to the home of Charles and Charlotte Calvert was the first of many similar visits to the small farms and plantations of the American South. In *A Tour of the Southern Slave States* (Olmsted 1856), and two subsequent books based on his tour, Olmsted proved himself an astute observer of buildings and fields, forests, and city streets. But he often colored his portrayals to make two points, "observations" that appear throughout his writings on American slavery: slaveholding undermined the moral and economic growth of the South, and slaves were inefficient and unreliable workers. He tried to convince both North and South that slavery should be abandoned for practical reasons, that the change would occur gradually and without the need for violent confrontation.

Having rehearsed his argument before leaving New York, Olmsted tried it on the Calverts. Charles Calvert did not sympathize: "Mr. C. is a large hereditary owner of slaves, which, for ordinary field and stable-work, constitute his laboring force . . . . He would not think of using Irishmen for common farm-labor, and made light

FIGURE 2. Restored Riversdale Mansion, north facade.

of their coming in competition with slaves. Negroes at hoeing and any steady field-work, he assured me, would 'do two to their one.'" Beyond this sentiment, we cannot tell how the Calverts felt, Charles being "disinclined to converse on the topic of slavery." Olmsted maintained a different view of slaves as laborers, noting that the Calverts's slaves often worked ineffectively and required Charles's frequent intercession. Theirs must have been a very curious conversation, taking place within, or in sight of, beautiful Riversdale Mansion, built by and maintained with slave labor, betraying skills and pride unacknowledged by either man.

Henri Stiers, a Belgian refugee, purchased more than 700 acres and arranged for the design and construction of a mansion near Bladensburgh, Maryland. Returning to Belgium under Napoleon's conditions of amnesty, Stiers left the property to his daughter Rosalie and her American husband, George Calvert. They oversaw the completion of the house and grounds, living there until Rosalie's death in 1821 and George's death in 1836 (Callcott 1991; Buonocore 1996; Glover 1996). Their son, Charles Benedict Calvert, inherited the property and lived there with his wife Charlotte until his death in 1864. Under Charles and Charlotte's administration, Riversdale grew to 2,000 acres by the 1850s, well-organized and planted, supporting scores of people in dozens of buildings. Only the brick and stucco mansion, an adjacent brick outbuilding, and archaeological deposits survive. Symmetry governs the placement of doors and windows producing a form and appearance typical of colonial-period mansions built a half century or more earlier than Riversdale.

Little documentation has surfaced regarding the construction of the mansion, the best published information appearing in Henri Stiers's letters to Rosalie Calvert (Callcott 1991). The exchange of letters between father and daughter tell the modern reader who designed the building and oversaw its construction, but not who actually made the bricks, erected the walls, and executed the fine interior woodwork. Likewise, Henri recommended a particular architect to lay out the grounds around the mansion, but neither he nor Rosalie say much about who executed the plan and maintained the terraced gardens, fountain, and ornamental pond.

Some details of the landscape survive in an 1853 map of the property, prepared by William Sides (Figures 3, 4). The map depicts several buildings adjacent to the mansion known, from other documentary sources, to include a kitchen, water tower, laundry, and smokehouse. Ornamental gardens appear in the north and south

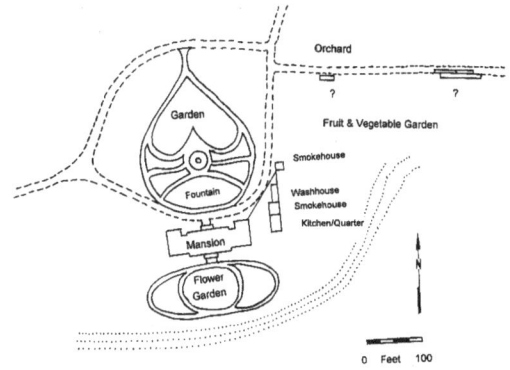

FIGURE 4. Detail of William Sides (1853) map of Riversdale [labels added].

yards, and an icehouse, barn, stable, and three dwellings lie further afield. The dwelling closest to the octagonal barn housed the overseer while the two unspecified dwellings probably sheltered household slaves (Callcott 1994). (See also Plummer's [1927] description of the slave house in which she was born and observations from her father's diary of 1841–1905.) The map also depicts two structures, probably agricultural, near the barn and stockyard.

Archaeological excavations along the east side of the mansion (sponsored by the M-NCPPC) revealed 10 structures, including several buildings depicted on Side's map (Figure 5). At least two brick foundations, however, mark the locations of probable garden buildings that do not appear on the 1853 map: an octagonal building and an irregularly shaped, but roughly square, structure (Figure 5, structures G and E, respectively). Both undocumented structures probably served as garden outbuildings dating to George and Rosalie Calvert's tenure (1803–1836). Limited excavations elsewhere on the property also uncovered probable evidence of the smokehouse, a garden wall, the fountain in the north yard, and one of the unlabeled structures noted by William Sides northeast of the mansion.

Taken together, the architectural, archaeological, and archival evidence reveal an elegant mansion and grounds that changed over the course of a half century. George and Rosalie's

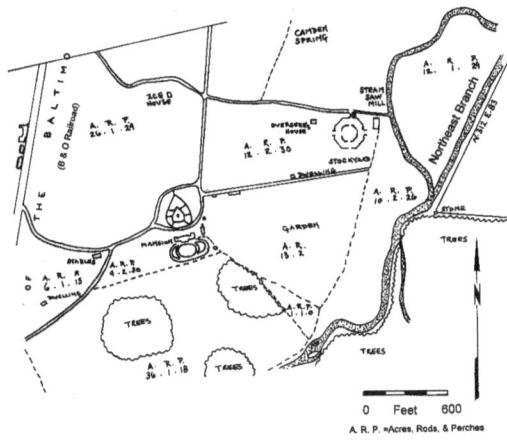

FIGURE 3. Enhanced view of the William Sides (1853) map of Riversdale.

home formed the heart of their plantation, but they also intended it as a place of repose and entertainment, surrounded by ornate gardens and secluded spaces. Charles and Charlotte, although no less the entertainers than Charles's parents, preferred a less formal, more pragmatically American setting. They probably razed the ornamental buildings, gone by 1853, but maintained the kitchen and laundry buildings. Charles prided himself on his scientifically designed octagonal barn, and published a description and plans in *The Country Gentleman* (Calvert 1854), a widely-read periodical. Visitors to Riversdale in the 1850s might have found the Calverts strolling about the ornamental gardens. More likely, they would find Charles and Charlotte inspecting the stables or laundry, re-evaluating drainage systems, or conducting an earlier visitor about the octagonal barn. Like Olmsted, any visitor expressing interest in Charles's agricultural ideas might spend the remainder of the day touring the farm and listening to Charles lecture on the need for scientific method in farming.

Archaeological and archival research reveals two plantations at Riversdale: an elegant mansion surrounded by ornamental buildings and gardens melding American and European designs at the heart of a traditional tobacco plantation, and a more distinctly American farm embodying new techniques and crop choices, and emphasizing simple, independent living with a minimum of ostentation and explicitly functional buildings and grounds. Both plantations, however, were built on slavery.

The high-quality bricks, the fine hand with which they were laid, and the many elegant details of house and gardens were products of slaves—both those owned or rented by the architect and building contractors and those owned by the Stiers-Calvert family. Enslaved women, children, and men built Riversdale. They raised the crops that paid for its upkeep, if not actual construction, and they built the splendid residence that survives to this day and the various garden features that survive only archaeologically. Given what we have learned from archaeological and archival research at Riversdale, let us return

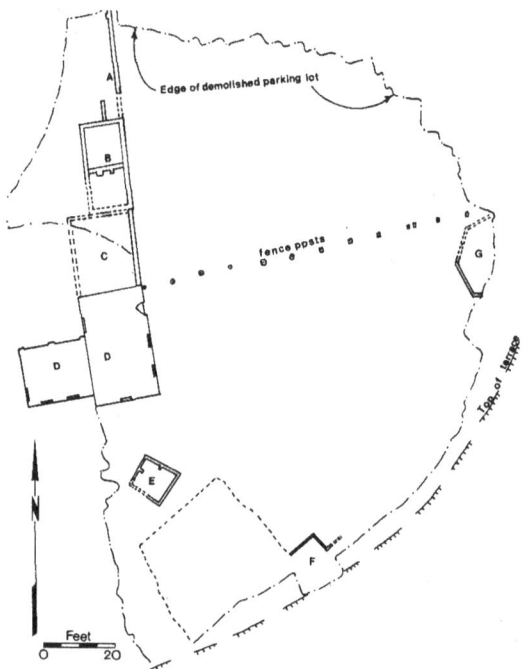

FIGURE 5. Archaeological evidence of structures at Riversdale: (A) garden wall; (B) washhouse; (C) water tower; (D) extant dependency and addition; (E) outbuilding of uncertain function; (F) possible terrace stairs; and (G) octagonal structure of uncertain function.

to the discussion between Olmsted and Calvert.

Calvert described his slaves as faithful, steady farm workers. Olmsted tells his readers that the slaves moved slowly and awkwardly, "difficult to direct efficiently," and "irksome and trying to one's patience." Neither looked about them and recognized the relationship between the stately manor and the people who worked on it. We know that Charles owned between 45 and 55 slaves from 1840 to 1860 and his parents owned 78 in 1810 (Buonocore 1996), most of whom we do not know by name. The Calvert slaves left no written account of their lives, but they did leave a monument to their skills and evidence of a pride in accomplishment, pride that survived and possibly thrived despite the pain and indignities of slavery. Riversdale was their mansion and their plantation.

Perhaps when we admire Riversdale and tour its restored interior we should think less of the Calverts and more of the people who built, maintained, and even occupied the mansion. The site memorializes the scores of men and women who built and preserved it, as well as the several families whose privileged positioned allowed them to leave a better documented—if no more enduring—mark on Maryland's landscape.

Dismantling "Riversdale"

This brief article aims at two objectives: relating some of the archaeological findings at Riversdale to a broadly defined, self-selected audience, and heightening that audience's awareness of contradictory views—past and current—of slavery in America. I remind my audience that Riversdale, and similar historic places, did not materialize directly from a series of plans. Labor, comprised largely of enslaved Africans, interpreted and executed those plans, turning them into enduring examples of the best in American design. Olmsted and Calvert did not, or would not, recognize that contribution. Their conversation took place on a stage that contradicted what they said. Their conversation also points out an important aspect of antebellum history, one that does not require archaeology to study: Americans did not agree on slavery, and even slaveholders like Charles Calvert had their doubts. Citizens will be well-served by archaeology and history if they learn that diversity of opinion was as much a part of the past as it is of the present.

There are problems with this article, partly attributable to the scope and nature of the original research, partly to the particular storyline. African Americans appear in the piece as nameless artisans and caretakers, while elite white men serve as the focal point. While such a focus undermines one of the two objectives—highlighting the African-American part in the Riversdale story, it also serves as an important point of departure, setting the conflicting perspectives of these two "positioned observers" against a backdrop that contradicted both. Additional research could have provided one or more named Africans who could have played a part in this one-act play, e.g., further study of

Adam Francis Plummer's life, as told by his daughter (Plummer 1927). The scope of work for this commissioned study focused on identifying and determining the historical significance of archaeological deposits on the grounds in advance of parking lot demolition and construction. Further research into the slaves of Riversdale would have been appropriate and, perhaps, integral to an argument for historical significance. More detailed analysis of the extant and archaeologically recovered architecture and landscape also might have shed greater light on African attitudes towards European aesthetics, revealing native meanings and leading to a greater understanding of antebellum African-American experiences.

I am also sensible of the effect that this article may have in promoting Riversdale as a museum of African-American history. As a contracted researcher, working within a narrowly defined scope of work, making such a policy recommendation probably would be inappropriate. I am comfortable in pointing out to larger audiences—larger than the government agencies managing the property—that enslaved women, children, and men built and maintained Riversdale, interpreting the plans and instructions of the Stiers-Calvert family and their contractors. The community may make use of this observation in current debates over the uses and interpretation of the site. Unfortunately, the technical report upon which I based the article contains little data or analysis pertaining to slaves at Riversdale, and little consideration of their experiences. Since I did not adequately explore the issue of slavery in the development of Riversdale in the technical report, I have not been able to make as convincing, or as useful, an argument as I might have made.

An ill-disposed person could use the Riversdale story to advocate the subjugation of African Americans by Euroamericans. Historically, according to the article, Africans were fine artisans and not the "awkward" workers described by Olmsted or the steady, but unskilled manual workers portrayed by Calvert. They played an important role in the architectural heritage of the nation, a role played in the context of slavery. Should this article include a disclaimer or warning against such an obvious, and illogical, misinterpretation? Potter (1991) advocates a clear statement of what is meant, and not meant. He suggests that such misuses can be predicted and preempted. Perhaps, but future generations will have their own predilections and prejudices and it would be naive to assume we can predict their misuses and misreading. A warning or disclaimer accompanying each paper seems overly defensive, cynical, and inappropriate. Potter (1991) offers better strategies: seek native meanings in larger historical contexts and, above all, take control over the presentation of data and ideas. Publish often and widely, and write material for specific audiences using, wherever possible, existing venues.

Conclusion

There are several points that I have made, and they bear repeating. Site tours grab the public's interest, but they do not send visitors away with substantiated results that can be used in the political arena. Those ideas are hammered out and supported through technical writing. Technical reports, although absolutely necessary to analyze and preserve data, are insufficient because they are physically and intellectually inaccessible to most people. Other suitable venues exist. Our job is to write interesting, responsible narratives for those venues, conveying our findings from technical reports to the public arena.

At the risk of offering a disclaimer, a practice derided above as defensive and cynical, I make three additional points, largely in response to issues raised by the anonymous reviewers of this paper. First, archaeologists do not exist outside of the communities in which they live and work, nor are they the only members of their communities studying and interpreting the past. Historians—professional and avocational—have been around far longer than archaeologists, and likely will continue in their capacity as respected historical interpreters. Second, our society educates and funds archaeologists. It expects leadership within the narrowly defined field of historical

inquiry, but does not bestow upon its archaeologists complete authority. We are responsible, however, for conveying what we have learned to our neighbors. Finally, while many people may be capable of reading and critiquing technical reports, most will learn about archaeological finds and interpretations through other media. Ideas presented through publications and exhibits enter the forum of community, and even national, debate. Whether or not the public accepts those ideas is not nearly as important as the positive role that archaeological and historical narratives play in promoting dialogue about contemporary issues. Third, cut free of the various ancillary issues that I have introduced, this paper encourages archaeologists to recognize that they are leaders within their respective communities, leaders with a responsibility to share their findings and insights, supported through rigorous data collection and analysis, in as clear and accessible a manner as possible.

Postscript

Callcott (1996) summarized for the membership of the Riversdale Historical Society the results of Gibb and Weiskotten's (1996) archaeological study, prior to the submission of the final report. Her summary clearly and succinctly describes what the archaeological team recovered, taking issue with the interpretation of one structure.

ACKNOWLEDGMENTS

I thank Carol McDavid and David Babson for their invitation to participate in the 1996 Society for Historical Archaeology symposium and to contribute to this special issue of Historical Archaeology. Their enthusiasm and commitment to public involvement in archaeology moved this paper to the top of my priority list. My apologies to those whose reports were slightly delayed as a consequence. I also thank Donald K. Creveling, Maryland-National Capital Parks and Planning Commission archaeologist, and Riversdale site managers Susan Wolfe and Ed Day for assisting in the archaeological study of Riversdale plantation. Daniel H. Weiskotten directed and reported much of the Riversdale research, and Susan C. Buonocore shared her thesis data. I accept sole responsibility for the conclusions and interpretations of Riversdale's past and future presented in this paper.

REFERENCES

ADAMS, WILLIAM H., AND SARAH JANE BOLING
1989 Status and Ceramics for Planters and Slaves on Three Georgian Coastal Plantations. *Historical Archaeology* 23(1):69–96.

BECKER, HOWARD S., AND PAMELA RICHARDS
1986 *Writing for Social Scientists: How to Start and Finish your Thesis, Book, or Article.* The University of Chicago Press, Chicago, IL.

BUONOCORE, SUSAN C.
1996 "Within Her Wall": Rosalie Stier Calvert and the Gardens of Riversdale (1803–1821). Unpublished M.A. thesis, Department of History, University of Maryland, Baltimore.

CALLCOTT, MARGARET LAW
1991 *Mistress of Riversdale: The Plantation Letters of Rosalie Stiers Calvert, 1795–1821.* Johns Hopkins University Press, Baltimore, MD.
1994 Slave Housing at Riversdale. *The Riversdale Letter,* Fall:2–4. Newsletter published by the Riversdale Historical Society, Riverdale, MD.
1996 First Stages of Riversdale Archaeology Completed: 1853 Plantation Map Aids Diggers. *The Riversdale Letter,* Spring:2–4. Newsletter published by the Riversdale Historical Society, Riverdale, MD.

CALVERT, CHARLES B.
1854 Plan of Farm Buildings for Animals. *The Country Gentleman* 4(7):108–109.

DAVIS, KAREN L., AND JAMES G. GIBB
1988 Unpuzzling the Past: Critical Thinking in History Museums. *Museum Studies Journal* 3:41–45.

EISELEY, LOREN C.
1958 *Darwin's Century: Evolution and the Men Who Discovered It.* Doubleday, NY.

GIBB, JAMES G.
1993a Publishing in Local History Journals. *Journal of Middle Atlantic Archaeology* 9:41–48.
1993b Chesapeake Bay Life: Finding History through Garbage. *The New Bay Times* 1(3):10.
1994 Railroad Ghosts. *The New Bay Times* 2(10):14–16.

GIBB, JAMES G., AND KAREN L. DAVIS
1989 History Exhibits and Theories of Material Culture. *The Journal of American Culture* 12(2):27–33.

GIBB, JAMES G., AND DANIEL H. WEISKOTTEN
1996 A Phase I Archaeological Survey and Phase II Site Examination of Riversdale Mansion (18PR390), Riverdale, Prince Georges County, Maryland. Prepared by James G. Gibb, Archaeological Consultant. Submitted to the Maryland-National Capital Parks and Planning Commission, Bladensburg, MD.

GLOVER, LORRI M.
1996 Between Two Cultures: The Worlds of Rosalie Stier Calvert. *Maryland Historical Magazine* 91(1):85–94.

HODDER, IAN
1992 *Reading the Past: Current Approaches to Interpretation in Archaeology.* Cambridge University Press, Cambridge, UK.

LOGAN, GEORGE C.
1992 Archaeology at Charles Carroll's House and Garden and of his African-American Slaves. Pamphlet. N.p., n.p.

McGUIRE, RANDALL H.
1992 *A Marxist Archaeology.* Academic Press, San Diego, CA.

McKEE, LARRY
1994 Commentary: Is It Futile to be Useful? Historical Archaeology and the African-American Experience. *Northeast Historical Archaeology* 23:1–7.

McMANUS, PAULETTE M.
1995 A Visitor's Guide to the Contents and Use of Guidebooks. In *Archaeological Displays and the Public: Museology and Interpretation,* edited by Paulette M. McManus, pp. 114–117. Institute of Archaeology, University College, London.

OLMSTED, FREDERICK LAW
1856 *A Tour of the Southern Slave States.* N.p., NY.

PLUMMER, NELLIE ARNOLD
1927 *Out of the Depths, or the Triumph of the Cross.* Published by the author, Hyattsville, MD.

POTTER, PARKER B., JR.
1991 What Is the Use of Plantation Archaeology? *Historical Archaeology* 25(3):94–107.
1994 *Public Archaeology in Annapolis: A Critical Approach to History in Maryland's Ancient City.* Smithsonian Institution Press, Washington, DC.

SHANKS, MICHAEL, AND RANDALL H. McGUIRE
1996 The Craft of Archaeology. *American Antiquity* 61:75–88.

SIDES, WILLIAM
    1853 Riversdale, Seat of Charles B. Calvert. Unpublished
          wall map. Special Collections, Library of the
          University of Maryland, College Park, MD.

JAMES G. GIBB
THE LOST TOWNS OF ANNE ARUNDEL PROJECT
PACE/PO BOX 6675
ANNAPOLIS, MD 21401

CAROL McDAVID

Descendants, Decisions, and Power: The Public Interpretation of the Archaeology of the Levi Jordan Plantation

ABSTRACT

Archaeological data from the Levi Jordan plantation in Brazoria County, Texas, indicate that the African Americans who lived on this plantation participated in many activities, several of African origin, that functioned to insure this community's survival in an increasingly oppressive outside world. Ethnographic data indicate that many descendants of the plantation's residents, African American and European American, still live in the Brazoria area, and that these descendants continue to negotiate issues of power and control. Any public interpretation of this archaeology will necessarily deal with diverse understandings of race and history in present-day Brazoria County. This paper will describe the political and organizational strategies being employed by a team of descendants, archaeologists, and other community members to plan and implement public interpretations that are "inclusive" of the various histories and archaeologies of the plantation's ancestors: pre- and post-emancipation African Americans as well as planters.

Introduction

This paper addresses the social character of theory and practice (Tilley 1989:114) when academics and local communities work together to plan the public interpretation of archaeology. In this case, the archaeology is that of the Levi Jordan plantation (Brown and Cooper 1990; Brown 1995). The primary question addressed here is whether or not it is feasible to create a public interpretation of this archaeology in the geographic vicinity of the (still standing) plantation house.

Three small towns—Brazoria, Sweeny, and West Columbia—are near the site, located about 60 mi. south of Houston, Texas. Many of the black and white descendants of the plantation's original black and white residents still live within 13 mi. of the site, either in one of these towns or in the rural area surrounding them. My collaborators in this project include several of these descendants as well as other community members; we are working together to decide how to interpret, publicly, the material culture of slavery, tenancy, and racism. This work is political because it reflects the ways in which contemporary people, descendants of people who owned and were owned by each other, continue to negotiate social and political power. It is also political because it incorporates ways that these people are affected, or feel that they could be affected, by the public presentation of "sensitive" archaeological and historical material.

Organization of the Research

The research for this project, which began after much of the archaeological work was complete, was designed to take place in two phases (McDavid 1994a, 1994b, 1995a, 1995b, 1995c, 1995d, 1996). The goal of the first phase, addressed here, was to determine if it would be feasible to interpret this archaeology to the public. This phase attempted to understand the ways in which local residents understood their own histories, in order to discover the constraints and opportunities, ideological and otherwise (Potter 1994:38) that might effect the public presentation of this archaeology. The second phase of the research was to involve members of the community in planning and implementing the public interpretation, with the particular goal of insuring that both black and white descendants of the original residents participated in the planning process. That phase is still underway and will be touched upon here, but only insofar as participation decisions continue to affect the feasibility question.

My goals were proactive; first, to outline a different, "inclusive" approach and, then, to apply it to the feasibility question in the study area. I conducted interviews, participated in community meetings, and took advantage of ongoing informal encounters to determine what the people in the study area thought of an "inclusive" approach and to find out how they viewed their own histories, and their places in those histories. How were their views of history con-

Historical Archaeology, 1997, 31(3):114-131.
Permission to reprint required.

stricted? Would a public interpretation of this archaeology exacerbate present-day social divisions, or assist in healing them? How did people who lived in the area surrounding the site of the interpretation deal with each other? How would the archaeology itself, rooted in a historical event that members of the community probably remember differently, affect how the archaeological story could be told?

"Public interpretation," "Public/s," and "Inclusivity"

This paper will use the terms "public interpretation," "public/s," and "inclusivity" throughout. Although they are commonly understood, they need to be clarified for this particular research. First, I refer to "public interpretation" as any museum, display, public talk, site tour, slide show, brochure, educational program, or other activity that attempts to "tell the story" of a site and the people who lived there. Second, "inclusivity" here means "mutual inclusivity"; that is, it refers to a public interpretation that encompasses the perspectives of *both* the plantation owners *and* its pre- and post-emancipation African-American residents.

Third, in using the term "public" or "publics" in Brazoria, Texas, I refer to several "publics": the descendants of Levi Jordan, the descendants of the African Americans who lived on the site, other European American and African-American members of the surrounding region, community leaders, local educators, people interested in history and archaeology, academics who study history and archaeology, and others. Occasionally people who identify with one of these groups also identify with others. Members of all of these groups form the social and political context surrounding the Jordan site, and it is hoped that to one degree or another all will participate and claim a voice in the creation of whatever interpretation takes place.

Some Brazoria "publics" were not invited to express an opinion in determining what happens at this plantation. For example, some interview data revealed a common assumption that white supremacist groups still operate in the area. No attempts were made to solicit opinions from people known to be members of these groups, nor will such attempts be made. However, I suspect that sometimes the people would not meet with me because they just "weren't interested" may have supported some of the ideas associated with white supremacy. Their opinions may surface if plans for a public interpretation progress; they, as well as more benign "publics," are elements of the social and political milieu in which people in Brazoria live.

The implications of reactions from these kinds of groups, as well as the reactions from the plantation's descendants and other community people, go beyond a simple decision about whether or not to publicly interpret these artifacts. The question is whether they can be interpreted *in Brazoria*, and, more specifically, at the site of the original plantation. The daily reality of confronting a physical manifestation of the history of the plantation south, in the form of a museum or whatever, could be uncomfortable for the descendants of the people who lived with the realities of slavery and tenancy. Most of this paper will deal with feedback from those descendants, black and white. However, a public interpretation at this site could also generate negative, potentially harmful reactions from people who may or may not accept the premise that the history of the South is something that should be looked at "inclusively."

Another group that forms a significant "public" for this study is the community of historical archaeologists. Historical archaeologists frequently deal with the archaeologies of disenfranchised peoples whose living descendants continue to negotiate issues of social and economic power. Some of these descendants have begun to realize that their lives can be changed by the ways that other people tell their family histories, and they are, increasingly, demanding a voice in presenting the archaeologies and histories of their ancestors. Although this paper deals with a particular community, and a particular social and political context, the ethical and practical concerns that apply to it could also apply elsewhere: to other archaeologies, histories, and communities.

Moving from Past to Present

Recent historical research (Powers 1994) has shown that the power relationships of 19th-century Brazoria, Texas, continue, in large measure, today. The local communities surrounding the plantation are still dominated by white descendants of 19th-century planters, while the African-American community is largely, though not exclusively, restricted to secondary positions in community leadership and social control. Powers (1994:122) has argued that this current situation springs directly from the particular history of the region and that after the Civil War, the "white power structure acted quickly and decisively to prevent any inversion of the antebellum social order. Southern whites were committed to retaining the status quo." She describes a number of strategies with which whites maintained their domination well into the present historical period, and points out how blacks reacted to this continued domination: they created a strong, insular, cohesive social system that operates largely outside the dominant white social and political system. Powers' analysis is also supported by recent oral history research in the area immediately surrounding the plantation (Wright 1994). According to Powers (1994:304), blacks "withdrew and isolated themselves from the Anglo residents of Brazoria; to some extent the retraction was voluntary, but overall it was in response to the treatment whites dealt them."

The separate, divided nature of present-day social and political Brazoria, rooted in the oppression and domination of the past, could well have an impact on the feasibility of creating a public interpretation of this plantation site. As the data will indicate, many people in the area derive at least part of their historical and social identities from an understanding of how they fit into the history of the region. In addition, I found that there was a great deal of local familiarity with the written histories of the region in the early 20th century, which spoke of slavery mainly in terms of economic loss, such as, "The freeing of the slaves deprived the Southern people of about two thousand million dollars" (Strobel 1926:15). These sources often characterized white supremacist groups, which were comprised of ex-confederate soldiers, as heroes who "stood like a stone wall for White supremacy and preserve and gave us our present civilization, to whom we owe a debt of gratitude that can never be repaid" (Strobel 1926:1). Indeed, it did not take formal research to realize that most of modern Brazoria is racially, socially, and economically segregated; there is a great deal of continuity between past and present power relationships in the area. The question of social and political continuity between the "old" and "new" South has been the subject of considerable debate among historians; Woodward (1951) and Weiner (1978) provide introductions to both sides of the question.

This is not to say that most Brazorians today have exactly the same racial attitudes as their 19th-century ancestors and early 20th-century historians. Some whites have reacted to earlier attitudes by rejecting them altogether, stating that they consciously attempt to avoid being "like" their ancestors. Others carry a burden of guilt, which, in part, drives their actions and decisions. Similarly, many black Brazorians speak of "moving on," and frequently they, too, consciously reject the attitudes of the past. However, the world that present-day Brazorians inhabit derives from a broader historical and social context, and it is likely that their deep-rooted assumptions about power are, in part, shaped by the historical milieu in which they live.

In addition, historical relations between the two main branches of Jordan's descendants, the Martin and the McNeill families, have been strained since the 19th century (Brown 1993, 1995). These strained relationships still form part of the present-day social and historical context of the community. Some members of each branch of the family still regard each other with attitudes ranging from mild mistrust to, in some cases, outright animosity. Complicating this, the archaeological deposit in the former slave and tenant quarters of the Jordan plantation indicates that the African-American tenants left their homes suddenly, and left in such a manner that they could take very little with them (Brown 1995:98). The site was owned by the Martins at the time of this "abandonment," and historical evidence suggests that the sudden departure of the tenants from the site was provoked by the actions of some of the Martin ancestors. In addition, these same Martins were among the most active in local white supremacist movements of the late 19th century (Powers 1994; Wright 1994). Therefore, "telling the story," in archaeological terms—that is, why the tenants' possessions were abandoned in the first place, entails discussing some rather unsavory behaviors on the part of some of the Martins. Some of their living descendants object to exposing any information about the past that would "rewrite history," as some have put it.

However, the people who support archaeological research at the plantation are also from the Martin side of the family, and they are among the most vocal in demanding that the "whole truth" be publicly told and dealt with, as interview data later in this paper will indicate. Nonetheless, plans for public interpretation have already been constrained by personal and familial agendas, even though some family members approve of an "inclusive" interpretation of the site, extending even to acknowledging and dealing with actions of some of their ancestors.

Theoretical and Ideological Perspectives

The intent here is to develop this research within the broad framework of what is known as a "critical" perspective and to incorporate a mutually inclusive *both/and*, as opposed to *either/or*, point of view.

Critical Theory

The use of critical theory in the public interpretation of history and archaeology has been addressed elsewhere (Wylie 1985; Leone et al. 1987; Handsman and Leone 1989; Potter 1994) and will not be discussed at length here, except

to point out how this approach has been useful within the context of this particular project.

Critical theory is concerned with the ways in which the production of knowledge is historically situated, and with understanding how archaeological findings are relevant to particular social and political interests, whether or not the archaeologist attempts to make those findings relevant (Tilley 1989:2; Potter 1994:39–40). Traditional public interpretations of plantation life, which have tended to focus almost exclusively on the lives of planter class, have the effect of reinforcing the idea that planter class values and ideologies were natural and inevitable. Expanding the focus to include the lives of *all* the people who lived on a plantation is one way of deconstructing the dominant planter ideologies. Doing so, and doing so in explicit terms, allows the consumers of archaeological and historical knowledge to see how our understanding of the past is, in part, a function of how it is presented (Tilley 1989:114).

A central element of critical theory is a concern with the particular (Potter 1989). A critical approach, therefore, requires that the social and political constraints (Leone et al. 1987) existing in any particular community be taken into account when deciding whether or not to do a public interpretation within that community. As mentioned previously, the social and political constraints in present-day Brazoria are very much a function of those that existed the past. A "critical" approach attempts to understand the "interests and conflicts" (Leone and Potter 1994) existing within the community of Brazoria, Texas, and to incorporate them into any public interpretations that take place—even if incorporating them means that the public interpretation does not take place on the site itself.

Critical theory also calls for self-reflection by the social analyst and, I would argue, by other participants in the public interpretation process; each social actor is a "part of the societal process analyzed" (Held 1980:191). The approach here has been for each actor (academic, community member, board member, volunteer, and visitor) to recognize how his or her individual bias influences the knowledge presented about this site, and to consider how this knowledge serves their own, or other, interests (Potter 1994:39, citing Geuss 1981:78). For example, my research method included asking several project participants to become familiar with my academic biases—with critical theory and its application to this project. Without exception, all agreed that a "critical" approach, as described here, was appropriate and useful. However, all also felt that dealing explicitly with the roots of this approach, and its derivation from Marxist and neo-Marxist thinking, would be counterproductive within the conservative context of present-day Brazoria, Texas. In Brazoria, ideas about individualism, family, work, class, race, and power are constructed within modern capitalist frameworks (Handsman and Leone 1989:119), even though they may be differently perceived within black and white segments of the larger community. Although any public interpretation of this site would work toward achieving enlightenment about past and present-day issues of domination and power, it would need to do so within local frames of reference to be accepted by the community in which it takes place.

Unlike some critical archaeologies, which call for a concrete plan of social action and emancipation (Handsman and Leone 1989; Tilley 1989) the purpose of a critical approach here is simply to create a path for a public interpretation that will challenge and expand traditional ways of understanding the history of the plantation South. As such, we are "willing to accept enlightenment as an adequate result" (Potter 1994:38). This is a rather broad view of critical theory, and some may find that this project is not sufficiently "critical," in that it does not deal with issues of "class interests and exploitation" only in terms of economic domination (Blakey 1987:292). While there may be economic ramifications of all forms of oppression, "particular situations of dominance may involve sexual, political, or social exploitation without any direct economic consequence" (Spencer-Wood 1992a:3).

Critical theory also rejects views that privilege the scientific method over other ways of producing knowledge. It does not say that stringent empirical-analytical methods should be rejected (Handsman 1981; Wylie 1985:141–142; Tilley 1989:112), only that by itself positivism produces an inadequate view of the world (Potter 1994:32). The archaeological investigations at this site have used the empirical methods of the "New Archaeology," applied within the contextual, interpretive theoretical frameworks of postprocessual archaeologies (Hodder 1986; Brown 1995). Related research (Wright 1994; Taylor 1996; Hill 1997) has employed interpretive anthropology, oral history, and genealogy to illuminate the same historical period as that addressed by the archaeology. The assumption among all project participants is that science is an important way, but not the only way, to understand the past.

A "both/and" Point of View

Besides critical theory, a *both/and*, rather than *either/or*, approach (Spencer-Wood 1991, 1992a, 1992b, [1993], 1996) has also been useful in this work. Put simply, this approach will attempt to develop ways to talk about *both* black history *and* white history in the plantation South, without doing either at the expense of the other. A *both/and* approach provides a framework to explore, publicly, the interaction of dominant and non-dominant groups, and to explore the many ways that people dealt with societal restraints to form ideologies, identities, and behaviors to empower themselves. It rejects simplistic definitions of non-dominant individuals as "victims who react, negatively motivated by dominance, without any positive viewpoints or ideology of their own" (Spencer-Wood 1992b:4). Similarly, it also rejects definitions of all dominant individuals as oppressors and villains. It is hoped that this approach to public presentation will provide a way for diverse "publics" in Brazoria to be comfortable with the expression of their divided, sometimes contested, histories and that it will promote an appreciation of the contributions of *all* the people who lived on this plantation.

Method

Several data-gathering procedures were employed during this study: fact-finding trips to other interpretive sites; formal but unstructured interviews with community residents; participation in community meetings and presentations to community organizations; informal encounters with respondents; and active participation in professional associations concerned with the presentation of historical materials. The fact-finding trips took place in the summers of 1992 and 1993 and will not be addressed here, except to say that they affirmed my initial impression that most public interpretations of the history of the plantation South—despite a few well-known exceptions, some of which are included in this volume—tend to focus almost exclusively on the owners' homes, furniture, and wealth. Formal taped interviews began in October 1993 and continued into the fall of 1994. In the fall of 1994 I determined that the formal interview process had ceased to be productive; the reasons for this will be explained later in this narrative. Many informal conversations and meetings took place during the entire time and are, even now, part of an ongoing research process.

I attempted to interview representatives from various "publics" previously described: descendants of Levi Jordan, descendants of the African Americans who lived on the plantation, members of communities surrounding the plantation, persons interested in Texas history and tourism, and community leaders. Selection criteria were based on my perception of family and community influence, such as family elders, community leaders, and people actively involved in historical interpretation, and on the respondent's willingness to participate.

As mentioned previously, part of my method was to state my personal and professional agendas very clearly. Interview transcripts reveal that I sometimes did almost as much talking as my respondents—explaining what I meant by a

both/and approach, talking about work being done at other sites, explaining what our goals were in terms of community empowerment, and so on. I usually revealed something of my own "baggage" during these interactions—there were many discussions about what it was like to grow up as southerners in a racially polarized culture, our feelings about the Civil Rights movement, how the legacies of slavery affect people in the present, and similar topics. I always made it clear that "we," meaning the core group of people initially involved in this project (the archaeological project director and two white Jordan descendants) wished to see if it would be feasible to create an inclusive, *both/and* public interpretation at this site. I made it clear that the core group would rely on community input to decide whether to support such a public interpretation. If it chose not to support it, then the public interpretation, if any, would take place elsewhere.

These transcripts revealed extremely interactive conversations, not one-sided "objective" question/answer sessions. I wanted my respondents to be able to trust me, but neither they, nor I, could ignore that I was a white, urban, university affiliated outsider—I was, and continue to be, "the other." If I had attempted to position myself as an insider, or to hide behind a mask of objectivity, I would have been seen as less trustworthy, not more. One African-American businessman commented, "Well, I don't want to interview *you*, but I think this has changed you . . . your attitude about things. And I really don't know what they were before, but I sense that since you've been doing this thing you see things differently, you know, as you really search and find out the truth about things . . . and, then, I do sense that you are sensitive, maybe more sensitive, to people since you've done this."

An African-American minister commented, after I asked for his support and told him why I felt that this project was important, that "the only way this will work is if people believe that you have a good heart . . . but I can tell you have a good heart." This kind of comment reassured me that my reflective, proactive approach had a direct and positive effect on the kind and amount of information I received during my interviews. My willingness to own my otherness—to talk about it openly and to reveal personal reasons for doing this research—led to franker, more open communication than would have been possible otherwise. It was sometimes essential in getting people to talk to me at all.

Data: Interviews, Community Meetings, and Informal Encounters

Data were gathered in several contexts: interviews, community meetings, and informal encounters. Each is discussed further below.

The Interview Process

Most of my early interviews were with Jordan's descendants; they had already been identified through attendance at family reunions and personal introductions. They were usually very eager to provide their ideas, and there was no difficulty in arranging meetings. The same held true for meetings with local community leaders—most were eager to hear about a new source of potential tourist dollars. I knew it might not be as easy to arrange interviews with African-American descendants and other community residents but had confidence that it would occur at some point. I did have some good contacts in the African-American community who had said they would be willing to introduce me to other people.

I have already mentioned that I stopped the formal interview process early in that stage of the research. To explain why, and to contextualize the summary of interview data that follows, I will now describe the legal entity that was formed to direct all public activities deriving from the plantation's archaeology. The formation of this organization was not intended to be a part of the feasibility phase of the research because it was not originally perceived to have much to do with the specific questions I was asking in my interviews—questions about how to talk about slavery and tenancy, how to teach

history, and the like. However, the existence of this organization and, more importantly, its composition, had a direct impact on my efforts to obtain candid feedback from the local African-American population.

In 1993 two Jordan descendants, including the site owners' representative, and the archaeology director, Dr. Kenneth L. Brown, set up the Levi Jordan Plantation Historical Society, a 501(c)3 tax-exempt, non-profit corporation. My role in the organization was to arrange for pro bono legal work, to serve as the organization's secretary, and to function as an unofficial organizer and "expediter." I did not serve on the board of directors because we all agreed that it should be dominated by local individuals; the only "outsider" on the board was the archaeology director. The job of the organization would include, but would not be limited to, planning the public interpretation, if it was determined to be feasible. It would also include house restoration, loaning artifacts to museums, fundraising, and similar activities. We all agreed that no substantive planning would take place—such as writing a mission statement, applying for National Register status, and so on—until the board had learned what it could from my interviews, and, more importantly, until it could expand to include people to represent the plantation's African-American ancestors. At that point we had not identified many of the African-American descendants and had no idea who might be willing and able to be involved; my research was seen as a way to get community input as well as to identify people who might be interested in participating on a formal basis.

So, I began to conduct interviews with people in the African-American community. Some interviews went very well, and the comments they generated were very useful in establishing themes that could guide us later in planning a public interpretation. During these interviews, I usually felt that I had been able to connect, to start forming a basis of mutual understanding and trust, and so on. It proved to be extremely difficult to arrange appointments, however. Only one person ever said "no" to an interview request, but many had some reason not to meet with me, citing reasons such as not having time, busy schedule, and illness. The people I interviewed were unfailingly polite and gracious, but I kept sensing a wariness, a reluctance to tell me what they really thought. One African-American respondent, who had been active in community affairs and local government, warned me that I would have trouble getting candid opinions from members of his community: "sometimes the people who would have real influence in the black community would be same ones who wouldn't want to be involved . . . you have to realize that people will tell you what they think you want to hear."

During these interviews I sensed that my own ethnicity was only part of the reason for this apparent wariness. When we started talking about racial issues, and about the shared aspects of our experiences as southerners in the late 20th century, my own openness seemed to reassure people that I was sincere and basically trustworthy. I knew there was "something else" besides my being a white, urban outsider that was affecting the success of arranging interviews in the first place.

In the summer of 1994 I finally got a glimpse of why people might have been skeptical when hearing my statements about "involving the African-American community early on." I started to hear, indirectly and never with specific examples, about other history-related community projects in which blacks had been asked to participate after most of the substantive planning had already taken place. One person mentioned a museum that had neglected to include blacks on its board, except in a token fashion, and another mentioned a parade in which blacks participated, but after most plans had already been made. Some also noted that the other local plantation museum had recently attempted to do some programming about African-American history, but that this effort had been restricted to a small display in one outbuilding on the site, and had been poorly funded by the state agency that manages the site. The blacks had been told they were "welcome" to do some kind of display, but

it was evident that there was no intent to change the more general planter-class focus of the site.

All of the African Americans who alluded to the history of tokenization in the community were very circumspect about mentioning names and specific events. Only one ever discussed the issue on tape:

> Well, [once] when we had a parade . . . the Negro was never just told "Okay, we want you all in this" . . . We live here . . . this is our home and we want to be a part of it. I told them that at meetings . . . that kind of thing, you know. But the persons who are in leadership . . . they forget about that . . . so for that reason, I think we're left out of whatever there is here to be . . . I think to a marked degree we have not been represented in the organizations as [much as] we should have been.

I started to realize that it was not surprising that my naive requests for interviews and appeals for opinion were regarded with suspicion. It became obvious that interviews were not going to be a productive way of getting input from the African-American community until members of that community were fully empowered to act on any suggestions they might make. One encounter, in particular, clarified this situation. In the fall of 1994 I attempted to make an appointment to speak with an African-American woman who is a retired educator. This individual had obviously come across university researchers before, and stated flatly that she would not meet with me until I had answered, in writing, the following questions: 1) What would I actually do with the results of our interview? Would the community be able to put it to use, or would I just get my thesis written and put the book on a shelf somewhere? 2) What would the university's role be in the process down the line? Would the archaeologist help plan the interpretation, or would he simply pack up his trowel and move on? and 3) What likelihood was there that the project would ever actually happen? Who would benefit from the project — the community or the university?

I finally realized that these kinds of questions must have been on the minds of many of the people I attempted to interview, even if they did not come right out and ask them. I did respond in writing to this individual, of course, and decided to terminate the formal interview process. I then recommended that the board of directors of the Levi Jordan Plantation Historical Society concentrate *all* its efforts on recruiting new members before any more planning, or talk of planning, took place. They readily agreed, and now, two years later, the society has a seven-person board that includes African-American descendants as well as other members of the black community.

It is important to point out that the original, three-member board did not identify and select the new members. The first new member was selected by a local African-American service organization whose membership includes several plantation descendants, including the person most active in helping us recruit. The new board member, who happens to be the same person who posed the questions above, then helped us to find additional volunteers.

So, even though the formation and composition of the Levi Jordan Plantation Historical Society turned out to have little to do with community opinions about archaeology museums and public interpretation, they had a great deal to do with community perceptions of empowerment, voice, and authority. I realized that I could interview as many white descendants, mayors, chamber presidents, and the like as I wanted to, but until African Americans were vested in the process, and empowered to make policy-level decisions, feedback from them would be extremely hard to obtain. Unless power was perceived to be held equally with the white descendants and other residents, I would probably continue to "hear what they thought I wanted to hear," to paraphrase the respondent mentioned earlier.

In spite of that difficulty, however, a number of themes emerged in interviews and other encounters which would have a direct bearing on whatever public interpretation could be created, provided that the issues of power and control discussed above are addressed. The rest of this section will highlight a few of these themes; their implications for the public interpretation of

this site, and the implications of the power question, will be addressed in the Conclusion. All names, of course, have been changed.

The Themes

Most respondents, black and white, had a strong sense of family and regional history, although it played out in different ways. One common theme was that geography seemed to play a significant role in how people defined themselves and their histories. The Jordan plantation, and the communities of Brazoria, Sweeny, and West Columbia, are located in western Brazoria County, in an area that was central to the development of early Texas history (Creighton 1975). The Brazos River divides the county into east–west sections; people living there frequently acknowledged themselves as having a "West of the Brazos" identity. There is a "West of the Brazos" phone book, for example, and a strong sense that people are keenly aware of their own history.

There also seems to be as much competition between these three small towns as there is solidarity. All have separate historical societies and separate historical museums, but there is also a museum association for the three museums that meets on a regular basis. People from West Columbia seldom neglect to mention that their town was the first capital of Texas, and people in Brazoria frequently refer, with some degree of resentment, to the time back in the 1930s that the present county seat was "stolen" in the "dead of night" and moved to Angleton (east of the Brazos). As one local resident put it after I made a presentation at a local Chamber of Commerce meeting, "this project would be a good idea — because, after all, "we" are more historical than those towns on the other side of the river."

As mentioned previously, many people I met were very informed about the early history of the county, and much of their pride had to do with the fact that the region was the locus of Stephen F. Austin's first settlement in the 1830s (Creighton 1975). The original white settlers formed what became known in this century as the "Old 300", and I heard this term many times when speaking with local residents. Once I saw a bumper sticker that declared proudly that the car's driver was "One of the old 300!," and one evening in a local bar/cafe I noticed that there were two mugs emblazoned with Austin's image nestled amongst the beers displayed for sale. The Brazoria County Historical Museum has a permanent exhibition about the original Austin settlement and lists the names of the "old 300" settlers on a prominently featured sign at the exit to the exhibition.

I also had the impression that while all respondents recognized the term "West of the Brazos" and identified themselves with being a part of that area, as opposed to "the other side of the river," the use of the term was regarded by many African Americans as more of a "white" thing, which is not surprising, since it seems to be connected to the "old 300" idea. From Mr. Alexander, a middle-aged African-American businessman: "Well, I think it is something distinctive . . . something their family has done to establish roots in this country . . . they want to say that they were part of the old 300, which I think is prestigious as a family who have developed this country . . . as well as it is for black Americans who have contributed things to this country . . . to have that same amount of prestige and distinction about what they've done . . . and so, that's why I say we have to balance the two."

My research showed that most African Americans in Brazoria were not interested in helping to plan a public interpretation that would perpetuate the stereotypic view that slaves and tenants were passive in their response to oppression and victimization. Some were skeptical when asked whether or not their community would accept a public interpretation that would focus on black history—some asked, "why do you want to stir all that slavery stuff up again?" Some expressed the idea that "just telling the truth" could be "dangerous," and several commented on the need to have interpretations that were, in their words, "non-polarizing." Again from Mr. Alexander: "You have to incorporate

the two [points of view] and then go from there . . . because otherwise it would be like all one of this and all one of that . . . you know, and it would polarize people . . . so I think that the only way you are going to really get the essence of the thing is . . . to let them work together . . . and maybe the authority would come from both . . . they can both say things about it, and they'll be more open to say it, and then I think there would be less criticism saying, well, it's all this black or all white."

When I began to talk about using a "*both/and*" approach, and to describe the kinds of inclusive programming underway at other sites, the response to the Jordan project warmed considerably. While most blacks I met frequently commented on the need to avoid emphasizing what they called "the punishments," they also talked about the importance of positive role models, and there was usually great enthusiasm as we explored ideas about incorporating this archaeology into history curricula in local schools. As one local African-American minister put it, when talking about how we might involve young people, "you have to show connections between what's in the ground and what people have accomplished since then." Earlier, Mr. Alexander commented that "I think it [the *both/and* approach] would be the only way it would survive . . . and what we need to focus on is how we're going to make it better . . . that's what I think of how it should work, and I think that's the way it would survive in the long run."

Later, Mr. Alexander and I also discussed how a public interpretation should address the "ugly" parts of history, and he said, "Well, if you did present that, it'd have to be real gentle . . . you know, something where a small kid, say six or seven, would understand it. I don't think it has to be . . . you wouldn't want to overblow that kind of thing, because some people are still sensitive about it . . . I think it would just have to be something gentle." This kind of conversation frequently led to discussions about the importance of black history and Black History Month. Whites sometimes commented that "well, it's OK, but maybe we should also have White History Month." Blacks, on the other hand, sometimes said "maybe it would be better if black history was studied all year, not just in February." The common thread in both kinds of responses, however, was that a public interpretation at this site could provide a way for students to learn about everyone's history all year long.

While whites did not generally criticize traditional interpretations, they did respond favorably to learning about the inclusive approaches being explored at other sites. Some whites expressed an enthusiasm for "telling the whole truth," although they also sometimes asked, "Is this [project] only going to be about black history"? This question may be especially pertinent to the Jordan descendants, because, as mentioned previously, the archaeological deposit itself suggests that the tenants were forcibly evicted by one of their ancestors, and because many ancestors were active in various white supremacist groups of the postbellum period. While most white descendants were quite willing to acknowledge the roles their ancestors played in the racial turbulence of the past, they also wanted to make sure that the other, "better" stories are told, such as the stories—recounted by both blacks and whites—about the friendships that sometimes developed between black and white plantation residents, and stories about the courage and fortitude of the women in the planter's family.

Most people I met thought that history, and learning about one's ancestors, was important and valuable. Mrs. Moore, a middle-aged African-American businesswoman and church worker commented that "I want my children to know all what happened during slavery . . . . I want them to get out there and know that we did this, we didn't do this, what was done . . . it's good education, and my daughter has grown strong in knowing these things." And Mr. Alexander, in his comments addressing the same issue, alluded to the importance of understanding the complex relationships that frequently existed between the enslaved and their enslavers: "Just the way these people lived . . . most of the things they had, you know, they had to do it in a creative way . . . you know, there were certain things they could do, certain things they couldn't do .

. . you know, and they survived. But . . . there were the relationships between the two [groups of people] . . . . I think there's a lot of things that we don't really see about what really went on . . . other than just master and slave . . . it wasn't just all, you know, Afro-American or European American."

Kay, an older college student and white McNeill descendant, was also asked how she felt about publicly interpreting the archaeological materials from the quarters area. She said that "learning about it could be very healing for both sides because I do believe there's a kind of collective guilt that I feel or just sort of a guilt for, you know, things wouldn't be where they were today if they hadn't been the way they were back then."

On the whole, community leaders, such as mayors, chamber of commerce members, and museum directors, liked the idea of a plantation interpretation that would involve all members of the community—one that would increase local appreciation of the African Americans who made the planters' fortunes possible. As one local (white) leader put it, "If planning this kind of project will help us to have better ongoing contact with the leaders of the black community, then that's reason enough to do it." However, I also heard, in non-taped interviews with African Americans, that some of the people who stated their support of an "inclusive" interpretation had exhibited very different attitudes when a local group attempted to build a public swimming pool. Some whites fought the swimming pool project, and the strong perception among blacks was that the whites did not want a pool because that would mean that black children would swim with white children. On the basis of non-taped conversations with some of these individuals, my guess is that this perception was correct.

However, while many whites' support of an "inclusive" interpretation was apparently sincere, there was also awareness of the difficulties that would be involved in creating such an interpretation. Margaret, an elderly white descendant, when asked "what do you think about having the project planned by descendants of both black and white residents of the plantation?," responded that "I think that's the only approach that you can take to get cooperation from everybody, and I think they're [the black descendants] are going to have to be convinced from the first that they're not token . . . and that's not going to be an easy time."

Discussion and Conclusions: Is a Public Interpretation of This Site Feasible?

On one level of decision-making, interview data and other community input revealed that it would be feasible to create a successful public interpretation of this site if, and only if, it is truly multivocal—inclusive of black, white, Martin, McNeill, diverse "public," and archaeologist viewpoints. There was a great deal of support for an "inclusive" approach to interpreting the archaeology and history of this site, and people I met and interviewed are now more aware of what a "different" kind of plantation interpretation might be like.

However, in the long run, feasibility will have more to do with how issues of power and control are resolved than it will with whether people like the idea of an "inclusive" interpretation. A major result of this work was the realization that, before the answer to the feasibility question can ever be an unqualified "yes," the following questions will need to be addressed: 1) How can the planning group (the Levi Jordan Plantation Historical Society) continue to find ways to share power in authentic, credible ways? And, no less important, 2) How can it find ways to convince its various "publics" that power and control are genuinely shared?

While my own awareness of the importance of the power issue was one result of this work, an even more important result was the increased awareness and articulation of it within the local planning group, the board of directors of the Levi Jordan Plantation Historical Society. This is not to say that local members of this group were not aware of how power was vested in their community; obviously they were, and more profoundly than I would ever be. However, knowing something on an intuitive, common-sense level is one thing. Expressing this knowledge in explicit terms, and incorporating it into the infrastructure of an organization, is very different. The collaborative nature of this project gave definition and vocabulary to the power/control issue; project participants now share a common understanding of its importance to the success, or lack of success, of this project. As one African-American descendant put it to me recently, "It's going to be a long journey . . . but at least we've started."

At some point it will be necessary for exhibit designers, including archaeologists, to understand how local people view themselves and their histories, how they think issues like slavery should be addressed, how young people should be taught history, and so on. These themes, which were explored in my interviews—for an in-depth analysis of interview data, see McDavid (1996)—will be useful in creating a public interpretation, but they will only be useful if the power issues can be negotiated successfully. Only in a setting of shared power can sensitive, "ugly" parts of history be dealt with openly and productively—*it is a question of what comes first.* In this case, the public perception and acceptance of shared power must come first, before any public interpretation can be implemented.

For example, some of the artifacts themselves will lead to difficult choices about how to present them publicly. One such artifact is a shackle, still embedded in the brick wall in which it was found. Handling the emotional reaction that this artifact initially provokes will be a difficult challenge for the people implementing a public interpretation. How can one be "multivocal" about a shackle? At first glance the shackle would seem to be a clear-cut, unambiguous testament to white oppression, offering little opportunity for public interpretation other than to acknowledge its painful origins and then move on. However, its presence, and its location *in the quarters area*, could also provide pathways to discuss other, related issues—How did people resist oppression? How were stereotypical attitudes toward blacks responses to strategies of black resistance to white domination?

If this part of the quarters was used at some point to confine people (Kenneth L. Brown 1996, pers. comm.), this artifact could provide an opportunity to discuss how blacks might have dealt with the presence of a "jail" in the midst of their living area, and could also offer opportunities to discuss the difficult, ambiguous roles of slaves and tenants who also functioned as overseers, drivers (Genovese 1976:365–388), and, in this case, possibly jailers. It is perhaps true that these related issues are just as difficult to deal with as the presence of the shackle, but using the shackle as a point of departure could offer possibilities to discuss how the lives of the people on this plantation "overlapped, combined, and changed in different cultural contexts and over time" (Spencer-Wood [1993]). The shackle could also be used to examine the ways in which oppression and domination take many different forms, and how people take individual actions to deal with that oppression and domination (Spencer-Wood 1994).

As previously mentioned, most present-day Brazorians, including descendants of the original slaveholders, do not agree with their ancestors' attitudes towards slavery. Most, though not all, as discussed below, are willing to discuss and acknowledge their ancestors' roles in the slave and tenant system. The common view is that the old attitudes were, simply, wrong, and there is no suggestion here that the viewpoints of oppressors and oppressed should be presented as equally valid. However, presenting "good" and "bad" parts of history in an open-ended, inclusive way, rather than a closed, "this is the way it was" fashion, could help people to see for themselves how much people and attitudes have changed. More importantly, it could also allow them the space to see for themselves, without preaching or polemics, how present-day attitudes are rooted in those of the past, and begin the process of acknowledging their own participation in the perpetuation of racist, classist, and sexist social attitudes (see Blakey's discussion of white denial of racism, this volume).

One historical artifact that has already been painful for local descendants to deal with relates to the manner in which African Americans appear to have left the plantation. The objects they left behind are a positive, compelling testament to the ways that African Americans coped with slavery and tenancy, but their very existence could well bring up questions of ownership. While the legal documents setting up the Levi Jordan Plantation Historical Society provide that all artifacts will be controlled by the planning group, not by the site's white owners, in the future, descendants of the people who left the artifacts behind could easily wish to contest the legal fact that they still do not own them.

It will also be necessary to deal with the demands of white descendants who have expressed angry reactions to archaeological interpretations that attempt to explain why the deposit exists. For example, one local newspaper, while generally supportive of local historical projects, occasionally tends to emphasize the negative, sensational aspects of the plantation's history—that is, the abandonment episode. A recent story, headlined "Excavation Slowly Uncovers History's Scars," began with the sentence, "The ghosts of former slaves are whispering of an injustice done more than 100 years ago on a plantation near Brazoria" (VanDerSlice 1996). Not surprisingly, several white plantation descendants reacted very angrily to this article; one commented that "just because you found some stuff in the ground doesn't give you the right to destroy [my] family." Most of them did not dispute the relative accuracy of the article—they are quite aware of the roles that their ancestors had in the turbulence of the past. However, they blamed the archaeology director, not the newspaper reporter, for the content and tone of the article, and have begun a campaign to stop plans to publicly interpret the site. The board of directors of the planning group (Figure 1), which, as already mentioned, is composed of both European American and African-American descendants, was also very unhappy about the inflammatory tone of the article, and recognized its potential to further polarize an already segregated community.

The only way that these kinds of situations will have any hope of being resolved is for the planning group to have credibility within the local communities of *both* African-American *and* European American descendants—for it to be publicly recognized as an organization in which power and control are genuinely shared. Whether this can happen is very much an open question. Its activities have only recently begun to develop this type of positive public recognition, and the damage caused by the recent newspaper article may not be able to be contained. In addition, given the dichotomized manner in which power is still distributed within the community, the public recognition of shared power will probably be only the first, most difficult,

step in dealing with these kinds of interpretation issues.

Despite these threats to the process of community empowerment and inclusive history-writing, I will close this paper by emphasizing the positive, productive aspects of the community story, and describe the present structure and work of the board of directors of the Levi Jordan Plantation Historical Society. It is in the work of this board that the ideas about critical theory and a *both/and* approach have been incorporated into the infrastructure of this project—*theory and practice have merged.*

Facts photo: Robert J. Reed

Historical Society looks to future

Directors of the Levi Jordan Plantation Historical Society stand in front of the plantation homestead in Sweeny. Pictured, from left, are Ginny Raska, Hazel J. Austin, Carol McDavid, Dorothy Cotton, Morris Richardson and Julia Mack. The Levi Jordan house was built about 1849 and is one of the few original plantation houses still standing in the county. The group plans a history day for the fall and is formulating plans for a membership drive which will begin Aug. 1. For more information on the plantation or the historical society, call Raska at 798-1628 or Austin at 964-3823.

FIGURE 1. Photograph of some members of the Levi Jordan plantation board of directors, taken in front of the plantation house (after *The Brazosport Facts*, 22 July 1995; reprinted with permission of *The Brazosport Facts*).

Last year the new seven-member board, described earlier, began to work together (Figure 1). Their first job was to write a formal mission statement. This statement was designed to be somewhat global in nature—to allow flexibility while giving an overall direction for the organization. This statement, in particular, embodies the *both/and* approach that I had proposed, and that the board adopted. It is as follows:

MISSION STATEMENT
The primary mission of The Levi Jordan Plantation Historical Society is to preserve and interpret the archaeologies and histories of all the people who lived and worked on this plantation after its inception in the mid-19th century.
The secondary mission of the Society is to preserve and interpret the history of Brazoria County and the surrounding region, to complement the primary purpose and to offer a more thorough understanding of contributions of the people of this plantation and of this region to the history of Texas and the United States.
The tertiary mission of the Society is to utilize the public interpretation of historical and archaeological research to promote understanding and appreciation of the diverse histories of the people who built this plantation, this region, and this country.

After writing the mission statement, and expanding it into a long range plan with many specific ideas about educational programming, restoring the plantation house, and the like, the group realized that these documents did not state, in explicit terms, the ideas that formed the basis of planning—the ideas embodied in the critical, "*both/and*" approach described earlier. Therefore, the long range plan now includes a section that outlines these ideas; they comprise in effect, an ideological statement in which each member of the group believes. Here is how the idea statement appears in the printed brochures (Figure 2) that are distributed at public meetings and similar occasions:

OUR MISSION STATEMENT STATES OUR "BIG GOALS," BUT WHAT OTHER IDEAS HAVE GUIDED OUR PROPOSED PLANS TO ACCOMPLISH THAT MISSION?
That there are many different, but complementary, ways of learning about the past—archaeology, history, genealogy, oral history, literature, and others—and that each offers a different kind of "lens" through which we can

The Levi Jordan Plantation
Historical Society

Long Range Plan

Preliminary Draft
for Community Review

BOARD OF DIRECTORS
Hazel J. Austin
Kenneth L. Brown, PhD.
Dorothy D. Cotton
Bruce Gotcher
Julia Mack
Ginny McNeill Raska
Morris Richardson

MAILING ADDRESS

P.O. Box 4011
Brazoria, TX 77422
(409) 798-1628

FIGURE 2. Cover of mission statement and long range plan document, including line drawing of a carved shell "cameo" found in the slave and tenant quarters of the site.

"see" the past.
That what we call "history" was not inevitable: that along the way individuals and groups made choices, and all of those choices affected what we are today.
That it is important to respect the idea that some objects from the past may have different kinds of spiritual and emotional importance to different people.
That historical truth may be defined in a variety of ways—what one person or family perceives as important about "what really happened" may be different from what another person or family perceives, and it is possible that these different perceptions may be, in some ways, equally true.
That people in the past were, in some ways, different from people now–that their decisions, conversations, and social relationships were different from ours today.
That people in the past were, in some ways, the same as people are now–that they too had work lives, family lives, spiritual lives, creative lives, and intellectual lives, and they made choices about those lives.

That the decisions we make now about how we present history will influence what we know about the past, and that all of our local communities should have a voice in making those decisions.

The people involved in this project hope that the diverse composition of the planning group, along with the mission statement, long range plan, and statement of ideas, will provide a way for people with different perspectives to see the Jordan project as something they can support and appreciate. We hope that public meetings held to present these documents, along with associated slide presentations and conversations, will offer testimony to local "publics" about how power is shared within the planning group, and will counter the negative public response to more divisive elements of the plantation's history. If this occurs, planning the public interpretation of this archaeology could begin to provide the public with "the intellectual means to assess, criticise, define, and redefine" the past (Tilley 1989:114). It could also provide a way to begin positive, meaningful communication between the various community groups who have a stake in the past, present, and future of this plantation and, in the most hopeful sense, could provide one context in which the real renegotiation of community power can finally begin to take place.

ACKNOWLEDGMENTS

Thanks to Kenneth L. Brown, for his ongoing support of my research, past and present. Thanks also to Norris Lang, Amilcar Shabazz, John McIntyre, and the board of directors of the Levi Jordan plantation (Hazel Austin, Ken Brown, Dorothy Cotton, Bruce Gotcher, Julia Mack, Ginny Raska, and Morris Richardson), for ongoing support during this research. Thanks to Parker Potter and Suzanne Spencer-Wood, whose work inspired the approaches applied here—with special appreciation to Spencer-Wood for insights on this paper; in particular, for comments about the both/and feminist perspective and its application to the conflict resolution and inclusivity issues discussed here. Thanks to Herman Kluge, Betty McDavid, Gene McDavid, Patti Jeppson, Mary Lynne Hill, Cheryl Wright, Cheryl LaRoche, Linda Derry , Ywone Edwards, and Amy Young for personal and scholarly support. All omissions and errors are, of course, my responsibility. Most of all, thanks go to the people who lived and worked on the Levi Jordan plantation from 1848 to 1892. I hope that this work helps make it possible for their stories to be told.

REFERENCES

BLAKEY, MICHAEL E.
1987   Comments in Response to Leone, Potter, and Shackel, "Toward a Critical Archaeology." *Current Anthropology* 28(3):292.

BROWN, KENNETH L.
1993   A Brief History of the Levi Jordan Plantation. Paper presented at the Antebellum Texas, Brazos Style, Conference. Center for the Arts and Sciences, Lake Jackson, TX.
1995   Material Culture and Community Structure: The Slave and Tenant Community at Levi Jordan's Plantation, 1848–1892. In *Working Toward Freedom: Slave Society and Domestic Economy in the American South*, edited by Larry E. Hudson, Jr., pp. 95–118. University of Rochester Press, Rochester, NY.

BROWN, KENNETH L., AND DOREEN C. COOPER
1990   Structural Continuity in an African-American Slave and Tenant Community. *Historical Archaeology* 24(4):7–19.

CREIGHTON, JAMES A.
1975   *A Narrative History of Brazoria County, Texas.* Brazoria County Historical Commission, Waco, TX.

GEUSS, RAYMOND
1981   *The Idea of Critical Theory: Habermas and the Frankfurt School.* Cambridge University Press, Cambridge, UK.

GENOVESE, EUGENE D.
1976   *Roll, Jordan, Roll: The World the Slaves Made.* Vintage, NY.

HANDSMAN, RUSSELL G.
1981   Early Capitalism and the Center Village of Canaan, Connecticut: A Study of Transformations and Separations. *Artifacts* 9:1–21.

HANDSMAN, RUSSELL G., AND MARK LEONE
1989   Living History and Critical Archaeology and the Reconstruction of the Past. In *Critical Traditions in Contemporary Archaeology*, edited by Valerie Pinsky and Alison Wylie, pp. 117–135. Cambridge University Press, Cambridge, UK.

HELD, DAVID
1980   *Introduction to Critical Theory: Horkheimer to Habermas.* University of California Press, Berkeley.

HILL, MARY LYNNE
    1997   *The Discipline of Social Corsets: Negotiation of the*
           Gender Typification of the Southern Lady by Female
           Descendants of Levi and Sarah Stone Jordan. M.A.
           thesis, Department of Anthropology, University of
           Houston, Houston, TX. University Microfilms
           International, Ann Arbor, MI.

HODDER, IAN
    1986   *Reading the Past: Current Approaches to*
           Interpretation in Archaeology. Cambridge University
           Press, Cambridge, UK.

LEONE, MARK P., AND PARKER B. POTTER, JR.
    1994   Historical Archaeology of Capitalism. *Bulletin of the*
           Society for American Archaeology 12(4):14–15.

LEONE, MARK P., PARKER B. POTTER, JR., AND PAUL A.
SHACKEL
    1987   Toward a Critical Archaeology. *Current Anthropology*
           28(3):283–302.

MCDAVID, CAROL
    1994a From Archaeological Context to Public Contexts:
           The Public Interpretation of the Archaeology of the
           Levi Jordan Plantation. Paper presented at the Annual
           Meeting of the Society for Historical Archaeology
           Conference on Historical and Underwater
           Archaeology, Vancouver, BC.
    1994b From Archaeological Context to Public Contexts:
           The Public Interpretation of the Archaeology of the
           Levi Jordan Plantation. Paper presented at the
           Southeastern Archaeological Conference, Lexington,
           KY.
    1995a Descendants and Decisions: Planning the Public
           Interpretation of the Archaeology of the Levi Jordan
           Plantation. Paper presented at the Southeast Region
           Annual Meeting of the Association of Living History
           Farms and Museums, Tallahassee, FL.
    1995b Descendants, Collaboration, and Consensus: The
           Public Interpretation of the Archaeology of the Levi
           Jordan Plantation. Paper presented at the 28th Annual
           Chacmool Conference: Archaeology into the New
           Millennium: Public or Perish. Calgary, AB.
    1995c Many Pasts and Many Presents: Collaboration in
           Planning the Public Interpretation of the Archaeology
           of the Levi Jordan Plantation. Paper presented at the
           Southeast Preservation Conference, Birmingham, AL.
    1995d The Importance of Archaeology in the Preservation of
           African American Heritage: The Levi Jordan
           Plantation Project. Paper presented at the African
           Americans and Heritage Preservation Conference:
           Practical Strategies for Livable Communities. Texas
           Historical Commission, Houston.
    1996   *The Levi Jordan Plantation: From Archaeological*
           Interpretation to Public Interpretation. M. A. thesis,
           Department of Anthropology, University of Houston,
           Houston, TX. University Microfilms International,
           Ann Arbor, MI.

POTTER, PARKER B., JR.
    1989   *Archaeology in Public in Annapolis: An Experiment*
           in the Application of Critical Theory to Historical
           Archaeology. Ph.D. dissertation, Department of
           Anthropology, Brown University, Providence, RI.
           University Microfilms International, Ann Arbor, MI.
    1994   *Public Archaeology in Annapolis: A Critical Approach*
           to History in Maryland's Ancient City. Smithsonian
           Institution Press, Washington, DC.

POWERS, BETSY J.
    1994   *From Cotton Fields to Oil Fields: Economic*
           Development in a New South Community. Ph.D.
           dissertation, Department of Anthropology, University
           of Houston, Houston, TX. University Microfilms
           International, Ann Arbor, MI.

SPENCER-WOOD, SUZANNE M.
    1991   Toward a Feminist Historical Archaeology of the
           Construction of Gender. In *The Archaeology of*
           Gender: Proceedings of the Twenty-Second Annual
           Conference of the Archaeological Association of the
           University of Calgary:234–244. Dale Walde and
           Noreen D. Willows, editors. Calgary, AB.
    1992a Introduction to Critiques in Historical Archaeology.
           Paper presented at the Annual Meeting of The Society
           for Historical Archaeology Conference on Historical
           and Underwater Archaeology, Kingston, Jamaica.
    1992b Class and Ethnicity in Domestic Reform. Paper
           presented at the Annual Meeting of The Society for
           Historical Archaeology Conference on Historical and
           Underwater Archaeology, Kingston, Jamaica.
    [1993] Toward the Further Development of Feminist
           Historical Archaeology. *World Archaeological*
           Bulletin 7, forthcoming.
    1994   Diversity and Nineteenth-Century Domestic Reform:
           Relationships Among Classes and Ethnic Groups. In
           Those of Little Note: Gender, Race, and Class in
           Historical Archaeology, edited by Elizabeth M. Scott,
           pp. 175–208. University of Arizona Press, Tucson.
    1996   Feminist Historical Archaeology and the
           Transformation of American Culture by Domestic
           Reform Movements, 1840–1925. *Proceedings of the*
           1991 Winterthur Conference:397–445. Lu Ann De
           Cunzo, and Bernard L. Herman, editors. Winterthur
           Museum, Wilmington, DE.

STROBEL, A.
    1926   The Old Plantations and Their Owners. In *A History of*
           Brazoria County, Texas, edited by T. L. Smith, pp.
           15–62. Union National Bank, Houston, TX.

TAYLOR, BARBARA
    1996   Genealogical Research in the Brazoria Community.
           Unpublished notes and interview data. On file,
           Anthropology Department, University of Houston,
           Houston, TX.

TILLEY, CHRISTOPHER
    1989   Archaeology as Socio-political Action in the Present.
            In *Critical Traditions in Contemporary Archaeology*,
            edited by Valerie Pinsky and Alison Wylie, pp. 104–
            116. Cambridge University Press, Cambridge, UK.

VANDERSLICE, PHILLIP
    1996   Plantation's Past Life: Excavation Slowly Uncovers
            History's Scars. *The Brazosport Facts*, 6 June:1A,
            5A. Brazosport, TX.

WEINER, JONATHAN M.
    1978   *Social Origins of the New South: Alabama, 1860–
            1885.* Louisiana State University Press, Baton Rouge.

WOODWARD, C. VANN
    1951   *The Origins of the New South.* Louisiana State
            University Press, Baton Rouge.

WRIGHT, CHERYL
    1994   *I Heard It Through the Grapevine: Oral Tradition in
            a Rural African American Community in Brazoria,
            Texas.* M. A. thesis, Department of Anthropology,
            University of Houston, Houston, TX. University
            Microfilms International, Ann Arbor, MI.

WYLIE, ALISON
    1985   Putting Shakertown Back Together. *Journal of
            Anthropological Archaeology* 4:133–147.

CAROL MCDAVID
CLARE HALL
UNIVERSITY OF CAMBRIDGE
CAMBRIDGE CB3 9AL, UNITED KINGDOM